# IMAGINATION AND THE SPIRIT

CLYDE S. KILBY

# IMAGINATION AND THE SPIRIT

***Essays in Literature and the Christian Faith presented to Clyde S. Kilby***

edited by
CHARLES A. HUTTAR

WILLIAM B. EERDMANS PUBLISHING COMPANY
Grand Rapids, Michigan

Library of Congress Catalog Card Number: 68-20591
Printed in the United States of America

# Foreword

A quiet man but never a dull one — such was my impression when I first met Clyde Kilby, how many years or decades ago, and such has been the deepening impression through the years upon seeing him many other times at Wheaton or Modern Language Association, and also upon coming to know him through his writings. A gentle man possessed of the quiet strength that goes with a particular kind of gentleness; a man more all one piece than most of us are, one long since dedicated to the God revealed and ever present through Christ, and dedicated also without confusion or conflict to man's knowledge of self and non-self through literature, most of all the "romantic theologians" whose literary works are peculiarly attuned to his sensibility.

Not every Festschrift is a happy event. Often there is a sense of strain, as though the authors had nothing in common, except perhaps a fleeting professional acquaintance with the person being honored. Such volumes may be interesting for individual contributions, but give the impression of a herd of horses mysteriously stampeding one horse at a time toward every point of the compass. The present Festschrift is more an organic outgrowth of the long and fruitful career of Clyde Kilby. Most of the authors have not merely studied under Kilby but in their interests and points of view, however varied these have become with the years, show the lasting impact of his thought and feeling. There is the further bond, implied if not explicit, that the contributors share a broad commitment to the Christian world-view, and that they refuse to put this in one private pigeonhole and treat it as irrelevant to matters of esthetics, literary analysis, and criticism.

It is fitting that C. S. Lewis should be the central figure in this book, treated in a number of essays and from an illuminating variety of perspectives. Clyde Kilby, by his book, *The Christian World of C. S. Lewis,* and by the growing collection of Lewis letters and other material he has assembled at Wheaton College, has established himself as among the half dozen most important Lewis scholars.

But more interesting even than any particular essay on a particular writer or question of philosophy is the way that certain questions weave in and out of the Festschrift. These are most often not treated directly, but are more the unspoken background against which specific matters are discussed. I am at a loss for a phrase that will briefly say what this is. Perhaps the word "spirit," in all its rich ambiguity, is as good an oversimplification as any. The Spirit of God — if one wishes, specifically the Holy Spirit — and man's spirit, particularly as revealed in works of literature and the other arts — what is one to believe about the relation of the two "spirits"? Is the writer or artist a rival to Deity, or a junior partner in the work of creation? Or is he engaged in an activity to which God grants total autonomy, so that the relation is merely one of God's benign neglect?

These are questions I raise not to seek answers from any of the contributing authors nor from my own speculative insights. I mention them to suggest that this book as a whole is collectively memorable for its open-ended quality. It opens many doors that it does not really peer into. It raises many questions on a radically theoretical level, leaving the reader less certain of his own middle-level answers to big questions, and more goaded to think through certain dilemmas that he has preferred to file away for consideration in some vague future.

Certainly, the Festschrift demonstrates — and it still needs demonstration in order to convince many literary scholars — that a factual background (and for that matter, an experiential background!) in the Christian faith is a powerful tool in unlocking a vast amount of major literature. I have often been astonished at the effrontery of scholars whose religious education terminated with eighth-grade Sunday School, but who assume that this modicum of knowledge is sufficient for exploring the religious dimensions of literature — or ruling that the dimensions aren't there at all. Many of the present essays are illuminating because the contributors can speak from inside a tradition shared, to one degree or another, by the author under consideration.

Now let me revert to some of the major questions the essays raise, where I think a whole frontier lies open for exploration by Christian scholars. What I am thinking of is a radically theoretical examination, seeking a model, if you will, of the relation between the religious and the esthetic (a term I use for lack of anything better, to indicate what it is about literature and the arts that sets them apart from purely practical or moral activities). Put another way, why do men indulge in esthetic activities — painting pictures, writing poetry, composing music, designing gardens? Still more, why does mankind consume the products of esthetic creation? It is a kind of miracle when a poet writes a poem, but a greater miracle when someone pauses to read it.

I suppose what I am asking is — how does esthetic activity (both production and consumption) fit into the total scheme of things established by God? More modestly, I am asking whether religion (faith, experience, formal theology, everything) can throw any light on esthetics, and conversely whether esthetics can illuminate and perhaps rejuvenate our understanding of religion.

One can answer all such questions briefly and with finality by taking an iconoclastic position, and indeed it has played a continuing role in the Christian tradition. The short answer then is to say that preoccupation with the arts is at best a rather infantile diversion, like children playing with a doll house, and at worst an idolatrous attempt to create and enjoy a world, ultimately illusory or even demonic, that is created in rivalry to the one real world, that of God's building. I personally would grant that among some artists and some esthetes there is occasionally an attempt to live entirely in the world of the esthetic, making it a substitute for religion, and that the iconoclastic either/or may be a wholesome corrective. But I cannot believe this situation to be normative. Sophocles and Shakespeare are doing something more important than juggling illusions or consorting with demons.

If scholars are to explore these further frontiers implied by some of the essays in the present book, I think they might start by the way of analogy, taking key concepts in esthetics and religion, and seeking parallels, then finally asking whether each discipline throws light upon the other.

That this is not an unheard of novelty is illustrated by Dorothy Sayers' *The Mind of the Maker,* which draws parallels between the doctrine of the Trinity and the creative process as experienced by writer and reader. Whether more than a loose analogy actually exists in the ultimate realm of what is most real is an unanswerable question, but in the process of developing the parallels Sayers at least makes the Trinity imaginatively plausible, and — as this writer can testify — throws a flood of light on the mysterious way that the first hazy concept of, say, a poem travels from mind to its painful incarnation on paper, and then is recreated with power in the mind of the reader.

Since this is a foreword and not a chapter, I have the privilege of suggesting approaches without carrying them through.

I shall jot down just a few possible parallels that haunt me, in the hope that a scholar here and there will choose the dangers of being a pathfinder.

For a starter, could someone take up where Sayers left off? Does the biblical doctrine of Creation hold an important key to the universality of esthetic activity and experience? It does seem odd that even the most "primitive" tribe, preoccupied with its daily survival, somehow finds time and energy to compose and transmit literature, to decorate baskets beyond functional requirements, to develop musical instruments. Does the *imago Dei* within us include an urge to carry on the work of creation? Is the earth rather like a newly built house and is God the kind of architect who encourages us to create the sort of interior we consider appropriate? If so, what does this do to the traditional concept (perhaps more Greek than Hebraic) of God as the immutable, perfect, and ever-all-knowing? Is it possible that God himself is sometimes surprised, because he has deliberately created beings with the capacity to surprise him?

I wonder also whether the story of Eden may not have something to say about the reasons for esthetic activity. Legends from all over the world seem to echo the theme of exile, the awareness that empirical human existence, even at its best, is not what was originally intended. The lost Eden was a garden of harmony before sin and self-awareness entered simultaneously. You can't go home again, human experience seems to say. But through the arts you can take all the ingredients of the fallen world and fit them together in such a pattern that the total thing is alive and serene with harmony and beauty. This can be seen most clearly in some types of modern sculpture, when the artist visits the city dump to get his raw materials, returns home and takes out the welding torch, and puts together a composition made of the broken and discarded things of existence — each individually ugly, the totality beautiful and evoking visions of the lost paradise. In such a work of sculpture a discarded coffee pot, blackened from long use, remains hideous as long as you look at it alone, but gleams like a Holy Grail when seen through the total esthetic context. Or take tragedy. Shakespeare stirs together an old man driven forth into the tempest, a man with eyes gouged out, a dutiful daughter hanged, and sundry other horrors, all of which remain horrible, but the total impact of the play is to send the audience forth, perhaps not kinder or more devout than they were before, but with a curious sense that though everything in particular is wrong, All is right.

I suspect that the arts function in more than one way for us, rather as certain parts of our bodies double up in function: lips to help in eating and drinking, to use for talking, adapted for kissing. It could be that something of God's passion for creating is in us, and that each new sonnet increases the fulness of the universe. And it may equally well be that memories of the lost Eden compel us, for our soul's health, to take occasional vacations in a secondary but real Eden constructed by esthetic magic. Perhaps the temporarily recovered Eden is more than a backward glance. Could it also be an eschatological sign, a goad to keep us from ever being permanently contented with the best ordered society and way of life, a tantalizing hint that in the ultimate culmination we shall know Eden again, but now a sophisticated paradise, not a naive one; and in knowing it will discover it was never at any moment totally absent from us?

As I think about basic Christian doctrines and come to justification, I do not see a direct analogy, though perhaps someone else will. At this point I discern more of a handmaiden-of-theology relation than at any other point. To accept God's acceptance and therefore be set right with him is not easy; uptight Paul had to be blinded into spiritual openness before God could get at him. I do not quite see how the esthetic experience as such produces the radical re-orientation that we call justification — but I do see how it prepares the way in some cases, by liberating the imagination from flat common sense, and by making a person open to new experiences and a transformed sensibility.

The doctrine of sanctification, sometimes unduly minimized lest it compete with justification, has interesting parallels with the arts. Here I am thinking of mankind's long collective history more than of the individual. If we imagine that the first inhabitants of the primal garden were minimal human beings, full in their sinlessness but empty in consciousness, scarcely aware yet of their own existence, it has been the arts as much as any one thing that have educated, guided, and goaded mankind into self-knowledge and the passion to know the Other-than-self. The process continues. There is much talk today of Consciousness Three, and speculations on a psychic mutation now taking place — perhaps an evolution from the emphasis on abstract reason, and a move toward intuition, feeling, the magic, the mysterious, the divine. With all its zigs and zags the gradual evolution of mankind's consciousness could prove ultimately to be toward a greater awareness of, and relatedness with, all things that be, supremely the Author of all things that be. Put another way, we are partially human and dare hope that the race will become fully so; the artists play their role in the humanization of the tribe, a process analogous to sanctification, and perhaps connected with it by more than formal analogy.

Finally, I should like to see Christian scholarship lose a bit of the high seriousness that too often accompanies it. Speculative scholars might loosen up by exploring, for instance, the meaning of play, and the possibility that it subsumes both the religious and the esthetic. Perhaps the child making a mud pie, the poet writing a sonnet, and God creating a universe are united by the simple fact that they are playing the particular game that each in his freedom has chosen. It could be that one ultimate word about theology and about the arts was spoken by C. S. Lewis in his vision of the Great Dance at the end of *Perelandra.* Whatever is ultimate may be closer to skipping rope or playing with a doll house than it is to a graduate seminar, the assembly line, or an edifying sermon. A child releasing a helium balloon into the sky, Jesus Christ ascending into heaven, Shakespeare composing the final scene of Lear — these may be echoes and remembrances of that primal impulse of a God who had no necessity to do anything, but decided to play at creating a universe in which beings in his own likeness could play their games too.

Enough of unfootnoted speculation. And I receive my proper punishment. When I finished reading this Festschrift and set about to write a Foreword, I was full of ideas for books that I hoped others would be inspired to write. I realize now that the one person I have probably stirred up is myself, and that I will have no peace until I responsibly think through some of the speculations I have set down above with the freedom of irresponsibility. If I am punished by finding myself eventually at the typewriter, composing a new book, it will be in large measure because this Festschrift somehow arouses in the reader some of Clyde Kilby's own patient and hopeful spirit of inquiry.

—Chad Walsh
*Beloit College*

# Contents

# Abbreviations

| | |
|---|---|
| *JEGP* | Journal of English and Germanic Philology |
| *MP* | Modern Philology |
| *OED* | Oxford English Dictionary (New English Dictionary) |
| *PQ* | Philological Quarterly |
| *RES* | Review of English Studies |
| *SP* | Studies in Philology |
| | |
| *ELH* | [English Literary History] |
| *PMLA* | [Publications of the Modern Language Association] |

# Introduction

It is characteristic of Clyde Kilby that, when his time came to retire, he should keep right on — relinquishing, it is true, the burden of administrative duties he had carried with such grace and vision, taking a half-load of teaching, but at the same time entering into new activities: the lecture circuit, the Lewis collection, the books one after another, and being generally as busy as ever if not busier, accomplishing as much if not more.

How can a book like this be offered to mark the retirement of a man who will not retire?

Perhaps we may call it (since round numbers are customary) an advance seventieth birthday present.

Here a representative cross-section of those who have been professionally associated with Clyde Kilby — students, colleagues, co-laborers in the fields of scholarship — join to pay tribute and to express gratitude. Professor Kilby has had a lifetime vision of what it means to be a Christian scholar. He has communicated that vision, by word and by example, to many a generation of students (unready at first and sometimes uncomprehending or even hostile, but as the years went on, as the climate of Evangelical opinion changed under the influence of Kilby and others, more and more receptive). For courage and persistence and skill and humility, which is the seedbed of continual growth, we honor him.

For largeness of mind also: the variety of subjects treated in this collection and the 38-year list of his own publications indicate something of the breadth of Professor Kilby's academic interests. That his interest in most of these subjects goes beyond the merely academic betokens another kind of breadth. Again, a broadened receptiveness to truth, from whatever quarter it comes, is one of the lessons he has taught to many a student bred to an exclusivistic, sectarian kind of Christianity. With such a narrowed perspective — and he, too, began there — it is not always easy to become aware of the richness of spiritual insight vouchsafed to those who dot their *i*'s or cross their *t*'s differently. But the clue to Professor Kilby's openness, as well as to the unity underlying his varied fields of interest and his many professional activities, is the concept of the Christian imagination. And from this notion our book takes its title.

* * *

The operations of the human mind are manifold. It works by thought, by sense and image, by faith, by passion. Denying any of these, a mind is incomplete: wholeness requires that they all work in harmony. Each operation has its proper sphere. Some feats, for instance, reason can accomplish. Other things reason cannot do but imagination can, or passion, or faith; and if reason tries to do them it doesn't merely fail but goes sour. The result might be Pangloss or Laputa or the terrible despair of Marlowe's Faust. The century that gave us two of those examples, discerning reason's limits and abuses, took an even harsher view of nonrational activity. Faith must grudgingly be let in (though the Deists made a way to be religious without it) so long as it didn't become foolish credulity. But as imagination did not share faith's theological credentials there was no need to harbor it: it could sour too easily into escapist fantasy to be trusted; it was much too close to enthusiasm to be safe. These are the roots, I believe, of the imaginal poverty of which Professor Kilby accused the fundamentalist ethos he was familiar with.

But *enthusiasm* means a god-indwelling, god-possession, and risky as it most certainly is, it is also, above all things, to be desired. Imagination opens a door on the ultimate. It "is permitted to enter the darkness of the divine mystery."[1] Imagination wells up from the abyss of personality where human spirit and Holy Spirit meet. It may seem to be overstating a case to imply that imagination *always* does these things. After all, poets expend their gifts on many quite mundane matters. Yet to discover a metaphor, however trivial, is to build a bridge and to find meaning; and all little meanings are part of the great Meaning. A closed door is always a mystery. It may lead to another room in a comfortable house — but it may reveal a breathtaking vista or a sheer chasm. One grain of sand may be only silicon while the next may reveal eternity.

Does one *discover* a metaphor or *invent* it? (Or has the latter word, in its centuries of development from Latin, taken on a polarity that did not always exist?) Does one *find* meaning or *make* it? The power to form images — to give visual and

[1] Richard Kroner, *The Religious Function of Imagination* (New Haven, 1941), p. 14.

bodily substance to thoughts — is of its essence creative. In these terms the earliest of all creative activity may be described. The Spirit broods over chaos, where no images are, where all is formless and void; the divine Essence brings images into being by a word, an utterance of the Word. The Spirit breathes into the mouth of man and he is alive; he too has words. He can name the animals, exerting on them the power of abstract thought, and by this means he is commissioned to subdue all things. But his destiny is not merely to subdue. Formed in the Image of the Creator, he too is given the power to create and is made a co-laborer with God in consummating the work of creation. By imagination he bodies forth the forms of things unknown. He conceives (perhaps the overtones of this word will reconcile the action and passivity implicit in the paradox of discovery/invention;[2] may one speak of the Holy Spirit as the fertilizing agent in a true imaginative conception?) — he conceives of aided travel, and behold! a wheel, a canoe, a saddled horse. The newest refinement in the perennial quest for better social structures, the latest example of better living through chemistry, the most recent revelation of unique personality in poetry or fiction or on canvas — all have their motive impulse and their first form in someone's imaginative mind.

Like God's other gifts to men, imagination descends alike upon the just and the unjust. Thus the present collection by design is not limited to examining Christian authors. Meaning is one; through the centuries and across cultural lines the ultimate Source of illumination is one.

Some of the essays that follow seek to place a literary movement in its historical context; some theorize more broadly about the nature of the artistic endeavor; some present detailed accounts of the artistic techniques by which an imaginative moral vision was given a local habitation and a name; some explore the ideas of an author or of several authors. The essays have been grouped together in the obvious sort of arrangement, but between one group and another surprising interrelationships of theme will be noted. Over and over the contributors recur to the themes of mystery and paradox; to such theological concepts as sin, incarnation, redemption, providence, myth; to concerns that lie at the heart of human existence such as destiny, exchange, love, and the quest for self-knowledge. For when the human spirit sounds its own depths and searches the heights of the universe for meaning, these are the things it wants to know about. And to honor the search (as well as having already

[2] Cf. Kroner, pp. 48, 54f.

impelled the search) the divine Spirit hovers, ready to reveal the images of truth.

* * *

As editor I wish to thank those who wrote articles for this collection; the editorial staff of Eerdmans for craftsmanlike cooperation; Chad Walsh for his Foreword; those (listed elsewhere) who have given permission for quotation of material; Mrs. Martha Kilby, Miss Ivy Olson, and Miss Agnes Horness for help with the bibliography; and my wife Joy (also a former Kilby student), without whose encouragement, patience, and acquired skill in numerous minor household repairs this book could never have become a reality.

—Charles A. Huttar

# I. Art and Philosophy

# Language, Symbol, and Truth

ARTHUR F. HOLMES

Language is a crucial ingredient in any culture. The richness of language enriches culture, its impoverishment impoverishes culture, and a static, dead language is evidence of a dead culture. In our day the problem of "two cultures" with the gap between the sciences and the humanities, between technology and human values, in measure results from a corresponding gap between two languages. On the one hand, language is regimented to scientific demands; on the other hand, it is the creative tool of the humanist.

The view one holds of language accordingly affects one's view of culture. Where scientism prevails — not the scientific study of language but the sort of scientism evident in the logical positivist's verifiability theory of meaning — there metaphysics is denounced as meaningless gobbledygook, art is relegated to the emotive, and ethics falls by default to the existential situationist. Religion meets all three fates, depending on whether it is regarded as wishful metaphysical thinking, as expression of feelings, or as a self-authenticating encounter that completely defies conceptualization. Even the secularization of society, as-

---

Arthur F. Holmes is Professor of Philosophy, and department chairman, at Wheaton College. He received the A.B. from Wheaton College in 1950, M.A. there in 1952, and Ph.D. from Northwestern University in 1957. His published work includes *Christianity and Philosophy* (Inter-Varsity Press, 1960; Tyndale Press, 1964); *Christian Philosophy in the Twentieth Century* (Craig Press, 1969); and *Faith Seeks Understanding* (Eerdmans, 1971); articles in *Journal of Philosophy, Journal of Religion, Philosophy and Phenomenological Research, Personalist, Gordon Review, Christianity Today,* and other journals; and "The Philosophical Methodology of Gordon Clark," in *The Philosophy of Gordon Clark,* ed. Ronald H. Nash (1967). He has held summer appointments at the University of the Pacific Summer Philosophy Institute (1966) and Garrett Theological Seminary (1967).

sociated as it is with a loss of the religious world view that has for centuries given meaning and cohesion to Western culture, is therefore related to the problem of language.

This essay is an attempt to focus certain aspects of the problem, not to solve it. We attempt (1) to set off the humanistic view of language in contrast to the scientific, (2) to develop as one of its key distinctives the use and meaning of symbols, and (3) to trace the resultant contrast between two approaches to truth. Our method will be one of exposition, not primarily of argument or arbitration. Our purpose will be achieved if the scientific and humanistic models are seen with greater clarity and in sharper contrast, and if the value of the humanistic is accordingly underscored. Our intent is not to deny all validity to the scientific model, nor to discuss the *science* of linguistics, but to point out that the scientific model applied universally and exclusively by certain *philosophies* of language produces a reductionistic scien*tism*. By the same token, we have not examined the constructive role of the scientific model in relation to the humanistic. This would require a further essay. We have contented ourselves with exploring the value of symbols and the notion of truth in the humanistic alternative.

## *I. LANGUAGE*

Ours is not the first cultural crisis in the history of the West. Plato was troubled by the crisis in his day. The Sophists precipitated it at the theoretical level by virtue of their relativism. What is the basis of truth and value? Is it in nature or in convention, in *physis* or in *nomos?* Whichever answer one gives, the Sophists argued, the same result accrues: if nature is the basis, and each man is by nature different, then each man is the measure of all things; but if convention is the basis, and conventions change with time and place, then relativism results. Plato discussed this dilemma with reference to various aspects of culture, including language. In the *Cratylus*, he asks whether words are arbitrary signs of experienced objects, deriving their meanings from purely conventional associations, or whether they are naturally appropriate names chosen because in themselves they convey the meanings we intend. Plato does not decide the issue all one way. On the one hand, words cannot be purely conventional, for then how would those who first use them come to associate them with their referents? Words are well chosen when they are appropriate. On the other hand, some words — notably the names of the numerals — cannot possibly be regarded as naturally appropriate; it is obvious that they are arbitrarily assigned.

Plato skirts a further problem: whether language is a physical phenomenon, a pattern of responsive behavior deriving its significance from its external stimuli, or a spiritual phenomenon, a way in which human persons create meaning for themselves and establish their place in the world. This amounts to the choice between a theory of language oriented to the sciences and one more indebted to the humanities. Gorgias the Sophist, whom Plato may well have in mind, exemplifies the former. He made himself famous by adding to the scepticism of Protagoras the startling conclusion that if anything exists and can be known, it still cannot be communicated. As a physical phenomenon, speech is apprehended solely by the sense of hearing, not by the wider range of senses used in knowing external objects. Speech is therefore ill suited to express what we know. For Plato, however, a well-chosen name participates in the nature of the known, either by onomatopoeia or by virtue of some etymological association. It is therefore well suited to express what we know and to give structure to our world. Plato prefers the humanistic model.

Augustine presses Plato's position further in his early dialog, *Concerning the Teacher*. Words, he argues, cannot communicate knowledge, for either we know what they mean or we do not. If we do know what they mean, then they convey nothing not previously known. If we do not know their meaning, then the words convey nothing at all. In either case, they communicate nothing. A sceptical conclusion to the dilemma is only avoided, he maintains, by recognizing that God's image in man means that *rationes aeternae* are innate in the human mind and are brought to birth by the stimulating Socratic midwifery of a verbal dialectic. In the final analysis it is not a man who teaches me, nor his words, but Christ the Logos who teaches within. Words are stimuli to knowledge by recollection, a knowledge we have independently of verbal signs, a knowledge that itself gives meaning to the world of daily experience.

Aristotle, meantime, had proposed that by virtue of their nonliteral uses, words serve as more than mere signs.[1] "Metaphor consists in giving the thing a name that belongs to something else." He includes here those uses of analogy whereby we speak meaningfully of otherwise nameless acts. "Thus to cast forth seed is called 'sowing'; but to cast forth its flame, as said of the sun, has no special name." Since it stands in the same relation to sunlight, however, as sowing does to seed,

[1] *Poetics* xxi. 1457b.

the poet speaks of "sowing around a god-created flame" and so talks meaningfully of what has not itself been so named. "Sowing," we may say, serves as a metaphor for something else. Sometimes a metaphor gives the name of one species to the whole genus, or of the genus to one species or of one species to another species. In similar fashion with other non-literal devices, the part may become a symbol of the whole or else the whole of the part, or else one sort of thing symbolizes another sort.

The Scholastics build here their doctrine of analogy. Not all predication is either univocal or equivocal; some of it is analogical. This is particularly the case in talking of God. Because he is *sui generis,* we cannot use of him universal predicates abstracted from our experience of the species or genus to which he belongs. We cannot predicate goodness and truth of him or of his creatures in any univocal sense. Yet neither do we talk equivocally using nonsense syllables. Rather we speak of him in terms that apply more directly to his creatures. We speak by way of analogy, as Aristotle put it, giving names that belong to something else. Our words are symbols rather than wholly literal descriptions, but they are cognitive symbols and there is "adequation" between their connotation and the reality they symbolize.

The nominalists strongly disagree, not only with realistic theories of universals whether in Augustine, Thomas or Scotus, but also with the belief that we think at all in general, abstract concepts of either univocal or analogical sort. Words, they maintain, are simply sounds, arbitrary signs that indicate particular mental events caused by particular physical stimuli. They derive their meanings from such experiences, not from innate ideas, nor from abstracted concepts. There may arise behaviorally based associations between particular experiences, but not analogies based on a knowledge of universals. Our knowledge can never reach beyond the world of experienced particulars. In the Renaissance, Thomas Hobbes pursues this line and bases it on a mechanistic psychology. The units of language are single words denoting atomistic sense-objects. The molecular structure of sentences parallels that of the world: particles of matter in mechanically ordered motion. As arbitrary signs, words are part of the behavioral-response mechanism that enables us to refer to things and to retain experiences for delayed reaction.

In the same tradition, we may cite the Cartesians. These words by Stuart Hampshire are remarkably apt.

> In the Cartesian and classical age the language of rational discourse had to be as far as possible free from figurative or metaphorical expressions; or at least the figurative or imaginative use of expressions must be recognized as purely decorative; such a style was in fact characteristic of the great French classical writers of the seventeenth century and of most of their successors both within and outside France before the Revolution. Philosophy in the age of Descartes, Spinoza, and Leibniz was in part written in a learned Latin which, having largely lost its poetical and conversational uses, could be made entirely formal and abstract and, therefore, in Descartes' sense, extremely clear; words could be given a precise technical meaning, comparatively unconnected with any of their shifting and figurative uses in ordinary speech. Descartes further wrote French prose which has always been a model of absolute clarity and simplicity and he exhibited an ease in handling abstractions which has never been achieved in any other modern European language. Leibniz, having himself written in the bare Latin and French which was the common currency of the learned world, actually proposed the creation of an artificial symbolic language in which every clear and simple idea would have a single symbol; so, all the symbols being governed by rules prescribing their possibile combinations, all abstract reasoning would be reduced to mere algebraical calculations. This project of what Leibniz called a *Characteristica Universalis* was the extreme and logical development of the common rationalist doctrine that error and uncertainty are due to the unclarity of ordinary spoken and literary languages, which are not designed to convey clear and distinct ideas.[2]

Bertrand Russell's logical atomism, inspired by Leibniz, is a more recent and sophisticated attempt in the same direction. Words are the atomic constituents of language; they denote the atomic constituents of experience which we order logically into a formal scheme. Ordinary language is not this way; it is illogical, informal and misleading. Russell helped develop symbolic logic as a more ideal language. By replacing verbal variables with mathematical symbols he hoped to dispel the logical confusion and linguistic connotations that prevent scientific clarity and rigor. Similar ideals are enshrined in logical positivism's verifiability theory of meaning, the theory that apart from formal utterances like tautologies and definitions, the only cognitive language is purely factual, and can be reduced to verifiable statements about sense data. All else is discarded as emotive. There is no room in cognition for the symbolism of literature and art and religion, nor for the abstractions of metaphysics, nor for any language that derives its meaning from something other than sense experience.

Arbitrary signs, denotational meaning alone, nominalism,

[2] *Spinoza* (Pelican Books, 1951), pp. 20f.

behaviorism, positivism, scientism — these are all relatives, members of the same family. They all interpret language exclusively on the scientific model. As philosophies of language they exhibit shortcomings. Not all factual statements consist of words that refer to particular data. John Wisdom points out that the sentence "England declared war in 1939" contains a collective noun ("England") and a performative verb ("declared war"), which defy such translation.[3] Statements about material objects are equally difficult unless one says that a material object is nothing but a collection of sense data, an assertion with which few epistemologists are altogether satisfied. And Strawson complains that ideal logical languages fail to take seriously the nonscientific concepts expressed "in law courts, in appraising people's characters and actions, in criticizing works of art, in recounting our states of mind, in getting people to fetch things, in narrating histories, in describing what things sound and feel like, in entering engagements with others, in identifying people"[4]— and, we may add, in articulating a world-and-life view. In fact, a purely denotational theory of language creates more problems of interpretation than it solves.

It is therefore not surprising to find richer views of language emerging in recent thought. Not all philosophical analysts demand conformity to the scientific ideal. Ordinary language analysts like Wisdom and Strawson reject such reductionism, claiming that it obscures distinctions preserved in common usage, truncates the depth and breadth of human concern, and cuts off creative thought and interpretive expression. It dismisses the mysterious and dissipates wonder. Language, they maintain, is far more variegated than has been supposed. As Ludwig Wittgenstein puts it, there are many "language games," not just one, and each has created its own rules in the course of its own development. William Frankena finds there are many kinds of cognitive use, and one cannot just label an utterance scientific or emotive, cognitive or noncognitive, without a great deal of explanation. Those easy dualisms do not fit.[5] As a result it is unjustified on any a priori basis to eliminate metaphysical

[3] "Metaphysics and Verification," in *Philosophy and Psychoanalysis* (Oxford, 1952); cf. Isaiah Berlin, "Logical Translation," *Proceedings of the Aristotelian Society*, L (1949-50), 157-188.

[4] P. F. Strawson, "Carnap's Views on Constructed Systems versus Natural Languages in Analytic Philosophy," in P. A. Schlipp ed., *The Philosophy of Rudolph Carnap* (Lasalle, Ill., 1963), p. 505.

[5] " 'Cognitive' and 'Noncognitive,' " Ch. vi in Paul Henle ed., *Language, Thought and Culture* (Ann Arbor, 1958).

discourse or to call art and ethics emotive. Even religious language must be examined *in situ* and understood as it is used.

In European thought, the neo-Kantians preserved the humanistic approach to language. Kant had taught that percepts without concepts are blind: it is our a priori categories and forms that give meaning to experience. Ernst Cassirer applies this to science, art, religion and language: each expresses in symbolic form the creative spirit of man. He rejects all positivistic, nominalistic and naturalistic theories of language, in favor of the view that man not only communicates by what he says but also builds his understanding and gives meaning to his experience. Experience is never purely objective and independent of the subject; it is only possible in any meaningful sense because of the form it receives from man.

> In language, in religion, in art, in science, man can do no more than to build up his own universe — a symbolic universe that enables him to understand and interpret, to articulate and organize, to synthesize and universalize his human experience.[6]

In this sense language is always symbolic; it is not pure objectification; nor is it pure subjectivity. It emerges from the pretheoretical subject-object continuum with other forms of cultural expression. Language consequently liberates.

> Human culture taken as a whole may be described as the process of man's self-liberation. Language, art, religion, science, are various phases in this process. In all of them man discovers and proves a new power — the power to build up a world of his own, an "ideal" world.[7]

This theme is paralleled in the existential philosophers. Martin Heidegger has developed the view that by means of language a man "establishes" his existence in the world. Far from being a collection of arbitrary signs and spiritless grammar, language is a mode of our being-in-the-world. In language the real essence of a thing shows itself amidst the tensions of the human situation — unless of course the language has been deformed or effaced by objectification or "substantivization."

> ...Words and language are not wrappings in which things are packed for the commerce of those who write and speak. It is in words and language that things come into being and are. For this reason the misuse

[6] *An Essay on Man* (Anchor Books, Garden City, 1953), p. 278. Cf. *The Philosophy of Symbolic Forms* (3 vols., New Haven, 1953-57). Also W. C. Swabey, "Cassirer and Metaphysics," in P. A. Schlipp ed., *The Philosophy of Ernst Cassirer* (Evanston, 1949), pp. 121-148. A similar point of view is evident in William Urban, *Language and Reality* (New York, 1939).

[7] *Essay on Man*, p. 286.

of language in idle talk, in slogans and phrases, destroys our authentic relation to things.[8]

Paul Tillich has something similar to say. Language is "the basic expression of man's transcending environment, of having a world."[9] Words have "meaning-creating power."

> Man is free, in so far as he has language. With his language, he has universals that liberate him from bondage to the concrete situation to which even the higher animals are subjected.[10]
>
> In language, communication becomes mutual participation in a universe of meanings. Man has the power of such communication because he has a world in correlation to a completely developed self. This liberates him from bondage to the concrete situation, that is, to the particular here and now of his environment. He experiences world in everything concrete, something universal in everything particular. Man has language because he has a world, and he has a world because he has language.[11]

For language to be confined to arbitrary denotations, tied to particular sense data which it passively signifies — this is the inauthentic existence of men alienated from true being. Tillich points us beyond this. By means of language a man "has a world" rather than being enslaved to one; he discovers the universal in the particular and so reaches beyond the here and the now; he participates with others in a "universe of meanings." This is authentic, free existence.

Jean-Paul Sartre similarly: language is not a phenomenon "added on" to being-for-others; it *is* our being-for-others. I *am* language. It is part of the human condition, of my freedom to create whatever meaning I choose in an otherwise intrinsically meaningless world.[12]

And Willem Zuurdeeg: language is the way we find our place in the world and establish our existence. Man is best defined as *homo loquens*.[13]

Here, then, are two models and two views of language. One, taken exclusively, requires all cognitive language to exhibit the precision and clarity and logical vigor of descriptive science;

[8] See Martin Heidegger, *An Introduction to Metaphysics* (Anchor Books, Garden City, 1961), p. 11. Cf. his *Being and Time* (New York, 1962), pp. 203-210.

[9] *Systematic Theology* (Chicago, 1951-63), I, 170.

[10] *Ibid.*, II, 31.

[11] *Ibid.*, III, 58.

[12] *Being and Nothingness* (New York, 1956), pp. 372ff.

[13] *An Analytical Philosophy of Religion* (New York, 1958), especially Part I. For a general treatment of the subject see Remy C. Kwant, *The Phenomenology of Language* (Pittsburgh, 1965).

the other sees language as an expression of the creative human spirit at work in the world. We have objected to the reductionism of the former: it embodies an essentially naturalistic view of man. We may also object to the latter — to Cassirer's idealism — and to Sartre's radical view of freedom. Neither the naturalistic nor the existential extreme is wholly satisfactory. We do well, with Plato, to decline to settle the argument one way or the other. Some words do amount to arbitrary signs, and denotative language does derive its meaning from the phenomena to which it customarily refers. Yet some language is not this way: it is far more creative. Nor need human creativity imply too radical a freedom — only the imaginative power to see things whole, to build world views, to devise symbols, to pursue and grasp and express meanings that are not given in fragmented sense data nor in perfunctory speech and conventional expressions. We must neither reduce man to a verbalizing response mechanism nor apotheosize him as the tragic creator of cosmic meaning. Finite man in God's image is neither mechanism alone nor absolute freedom. He is a created creator: as created he is part of nature, subject to nature's law; as creator he transcends nature and establishes a world of his own. Created to create, his freedom is at best but a finite image of God's.

## *II. SYMBOL*

How does language create meaning? How does it authenticate existence and free a man from the tyranny of the particular? It is by other means than those to which nominalism, behaviorism and positivism reduce language. It is by means of language such as we use in the humanities. The role of the humanities — literature, the arts, philosophy — in human culture and in liberal education is just this: to make men more fully human, to liberate them from the mundane, the trivial and the trite, to open up new dimensions of personality and richer aspects of life, to cultivate an appreciation of truth, of beauty, of goodness, to provide a perspective on life that makes it whole. The humanities do not just describe life and objectify it, they involve a man in it, they interpret it, and in interpreting it they express ideas and values that make up a world-and-life view and make a man what he is.

The language of the humanities is the language of men with wondering eyes; their wonder and their quest for meaning find creative expression in their words. What is it about their words that possesses this meaning-giving power? Surely not denotations, nor just correct grammar. New insights and understanding are developed more by creative uses of language than by habitual reference, more by connotation than by denotation, more by suggestion than by description, more by symbol than by sign.

1. The meaning of a sign is its particular referent. A symbol also has a referent but this does not exhaust its meaning. It uses a direct literal referent as a vehicle for grasping something else. This is the case with various sorts of symbols. Take the flag. It is more than a banner; it has become identified with the larger meaning and value of a country, and symbolizes all that for which the country stands. It may be trampled and burned or it may be raised and saluted, but in any case it is so treated because, as Tillich says of all symbols, it participates in the meaning and reality and power of that for which it stands.[14] Among religious symbols the cross has a meaning that transcends its literal reference to an event in the year 27. It is the symbol of faith and hope because it expresses the whole of God's redemptive work in history. Similarly the term "blood" in Christian hymnody is more than an allusion to liquid that flowed from the wounded Jesus of Nazareth. It is a symbol for the meaning of his death, for grace, atonement and forgiveness. "There is a fountain filled with blood, drawn from Immanuel's veins"— these lines persist because their symbolism is meaningful. Any literal explanation that reduces them to their direct referents without the larger meaning becomes crude and superstitious rather than being religiously meaningful or theologically correct. Jung has written about the symbolism of dreams, and we speak nowadays of "status symbols" — things that people desire not for their own sake but because they speak of something else and indirectly provide that something. Art and architecture and liturgy have their symbolism. And we prize our "good name," we keep our family's name or that of Alma Mater from disgrace. We pray "in the name of Jesus," because a name symbolizes personal prerogatives just as the command "Open in the name of the king!" used to be an order immediately obeyed. Whether or not a name is arbitrarily assigned or naturally appropriate, it comes to refer to more than the individual it names; it participates in the power of that to which it refers.

Symbols, whether verbal or nonverbal, whether artistic or religious or cultural or psychological, tell us more than signs. A symbol points beyond itself and its immediate referent;

[14] For this point amid other fruitful discussion of symbolism, see his *Dynamics of Faith* (Harper Torchbooks, New York, 1958), Ch. iii, and *Theology of Culture*, ed. R. C. Kimball (New York, 1959), Ch. v.

it interprets and evaluates and expresses created meanings. As William Urban puts it, a symbol has dual reference, to an original object and to an object for which it now stands.[15] Leroy Loemker proposes that between the symbol and its further referent, such as between a name and a person, there is not only the functional correspondence of a sign but also a conscious conceptualization that frees the speaker from bondage to the isolated and concrete object.[16] Philip Wheelwright is even more direct: a symbol invites consideration and interpretation rather than observation or overt action alone.[17]

A sign is static: it points to something familiar, which can thereby be clearly recognized and readily noted. A symbol is dynamic: it opens up new vistas of thought and new levels of reality. It is an exploratory probe, part of a living and growing language, an attempt to capture an elusive idea, to pin down a general conception, to focus on a certain kind of experience. Like a metaphor or analogy it gropes toward what cannot be literally stated. Because it speaks indirectly, by means of words that taken literally refer to something else, it may seem vague and opaque. Yet it is still revealing and it elicits insight.

Among nonverbal symbolism we have the example of a painting. We say it "portrays." Yet a landscape portrays much more than is apparent on the surface of the canvas. We ask what it "means"—something about nature or about life as a whole. Some of it could perhaps be verbalized, yet the painting presents it "powerfully" and as a whole. Or take poetry. It is not by accident that Romanticists used the poetic symbolism they did. If Wordsworth's daffodils did not flutter or dance in the breeze we would not get as close to seeing life his way as we do, for the sprightliness of flowers is symbolic of nature as a whole, and he conveys it far more clearly and more persuasively than prosaic literalisms ever do. The symbol, then, opens up to our sight a reality far larger than itself.

The paradox analogously opens up the uniqueness of an event or person that bursts the bounds of our ordinary expectations. It is *para-doxa*, contrary to opinion, to call anyone the "*wisest fool* in Christendom." An expression like this enables us to grasp something peculiar about a man that more direct and strictly logical statements shun. If there is "paradox" in

[15] *Language and Reality*, p. 422.

[16] "Symbol and Myth in Philosophy," *Truth, Myth and Symbol*, ed. Thomas Altizer *et al.* (Englewood Cliffs, N. J., 1962), p. 112.

[17] *The Burning Fountain* (Bloomington, Ind., 1954); cf. *Metaphor and Reality* (Bloomington, Ind., 1962).

human freedom, it is because man is unique in creation: categories like chance and necessity derived from mechanistic science do not fit; man is different. And if there is "paradox" about the ways of God, it is because he contradicts not himself but us: our empirically built concepts are shattered by him who is *causa sui* and *sui generis*. The paradox points up such uniqueness better than more formal statements; symbol captures levels of reality and experience better than do arbitrary signs.

We use paradox and we use symbol when more literal language and more abstract categories fail to embrace the experience we face. Symbol is more imaginative than logical abstraction just as paradox is more adaptable to logical surprises than is a set of self-consistent propositions. A symbol does not indicate incommunicability any more than a paradox indicates ultimate logical contradiction, but both symbol and paradox express the limitations of more prosaic language and abstract thought. They respond creatively to concrete novelty rather than denying its possibility on a priori logical or scientific grounds. They recognize elements of mystery which a scientistic view of language precludes from both life and thought.[18]

2. The symbol is distinguished from the sign not only by this cognitive power of opening up new levels of reality but also by disclosing new levels of the self. As an interpretive, meaning-adducing expression, it is not purely objective. It reveals an object in relation to the particular subject "I," and it reveals the self as subject always in relation to objective situations. At such a preobjectifying level of consciousness there is no object-in-itself apart from a subject, nor subject-in-itself apart from an object. Subject and object are correlative terms and correlative realities. A person is most fully personal when he makes the world his own, and the world is most meaningful when it becomes *his*. This is uniquely true of our relationship with other persons. A man comes to know himself most fully not in isolation but in relationship to others, most of all in relationship to God. A symbol such as "Father" illustrates this point. It is a correlative term. God is a Father-to-his-people, a Father-for-me. This symbol opens up not only the character of God but also the creatureliness of man. To know Him as "Father" helps me to know myself more truly as "child." Subject and object are always correlative.

[18] This view of paradox finds its classic expression in Søren Kierkegaard's *Concluding Unscientific Postscript* and *Philosophical Fragments*. See also I. T. Ramsey and Ninian Smart, "Paradox in Religion," *Aristotelian Society Supplement*, XXXIII (1959), 195; J. V. L. Casserley, *The Christian in Philosophy* (New York, 1958), pp. 177-182.

The adequacy of a symbol is not that of a one-to-one copy, like a photostatic copy of what is already public and patent. Its adequacy is determined by both poles. On the one hand, it must represent faithfully what is known more literally of the object, and must also further disclose the object by suggestion, by imaginative stimulus, by the creative use of analogy, etc. On the other hand it must have disclosure value for the subject, for me at this juncture of history; it must give meaning for me to the object of which it speaks; it must enable me to understand myself and my world more intimately and to find my place more effectively in life; it must have the power to communicate, to elicit response, to create action.

What does it reveal about the self as subject? It shows the stuff I am made of. It enables me to be authentically and freely myself. It discloses my ideas and values, my perspective on life, my attitudes and hopes and fears — those things that make me the unique person I am. Here, of course, depth psychology becomes interested not only in symbols of the imagination but also in those of dreams. Yet there is an important difference between dreaming and the deliberate use of creative expression. The verbal symbol is not an illusory projection of fear or the fulfillment of a wish, and nothing more. J. O. Wisdom and Morris Lazerowitz take such a view of metaphysical symbols, regarding them as linguistic proposals generated by psychological causes. George Berkeley's immaterialism becomes a symbol of his pathological aversion to physical things and especially to human excretion.[19] But this presupposes a thoroughly emotivist view of man and the naturalistic view that language is complex behavioral response rather than a creative conceptual vehicle. And unless this is a literal, scientific account, not itself metaphysical, it backfires on its own proponents: for what then is the account they give but a symbolic expression of their own pathological condition? *Et tu, Brute!* But if we wish to take seriously both language and the humanities (including metaphysics), then we will not explain them away. We will recognize them as truly human creations and start to explore them on their own terms, looking through them at both the objective and the subjective worlds they reveal, and recognizing their ability to elicit creative response.

3. On the basis of the foregoing distinctives — that symbols participate in the reality of which they speak and that they

[19] J. O. Wisdom, *The Unconscious Origins of Berkeley's Philosophy* (London, 1953); Morris Lazerowitz, *The Structure of Metaphysics* (New York, 1955).

open up new levels of both the objective and the subjective world — it follows that they cannot be replaced by more literal, objective language nor reduced to univocal and more direct utterances. In time it often happens that what was once a fresh, meaningful symbol becomes hackneyed and effete. As Tillich points out, it "dies." For symbols are not arbitrarily assigned static indices; they are born for living people in a dynamic culture, and sometimes they die. The way to keep them from dying is to keep them alive and growing, to relive their suggestiveness, to enrich and deepen their meaning, to expand them and from them to generate further symbols, to press back still more the frontiers of understanding and elaborate more fully a living vision of the meaning of things, to enrich by means of them our own selfhood and self-understanding.[20]

Religious symbols are subject to the same processes. Bishop Robinson, in his popular *Honest to God,* rejects an overliteralized theology for an existential one. The overliteralized theology — caricature though it is — fails to give meaning to God for men today. Robinson's successors tell us God has died in our generation. The symbols have lost their meaning. Part of the trouble, I suspect, is the lack of creative and exploratory religious literature. When the church freezes its language and its theological *status quo* in a world where language and culture change and knowledge grows, it allows God to die. But when the church rediscovers the meaning of language and so values aright the written revelation, it becomes a creative, redemptive force in society and in the world of thought. The Bible is a corpus of literature of various forms, and its language is rich in symbolism. Its words must not be reduced to static signs; they are creative expressions, part of a living literature that is pregnant with meaning for men in every day.

The credal affirmation that God is "Father Almighty, Maker of Heaven and Earth" is one example. As a literal, scientific description it is inadequate. "Father" does not signify one who either begets children or works to support them. But it suggests analogous things about God the Creator that are uniquely appropriate to him. It opens up to us glimpses of the unique character of the Almighty and his distinctive relationship to the creation of which we are a part. The theology of the early church attempted to explore the meaning of the symbol, to expand it. In the process other symbols were introduced and in-

[20] See Urban (cf. note 6), p. 434 *et passim.* Cf. James Edie, "Expression and Metaphor," *Philosophy and Phenomenological Research,* XXIII (1963), 538-561.

terrelated. The *Logos* concept, for instance, played a leading role in the drama. God the Father, creation, logos — these were key symbols in Patristic theology. They helped the church understand and communicate the Christian message in a world that knew about emanations from the One but not about *ex nihilo* creation, and whose logos was an impersonal cosmic necessity.[21] These symbols may still live. Their meaning is open-ended, not closed and exhausted. Men still seek the logos that gives meaning to human existence and history, for they must still live with life's mystery.

## *III. TRUTH*

In the first part of this essay we distinguished two kinds of philosophy of language; in the second part we elaborated one of the distinctives of the humanistic kind, namely its use of symbolism. We shall now attempt to show that the two approaches to language correspond to two approaches to truth and its relation to beauty.

1. On the scientific model, language is a form of behavioral response that uses arbitrary signs in order to indicate and communicate factual information. The locus of truth accordingly is the factual assertion, and the essence of truth is a relationship between assertion and fact that is labelled "correspondence" in the British empiricist tradition, or "adequation" in the Thomistic tradition. In its crudest form this theory of truth requires a one-to-one correlation between the signs and syntax that make up the statement and the objects and their relationships that constitute the referent. When linked with a purely denotative theory of meaning, as in positivism, the theory implies that both the meaning and the truth of our statements can be determined by empirical means.

Factual correspondence may be appropriate to the truth of purely factual statements, and may be ascertainable when the referent is sufficiently limited and specific. But (1) are any statements "purely factual"? Even scientific statements presuppose mathematical schema and operational or conventional definitions. And the more a statement is concerned with general ideas, interpretations and evaluations, the less "purely factual" does it become. The language of the humanities, like that of ordinary life, is "loaded" in this way: bare facts give way to "interprefacts," and the meaning of "interprefactual statements" is not limited to empirical referents.

[21] See Langdon Gilkey, *Maker of Heaven and Earth* (Anchor Books, Garden City, 1965).

(2) Interprefactual statements are not as specific as an empiricist requires. They are "world-viewish," either explicitly or by implication; and world views are neither confirmed nor disconfirmed empirically. They fit the facts, illuminate and explain them; but this is in itself neither proof nor disproof: the explanation and evaluation they offer is in terms of nonempirical beliefs that are *adduced* to the world of direct experience rather than being derived inductively therefrom. Wordsworth's language about daffodils is not only apt and descriptive, it is also interpretive — of nature and of life as a whole. So is Tchaikovsky's *1812 Overture:* it is more than a description of victory celebrations; it evaluates and interprets events from the viewpoint of the Russian spirit. So too a Renoir or a Monet. So too religious affirmations. "God commendeth his love toward us" functions as more than a historical assertion about certain first-century events. It interprets the meaning and value of those events in the light of the Judeo-Christian understanding of God, of man, and of history. It discloses this meaning *for us.* The truth of the assertion is not seen empirically, but in the plausibility of its world-viewish explanation of enigmatic historical occurrences; the explanation "makes sense" in the context of the Judeo-Christian view as a whole; it illuminates and authenticates the impact Jesus Christ has on *me.* If the meaning of language is more than denotative, then truth is more than factual correspondence.

(3) If truth is no more than factual correspondence, then artistic and literary expressions convey no more truth than the most prosaic factual assertions. On the scientific model of language and truth, the aesthetic becomes emotive and decorative. Beauty and truth have no essential connection. Wordsworth could have said as much as he did apart from poetry, Renoir and Monet apart from painting, and the Bible as a revelation of the truth need have used no other literary forms than historical description and didactic exposition. Metaphor and symbol, poetry and apocalypse become superfluous, and their "emotive" appeal, being irrelevant to the truth, is therefore dishonest.

In summary, since even science is not purely empirical factual description, since interprefactual statements are world-viewish rather than descriptive, since the humanities would be an emotional luxury rather than a cognitive necessity, I suggest that the scientific model for language and truth does not offer adequate perspective.

2. On the humanistic model, language creates meaning rather than just fixating facts. It captures the unique and revealing and so opens up the mystery of life; it gives birth to the

symbols that express what I really am, the ideas and values that structure my being. The locus of truth, then, is not in the factual statement but in the meaning-giving perspective. Truth becomes an ideal for which men strive, the ideal of mystery unravelled, of life made whole. It allures men and in doing so draws from them their most creative expression and far-reaching thought. "Ye shall know the truth, and the truth shall make you free." Truth reveals itself in response to a man's self-disclosure and a man reveals himself in response to the disclosure of truth. Knowing the truth depends upon our openness to it and upon being willing to act on it (John 7:17). Subject and object cannot be separated.

Plato was one of the first to state this in the history of Western thought. To bring truth to birth is like bringing a baby into the world. It takes Socratic midwifery. The Socratic dialog that Plato used as his literary form is more than a decorative or rhetorical device, more than an emotively appealing substitute for direct exposition. Dialog opens minds to the truth. Its aesthetic value includes the cognitive, for as far as Plato is concerned the truth discloses itself in response to open-minded inquiry in the give and take of a dialectic that is free from the tyranny of the empirical, free to grasp truth that enlightens the mind. Admittedly Plato did not sufficiently appreciate the role of the empirical in the quest for truth; yet tacitly at least he insists that the truth must fit the facts, for it illuminates the world of experience and makes it meaningful.

The same viewpoint appears in the Socratic dictum "Know Thyself" and in the claim that the unexamined life is not worth living. I know myself in relation to the truth as a whole, and I know the truth as I know myself. Subject and object cannot be separated. To know the truth is primarily to see what life is really about, not to objectify certain factual occurrences and fixate them linguistically.

The same view appears again in Plato's conception of love. Love is contemplative longing, not irrational passion. It is a desire for Beauty-itself, the universal, not for particular emotional satisfactions nor for the possession of some individual. Since beauty is intelligible unity and form, the aesthetic is an aspect of truth. And since beauty and truth are one, love for beauty and longing for truth amount to much the same thing. Knowledge, like love, reveals both the truth to me and me before the truth. It is therefore not surprising that Plato used myth in developing his philosophy. Myth is symbolism extended into narrative, an art form that instead of objectifying facts attempts to create a unified world of meaning that factual representation alone does not cover, and to which even a conceptual dialectic could not penetrate.

In the subsequent Platonic tradition, truth has been conceived more in terms of coherence than of correspondence. Coherence involves not only self-consistency but also unity — the cohesiveness of a body of knowledge which is more than the sum of its parts. It is not at all surprising in view of the relation between truth and beauty, and between the love of truth and the love of beauty, that coherence has been called an *aesthetic* criterion of truth. The surprising thing is that this is sometimes regarded as a criticism, as if aesthetic experience is noncognitive and ordered unity is a seductive delusion. But if all truth is ultimately one, coherence is as legitimate a criterion of truth as it is of beauty, and to it the love for truth rightly responds.

Truth, we have said, is an alluring ideal, a value to be pursued. It is something dynamic and self-revealing, not a static relationship. Gabriel Marcel, in his Gifford Lectures, *The Mystery of Being,* has a chapter entitled "Truth as a Value." He asserts that the theory of truth as adequation of thing to intellect fails to throw light on what we mean when we say that we are guided by the love of truth, or that someone sacrificed himself for the truth. He did not die for the adequation of thing and intellect but for truth as a value that was "at stake." We say further that the truth enlightens us, yet it can also dazzle and wound us, and to it some people are deliberately blind. Adequation and the empiricist theory of truth do not account for such phenomena. It is more plausible, suggests Marcel, to say that all intercourse between persons takes place against a kind of intelligible background which we refer to when we speak of being "within the bounds of truth." What we call the love of truth may be a sort of joy at living meaningfully against this intelligible setting. In this sense the truth shows itself in what we are, as well as in what we say. We should *be true* too.[22]

Martin Heidegger discusses the notion of truth in a similar vein. He criticizes the traditional notion that the primary locus of truth is the assertion and that the essence of truth is an agreement between thought and object. He argues that such a notion is foreign even to Aristotle. Phenomenologically, truth becomes explicit when knowing *shows itself* as true. Truth is

[22] See Marcel, *The Mystery of Being* (Gateway ed., Chicago, 1960), I, 70-94. On the notion of "being true" see also E. J. Carnell, *Christian Commitment* (New York, 1957), Ch. ii.

dynamic, a disclosure, not static. And what is disclosed or shown, and in this sense "demonstrated," is "not an agreement of knowing with its object" but the being of the entity itself. An assertion is true when it uncovers the entity as it is in itself.[23] But an assertion is founded upon interpretation and understanding and language, and these are modes of *our* being-in-the-world (*Dasein*), means by which we establish our existence and create meaning. The truth of our assertions is therefore rooted in our self-disclosure as well as that of the entities concerned. An assertion is not the primary locus of truth, but rather the being we have in the world.

This leads the early Heidegger to the rather extravagant claim that apart from man there is no truth; there can be no eternal truths unless *Dasein* has been and will be for all eternity. This does not mean that Newton's laws, for instance, insofar as they are true, uncover no real entities as they already were before Newton. Truth is not subjective in that sense; nor is it left to every man's discretion to believe whatever he will, regardless. Rather our openness to the truth is needed in order to free things from their hiddenness. Truth (*alētheia,* disclosure) is mutual.

In his later essay "On the Essence of Truth"[24] Heidegger is less anthropocentric, and speaks of man in relation to what-is-in-totality. Being-itself is disclosed in our being: consequently the truth-for-me is not just mine, nor just truth-for-man. Yet truth is still the openness of being in a subject-object matrix.

Tillich relates the bipolarity of truth to the use of symbols. From the subjective side faith is true if it *adequately* expresses ultimate concern; from the objective side, it is true if its content is really *ultimate.* Adequacy and ultimacy — these are essential. Adequacy is the power of expressing an ultimate concern in such a way that it creates reply, action, communication: symbols that do this are alive. Ultimacy, the objective side, precludes the idolatrous worship of theological symbols; for no symbol portrays God exhaustively. The truth of faith extends beyond the limitations of concrete symbols,[25] for they themselves stand under the "yes-or-no judgment" of the Christ-event.

So also Philip Wheelwright. He asks what truth and falsity mean when applied to statements that are not only declarative as in science but also expressive, statements that express our

[23] *Being and Time,* p. 261.
[24] *Existence and Being* (Chicago, 1949), pp. 292-324.
[25] *Dynamics of Faith,* pp. 96f.

depth-interests in religion, philosophy and art. Such statements are not simply emotive nor simply a report on ideas I happen to like. Evaluations and affirmations of belief affirm what I, and by implication others, *ought* to affirm. They express our basic loyalties. In similar fashion, a poetic utterance invites our imaginative depth-assent, a person-response to what is disclosed.[26]

The point is that truth on the humanistic model stretches between two poles: the personal — being true to myself and my most ultimate commitments, to the beliefs and values that make me what I am; and the more objective — being true to things as they are and as a whole. Scripture exhibits this bipolarity: it speaks of our being "in the truth" as well as of our "knowing the truth."

This bipolarity has sometimes been taken as a denial of absolute truth. For two reasons this is a mistake. First, it is primarily the recognition that truth is a value, an object of personal concern rather than of detached indifference. Soren Kierkegaard says this dramatically: truth is subjectivity. He does not mean that it is private, relative, a matter of individual preference; he never denied the objectivity of truth, nor the appropriate role of scientific investigation. He meant rather that a man makes the truth his own by embracing it with passionate concern.

Second, Paul Ricoeur, the French Protestant philosopher, points out that truth and hope are related concepts. Truth for man-in-history is always incomplete. Our foreglimpses are but "earnests" which look beyond the limitations of the present; truth remains an "eschatological ideal" which we cannot yet articulate completely.[27]

On the humanistic model, then, truth is a value, an object of personal concern as well as careful investigation; truth is dynamic; it shows itself to those who are open to the truth; it has a bipolar structure, an objective reference and a personal perspectival nature. Response to the truth is not a mechanical assent or a mathematical "Q.E.D." but a confession of faith: "I have heard about this, but now I see and know for myself."

The man who views truth this way is saying that philosophy is not so much a science as one of the humanities. Like literature and art it attempts to look at life and to see it whole

[26] *The Burning Fountain,* Ch. xiii.

[27] *History and Truth* (Evanston, 1965), pp. 41-56. Cf. Herman Dooyeweerd, *A New Critique of Theoretical Thought* (Philadelphia, 1955), II, 565-582.

from a personal perspective, which is taken to be true because of its meaning-giving power. Metaphysics is like poetry.[28] The point may be illustrated by considering the history of philosophic inquiry. It is sometimes objected that no progress is made such as science can boast. One response is to point out that philosophy is not a special science, dealing with a particular area of data. It is scientific in two other senses only, that it methodically seeks theoretical understanding and that its conclusions must do justice to scientific knowledge. It makes progress accordingly by adjusting its categories and developing its conceptual schemes so that they can cope adequately with scientific developments. Descartes kept up with mechanistic science, Locke with Newtonian science, and Whitehead with energistic physics.

In other regards, however, philosophy is closer to the humanities than to the sciences, and its progress should be judged accordingly. For centuries the humanities have continued to reflect on life and its meaning, to express man's longings and portray his ideas. The history of literature and art depicts changing world views — classicism, romanticism and so forth. Good work in the humanities is marked by creativity in method and clarity in expression, and by the penetrating insights its symbols afford. Philosophy similarly makes progress in improving old methods and creating new ones, in clarifying concepts of lasting value and elucidating current views of life and the world, in its revealing insights into things that do not change — the nature of man and God, the structure of the world and of history. And within any one tradition a philosophy makes progress by keeping its perennial themes in up-to-date form. Homer and Bach and Plato are therefore not surpassed by scientific progress as are Galen and Ptolemy and even Newton. We continue to value them for their own sake long after we refer to Galen "for historical reasons only." The progress represented by T. S. Eliot and Rachmaninoff and Whitehead is real, but it is not intended to "settle" once and for all whatever it was their forebears grappled with. We still learn directly from Homer as well as Eliot, from Bach as well as Rachmaninoff, and from Plato as well as Whitehead, even if science today has no reason to read Galen or Grosseteste or even Newton "in the original."

The dogmatist tends to look upon philosophy as an extraspecial science that settles things once and for all, and the history of that science as the inevitable road to final truth. The sceptic too expects philosophy to be scientific, and when

[28] See, for instance, Martin Heidegger, "Hölderlin and the Essence of Poetry," in *Existence and Being,* pp. 270-291.

it fails to meet his expectation of scientific progress by not answering questions in publicly confirmable or generally agreeable fashion, he gives up. In both cases the model imposed on philosophy is that of a science rather than the humanities. Maurice Merleau-Ponty expresses the outcome this way:

> From now on the tasks of literature and philosophy can no longer be separated. When one is concerned with giving voice to the experience of the world and showing how consciousness escapes into the world, one can no longer credit oneself with attaining a perfect transparence of expression. Philosophical expression assumes the same ambiguities as literary expression, if the worth is such that it cannot be expressed except in "stories," and, as it were, pointed at. One will not only witness the appearance of hybrid modes of expression, but the novel and the theater will become thoroughly metaphysical, even if not a single word is used from the vocabulary of philosophy.[29]

Literature, along with philosophy, is a means of apprehending reality. The beauty of the symbols opens up the truth it "shows" and helps men to see, to be truly human and authentically themselves.

[29] *Sense and Non-Sense* (Evanston, 1964), p. 28.

# Either : Or

## OWEN BARFIELD

### I

Everyone who knows anything about Coleridge is more or less familiar with two of the three concluding paragraphs of Chapter xiii of the *Biographia Literaria* ("On the Imagination"). They are brief enough to permit my beginning this article by quoting them:

> The IMAGINATION then, I consider either as primary, or secondary. The primary IMAGINATION I hold to be the living Power and prime Agent of all human Perception, and as a repetition in the finite mind of the eternal act of creation in the infinite I AM. The secondary Imagination I consider as an echo of the former, co-existing with the conscious will, yet still as identical with the primary in the *kind* of its agency, and differing only in *degree,* and in the *mode* of its operation. It dissolves, diffuses, dissipates, in order to re-create; or where this process is rendered impossible, yet still at all events it struggles to idealize and to unify. It is essentially *vital,* even as all objects (*as* objects) are essentially fixed and dead.
>
> FANCY, on the contrary, has no other counters to play with, but fixities and definites. The Fancy is indeed no other than a mode of Memory emancipated from the order of time and space; while it is

---

A retired lawyer who lives near London, Owen Barfield is the author of several distinguished and original books in philology and philosophy, from *History in English Words* (1926) to *Speaker's Meaning* (1967). Forthcoming is *What Coleridge Thought,* a full-length study of Coleridge's philosophy, which is closely related to the subject of the present article. Since his retirement Mr. Barfield has held visiting lectureships at Drew and Brandeis Universities, the State University of Missouri, and Hamilton College, which conferred on him the honorary degree of Doctor of Humane Letters. One of his close friends was C. S. Lewis, who once referred to him as a man who "cannot talk on any subject without illuminating it."

> blended with, and modified by that empirical phenomenon of the will, which we express by the word CHOICE. But equally with the ordinary memory the Fancy must receive all its materials ready made from the law of association.[1]

The concluding paragraph is still shorter and we need not trouble with it. It is the two I have quoted that have been praised, criticized, confuted, confirmed, argued from, argued against, blessed and cursed ad nauseam since the day they were published. It is all the more remarkable, and indeed deplorable, to reflect how few there are who know anything about the *first* three paragraphs of the same chapter. The interval between these first three paragraphs and the last three contains only the well-known "letter from a friend" advising the author not to proceed with it because it is too alien to the trend of contemporary thought, but to reserve its content for his projected great work on the Constructive Philosophy. Instead therefore of continuing his exposition from the point he had reached by the conclusion of paragraph three, Coleridge suddenly closed it with the terse epitome that constitutes the two paragraphs already quoted, containing (he says) "the main result of the Chapter, which I have reserved for that future publication."

Later in his life Coleridge disclosed that the "friend" was a fiction and the "very judicious letter" had in fact been composed by himself. I do not propose to go into the practical difficulties under which he was laboring when the *Biographia Literaria* was being written; but it was certainly these, together with the discouraging reception his contemporaries had hitherto accorded to his heterodox philosophy, that induced him to give up. The "letter" is chiefly important for the information it lets drop that the intended length of the chapter was not less than a hundred pages. Its actual length is a bare seven or eight, of which two or three are taken up by the "letter."

Although the chapter "On the Imagination" was never written, the substance of it was clearly present in Coleridge's mind and his constructive, or "dynamic," philosophy can be elicited from his other prose writings. This is possible, even if we limit ourselves to the published writings (Chapter xii of the *Biographia* already contains it in a highly condensed form); but much help is also to be found among the unpublished literary remains, which will someday be made available in the *Collected Coleridge* now in preparation under the able supervision of Professor Kathleen Coburn of the University of Toronto.

Meanwhile the premise on which his theory of imagination

[1] Ed. J. Shawcross (Oxford, 1907), I, 202.

is systematically based, and which has been as systematically ignored by all but one or two of his would-be interpreters, is firmly posited in the three long opening paragraphs of Chapter xiii. I draw attention to it, as will be seen, for a particular and limited purpose; but it would be well worth doing on general grounds. In the first place Coleridge's theory of poetic imagination does not make sense without it, though valiant attempts have been made to make it do so. And then there is the fact that he was so much more than a literary critic. The influence of his theological thought (through F. D. Maurice, for instance, in England, and Horace Bushnell in America, but still more through numberless unidentified channels) was far deeper and more lasting than is commonly realized.

Lastly, if his premises are supportable (and, if they are not, his theory of imagination falls with them), much that he had to say is relevant today in the domain of philosophy, including the philosophy of science.

Now the first word in Chapter xiii is the name of the philosopher Descartes and the chapter goes on at once to state Coleridge's premise as an *alternative* to that on which the Cartesian philosophy is based. Descartes had said: "Give me matter and motion and I will construct you the universe." Coleridge substitutes for matter and motion, "two contrary forces, the one of which tends to expand infinitely, while the other strives to apprehend or *find* itself in this infinity." And he adds that the two forces are forces "of one power," that they "counteract" each other, and that they are "both alike infinite and both alike indestructible."

Moreover these two "forces" differ sharply from the Cartesian matter and motion in this: that they are operative both "in the living principle and in the process of our self-consciousness." Matter and motion — and this applies no less to whatever is substituted for them in contemporary physics — are phenomena. They are exclusive to the world of *res extensa* (extended substance) — whereas the "two forces of one power" are prephenomenal. If it is asked how, then, we can know anything about them, the answer lies in the fact that although they underlie the phenomenal world and constitute its ultimate being, they are also to be found "in the process of our own self-consciousness."

This is not primarily a philosophical essay and I make no attempt in it to meet the various objections that may be raised at this point,[2] beyond surmising that they are likely to be based

[2] Still less to enter into the academic question of Coleridge's "originality"

on the Cartesian dichotomy between matter and mind, which Coleridge expressly repudiated, and on the tacit assumption that that is absolute. I concede at the outset that it is wildly impossible to fit a non-Cartesian psychology into a Cartesian cosmos, and remain chiefly concerned with the relation which Coleridge adumbrated as subsisting between the two forces, and to which he gave the name of "polarity."

Now the word polarity is fairly frequently used in our time without much understanding of what it really signifies. We probably owe to Coleridge himself its adoption into the general vocabulary[3] within such realms as psychology and literary criticism. According to him, polarity is a "law"; it is a law that reigns through all nature; in it the duality of the opposite forces is the *manifestation* of a prior unity; and that unity is a "power." It is a "productive" unity. It is not, that is to say, any abstract "principle" of unity or of identity. Moreover, most of the much that has been written in the last few decades concerning the "reconciliation of opposites" in literature, and often with express reference to Coleridge as its putative father, betrays a lamentable failure to understand what "opposites" and their "reconciliation" actually signified in Coleridge's vocabulary. There is a world of difference, for example, between Coleridge's polarity and those "gorgeous ballets of dialectical opposition, combination and fruition,"[4] to which we have been treated not only by literary critics theorizing about poetry, but also by psychologists, and more lately by theologians seeking to "reconcile" the sacred and the profane.

Polarity is dynamic, not abstract. Where logical opposites are merely contradictory, polar opposites are generative of each other — and together generative of new product. They are thus agents of genuine transformation, as distinct from a Democritan rearrangement of existent entities. The two forces do not rearrange entities, they bring them into being in the first place. Polar opposites exist by virtue of each other *as well as* at the expense of each other; "each is that which it is called, relatively, by predominance of the one character or

and adjudicate on the extent to which his insight may have been derived from, or shared with, Heraclitus, Giordano Bruno, Jacob Boehme, Kant, Hegel, Schelling and other claimants. The reader may refer to the Introduction to Shawcross's two-volume edition of the *Biographia Literaria* and to J. A. Appleyard's *Coleridge's Philosophy of Literature* (Cambridge, Mass., 1965).

[3] See the *New English Dictionary.*

[4] With acknowledgments to Richard Foster, writing on R. P. Blackmur in *The New Romantics* (Bloomington, Ind., 1962), p. 100.

quality, not by the absolute exclusion of the other."[5] Moreover each quality is present *in* the other. We can and must distinguish, but there is no possibility of *dividing* them.

When one has said all this, how much of use has one succeeded in conveying? The point is, has the imagination grasped it? For nothing else can do so. What other helps then can we find for the imagination? We can try a simile; we can picture, for instance, two nations at total war, each with a network of spies and an effective resistance movement distributed throughout the other's territory — and each with a secret underground passage opening into the citadel in the heart of its enemy's territory. Or we can turn aside from simile and go direct to nature, leading the mind into the invisible process by letting the mind's eye rest (and I mean *rest*) on the visible product evinced by the process. (This is what we must in fact have done before we can meaningfully use such words as "tendency.") With this aim in view we can look, for example, at the further meaning for "polarity" given by the *New English Dictionary* in its 1926 Supplement:

> The tendency observed in some animals of a severed head-piece to develop a tail or of a severed tail-piece to develop a head; a similar tendency in parts of plants.

For many, a better way still will be to think of the nature of metaphorical language; to see how many of the characteristics of polarity enumerated in the previous paragraph can be applied to the two parts of a poetic metaphor —"tensive" utterance, as Professor Philip Wheelwright has well called it — by contrast with the "steno-language" of strictly logical discourse.[6] Yet, when all is said, in order to grasp the nature of polarity we are called on not to think about imagination but to use it. Indeed, it is my contention that the apprehension of polarity is *the* basic act of imagination, that it is the fundament of imaginative thinking, in the same way that the apprehension of identity is the fundament of discursive thought. And the two ways of thinking, with their two bases, are parallel, not serial; or rather they are themselves polarically "counter." The one cannot be reduced to the other.

In a word, where logical contradictories, like solid objects in space, *exclude* one another, polar opposites *contain*, and, in doing so, enhance, one another. Moreover this mode of duality

[5] *Church and State*, Ch. iii, in *The Complete Works of Samuel Taylor Coleridge*, ed. W. G. T. Shedd (New York, 1884), VI, 46. The title *Works* in succeeding notes refers to this edition.

[6] In *The Burning Fountain* (Bloomington, Ind., 1954) and elsewhere.

— concrete in place of abstract — is always at the same time a trinity. A "paradox" is a bare, logical abstraction; but the "tension" between two concrete and energetic opposites is a process and, as such, is itself a third reality. For nature, indeed, it is the paramount reality, because it is this process of energetic interpenetration that underlies the sense world as a whole. In his *Hints towards a more Comprehensive Theory of Life* (usually called the *Theory of Life*)[7] Coleridge developed this in some detail in its relation to the science of biology and it is there, incidentally, that we find the fullest exposition of the concept of polarity itself. Here however the point is that that concept, or rather that "imagination," was integral to his thinking on every topic — and there were many — on which he attempted to throw light. So much so, that, in his Notebooks and often in his private correspondence, he habitually employed the symbol ")-(," instead of writing out in full some such phrase as "is polarically related to" or "is the polar opposite of"— just as more conventional thinkers will substitute "=" for "is equal to" or "is identical with."

As far as his philosophy, with its correlative psychology, is concerned, we need not go beyond the *Biographia Literaria* if we are prepared to read it (and particularly Chapter xii) intensively; though the task is certainly made easier if we supplement from parts of *The Friend* and the *Aids to Reflection.*[8] But Coleridge's theological insight, though it is even more dimly surmised in most quarters, is, I believe, at least not *less* important than his philosophy, and perhaps especially so in our own time. For this we can turn to such works as *Aids to Reflection, Church and State,* the *Statesman's Manual* and *Confessions of an Inquiring Spirit.*[9]

The Cartesian cosmology, with *its* correlative psychology, has been found to be specifically opaque to any but the most abstract and subjective Christian theology. It is opaque, for example, to the concept of sacrament; and it is opaque ("the ghost in the machine") to the concept of the Incarnation, because it is opaque to *any* concept of incarnation. And it is both these things because it is opaque to the concept of a triune God. It may be noticed in this connection that the theologians of the "Death of God" school, which is, I suppose, the apotheosis — or rather the "ec-theosis"— of all theology in an *either : or* strait waistcoat, seem never to have heard of the Trinity. Or,

[7] *Works,* I, 373ff.
[8] *Works,* II; I, 117-366.
[9] *Works,* I, 117-366; VI, 29-116; I, 419-451; V, 576-623.

if they have heard of it, they write it off in a sentence as an incomprehensible, because self-contradictory, dogma.

This was not how St. Augustine saw it, though he seems to have been as good at spotting a contradiction in terms as any modern professor that I at least am acquainted with. On the contrary, in his book *On the Trinity* we are led to perceive tri-unity, not only in heaven, but also on earth, where it is basic to the structure and function of human consciousness.[10] For him it was not a question of being unable to comprehend tri-unity, but of being unable to comprehend anything without it.

So it was with Coleridge. For him the doctrine of the Trinity was "the one substantive truth, which is the form, manner, and involvement of all truths."[11] Again "... There neither is, nor can be, any religion, any reason, but what is, or is an expansion of the truth of the Trinity.... As soon as I discovered that these doctrines were not only consistent with reason, but themselves very reason, I returned at once to the literal interpretation of the Scriptures, and to the Faith."[12] He praises the seventeenth-century theologian Richard Baxter for having discovered a century before Kant the need to think in terms of Trichotomy rather than Dichotomy;[13] and he was particularly fond of quoting Baxter's remark that "The Divine Trinity in Unity hath expressed itself in the whole frame of Nature and Morality."

But then Coleridge had accustomed himself to perceive the working of tri-unity throughout the whole of life — for instance, in "the germinal power of every seed."[14] Here too, underlying the series of mensurable events perceptible to the

[10] See, for instance, Book XI, Ch. xi.

[11] Quoted by Sara Coleridge in her *Note* to *Confessions of an Inquiring Spirit* (London, 1849).

[12] *Literary Remains*, in *Works*, V, 404-5.

[13] An element in the Kantian system, which is a good deal overlooked. On Baxter see *Works*, V, 355. Coleridge himself once contrasted the two kinds of logic as follows. In the logic of dichotomy, "two terms in manifest correspondence to each other are yet opposed as contraries, without any middle term; the consequence of which is, that one of the two becomes a mere negation of the other..."; whereas in the logic of trichotomy (which he also called "polar logic") "we seek first for the Unity, as the only source of Reality, and then for the two opposite yet correspondent forms, by which it manifests itself — For it is an axiom of universal application that 'Manifestatio non datur nisi per Alterum'" (there is no manifestation except through another). Marginal Note to Swedenborg's *De Infinito et Causa Finali Creationis;* MS in the possession of Victoria College, University of Toronto, Coleridge Collection, MS. B. T. 21, fol. 10 (note to pp. 264, 265).

[14] *Aids to Reflection,* in *Works,* I, 219.

senses, and evincing them, there is an "ipseity" that begets its own "alterity" and a process ("life") that proceeds from that begetting. A mind already accustomed to the contemplation of two contrary forces, "the one of which tends to expand infinitely, while the other strives to apprehend or *find* itself in this infinity," and both of which cohere in an antecedent unity, will not automatically cease to function when confronted by the kind of language in which the Church Fathers — or any religious writer who lived before the scientific revolution — were wont to express their thoughts. Rather it will divine the truth in an unaccustomed dress and then seek to reclothe it in the language of today.

## II

The experience of oneself over against that which is not oneself is a *sine qua non* of human consciousness. But there are three different ways in which that experience is undergone. There is firstly the experience of myself here, and the world, or "nature," out there. This is given to or thrust on us without any effort on our part. Secondly, there is the experience of myself on the one hand in the midst of my fellow men on the other. This is also normally "given," though it is avoidable by deliberate choice, or a series of deliberate choices, on our part. We may live the life of a hermit, or we may acquire the habit of treating our fellow men as mere objects, and thus as mere parts of "nature." Of a third way in which this second experience may be lost something will shortly be said. Lastly there is the experience of the self as other than the creator of the self and the ground of its being, that is, the experience of the self over against God. This may, by misfortune, never be realized and in our time is easily avoided.

All these three ways of experiencing selfhood have been found to be equivocal, or (to use the vogue-word) "paradoxical," inasmuch as the separateness from its opposite (not-self) on which selfhood depends is also felt, first as desolation, and then as threatened extinction. We cannot fully experience the separateness without at the same time longing to overcome it. It grows more and more obvious that the unspoken dilemma dimly underlying our contemporary malaise runs something like this: Either I am my separate, excluded self or I am not. If and so far as I am not, then I am another (whether that other is nature, or instinct, or my unconscious, or my fellow man, or Being generally). The sound "I" comes out of this mouth, but it is a lie, for something or somebody else is pulling the strings.

But if I *am,* up to the hilt, only my separate excluded self; if I experience *everything* as other and external to me, then I am nothing — a mere null-point of awareness, which I shall not even be able to maintain, because there is no "I" to do the maintaining.

Therefore, it seems to me to be worthwhile pointing out that it was Coleridge's lifelong conviction as a philosopher and (as he hoped) his message to posterity that none of the three ways of experiencing selfhood can in fact be comprehended without the concept — or rather, as I have said, the "imagination"— of tri-unity. As a philosopher he discovered, or rediscovered, for himself the remedy for a disease that has become even more chronic in our time than it was in his — in spite, or perhaps even *because,* of the fact that in his life as a poet he himself suffered so acutely from that very disease.

Of the three relations between self and not-self we have been considering, the one with which Romantic poetry is primarily concerned is the relation to nature. And, speaking as a poet, Coleridge had a name he frequently used for one extremity (we may call it the negative one) of that equivocal relation to nature, which is the predicament of modern Western man. He called it "joy."

*Joy, Lady! is the spirit and the power,*
*Which, wedding Nature to us, gives in dower*
*A new Earth and new Heaven,*
*Undreamt of by the sensual and the proud —*
*Joy is the sweet voice, Joy the luminous cloud —*
*We in ourselves rejoice!*
*And thence flows all that charms or ear or sight,*
*All melodies the echo of that voice,*
*All colours a suffusion of that light.*

The "message," and to a considerable extent the language, of these well-known lines from the *Ode to Dejection* are frequently echoed in his letters to his friends, especially in the opening years of the nineteenth century. Joy was that sense of blissful union with the being of nature which, in his case at least, was so swiftly followed by "the journey homeward to habitual self."[15]

In his interesting and illuminating Essay " 'Rasselas', Romanticism and the Nature of Happiness"[16] Professor John Law-

[15] Lawlor (see note 16), I, 252, 253 and 264; a line sometimes quoted by C. S. Lewis from Keats's *Endymion* (II, 276).

[16] *Friendship's Garland: Essays presented to Mario Praz on his seventieth birthday,* ed. Vittorio Gabrieli. Storia e Letteratura, 106-7 (Rome, 1966), I, 243-270.

lor points up the similarity between this joy of which Coleridge wrote as a poet, and which he valued so desperately, and the "joy" that is so essential an ingredient in the Christian philosophy of that little group of English writers who are sometimes referred to as "romantic theologians," and especially of their best-known representative, C. S. Lewis. It may be recalled that Lewis's autobiographical account of his conversion to Christianity bears the title *Surprised by Joy.* In that book he has given us an analytical as well as a biographical account of what he means by joy, as in his much earlier *The Pilgrim's Regress* he had combined the analytical with an imaginative or symbolic approach to the same concept. The longing for a "paradisal" reunion with the Absolute, or with the spirit informing the life of both man and nature, is, he contends, native to the human spirit and is one that embodies itself in symbols at all levels (including of course the sexual one). It is a crucial element in man's faculty of imagination, and it is by its nature unattainable — except at the price of a pantheistic surrender of the very existence of the individual spirit. The longing was a basic element, throughout his life, in the whole man, C. S. Lewis, and forms the link between his early poems and the matured Christian philosophy of his final years.[17] The solution of the irreconcilable antagonism implicit in this longing, without which we are less than men, but which we can only satisfy by ceasing to be men — or (to put it another way) the right way to "handle" a desire by its nature unattainable — lies (so Lewis gradually discovered for himself) in taking a further step. The further step consists in discovering for oneself that the very presence of the desire is its own fulfillment; that "what we really wanted" all the time was not any one of the many successive objects to which the desire deludes us by appearing to point — but the desire itself, or rather an essential *quality* in it. Symbols are symbols of each other, as well as of that which both symbols embody; and the longing for reunion with nature, though it is archetypal to most other longings, is itself only a kind of symbol for the ultimate archetype, which is precisely that quality. It is only when we experience that indefinable quality, as and for itself, that we experience what Lewis called joy.

Lawlor treats this as a kind of dialectical extension from

[17] See, for instance, several of the poems in *Spirits in Bondage* (London, 1919) (published under the pseudonym Clive Hamilton) and the conclusion of *The Queen of Drum* written a few years later and published posthumously in *Narrative Poems* (London, 1969).

the "romantic agony" of the felt exclusion from nature (that exclusion being, at the same time, the very thing that made romanticism possible at all). And it is true, I think, that if the Romantics as a whole, and Coleridge in particular, not merely discovered, but had somehow to *live* the discovery of the inevitableness of the exclusion, so the romantic theologians, and Lewis in particular, have lived the discovery of this particular way of dealing with (for one cannot quite say "transcending") those irreconcilable opposites. Lewis himself once called it "the dialectic of Desire."[18]

There is of course another way of dealing with irreconcilable opposition, and particularly the irreconcilable opposition between man at one with nature and man cut off from nature; a way with which we are much more familiar. It consists in placing the two opposites side by side, treating them as contradictories, and contemplating the result with ironical detachment. It would probably be going too far to say that this other way "originated" with T. S. Eliot, though it was certainly popularized or disseminated by his style in poetry and was formulated in his critical theory of the "dissociation of sensibility." It was well argued for by Cleanth Brooks in his *Modern Poetry and the Tradition* and need not here be pursued further.

One can say, of both these ways, that they are based on a sharp awareness of the principle of logical contradiction. When the understanding is faced with two propositions that contradict each other, that is its *ne plus ultra* and (however it may be for the *feelings*) human thinking has reached its all-time terminus. Our understanding tells us, in no uncertain terms, that they cannot both be true, though one or the other may be. It is *either : or.*

This sharp apprehension of *either : or* as the *terminus ad quem* of the human mind began with Greek philosophy and culminated in the seventeenth century in the great Cartesian *either : or* between matter and mind — *res extensa* and *res cogitans* — on which the whole of modern science is implicitly based. We have an example of it in Professor I. A. Richards' thoughtful and original treatment of Coleridge in his *Coleridge on Imagination.*[19] Professor Richards is among the small number of critics who have realized that it is impossible to expound Coleridge's doctrine of imagination without coming to grips

[18] *The Pilgrim's Regress* (London, 1943), p. 10 (quoted in Lawlor, p. 263).

[19] (London, 1962).

with his psychology of the reciprocal relation between subject and object; and he takes pains to set this out in terms as clear and simple as possible, impressing on the reader the value of Coleridge's terminology as well as his preciseness in the use of it. At the same time however he believes he can coolly amputate Coleridge's philosophy from his psychology. A man's philosophy of the relation between subject and object will depend (says Richards in effect) on his view of the relation between man and nature. If he is an idealist, his philosophical interpretation of Coleridge's psychology will accord with Coleridge's own; if he is a materialist or a behaviorist, it will be exactly the opposite, conceding to the object the same ultimate priority that the idealist concedes to the subject. He does not pronounce judgment between the two, though he does, with a view to presenting the psychology itself with the maximum of impartiality, inform the reader that he himself is of the latter persuasion. It is, to my mind, this detached sympathy that gives this particular book on Coleridge its unique value.

But of course, it presents the reader with yet another *either : or*. And in view of this it is not surprising to find that, with all its penetration and its many solid merits, this presentation of Coleridge's psychology of imagination has one very grave defect. It takes no account of, in fact it hardly mentions, the concept that was central to all Coleridge's thought, whether about man or nature, about psychology or science, or about the activity of imagination; and that is the concept of a polarity between two opponent energies. Yet, if I am right, this is crucial, not only for the purpose of understanding Coleridge's system, or "dynamic philosophy," as a whole, but also for grasping his psychology of imagination. I have called it a "concept"; but it is not a concept in the ordinary sense of the word. For concepts themselves are the product of the *either : or* psychology; whereas the mere apprehension of polarity, the meaningfulness of the word itself, demands an act of imagination. Indeed it demands *the* primary act of imagination; and, as such, the philosophy of it was Coleridge's way out of the great *either : or* with which contemporary humanity is confronted; no less than the philosophy of "joy," or something like it, is the way out for "romantic theology," and the philosophy — or nonphilosophy — of irony has been the way out for postromantic literature and art as a whole.

In speaking of a "way out" I mean of course a way out for the mind as well as for the heart. We may see it as a stroke of destiny — a hard and heavy one, as they often are —

which denied to Coleridge, when once the *annus mirabilis* of 1799 was over, that way out for the heart (the Wordsworthian way) with which he felt himself most in tune, since it was this above all that led to his spending so much of the rest of his life in developing a way out for the mind. But, even from the mind's point of view, the question may arise whether a satisfactory solution of the relation between man and nature is all that important; or at least whether it is all that important in the context of religion, "romantic" or otherwise. Of its *theological* significance I endeavored to say something in Section I; but it is mainly in its bearing on the relation between man and nature, as such, that I have so far been considering the implications of an *either : or* philosophy and the exclusively *either : or* psychology that is inevitably based on it. Have these the same, or any particular, significance for the third of the three basic relations that constitute man's life on earth: his relation to his fellow man?

To this question I believe the answer is Yes. Let us take, for example, a recent work on psychiatry, the existential psychologist R. D. Laing's *The Divided Self*,[20] and particularly the chapter entitled "Ontological Insecurity." "A man who says that men are machines," he demurely remarks in his Preface, "may be a great scientist. A man who says he *is* a machine is 'depersonalized' in psychiatric jargon." This experience of depersonalization, and consequently of disintegration, is the outstanding feature of psychosis, especially in its prevalent modern form of schizophrenia; and Laing makes it his task to give the best account he can of it at a time when "the discovery of 'the logical form through which the unity of the personal can be coherently conceived' is still a task for the future" (p. 23).[21]

When two sane persons meet, "there is a reciprocal recognition of each other's identity"; and it is really on that reciprocity that our humanity depends. Yet it is just that reciprocity of which the schizophrene, under the despotism of an *either : or* approach to reality, is incapable:

> ...Instead of the polarities of separateness and relatedness based on individual autonomy, there is the antithesis between complete loss of being by absorption into the other person (engulfment) and complete aloneness (isolation). There is no safe third possibility of a dialectical

[20] [Baltimore, 1965 (first published in 1960)].

[21] Laing quotes from J. Macmurray's *The Self as Agent* both the formulation included above and the following observation: "We should expect that the emergence of a scientific psychology would be paralleled by a transition from an organic to a personal... conception of unity."

relation between two persons, both sure of their own ground and, on this very basis, able to "lose themselves" in each other.[22]

Earlier in the book Laing has quoted with approval the existential formula of man's *being-in-the-world,* and it is within this parameter that he presents his case for a kind of "built-in" psychosis, afflicting contemporary man as a whole and of which the schizophrene is only an extreme instance. I find it convincing; and it will be noted that "world" here means, not the world of nature, but the world of one's fellow men.

In a wider context do we not observe the same tendency — a tendency to assume that the antithesis between "isolation" and "engulfment" is irreconcilable, and even to construct systems upon that assumption? An example here would be the evolutionary sociology of Marshall McLuhan, supported by a wealth of acute observation and analysis and presenting individual man with the alternatives of the isolation that arises from "cool" media of communication, and an engulfment in a kind of tribal or neotribal mass-existence, which their supersession by the "hot" media is to bring upon us.

Again, at a more metaphysical level, in the contemporary tendency of the more advanced among Western thinkers to rebound the whole way into typically Oriental conceptions of the exclusively superindividual unity, not only of being itself, but of anything that can be dignified by the name of "reality," I see the same assumption that the major antitheses are irreconcilable, and that *individual* being must *either* amount to a deplorable illusion because it is "isolated" from universal being *or* must be "engulfed" in universal being and disappear altogether. Coleridge, as has perhaps become apparent, would have agreed that this must be man's predicament — if God were only God the Father.

In other words, if (as I believe) it is just those most alert today to the signs of the times, or to the requirements of evolution, who are also most keenly aware of a kind of arbitrary and limiting parochialism in the Aristotelian and Cartesian *either : or;* if it is just these thinkers who are inclined to treat that whole way of thinking as a historical interlude rather than as a psychological absolute for all time; if it is just these pioneers in the domains of literature, psychology, theology and even science who bravely maintain that there are antitheses apparently irreconcilable, which must nevertheless be reconciled, opposites that must be dealt with, not by clash-

[22] Laing, p. 44.

ing them and then exercising our option, but by living out the tension between them, yet there is one point at which these thinkers do not measure up to their own insight.

For there is *one* pair of opposites, and that the most important of all, that they do still treat as contradictory and irreconcilable. And that is their own antithesis between the one way of thinking and the other; namely between the *either : or* syndrome *itself,* and the alternative to it with which they present us — whether that alternative is put forward as a desideratum, as in the case of Heidegger's "silence," or (with McLuhan) as a next development in social evolution, which is coming on us whether we like it or not. Just here, where the concept, or rather the active imagination, of polarity is most desperately needed, it is allowed to drop out of sight. Just here, in my submission, in spite of their highly contemporary flair, these pioneers have not yet caught up with Coleridge.

For Coleridge, the basic polarity between two forces or energies, one of which strives to apprehend or *find* itself, while the other tends to expand infinitely, is not only the source of nature's life — both her visible life at any moment and her evolutionary life as the biological tendency to individuation; it is also the source of man's individual consciousness. Indeed it is the one because it is, and by being, the other. But, at this latter level, it reappears as a *psychological* polarity; and the two forces are now recognizable as, on the one hand, the *either : or* way of thinking, to which we owe our separate existence (though not our being) as individuals — the way that Coleridge labelled "understanding"— and, on the other hand, the undifferentiated and undifferentiating (and therefore unconscious) mental activity that stems from "Reason." Because they are inseparable, the two are not therefore indistinguishable; indeed to be distinguishable without being separable is the very hallmark of the relation of polarity.

One of the distinctions Coleridge himself drew between understanding and Reason was to point out that the mental activity that is Reason is no less an act of will than it is an act of thought. And here the function of understanding is to convert the act of Will into acts of individual wills. Thus, the *source* of individual human self-consciousness is the "productive unity" of this Willing-thinking Power, operating through the "separative projection," which leads to its polarization into two contrary forces. And this genetic process is observable, not only phylogenetically in the evolution of the race, but ontogenetically also in the case of every child growing up and learning to speak. In either case there must be the "repetition in the finite mind" of the infinite I AM, in order for self-consciousness to come about. In other words, a human being cannot be really self-conscious without himself exercising "separative projection"; that is to say, without doing the very thing Laing's schizophrenes have failed to do. Laing concerns himself with insanity as involving "depersonalization," that is, the loss of consciousness of a single self. In doing so, he affirms that sanity depends on "a third possibility of a dialectical relation between two persons, both sure of their own ground and, on this very basis, able to 'lose themselves' in each other." Coleridge in his *Essay on Faith* observes that "the equation of Thou with I, by means of a free act, negativing the sameness in order to establish the equality, is the definition of conscience."[23] On the one hand, we must objectify our fellow man (for otherwise we cannot be separate from him, and he is not a "fellow" at all), and this we can only do by bringing to bear on him the whole syndrome of *either : or* thoughts and perceptions. But on the other hand we must recognize that he is not merely an object, but also a subject like ourselves. And this we can really only do by repeating the divine act of "separative projection," which in human beings is imagination. This we can only do by "a repetition in the finite mind of the eternal act of creation." Thus, the further step from primary to secondary imagination is, to say the least of it, not *less* important here than in the making of poetry. For it is only so that we can come to acknowledge, not merely another person but an autonomous independent spirit of equal status and equal value with ourselves. Moral imagination is the dialectic, or rather the polarity, of love. Furthermore it is only through moral imagination that we can become fully aware even of *ourselves* as subjects. By preserving their separate existence, and at the same time exercising mutual respect, human beings offer to one another the gift of the possibility of self-consciousness; and it is in this sense that consciousness and conscience are inextricably one. For "as without a Thou there can be no You, so without a You no They, These, or Those; and as all these conjointly form the materials and subjects of consciousness, and the conditions of experience, it is evident that the conscience is the root of all consciousness."[24]

Today therefore, more than a hundred and thirty years after Coleridge's death, if I am to look for a thinker whom I can really describe as "contemporary," I must look for one

[23] *Literary Remains,* in *Works,* V, 560.
[24] *Ibid.*

who has not merely caught up with Coleridge in this matter of the two forces, but gone beyond him. There are plenty who tell me that *either : or* is not the last word; that the individual soul is amputated by it both from the world of nature and from the world of its fellow men; that there must be a silent world of "primordial discourse," prior to all human language, and thus the source from which language springs, prior also to the world of natural objects and (through language) the source of that also. But they also tell me that that world and the one I live in are incommensurate, and that the "primordial discourse" in which we originated is wholly incommunicable.

The truly contemporary thinker for whom I must look will be the one who has found that this antithesis, too, is bridgeable, that this major pair of irreconcilables is in fact reconcilable if we are prepared to pursue further, with the imagination-based thinking that alone is capable of grasping them, those two prephenomenal forces, and the relation between them, to which Coleridge pointed again and again, and whose productive operations he himself had at least begun to study *in detail,* alike in his philosophy of nature and in his philosophy of man. It will not signify what names he chooses to apply to them, whether "etheric" and "astral," or some other two. (Coleridge himself never got as far as naming his two forces; he sometimes characterized them as negative and positive, sometimes as centrifugal and centripetal, and sometimes otherwise.) What will matter is that he should have a mind capable of familiarizing itself, and of working, with them; and then of communicating the results of his work in intelligible language. It is because I have found that capacity in Rudolf Steiner, and because I have not so far found it elsewhere, that I am bound to regard his as the one fundamentally "contemporary" mind that the first two-thirds of the twentieth century has produced.

I have sometimes wondered whether it might have been otherwise in England if, for example, the "romantic theologians," or some of them, had chosen to explore the path Coleridge opened up for the English-speaking world; if they had sought a reconciliation between reason and imagination, not only in the religious, or semireligious, experience of "joy" as "the dialectic of Desire," but also by penetrating inward to the point at which logic itself becomes "polar logic" and the two are actually one. I have wondered if Lewis might have been led to mitigate his occasionally Talmudic emphasis on the divine transcendence, and if Charles Williams' brilliantly mystical doctrine of "co-inherence" might have gained something in depth and his account of the Descent of the Dove have lost something of tautness, something a little strained, if either of them had pondered the mystery of "separative projection" as it is expounded in the *Theory of Life*, the *Essay on Faith* and elsewhere sporadically throughout Coleridge's writings.

What seems certain is that, had they done so, they could hardly have developed the particular quality, unique, valuable, irreplaceable (as all positive qualities are irreplaceably valuable in a world we would have as rich as possible) that they did in fact develop.

> In the nineteenth century [concludes Professor Lawlor] the former rebels embrace authority as revealed religion. But if I am right it is not until the middle twentieth century that a working reconciliation is offered not simply between mythology and Christian story, not merely between the ethics of duty—"the bare willing obedience"—and the ethics of virtue, but between reason (mistakenly thought to be the enemy of both romanticism and revealed religion) and the nature of intense awareness, when that awareness is understood neither as the "luscious falsehood" of idle delusion nor as the sole entry upon ultimate reality. . . .[25]

Well, I do not think he *is* quite right at this point. Nor do I think he is right when he maintains, a page or two earlier, that "in Coleridge's . . . acceptance of Christianity . . . the long quarrel between reason and romanticism is not made up." I have tried to make it clear that, in my view, there is another "way out" of the apparent contradiction between understanding and imagination, and consequently between an obedient and a creative virtue, and that Coleridge, for one, had found that way. I think, too, as I have always thought and have from time to time sought in various ways to demonstrate, that it is a way forward that will have to be ensued if the territory won for the human spirit by the Romantic Movement is ever to be consolidated and occupied. But, whether I am right or wrong about this, it was not the way that was found, or perhaps even sought, by the Romantic Theologians. Professor Lawlor has earned our gratitude by drawing our attention to the alternative way on from romanticism, which these writers discovered and hewed out for themselves; and amid all the riches that we have received from them, it is to this discovery that we owe the peculiar quality of combatant gaiety and astringent sweetness that some of us admire and love so well in their work.

[25] Lawlor, pp. 269-270.

# Mimesis and Incarnation

THOMAS HOWARD

There has, perhaps, never been an epoch in which the hiatus between serious artistic activity and common taste has been wider. What appears in the galleries and in the journals of poetry is addressed frequently to the cognoscenti, and leaves the public murmuring confusedly. Historically, this was not the case. Much of what we now call "great art" appeared in response to a direct commission from a patron or church, or, in the case of epic poetry, was addressed to a listening audience of mostly uneducated people. The assumption was that everyone would understand what was being offered. There were not two worlds — the one of the artists and the few, and the other of the masses. Even into the eighteenth and nineteenth centuries, the novels and poetry that are now read only in graduate studies were written for anyone who cared to buy a book.

The cleavage between artist and public is so total now, however, that it is doubtful whether the name of a single serious painter or poet is familiar in at all the same sense as are the names of popular entertainers. This, of course, raises the question of blame: has the public rejected the artist, or the artist the public?

This is a question that cannot be answered one way or the other, since both answers are right. Something can be said, however, about the present state of affairs. It is worth asking whence it arose and what sort of criticism is possible in the light of historic notions concerning the office of the artist and the nature of his world.

---

Thomas Howard is Assistant Professor of English at Gordon College. He holds the B.A. from Wheaton College (1957), the M.A. from the University of Illinois (1965), and the Ph.D. from New York University (1970). He is the author of *Christ the Tiger* and *An Antique Drum.*

The public is understandably bewildered when it encounters soup tins, ropes, burlap, crumpled auto parts, plaster hamburgers, flags, and comics in the art museums, and is told by the critics that it ought to be impressed and moved. The popular response is, often enough, disgust, fear, embarrassment, or blankness.

The rationale offered by its practitioners for much of current art may itself follow various lines of thought. There is the dogmatic nonhumanism of Ad Reinhardt, for example, who insisted on the entire independence of the artistic endeavor, and disallowed most of the canons of nonrepresentational as well as representational art. The "op" artists employ their stripes, checkerboards, swirls of color, and dots with a rigor and exactitude second to none in the history of art, seeking not so much for images to be looked *at* as for forms that will arouse perceptual responses. The idea is to engage the viewer in an act that will, it is hoped, increase his awareness of his visual capacities, and hence contribute to that great end of all high art, the heightening of consciousness.

Other artists, angrily or happily aware of the metamorphosis of American life into a vast travelogue of cola billboards, parking meters, ribbons of macadam, and gleaming formica-and-steel drive-ins, urge that, since this is the stuff of our existence, this is to be the stuff of the mimetic arts. Insofar as the Greek vision involved the glory of the human form, that is what one sees in the iconography of the epoch; insofar as the medieval involved annunciations and pietàs, that is what is figured; insofar as ours involves hamburgers, that is what we shall have. The artist is the seer who gives its own existence back to his age, transfigured for contemplation. Traditionally, the images in which he gives that existence back to the world are those that speak of the eternal, whether that be a religious eternity as in the Christian vision, or a nonpersonalistic eternity of pure form as in post-Enlightenment vision. Given the modern world, say these artists, we will give you your bibelots, which speak of nothing.

The "primary structuralists," whose work takes the shape of immense rhomboids, cubes, and hexahedrons, are seeking a nonillusive form. Since, in their view, the world is neither meaningful *nor* absurd ("It simply is," says Alain Robbe-Grillet[1]), the effort is to create solid, immediate objects that are nothing but what they are. They are "presences," it is urged, without meaning or referent.

[1] As quoted in "The Shape of Art for Some Time to Come: Primary Structures," *Life*, LXIII, iv (July 28, 1967), 44A.

It may help us see what is occurring in contemporary painting and sculpture if we inquire into the notions from which the mimetic activity of the last one hundred years derives.

Historically, it was felt that there is an onus of sublime affirmation laid upon high art. That is, that the office of the poet and artist is to "see life steadily and see it whole," in all of its beauty, ambiguity, and horror, and to find an imagery that not only figures that life truly, but takes the stuff of that life and transfigures it into forms that speak of ultimacy.

It is, perhaps, in the notion of sublimity that the discontinuity occurs between the art of earlier epochs and that which has arisen in the last century. Art traditionally proceeded on the assumption that there is an equation between Beauty and Truth, and had for its aim the figuring of Beauty in images faithful to human experience. In the nineteenth century this aim was forsworn in the name of Reality. There had been, in the wake of postmedieval methods of describing the world, a gradual dissolution of confidence in myths and other ideas that were not verifiable according to the terms of the new methodology.[2] Sibyls, prophets, angels, priests — everyone who tried to bring tidings from outside to the human situation — had been discredited. The field for investigation and for imagination was to be the one at hand. Since we see no titans, fauns, heroes, devils, or archangels at play there, we must assume, until they appear in our lenses, that there are none. Thus a positivistic view, and thus the *Zeitgeist* that ensued.

Since we are to scrutinize our world dispassionately, we will posit Reality in our own terms as our starting point, and leave the erstwhile notion of Beauty to fend for itself. If it emerges from our experience, *tant mieux;* if not, *tant pis.* We will not conjure it from a realm about which nobody knows anything. The point was that the sublime is a notion referring to nothing that we can verify in our terms, and hence is inappropriate as a referent for modern imagery.

The man who announced the emancipation of painting from anachronistic notions of beauty and sublimity was Gustave Courbet. Reality is to be the province of the artist from here on, he declared. At about the same time, Whistler announced his attempt to "divest the picture from any outside sort of interest," in answer to Ruskin's charge that he had "flung a pot of paint in the public's face."

[2] See, in this connection, Walter J. Ong, S. J., *Ramus, Method, and the Decay of Dialogue* (Cambridge, Mass., 1958), and Owen Barfield, *Saving the Appearances* (London, 1957).

Proceeding from Courbet, Edouard Manet focussed attention on the medium itself. In his view, the province of the artist is paint and canvas, not what they "stand for." His "Fifer" aroused dismay when it appeared, for it was clear that the artist had made no attempt to subject his paint to the demands of three-dimensional illusion: on the contrary, here was a brightly colored doll, in effect pasted flat onto the canvas. The focus was on the thing itself, not on the idea of a real little boy with a fife. Manet and those who followed him tried to get a scientifically exact record of the patterns of light that the retina registers, not the image we construct in our imagination in response to the phenomenon. They felt that artistic activity must become less and less servile to our figuration of the external world, and more and more independent. The work of Renoir, Cézanne, Monet, Pissarro, Seurat, and Degas evinces this effort.

In the twentieth century, painting went in three directions from this beginning: toward Expressionism, toward Abstractionism, and toward Fantasy.[3] Each exhibits its own special effort to discover significance in the world without reference to a discredited transcendence. Expressionism concerned itself with the emotional world, Abstractionism with questions of formal structure, and Fantasy with imagination, especially irregular imaginations and dreams.

The fathers of Expressionism were probably the "fauvists" (wild beasts), who aroused critical ire by appearing to do violence to human perception. Matisse, with his dancing curlicues, wanted to pursue the formal demands of design and color further than had been done up to that point. Rouault saw vividly the corruption of the world and figured this in his "ugly" portraits, hinting nonetheless at a residue of nobility in the human face. Kokoschka, Kirchner, and Beckmann assailed the public eye with images of vacuity and damnation.

Picasso, Braque, Leger, and Mondrian became occupied with formal questions, abstracting from the apparent world suggestions of geometric structure. Picasso scandalized everybody with his "Les Demoiselles d'Avignon," which represents the methodical and violent break-up of classical notions of beauty. This sort of thing (known as Cubism) attempts to find an alternative to the external world by discovering a "building material" of angular chunks of voids and spaces (one cannot help but recall some

[3] I owe this classification and much of my view of what was occurring in early twentieth-century painting to Professor H. W. Janson of New York University. See his *History of Art* (Englewood Cliffs, N. J., 1964), pp. 489-537. See also Alan Gowans, *The Restless Art* (Philadelphia, 1966).

of Cézanne's work here). Braque worked with scraps of this and that (wood, fabric, newsprint, tickets), calling attention to texture itself rather than to anything scenic perceived through the "window" of traditional painting.

Up to this point there was still a reference to the external world. Whether in terms of texture or form or image, the matrix from which the imagery arose was still perceptibly of that world, although it was sometimes in the form of disavowal. But Wassily Kandinsky made the disavowal final. He abandoned representation entirely, and sought to present emotion directly on the canvas. He sought to invest pure form and color with a spiritual meaning quite apart from the familiar world of appearance, so that not only is it impossible to discover any imagery in his composition: it is a mistaken effort. There is none. Likewise, Piet Mondrian set about to apprehend "pure reality" in wholly nonrepresentational modes. He saw this reality to consist in an equilibrium achieved in terms of a balance of forms, and his blocks of primary color divided by heavy ruled lines are among the most familiar and pleasing objects of twentieth-century painting.

The third major stream in the painting of this century is that of Fantasy. The doctrine involved is that imagination is a more significant source for mimetic imagery than is the external world. It posits the psychoanalytic idea of a commonalty of subconscious images in all of us, although in its handling of these images it frequently becomes entirely private, so that the viewer may bring his own interpretation to the painting. In the dream visions of De Chirico, in the fairy-tale childhood memories of Chagall, and the "language of signs" of Klee, this sort of thing is visible. It is visible in the Dadaism of Duchamp and others, who declared that, as of the Great War, *all* value systems had become otiose and who preached nonsense as the desideratum, and in the Surrealism of Dali and Miro, who sought to explore "pure psychic automatism," that is, thought free from the trammels of reason, morals, or aesthetics.

A drastic departure from even these iconoclastic activities occurred in the work of Jackson Pollock, who announced the centrality of the *act* of painting. He forswore the attempt to figure anything at all on the canvas (dreams, pure form, signs, nonsense), substituting for these traditional activities an interest in the dynamics of the paint itself. It is not insulting to him to say that he poured and dribbled and threw the paint: that is precisely what he did. He moved, perhaps, as far as it is possible to move from the view of the painter's office as having anything to do with human existence.

We have already noted some of the post-Pollock activity, and it is possible to see in some of it a return to the world of appearances, albeit a return that insists that things are what they are, period.

The mimetic activity of the last century derives, then, directly from doctrines that attended the intellectual activity of the era. The doctrines entail, again, a final confidence in an analytic and descriptive methodology as the sole approach to the world. There is a circular movement involved, in that the early decision to exclude from inquiry all realms not scrutable by the methodology is followed by the dogma that there *are* no such realms, since the method does not perceive them. Corollary to this is the view that it is not possible to discover any principle of *significance* in appearances, in that there is nothing else to be signalled.

There is an alternative view possible, of course. It is the view, once universal, that the data of our world are significant. The human consciousness has, from the beginning, figured its intimation of this in its mimetic activity. The method involved was synthetic and anagogical rather than analytic and descriptive. The notion was that one thing signals another, that there is a continuum of significance from the lowest worm to the highest seraph, that there is a form, an order, a harmony, a dance in which all participate. It tended to feel, in contrast to our own epoch which urges that nothing means anything, that everything means everything. It believed in the image as a mode — perhaps *the* mode — of articulating what it suspected. It is visible in the imagery of all times and all places. And it uttered itself variously in the doctrines of Aristotle, Caxton, Sidney, Shelley, Wordsworth, Arnold, and Emerson — that the poet has upon him the high task of perceiving the myriad hierarchic interchanges among all things, and of figuring that perception in noble images.

This notion has, often enough, attended the religious view of the world. In the Egyptian, Assyrian, Greek, and animistic worlds, it was inseparable from religious vision: the imagery *was* religious. The conjunction of aesthetic and religious vision is, of course, most familiar to us in the West in medieval and Renaissance — that is, in Christian — imagery.

The Christian vision affirms the significance of the mimetic act. It does so because it sees here the human echo of activity connate with the origins of things, and because its own understanding of the world is one that involves the notion of the Incarnate Word.

It sees the original creative energy as describable by the term "Word." It understands this energy as tending toward utterance, that is, toward the articulation of significance, and indeed toward being, from nonsignificance and nonbeing (cf. human language, which, far more than serving merely as the mode by which we exchange ideas, in effect calls our world into being for us by *naming* it). It is an articulation tending always toward concretion and identity, and not, as might be supposed, toward abstraction and anonymity. The energy utters itself in terms that we apprehend as soil and rock and fire and flesh. It uttered its form most nobly in man, and eventually in The Man — Immanuel. Which is to say that this Word, the Ground of all form and significance, the Referent for all phenomena and imagery, is such that its self-articulation tends finally toward Incarnation.

And the Incarnate, called Logos, embraced the limitations of this world and proclaimed authenticity and freedom and glory to us not, as many prophets have done, via escape into the ether, but via participation in the actualities of human existence. The vision of glory declared here is one, not of dissolution and a denial of carnality, but on the contrary, of a restoration of concretion and specificity and flesh in the unity and harmony for which it was made. The Christian agrees with Plato up to a point, but, unlike Plato, he suspects that the Ideal, far from being an abstraction, is harder and "knobblier" (C. S. Lewis) than anything we knock our shins on here. He sees this world, not as illusion, but as figure — that is, as the species under which we now apprehend Actuality. And, because he understands the Incarnate to be the finally authentic utterance of Actuality, he must affirm the validity of the world which that Incarnate affirmed.

The Incarnational view, then, would entail at least the following notions: it would affirm the immediate (because it believes in the Incarnation); it would affirm the transcendent (because it believes in the Logos); it would see the commonplace as the vehicle of ultimacy (n.b. the common manhood of the Incarnate, and also his pedestrian *modus vivendi*); and it would insist on the public character of significance (again, because it believes in the Word).

A person who takes this view would have, then, various questions to ask concerning aesthetic theories and the imagery deriving from those theories. He would find himself, for a start, at a point midway between the two eternal human inclinations — the one that seeks Reality in an escape from this existence, and the other that disavows the transcendent in its effort to apprehend the actuality of this world. Historically, the former view is the one that has issued most often in sublime images: indeed, there is an element of this escapism in most religious imagery.

But in its final form, the tendency is gnostic, and leads to a vision that becomes more and more ethereal and less and less congenial to any imagery at all, and hence leaves the province of art altogether, since mimetic activity must presuppose a robust affirmation of the concrete if it is to have any matrix from which its images are to rise. (Hence the poor artistic yield of religions and cults that seek Actuality in purely spiritual terms: their categories reduce the possibility of imagery; the Reformation faith might ask itself some hard questions here.)

The view that, on the other hand, seeks Actuality in the stuff at hand has much to be said for it. Besides giving an impetus to scientific inquiry, it has given us the great vision of the Impressionists. However, at the point at which this view excludes the transcendent altogether, and seeks Actuality *solely* in the world investigated by the sciences — at that point its grasp upon even *that* world begins to slip. For it becomes increasingly difficult to posit the notion of significance, and hence to draw images of power and sublimity from this matrix. Ironically, the quest for Actuality in these terms leads eventually either to a retreat from the recognizable into abstract and arcane forms (since the thing-as-it-appears-to-us is nonsignificant) or to a myopic crawl into an inner universe of fantasy which yields images of greater and greater grotesquery and inanity. Often enough, the early stages of this quest yield compelling and powerful images. The work of Duchamp, Mondrian, and Braque has surely opened our eyes to provinces of form and texture that we would have missed. And who can gainsay the power of the visions of horror in the work of Kirchner, Beckmann, and Grosz? Perhaps it took an antitranscendentalist view to make this imagery possible. But, however compelling or intriguing or unsettling or shocking or amusing or engaging or diverting the imagery may be, it is difficult to find in it that troubling thing we call, vaguely, greatness, which seems to rise from the simultaneous awareness of limitation and sublimity, and sees them both figured in the human situation. The mighty vision of a Michelangelo took the *donnée* (the human form) and transfigured (not twisted) it into forms that spoke of the eternal. Perhaps we need the twisting as an image of perdition; but perdition is of proximate interest only. Sublimity alone is final.

Again, the Incarnational view, with its celebration of the commonplace, would have to inquire into the worth of the bizarre and arcane as appropriate vehicles of authenticity. For it would suspect, unlike the more intoxicating view that freedom and fulfillment lie in the bacchic and the occult, that this freedom and fulfillment lie in the obvious, and that participation in the given rhythms of existence (dawn and twilight, spring and fall, birth, marriage, work, eating and drinking) is the beginning of glory. Vermeer is the colossus towering above those who, on the one hand, seek increasingly peculiar images, and those who, on the other, insist flatly on the nothingness but inevitability of what is at hand (hamburgers and rubber tires). In contrast to the former, Vermeer found luminescence and sublimity in a *room corner;* against the latter, he found *luminescence and sublimity* in a room corner.

Finally, the Incarnational view would suspect that the truly significant is public in its nature, and that the private is of limited interest only. Because of the universal utterance of the Word, and because of the response to this in the great "Benedicite, omnia opera Domini," this view would look with suspicion on mimetic activity involving any esoteric doctrine or the tendency toward solipsism. Hence, while it is surely entirely permissible (and perhaps helpful to himself) for an artist to see his task to be the figuring of private visions and emotions directly on the canvas, the result is of minimal significance. High art is an eminently public thing, for, like the Word, it calls form from havoc and utters it in universal terms.

The criticism that this view would urge, then, against our own epoch, is one that will raise again the questions that are not asked. It will urge no atavistic return to the manageable ages of supposed ignorance. Nor will it be nostalgic for some twelfth-century equilibrium of sensibility.

But it will ask whether the dogmas deriving from postmedieval methodology are quite axiomatic after all. It will ask whether the exclusion of the ghoulies and ghosties and long-legged beasties (and Apollo and the Virgin of Chartres and Immanuel) from categories of inquiry is not abortive. It will doubt whether the human imagination will ever be satisfied with the edict that declares that man comes of age to the extent that he disavows the notions celebrated in the imagery of other ages — candor, valor, *caritas,* beauty, glory. It will test with inquisitorial rigor the sensibility of an age whose imagery can speak truthfully only of banality and perdition and the immediate. And it will urge that only that mimesis rises beyond cleverness and topicality whose imagery figures the sublimity and fear in a handful of dust.

# II. Writers in the Christian Tradition

# Forms of Spirituality in the Middle English Lyric

DAVID L. JEFFREY

The language of the Middle English lyrics has long since grown quaint and old. Refrains that perhaps more than any other echo in the verse of later English poets now fall strangely on our ears. Yet anyone who will still cup his ear in patience to listen can scarcely fail to be moved by the beauty of their more distant melody. The haunting mood of "Wynter wakeneth al my care," the lissom cadences of "Lenten ys come with loue to toune," and the haiku-like intensity of "Sunset on Calvary" are among the finest notes in English poetry.

Unfortunately, for the modern listener the enchantment is too often suddenly broken, when he is disturbed to uncover firmly woven into the rich musical fabric of the lyrics a pervasive woof of religious message. For an age in which the functional use of art is often heresy, and for which terms like "didactic" (and sometimes even "meaning") have become nearly pejorative, it is difficult to understand a former age of poets who thought it heresy *not* to marry a message to the means, and so to render aesthetics a helpmeet to philosophy. But as students and would-be-informed readers of English literature, we have enjoined an

---

David L. Jeffrey graduated from Wheaton College in 1965 and proceeded to Princeton University, where he took an M.A. in 1967 and in the following year won the Harold W. Dodds senior graduate award. Following research in Italy and in England on a Woodrow Wilson Dissertation Fellowship and Canada Council Doctoral Award, jointly held, he completed his Ph.D. at Princeton in 1968 and joined the English Department of the University of Victoria, British Columbia. In 1969 he was appointed Assistant Professor of English at the University of Rochester, where he now teaches. He is the author of articles on Chaucer, Shakespeare, and medieval drama, and a forthcoming book on the Middle English Lyric.

obligation to reach backward in an attempt to grasp the significance of that marriage if we are fully to appreciate our own poetic heritage. More immediately, our reading of the Middle English lyric poets themselves may be greatly enriched through even a limited awareness of the rich context of medieval spirituality which was — aesthetically and ideologically — the informing principle of their poems.

In the course of what follows, I hope to suggest something of the superb adaptation of the Middle English religious lyric to the purposes and audience for which it was intended. To do this, I will try to indicate significant aspects of the Middle English lyric heritage that lie in the *historia ordum* of its effective inventors and most successful practitioners, the Franciscan friars. At the same time, to provide a fuller historical perspective from which to view Franciscan poetic development, I will endeavor to show that the adaptation of poetic means by the Vaudois, another movement of spiritual reform rooted in the same socioreligious conditions, is parallel to, if not itself generative of a similar development in the evangelical methodology of St. Francis. Both of these groups, I will argue, though sometimes employing different poetic genres, manifest as primary traits of their spirituality the two distinct themes that most characterize the Middle English religious lyric: penance and identification with the passion of Christ. Through the exigencies of history it is the Franciscans who physically touch the English lyric. Therefore it is to them that this discussion will ultimately return.

## I

Of all the Middle English lyrics left to us, seventy-five to eighty percent are "religious"; that is, their main purpose is the making of a specific religious point. Many of these are technically "carols," and nearly all were meant to be sung rather than merely read or recited. Today we might think of them as popular hymns, or religious "folk music." Most were written for what might loosely be called "teaching" purposes, and nine-tenths of the 450 poems of known authorship were by men in holy orders.[1] When the sources of the poems with identifiable provenance or authorship are counted, the Franciscans stand out above all others as the order of English lyric poets.

The chief places in which Middle English lyrics have been found are in collections of sermon material (sermons and sermon notebooks), and in certain collections of proverbs, treatises and

[1] Rossell H. Robbins, "The Authors of the Middle English Religious Lyrics," *JEGP*, XXXIX (1940), 230.

poems known as "miscellanies." Other sources, such as devotional or prayer books, flyleaves in aureate collections and commonplace books, are much less significant, though for such secular lyrics as remain a few minstrel and song books are important. Of the extant collections of sermon materials from the Middle English period, the majority and the most important are of unquestionable Franciscan provenance. The thirty manuscripts of the best known of these collections, the *Fasciculus Morum*, show an organized attempt by the Franciscans to utilize the English lyric "for the very practical purposes of religious instruction" (Robbins). The numbers of manuscripts of this kind of collection that still exist argue for a wide circulation. The miscellanies, though not so well preserved, again show Franciscan poets figuring strongly in the materials as we have them. Of the eight manuscripts in this group, five are known to have been compiled (and probably composed) by friars (Robbins, p. 234). And, in those sermon collections and miscellanies not proven Franciscan, many poems recur that are in known Franciscan collections, a fact that suggests possible Franciscan authorship for yet other manuscripts. That there is Franciscan influence on the Middle English religious lyric is thus obvious. What has been hinted at, but not yet stated, is the nature and form of that influence.

Certain characteristics of the English lyrics[2] are immediately apparent to even the casual reader. The most obvious has already been mentioned: their religious quality. More specifically, the lyrics tend to be of two varieties; they are either songs of praise, or of doctrinal instruction.[3] One poem by the fifteenth-

[2] The best collections of Middle English lyrics for the general reader are the five volumes in the Clarendon Press and Oxford Series: *English Lyrics of the XIIIth Century*, ed. Carleton Brown (corr. ed., 1962), hereafter referred to as Brown XIII; *Religious Lyrics of the XIVth Century*, ed. Carleton Brown, 2nd ed. rev. by G. V. Smithers (1956), hereafter referred to as Brown XIV; *Secular Lyrics of the XIVth and XVth Centuries*, ed. Rossell H. Robbins (2nd ed. 1959), hereafter referred to as Robbins, *Secular Lyrics; Historical Poems of the XIVth and XVth Centuries*, ed. Rossell H. Robbins (1959); and *The Early English Carols*, ed. Richard L. Greene (1935).

[3] This is true both of what is technically called the "carol" and of the "lyric," both of which in any case were written to be sung, so rendering the distinction somewhat ambiguous. What is usually intended by the term "carol" is the preponderant stanzaic form *aaab* plus burden, or variations thereof. The history of this form is a highly interesting study in itself, and I am presently preparing for an article on its development in connection with the Franciscan poets. For the sake of convenience here the terms "lyric" and "song" will be used to signify all of the lyrics, regardless of their stanzaic form.

century English Franciscan poet, James Ryman, particularly illustrates the doctrinal emphasis. Ryman there tries to compress the entire life of Christ with all of its traditional points of theological significance into seven four-line stanzas. Most other attempts are less ambitious, usually settling for limitations more easily compassable in lyric form. Typically, as in the poem that follows, these end in a note of penitence and supplication.

*A Roose hath borne a lilly white,*
*The whiche floure is moost pure and bright.*

*To this roose aungell Gabriell*
*Seide: Thou shalt bere Emanuell,*
*Both god and man with us to dwell;*
*The which floure is most pure and bright.*

*This roose, the prophete Ysaye*° (Isaiah)
*Seyde, shulde conceyve and bere Messy*° (Messiah)
*Withouten synne or velonye;*
*The which flour is moost pure and bright.*

*As the sonne beame goth thurgh the glas,*
*Thurgh this roose that lilly did pas*
*To save mankynde, as his wille was;*
*The whiche floure is moost pure and bright.*

*This roose so myelde aye undefielde*
*Hath borne a childe for man so wilde*
*By fraude begiled, from blis exiled;*
*The which flour is moost pure and bright.*

*This roose so good at the cros stode*
*With wofull moode, when Crist, oure foode,*
*Shed his hert bloode for man so woode*°*;* (mentally deranged)
*The which flour is moost pure and bright.*

*This swete roose pray bothe nyght and day.*
*Withoute denay*° *that we come maye* (doubt)
*To blis for ay the redy waye;*
*The which flour is moost pure and bright.*[4]

Songs of praise, or "orisouns" are more to the point of private devotional worship, though many were incorporated into the liturgy as well. Often they are addressed to Mary.

[4] By James Ryman, from Cambridge Univ. Lib. MS. Ee. I. 12; Poem No. 19 in the edition of this MS by J. Zupitza, "Die Gedichte des Franziskaners Jakob Ryman," *Archiv für das Studium der neueren Sprachen und Litteraturen,* LXXXIX (1892), 166-388. In my quotations abbreviations are expanded and *i/j, u/v,* and the ME thorn silently conformed to modern usage; otherwise the orthography of the copy-text is preserved.

*Mayde and moder mylde,*
*vor loue of thine childe*
*thet is god an man,*
*Me thet am zuo° wylde* (so)
*vram zenne° thou me ssylde°* (sin, shield)
*ase ich the bydde can.* *Amen*
[Brown XIV, No. 33].

There are also a few poems of practical merit for daily life. In one of the more popular of these (existing in many variations) a woman asks her broom what to do to gain her husband's love (Brown XIII, No. 21). The broom's answer is time-honored:

*Hold thine tunke° stille* (tongue)
*& hawe al thine wille.*

To the characteristics suggested by these examples could be added a characteristic "dramatic" form, for many of the lyrics consist of monologues, dialogues (e.g. between Christ on the cross and Mary in the "Stond wel, moder, ounder rode" of MS. Digby 86),[5] or debates — usually doctrinal. In the poem "Stond wel, moder, ounder rode," the guise in which the doctrine is delivered is that of Christ "explaining" to Mary the significance and the necessity of the Atonement. But in each of these cases, the object of the poem is not only instruction and worship, but *penaunce* and *amendement.* The Franciscan poet's motivation is uncompromisingly evangelical, emphasizing the gravity of man's sin, his need of penance, and the avenue provided by Christ through which repentance may become efficacious, and often, as in "Amende we us, while we have space" (printed in section vi below), carrying a feeling of urgency in the matter not uncommon to the early Franciscan movement. There are many such warnings against procrastination:

*Loverd, thu clepedest° me* (called)
*an ich nagt° ne ansuarede the* (naught)
*Bute wordes scloe and sclepie:°* (slow and sleepy)
*"Thole° yet! thole a litel!"* (allow)
*Bute "yiet" and "yiet" was endelis,*
*and "thole a litel" a long wey is*
[Brown XIV, No. 5].

Men should repent, "for why nowe is the tyme of grace." The Franciscans, as we shall see, felt some reason to believe that the "tyme of grace" was drawing to a close.

[5] Brown XIII, p. 87.

## II

The English Franciscans, however, were not the first of their Order to use poetry as a channel for evangelical purposes. The first of the celebrated *joculatores dei* was St. Francis himself. But to profit best from a look at St. Francis and his early followers as we trace the Franciscan poetic tradition, we should first go back one step to examine the general conditions that produced not only the revolutionary Franciscan response to traditional Christian gospel, but the response of other movements of reform spirituality at the close of the twelfth century that employed poetic devices as well.

At the beginning of the eleventh century, the organized church was showing signs of an encroaching cancer. Nowhere was this more true than in Languedoc and northern Italy.[6] For years it had been common and widespread for priests to practice concubinage and simony; and however much the people of the parishes despised such conditions, there was little they could do except refuse to attend mass and the sacraments, which in any case were offered with remarkable infrequency. Despite attempts to control the many excesses, the situation continued largely unaltered to the end of the twelfth century. St. Bernard's description of the churches of his own time is stark enough:

> The churches are without preachers: the priests do not have the respect which is their due, Christians deny Christ, and their temples pass for synagogues. They disavow the sanctity of the sanctuary of God, and the sacraments are no longer regarded as sacred. Holy days pass without solemnity; men die in their sins, and their souls are born before the redoubtable tribunal without having been reconciled to the Saviour by penitence, and without the aid of the final sacrament. The children of Christians no longer learn to know Christ, and they are no longer permitted to walk in the way of Salvation.[7]

In a society that centered itself so completely around the church, such abuses were bound to produce unrest. Since the first quarter of the tenth century heretics had been increasingly a problem, and some had been burned (Runciman, p. 117).

Against this continuing confusion Pope Gregory VII, already disturbed by the lack of papal control over France, considered an encyclical against simoniac and adulterous bishops, one that would sever the responsibility of obedience incumbent

[6] See Steven Runciman, *The Mediaeval Manichee* (Cambridge, 1947).

[7] *Epistle* 241, my translation of the Latin text in *Patrologia Latina*, ed. J. P. Migne (*PL* in future references), CLXXXIII, cols. 386-387.

upon those under their sinful example.[8] For a while his action was staved off by the efforts of a few clerics, notably Sigebert of Gembloux, a Belgian, who urged that there should be some other way of negotiating reform of the churches than such a decree. In his *Chronics* (1074) he expressed the fear that it might push the people to "Donatism"—i.e. a willful rejection of the established church on the basis of the quality of its local representatives (*PL*, CLX, 217). Sigebert apparently knew the condition of the European churches better than the Pope.

In the same year, Gregory issued his proposed encyclical requiring all to renounce their obedience to those bishops who showed indulgence to the clergy in the matter of celibacy. In the following year he commanded the laity to accept no official ministrations from married priests, to refuse the sacraments from them and to "rise against all such"; he also deprived reprobate clerics of their revenues (Jaffe, pp. 598ff.). In 1109 he declared consecration by a simoniac to be null and void. Needless to say, these changes met with no little protest on the part of the affected clergy. Of more consequence, the number and extent of infected parishes were so great that the decrees served as a warrant of license for whole populations to disown the hierarchic church. With papal authority on their side, long repressed feelings of animosity toward the clergy burst from the people. Some did indeed refuse the sacraments; some stoned and even killed accused priests, literally taking the law into their own hands. Laymen whose sincerity of faith was respected by their peers began to fill the function of priests—in open defiance of worried injunctions against their doing so—even to the administration of sacraments. Priests were burned in their own money, and communion elements "blessed" by married priests were overturned. Sigebert of Gembloux wrote a pamphlet crying, "Where is the Catholic who would not be grieved . . . at the beauty of the Church being turned into folly. . . . Clerics are objects of public derision and persecution, they are castrated, mutilated. . . ," he adds, "as evident testimony to the considerable wisdom of their chastisers." Yet "some priests do not repent if they are so fortunate as to escape public violence, and therefore . . . dealing fiercely with their pastors is now regarded as 'good works' by the people."[9] It is

[8] P. Jaffe, *Regesta pontificum*, 2nd ed. (Paris, 1865), I, 594-649.

[9] Some confirmations were performed with a substitute oil of confirmation made from ear wax. G. H. Pertz, T. Mommsen, *et al.*, *Monumenta Germaniae Historiae*. Auspiciis Societatis Aperiendis Fontibus Rerum Germanicarum Medii Aevi, 1826-19— (hereafter cited as *MGH*), ser. LL., II, 436.

small wonder that in such a climate "heresies" should have sprung up.

Other conditions, many of the same which favored the development of art and literature, also nourished the tendency to rebellion. No country offered a more favorable soil to the growth of heresy than the south of France. Wealth, practical independence from the central power of the French kings, a broadly based merchant trade, the natural spirit of the inhabitants — all of these had fostered a degree of freedom scarcely equalled in other parts of feudal Europe. Much the same could be argued for northern Italy.

At first the heretics were largely "nondoctrinal" and were principally manifestations of two phenomena: anti-clericism and religious "zealotism."[10] People like Tancheln, Pierre de Bruis, Henri de Lauzan, Clement and Edwardus, Eudes, or Eon de l'Etoile, the Publicani, the Paulicians, the Patarenes, the Poor Men of Lyons, and their brothers the Poor Men of Lombardy,[11] were basically people who would have much preferred to stay in a purified Catholic church. Many of them, in fact, continued to seek out "pure" clergy from whom to obtain the sacraments.[12] Inevitably doctrinal differences of varying importance did creep in, but for the Inquisition, the principal charges remained insistence on holy poverty and failure to submit to ecclesiastical authority.[13]

That there were many of these groups with doctrinal tendencies often quite distinct from one another is a fact that has been confused (even by the Inquisition) through lumping

[10] J. Guiraud, *Histoire de l'Inquisition aux Moyen Age* (Paris, 1935).

[11] For Tancheln and Pierre de Bruis see the account of Peter the Venerable in *PL*, CLXXXIX, cols. 719, 850; for Henri de Lauzan see the account of St. Bernard of Clairvaux, *PL*, CLXXXII, cols. 434ff.; for Clement and Edwardus see Guibert de Nogent, *Histoire de Sa Vie*, ed. Georges Bourgin (Paris, 1907), Book III; for Eon de l'Etoile see *MGH*, ser. Scriptores, XIX, 131ff.; for the Publicani see William of Newburg in *Rerum Britannicarum Medii Aevi Scriptores* (London, 1858-1898) 82, I, 60; and for the Poor Men of Lyons see Jean Jalla, *Histoire des Vaudois des Alpes* (Paris, 1904), Ch. i.

[12] See Runciman, *passim;* also Étienne de Bourbon, *Anecdotes Historiques Legendes et Apologues*, publiée pour la Société de l'Histoire de France, par A. Lecoy de la Marche (Paris, 1877), pp. 327ff., 274-314. Étienne was a Dominican of the early thirteenth century, and serves as a good source for this kind of study in that his is probably the closest thing to an objective account of the heretics in an Inquisition-minded age. Though a Dominican, he took considerable interest in the heretics, even to the point of later being among the first to imitate them in the use of verse from the pulpit.

[13] C. Schmidt, *Histoire et Doctrine de la Secte des Cathars Albigeois* (Paris, 1848), I, 7-24.

all heretics under the title "Albigensians."[14] Collectively the heretics provided an extreme problem for the church. For a brief period they eclipsed the church as the major religious power in an area extending from Padova to the Loire, and opposing them was often difficult because of the remarkably exemplary lives many of them led. It is in this latter respect that the heretics had much in common: high ideals, a professed love of absolute honesty and truth for its own sake, a stated emphasis on *caritas* as the basis for human conduct — effectively an attempt to live the *vita apostolica* (Turberville, pp. 20-21).

## III

One of these groups, the Waldensians, or Vaudois, is of particular interest. In 1173, in Lyons of Gaul, a burgher named Peter Valdesius (Valdes), or Waldo, had accumulated great wealth through the "iniquitous practice of lending money at interest," and was living in enjoyment of his success. As he walked along the road one day he stopped to listen to a jongleur telling the story of St. Alexi. It had a profound effect upon him. Waldo invited the jongleur to his house, talked with him, and later went to the school of theology to seek advice for his soul's struggle toward God. The advice was, "Go and sell all that you have, and give to the poor." Waldo did just that. The poor rejoiced, his wife left him in disgust, and to this point he was regarded by the church as favorably as any "religious" — except that they were concerned about his indiscriminate distribution of his money.[15] By 1177, the *Chronique du Canon de Lyons* reports of Waldo that he had taken vows of "eternal poverty," and had gathered around himself several enthusiastic followers who had vowed the same. Soon the group increased enough to be known as a sect, called at first not Waldensians or Vaudois, but Poor Men of Lyons (a later branch were called the Poor Men of Lombardy).[16] Little by little they began to

[14] A. S. Turberville, *Mediaeval Heresy and the Inquisition* (London, 1921), p. 22. (This tendency has behind it St. Augustine's treatment of Manicheanism, thus Runciman's title "The Mediaeval Manichee.") Pierre Belperron (*La Croisade contre les Albigeois et l'Union de Languedoc à la France* [Paris, 1948], pp. 61ff.) does not make this mistake. He divides the Albigeois into their constituents — principally Cathars and Vaudois, plus the many unassociated groups.

[15] Étienne de Bourbon, pp. 290ff., Jalla, pp. 121ff. The St. Alexi referred to is the anchorite who died in 412.

[16] Jalla, pp. 13ff. The Third Council of the Lateran in 1179 (Pope Alexander III) condemned many heresies (Cathar, Publicani, Patarenes, Albigensians of Toulouse, etc.) but not the Valdes. The Pope approved the

inveigh against the sins of others, preaching penance. The Bishop of Lyons, despite the decree of the Holy See, conceived a dislike for their disturbing insistence on holy poverty, and inverted any possible cooperation of the church to intense scrutiny and disfavor. This hostility only served to cause a more rapid expansion of the Vaudois.

The Vaudois doctrine was much less unorthodox than that of most other "heretical" groups. The principal deviation derived from a heavy emphasis on poverty, on chastity, and particularly on the Holy Scriptures: God's word was regarded as more authoritative than man's, consequently there was a doubled tendency toward disobedience of ecclesiastical authority when it could be seen apparently to contradict Scripture. The specific doctrinal deviations that developed later on were a rejection of belief in prayer to the saints, in prayer for the dead, and in infant baptism. At first the poor men of Lyons had preferred to have all sacraments administered by the church; they wanted only to live and to preach the *vita apostolica*. Theirs was a distinct attempt to return to what they conceived of as primitive Christianity.[17]

In order to effect a program of spreading their belief to others, the early followers of Waldo turned to the means that seemed to lend itself best to the problems of transmitting scriptural and doctrinal instruction to a basically illiterate (un-Latinate) people — vernacular poetry. The idea was not wholly original: Waldo himself had first been moved to repentance by the song of a jongleur, and the process of vernacularization had had an early start in Provence. As early as 840 there are records of monks inserting vernacular pieces into antiphons and the liturgy, some of these described by the more traditional clergy as of "indecent character." In the tenth and eleventh centuries the practice had become common, and critics were complaining of the "prodigious ignorance" and "astonishing liberty of imagination" of the priests who rendered scriptural tales into poetical narrative. The monks were known to have written amatory and Song of Solomon-styled poems as well as

Waldensians and their vows of poverty, but forbad them to preach except by invitation of a priest. This was obeyed for a short time only.

[17] See documents in S. R. Maitland, *Facts and Documents Illustrative of the History, Doctrine, and Rites, of the Ancient Albigenses and Waldenses* (London, 1832), pp. 342ff. Lucie Varga, "Peire Cardinal était-il hérétique?" *Revue d'Histoire des Religions*, CXVII (1938), 213, says that they were trying to return "vers un catholisme primitif."

hymns on the nativity.[18] We know that there was already a healthy tradition of Christian Latin poetry by this time,[19] and it may seem that this new poetry was a natural development from it. But there are other factors that should be taken into consideration. Trade routes, fairs, travellers, the popularity of jongleurs and travelling groups — all of these indicate a widespread public taste for entertainment. This taste coupled with a substantial number of jongleurs and minstrels within the native population seems to have ensured that entertainment was available. Some have thought that monastic poetry in the vernacular gave rise to *la poésie populaire,* and this may have been partially the case.[20] It is clear, however, that by the late twelfth and thirteenth centuries the church was resorting to the vernacular, both in sermons and in poetic inserts, to compete with a popular tradition already geared to meet a popular demand (Fauriel, pp. 162-163). We shall look more closely at the nature of their borrowing in a moment. How far back it reaches we can only guess — presumably at least to the last quarter of the eleventh century.[21]

The very earliest troubadour poetry apparently was mainly religious (Bayle, pp. 241ff.), a fact that fits in with the picture we have of a very strong desire among the people for a practical knowledge of Scripture — something very difficult for the non-Latinate to have obtained from the church. We have seen that masses, let alone sermons, were in remarkable scarcity for close to two hundred years in Provence. Presumably, how-

[18] See C. C. Fauriel, *History of Provencal Poetry* (trans., New York, 1860), pp. 155, 158-163.

[19] As demonstrated in F. J. E. Raby, *A History of Christian-Latin Poetry from the Beginnings to the Close of the Middle Ages* (Oxford, 1953).

[20] "La poésie monastique devait produire la poésie populaire. Les jongleurs après avoir répété les hymnes et les récits qu'ils avaient appris dans les cloîtres, composaient euxmêmes des chants naïfs qui bientôt passaient de bouche en bouche, voyageaient d'une province à l'autre, étaient répétés dans toutes les campagnes par les patres gardant leur troupeau, par les laboureurs poussant leur charrue, par les femmes rassemblées autour du lavoir ou occupées a la cueillette des olives. On ne savait pas quel était l'auteur de ces couplets si promptement graves dans toutes les memoires. Inspirés par le peuple, ils retournaient au peuple, après avoir reçu d'un menestrel ambulant une forme rythmique et un air facile a retenir." L'Abbé A. Bayle, *La Poésie Provençal* (Aix, 1876), p. 194.

[21] This is where Fauriel (pp. 351ff.) places the real upsurge of vernacular poetry in Provence. It is fair to suspect that among the travelling jongleurs and minstrels this kind of material existed even before this time. However, since it was orally carried more often than written we do not have extant MSS (see Ernst Hirsch, *Beiträge zur Sprachgeschichte der württemburgischen Waldenser* [Stuttgart, 1962]).

ever, the popular taste for biblical knowledge may have been developed and preserved by adaptations into the vernacular: the jongleur who "converted" Waldo is a case in point. Nor is this the only record of such an occurrence.[22] Waldo himself worked to obtain translations of parts of Scripture almost immediately (Jalla, ch. ii); his Poor Men of Lyons went about preaching on the basis of their translated passages, chanting religious verse based on scriptural paraphrase (in the style of the wandering jongleurs)[23] in order to learn the material better themselves and so impress it on the memory of their hearers.

The Vaudois, as we have seen, were in theological dispute with the church at one primary point — their belief in each man's efficacy as his own priest in approaching God directly, opposed the church's insistence on the primacy of the hierarchic priesthood. Since this deviation and others less significant were said to be derived by Waldo from recourse to the Bible in his own language, it soon became a primary objective of the Vaudois to get either vernacular Scripture or a reasonable facsimile thereof into the hands of their followers and would-be converts as quickly as possible. Official opposition to translation of the Bible rendered the production of more than a few passages impossible, so that in place of translation, the Vaudois seem to have turned to narrative paraphrase or to doctrinal sermonizing in verse based upon Scripture; and such is the substance of what is left to us of their poetic corpus.

[22] Étienne de Bourbon records another instance, where a jongleur meets a woman known for her beauty and concupiscent love of many suitors, and converts her to the love of God, a Love greater than all others: "Audivi quod, cum quidam domina pulcritudine speciosa, a multis impetita, multos amore pernicioso adamasset, et multi eam, quidam joculator per hanc viam eam ad amorem Dei convertit. Sollicitabat eam quod amorem suum poneret in quemdam magnum maxime pulcritudinis, probitatis, largitatis, curialitatis, etc. Cum autem illa diceret quod ipsa habuisset tot impetitores et habuisset amatores tam magnos et divites et probos, cum ille intulisset quod ille pro quo rogabat omnes gracias aliorum excedebat, illa tandem consenciente quod, si talem eum probaret, amorem suum ei daret, intulit: 'Nullus nobilior, divicior, curialior Virginis filio, in quo sunt omnes gracie sine defectu.' Cum ergo ostendisset ei eorum quos ipsa dilexerat defectum et christi complementum graciarum omnium, movit eam ad contemptum vanitatis et amorem veritatis" (p. 186).

[23] It is an Inquisitor who indicates the object of these rhymes, and he adds that they are not the only attempts of this kind: "Callide inserunt ibi ritus suos et heresses, ut melius alliciant ad ea discenda et forcius inculcent ea memoriter, sicut nos laycis proponimus symbolum, oracionem dominicam, et alia pulchra huius modi causa cum inexerunt carmina." David of Augsburg, as quoted in Emilio Comba, *History of the Waldenses of Italy* (London, 1889), p. 338, n. 801.

Aside from Scripture, parts of the liturgy,[24] and perhaps a commentary on the Canticles, little religious poetry of the Provence Waldensians has escaped the fires. Chief among the remnant are *La Nobla Leyczon, The Scorn of the World, The Bark, The New Comfort, The New Sermon, The Lord's Prayer, The Parable of the Sower,* and *The Father Eternal.* An account of these may be had elsewhere;[25] for economy's sake I should like to indicate only two or three of the most interesting aspects of the poems.

First of all, this is all religious poetry in the tradition of what Bayle (p. 193) has called *vrai poésie populaire* — poetry of penitence, praise, narrative instruction, and adulation. There is evidence that a large body of poems no longer extant, like those mentioned above, concerned themselves with paraphrasing "les plus touchantes histoires de la Bible." Secondly, the poetry is not properly lyric: the pieces range from two lines to over four hundred, and since most are fragments, there were presumably some that were longer. *La Nobla Leyczon* in particular resembles the sort of thing seen in parts of the English *Cursor Mundi.* Others of the poems are reminiscent of Old English Christian poetry (Caedmonian) far more than of the Middle English Franciscan lyrics, although there is frequent use of lyric stanza forms. Since these poems were primarily constructed as rhetorical teaching devices, there is every reason to believe that they were delivered in the manner of a sermon. *La Nobla Leyczon,* written between 1190 and 1240 (Comba, p. 233), has a clearly didactic, rather than simply narrative thrust, emphasizing that the true follower of Christ will practice the three virtues of spiritual poverty, chastity, and humility. This emphasis on a life consistent with that of Christ and the apostles runs throughout the poetry; *The New Comfort* (as printed by Comba, pp. 219-221) begins with an injunction to abandon self and serve God with fear, "per l'amor del Segnor." Then follows a description of the wretchedness of this fleeting life, and after that a series of quatrains on faith and works. These verses lay heavy stress on the doctrine which

[24] One early Waldensian MS contains "the Gospels appointed for the last fortnight in Lent, with some Epistles for the same season, and the gloss attributed to Haimon" (Comba, p. 171). It should be noted that the Waldensian MS language is definitely Provençal (Comba, pp. 163-166, and notes 327, 328; and Raynouard, *Choix des poésies des troubadours* [Paris, 1817], II, 140).

[25] Comba, pp. 215-231ff.; a reproduction of most of these exists in Antoine Monastier, *Histoire de l'Église Vaudoise* (Lausanne, 1847), pp. 245-379. See also his catalogue of "known" Vaudois items, most of which are not now extant (pp. 232ff.).

*San Jaco° mostra e aferma clarament,* (St. James)
*Qu l'ome non se salva per la fe solament*
*Se el non es cum las obras° mescala fidelment.* (works)

*The Parable of the Sower,* in the same stanza form, is a clear attempt to tell a biblical story in the vernacular poetic idiom, with a highly interesting attempt to enhance immediate and local application through allusions to contemporary places and events. There is no reason to think that this was the first instance of poetic doctrinalizing in the vernacular; it is entirely possible that Waldo's followers learned it from a tradition, primarily oral, perhaps like that of the jongleur who had sung to Waldo the life of St. Alexi. This likelihood seems the more probable in that while Waldo's followers sang such songs and told such tales, we also know that they themselves were for the most part illiterate and there is no record of "trouvering" among them. The application of these poetic traditions to their own proselytizing purposes may have been chiefly the work of a learned minority, especially since the first converts were mostly among the laity.

As for the balance of early Vaudois poetry which we know about but do not have, it was apparently of a typically religious variety: hymns to the Trinity, "reminders of the miraculous life of Christ," legends adapted from prose Latin sources, acts of ancient heroes, saints' miracles, and pieces where "under the pretext of an invocation to God the poet recounts the principal events of the Old and the New Testaments."[26] The point here is that Waldo and his followers seem to have regarded the instrument of vernacular poetry as a means to the end of learning more Scripture — when they could not obtain copies of translations they often passed on the passages orally, committing them to memory.[27] Reinerius Saccho tells us that out of six causes to which he ascribed heresy, four were directly involved with the *learning* of the heretics. "They teach and learn, without books . . . night and day. . . . To those who would excuse themselves, as not being able to learn, they say, 'Learn only one word every day, and in a year's time you will know three hundred, and you will get on.' " The result was that Saccho had "seen and heard a certain lay countryman, who repeated the book of Job word for word, and many who perfectly knew the whole New Testament."[28] Saccho reports that their "learn-

[26] Joseph Anglade, *Les Troubadours* (Paris, 1908), pp. 203ff.; see also Bayle, pp. 193ff.

[27] Étienne de Bourbon, pp. 307-308.

[28] Maitland, pp. 400ff. The early prose translations attempted to be "word

ing" (he means practical theological knowledge) was in fact often superior to that of the clergy. The instrument apparently served its masters well.

My purpose in introducing the Vaudois into a discussion of the heritage of Middle English poetry is not to suggest that Peter Waldo and his followers are to be equated with the movement of Francesco Bernadone. Despite some obvious similarities, there are marked and important differences. What the Poor Men of Lyons do teach us is that with respect to the conditions of the time, the essential spirituality and orientation of St. Francis was not unique. Like Waldo, Francis was interested in the spiritual regeneration of men. In his methodology (and this particularly is why Waldo's methodology of one generation earlier has been introduced), he too employed poetry for teaching. A noteworthy difference is that the early Franciscans, not under the same pressure from official ecclesiastical authority as the harried Vaudois, developed another poetic form — the popular song — more suited to their characteristically different needs and approach, while the suppressed Vaudois poetry more quickly went the way of all things. The Franciscan form, produced by an essentially similar climate of reform spirituality, became, by virtue of a trick of history, the major shaping influence in Middle English lyric poetry.

## IV

St. Francis was born and raised in Assisi, a town that in 1203 had chosen an "Albigensian" for *podesta,* a fact suspicious enough to have aroused some of the Pope's advisors.[29] While the Franciscan movement is not to be confused with that of the Vaudois, almost all of its basic objectives were the same.[30] Like the Poor Men of Lyons, St. Francis demanded absolute poverty; like them, his group were wandering preachers and singers — the *joculatores Dei* who sang men into the kingdom of heaven.[31] The Franciscans likewise considered themselves an apostolic and penitential order, and the scriptural passage that

for word" and were given this kind of literal interpretation as well (Comba, pp. 187ff.).

[29] Johannes Jorgenson, *St. Francis of Assisi* (Image Book, New York, 1955), p. 81.

[30] One notable exception is the emphasis on Scripture translation into the vernacular, although even in the thirteenth century Franciscans were interested enough in the Scripture to make translations directly from the Hebrew text; see Beryl Smalley, *The Study of the Bible in the Middle Ages* (Notre Dame, 1954), p. 341.

[31] *Speculum Perfectionis,* ed. Paul Sabatier (Paris, 1898), p. 197.

had convinced St. Francis of the necessity of poverty was the same as that proclaimed by the Vaudois.[32] Theologians have said St. Francis himself may have reflected a "heretical" influence in some of his teachings; and some sympathy in that direction — though I suspect for reasons of Christian charity and not of heresy — may be suggested by the "Portiuncula Indulgence."[33]

St. Francis began with an intense mystic adoration fixed on the person and passion of Christ, an adoration revealed equally in the early biographies and in the songs of his followers. Along with the post-Inquisition tide, Franciscans began to evince an interest in the cult of the Virgin which is reflected in Franciscan poetry as late as that of James Ryman, in England. But in other of their themes, and perhaps especially in their poetic forms, sources antedating St. Francis may have some part. We know that in the years of the most severe persecution of heretical and unorthodox groups, many of the returning "fraternities" as well as individual heretics, mystics, and vagrant clerks, did attach themselves to the Franciscans.[34] Many of these, especially the clerks, were likely jongleurs. As for St. Francis himself, we learn from his early biographers that he first learned to write poetry in Provençal, and that for many years whenever he composed songs it was in the tongue of Languedoc and not in his native Umbrian.[35] Perhaps, in view of these considerations, it would not be entirely unjustified to study the Franciscans — especially of the time just after St. Francis' death — for evidences of religious and even literary influences of diverse origin.

32 Matt. 10:7-13 (Jorgensen, p. 145). St. Francis heard it read and expounded by a priest.

33 See Runciman, p. 129; Portiuncula was the town where St. Francis had heard the Scripture just referred to. In 1216, in the height of the anti-heretical activity, St. Francis came to the Pope (Honorius II) and begged for the Portiuncula church the same indulgence granted to the Crusaders in the Holy Lands: "That everyone who, with penitence for his sins, comes into this church and confesses his sins and is absolved by the priest, shall be free from all guilt and *punishment* [italics mine] for the sins of his life from the day of his baptism to the day when he entered the said church" (as quoted in Jorgensen, p. 145). Not surprisingly, Honorius depicted the injury it might do to the Indulgence of the Crusade, but grudgingly let it pass in a modified form. This sort of indulgence would naturally be of great benefit to former heretics wishing to escape reprisal.

34 See R. W. Emery, "The Friars of the Blessed Mary and the Pied Friars," *Speculum*, XXIV (1949), 218-228; also G. Meersseman, "F. F. Précheurs et Mouvement Devôt en Flandre au XIIIe siècle," *Archivum Fratrum Praedicatorum*, XVIII (1948), 73ff.

35 *Legende Trium Sociorum*, trans. in Otto Kerrer, *St. Francis of Assisi* (New York, 1948), pp. 14, 18.

In the first years of the thirteenth century a steadily mounting papal pressure succeeded in launching an offensive against numerous heretical groups, principally the Cathari and Vaudois who populated southern France and northern Italy. Significantly, recriminatory actions were taken at the same time against the "spiritual" Franciscans, who, despite the opposition not only of the Holy See but of the majority in their own Order ("Conventuals"), persisted in their insistence on holy poverty, mendicant evangelism and Joachimite (see below, section V) apocalyptic speculation. (Notable among the *zelanti*, who unless they repented were forced to flee into hiding as heretics, was the English Franciscan theologian William of Ockham.) On the whole, the disciplinary efforts were generally successful in reestablishing Roman control. During and immediately after the Inquisition and the "crusades" the popes were successful in obtaining the reintegration of many of the heretical groups back into the church. The reconciliation was accomplished in a variety of ways. In 1208 and 1209 some Franco-Hispanic Vaudois under the urgings of Innocent III were led back into the fold by their poet-preacher Durandus de Huesca. Many of the Lombard Vaudois, despite their intense emphasis on the personal relationship between man and God and the "priesthood of believers," were nevertheless won back to local parishes in Lombardy. The Humiliati, a heretic group with much the same emphasis on poverty and spirituality as the Franciscans or the Vaudois, were reclaimed under Innocent III as an entire order, and remain so today. Confraternities like that of the Rosary evidently met a need in this regard also. For that matter, of course, the crusade was not entirely effectual. Many of the ordinary laity among the heretics, especially in the more isolated areas, simply went underground, only to reassert themselves later on.[36]

Altogether, the number of "heretic" poets who ended their life in reconciliation with the church, or died in cloisters, is considerable.[37] But perhaps more important to our immediate concern is the tremendous amount of borrowing from materials of the errant poets by either sympathetic or competitively

36 Jalla, Chs. xii, xiii; Belperron, Ch. iv. It is even suggested by Jeanroy, *Savaric de Mauleon: Baron and Troubadour* (Cambridge, 1939), p. 49, that by 1224 the Albigensian heretics had for all practical purposes regained almost all ground lost in the crusade.

37 Anglade devotes a whole chapter to this (iii). There were a few also who had been reclaimed long enough before their death to do some damage. Folquet de Marseilles, the one-time bishop troubadour, became the most zealous of antiheretical persecutors.

minded clergy as well as by Franciscans. The sudden prevalence of the use of rhyme in the thirteenth-century French sermons and the new emphasis on religious poetry did not develop out of thin air. Lecoy de la Marche, *La Chaire Francaise au Moyen Age* (Paris, 1886), p. 479, describes the situation: "La chaire n'échappe pas a la contagion: tantôt le prédicateur s'empare d'un texte de chanson vulgaire pour en faire un commentaire de fantaisie, tantôt il revêt son discours même d'une forme rythmique." A case in point is Étienne de Bourbon, Dominican priest and Inquisitor. Faced with the success of his opponents, he began to adapt and compose verses, making them "objets que de rappeler a l'orateur les principaux points de son sermon." What he used for this purpose was four or five rhymes which he called *versus colorati:* others of his compatriots we know began to use longer poetic insertions or even metrical sermons.[38] It is in these forms, of course, that the real influence of the suppressed poetic tradition of the Vaudois and other heretic groups survive. Soon both poetic sermons of the type first used by groups like the Vaudois 150 years earlier and the sermon-tag lyrics of the Franciscans had spread over France and appeared also in England.[39]

As late as the Irish Red Book of Ossory (started by the Franciscan Richard de Ledrede in 1316, and continued by his successors till the sixteenth century) the reorientation of actual vernacular songs was a short route to providing religious music on short notice — in this last case for the use of the clerics themselves. Among the Latin songs and scraps of vernacular verse in the book is a Latin rubric that explains the presence of the early fourteenth-century songs. As Robbins has observed, in the course of their contact with the local people the clergy had picked up various *cantilene teatrales turpes,* and their bishop, not wishing to forbid what was enjoyed, "substituted pious words for the secular, and thereby reproduced in Latin the original form of the vernacular pieces. So that his clergy would recognize the tune for the new Latin verses, Ledrede headed some of his sacred parodies with lines of the corresponding

[38] Lecoy de la Marche, pp. 479-480, feels that Étienne's use of the term *versus colorati* was "sans doute par opposition aux vers *blancs,* et qui ne sont qu'une suite de récits ou de citations a l'appui." Étienne had been a member of the Inquisition for twenty years, yet the tone of his *Anecdotes* and the type of material he covers indicate that he was, if not a sympathizer with the heretics, interested in them on a slightly more academic level than most of his colleagues.

[39] Homer G. Pfander, *The Popular Sermon of the Mediaeval Friar in England* (New York, 1937), pp. 20ff.

vernacular song."[40] One is reminded of the story told by Gerald of Wales in his *Gemma Ecclesiastica:* one day an absent-minded priest got up before his congregation and began to chant — but the words that first came to the music were "swete lemman, dhin are". That kind of "are" (mercy, favor) not being the sort of thing his bishop thought the church should be dispensing, a ban on the song ever being sung again within the parish was promptly proclaimed.[41] So while the borrowing of poetic forms for *de nouveau* religious composition by friars and others was distinctly a more common occurrence in the thirteenth century, the examples here adduced show that when occasion suited, the church itself was not entirely averse to borrowing tavern songs to meet the competition.

Indeed, flexibility for the adaptation of whatever most effective materials are at hand has always been a singular mark of effusions of Christianity at their moments of greatest spiritual strength. The history of liturgical music is replete with instructive examples. The organized introduction of music into Christian worship has been claimed for Arius, now known as a heretic. He collected songs of sailors, millers, and travellers, setting to them liturgical texts. Gibbon (*Decline and Fall,* Harper, New York, 1845, II, 537) tells how Arian singers paraded the streets of Constantinople, beguiling the ignorant by spreading their doctrine on the wings of popular song, until Chrysostom effectively countered them with his own band of choristers. Many dance tunes of the Renaissance have been preserved to us through their incorporation into a Mass. For example, the tune "L'homme armé" ("The armed man") was a popular French folk song of the fifteenth century. Antoine Busnois made a polyphonic song of it. Over the ensuing generations thirty writers adopted it for newly polyphonic liturgical music. Pales-

[40] Robbins, *Secular Lyrics*, p. xxxv. A graphic modern example of how this sort of thing probably worked out in practice is afforded by a modern novel, John Steinbeck's *Grapes of Wrath.* Steinbeck introduces the preacher Jim Casy sitting under a tree "whistling solemnly the tune of 'Yes, Sir, That's My Baby.' His extended foot swung slowly up and down in the tempo. It was not dance tempo. He stopped whistling and sang in an easy thin tenor:

> 'Yes, sir, that's my Saviour,
> Je-sus is my Saviour
> Je-sus is my Saviour now.
> On the level
> 'S not the devil,
> Jesus is my Saviour now!' "

Compass Book ed. (New York, 1958), p. 25.

[41] Giraldus Cambrensis, *Opera,* Rolls Series, II, 120.

trina's *Missa quarta* of 1582 is based on "L'homme armé." During the Reformation, likewise, many popular tunes found their way into hymns. Sigemund Levarie, in his book on the fourteenth-century French composer *Guillaume de Machaut* (New York, 1954), p. 57, describes one such process:

> Students used to sing a ditty when leaving their university town at the end of a term; substitution of one word changed "Innsbruck, I now must leave thee" to "O world, I now must leave thee," and religion gained new adherents by the adoption of a melody. A popular tune, "Mein mut ist mir betrubet gar" ("My heart is very sad") opens a song collection written down by a Nürnberg citizen around 1450. The composer Hans Leo Hasler, of the same town, used the melody in a small piece for chorus, which was widely sung around 1600 as a lament to the words "Mein G'mut ist mir verwirret" ("My heart is all confused"). For this secular "hit," the Protestant poet Paul Gerhardt found a new text by freely translating St. Bernard's mystical "Salve caput cruentatum" into "O Haupt, voll Blut und Wunden" ("O head, full of blood and wounds"). And in this version one hears it today, as the often recurring and deeply moving chorale in Bach's *Passion According to St. Matthew.*

Many more highlights could be cited, including one to which Protestants are still heir, the eighteenth-century revival hymns adapted under the influence of the Wesleys. One wonders how many modern congregations are aware that "Rock of Ages" is a pastorale, Handel's "And the Glory of the Lord" a minuet, and "Oh That Will Be Glory For Me" a waltz. The history of Christian music shows in general, however, that since the eighteenth and early nineteenth centuries, serious adaptation of secular music to Christian uses has with a few exceptions been on the wane. In fact, in a notable recent interchange, Negro spirituals and modern jazz, the adaptation has been of sacred to secular.

But in the thirteenth century secular adaptation was a thriving enterprise, and while Franciscans and groups like the Vaudois were chiefly catalytic to the process, the secular clergy were quick to respond to the challenge. Indeed, they soon saw that here too, just as in the more exalted genres of narrative poetry, there was ample justification for such a methodology in the early Fathers. St. Augustine, in particular, commenting on the Exodus, notes that "just as the Egyptians had not only idols and grave burdens which the people of Israel detested and avoided, so also they had vases and ornaments of gold and silver" which the Israelites took with them, on God's commandment, to put to a better use (*On Christian Doctrine* II.xl.60). This passage, along with passages in Origen and St. Jerome

(*Epistle* 70 in particular), received a popular audience through preaching guides like John Bromyard's *Summa Praedicantium* and became for the centuries that followed a cautious injunction to borrow from the world whatever could be rendered serviceable to furthering the message of God's love *(caritas)* found in the Bible.[42] It is interesting that at the very time when certain elements of the church, particularly in northern France, were rediscovering this principle, it was already being implemented far more pervasively at the popular level in the south of France and in northern Italy, and by groups most of whom would prove eventually to be an actual threat to the established church. The threat, however construed, was the motivating force behind not only extensive competitive borrowing of the poetic medium, but also the various reclamation movements (e.g. confraternities like those of the Rosary and Puy,[43] and the ordo Humiliati) already mentioned.

## V

It is as the most significant of the Catholic "reclamation" groups that we now regard the Franciscans. That they were able to fulfill this role is due in great part to their natural affinity to the heretical sects, with their emphasis on *vita apostolica* and evangelical spirituality.

When St. Francis was recognized by Innocent III in 1210, it was in an attempt to bring his group under the wing of the church before it, too, went the way of the Vaudois. Based like that of the Cathari and Vaudois on poverty and renunciation, while emphasizing a thoroughly personal and evangelical content, his belief was saved from the charge of heresy only by its utter lack of theological speculation and its simple obedience to the constituted powers of the church. There is however substantial evidence to suggest that if not St. Francis himself, then certainly those who continued to insist on following his "pure rule"— the *zelanti* — were profoundly influenced not only by many of the same conditions as the Vaudois, but also by the perhaps more dangerous apocalyptic teachings of Joachim of Fiore.

Joachim, a sometime Cistercian abbot who died in Calabria in 1202, had brought into the world of St. Francis' time a startlingly new conception of history. Derived from a historio-

[42] For a concise study of the "Egyptian gold" concept, see D. W. Robertson, Jr., *A Preface to Chaucer* (Princeton, 1962), pp. 337ff.

[43] Puy, a French-English confraternity of jongleurs who held an annual singing contest; see art. in *Dictionnaire de Spiritualité*.

graphical exegesis of the Apocalypse, its main tenet was the now famous theory of the three ages of man, a "trinity of ages" corresponding to the divine Trinity. The period of the Old Testament was the age of the Father; the period from the time of Jesus down to Joachim's time was roughly the time of the Son; and the third and final age would be that of the Holy Ghost, under whose aegis the Saracens and Jews would be converted and the world returned to a prelapsarian harmony.[44] Joachim's predictions had led to the belief that the age of the Son would draw to a close forty-two generations after Christ — which suggested 1260 as a possible date for the *terminus ad quem* of the "tyme of grace." Many of those influenced by his teaching, including many Franciscans, thought Frederick II was to be the Antichrist. Unfortunately, Frederick had the discourtesy to die in 1250 and thus frustrate their expectation. Nevertheless, recalculations were continually made to show that the Apocalypse was just around the corner,[45] and to groups like the spiritual Franciscans this added an acute urgency to their mission of evangelization. Moreover, they show evidence of having regarded themselves as the very harbingers of the new age. Joachim had prophesied that just as there were twelve prophets in the First Age, and twelve apostles to proclaim the Second, so there would be twelve pure monastics — much more devoted to poverty and the imitation of Christ than his own Cistercians — who would usher in the Third and Final Age.[46] The early biographies of St. Francis, particularly those of Brother Leo, the *Trium Sociorum* and the *Fioretti,* are replete with suggestions that many early Franciscans regarded themselves as fulfilling such a role.

Yet for practical purposes, St. Francis was not in any doctrinal dispute with the church. One could almost say in fact that he and most of those who followed his example were "sublimely ignorant" of strictly theological questions. For him the

[44] Joachim de Fiore, *L'Évangile Éternel,* Des texts du Christianisme, IV (Paris, 1928), pp. 90-115.

[45] Edmund G. Gardiner, "Joachim of Fiora," *Catholic Encyclopedia,* VIII, 407b. This did not destroy apocalyptic expectations by any means. Predictions of actual dates were merely advanced to years like 1333, then 1366, and so on — thus perpetuating the urgent spirit of apocalyptic fervor into the late fourteenth and early fifteenth century. Wycliffe, too, thought he lived in the "final times." Recently Morton W. Bloomfield, *Piers Plowman as a Fourteenth-Century Apocalypse* (New Brunswick, N. J., 1961), has demonstrated the effect of this electric atmosphere on William Langland.

[46] Joachim de Fiore, *Concordia Novi ac Veteris Testamenti* (Venice, 1519; facs. repr. Frankfurt a.M., 1964), sig. G3$^{r}$ (II.ii.7).

issue at hand was the urgency of repentance and conversion in face of what seemed to be the imminent end of the "tyme of grace" and the coming of Judgment. Therefore, doctrinal content in the songs, whether traced in Umbrian, Provençal, or English, is as simple as the songs are popular — a "mass media" approach directed toward moving hearers to spiritual reform. Generally unhindered by official persecution, the friars could wander from town to town in the manner of minstrels, singing from marketplace or street corner the old songs which had become new, and thus drawing townsfolk for a characteristically simple penitential sermon. Poetry was the waysong, the appetizer as it were, but not always the main course. For this reason the poetic tool they developed was lyric, and not narrative like that of the Vaudois.

St. Francis, schooled in the language and forms of the Provençal poets, himself wrote the earliest Umbrian lyric in the vernacular ("The Canticle of the Sun"),[47] and one of his original followers, Brother Pacifico, had in the world composed wanton songs and been crowned by the emperor as *Rex versum* before joining the Order. Talent was not lacking even in the early movement to adapt popular song forms to higher purposes. In Umbria and elsewhere in Italy, lay brotherhoods of *Laudesi* sprang up which gave employment to jongleurs and poets who would "with more devotion than art . . . frame rude songs or dramatic pieces on the ever-popular events of the Gospel story, especially on the Passion, the miracles of the Virgin, and the joys of Paradise" (Raby, p. 430). Out of these groups also came Latin hymns of lasting fame: the *Dies Irae* of Thomas of Celano, the *Stabat Mater* of Jacopone da Todi, and the *Philomena* of John of Pecham, the brother minor who became Archbishop of Canterbury in 1279. But the vast body of Franciscan poetic production remained popular and in the vernacular dialect. In it the emotional atmosphere of early Franciscan Christianity is continually present. The two principal themes of Franciscan spirituality remained repentance and identification with the passion of Christ.

Jacopone da Todi, like Franciscan poets after him, was aware of the impetus given to repentance by knowledge of the decay of the flesh. In his vernacular poems, like the dialogue between the Soul and the Body, or the even more horrible *Quando t'allegri* (an address to a decaying corpse), we see a rationale behind the call for spiritual reorientation which is

[47] J. R. H. Moorman, *The Sources for the Life of St. Francis* (Manchester, 1940), p. 17.

more succinctly stated in the first stanza of his Latin *De Contemptu Mundi:*

> *cur mundus militat sub vana gloria,*
> *cuius prosperitas est transitoria:*
> *tam cito labitur eius potentia,*
> *quam vasa figuli, quae sunt fragilia,*

or in the translation of a Middle English poet (Brown XIV, p. 237):

> *Whi is the world biloved, that fals is and vein?*
> *Sithen that hise welthis ben uncertein.*
> *Al so soone slidith his power away*
> *as doith a brokil pot, that freish is and gay.*

Yet penance is not the ultimate goal, but rather the crucial turning point after which, by grace, man may identify himself with Christ and so attain unto salvation. Identification with Christ in his death on the cross is the means, as St. Paul said, of death to the old man in ourselves, and rebirth into the new life which is Christ in us (Galatians 2:20). This kind of identification is ultimate, and in his *De Passione Domini,* Jacopone's final cry epitomizes the point of his whole poem:

> *in hac tua passione*
> *me agnosce, pastor bone.*
>
> *[In this your passion*
> *recognize me, good shepherd.]*[48]

Traditionally, Franciscan poets saw the most powerful appeal of the Atonement as emotional, and in turn saw the basis of that appeal as concretely manifested in the details of the crucifixion itself. In this they departed substantially from all previous tradition, taking the sometimes remote biblical doctrine and infusing it with vivid, even gruesome descriptions of the pain and suffering of Christ. Almost always, the physical dolor of Christ was made to stand for the infinitely greater magnitude of his spiritual suffering on behalf of sinful mankind; but to drive the spiritual message home the *physical* point was graphically made as never before in Christian art. The appeal of this new approach was explosive, ultimately creating a sty-

[48] The phrase in the second line is often trans. "know me," but has connotations of an ultimate metaphysical nature. Thus in the Vulgate trans. of John 10:27, 28 we read: "Oves meae vocem meam audiunt et ego Dominus agnosco eas, et sequuntur me; et ego vitam aeternum do eis. . . ." The same verb is also used in vv. 14 and 15. The force of this kind of knowing is connected with the context of Christ's giving of *novam vitam,* so that St. Bernard (*PL,* CLXXXII, col. 413) and others in discussing the "new birth" play on this connotation of *agnoscere.*

listic revolution that changed the course of European art.[49] In all of this, in psychology and motif as well as in theme, the spirituality manifested in Franciscan poetry is double-edged: vividly portrayed, the fear of death moves toward penance, and vivid expressions of the greatest love and pity move toward love. As was noted before, the latter response may be evoked through a vision of the passion of Christ as seen through the eyes of Mary, who in the literary iconography of Franciscan poetry is often given the attributes of the *sponsa* of the *Song of Songs,* and thus serves as a figure for the Bride of Christ, his church. F. J. E. Raby has aptly said that "the Franciscan singers, from Bonaventura to Jacopone, sang always with their faces set to the scene of this double passion, where

*Under the world redeeming rood*
*The most afflicted mother stood*
*Mingling her tears with her Son's blood."*
[p. 421]

He might have as easily made the boundaries larger — from St. Francis to James Ryman.

## VI

On September 10, 1224, during the same week in which St. Francis received the stigmata, Fra Angello of Pisa and eight companions landed at Dover. Within six months they had established friaries at the three centers — ecclesiastical, civil, and intellectual — of national life (Canterbury, London, and Oxford), as well as at Northampton. Within five years a dozen more houses were added in major English towns and by 1240, thirty-four strategically located friaries extending past the Scottish border were a testimony to the spiritual and administrative *blitzkrieg* effected by the first English Franciscans.[50]

The English province remained longer than the continental provinces in the camp of the "spiritual" Franciscans, so we might anticipate that the "evangelical" methodology they employed would have had good opportunities to take root. The evidence supports this view. The Franciscan friars, it will be remembered, were mistaken for minstrels when they first came

[49] For concise treatment of this revolution in style see Émile Mâle, *L'Art religieux du XIIIe siècle en France* (Paris, 1935). One of the most significant Franciscan documents for study of the "new style" is the *Meditations on the Life of Christ,* translated and edited by Isa Ragusa and Rosalie B. Green (Princeton, 1961).

[50] Dom David Knowles, *The Religious Orders in England* (Cambridge, 1962), I, 127-145.

to England in 1224. It was with considerable disappointment that the mistake was first discovered — and the erring priory promptly ejected the bewildered friars (Pfander, p. 23). But these same wandering friars were very likely the first in England to use vernacular verse in their sermons. In fact, it may be through them that England of the thirteenth century was introduced to the religious lyric and verse sermon.[51] There is obviously not time to recount here the evidence of Franciscan influence in all these areas. But from the point of view of Middle English poetry, it is difficult to overlook the fact that while we have almost no record of lyric production before 1225, there is abundant evidence of a flourishing tradition immediately after that time. In the many poems that do remain to us of that tradition, we see the unmistakable themes and even forms of the first Franciscan *joculatores dei*. And it is now clear that the provenance of most Middle English Lyrics written before 1350 is Franciscan.[52]

As I have tried to indicate, the most characteristic of these poems attempt to be either expressions of the nature of Christian *caritas* through praise and prayer, or injunctions to repentance, or both. A late fifteenth-century poem of James Ryman can do more than any further explanation on my part to render explicit the manner of their appeal.

*Amende we us, while we have space,*
*For why nowe is the tyme of grace.*

1.

*That holy clerke, seint Augustyne,*
*Seith, now is tyme for to inclyne*
*To vertue and synne to resyne,*
*For why now is the tyme of grace.*

2.

*Now, while we lyve, to do penaunce*
*It is oure soules to avaunce*
*And into blisse for to enhaunce,*
*For why now is the tyme of grace.*

3.

*Are° we departe this worlde fro,* (Before)
*Oure soules we may save fro woo;*

[51] G. R. Owst, *Literature and Pulpit in Medieval England*, 2nd ed. (Oxford, 1961), p. 10.

[52] Robbins. A fuller treatment of the provenance MSS of Middle English Lyrics to 1350, including Harley MS. 2253, will appear in Ch. v of my forthcoming book *Franciscan Spirituality and the Middle English Lyric*, where it is shown that the number of MEL MSS of Franciscan provenance is actually much higher than even Robbins supposed.

*Whenne we be gone, we may not so,*
*For why now is the tyme of grace.*

4.

*Do we so now, while we here be,*
*In worde and dede, that we may see*
*Almyghty god in mageste,*
*For why now is the tyme of grace.*

5.

*In wille, in dede, in worde and thought*
*Axe we hym grace, that us hath bought,*
*Ayenst his wille that we have wrought,*
*For why now is the tyme of grace.*

6.

*Criste, that ay was, shall be and is,*
*Graunte us forgevenes of oure mys*
*And graunte us grace to swell in blis,*
*For why now is the tyme of grace.*

[Zupitza, No. 49]

He would be a dull fellow who missed the point of this poem: "Let us amend ourselves, while we have opportunity, for now is the time of grace." While Ryman's poetic abilities are hardly distinguished among his kind, his poem serves to show us much. Here we have the popular *aaab* carol form developed in Provence and adopted by the earliest Franciscans to sing the gospel; here too we have the characteristic expression of medieval spiritual movements of the urgent need for repentance; and here is an explicit recounting of the traditional doctrinal reasons for penance. These reasons arise naturally from the nature of man's sin against God's "wille" and from the enabling grace purchased in Christ's atoning death which alone makes penance effective (stanza 5). The well-known Augustinian idea of the six ages of man, of which the last, that of grace, began with Christ, is invoked by reference to "that holy clerke" in the first line of the song. The great *lifes laene* theme of medieval poetry is sounded in the first lines of stanzas two, three, and four, where together with the reiterated message of the two-line burden or refrain, the song receives a unifying emphasis on the urgency of repentance in the face of fleeting "tyme." The first line of stanza five underscores the totality of commitment involved in the prayer for grace: it is an action of *wille* foremost, followed by *worde, dede,* and *thought.* Thus both the aspect of works consistent with faith, introduced in the preceding stanza, and the aspect of grace amplified in the last stanza are compactly stated in one stanza. In addition, the factor of free human will is introduced in the same sentence as God's will, in terms of which it chooses. There is much theology here in little space; in fact the fifth stanza capsulizes the message of the poem. But the last is not then anticlimactic or nugatory, for it, again in an apt first line, strikes the note that prevents Christian despair over the transitoriness of human existence: it is Christ's eternality that guarantees that our true "blis," toward which we are called to travel, is not the sort that moth or rust may corrupt.

No one could miss the obvious doctrinal nature of such a poem, or fail to infer its pragmatic value, even if he did not know the history of its development and use. But there are many other poems, just as much a part of the same spiritual tradition, whose superior artistic merit may for the modern reader cloud the nature of their "evangelical" intent. Here is a poem from the well-known Harley MS. 2253 to illustrate the point.

*Wynter wakeneth al my care,*
*nou this leves waxeth bare;*
*ofte y sike ant mourne sare*
*when hit cometh in my thoht*
*of this worldes joie hou hit geth al to noht.*

*Nou hit is ant nou hit nys,*
*also hit ner nere ywys.*
*that monie mon seith soth hit ys:*
*al goth bote Godes wille,*
*alle we shule deye thah us like ylle.°* (though it please us ill)

*Al that grein me graveth grene,*
*nou hit faleweth al bydene;*
*Jesu, help that hit be sene,*
*ant shild us from helle,*
*for y not° whider y shal ne hou longe her duelle.*[53] (know not)

[53] Fol. 75v; Brown XIV, No. 9. Since most of the friars' audience had only generalized theological knowledge, in the ensuing explication I do not employ the following literary sources, although they were certainly known to the friars who composed the poems and to their more educated audience. For example, Gregory the Great interprets winter as the present life, and the austerity of the Old Law (*PL*, LXXIX, col. 498). Honorius of Autun says winter signifies *infidelitas;* for just as winter fetters the earth with ice so that nothing grows, so infidelity fetters men's hearts with the coldness of sin so that they do not bear the fruit of faith (*PL*, CLXXII, cols. 391-392). The advent of winter and its coldness are also seen as images of the Last Judgment and the end of the world (see *Allegoriae in sacram scripturam, PL*, CXII, cols. 937, 954, and Rabanus Maurus, *De universo, PL*, CXI, col. 303). All those familiar with the liturgical calendar, of course, know that the time of the coming of the winter solstice, as the leaves "wax bare," is the time of Advent, which is associated with penitence in preparation for the birth of Christ as a spiritual event in the human heart (see for example St. Bernard, *De Adventu Domini,* parts of which are translated in *St. Bernard on the Christian Year* [London, 1954]).

If the beautiful, haunting tone, the deft strokes of vernal imagery, and the semialliterative whisper of its cadence seem to obscure the doctrine, look closer; it is still there. Winter, the time of old age, barrenness, and remembrance of misspent summers, has a solidly traditional iconography traceable to earliest Christian times. Both in the visual and literary arts, the season is associated with old age and sin, which in turn is identified with St. Paul's "old man" (Ephesians 4:22). This motif, coupled with the reiterated idea of the utter impermanence of temporal, tangible things in the fifth, sixth, seventh, and tenth lines, is contrasted to the poet's starkly effective realization at the exact center of the poem: "What many men say — truth it is: all goeth but God's will." (Note how in stanza five of Ryman's poem God's "wille" also becomes the enduring and pivotal concept with which man in his transitory world is confronted.) The lines are uttered in a dramatically perfect sigh of self-perception: as the leaves of life begin to fall, there is no use thinking that the earth will not receive its own. There is no hope in things deciduous. But as every medieval person knew from a common image in parish sermons and other religious poems, that which was ever green (often the holly) was a symbol of the eternality of the resurrected Christ, the perpetual spring of Paradise, and Christ's own resurrection which is reflected in the greenness of springtime.[54] As this saving note is sounded at the beginning of the third stanza, another reference is directly called forth by its first two lines. "All that seed I bury unripe, now it withers already: Jesus help that it be seen." The source idea is of course John 12:24, 25: "Verily, verily, I say unto you, Except a corn of wheat fall into the ground and die, it abideth alone: but if it die, it bringeth forth much fruit. He that loveth his life shall lose it; and he that hateth his life in this world shall keep it unto life eternal." This also is a popular passage with medieval commentators, who use it to point up the very theme of both these poems, that man's proper movement is not toward the things of this life, but toward the love of the New Jerusalem which is to come (Augustine *De civitate Dei* xiv, 28). He that loves his life more than he loves God is guilty of *cupiditas,* the self-love that leads to destruction and death. But as St. Augustine and scores of later medieval writers were wont to stress, he who loves with *caritas,* the crucial virtue of Christian character

[54] See St. Augustine on Psalm 1, *PL,* XXXVI, col. 68. For a fuller treatment of spring imagery in medieval poetry see D. W. Robertson, Jr., "The Doctrine of Charity in Mediaeval Literary Gardens," *Speculum,* XXVI (1951), 24-49.

(without which St. Paul says all the rest of life's efforts are irrelevant), despises the cupidinous desires of his temporal body that he may attain "unto life eternal."

Here again, as in Ryman's poem, the poet's goal is to move his hearers toward that *caritas* which loves God rather than self, emphasizing the dire urgency of repentance before the seasons of this life conclude their course. Thus, he too does not close on the note of comfort at the first of his final stanza, and lacking the two-line "burden" to reemphasize his theme, employs another technique. Referring to the "grein" (seed) again, he says, "Jesus, help that it be seen," that is, he prays that Christ may notice that he has become "dead to the things of this world" and laid down his life so that he might not ultimately lose it. The implication is clear: winter is not the usual time for planting seeds, and perhaps Christ might not be looking for grain committed so late. The poet's final lines therefore combine beautifully both the urgency of his belated plea and the poignant air of insecurity he shares with all who are not new men, renewed in the grace which is of Christ.

*ant shild us from helle,*
*for y not whider y shal ne hou longe her duelle.*

The sudden, momentary shift from first person singular to plural in the second-to-last line comes at precisely the right psychological moment to deftly identify the poet's listeners with his own song.

## VII

It is now possible, I think, to perceive certain relationships that have not been commonly recognized before. Foremost, the emphasis of medieval spirituality, particularly of the late twelfth and thirteenth centuries, and particularly as represented by Franciscan poets, may be of primary significance for the development of the Middle English lyric. Also, while these lyrics are emotionally oriented by comparison to most medieval Christian literature, we can see that their emotional quality derives from the salutary effect of mendicant methodology on an essentially standard New Testament theology. Whether composed *de nouveau,* or from existing models, or borrowed from secular tunes, the Middle English lyrics were primarily conceived as vehicles for transmission of the gospel, and notably are directed toward the practical goal of penance. Some of the poems, like "Wynter," convey their theology subtly and beautifully, yet just as explicitly as some of the more obviously doctrinal poems.

It is not possible to dismiss the Middle English religious

lyrics as either trite or merely polemic. True, they were often intended to teach in the most strictly didactic sense the lesson of penance and the propriety of response to Christ, but the form in which the lesson came was contrived to produce through words and music an aesthetic and emotional response that would etch the message on the total personality. Some individual lyrics, indeed, are as poetically powerful as the best of their kind in later English verse. What sets them off for our particular interest is that they are a remarkable adaptation of artistic means to what was considered to be the highest and imperative end, a conception that in the mind of poet, singer, and audience rendered their burdens far from trite. The Middle English religious lyrics were the stuff of apocalypse, of religious and social revolution, and of a pervasive religious commitment carrying depth and sincerity.

More than anything else, this poetry is an expression of the readiness of men as diverse and yet as similar as Waldo and Francis to forge from the "Egyptian gold" at hand vessels best suited to carry the message of God's love to their people. As perhaps the most vibrant popular expression of medieval spirituality, the Middle English lyrics served to marry the message of God's love for fallen men to the aesthetic of popular song. So doing, they met the people where they lived and played, and became the most widely sung religious songs in the history of our tongue.

# Chaucer's Precarious Knight

DEAN EBNER

In the dramatic give-and-take that occupies the travellers to the shrine of Thomas à Becket in Chaucer's *Canterbury Tales,* there occurs a relatively minor episode which may open a very large window on the character of the Knight as he confronts a most human problem, the insecurity of prosperity. I refer to the Knight's interruption of the *Monk's Tale.* The Monk has droned on through seventeen stories, giving historical and legendary examples of men and women who illustrate a tragic vision of life, couched in distinctly medieval terms. Nebuchadnezzar, Caesar, Nero, Alexander, to name only a few, were noble and prosperous people who fell from "heigh degree" to irreversible adversity and poverty. They were wealthy, powerful, and famous rulers who, despite varying degrees of moral worth, were forced to give up a life of repeated physical pleasures by the sudden and irrational changes of Fortune's wheel:

> *I wol bewaille, in manere of tragedie,*
> *The harm of hem that stoode in heigh degree,*
> *And fillen° so that ther nas no remedie* (fell)
> *To brynge hem out of hir adversitee.*
> *For certein, whan that Fortune list° to flee,* (desires)
> *Ther may no man the cours of hire withholde.*

The moral is clear:

---

Dean Ebner is Chairman of the English Department, Whitworth College. He received the A.B. degree from Wheaton College in 1959. Pursuing graduate study under Stanford University and Woodrow Wilson Fellowships, he received the Ph.D. degree from Stanford in 1965, specializing in English literature of the Renaissance. Since 1964 he has taught at Whitworth, where he is now Associate Professor of English. He has published articles on aesthetics in *The Gordon Review* and on *The Tempest* in the *Shakespeare Quarterly,* and his book *Autobiography in 17th Century England: Theology and the Self* is forthcoming from Mouton and Co. (The Hague; Paris).

*Lat no man truste on blynd prosperitee;*
*Be war by thise ensamples trewe and olde.*
[VII, 1991-98][1]

In modern colloquial terms these were people who "had it made," successful people occupying positions of status in the "Establishment" who had a streak of "bad luck" and "lost out," experiencing the futility of depending upon a stable social order in an absurd universe. But the Monk's moral, that pilgrims through life should shun prosperity and the mental perspectives inevitably connected with it, is as lost on the modern reader as it was on the Knight. For we seem no more able to escape a kind of "truste" in our own affluence than he. Thus it is that in his silencing of the Monk with a plea for more cheerful tales (VII, 2767-79), the Knight becomes the archetypal spokesman for our whole culture, a culture that answers the darker and ultimately more realistic tragic vision of medieval man with a swift change of subject and an anxious redoubling of the pleasures of life.

The Knight is an active and ambitious man. His quest for glory, fame, and profit through military adventure requires a God who will reward effort and guarantee a stable prosperity. For this reason he much prefers his own tale of romance with its contrived happy ending to the Monk's tragic vision. And for this reason he feels compelled to interrupt the Monk. The Knight, in short, is afraid. If the moral universe constructed by the Monk reflects the way things are in the real world, then through his own choice the Knight is embarked upon a false and unstable way, highly vulnerable to the whims of irrational forces. He perceives, as does modern Western man, in the example of those who have already fallen, a threat to his own personal good fortune. To be high on the Wheel of Fortune is to invite adversity. The Knight's uneasiness is akin to ours. It might be well, therefore, to understand in somewhat greater depth the opposing pictures of the universe and man's place in it given in the *Monk's Tale,* on the one hand, and the character and tale of the Knight on the other.

Chaucer drew the Monk's view of Fortune from both Boccaccio and Boethius. Boccaccio's *De Casibus Virorum et Feminarum Illustrium,* the *locus classicus* of the Fall of Princes theme, was his chief source. In using the *De Casibus,* however, Chaucer caused the Monk to be truer to the formula than even Boccaccio

[1] All references to *The Canterbury Tales* employ F. N. Robinson's numerical system, and the translation of key terms draws upon his glossary and notes. *The Works of Geoffrey Chaucer,* 2nd ed. (Boston, 1957).

had been. Boccaccio had included a brief defense of worldly activity in recording the case of Alcibiades. Some striving after measurable success seems justifiable even in an insecure cosmos. This qualification is eliminated in the *Monk's Tale.*

Chaucer's indebtedness to Boethius stems primarily from Book II of *The Consolation of Philosophy,* a work Chaucer translated into English prose. Here we learn that Fortune deceives with fake prosperity. She stacks the outcome of events decidedly in her favor. "Richesses, honours, and swiche othere thinges," she boasts, "ben of my right." For this reason Dame Philosophy must warn against the vanity of riches, power, and glory, and "covetise of mortel thynges."[2]

The moral of the *Monk's Tale* and its sources, then, is that man is not to trust in the changeable prosperity of this world but to prepare for the next. In this way, the Fall of Princes motif was a primary expression in literature of the "contempt of the world" theme which heavily influenced medieval sensibility during and after the twelfth century. Such an emphasis served to undercut the desire for a life of worldly action and the search for fame, and to reinforce the church's underlying conviction that in the final analysis the ascetic life is really the most acceptable to God. To give up is the way to possess what really matters. This is why the Monk tells us he has a hundred such tragedies in his cell. They were among the favorite persuasive devices used to encourage monasticism. And so compelling was the monastic style of life in the Middle Ages that the medieval man who was not an ascetic knew that he jeopardized his soul in concentrating on the broader secular affairs of an active life. Since the Wheel of Fortune governed chiefly those men who attached themselves to worldly ambition, the irrationality of life increased with the choice of a wrong goal. Certain protection from the fickle goddess could only be achieved by withdrawal from the active life altogether[3] and, as Boccaccio suggests in the *De Casibus,* by the choice of poverty. "For Contempt of the World," Farnham says, "the theoretically right story of misfortune is that of a great and good man overwhelmed through absolutely no fault of his own, always excepting the initial fault of choosing the active life. The greater and better the man the righter the story, since the aim is to show that neither eminent power nor eminent virtue can

[2] Robinson, pp. 331-338.

[3] Willard Farnham, *The Medieval Heritage of Elizabethan Tragedy* (New York, 1936), pp. 32, 41-46, 79, 107.

achieve security here below nor make this evil world into a good world. . . ."[4]

In other words, something inherent in the nature of things is set in motion to destroy us if we dedicate our energies to constructing a circle of comfort and prestige for ourselves in this fallen world. The enterprise is always doomed to disappointment. The circle can never hold out for long the dark side of life. The underlying fear of the medieval man who found attraction in a life of worldly activity is expressed in Petrarch's *Secretum,* in which we are warned of the danger of trying to combine two irreconcilable opposites. When Petrarch suggests that man might seek worldly glory while here and glory in heaven at the proper time (a solution later advanced by Thoreau in his famous quip that we should tackle one world at a time), the imaginary St. Augustine replies: "O man, little in yourself, and of little wisdom! . . . That delusion has betrayed thousands of men thousands of times, and has sunk into hell a countless host of souls. Thinking to have one foot on earth and one in heaven, they could neither stand here below nor mount on high. Therefore they fell miserably and the moving breeze swept them suddenly away."[5]

It was inevitable that similar otherworldly ideas, as they came to be expressed in the Fall of Princes literature, should come into sharp conflict with the ideal of knighthood, the code of manliness that led Western civilization into the modern era. Knighthood was an active life, open to all the temptations of high position, fame, and worldly riches — just those things which the church labeled vainglory and which it placed under the control of unstable Fortune. Attempts to reconcile the knightly ideal with the true Christian life in the Crusades and the military orders were partially successful, but they were accompanied by an uneasy conscience. St. Bernard, for example, condemned the knighthood of his youth after his conversion: "What, then, ye knights," he questions, "is this gigantic error, this intolerable madness, to fight with such expense and labour for no reward, save the reward of death?" When he finally approved of the knight-monk Templars, he did so with the clear injunction that such Christian warriors were to eschew the elaborate equipment of the secular knight. John of Salisbury sounds a similar note in *Policraticus.* Knights should avoid luxury and display and be quite certain that the desire for worldly glory is not the motive behind their deeds. Even the popular romance reflects the same

[4] Farnham, p. 89.
[5] Farnham, pp. 49-50.

uneasiness, as when Guy of Warwick decides that his knightly life is vanity and becomes a guide to pilgrims.[6] Thus, when we understand the view of the world that the tragic tales told by the Monk recalled to the medieval mind and the latent issues that they raised in the conscience of any prosperous nobleman immersed in a life of worldly activity, we are ready to examine the Knight's interruption with a new dimension of insight. This frequently overlooked episode becomes a magnifying glass through which we can see more clearly the Knight both as literary character and as exemplar of our own frustrations.

*"Hoo!" quod the Knyght, "good sire, namoore of this!*
*That ye han seyd is right ynough, ywis,*
*And muchel moore; for litel hevynesse*
*Is right ynough to muche folk, I gesse.*
*I seye for me, it is a greet disese,°* (discomfort)
*Whereas men han been in greet welthe and ese,*
*To heeren of hire sodeyn fal, allas!*
*And the contrarie is joye and greet solas,*
*As whan a man hath been in povre estaat,*
*And clymbeth up and wexeth fortunat,*
*And there abideth in prosperitee.*
*Swich thyng is gladsom, as it thynketh° me,* (seems to)
*And of swich thyng were goodly for to telle."*
[VII, 2767-79]

There are, of course, some obvious reasons why Chaucer has chosen the Knight to end the *Monk's Tale*. If the order in which the Host asks the Pilgrims to recite may be regarded as significant, then the Knight is the only one of higher social status than the Monk and is therefore suited to the role.[7] Chaucer could have used the Host, as he does in two manuscripts, but in moving the interruption to its final position at the end of Fragment VII, he found it necessary to avoid a monotonous repetition. He had used the Host to interrupt before *Melibee*.[8]

But viewing the content of the interruption as it stands, critics have not been satisfied with these external explanations. There seems to be some internal motivation in the Knight's character that makes it natural for him to react in this way to the tales the Monk is telling. Lowes is certain that we learn something new about the Knight from this passage, but he is

[6] F. J. C. Hearnshaw, "Chivalry and Its Place in History," *Chivalry*, ed. Edgar Prestage (London, 1928), pp. 47-48.
[7] R. E. Kaske, "The Knight's Interruption of the *Monk's Tale*," *ELH*, XXIV (December 1957), 249-250.
[8] Robinson, p. 750.

not certain what it is.[9] Malone is more specific. He thinks that the Knight interrupts the Monk in a rude manner and is no longer the courteous example of chivalry described in the *General Prologue*. Further, in desiring tales with happy endings, he expresses the taste of a child or of an unsophisticated soldier revealing his literary naiveté,[10] or, we might wish to add, the naiveté of an American television audience. Malone's reading, however, seems to raise more problems than it solves. Does the Knight really become rude and thus inconsistent with our earlier view of him? " 'Hoo! . . . good sire, namoore of this!' " seems more like the friendly jest of a social superior intent upon changing the subject than a rude denunciation. And are we to assume that Chaucer is so dramatically inconsistent that the narrator of the highly sophisticated *Knight's Tale* is now to be regarded as a naive critic of literary effort?

A simpler explanation of the Knight's interruption is surely evidenced by the text, one that preserves the consistency of his character throughout the poem while revealing a depth of motivation previously overlooked. From our understanding of the place of *De Casibus* tragedy in medieval thought, we may easily detect a certain anxiety in the Knight's mind, occasioned by his opposition to the view of Fortune that the Monk has set forth[11] and mixed with a certain suspicion that the Monk may be right. The Knight tells us directly that tales of people who have fallen from riches into poverty make him uneasy. Granting the need for most people to consider at least temporarily the darker side of life as appropriate to their condition, he would rather view his own existence from a more optimistic perspective, and hear of those who have risen from poverty to prosperity and have remained secure in that fortunate condition. We do not have to search far for the personal reason behind his preference for such tales. He is in a position of prosperity himself and hopes to remain there. He is a successful man who has nowhere to go but down. And if the Monk is right, the Knight's position on Fortune's fickle wheel is indeed precarious. A glance at his portrait in the *General Prologue* will confirm just how high that position is and support this reading of the interruption.

[9] J. L. Lowes, *Geoffrey Chaucer and the Development of His Genius* (Cambridge, Mass., 1934), pp. 202-203.

[10] Kemp Malone, *Chapters on Chaucer* (Baltimore, 1951), pp. 169-170.

[11] R. E. Kaske has noted the difference between the Knight's view of Fortune and the Monk's as seen in their respective tales. In "The Knight's Interruption of the *Monk's Tale*," he develops the thesis that the interruption is due to this difference. He does not, however, suggest the dramatic motivations behind the Knight's view.

The normal view of the Knight's character is often distorted because some readers make the mistake of assuming that a "verray, parfit gentil knyght" (I, 72) who has fought mainly in religious wars is somehow to be set apart from the normally more worldly members of his profession. Our Knight, they say, is not only an ideal knight (which he certainly is), but he also embodies the very highest standards of spiritual excellence. He (unlike other knights, we are to assume) is pious, courteous, and humble; and he (unlike the Monk and Squire) has eschewed vain apparel. We can conclude from his portrait, Kaske tells us, that "the Knight, in the impression of the austerity of life that he creates, is rivalled only by the Clerk and the Parson."[12] Such a reading, however, simply cannot be supported from the text of the poem, if one remembers that the ideals of courtesy and outward piety were attained by many fourteenth-century knights, that knighthood was not the church's idea of the highest spiritual excellence, and that Chaucer's words do not necessarily mean what they suggest to the modern reader. Let us reexamine the *General Prologue,* then, noting particularly those lines that will give us a corrected view of the Knight's character and establish the preference for worldly wealth and fame that trigger his opposition to the *Monk's Tale.*

We learn first that the Knight is famous: "evere honoured for his worthynesse" (50). Many times his military prowess has won for him the place of highest honor at the banquet table: "Ful ofte tyme he hadde the bord bigonne / Aboven alle nacions in Pruce" (52-53). The reference to Prussia suggests something akin to the Prussian "table of honor" held in 1377. Peter Suchenwirt, a wandering minstrel, describes the days of feasting that accompanied such a noble event:

> Thence they made their way to Königsberg, where each nobleman emptied his sack in feasting the others. But the Duke's banquet excelled all the rest. Before each course was heard the sound of trumpets and pipes. Of viands there was no lack; for one course alone were served baked meats and roast, spiced and gilded. With these went wine of Italy, of Hungary, and of Istria, served in vessels of gold, silver, and precious stones. Before the meal was ended, the Duke, of his bounty, had gold and silver borne in and bestowed upon two knights and one squire, each the best of his own land according to the law of arms, and one whom reproach had never sullied. . . .[13]

Such was the nonascetic world in which our Knight moved, for

[12] Kaske, p. 252.

[13] Quoted in Muriel Bowden, *A Commentary on the General Prologue to the Canterbury Tales* (New York, 1954), pp. 64-65.

in summarizing his successes in battle Chaucer tells us that "everemoore he hadde a sovereyn prys [obtained a very high reputation]" (67).

We come next to the line most often responsible for the false impression of the Knight's character: "He was a verray, parfit gentil knyght" (72). This line does not mean that he is "very perfect," nor that in contrast to most knights, he alone is of gentle behavior. That he is indeed "meeke as is a mayde," we learn earlier (69). This was the standard rule of behavior expected of all knights, at least toward their friends. The line states merely that he is a true ("verray") knight, and, punctuated as Robinson suggests, that his noble birth is of a perfect quality ("parfit gentil" — perfectly genteel). He is, in other words, a code hero of medieval chivalry.

We learn next of his array:

*His hors° were goode, but he was nat gay.°* (horses) (showily dressed)
*Of fustian he wered a gypon°* (he wore a tunic of thick cotton cloth)
*Al bismotered° with his habergeon,°* (besmutted) (coat of mail)
*For he was late ycome from his viage,°* (expedition)
*And wente for to doon his pilgrymage.*
[74-78]

This passage indicates neither a renunciation of worldly goods nor unusual piety. In fact, a close reading indicates precisely the opposite. First, he has with him at least one extra horse for no apparent reason other than the fact that he is used to travelling in a manner appropriate to his high station in life. Here is a man whose self-image requires a rather high and public standard of consumption. We should also note the significance of the conjunction in the same line: "His hors were goode, *but* . . .," i.e. in contrast to what one might naturally expect of a man with such fine horses, he is not gaily dressed. The remainder of the passage is devoted to explaining this surprising situation. He is wearing his battle tunic rather than the expected showy costume which would match his fine horses, not because he has renounced worldly goods, but because he was in such a hurry to perform the normal duty of a pilgrimage of thanksgiving expected of a knight (military success being closely connected to the blessing of God) that he only removed his expensive armor and did not take the time to change into anything better than the garments underneath. Perhaps he felt that showy dress was inappropriate for a pilgrimage. In any case, his party indicates that he has no opposition to worldly splendor. He has allowed his son, the Squire, to remain dressed in a manner befitting his occupation as a court dandy. The Squire's hair is curled, and he is dressed gaily. The Ellesmere miniature shows his coat and cap much decorated with embroidery. Even the Knight's servant, the simple Yeoman, carries "a gay dagger," perhaps evidence of his lord's generosity.

With these highly selected descriptive details, Chaucer builds an unquestionable impression of the Knight's successful position. He has fought for the Christian cause, and for his reward he has earned (ironically) wealth, power, and fame. With Alexander and Caesar he possesses "knighthood," "fredom" (liberality), and "gentillesse" (gentility). Like Hercules, Cenobia, Alexander, and Caesar, he is a conqueror. He has riches and fame like Sampson and Nebuchadnezzar; he would be at home at Balthasar's blithe feast; he is "large" (lavish) like Cenobia; and he probably possesses at home some jewelled clothing not unlike Nero's. No wonder he interrupts the Monk! Although he is not at the very top of Fortune's Wheel in being the ruler of a land, he is close enough to sense what a plunge into adversity would mean. It is not difficult to understand why he is restless in the presence of *De Casibus* tragedy, and why he prefers tales "As whan a man hath been in povre estaat,/And clymbeth up and wexeth fortunat,/And there abideth in prosperitee." How personally reassuring a tale of stable affluence would be compared to the Monk's dreary, ascetic moralizing!

In order to confirm this view of the Knight's motivation in interrupting the Monk, we have yet to examine his most significant appearance in the poem, the tale he tells of Palamon and Arcite. In the *Knight's Tale,* universally acknowledged to be subtly matched to its teller, we have both additional evidence of his love of splendor and a clear example of the kind of cosmic arrangement he prefers, one that will guarantee him a permanent appointment to the state of prosperity he now enjoys.

In keeping with the Knight's character as we have seen it develop thus far, Chaucer has assigned to him a tale in which description of the pomp and circumstance of the chivalric life receives more emphasis than even characterization.[14] The splendor of the backdrop, in other words, rivals the persons and their relationships for our interest. Much of this descriptive attention is focused upon Theseus, governor of Athens, who seems to fit the Knight's concept of the true nobleman: "Ful many a riche contree hadde he wonne;/What with his wysdom and his chivalrie"

[14] Charles Muscatine, "Form, Texture, and Meaning in Chaucer's *Knight's Tale,*" *Chaucer: Modern Essays in Criticism,* ed. Edward Wagenknecht (New York, 1959), pp. 69-71; R. K. Root, *The Poetry of Chaucer* (Cambridge, Mass., 1922), pp. 171-172.

(864-65). He pictures Theseus entering Athens with great glory and pomp "in al his wele [success] and in his mooste pride" (895). We learn, further, that it is Fortune that has made it possible for him to be a conqueror (915-16) and that he lives in an abiding state of joy and honor (1028-29). The Knight pauses to delineate

*The mynstralcye, the service at the feeste,*
*The grete yiftes to the meeste° and leeste,* (highest)
*The riche array of Theseus paleys,°* (palace)
*...who sat first ne last upon the deys,*
*What ladyes fairest been or best daunsynge.*
[2197-2201]

The extent to which Chaucer was interested in making these descriptions a revelation of the Knight's own love of splendor and of fame is seen in the fact that the fourth line of the passage above, concerning the place of honor at celebrations, does not appear in the source of the *Tale*, Boccaccio's *Teseida*. Chaucer was careful to expand upon the Knight's native interests.

The emphasis on rich display continues throughout the *Tale*. There is the description of Diana's temple, for example, also missing in the *Teseida:*

*And northward, in a touret° on the wal,* (turret)
*Of alabastre whit and reed° coral,* (white and red)
*An oratorie, riche for to see,*
*In worshipe of Dyane of chastitee.*
[1909-12]

King Emetreus appears on the scene in another addition to the *Teseida* story; he

*Upon a steede bay trapped° in steel,* (furnished with trappings)
*Covered in clooth of gold, dyapred weel,°* (decorated well)
*Cam ridynge lyk the god of armes, Mars.*
*His cote-armure was of clooth of Tars*
*Couched with perles white and rounde and grete;*
*His sadel was of brend° gold newe ybete°;* (bright) (beaten)
*A mantelet upon his shulder hangynge,*
*Bret-ful of rubyes rede as fyr sparklynge;*

. . . .

*Upon his heed he wered of laurer° grene* (laurel)
*A gerland, fressh and lusty for to sene.°* (pleasant to look upon)
*Upon his hand he bar for his deduyt°* (bore for his delight)
*An egle tame, as any lilye whyt.*
*An hundred lordes hadde he with hym there,*
*Al armed, save hir heddes, in al hir gere,*
*Ful richely in alle maner thynges.*
[2157-64, 2175-81]

Even in describing Arcite's funeral, the Knight dwells upon the richness of his armor (2887-98), the costly clothing he wears, the array on the pyre (2935-40), and the expensive items cast into the fire (2945-50). He even pauses to include the detail that the case and decorations of Arcite's Turkish bow are made of burnished gold (2896).

On earth, Arcite, one of the lovers in the *Tale,* had learned to renounce the vanity of wealth, but it is highly important to note that his speech (1251ff.) is countered strongly by Theseus at the end of the *Tale,* and Chaucer decided to save for *Troilus and Criseyde* the *Teseida* passage in which Arcite's soul ascends into the heavens and scorns from a superior perspective those who seek earthly happiness. In this way the Knight is allowed to go unhindered in his presentation of earthly wealth as the normal and abiding accompaniment of the noble life lived in the activities of this world. Even while using Boethius for a more optimistic view of Fortune than the Monk has presented, he is allowed to ignore whole passages in Books II and III of *The Consolation of Philosophy* which warn of the inherent instability of wealth, power, and position (2987ff.).

It is this more optimistic view of Fortune that finally confirms our reading of the Knight's character and the reasons behind his interruption of the Monk. Kaske has noted that in Boethian terms the *Monk's Tale* is an incomplete account of "evil" Fortune, while the *Knight's Tale* rounds out the picture. The losses experienced in the course of one's life are only temporary and apparent evils. As the Knight dramatizes it for us in this tale, we are led to contemplate a human order controlled not by chance but by the Christian Deity. An orderly Providence finally directs the actions of human life, although Destiny and Fortune (here, the astrologized pagan gods) are its ministers. In this manner evil is only a short-lived illusion, for God converts all things back to the good from which they derive and gives a man better things than he could devise.[15] This is why the Knight cannot tell a tale of tragedy as does the Monk. How can there be a genuine tragic vision of life in these terms? Human existence is, for Boethius and the Knight, as for Dante, ultimately a divine comedy.

Even before reading the first line of the story proper, we are prepared for its eventual happy ending: "And he bigan with

[15] Farnham, p. 114; B. L. Jefferson, *Chaucer and the Consolation of Philosophy of Boethius* (Princeton, 1917), pp. 142-143; Paul G. Ruggiers, "Some Philosophical Aspects of *The Knight's Tale,*" *College English,* XIX (April, 1958), 299.

right a myrie cheere/ His tale anon, and seyde as ye may heere" (857-58). As we follow the adversity through which Palamon and Arcite move in their imprisonment and lovesickness, we are frequently reminded of "the destinee, ministre general,/ . . . that God hath seyn biforn [seen before]" (1663-65). We know that somehow an omniscient Providence is working out all things for good and that there shall be "joye after wo." We can maintain a cheerful expectancy knowing that everything is going to be all right.

Hulbert has shown how Chaucer modified the character of the *Teseida* so as to leave the Knight with a tale that could arouse no tragic emotions.[16] In Boccaccio's work, Arcita and Emilia are individuated and Palemone made such a secondary character that the reader can feel genuine pity at Arcita's death. In the *Knight's Tale,* on the other hand, Chaucer makes the heroes indistinguishable and the heroine only a name, thus eliminating the possibility of there arising in the reader any deep feeling of tragic sympathy for Arcite. The price for such characterization was high in literary terms, but the Knight's consistent optimism is thereby assured.

Muscatine points out several additional antidotes to tragic implications in the fate of Arcite. First, there is the touch of lightness in lines 2759-60: "And certeinly, ther Nature wol nat wirche,/ Fare wel phisik! go ber the man to chirche!" Secondly, there is the lack of any moral evaluation that would place Arcite lower in virtue than Palamon and make his death a sort of tragic example. Rather, the description of his death centers upon physical realities. Finally, there is the noncommittal disposal of the question of heaven or hell:[17]

> *His spirit chaunged hous and wente ther,*
> *As I cam nevere,° I kan not tellen wher.* (where I never come)
> *Therfore I stynte,° I nam no divinistre;°* (cease) (theologian)
> *Of soules fynde I not in this registre,°* (table of contents)
> *Ne me ne list thilke opinions to telle*
> (Nor does it please me to tell such opinions)
> *Of hem, though that they writen where they dwelle.*
> *Arcite is coold, ther Mars his soule gye!*
> (In that case may Mars guide his soul!)
> [2809-16]

It is not Chaucer who is in serious doubt at this point as to the immortality of the soul or the destiny of virtuous pagans. He

[16] "What Was Chaucer's Aim in the *Knight's Tale?*" *SP,* XXVI (1929), 375-377.

[17] Muscatine, p. 76.

uses the passage, as Robinson suggests, for "a jest relief from the strain of pathos."[18] It is the Knight, his persona, who is the chief one in need of such relief.

The full nontragic import of the tale is brought out by the lengthy concluding speech of Theseus (2987-3074). In this philosophical monologue, the Boethian interpretation of events is clearly stated. The "Firste Moevere of the cause above" has knit the universe into a chain of love. Under Jupiter's wise rule it is perfect and stable. Furthermore, since death must come to all men Arcite has done well in departing in duty and honor. Palamon should now marry Emelye and give events a genuinely happy ending:

> *What may I conclude of this longe serye,°* (argument)
> *But after wo I rede° us to be merye,* (advise)
> *And thanken Juppiter of al his grace?*
> *And er that we departen from this place*
> *I rede that we make of sorwes two*
> *O parfit° joye, lastynge everemo.* (one perfect)
> *And looketh now, wher moost sorwe is herinne,*
> *Ther wol we first amenden and bigynne.*
> [3067-74]

So it is that Arcite's earlier protest (1219ff.) that man is the victim of irrational Fortune (a parallel to the Monk's view) is countered in Theseus' speech by the description of a universe bound together by love in which nothing is left to chance, and evil has no absolute existence.[19] What is more, the Knight concludes his tale by reducing this cosmic solution to human suffering to an earthly level. What we are given at last is another experience of the comic mode in literature, the archetypal wedding which will bring an end to all our woe and a return of our prosperity:

> *And thus with alle blisse and melodye*
> *Hath Palamon ywedded Emelye.*
> *And God, that al this wyde world hath wroght,*
> *Sende hym his love that hath it deere aboght;*
> *For now is Palamon in alle wele,°* (good fortune)
> *Lyvynge in blisse, in richesse, and in heele.°* (health)
> [3097-3102]

It is, after all, this view of man's earthly existence from which the Knight has most to gain.

Now that we have explored each major appearance of the Knight in the poem and its bearing upon his interruption of the

[18] Robinson, p. 682.
[19] Ruggiers, p. 301.

*Monk's Tale,* it might be well to summarize. Assuming that a dramatic interpretation of the *Canterbury Tales* is valid, that is, that one of the functions of the tales is to expose the soul of the Pilgrim who speaks, I have placed the Knight's interruption in the context of the entire poem in order to understand the motive behind his action. When this is done, some interesting perspectives emerge. The outlines of a basic opposition become clear. On the one hand, we have the world of the Monk, a world governed by the irrationality of the Wheel of Fortune, the medieval metaphor for the seeming absurdities of the human condition. The fickle goddess renders unstable and false the active life spent in the pursuit of riches, power, and fame. To such a view of the world the Knight, if he is to be a consistent character, must object both for philosophical and personal reasons. When we reconstruct his personality and philosophical views from this brief interruption, the *General Prologue,* and his own tale, we gain a new interpretation of his character.

Here is not an austere and pious saint turning from the grimness of warfare to seek spiritual solace in a company of pilgrims, but an ambitious man of the world engaged in the active life of seeking glory, power, fame, and profit from the holy wars against the Infidels. He has come with his fine horses, his dandy Squire, and his green-clad Yeoman to pay his respects to the god of stable prosperity. Along the way he will tell a tale of romance with a happy ending to support his outlook, a tale of people who live "in blisse, in richesse, and in heele." And if a sour and hypocritical Monk begins a seemingly endless sequence of dismal tales which recount with didactic pointedness the tragic fall of people in the Knight's position, then he will feel his own security threatened enough to intervene and cut short such a one-sided view of things. "Namoore of this!" Too many of these tales can unsettle one's conscience. They can raise the fear that perhaps one has chosen a precarious way of life after all, that cosmic forces may not second one's career pattern. They smack too much of the cloister. Thus the Knight finds it necessary upon several occasions to intervene for the sake of cheer. "Lat us laughe and playe," he tells the Host and Pardoner at one point (VI, C, 967), expressing his true character and freezing for all time the portrait of a man whose own continued successes have caused him to dodge, at least for the present, the imminent and tragic reversals of affluence and the pride of life.

# Samson's Identity Crisis and Milton's

CHARLES A. HUTTAR

*When I read the book, the biography famous,*
*And is this then (said I) what the author calls a man's life?*
*And so will someone when I am dead and gone write my life?*
*(As if any man really knew aught of my life,*
*Why even I myself I often think know little or nothing of my real life,*
*Only a few hints, a few diffused faint clews and indirections*
*I seek for my own use to trace out here.)*

—*Whitman,* Leaves of Grass

One of the dominant themes of *Samson Agonistes,* as indeed of all Milton's writing, is the mystery of divine call and human response. The question of the meaning of his own existence engaged Milton in a lifelong *agon.* This meaning was something to be *discovered,* a preexistent divine purpose which he could know by being sufficiently attentive to clues. But even God's call did not absolutely define his life. Equally important was Milton's answer: this meaning was something to be *worked out.* Only by the nature of his response could it finally become apparent who he, Milton, was, whether a great man or a great failure. On notions like these was Milton reared, and his sensitive nature took them to heart and dutifully tried to live with the tension of their double vision of man's passive and active roles.

---

Charles A. Huttar is Professor of English at Hope College. After studying at Wheaton College (A.B.) and Northwestern University (M.A., Ph.D.) he went to Gordon College to chair the Department of English. He moved to Hope in 1966. The author of several articles, he has also served as Editor of *The Gordon Review* and President of the Conference on Christianity and Literature, and currently heads CCL's bibliography project. He has also been a local chapter president in both the American Association of University Professors and the American Recorder Society.

It was an introspective age. Countless manuals of devotion, Protestant and Catholic alike, prescribed regular close self-examination. The Elizabethan homilies had taught that "the true knowledge of ourselves is very necessary to come to the right knowledge of God."[1] *Know thyself,* Sir John Davies had counselled in a long poem, appropriating the full weight of classical authority and harmonizing with it the Christian ideal. The Puritan in the seventeenth century "was haunted by the desire to survey his whole life in one glance, to hold his soul in his hands, the better to possess himself."[2] It is not by accident that in this century the autobiography came into being. And this spirit of introspection brought other tensions related to the first. Self-examination, for example, might turn out to be narcissism. By what ocular jugglery is the Christian supposed to fix his eyes upon God while constantly examining himself? What prevents "Who am I?" from being a most egoistic obsession? What subtle line separates the desire for self-fulfillment that rightly motivates obedience to the divine call from that desire for self-fulfillment which is Satanic? It is by giving talents appropriate to a certain use that God calls to his service.[3] Yet extraordinary talents are a sore temptation to pride. Ambition is a sin; lack of ambition is a sin. Milton's thin-skinned and elaborate self-defence against the charge that his pamphlets sprang from "some self-pleasing humor of vain-glory"[4] argues that the tensions suggested above were very real to his mind.

## I

In *Samson Agonistes* Milton portrays a man who has come to feel, as he himself did, the agony of these dilemmas. In doing so he raises at the outset the question of identity, and does not resolve it until the end. The chorus of Danites, catching sight of their degraded and enslaved tribesman, are shocked into the question, "Can this be hee, / That Heroic, that Renown'd, / Irresistible Samson?" And though told in the title that it is

1 Quoted in Sidney Warhaft, "Bacon and the Renaissance Ideal of Self-Knowledge," *Personalist,* XLIV (1963), 455.

2 Henri Talon on Bunyan, quoted and shown to be true of "Puritanism at large" by U. Milo Kaufmann, *The Pilgrim's Progress and Traditions in Puritan Meditation,* Yale Stud. in Engl., 163 (New Haven and London, 1966), p. 200.

3 Milton, *Christian Doctrine* (hereafter *CD*), I, xxix: ". . . these gifts constituting his mission." *The Student's Milton,* ed. Frank Allen Patterson, rev. ed. (New York, 1933), p. 1038. (All quotations of Milton are from this ed., which will hereafter be referred to as *SM.*)

4 *Reason of Church Government,* II; *SM,* p. 524.

Samson, the audience has already felt the same absurd doubt. When the chorus describes him:

> *See how he lies at random, carelessly diffus'd,*
> *With languish't head unpropt,*
> *As one past hope, abandon'd,*
> *And by himself given over;*
> *In slavish habit, ill-fitted weeds*
> *O're worn and soil'd,*

they merely verbalize what the imagined audience noticed in Samson's demeanor as soon as he came onstage. From the opening lines, "A little onward lend thy guiding hand / To these dark steps," Milton enforces on us Samson's unheroic state, blind, dependent on others for the common offices of life, at the mercy of his captors, brutalized by hard labor, daily afflicted by the jeers of his sighted and staring enemies (112-114), weighted with miseries "So many, and so huge, that each apart / Would ask a life to wail" (65-66). As in body, so in mind: his "restless thoughts" (19) swarm and sting like hornets; his sin of "weakly" revealing his secret argues an "impotence of mind" (50-52); and he is nearly given over to futile questionings not merely of his own fate but of the natural order (93-94). The whole direction of his psychic energy, as measured by the growing eloquence of his first speech, is toward an excess of self-pity that thwarts any inclination we might have had to view him as a hero. Though the physical identity of this unkempt prisoner is never in question, we feel uncomfortable about applying to him that glorious name, Samson, that belonged to God's Champion, the heroic Nazarite. And no one feels more uncomfortable about it than Samson himself. Facing the question "Who am I?" he can only say, in effect, "Alas, I am the man who *was* a hero." As for the present, he is "proverbd for a Fool" (203) and other like identities.

In the last scene, by contrast, the chorus after hearing of Samson's death pronounces him "victorious" (1663), and the earlier question "Can this be . . . that Heroic . . . Samson?" is explicitly answered by Manoa:

> *Samson hath quit himself*
> *Like Samson, and heroicly hath finish'd*
> *A life Heroic.*

He is to have a hero's remembrance, a monument where his trophies are hung and his deeds recited and where "the valiant youth" may "from his memory inflame their breasts / To matchless valour, and adventures high" (1738-40).

Jean-Paul Sartre has one of his dramatic characters affirm,

"It's by your whole life that your individual acts will be judged."[5] Just so Samson is, by final definition, a hero. It is indeed permissible to "survey his whole life in one glance," to grasp as a single unique thing the totality of his apparently fragmented career. Manoa is groping toward this insight when he demands of the Messenger, "How dy'd he? death to life is crown or shame" (1579); but the sententious tone of this remark, and his willingness to rely at such a critical moment on his stock of learned tags,[6] suggest he does not yet fully appreciate what it means for the past to be redeemed, for the unheroic Samson to be blotted out, absorbed up into the Samson who *is* a hero.[7]

Samson, who while onstage does not reach this appreciation either (and who thus must walk by faith almost if not quite to the very end of his life), is greatly concerned throughout the play over his *image*. That term is modern — but the idea returns us to the seventeenth-century Christian concept of self-knowledge.

In early life — before the action of the play — Samson had enjoyed in his own mind a sure sense of vocation; and what others might think of him was secondary. Milton provides adequate hints of this period. There were from the beginning clear outward signs of Samson's special commission from God: his "birth from Heaven foretold / Twice by an Angel" (23-24), his consecration as a Nazarite, his unshorn locks the badge of separateness, and finally his unexampled strength. These things constituted what we might call his "public image." Coupled with them were inward promptings and assurances — "divine instinct," Samson says (526), so that he grew "great in hopes / With youthful courage and magnanimous thoughts" and sought "after some proof / Of acts indeed heroic." For while his call to deliver Israel was manifest, just how he was to achieve this task had not been made explicit, and he naturally assumed it would be by the most obvious and direct use of his great gifts in exploits against the Philistine oppressors. Yet in the first of these exploits outward appearances were against him: judg-

5 *The Victors,* Act IV, in *Three Plays by Jean-Paul Sartre,* trans. Lionel Abel (New York, 1949), p. 268.

6 Cf. "A fair death honors the whole life," which appeared in a number of 16th- and 17th-century proverb collections, some of which are cited in M. P. Tilley, *A Dictionary of the Proverbs in England in the Sixteenth and Seventeenth Centuries* (Ann Arbor, 1950), No. D151. The quot. for 1616, like Manoa, uses the word "crown."

7 For another parallel to this idea in contemporary literature see Mary McDermott Shideler, *The Theology of Romantic Love: a study in the writings of Charles Williams* (Grand Rapids, 1966), pp. 182-183.

ing by the "public image" alone, what business had an Israelite, especially a Nazarite, marrying a woman of the Philistines? This time the inner voice contradicted the "image," and Samson (quite properly, Milton implies) gave it priority. He overrode his parents' objection, for

> *what I motion'd was of God; I knew*
> *From intimate impulse, and therefore urg'd*
> *The Marriage on; that by occasion hence*
> *I might begin Israel's Deliverance,*
> *The work to which I was divinely call'd.*[8]

The successes that followed might have seemed to give his decision a seal of approval, but again Samson's inward assurance of vocation was put to the test by circumstances. His countrymen, "servile" (1213), "corrupt" (268), always failed to take advantage of the confusion Samson was creating among their overlords, and however astounding his personal victories, the promised deliverance never materialized. Here might well have arisen a crisis in self-knowledge. Was the divine prediction false? Had the forecast of "deliverance" been misinterpreted? But there is no evidence Samson was troubled by such thoughts: he went on doing his "part from Heav'n assign'd" (1219). Looking back even from his valley of despair, he still refused to permit that failure, for which "Israel's Governours, and Heads of Tribes" (242) were culpable, to cast doubt on his own divine commission.

Thus far in his career, as Milton presents it by backward glances, Samson possessed a self-image which was (1) based on inward knowledge as well as externals, and therefore distinct from the misleading public image, and (2) accurate, and therefore not distinct from true self-knowledge. But then Samson's self-image and true self-knowledge diverge, for he becomes "swoll'n with pride" (532). Exempted once by divine authority from the ban on intermarriage, he tries the same thing a second time on his own (231ff.). Other errors follow and eventually disaster. By overestimating his powers Samson brings about their destruction. Thinking himself better than he is, he becomes worse. The degeneration begins inwardly, later becomes manifest — but not to Samson, for we are told that, after losing his hair, "he wist not that the Lord was departed from him" (Judges 16:20). But finally even he knows. The failure in self-knowledge is made explicit when Samson refers to "that blindness worse

[8] Lines 222-226. There is no reason to doubt the validity of Samson's sense of a special dispensation in this instance. The chorus, for one thing, accepts it (315-321).

then this, / That saw not how degeneratly I serv'd" (418-419).

This brings us to the opening of Milton's play, where the awful alteration is the first thing that strikes the chorus: "O change beyond report, thought, or belief!" With these words, in effect, the drama proper opens. They are strikingly like the words that begin the drama of *Paradise Lost,* when Satan "breaking the horrid silence" of the burning lake addresses Beelzebub in words whose grammatical discontinuity signals the extent and the shock of the change he sees: "If thou beest he; But O how fall'n! how chang'd..." (I, 84). The word *change* tolls like a knell through Milton's poetry. "Is this the Region," Satan asks rhetorically, "... That we must change for Heav'n, this mournful gloom / For that celestial light?" (I, 242-245). Soon he is boasting of "a mind not to be chang'd by Place or Time" — implicit evidence of the change already suffered by this being who was once too intelligent to have believed such a boast. Already he is "chang'd in outward lustre": that much he has admitted (I, 97). The process thus begun goes on until in another moment of boasting Satan and all his followers are "transformed / Alike, to Serpents" (X, 519f.). Milton is equally insistent on the change Adam and Eve undergo after the fall. After a night of "grosser sleep" they awaken "naked left / To guiltie shame" (IX, 1049, 1057f.). Here is the simile the poet uses:

*So rose the Danite strong*
*Herculean Samson from the Harlot-lap*
*Of Philistean Dalilah, and wak'd*
*Shorn of his strength, They destitute and bare*
*Of all thir virtue.*

Years before, Milton had told how Comus unmanned all who yielded to his allurements:

*Soon as the Potion works, their human count'nance,*
*Th' express resemblance of the gods, is chang'd*
*Into som brutish form...*
. . . . . . . . . . . . . .
*All other parts remaining as they were.*
[*Comus,* 68-72]

And in "Lycidas" we hear the knell again,

*But O the heavy change, now thou art gon,*
*Now thou art gon, and never must return!*

Whatever the immediate setting, the word *change* in Milton often opens a door upon dark vistas of disaster and loss, and in the shadows, never far off, is that archetypal metamorphosis, the fall of the angels and of man, "death . . . and all our woe."[9]

So it is that Samson's first visitor comes to the Gaza jail-yard and unwittingly reveals what a great change has befallen his son. Ignoring the bent, manacled figure standing there, he asks the Danite chorus where Samson is. Can it be that his own father does not recognize him? When the tribesmen point him out, Manoa breaks forth in lament:

*O miserable change! is this the man,*
*That invincible Samson, far renown'd,*
*The dread of Israel's foes. . . .*
[340-342]

One reason for Samson's dejection, of course, is that he has long been aware of the "miserable change" and brooded on it. His self-image has received a rude shock, as a result of which he has swung violently from a self-knowledge that was faulty by being too exalted to a self-knowledge that errs by being too low and despairing. Early in the play he complains of the

*restless thoughts, that like a deadly swarm*
*Of Hornets arm'd, no sooner found alone,*
*But rush upon me thronging, and present*
*Times past, what once I was, and what am now.*

Between these two identities, the past and present Samsons, he sees no continuity. He can no longer believe himself God's chosen deliverer, having by his own folly forfeited that identity and thus nullified the prophecy. That last absurdity will serve later in the play to help him regain a true self-knowledge, but at the beginning, blind as he is, the world of appearances — the public image — is all he is willing to accept. The "action" of the play, which some critics have called Samson's "regeneration," consists of his return to true self-knowledge — restoring the balance from the two extremes he has experienced — and his resulting ability to act rightly. The drama is bracketed, as it were, between Samson's false notion that "what once I was, and what am now" are irreparably distinct, and the true summation of his total career as "a life Heroic."

In his opening soliloquy Samson complains of being his enemies' "scorn and gaze." He needs no reminding, and there-

[9] The chorus goes on (164ff.) to find in Samson's condition an emblem of the "fickle state" of man — not in lapsarian terms, however, but in the commonplace figure of Fortune's wheel. This is classical wisdom — adopted though it may be by Christian culture and baptized. Lines 170-175 may echo the sentiments of the third chorus in *Agamemnon*, as they certainly echo (it seems to me) the tone of it.

fore feels the more pained when Manoa tells him, of his "Foes' derision" (366) and the "reproach" that he has brought "with shame" not only on himself but on his "Father's house" by giving the heathen grounds to praise their god above Jehovah (446f.). More salt is rubbed in when Dalila reminds him of the public "censure" of his "weakness" (785-787), for he has already realized "with what contempt" (400) she must have regarded him even while he was still in love with her. Now he feels "inferior to the vilest . . . / Of man or worm" (73-74). Blind though he is, he knows too well the physical image he presents, fettered, utterly dependent, "dark in light expos'd / To daily fraud, contempt, abuse and wrong, / Within doors, or without, still as a fool" (75-77).

The reputation for folly is perhaps what troubles Samson most, as moral realities outweigh physical.

*Am I not sung and proverbd for a Fool*
*In every street, do they not say, how well*
*Are come upon him his deserts?*
[203-205]

He accepts this reputation as deserved. Even for betraying the secrets of men, one would merit "the mark of fool set on his front" (496); how much more for the "vile . . . folly" which has "profan'd / The mystery of God" (377-378), for "my folly who committed / To such a viper his most sacred trust" (1000-01), "who like a foolish Pilot have shipwrack't / My Vessel trusted to me from above" (198-199). Now, the superficial glories of his earlier life wiped out, Samson is ready to accept this as the final verdict on who he is. No more unforgiving stance can he take toward Dalila than to treat her as he does himself, offering only "such pardon . . . as I give my folly" (825). These quotations, scattered all through the work, show how insistently Milton identifies Samson with folly. However, as we shall see, Milton also is working with a full awareness of the ambiguity of "folly," as St. Paul had written to the Corinthians.

In the abyss of self-knowledge into which he has now plunged, Samson heaps upon himself still other moral judgments. He has acted "presumptuously . . . impiously, / Weakly . . . shamefully"; his "crime" is "shameful garrulity," he deserves to be "avoided as a blab" (490-499). His deeds have also been "unmanly" (417)—realizing so must have been a severe blow to the self-image of the strong man. The conqueror of hundreds at a sweep was "effeminatly vanquish't" (562); even before his present bondage at the grinding mill, "foul effeminacy held me yok't" (410). From being "swoll'n with pride" it was but a short step to being

*Softn'd with pleasure and voluptuous life;*
*At length to lay my head and hallow'd pledge*
*Of all my strength in the lascivious lap*
*Of a deceitful Concubine who shore me*
*Like a tame Weather*

— with what harsher name could Samson lacerate himself than that of a gelded sheep? —

*all my precious fleece,*
*Then turn'd me out ridiculous, despoil'd,*
*Shav'n, and disarm'd among my enemies.*[10]

The two most obvious features of Samson's physical condition bear in upon his mind with terrible symbolic force. The chorus has begun the tying of them together (151-154):

*Which shall I first bewail,*
*Thy Bondage or lost Sight,*
*Prison within Prison*
*Inseparably dark?*

"The Dungeon of thy self," Samson is called.[11] But the poet was content there to use the metaphor of bondage simply to make us who have sight imagine more sharply what it is like to be blind. It remains for Samson to make the moral application (414-419):

*The base degree to which I now am fall'n,*
*These rags, this grinding, is not yet so base*
*As was my former servitude, ignoble,*
*Unmanly, ignominious, infamous,*
*True slavery, and that blindness worse then this,*
*That saw not how degeneratly I serv'd.*

Here both conditions are used metaphorically, and the metaphors are tossed back upon one another so that we cannot tell which is to be considered worse, slavery or blindness. Each in its way is a betrayal of the human (to which it pertains to be free and to know), and so the term "unmanly" is fitting in a wider sense, of which the narrower concept of effeminacy stands also as a metaphor.[12] And closely related to these images in moral

[10] Lines 532-540. Particularly ironic in the context is the claim to masculinity implicit in the word "swollen." Also note line 55. The image of line 567 also is symbolic of castration.

[11] Line 156. Cf. a similar ironic use of the reflexive pronoun in 102, "My self, my Sepulcher, a moving Grave." Here the metaphor for blindness is not bondage but death — with which Samson is also obsessed: see the following note.

[12] Elsewhere Samson links with these images still another, as his loss of

sayings, of course, is the notion of folly.[13] So the chorus generalizes at the end:

*So fond are mortal men*
*. . . . . . . . . . . . . . .*
*As thir own ruin on themselves to invite,*
*Insensate left, or to sense reprobate,*
*And with blindness internal struck.*
[1682-86]

It is the fall of the Philistines they are speaking of here, and they proceed to contrast the enemies' blindness with Samson's inward illumination.[14] But we have other things to consider before we can reach that triumphant moment.

What caps Samson's self-definition in the first half of the play, and what he himself sees as the greatest change of all, is his loss of vocation.

*Promise was that I*
*Should Israel from Philistian yoke deliver;*
*Ask for this great Deliverer now, and find him*
*Eyeless in Gaza at the Mill with slaves,*
*Himself in bonds under Philistian yoke.*
[38-42]

He sees no choice but to abandon the title of Deliverer which he once proudly bore. None of the dreadful irony escapes him. The Deliverer is now in bonds; he who should have saved others cannot save even himself. Especially ironic is the fact that now his strength has returned — only to be "put to the labour of a Beast, debas't / Lower then bondslave!" (37-38). Manoa offers to buy his freedom, but

*Now blind, disheartn'd, sham'd, dishonour'd, quell'd,*
*To what can I be useful, wherein serve*
*My Nation, and the work from Heav'n impos'd,*
*But to sit idle on the houshold hearth,*

sight seems to forebode a "double Darkness," "th' other light of life" soon passing away also (592f.).

13 That self-knowledge is an essential part of wisdom is a Renaissance commonplace. See Eugene F. Rice, Jr., *The Renaissance Idea of Wisdom* (Cambridge, Mass., 1958), pp. 110, 206, Pl. II and IV.

14 That the Philistines were "drunk with Wine, / And fat regorg'd of Bulls and Goats" (1670f.) is a detail Milton adds to the account in Judges — perhaps to contrast with the Spirit-filled Samson. Most contemporary pictorial representations do not include this idea. One that does (Fig. 1) belongs to a set of Bible engravings executed in France about 1564, for publication in texts with several different language editions. The reproduction here is taken by permission of The Folger Shakespeare Library from *Figure de la Biblia, Illustrate de Stanze Tuscane,* per Gabriel Simeoni (Lyon, 1577).

DE GIVDICI CAP. XVI.

*Staua Sanſone innanzi à Filiſtei*
*Priuato d'occhi, e di ſua viſta pria,*
*Di che volendo gaſtigare i rei*
*Di vendicarſi troua modo, e via.*
*Muoia hor Sanſon con tutti i Filiſtei*
*Diſſe, e le due colonne ſuelſe via:*
*Onde caſcando l'edifitio aterra,*
*Tre mila anime con ſe egli ſotterra.*

Figure 1

*A burdenous drone; to visitants a gaze,*
*Or pitied object,*

— he is still worried about his public image —

*these redundant locks*
*Robustious to no purpose clustring down,*
*Vain monument of strength; till length of years*
*And sedentary numness craze my limbs*
*To a contemptible old age obscure.*
*Here rather let me drudge....*
[563-573]

Samson is convinced of "Heav'ns desertion." God had chosen him as his "nursling," "destin'd from the womb," had overseen his "abstemious" growth, had directed him to "mightiest deeds / Above the nerve of mortal arm" — "But now hath cast me off as never known" (632-640). Worst of all is the knowledge that no one else can be blamed. "Sole Author I, sole cause" (376; cf. lines 44-46, 234). To Dalila he is forced to reply, "Bitter reproach, but true, / I to my self was false e're thou to me" (823-824; cf. line 784). To Harapha's taunts his reply is meekly to acknowledge "all these indignities" as "inflicted" by God "justly" (1168-71). The Samson that might have been, the mighty hero, is a phantom, the real Samson is this pitiful emblem of divine justice, and he is no longer "in the list of them that hope" (647). He feels death coming on and is ready for it, summing up his two lives in these words: "My race of glory run, and race of shame."[15]

But the reply to Harapha just quoted goes on to give us a glimpse of the stirring to life of a new Samson, for he adds, "[I] despair not of his final pardon ... / In confidence whereof I once again / Defie thee." Samson is now willing to admit again a world of reality beyond that of appearances and to assert that there is more to him than simply what the world can see. By implication the chorus has unwittingly indicated this change rather early in the play, in the well-known lines (293ff.),

[15] The cadences of this whole passage (590-598) beautifully reinforce its mood of weariness and death-longing. It is worth noting that the same language of light and darkness, weariness and rest, bondage, servitude, and liberty may be found in Job 3 (esp. vv. 4-5, 13, 17-20, 23), where Job, like Milton's Samson, has lost his previous identity and would fain relinquish his life. J. H. Hanford has written more generally on similarities between *Samson Agonistes* and Job in "The Temptation Motive in Milton" (1918) and "*Samson Agonistes* and Milton in Old Age" (1925), both repr. in *John Milton, Poet and Humanist* (Cleveland, 1966), pp. 262, 270f.

*Just are the ways of God,*
*And justifiable to Men;*
*Unless there be who think not God at all,*

but (alluding to Psalm 14:1) the only "School" of that "Doctrine" is "the heart of the Fool." Since it is clear that for all his shortcomings, Samson does not at any rate belong to this "School,"[16] we see implanted before the action has fairly got under way a subtle counterthrust to what appeared to be an accurate judgment on Samson conveyed with great emphasis by the overt dominant imagery, that he was a fool. But "this is not all fool, my lord": without abating our awareness of his folly, we realize as well that a residue of wisdom remains in him. We see this before Samson does. Thus the pattern of inadequate self-knowledge is repeated, but this time in the opposite direction. Misled by appearances Samson had held too high a view of himself and felt falsely secure; now, again misled by appearances, he has plunged to a self-image too debased.[17] But his two unfriendly visitors — quite contrary to their intention — raise him out of it. Proof of his folly, he has felt, was his failure to be on guard against Dalila's cajolery, since he should have learned a lesson from his first wife's betrayal in the matter of the riddle. Yet a few minutes with Dalila demonstrate that he need no longer be entranced by her "fair enchanted cup" and is not "so unwary or accurst / To bring my feet again into the snare / Where once I have been caught" (930ff.; cf. lines 381ff.). Then the encounter with Harapha brings Samson a tremendous excess of self-assurance (1123ff.) as well as a reaffirmation of his "trust . . . in the living God" (1140). Samson's confidence in God is, in fact, seen quite early: God "will arise and his great name assert: / Dagon must stoop" (467-468); but there it is utterly divorced from any thought that *he* is still eligible to be God's instrument. Only later does his assurance in God expand to make room within its scope for self-assurance.

Manoa, with an optimism at once sublime and ridiculous, serves to keep before us the possibility of Samson's return to heroism, but without anticipating Samson in the equally heroic mental feat of understanding what it is all about. Manoa speculates on what God might yet do with his destined Champion

[16] Cf. lines 43ff., 60ff., 373, 465ff.

[17] The difficulty of judging a person's spiritual state from outward appearances was a common theme in contemporary religious writing. Cf. Ludwig Borinski, "Puritanische und anglikanische Lebensideale im Zeitalter der englischen Revolution," *Festschrift zum 75. Geburtstag von Theodor Spira*, hrsg. H. Viebrock und W. Erzgräber (Heidelberg, 1961), pp. 202-204.

(581ff.). To Manoa, Samson's whole life (before his fall) was a divine miracle; why cannot God now restore sight to the blind? He persuades himself that God will do just that: why else should Samson's strength have returned? For God's "wondrous gifts" shall not, cannot, "be frustrate."[18] Manoa is incapable of thinking tragically. After Samson has gone to the Philistines' feast, Manoa reiterates his belief that his son's sight will be restored (once again displaying his shallow conception of divine activity), and even persuades the chorus that this might be the outcome (1495ff., 1527f.).

The chorus meanwhile has had other thoughts. After Harapha's departure, noting Samson's renascent self-respect, the chorus enumerates the two ways he may yet achieve the title of hero, by violent triumph as before or by patience. Either is possible, but because of his blindness, patience is now his more probable path to the ultimate victory, which is self-conquest (1268-96).

These speculations by Manoa and the chorus serve merely as a backdrop for the real drama, which takes place in Samson's mind. Now comes the second great reversal in his self-image. It does not depend this time on a change in appearance, for the chief outward features, blindness and bondage, continue. The change is all internal as Samson goes into this third stage of his life, and the heroic action of the first stage is united with the physical distress of the second to produce an outcome that includes, appropriately, *both* of the possibilities considered by the chorus, patience and violent triumph.[19]

It is a concern for his public image that immediately stimulates Samson's heroic self-image. He has a wide reputation for superhuman strength and the revelers want "some public proof" of it (1314). Samson refuses to go to them. "Regard thyself," warns the officer, "this will offend them highly." He answers (1334-37):

*My self? my conscience and internal peace.*
*Can they think me so broken, so debas'd*

[18] Cf. Manoa's earlier optimistic response (472ff.) to the assertion of Samson quoted above.

[19] On the same union of the active and contemplative elsewhere in Milton see M. Y. Hughes, "The Christ of *Paradise Regained* and the Renaissance Heroic Tradition" (1938), collected in *Ten Perspectives on Milton* (New Haven and London, 1965), pp. 35-62, and E. M. W. Tillyard's reply, collected in *Studies in Milton* (New York, 1951), pp. 100-106. Cf. T. S. Eliot's use of the idea, also in connection with martyrdom, in *Murder in the Cathedral* at Thomas's entrance: "Acting is suffering / And suffering is action" (cf. *patior* 'I suffer').

*With corporal servitude, that my mind ever*
*Will condescend to such absurd commands?*

This wordplay on the reflexive pronoun clearly marks the new tone that has entered Samson's voice. For the first half of the drama it was used most often in an ironical connection — "himself in bonds," "himself an Army, now unequal match / To save himself."[20] But now Samson has regained an heroic, not ironic, sense of self. He who has bathed his mind in the sense of his folly now refuses to play the "fool," the court "jester," for a band of drunken idolaters (1338). He who has accepted public derision even while complaining of it now calls a halt: "They shall not trail me through thir streets / Like a wild Beast" (1402-03).

Together with his recovered sense of self Samson has a new awareness of his relationship to God. He begins to think of his returning strength as a sign of "favour renew'd" and a "Consecrated gift" which he may not "prostitut[e]" to honor Dagon (1354ff.). He achieves an ethical insight far more subtle than the chorus's easy assurance that performing for the Philistines would be no sin "where the heart joins not" (1368). That excuse holds, says Samson, only where there is no choice — in an absolute, not the habitual hyperbolic, sense. In response to this moral imperative he determines to do "nothing dishonourable, impure, unworthy / Our God, our Law, my Nation, or my self" (1424-25). This is an important speech. At long last Samson can again see his own best interests and his responsibility toward God as coinciding: he gains a perspective that brings into proper focus the term *honor*. So long as he felt himself cut off from God, the concern over his public image was obsessive and blinding; now that he can link "our God" and "my self" in the same phrase, "honor" and "worth" have become larger concepts than just the public image. As a result that lesser concern, by being made subordinate, is made legitimate.

Finally, Samson has a renewed sense of vocation — possibly (he is not sure) even of the fulfillment of the old prophecies. The message that comes to his inner being brings its own confirmation in the very fact that the Spirit of God, which spoke to him of old, has returned.

*I begin to feel*
*Some rouzing motions in me which dispose*
*To something extraordinary my thoughts.*

[20] Lines 42, 346f. There are other examples as well: 121, 304, 375, 401, 789, and 844, besides those cited on pages 109n. and 112 above.

. . . . . . . . . . . . . . . . .
*If there be aught of presage in the mind,*
*This day will be remarkable in my life*
*By some great act, or of my days the last.*[21]

This speech is like the speculations of the chorus in that the two possibilities here presented as alternatives are, in the event, joined together. To reinforce the point that Samson does not yet know what will happen — and to obliterate completely the idea that his suicide has resulted from despair — Milton has him remark on the great value of life, a far cry from his attitude (595-596) when "nature" had seemed "in all her functions weary of herself." Now (1406) he says, "And for a life who will not change his purpose?" Clearly he does not yet plan to die: his self-knowledge is incomplete, he does not yet fully know his destiny. This suggests that, to Milton, there is something higher than such knowledge. It is not necessary completely to know (perhaps because one cannot); it *is* necessary to be.

The verdict of Manoa and the chorus is that Samson has been true to the self he started out to be and that his *whole* life — the second stage included — is to be defined by the word "Heroic." Manoa's words to this effect I quoted earlier. The chorus says: "Living or dying thou hast fulfill'd / The work for which thou wast foretold" (1661-62). If there were any doubt of the essential unity of Samson's whole life, that doubt is dispelled by the imagery two stanzas later:

*But he though blind of sight,*
*Despis'd and thought extinguish't quite,*
*With inward eyes illuminated*
*His fierie vertue rouz'd*
*From under ashes into sudden flame.*

To all appearances, the heroic Samson was burnt out, just dead ashes; yet the fire smoldered. It is an apt image for the continuity of personality. "Vertue" has, of course, primarily a moral meaning. Yet the "fierie vertue" can also refer to the power of the eyes, and this provides the transition to the next figures of speech, in which Samson is compared to two creatures whose superior sight helps them to surprise their prey.[22] Then the chorus proceeds to yet another figure from the Bestiary:

*So vertue giv'n for lost,*
*Deprest, and overthrown, as seem'd,*

[21] Lines 1381-89; cf. 1435ff.

[22] Cf. Lee S. Cox, "The 'Ev'ning Dragon' in *Samson Agonistes:* A Reappraisal," *Mod. Lang. Notes,* LXXVI (1961), 577-584. As for the eagle, his keenness of eye is proverbial.

*Like that self-begott'n bird*
*In the Arabian woods embost,*
*That no second knows nor third,*
*And lay e're while a Holocaust,*
*From out her ashie womb now teem'd,*
*Revives, reflourishes, then vigorous most*
*When most unactive deem'd,*
*And though her body die, her fame survives,*
*A secular bird ages of lives.*

By the end of the second century this classical myth had already become identified with the Christian idea of resurrection, both the resurrection of Christ and that of his followers.[23] By the sixteenth century it was an emblem also for regeneration, in Pauline terms of the dying of the old man and coming to life of the new.[24] The phoenix myth is, in fact, a germinal idea from which a great variety of fruits have sprung. In one Renaissance application the bird was a symbol for fame;[25] in another, for the triumphant progress of the divine purposes despite opposition and persecution;[26] in another, for virtue. The last, given wide circulation in Milton's earlier years, portrays a robust phoenix rising out of the flames, with a motto strikingly close to the lines just quoted from Milton: *Ex igne resurgit virtus* (see Fig. 2). In composing the passage likening Samson to the phoenix, Milton had at his disposal a vast tradition of interpretations, with which, considering his reputation for learning and the availability of encyclopedic compendia like Filippo Picinelli's *Mondo simbolico* (1653), we may well suppose he was familiar, and many of which he here montages. It is perhaps a quibble to observe that strictly it is not Samson himself but his virtue that springs to new life, and if we try to read with exact literalness we see that the line "And though her body die, her fame survives" applies also to virtue. This line, however, gives the cue for Manoa's speech in which he arranges for the care of *Samson's* dead body and the monument to *Samson's* fame. Clearly the man and his virtue are inseparable, and the lines are best understood if we read them as a reference to Samson himself who "revives" and is again "vigorous" on God's behalf.

[23] M. F. McDonald, "Phoenix," *New Catholic Encyclopedia* (New York, 1967), XI, 326, and "Phoenix redivivus," *Phoenix*, XIV (1960), 187-202.

[24] Eph. 4:22ff. provides the basis for the treatment in Arnoldus Freitag, *Mythologia Ethica* (Antwerp, 1579), p. 249. Cf. also the paronomastic motto of Ignatius Loyola, *Muero y nacio* (I die and am born): Mario Praz, *Studies in Seventeenth-Century Imagery*, 2nd ed. (Rome, 1964), p. 72.

[25] Rosemary Freeman, *English Emblem Books* (London, 1948; repr. New York, 1966), pp. 76-77.

[26] Praz, pp. 188-189.

Figure 2 (from *The Whole Booke of Psalmes* [London, 1632], title page, by permission of the Henry E. Huntington Library and Art Gallery)

Milton speaks of both vigor and virtue in a double sense, moral and physical. *Virtus* is the whole array of qualities belonging to the *vir*. In short, Samson's manliness has returned.[27] So reliance on outward appearances is confounded. For much is made in these lines of the public image: consider the words "seem'd," "deem'd," "despis'd," "thought extinguish't," "giv'n for lost." (In the last of these phrases the chorus neatly balances off its first observation of Samson "as one . . . by himself given over.") Against this false image Samson is vindicated. And then, strikingly, the seal is set on this vindication by translating it into — a public image! For the "fame" spoken of here is only that. Thus our examination of this passage has illuminated some points but raised others; "fame" needs further discussion, and we shall return to it in Section iii. There remains one observation to make about the phoenix symbol. This bird is unique; it "no second knows nor third." This commonplace was interpreted sometimes to mean that there was never more than one phoenix in the world at a time. When one dies, another is born. Ovid calls the dead bird the "father" of the new one.[28] But though later in the same passage he borrows a phrase from Ovid, Milton here deliberately follows a different tradition in which the phoenix that dies and the phoenix that rises from the ashes are *the same*.[29] His is a "*self*-begott'n bird." Obliquely, through the symbol, the chorus has reinforced its earlier hints of the continuity of Samson's identity throughout the various stages of his life. Manoa now picks up this cue and identifies the actual Samson with the ideal Samson, pronouncing his entire life "Heroic." Both Manoa and the chorus have attained a perspective from which they can "survey his whole life in one glance."

## II

In attempting to formulate the concept of identity which

[27] According to Erwin Panofsky, *Renaissance and Renascences in Western Art* (Stockholm, 1960), p. 37n., the growth of Samson's hair after his blinding was also taken as a rebirth symbol.

[28] *Unica semper avis* was an emblem that had wide currency. See Geffrey Whitney, *A Choice of Emblemes* (Leyden, 1586), p. 177; Claude Paradin, *Heroicall Devices* (London, 1591), p. 110; F. Picinelli, *Mundus Symbolicus . . . Nunc . . . in latinum traductus* (Cologne, 1687), I, 323. The reference to Ovid (*Met.* xvi.40) I owe to Panofsky, *loc. cit.*

[29] Evident for example in Picinelli, I, 322, where the emblem of the young phoenix springing up from the ashes has the motto *Mox eadem.* Ancient citations for both traditions, and Milton's borrowing from Ovid, are noted by C. G. Osgood, *The Classical Mythology of Milton's English Poems*, Yale Stud. in Engl., 8 (New Haven, 1900; repr. New York, 1964), pp. 69-70.

Phoenix, fire and resurrection all connect too with the probable solar reference in the etymology of 'Samson.'

Milton embodies in *Samson Agonistes,* we may profitably look first at several examples of that class of literature whose value, for Milton's age, lay in the terse expression of profound moral lessons. Wise men of old had uttered apothegms; Milton's models, the Greek tragic writers, had woven them into their works; schoolmasters had transmitted them to pupils as precious mottoes to live by, thus doing in quotidian fashion what Milton considered it the poet's task to do more exaltedly; and now, far from their origins and fully naturalized as part of a Christian culture, they represented not merely the cream of classical wisdom but an amalgam of human thought with that which was divinely revealed.

*Know thyself.* We have already alluded enough times to this *gnomos* that its central relevance to the theme of *Samson Agonistes* should be quite evident. It seems at first to have been a maxim against pride: man should know his place and powers, especially in relation to the gods, and neither presume too much nor dare too little. Socrates read it as directed especially against pride of intellect; to know oneself is to recognize that one knows nothing. For the Renaissance, Erasmus summarizes the various interpretations in his *Adages.*[30] But meanwhile a different kind of self-knowledge had flowed together with the classical stream. In recounting his conversion St. Augustine is aware of "a maimed and half-divided will," or rather "two wills, one new, and the other old, one carnal, the other spiritual," which fought within "and by their discord, undid my soul" (*Confessions,* viii. 8 and 5).[31] How great a barrier to self-knowledge this division of the self can be Augustine sets forth vividly (viii. 7):

> Thou, O Lord, . . . didst turn me round towards myself, taking me from behind my back where I had placed me, unwilling to observe myself; and setting me before my face, that I might see how foul I was, how crooked and defiled, bespotted and ulcerous. And I beheld and stood aghast; and whither to flee from myself I found not.

The African saint could have found in Plato the idea of the schizophrenic warfare of flesh and spirit, but instead his source is, of course, St. Paul. Erasmus brings both sources together, classical and Christian, in that section of his *Manual of the Christian Soldier* (iv-viii) where he affirms the maxim *Know thyself* to be "the chief point of . . . wisdom."[32] It scarcely needs

[30] See M. M. Phillips, *The Adages of Erasmus, A Study with Translations* (Cambridge, 1964), pp. 11-12.

[31] I use the translation of Edward B. Pusey in the ed. of Harold C. Gardiner (New York, 1951), pp. 141, 134-135.

[32] *The Enchiridion of Erasmus,* trans. and ed. Raymond Himelick (Bloomington, Ind., 1963), p. 62.

to be added that both Plato and Paul stood side by side likewise in Milton's mind.

The quest for self-knowledge, then, is made more difficult by a multiplicity of selves. Whether the lower self is seen in Pauline terms as the old Adam or in Freudian terms as the subconscious of memory and instinct, it insists upon being taken into account. Turning once again to St. Augustine, we find a hint that these two viewpoints may not be so far apart. "When asleep," he testifies (*Confessions*, x. 30), "false visions persuade to that which when waking, the true cannot. Am I not then myself, O Lord my God? And yet is there so much difference betwixt myself and myself, within that moment wherein I pass from waking to sleeping, or return from sleeping to waking!"

Even apart from the formidable task of knowing oneself at any moment — a task which, to use a favorite Miltonic image, is like the seeds given Psyche to sort out — even if all that is accomplished, the question "Who am I?" remains. For what is the relation among the infinitesimal moments strung out along the whole length of a man's life? Many today feel there is no relation — we are constantly changing into that which cannot be identified with anything but its instantaneous self. The separate moments making up what we casually call a "life" are seen as radically discontinuous. "In a world where all is 'chance, accident, absurdity,' the notion of a 'continuous personality which is identical with itself through all the changes it suffers in time' is an illusion. . . ."[33] "How do we read a human life? As a series of disconnected accidents or as the unfolding of a drama with an inner unity?"[34] Pirandello thought the former and wrote plays to say so. Proust thought the latter and composed an enormous work in which he claimed to find in memory the principle of continuity of personality. So had Augustine centuries before: "In that vast court of my memory . . . meet I with myself, and recall myself" (*Confessions*, x. 8). Although skepticism on the matter was not unheard of in the seventeenth century — Donne could even be playful about it[35] — the received

[33] "and . . . hence conventional autobiography is a 'trick.' " John N. Morris, *Versions of the Self* (New York and London, 1966), p. 11, describing the position of Goronwy Rees, *A Bundle of Sensations* (New York, 1961), pp. 15-16. The success of modern medicine in transplanting organs has seemed to some to raise in a new way the problem of personal identity. For an interesting discussion see Jonathan Miller, "Death," *The Listener*, LXXVIII (Oct. 19, 1967), 487.

[34] Harold G. McCurdy, ed., *Barbara: the Unconscious Autobiography of a Child Genius* (Chapel Hill, 1966), p. v.

[35] "Womans Constancy," 4-5.

opinion in Milton's time, to which he adhered, was that a man's life from beginning to end is an entity, which can be evaluated — once it is complete.[36]

*Call no man happy until he is dead.* Traditionally this was the advice spoken by Solon to Croesus (to whom in Xenophon's account the Delphic word *Know thyself* was also given), the fabulously rich king whose legendary immolation by his conqueror Cyrus gives a grim point to the proverbial advice.[37] Again, however, we are faced with a variety of interpretations. On the lips of Solon and Agamemnon, *Call no man happy until he is dead* is a warning that premature boasting of good fortune, whether verbally or just implicitly by one's behavior, may arouse the envy of the gods and thus bring disaster.[38] Leaving the personality of the gods out of it, much the same idea is expressed in the proverbs which see a man as especially vulnerable when he feels himself most secure. From this Milton derives Samson's words for the plight of strength without commensurate wisdom, "Proudly secure, yet liable to fall."[39] The wisdom Solon tried to teach Croesus is exactly the kind Samson needed alongside his strength. But there is another reason, perhaps less sinister, for not pronouncing a man "happy" or "fortunate" until he is dead. He may be so now, but who knows what changes of fortune will take place before the fatal day? The chorus sings at the end of the *Oedipus Rex:*

*Look to the end of mortal life. In vain*
*We say a man is happy, till he goes*
*Beyond life's final border, free from pain.*

In the Christian era a further complication entered. This

[36] On this proverb see further Albert W. Fields, "Milton and Self-Knowledge," *PMLA*, LXXXIII (1968), 392-399. Again the contemporary thought of Sartre offers an interesting parallel. See Alfred Stern, *Sartre, His Philosophy and Psychoanalysis* (New York, 1953), p. 140.

[37] Herodotus i. 32, 86; on Xenophon see Phillips, p. 11. Several significant 16th- and 17th-century references are provided in Tilley at M333.

[38] Aeschylus, *Agam.* 891f., where the king explains why he should not tread the tapestries. Cf. the saying attributed to Publilius Syrus, one of the Seven Sages, familiar to Renaissance schoolboys: "To call yourself 'happy' is to provoke disaster." Charles G. Smith, *Shakespeare's Proverb Lore* (Cambridge, Mass., 1963), p. 108.

[39] Line 55. See Tilley, W152 and P612, and I Cor. 10:12. Cf. Daniel Dyke, *The Mystery of Selfe-Deceiving. Or A Discourse and discovery of the deceitfullnesse of Mans Heart* (London, 1614), p. 275: "The *eigth deceit* is, when having performed some good service to God, we thereupon take occasion to be the more carelesse and secure." As this book was reprinted at least nine times before the middle 1630s, when it appeared in Dyke's collected *Works,* it seems likely that Milton would have known it.

*gnomos* became linked with Ecclesiasticus 11:27-28, which reads (in the Geneva translation):

> The adversitie of an houre maketh one to forget pleasure: and in a mans end, his workes are discovered.
>
> Judge none blessed before his death: for a man shalbe knowen by his children.

These reflections help us understand the plaintive words of Manoa during his first appearance in *Samson Agonistes.* After years of childlessness God had acted wondrously on his behalf — but to what avail, considering his old age now, and Samson's degradation?

> *I gain'd a Son,*
> *And such a Son as all Men hail'd me happy;*
> *Who would be now a Father in my stead?*
> [353-355]

*Respice finem,* "Regard the end." This adage, too, carries a double or even triple meaning. It may mean about the same as the proverb we have just considered.[40] It may be a call to purposeful action, with "end" as "goal," as in the analogue "The end crowns all" for which numerous Renaissance citations may be given.[41] More often, however, it reminded the reader to make all decisions with an eye to the rendering up of his final accounts. So much did this emphasis prevail that in Erasmus' *Adages* the proverb comes out *Finem vitae specta,* "Marke the ende of the life," as Taverner translates it (1552). Here too Scriptural influence may be at work; Lamentations 1:9 bewails the city that "remembereth not her last end." In any event, in the light of the insistence of late medieval devotion on remembering the "last things" it is easy to see how *Respice finem* came to be bred in the bone of the English schoolboy of Shakespeare's day, and probably Milton's too, as a warning to keep short accounts with God.[42] This proverb offers, to the warfaring or wayfaring Christian of Milton's day seeking direction for his life, a sort of antidote to the one preceding. Presumably if he goes through life faithfully "regarding his end," he will manage

40 Whitney, p. 130: "And SOLON sai'd, *Remember still thy ende, /* Before the which, none can have perfect joyes" — an evident reference to the advice of Croesus cited above.

41 Tilley, E116; cf. Smith, p. 44: "The end and issue of a thing is ever to be looked at."

42 Tilley's citations (E125) go on well into the 17th century. We may also note the chorus's rhetorical repetition of *end* in lines 704, 709; and Deut. 32:29, which was given currency among politically minded readers in 1639 by being quoted on the title page of Jean Puget de la Serre, *The Mirrour which Flatters not,* trans. T. C. (London, 1639).

Figure 3

to retain right up to death his right to the epithet "happy." By following this course he will be ready, as Everyman in the play was not, to obey Death's call. For the Englishman who saw *The Summoning of Everyman* there was comfort in the current proverb "He that lives well cannot die amiss."[43] There was also a vast literature of preparatives for death, which after waning

[43] Tilley, L391, with examples from 1506 to 1648.

somewhat in Elizabethan days burgeoned anew in the seventeenth century. Taylor's *Holy Dying* was only one of many.[44] Both the earlier and later appetites for death literature are sometimes explained by reference to the outbreaks of plague, but as many of those books in Milton's time antedated the plague years, it is safer, if less satisfying, to ascribe them simply to the "spirit of the age." Life was uncertain enough even under normal circumstances—and is; that is why *Respice finem* is perennially valid.

*Nescit homo finem suum.* When Robert Greene wrote, "Wee have nothing more certaine than to dye, nor nothing more uncertaine than the houre of death," he too was only reminding his audience of a commonplace they well knew (Tilley, N311). "For man also knoweth not his time" was the observation of the Preacher (Ecclesiastes 9:12), and this (in the Latin form which heads this paragraph) sometimes formed the motto for a popular seventeenth-century emblem that neatly drew together classical and Christian wisdom. This emblem seems to have been originated by Otto van Veen, a Dutch artist who studied in Italy and became the teacher of Rubens. In 1607 he issued a set of 103 copper-engraved emblems based on extracts from the poet Horace. During the century and more following, the work was often reprinted and much imitated.[45] In the thirteenth ode of his second book, Horace tells how he narrowly missed being struck on the head by a falling tree on his Sabine farm, and comments on the unexpected occasions and forms in which death can come. Veen's engraving for this ode pictures another ancient poet at the moment when he is about to meet his unexpected end (Fig. 3). Aeschylus, white-bearded and venerable, sits beside a brook some distance from a city, pencase and ink beside him, codex and quill pen in hand. He has been writing verse, has left off in the middle of a line—waiting perhaps for further inspiration from above. The facing text recounts the familiar legend, how the poet, warned that he would soon be killed by a falling arch, left the city in haste and went out into the open field in order to foil the prophecy.[46] Overhead flies an

[44] Sr. Mary Catharine O'Connor, *The Art of Dying Well: The Development of the Ars moriendi*, Columbia Univ. Stud. in Engl. and Comp. Lit., 156 (New York, 1942), pp. 191-212.

[45] The ed. I have used is *Quinti Horatii Flacci Emblemata* (Antwerp, 1612). I am grateful to The Folger Shakespeare Library for permission to reproduce the picture and also the MS verses from its copy. Praz, pp. 99, 523f., gives full information on this work and its various edd. up to 1777.

[46] P. 184. The detail of the falling arch is not found in Veen but is mentioned by one of his many imitators, Marin le Roy, Sieur de Gomberville,

eagle carrying a tortoise, looking for a rock on which to break the arched shell of his prey. He mistakes the poet's bald head for a rock, and thus the prophecy of his death proves accurate and inescapable. Following Veen's account of the Aeschylus legend, for which his immediate source appears to be the first-century anecdotist Valerius Maximus, we are given quotations from Menander, Cicero, and Seneca containing appropriate moral observations. These are followed by verse comments in Spanish, Dutch, Italian, and French — for emblem books enjoyed a cosmopolitan sale. This general pattern of text is followed on all the pages facing engravings. In addition, in the Folger copy there have been inserted by hand at the foot of several of the pages quatrains in English, evidently by a seventeenth-century owner of the book. His comment on the Aeschylus emblem (p. 184) contains interesting contemporary allusions:

*Could man foretell what Things would come to pass*
*Thy head Proud Stafford had not hung so Lowe*
*Nor thou Poor Coleman suffered like an Asse.*
*But Fates obscure, and Death comes sure though Slow.*[47]

There is no evidence that Milton ever saw this picture or one like it, but knowing the scope of his studies it would be foolhardy to say he did not. Certainly he knew the legend and he knew his Horace. Whether he saw the picture is not important. The stories of Aeschylus and Horace belong to a class of literature in which Milton took particular interest, the anecdotes of poets, their rewards and sufferings, the treatment accorded them by the world and by fate. Of Homer blind and Orpheus slain he wrote often, and more than once of Ovid homeless.[48] And nearly always, when Milton alludes to the fate of poets of old — whom he thinks of as his colleagues in a small, select band — hovering close in the context are his uncertain plans and hopes for his own future. "When the assault was intended to the city" is the title of one of Milton's sonnets, a playful appeal to an imagined Royalist soldier advancing on the poet's house, urging him to spare it out of regard for the Muses; in support Milton

*La Doctrine des Moeurs* (Paris, 1685), p. 372, and finds its way thence into an English translation, *Moral Virtue Delineated* (2d ed., London, 1726), p. 190. The curious similarity to the manner of Samson's death I assume to be pure coincidence.

[47] Edward Coleman and William Howard, Viscount Stafford, were among those implicated in the alleged "Popish Plot" and were executed in 1678 and 1680 respectively. Subsequently the proceedings were discredited and the chief informant convicted of perjury.

[48] *Elegies*, i, 21-22; vi, 19-20. Note also the references to blind Teiresias and exiled Calchas, vi, 68-69.

cites the respect paid by ancient commanders to places associated with Pindar and Euripides. But these two astonishing anecdotes tell of the exceptions; who today can imagine a reputation for poetry exempting anyone from the barbarities of war? — let alone of death. "What could the Muse her self" do to save Orpheus from his horrible end? Death (as his dancing figure had reminded an earlier generation) is no respecter of persons. Even though a poet be in the midst of his creative labors — like Aeschylus in the picture — still may come "the blind Fury" who "slits the thin-spun life." It is common knowledge that when Milton in "Lycidas" linked the helpless fate of Orpheus with the premature drowning of Edward King, what he had in mind as much as either of those was the uncertain future of John Milton: uncertain because (among other reasons) *Nescit homo finem suum.*[49]

This brings us close to Milton's private "identity crises." Before going on, however, it is well to conclude our attempt to formulate his concepts as found in *Samson Agonistes.* We have presented four classical commonplaces that have a bearing on the question "Who am I?" All four have this in common, that they emphasize the inadequacy of mortal vision. To recognize one's position in the universe, to penetrate beyond the curtain of appearances that constitutes one's public image, to know oneself in the deepest springs of motivation, to apprehend the unity amid all the vacillations of one's life — these are difficult tasks; but still they do not exhaust the question "Who am I?" To be able to complete the defining statement "I am the man who . . ." a person would have to see into the future, becoming aware of the fulfillment or failure of vocation, the vagaries of fortune, and the state of the soul at the hour of death.[50] This no man can do.

Those are the terms in which Milton's Samson, and Milton himself, faced the question of identity. They are human terms: a necessary starting point, but doomed, like all merely human reasonings "by thir own perplexities involv'd," to "never find self-satisfying solution" (304, 306). Milton pointed his Samson toward a solution to be found in different terms, because it was upon different considerations he had found his own.

There is little need to pass in review all the evidence in

[49] For an association of this particular motto with the Aeschylus emblem see Ioh. Weichardus Valvasor, *Schau-Bühne dess Menschlichen Todts* (Leybach, 1682), sig. Q2; reproduced in Robert J. Clements, *Picta Poesis* (Rome, 1960), Pl. X.

[50] The *locus classicus* for this last point is, of course, the *Divine Comedy.*

*Samson Agonistes* for the inadequacy of human vision. We are kept conscious of it by the metaphor of the hero's blindness. Still, it would be well to attempt an ordering of the material. We are shown that the image formed by the public is not to be trusted, for the people are wont to "gaze" (36), "stare" (112), and look askance with suspicion (272), while even the "wisest and best" are "full oft beguil'd" (759). Those who attempt to order their lives without taking God into account have only "vain reasonings" (322) and "blindness internal" (1686). Even those who believe in God may make the mistake of passing judgment on his doings from their human perspective. It is the chorus, true Israelites all, who complain of God's "contrarious" dealings with men (667ff.). Why does he suddenly bring low those to whom he had shown favor? Such are "unseemly falls *in human eie*" (690, my italics). Even though the chorus and Manoa believe in God's power, they do not really understand. In his assurance that God will not permit Dagon to triumph Manoa shows his faith, but he goes astray in placing too much confidence in his own ability to foresee the methods God will use.[51]

Samson's vision of the future is clearer than his visitors', once he is past the despair which can foresee only bondage and death.[52] Even in the midst of that despair, he is ready to acknowledge the superiority of God's vision; and when this acknowledgment becomes no longer academic but something he can live by, it is his salvation. His checking himself,

> *But peace, I must not quarrel with the will*
> *Of highest dispensation, which herein*
> *Happ'ly had ends above my reach to know,*
> [60-62]

and admonishing his father to "appoint not heavenly disposition" (373), spring from a theological orthodoxy that is purely academic: he does not belong to the Fool's school, but on the other hand he fails to see that it can still apply to him. While he was growing up "under [God's] special eie" (636), the divine insight had been a personal reality, but now he feels "cast . . . off as never known" (641) and is utterly without hope. Later, however, there comes a moment in the play when he can meet Harapha's taunts by admitting he had sinned but adding that he does not "despair" of pardon from a God whose "eye" is "gracious to re-admit the suppliant" (1171ff.). He has just told Harapha, "My trust is in the living God" (1140), and in so

51 Lines 516, 582ff., 1500ff., 1527; on the chorus, 708-709.

52 See especially 1265-67, 1388-89.

doing affirmed for the first time the relevance of his impeccable theology to his personal need. God (not magic) is his source of strength. But there is yet another step to be taken, for strength (as he had observed in his entering speech) must be accompanied by wisdom, and both must be from God. When Samson finds it possible, in the scene with Harapha, once again to claim the divine presence, in effect rediscovering a portion of his lost vocation, the way is paved for him to receive the gift of divine wisdom as well. That comes suddenly, just when Samson has been employing his human wits in a ringing refutation of the officer who has come to summon him. He neatly ticks off the reasons he cannot go: Jewish law forbids it, he is "tir'd" and "over-labour'd," this is just a trick to stir up "new quarrels," he need not subject himself to public contempt. They are all good reasons; the first is evidently the most important to him, as he elaborates on it for the chorus's benefit. Despite a theoretical faith in a God whose knowledge and methods are both higher than man's, Samson is still up to this point employing his own reasoning. Abruptly there is a change. The Spirit whose inward witness had been the source of his true self-knowledge in youth, the Spirit that had departed from him when his hair was cut, returns. And because he has already reestablished his openness to God on the level of physical strength, he is now able to respond properly to these "rouzing motions" (1382) that mark the influx of divine wisdom. The suddenness of the change is important. The highest reaches of which his own vision was capable are willingly abandoned and God's vision is accepted instead. "With inward eyes illuminated" Samson can now proceed to his destiny — to discover, by enacting it, who he is.

The solution to his identity crisis comes by a trust in God so complete that it is no longer a crisis. He goes out with the officer, freely acknowledging he does not know what will happen; that ignorance, however, obviously does not worry him. His agonizing question can be answered only when he ceases to ask it.

The shift from human to divine perspective entails two interesting consequences. I said before that Samson's *whole* life is rightly evaluated as "Heroic," the middle period of degradation being somehow redeemed by his spiritual victory at the end. Something analogous occurs in connection with other evaluations that must be made. Milton presents God as the source not only of true knowledge and true guidance, but also of true judgment. (1) In his final acts Samson violates a whole series of religious taboos. On one level of human reasoning this can be justified (e.g. the chorus's argument from compulsion). On a higher level such reasoning is invalid, for when the law of God comes into conflict with human reasoning, the former must prevail. But once that conflict is settled, then God from a still higher level — that is, from his own perspective — can, without jeopardizing the principles asserted in his "law," by special decree sanctify those things which would otherwise be sinful or unclean. He did it in connection with Samson's first marriage — Milton alludes to this point more than once — and again in allowing him to go with the officer, and perhaps this is the most fruitful approach to take in dealing with the problem of Samson's suicide.[53] The second of these three levels is an accommodation to human weakness. All this is related to Milton's pronounced views on the distinction between Law and Grace and on Christian liberty.[54]

(2) On the lowest level of human vision a "public image" of a person is easily formed. We have already noted its susceptibility to error. On this frail basis one may receive, and even be puffed up with, public acclaim, on the dangers of which Milton has much to say — but he is also well aware of its strong allurement. He has his chorus "reckon" the man to be "in high estate" who by a combination of strength and virtue wins the

[53] On the suicide cf. F. Michael Krouse, *Milton's Samson and the Christian Tradition* (Princeton, 1949), pp. 75, 107, and H. J. C. Grierson, *Milton & Wordsworth* (Cambridge, 1937), p. 139. The importance of the point to Milton may be judged by the space devoted in his first *stasimon* to God's right "with his own Laws" to "dispence" (307-324). As to Samson's two marriages Arnold Stein, *Heroic Knowledge* (Minneapolis, 1957), p. 146, makes the acute observation that his decision to marry Dalila was a rationalistic error; the first marriage had been truly justified, by divine intuition, but the second falsely, by a merely human logical process of analogy.

[54] Cf. *CD*, I, xxvi-xxvii. Some weighty critics have argued, however, that because he was dealing with an Old Testament character Milton deliberately avoided a Christian viewpoint and, further, that this proves his temper was essentially Hebraic, not Christian. Time serves not now to argue in full this vexed question. Let it suffice to record my agreement with John M. Steadman, "'Faithful Champion': The Theological Basis of Milton's Hero of Faith," *Anglia*, LXXVII (1959), 12-28 (esp. 17f.), that the Samson of Milton's play is the hero as seen not only in Judges but also in Heb. 11. Different but complementary approaches to the same conclusion that the poem is a Christian one are explored by A. S. P. Woodhouse, "Tragic Effect in *Samson Agonistes*," *Univ. of Toronto Quart.*, XXVIII (1959), 205-222; Arthur E. Barker, "Structural and Doctrinal Pattern in Milton's Later Poems," *Essays in English Literature . . . Presented to A. S. P. Woodhouse*, ed. M. MacLure and F. W. Watt (Toronto, 1964), pp. 175-179; and William G. Madsen, *From Shadowy Types to Truth* (New Haven and London, 1968), pp. 199-202.

right to be "universally crown'd with highest praises" (170ff.). Yet appealing as this crown may sound, we are not meant to take it as a worthy motive. Dalila's parting words of reliance on this kind of fame as her reward (980-993) are easier to see through, unintentionally qualified as they are by her own description of Fame as "double-mouth'd" (971). The chorus finally proceeds to a second level of human vision where it can speak of a higher "crown" (1296), and Samson declares he would sooner displease Man than God (1373ff.). This is the perspective where the divine vision is accepted by man as authoritative. But again there is a third level, the perspective of God himself. Samson's final restoration to the "wondrous glory" from which he had "fall'n" (167ff.) indicates that public acclaim, so long as it remains duly subordinated to the true evaluation of God's eye, need no longer be rejected as unworthy. "What God hath cleansed, that call not thou common." Manoa's plan to erect a monument to his son's fame, though parallel in some details to Dalila's quest for spurious glory, in no wise betrays a lack of judgment on his part. God "to his faithful Champion . . . / Bore witness gloriously" (1751-52).[55] In the words "bore witness" we find the conjunction of the divine and human perspectives; and the word "gloriously" is the last of many examples of *light* imagery in the poem.

## III

In the life of John Milton we may trace a quest for self-knowledge that follows a similar pattern. Through introspective assessment combined with an implanted sense of moral duty he conceived certain goals for his life. The motive power to reach these goals was supplied, in varying degrees, by a fondness for acclaim, great personal ambition, and a sense of divine vocation — a troika whose latent conflicts spelled trouble. In the course of his life the self-image that he formed received a series of shocks. Might he fail to reach his goals — that is, turn out not to be the person he thought he was — either because changing circumstances would bar his way or because he had been mistaken after all in thinking he had the capacity? The former cause might result either from external forces entirely or, more unsettling, from his own acts; the other might be a matter of lacking either the necessary talent, or the moral

[55] Thus marking the hero's death with a *figurative* splendor symmetrically answering to that which *literally* attended his conception (24ff.) and perhaps meant to indicate the Shekinah presence of God himself (cf. 28, 1673-74).

capacity. Milton's resolution of each of these crises matches the paradigm we find in *Samson Agonistes.* Faced with doubts whether his self-image was true self-knowledge, he sought to correct it insofar as he could, but beyond that learned the lesson to be content with not knowing. More important ultimately than self-knowledge was the knowledge that he was known, that though he might seek in vain to grasp fully his identity there was One who did know him, future as well as present, and in whose guidance and true evaluation he could set his doubts at rest and find not only peace but power.

From the start Milton considered his calling to be, somehow, that of a servant of God. Given his religious upbringing, this was almost a foregone conclusion. Over the years he was able to bring more sharply into focus the role in which he saw himself. His service was to be nothing ordinary but rather would be distinguished by notable achievements. More specifically, he would serve God and his nation together by doing the work of a moral teacher and guide — a role somewhat analogous to that of a shepherd leading a flock. This was still pretty general: such a role could assume several different concrete forms. A church career, for instance, would be one possibility, and remained so for Milton till he was nearly thirty. Finally he settled on poetry,[56] and what had all along been an important part of his life now became its focus. The self-image of poet meant to Milton the achievement of excellence in the highest genres. The work of forced fingers rude might be enough if poetry were merely an avocation, but as a career it required more. It was as an English Virgil, at the very least, that Milton came to see himself. The familiar account in his *Reason of Church Government* nicely summarizes the considerations that combined to produce this decision:

> I began thus far to assent both to them [in Italy] and divers of my friends here at home, and not less to an inward prompting which now grew daily upon me, that by labor and intense study, (which I take to be my portion in this life,) joined with the strong propensity of nature, I might perhaps leave something so written to aftertimes, as they should not willingly let it die.

Together with "these thoughts" he was "possessed" by the conviction that, if he could write with any hope of permanence, his prime concern should be for "God's glory, by the honor and instruction of my country" (*SM,* p. 524).

Autobiographical statements like this, which occur frequent-

[56] Cf. John T. Shawcross, "Milton's Decision to Become a Poet," *Mod. Lang. Quart.* XXIV (1963), 21-30.

ly in Milton, are fascinating. They reveal, perhaps more fully than the author intended, the persistence within his mind of the tension described in the introductory paragraphs of this essay. It is clear that the "noble mind" still suffers its "last infirmity" even in the very moment when, surely with the deepest sincerity, the selfless motive of "God's glory" is declared. This doubleness, and its resolution, form the central concern of the present study.

Milton cared greatly what image he presented to the world. In the *Reason of Church Government*, just before the passage I have quoted, he unabashedly hints at the psychic support he received from the "acceptance" accorded him and his works on his Italian journey — especially since the Italians were known to be sparing in their praise of northern cultures. Sustaining him earlier in life was the opinion of "sundry masters and teachers" that his style in prose and verse, especially verse, "by certain vital signs it had, was likely to live." Not that he was excessively dependent upon his public image (like Samson at the beginning of the play): he had enough self-assurance to be able to preserve his self-image in the face of adverse public opinion, appearing to ignore the latter or rationalizing it away. "The mind is its own place." The nickname of "Lady" given him at Cambridge, for example, did not cause him to regret his fair complexion or change his fastidious behavior. Yet the detraction did sting him into a rejoinder, and that fact is significant, particularly as we see the pattern repeated in the Hall and Salmasius controversies.[57] Another example might be Milton's disappointment in the public reception of his teachings on divorce. The strategy displayed in the two sonnets on this subject is typical. He is not unwilling to be Milton *contra mundum* — if necessary — but prefers to retain some sense of the judicious approval of the *aristoi* while dismissing popular objections as the "barbarous noise" of "Hoggs" (along with a few other choice epithets), of unlettered anti-intellectuals, of the "wilde Rout" as he put it in a parallel passage in *Paradise Lost* (VII, 30-39). His self-image is firm enough that he can dispense with the plaudits of the mob; nevertheless he yearns to find acclaim among his "fit audience

[57] On the "Lady" nickname see *Prolusion* vi and E. M. W. Tillyard, *Milton*, rev. ed. (New York, 1967), pp. 26-27. On the later tracts John S. Diekhoff, *Milton on Himself* (New York, 1939), pp. xiv-xv, questions whether Milton "is as unconcerned as he thinks when he discusses his own personal appearance in reply to his enemies' descriptions of him." Something of the importance Milton attached to facial appearance may be caught in *Comus*, 526-530; Son. xxii, 1-2; *PL*, III, 44; and "Lycidas," 62, "goary visage" (altered in MS from the less horrific "goarie scalpe").

. . . though few."[58] The loss of their esteem, and even at times more general public detraction, will put on him repeatedly the psychological requirement of reexamining his concept of identity.

Milton was nothing if not ambitious. His desire to excel all rivals apparently reflects two purposes, the glorification of others (God, country) and the glorification of himself. Perhaps these two are interrelated; we shall see.

I have already quoted Milton's account of his resolution to write for "God's glory, by the honor and instruction of my country." He proceeds in further detail (*SM*, p. 525):

> . . . That what the greatest and choicest wits of Athens, Rome, or modern Italy, and those Hebrews of old did for their country, I, in my proportion, with this over and above, of being a Christian, might do for mine; not caring to be once named abroad, though perhaps I could attain to that, but content with these British islands as my world; whose fortune hath hitherto been, that if the Athenians, as some say, made their small deeds great and renowned by their eloquent writers, England hath had her noble achievements made small by the unskilful handling of monks and mechanics.

Others have explained the literary means by which Milton hoped to achieve this patriotic end; I am primarily interested now in that telling phrase, *with this over and above, of being a Christian*. There is due humility in what goes before, "in my proportion," but here is great audacity, as also in what follows comparing England with Athens.

The superiority of Hebrew culture over Greek and of Christian over both is a frequent theme in Milton's works. Sometimes all three members of the triad are involved, sometimes only two. Milton's ensuing discussion of the various possible kinds of poetry he may undertake is of the latter sort. Each Greek example is matched by one from the Bible, whose "songs" excel "not in their divine argument alone, but in the very critical art of composition."[59] *Samson Agonistes* has only two

[58] See Diekhoff, p. 150 & n., and index s.v. "Audience." To seek the plaudits of the great while disdaining those of the mob is a trait of that classical paragon, the Magnanimous Man of Aristotle. See Maurice B. McNamee, *Honor and the Epic Hero* (New York, 1960), p. 2.

[59] In this last phrase Milton may well have had in mind the contemporary analysis (elaborating on Patristic sources, but thoroughly mistaken, as Bishop Lowth was later to show) of Hebrew poetry as composed in a great variety of classical quantitative meters. The subject has been fully set forth by Israel Baroway in a series of articles in *JEGP*, XXXII (1933), 447-480, and *ELH*, II (1935), 66-91; VIII (1941), 119-142; XVII (1950), 115-135. Leo Spitzer sees in the *Reason of Church Government* passage the full Hebrew-Greek-Christian triad: *Classical and Christian Ideas of World Harmony* (Baltimore, 1963), p. 205; cf. pp. 103-107.

allusions to classical myth (apart from the christianized phoenix) and both follow this pattern. The "Gentiles" have their stories reminiscent of Samson, but strong as Atlas may be, he is inferior because they only "feign" him (150); and the tortures assigned in Hades for betraying secrets are mere "Parables" (500). Something similar happens in *Paradise Lost* near the beginning, perhaps while the poet's mind is still echoing with the thought of soaring "above th' Aonian Mount" or wondering "if Sion Hill / Delight thee more." Requiring a simile to describe Satan's vast "bulk" he turns first to the Greek Titans — who, he immediately recognizes, are only "Fables." So he tries again, this time looking to the Old Testament for "that Sea-beast / Leviathan, which God" (contrasting with "Jove" three lines before) "of all his works / Created hugest" (I, 200-202). It was, of course, in *Paradise Regain'd* (IV, 221-364) that Milton finally made his most extensive comparison of Hebrew and Greek culture.

His comparison of classical and Christian follows similar lines, but goes further. In passages too numerous and too familiar to require listing, he holds Christian culture, too, superior to Greek. But there is also a set of passages revealing his belief that Christianity excels *both* Judaism and Hellenism: these passages have to do with the hope of life after death. The Mosaic law and the gospel, he writes in the *Christian Doctrine*,[60] have this in common, that both belong to the Covenant of Grace. But the law offers man promises which relate to "temporal life," while the promise of the gospel is one "of eternal life" (*SM*, p. 1024). So far as the Christian-classical distinction is concerned, Milton thinks immortality as conceived, say, by Plato pretty thin stuff beside Christ's conquest of death seen by the church as historic fact. In his youth particularly, Milton's imagination was so stirred by the Christian doctrine of resurrection that in several poems he contrasted it with the less adequate classical response to death.[61] Nor is the theme confined to his youth. Indirectly the comparison enters into Sonnet xiv, "On the Religious Memory of Mrs. Catharine Thomason."

*Meekly thou didst resign this earthy load*
*Of Death, call'd Life; which us from Life doth sever.*

Here is the Christian parallel to the Greek proverb *Call no man*

[60] See above, note 54. Cf. also Arthur Sewell, "Milton and the Mosaic Law," *Mod. Lang. Rev.*, XXX (1935), 13-18, 218.

[61] *Elegies*, iii, 56-65; *In ob. Praesulis Eliensis*, 41, 49-50; "Fair Infant"; "Lycidas," 172-181; *Ep. Damonis*, 212-219.

*happy before his death,* but the reasons behind the injunction are entirely different: not because the man may yet plunge into unhappiness before he dies, but because he cannot know fullest happiness till then. And in that most moving sonnet, his last, he brought all three isms into comparison (just as in the prose passage, "choicest wits of Athens . . . Hebrews of old . . . , I, . . . a Christian"), using as a basic structural principle the triad classical-Hebrew-Christian, arranged in that rising order. In the first four lines of the sonnet the dead wife brought back to him in a dream is compared to Alcestis whom Hercules "rescu'd from death." But that rescue was imperfect: Alcestis had to be brought "by force" and even so remained "pale and faint." Next she is compared to a woman "saved" by the ceremonies of "the old Law" from the symbolic death of parturition: that is, to one who has in the pains of childbearing — associated in Genesis 3:16 with the curse of death following the fall[62] — experienced a descent into the mysterious realms from which man enters earthly life and to which he returns at its end, and has re-ascended with her child, but can only be fully restored to "life" as a member of the worshipping community through the Levitical rite of purification. This death, to be sure, is only symbolic; and the salvation is, to employ again the language of the *Christian Doctrine,* only temporal. But it comes through sacrifices, not "by force," thus in one respect correcting the Greek error and pointing toward the still more fully realized Christian solution. It remains for Christianity to offer a complete conquest of real, not symbolic, death. Through the sacrifice of him to whom "Joves great Son" is a mere pagan shadow, Milton can hope for "full sight . . . without restraint" of his loved one (as opposed to the attenuated vision of Alcestis), "in Heaven" (as opposed to the mere earthly and temporary restoration in both the other examples).[63]

[62] As John Calvin had observed in his comment on Lev. 12. *Commentaries on the Four Last Books of Moses,* ed. C. Bingham (Edinburgh, 1852-55), I, 499.

[63] Since developing this analysis of Son. xxiii I have noted some of these points also made by Leo Spitzer, *Essays on English and American Literature* (Princeton, 1962), pp. 124-126; and by Martin Mueller, "The Theme and Imagery of Milton's Last Sonnet," *Archiv,* CCI (1964), 267-271, who, however, I think mistakenly, splits the third member of the triad in two, distinguishing the veiled saint of the dream from the glorified saint in heaven. But the dream image is really not part of the triad at all; it is to her that all three comparisons apply. Each represents a restoration and transformation after death, and they are arranged in order of increasing perfection. The veil has not nearly the significance given it by Mueller (and several other critics!). Explicable simply as one of the facts of his

It is clear that Milton's hierarchical arrangement of the three cultures that together formed his mind was a powerful stimulus to his imagination. Even in a more playful mood he voices the ambition to surpass the ancients — sure sign that its root went deep in his psyche. At the close of "L'Allegro" he can imagine music sweet and strong enough to raise the dead, thus — boldest stroke of all — thus succeeding where Orpheus failed. He would not only bring back Eurydice, but waken the archetypal singer himself from Elysian slumber — exerting over Orpheus the same power Orpheus had had over lesser dead things such as rocks and trees. Not that the poet can of himself compose such music; it comes from the goddess. Yet it is her gift to *his* imagination. This passage, of course, is somewhat fanciful and cannot be read as deliberate self-description like that we find in the autobiographical prose or the epic invocations. And therefore I consider it all the more revealing.

Further, it may be significant that the music in "L'Allegro" is not explicitly Christian in origin.[64] For if Milton's sense of superiority derived solely from his awareness of the greatness of the gospel, his own role being only that of a messenger proclaiming it for God's glory, we could hardly charge him with personal ambition. In "L'Allegro," however, the message itself appears to be omitted yet the imaginative force of the concept remains, which suggests that this force may derive from a different motive, one that vies in Milton with his genuine desire to glorify God. Pointing toward the same conclusion are the passages in *Paradise Lost* where he invites comparison between himself and the ancient poets. In Book III he hopes through his "nightly" visits to "Sion" to be "equal'd . . . in renown" with the legendary blind bards and seers of Greece. And if earlier in the same passage (13-21) he again outdoes Orpheus,

dream (for no convincing reason has been offered to think the whole poem a fiction), the veil, as the poet is at pains to say, does *not* denote any inferiority of the dream figure to the heavenly. Despite the veil and despite his blindness, the dreamer sees the real essence of his loved one with clarity and "delight." ("Her person" is a neat *double entendre* suggesting her essential qualities — "love, sweetness, goodness" — and also, by its Latin cognate, a *face* which, even though veiled, "shin'd / So clear.")

[64] On the other hand, one dare not dogmatize that it cannot be Christian; and in the parallel passage of "Il Penseroso" (161ff.) the Christian nature of the music is explicit. Further, the lines in "L'Allegro" may owe something to the tradition of Orpheus as a type of Christ. See V. de Sola Pinto, *Peter Sterry, Platonist and Puritan* (Cambridge, 1934), p. 181; Austin Warren, *Richard Crashaw: A Study in Baroque Sensibility* (Ann Arbor, 1939), p. 72; and D. C. Allen, "Milton and the Descent to Light," *JEGP*, LX (1961), 616ff.

*Taught by the heav'nly Muse to venture down*
*The dark ascent, and up to reascend,*
*Though hard and rare,*

it is still no more than a Roman poet has accomplished before him. In Book VII, however, he not only hopes for a better fate than Orpheus, whom the Muse could not defend ("For thou art Heav'nlie, shee an empty dreame" [39]), but speaks of soaring "above th' Olympian Hill" and "above the flight of Pegasean wing" (3-4). In Book IX — again depending on the favor of his "Celestial Patroness" — he undertakes a theme "more Heroic" (14ff.) than anything sung in ancient epic. And from the beginning he has disdained any mediocre ambition. His song is "adventrous," satisfied with "no middle flight" but soaring "above th' Aonian Mount," pursuing "things unattempted yet."[65] Charles Williams calls attention to the "humility" which pervades the tone of this opening invocation, but his purpose is not to deny the pride and ambition which are in it — only to insist that the lines possess *both* humility and pride.[66] That is just the point. John Milton was driven by an enormous personal ambition, and at the same time he possessed a great sense of dependence on divine aid and commitment to the divine will. If in the invocation to *Paradise Lost* the latter force in him has got the former under control (as I believe it has), it is just barely so.

But perhaps in all this Milton was only employing a rhetorical device? Emulating or "outdoing" one's predecessors is one of the *topoi* that Milton's age inherited from late antiquity. However, as Hallett Smith points out in this connection, it is thoroughly characteristic of Milton "to use conventional forms when he is being most intimate and personal." And the instances of "outdoing" found in Milton seem to me to bear this out. All the way from the "Nativity Ode," where with his small gift for the Christchild the poet "would outstrip any who come bearing

[65] Concerning Milton's idea of Christian superiority see W. R. Parker, "On Milton's Early Literary Program," *MP*, XXXIII (1935), 49-53, and R. J. Beck, "Milton and the Spirit of His Age," *English Studies*, XLII (1961), 288-300. In contrast to "th' Aonian Mount" Milton has in the preceding lines identified as the source of his inspiration mountains associated with Moses or, better still ("delight thee *more*"), with Christ. Thus he implies again the hierarchical triad noted above in Son. xxiii and elsewhere. See Jackson I. Cope, "Milton's Muse in *Paradise Lost*," *MP*, LV (1957), 7. (George W. Whiting and Ann Gossman, *SP*, LVIII [1961], 193-205, while they say much that is true, do not, in my opinion, succeed in their effort to refute this interpretation.)

[66] *The Image of the City and Other Essays* (London, 1958), pp. 24-25. See also Joseph H. Summers, *The Muse's Method* (Cambridge, Mass., 1962), pp. 21-22.

the secular wisdom and power of all the earth," to the latter part of *Paradise Lost* and all of its sequel, where he will outstrip the other epic poets by leaving behind "warrs, hitherto the onely Argument / Heroic deem'd" to treat "the better fortitude / Of Patience and Heroic Martyrdom / Unsung" and tell of "deeds / Above Heroic," Milton may use the *language* of hyperbole — but he means every word of it![67] For this is the way Milton's mind works — always thinking in terms of opposition, conquest, triumph. Here it springs, of course, from his sense of Christianity as superior to the best of ancient thought. It is, in fact, Christ himself whose deeds are "above Heroic." Yet while glorifying the subjects of his verse Milton expects also to glorify himself: he would attain to the height of style "which justly gives Heroic name / To Person," that is, to those of whom he writes, and also "to Poem." Still in the very moment when he reaches out for the fame which will be his proper reward, the poet recognizes that if he achieves such a style it will not really be his doing but "Hers who brings it nightly to my Ear."[68] Thus we find again in Milton's verse that tension of ambition and humility which was such a constant element in his personality.

In sum, Milton's ambition to excel, his eagerness to obtain recognition for that excellence, and his sense of duty as a servant called and fitted by God for a certain task all combined to impel his quest of the highest literary achievements. But there were times in the poet's life when the quest as he had understood it till then seemed impossible of fulfillment, and he was thus forced to reexamine that understanding — his self-image, that is — and reshape it in such a way as to take the new circumstances into account. Each of these occasions may fairly be referred to, in the sense in which we have been using the term, as an identity crisis.

It will be well to survey these crises before examining how

[67] E. R. Curtius, *European Literature and the Latin Middle Ages* (New York, 1953), pp. 162-165 ("Outdoing"); see also Gilbert Murray, *The Classical Tradition in Poetry* (Cambridge, Mass., 1927), p. 11; H. O. White, *Plagiarism and Imitation During the English Renaissance* (Cambridge, Mass., 1935), pp. 3-37; and Chaucer, *Merch. T.*, E1715-17. Hallett Smith, "No Middle Flight," *Huntington Lib. Quart.*, XV (1952), 160. "Nat. Ode," 24, as interpreted by C. G. Osgood, *Poetry as a Means of Grace* (Princeton, 1941), p. 86. *PL*, IX, 28-33; *PR*, I, 14-15. The word "Patience" in the quot. from *PL* may remind us of similar passages in *SA*, which however pre-Christian in the way the idea is presented by the chorus (for Milton would tolerate no anachronism), are nevertheless fully Christian: the chorus's comprehension, by design, is not so profound as the poet's. Cf. Stein, p. 141.

[68] *PL*, IX, 40ff.

the poet dealt with them: (1) the lack, even as late as the age of twenty-three, with his university studies completed or virtually so, of evidence that his promised development was actually taking place; (2) the death of Edward King and the immediate awareness it brought of the uncertainty of life; (3) the failure of his first marriage, accompanied during the same years by increasing eye trouble and by the inability to write poetry (except occasional verse), either because of the pressure of public duties or, as some have suggested, through a failure of inspiration; (4) his total blindness; (5) the final collapse of his hopes for England, accompanied by personal danger, at the Restoration.

It was not always in the same way that these crises threatened Milton's self-image. In the second and last instances what he feared was falling victim to forces quite outside his control — the "blind fury" of "Lycidas" or the avenging lackeys of Charles II who, if they failed to send Milton to the block or to jail as they had some of his colleagues, might nevertheless find ways to afflict him.[69] The loss of his sight was also an unalterable fact that required him to redefine his identity, but at the same time he thought of it as containing an element of choice: the new self-definition that emerged from this crisis included the notion of a deliberate sacrifice of his eyes "in libertyes defence, my noble task." Similarly the putting aside of his "singing robes" at the long-awaited outset of his career to employ only his "left hand" in "the cool element of prose" was a matter of deliberate choice. Formerly he had seen himself as both a poet and a faithful steward of the divine gifts: the two had seemed one and the same; but now "in a crisis of so much danger" to his country, it was apparent that he must choose. Which role was really his "identity" and which was expendable? To continue on a poetic career was tantamount to renouncing any claim to the title of faithful steward. To serve God it might not be necessary to abandon the hope of becoming a poet — but certainly to postpone it indefinitely and, for now, put it quite out of his mind. "I therefore determined to relinquish the other pursuits in which I was engaged, and to transfer the whole force of my talents and my industry to this one important object" — namely, "the establishment of real liberty" through a systematic exposition of its principles.[70] The tracts of the 1640s were the

[69] The biographer Richardson adduces contemporary evidence that Milton "was in perpetual terror of being assassinated; though he had escaped the talons of the law, he knew he had made himself enemies in abundance. He was so dejected he would lie awake whole nights. He then kept himself as private as he could" (*SM*, p. xlvi).

[70] *Second Defence: SM*, p. 1147. The reference to "libertyes defence" is

impressive result. A long autobiographical passage in one of them, the *Reason of Church Government*, from which we have already quoted, indicates that he maintained for a time the hope that the two roles might prove after all compatible: though "God by his secretary conscience" had directed him for now to "the meanest under-service," yet he was willing to describe his poetic aspirations at length and "covenant" with the reader for their eventual fulfillment (*SM*, pp. 526-527).

Later, however, after the fiasco of his marriage to Mary Powell, such hopes may have come to seem much more tenuous, and that brings us to a different sort of identity crisis. In the crises commented on above, the threat to his self-image came from without or, if brought on by his own choice, betokened a nobility of character which might serve to offset the sense of loss. But if those scholars are correct who interpret the "prose period" as a time of dryness when "his Heavenly Muse stayed away," until the poet was constrained to worry lest "she should never come again,"[71] such a crisis would imply an altogether different kind of failure in self-knowledge. Instead of merely having to add to the definition of himself some unforeseen contingency — death, imprisonment, or blindness — he would have to acknowledge a radical error in the assessment on which his whole self-image had been based. Perhaps a failure of inspiration meant that he had been deceived in ever thinking he had the makings of a great poet. Similar doubts evidently were at the root of that earlier crisis associated with his "three and twentith yeer." As he concluded at that time, this if true would be a great disappointment, but would at least leave his role of God's servant intact. But what if he had misjudged not his talent but his moral character? Then both roles were threatened. And so closely related were they in his mind that it is in this direction, sooner than to the more comforting notion of a loss of talent alone, that his thoughts would have turned. He would be far more likely to see the loss as a punishment than as a mere fortuity. The incredibly learned Milton recognized the dangers inherent in mere erudition without goodness or wisdom[72] and perhaps feared, when his inspiration seemed taken away, that this destiny had come upon him. Indeed, lack of wisdom may well have seemed the inescapable verdict on Milton's hasty

from Son. xxii, and those in the following sentence from *Reason of Church Government*, II: *SM*, p. 524.

[71] Osgood, *Poetry as a Means of Grace*, p. 91.

[72] *Ibid.*, pp. 87-88. Cf. the context of the quotation which closes the preceding paragraph; the portrait of Belial in *PL;* and Christ's view of learning, *PR*, IV, 321-330.

and ill-advised marriage; it is even suggested that the description of Samson as "sung and proverbd for a Fool / In every street" springs from Milton's own bitter experience then.[73] Worse yet, Milton perhaps saw the marriage (it is argued) as not just folly but rebellion, abandoning the complete dedication to God's service which he had vowed some five or six years earlier, and in consequence being abandoned by God.[74] This, of course, can never go beyond conjecture; but the fact we are compelled to suspend judgment in no way reduces the possibility of its being true. If true, it indicates that Milton faced in his late thirties a complete devastation of the image he had formed of both his destiny and his character. Such a crisis, if it occurred, obviously did not prostrate him, for he was productive during that decade, if not inspired (and some would call *Areopagitica* inspired), and he emerged from it so fully as to be able to testify in the *Second Defence* that after scrupulous soul-searching "I am not conscious . . . of having committed any enormity, which might deservedly have marked me out as a fit object for such a calamitous visitation," referring here to his blindness (*SM*, p. 1140). But even if his conviction of moral integrity never was shaken, yet those years may be viewed as a crisis period of one sort or another. Whatever the threats to his identity, we know that he successfully met them. We lack, however, anything like a full literary record of the means whereby this crisis, number three in the above list, was resolved.

In seeking the pattern of Milton's resolution, then, we must turn our attention to the three crises of which a detailed account is available in his poetry. These are the first two in the list, and the fourth. The poems, of course, are the sonnet "How soon hath Time" for the first crisis, "Lycidas" for the second, and the sonnet generally entitled "On His Blindness" for the third. But to say that these works provide an "account" of how Milton met his crises is misleading unless we recognize the special strategy employed by the poet in transmuting his experience into art. For these poems are not spontaneous outbursts of the tormented soul who in the process of his anguish and recovery commits to writing a play-by-play account of that process. Nor are they cool retrospective analyses of what the poet has gone through, as viewed from some Olympian height of attainment. They are retrospective, yet deliberately re-creative of the event.

[73] R. M. Frye, "Milton's First Marriage," *Notes and Queries*, III (1956), 200-202. Cf. also A. S. P. Woodhouse, "*Samson Agonistes* and Milton's Experience," *Proc. Roy. Soc. Canada*, ser. 3, XLIII, ii (June 1949), 172.

[74] Ernest Sirluck, "Milton's Idle Right Hand," *JEGP*, LX (1961), 749-785.

But the process they describe is not so much the raw historical sequence of events that took place in Milton's mind, as a patterned sequence that symbolizes those events and reveals their essential meaning as the poet has come to understand it.[75] (Thus in the following analyses, when I speak of "the poet," I may refer to the "I" of the poem, who in a sense is only a fictional character.)

And in all three cases, Sonnets vii and xix and lines 64-84 of "Lycidas," the passage on Fame, the pattern is basically the same. Each begins with a question which is really an outcry, distilling the particular threat which the current circumstances offer to what has served the poet up till now as an ordered and satisfactory way of viewing his existence. Each concludes with a gnomic statement reflecting "higher wisdom" which enables him to restructure his collapsing self-image so that even tardy development or blindness or death ceases to be seen as ultimately threatening. The link between these two parts is in each case a word or concept which is central to the opening outcry ("Time," "Fame," and the concept of what God will "exact"), or rather, the *misapprehension* of which makes the speaker's outcry possible. The ensuing response then picks up this word or concept and solves the problem by correcting the misapprehension. In effect, the resolution is achieved in each case by the speaker's being brought to a higher level of understanding — being made to substitute for his limited, earthly vision a new and heavenly one. The pattern here is thus the same as that which we have observed in *Samson Agonistes*.

The first of Milton's documented identity crises came about as a result of the stock-taking in which he would quite naturally have engaged at such a major landmark as the close of his Cambridge career. Already at twenty-one he had made a sort of "mental dedication of himself to the high calling of epic poet"[76] (although the final casting of the die was not to come until later). From that time until he left Cambridge his actual achievement as a poet was disappointing and may well have caused him to doubt the rightness of his tentative decision. His ambitious attempt to follow up the "Nativity Ode" with a poem on Christ's passion fell so flat that he gave it up, and if "L'Allegro" and "Il Penseroso" afforded satisfying evidence of continued mastery, his success in these highly introspective poems was no proof at all that he could handle the more objective

[75] Cf. Aristotle, *Poetics*, ix.

[76] Tillyard, *Milton*, p. 35; for the qualification, see Shawcross (above, note 56).

genres which by the examples of Virgil and Spenser were the prescribed steps for the apprentice poet. This failure to get quick confirmation of his poetic leanings set Milton to brooding, in terms (characteristically) of the warnings of Christ in the gospels. To "a friend" (anonymous and perhaps fictional) he wrote, "The howres of the night passe on (for so I call my life as yet obscure, & unserviceable to mankind) & . . . the day with me is at hand wherin Christ commands all to labour while there is light" (*SM*, p. 1127). Attached to the letter in the Cambridge MS is the sonnet —

*How soon hath Time the suttle theef of youth,*
*Stoln on his wing my three and twentith yeer!*

He is near manhood, though he may not look it, for his ladylike facial characteristics[77] make him look younger and even raise in his own mind doubt of his real maturity. For there is still greater disparity between the "inward ripeness" appropriate for his chronological age and the evidence he has been able to show so far — not even a "bud or blossom," let alone fruit! Words like "shew'th," "semblance," "appear" demonstrate how much the struggle was to Milton one of reconciling image and reality. The intensity of his worry is apparent from his devaluation of those early poems which we see now as unmistakably the work of genius. He devotes the octave of the sonnet to defining his crisis, in three loose sentences (line 1 is the only line requiring something more to complete the grammar) whose intermixed polysyllables cause the verse itself to "flie on with full career." Then with the word "yet" the tone shifts, and a line of ten monosyllables, ending with "slow," introduces a ponderous four-line period, after which he concludes with an aphorism, still personal in tone yet heavy with the weight of Pindar and the sententious tradition. And Time itself, whose rapacious "wing" lent the octave its rapid movement, has been harnessed (together with "the will of Heav'n") to "lead" the poet "in strictest measure" — words which aptly describe the verse as well — to his destiny. Rooted in self-doubt, the poem ends in serene confidence. "Time" is the word which links outcry and answer. The sestet demonstrates that the poet's initial concept of time was wrong: a human way of seeing it, to be sure — but time, in fact, can in some mysterious way be caught up into and identified with eternity.[78] It can be; whether it is, will depend on how

[77] OED, s.v. *semblance.* Again we may observe Milton's sensitivity, commented on in note 57 above, about his facial appearance.

[78] It is only fair to point out that the clause "All is . . . / As ever" is pretty obscure and has consequently been accorded a wide variety of interpre-

the poet uses time; yet even in that, his own responsibility, he is also dependent on "grace." It can be — but only in a vision that is not human but divine: "in my great task Masters eye." The poet himself does not manage to exchange his lower vision for that higher one; he attains only a middle level of understanding, one where he can recognize the inadequacy of his lower vision and accept by faith the existence of the higher. The basis for his trust is the realization that the Possessor of this higher vision and the Determiner of his lot are one and the same; if God imposes a "task" that to human vision produces only anxiety, it is God also who offers the divine vision to relieve the anxiety. Because it is the "task Masters" own "eye" which sees, the poet can rest content.

In the summer of 1637 came a second crisis, not a question this time of *how* he should most properly fulfill his divine calling but of *whether* he would be able to. The negative possibility appears in its starkest form as Milton *sees himself* in the image of his dead classmate Edward King. Not that he literally visualizes his own "beautiful and well-proportioned body"[79] "flot[ing] upon his watry bear / Unwept, and welter[ing] to the parching wind," or "perhaps under the whelming tide / Visit[ing] the bottom of the monstrous world" — though his imagination was powerful and he may have done exactly that. The undebatable evidence is that (garbed in the thin disguise of a rustic "Swain") he spoke of his own "destin'd Urn" and "sable shrowd," and of the "blind Fury" whose "abhorred shears"

tations. The one offered here (*All* meaning 'time,' and *ever* as a noun) is expounded by Donald C. Dorian in *Explicator,* VIII (1949), art. 10, and developed further by E. A. J. Honigmann, ed., *Milton's Sonnets* (London and New York, 1966), pp. 99-100.

Milton's idea of time as eternity may interestingly be compared with a similar notion presented by T. S. Eliot in *The Cocktail Party* — there, too, in a context whose central theme is the problem of personal identity. Past, present and future of an individual's life exist all at once in a transcendent Now; since the future already exists it is accessible — though not to ordinary vision; and the past by itself is neither complete nor fixed but depends ultimately upon the whole for its reality. "When I first met Miss Coplestone," says Reilly in Act III, "I saw the image, standing behind the chair, / Of a Celia Coplestone whose face showed the astonishment / Of the first five minutes after a violent death." (One is reminded of the 17th-century dramatist who, according to Eliot's "Whispers of Immortality," "saw the skull beneath the skin.") Several lines later Reilly tells the Chamberlaynes, "Only by acceptance / Of the past will you alter its meaning." (Cf. above, note 7.) I mention Eliot in connection with the ending of Son. vii because in order to understand Milton here we must recognize that he is very much in the Christian mainstream.

[79] Aubrey's description. *SM*, p. xxiv.

end a poet's life "ere his prime" and under circumstances of asceticism remarkably similar to Milton's own; and that he imparted to the entire poem a fervor of expression quite beyond that demanded by the occasion or the pastoral form.

In the twenty-one lines on which our attention centers he expands the question-answer pattern described above by adding a prelude, also in question-answer form. This first question is a lesser one, readily answerable by the unaided human vision. What incentive could justify the young poet's forsaking the pleasant company of flesh-and-blood girls for the austere contemplation of a "thankles Muse"? "Fame is the spur." Though he couches this reply in terms drawn from the tradition of classical wisdom,[80] nevertheless Milton is here expressing deep personal feelings. Indeed we have already noticed his passion for approval — if not that of the mob, at least that of the select few qualified to judge. When he testifies in "Lycidas" to the power of Fame to impel austere labor, he is in effect repeating an acknowledgment of motive made some years earlier when he wrote of "a desire of honour & repute & immortall fame, seated in the brest of every true scholar; which all make hast to by the readiest ways of publishing & divulging conceived merits" ("Letter to a Friend," *SM*, p. 1128). The desire for fame belongs to the order of merely human vision, with all its limitations — this Milton readily grants — but within that order it represents the highest possible achievement of exalted motive: "not of pure, yet of refined nature" as he puts it in the letter just quoted, or as it appears in "Lycidas," the "last infirmity of Noble mind." The phrase "Noble mind" hints at the Aristotelian virtue of magnanimity, which is the crown of all the virtues and whose essential quality is a determination to be accorded due honor and glory. To Aristotle, of course, this determination was far from being an "infirmity"; so by this description Milton acknowledges his debt to the classical concept and in the same stroke his radical departure from it.[81]

[80] See B. G. Koonce, *Chaucer and the Tradition of Fame* (Princeton, 1966), pp. 20-21n., and John S. Coolidge, "Boethius and 'That Last Infirmity of Noble Mind,'" *PQ*, XLII (1963), 176-182. Cf. also Rudolf Wittkower, "The Vicissitudes of a Dynastic Monument," *De Artibus Opuscula XL*, ed. M. Meiss (Zurich, 1960), I, 507-508; II, 170; and T. E. Mommsen, "Petrarch and the Story of the Choice of Hercules," *Jour. Warburg and Courtauld Inst.*, XVI (1953), 189-192.

[81] McNamee (above, note 58), pp. 122, 160-175; John M. Steadman, *Milton and the Renaissance Hero* (Oxford, 1967), Ch. vi, "The Critique of Magnanimity." Milton had earlier, while at university, observed this same distinction of earthly and heavenly Fame: see D. C. Allen, *The Harmonious Vision* (Baltimore, 1954), pp. 66-68. Roy W. Battenhouse, *Shakespearean*

But to stress, at this stage, the desire for fame as an ethical weakness or "infirmity" would be to move ahead of the poem's own dialectic. For that is not the reason the pseudo-solution of fame proves inadequate. In the doctrine of magnanimity the due reward of excellence in all the virtues is glory, which the great-souled man is not merely permitted to accept but bound to seek as an integral part of his greatness. He must recognize his own worth and demand that others recognize it. So closely is glory linked to virtue that if he should fail to make good his claim, it could only mean the claim was unjustified. True worth *will* be praised; success is a part of heroism. This was the Greek attitude, which existed long before Aristotle: Achilles in the *Iliad* was an embodiment of it.[82] Hidden virtues, however, do not evoke fame; they must be displayed; glory is the reward of noble *deeds* and high *achievements*. Milton sees an inevitable time lag, a period when a great-souled man does recognize his worth and undertakes a plan of achievements calculated to bring him deserved glory — if all goes well. What if during this period, spurred by the hope of fame but not yet rewarded by its fulfillment, he falls victim to "the blind Fury"? Does this failure then prove his self-appraisal of worth to have been in error? It is the same question "Who am I?" agonizingly restated. Once obtained, fame can even conquer death — so the poets from Petrarch in his *Trionfi* to Shakespeare in his *Sonnets* have sung — but what if death comes sooner, comes after all the hopeful labor but before we "burst out into sudden blaze"?[83] Here is the real "outcry" of the poem, formed out of a high ambition or potentiality plus an absolutely unpredictable future. Its anguish is all the greater because of the prelude in which the noblest motive discernible by human vision has been asserted. Now this very ultimate proves not enough.

It is only through this dark night of anguish that the poet allows himself to move to a discovery of the higher vision which can transform the failure of fame from a blind fortuity to an explicably necessary fact. That motive had already been

*Tragedy, Its Art and Its Christian Premises* (Bloomington, Ind., and London, 1969), pp. 10-17, discusses the Augustinian background of the Renaissance critique of the quest for glory.

[82] McNamee, Ch. ii, "Proud Achilles, the Noblest Achaean of Them All." Aristotle himself modified this position somewhat. In fact, he glimpsed the paradox of ambition vs. humility/sloth which is the subject of this essay, but, bound to his own logic, lacked the equipment to handle it. *Nic. Ethics*, IV, iv, 4-6.

[83] Cf. the metaphor of smoldering ashes in the penultimate chorus of *SA*, discussed above (p. 116).

seen, wryly and helplessly, as an "infirmity"; now it can be helped; the noble mind can, by a new way of seeing, be made whole. The help is brought this time by another persona, a heavenly messenger. He strikes at once to the very center of the poet's disturbance — his misapprehension of the concept *fame.* This corrected, all the other misunderstandings which made the outcry possible are set right. The poet had mistakenly identified fame with the world's "praise," the mere glitter of earthly glory; but true fame is not a plant whose roots are in "mortal soil," where death could entirely blight it, but one which

> *lives and spreds aloft by those pure eyes,*
> *And perfet witnes of all judging Jove.*

Implicit in this redefinition are the answers to the questions posed above. Aristotle was right in one respect: fame is so essential a concomitant of virtue that any claim of worth which is not accompanied by fame to back it up is invalid. But now the same identity may be expressed in reverse fashion: any praise which does not ensue immediately upon praiseworthiness but must wait for a display of it is not true fame. There was another alternative available to Milton: he could have asserted simply that praiseworthiness itself *is* praise; that praise is an inherent quality rather than an external pronouncement.[84] It is significant that he does not choose this approach. To him praise *is* external — but not earthly. It is God's pronouncement — God's creative pronouncement, one may say — that declares a man worthy and it is *by* that declaration that he is worthy.[85] True fame is immediate. Even while the young man is striving to become a poet, he is already a poet; even while he is getting ready to achieve something worthy of fame, his fame exists, for he has already achieved one thing: to *be.*[86] His fame exists, in a realm where premature death or any other accident cannot touch it; it exists already, though he must "expect" its fruition

[84] Walter J. Ong, *Ramus, Method, and the Decay of Dialogue* (Cambridge, Mass., 1958), pp. 278-279.

[85] Cf. John Arthos's interpretation of the poem as a whole: "Lycidas takes his place in God's order by the very fact of his being seen by Him." *Dante, Michelangelo, and Milton* (London, 1963), p. 115; and cf. p. 90 on the Platonic background.

[86] Cf. *An Apology for Smectymnuus* (1642): "I was confirmed in this opinion, that he who would not be frustrate of his hope to write well hereafter in laudable things, ought himself to be a true poem . . ." (*SM*, p. 549). Stanley E. Fish in a brilliant discussion of Abdiel has shown how Milton, having learned the lesson that divine vision sees heroism not in deeds but in the state of being from which deeds may spring, undertook in *PL* to convey it to his readers (*Surprised by Sin* [New York, 1967], pp. 180-196).

when he himself is "in Heav'n"; it exists moreover as an absolutely accurate gauge of worth, free of the distortions that accompany human judgment; and it not only exists but "spreds."[87] And as in Sonnet vii it is the divine eye which both judges and guides, thus in a union of seemingly conflicting roles restoring the poet's wavering confidence, so here the reference to God's "pure eyes" not only assures him explicitly of accurate and fair judgment, but also corrects his allusion to a "blind Fury" and implicitly sets that misapprehension straight as well: having established that even if Edward King's or anyone's death were an accident, his true fame would not be impaired thereby, Phoebus now hints that the issues of death belong not to some sightless, malign being but to One whose "pure eyes" exclude evil (cf. Habakkuk 1:13) and who can guarantee immortality "in Heav'n." If there was any real blindness in what the poet said about the Fury's shears, it was his for thinking so. Once again, he must learn to repose his trust in a vision which, being human, he cannot share. (In the same way, the "trembling ears" of Midas-Milton cannot appreciate the divine harmonies — or is Phoebus' touch intended this time not to elongate but to open them?)

By 1652 Milton was totally blind. What he had at one time conceived to be his life's work still lay ahead of him. Eventually the loss of sight too would be fitted in place in the poet's developing self-image — a picture not so much radically redrawn to accommodate new contingencies as progressively working toward

[87] This word, hinting of a breadth of fame in heaven, is the heavenly counterpart to the "broad rumour" associated with false fame in the preceding line. The line following also picks up the idea, equivocally, in the word "witnes": cf. *SA*, 1752. As to the future fruition of "fame in Heav'n" — the "immortal garland" of *Areopagitica* (*SM*, p. 738) — something of what Milton had in mind may be discerned in a scene in *PL* (VI, 29ff.) in which the awarding of heavenly fame is actually described. The terminology of "Lycidas" is echoed in the commendation given Abdiel: "for this was all thy *care* / To stand approv'd in *sight* of God, though *Worlds* / *Judg'd* thee perverse" (my italics). The speech begins with the salutation, "Servant of God, well done," a quotation from the parable of the talents in Matt. 25, suggesting that here, and in "Lycidas" as well, Milton drew his conception of heavenly fame from the same sources as influenced his image-making in those two other crises we are considering. (The link with Son. xix is obvious; that with Son. vii may be seen in the accompanying letter from which I have already quoted, and in which he refers apprehensively to "the seasing of him that hid the talent" [*SM*, p. 1128].) See M. Y. Hughes, "Milton and the Sense of Glory" (1949), collected in *Ten Perspectives*, pp. 12-34, and cf. also the parallel in *PR*, III, 60-64, and the discussions in McNamee, pp. 170-172; Stein, pp. 78ff.; and Hughes (above, note 19).

true self-knowledge by a stripping away of the superficial badges of identity so as to reveal the very essence of the self unchanged. Between crises the lesson seems forgotten; each time the prospect of change is felt as a genuine threat whose emotional impact is great. Each time essentially the same lesson must be relearned: rely on the Taskmaster's eye. The sameness of the lessons, as well as the survival through each crisis of the essential self, bore witness to a continuity of identity. Milton might have to give up the image of himself as a great epic poet, or even as a guide and teacher of any sort to the English people, or even — greater loss — as a man distinguished in any way by notable achievements; but the core of his identity, out of which all these ambitions had grown, must still, if they were cut off, remain: he was still a servant of God.

But this irreducible identity opened onto two alternatives. He must be a servant: what kind would he be, "faithful" or (in the uncompromising categories of Scripture) "unprofitable"? Perhaps that decision had already been made, and his blindness was both determinant and token of his inability to undo a rendered verdict of "unprofitable." That at least is the poet's fear at the outset of Sonnet xix, a fear that even the heavenly fame, which in "Lycidas" had resolved his difficulty, might finally elude him. As with the foolish virgins whose story is told in Matthew 25, his "light is spent," and their fate of being locked out at midnight from the bridal feast (out in "this dark world and wide") looms before him. Moving on in the chapter to the next parable, he thinks of himself in the role of the servant who, entrusted with a single talent, fearfully buries it in the dark earth instead of investing it for "usury." But Milton sees a subtle difference between himself and that servant. The servant, "wicked and slothful," deserved his punishment; but it is not Milton's fault that his "Talent" (an obvious pun) is "useless" (another pun, on *use* in its ordinary and commercial senses) — he *wants* to serve God (he is "bent" perhaps for the yoke we will hear of shortly) and "present" an "account" of himself as a faithful ("true") servant. Or perhaps the phrase "my true account" is intended to suggest a disparity between what he considers his real inner being and the false picture given of him by his enforced idleness. Yet in the harsh retributive climate of the parable he can see no room for such subtle casuistries. Hence his outcry: "Doth God exact day-labour, light deny'd[?]"

It is, as he admits, a foolish question. Even though the obvious and easy answer, "No, God is merciful," seems ruled out by the parable itself, the question is absurd because it is thoroughly based on misunderstandings. Therefore it cannot be answered directly, and in the poem it is not; correct the misunderstandings and it will answer itself. What Milton gives in the sestet, or has given to him, is a much greater vision, not alternative either to God's exactions or God's mercy, but inclusive of both and more. Like the answer given to Samson, it involves patience. In fact, it is given by "patience," thinly personified, which both is and is not an aspect of Milton's own mind.[88] It is a message from God, but the instrument he uses is the human mind, so that the discovery the poet makes in the sestet is self-transcending and at same time self-authenticating.

*God doth not need*
*Either man's work or his own gifts, who best*
*Bear his milde yoak, they serve him best, his State*
*Is Kingly. Thousands at his bidding speed*
*And post o're Land and Ocean without rest:*
*They also serve who only stand and waite.*

To the poet's question Patience gives no answer but an explanation. As Job discovered, God will not spar with men. He is beyond their comprehension. A parable, reflecting one facet or another of his infinite being, is an accommodation to human finitude. A valuable truth is taught in the story of the capitalist

[88] The same may be said, of course, of Phoebus in "Lycidas." Milton's externalizing as two personae the two states at war within his mind is an obvious instance of the poet's transmutation of personal experience into art — the process that made these poems not autobiography but a patterned re-creation of experience (see above, note 75 and text). Another instance is the clarity with which in the present sonnet his outcry is articulated, for he builds a tremendous 7-line period here out of what I think would have been in real life half-conscious ranklings to which in the very moment of articulation a cancelling answer would have begun to form. The rhetoric of discourse requires that question and answer be given *seriatim;* only in the word "prevent" does Milton take formal note of the fact that he is here artificially separating a "murmur" and reply actually telescoped. And this might have happened to him not once but several times. That is why I have avoided discussing the date of the sonnet. In writing of it I have accepted the traditional dating, 1652, but my argument is essentially unchanged if the sonnet was written in 1644 or 1655 (see Honigmann, pp. 169-174). And I do not see how, on present evidence, the date can be known. Most writers on this question seem to assume that once Milton faced and conquered the despair over his blindness — as some think the *Second Defence* (1654) shows signs of his having done — it could not have returned. I question this assumption. Milton was in the process of going blind for a long time, and the temptation to despair might well have recurred more than once, irrespective of previous victories. (The root question was not so different from that he faced in the other two crises we have examined, and his success in reaching a solution then did not prevent the temptation's returning in the new context of blindness — *sometime* between 1644 and 1655.)

who demands a return on his invested talents, but it is a mistake to think that God needs anything from man, even the gifts he has lent. If the parable of the talents demonstrates God's absolute freedom of activity, so in an opposite way does that of the workers in the vineyard,[89] to which Milton alludes in lines 7 and 14 of the sonnet. Thus is mercy set alongside justice. His "milde yoak," in the words of Jesus, is "easy" (Matthew 11:30), and in bearing it "ye shall find rest unto your souls." Milton says in the sonnet that those who do this "best / . . . , they serve him best." Now if in the service of God, in accomplishing his will, his servants find rest, that is because — to paraphrase Dante — their rest *is* His will. Here is subsumed that merciful aspect of God's nature which a more impatient mind would have grasped for at once — and been the poorer. The legalistic rigor of the poet's outcry is patiently corrected by Patience in a manner consonant with Milton's teachings on the relationship of Law and Gospel (*CD,* I, xxvii). One of the law's purposes is to "impress us with a slavish fear through consciousness of divine enmity." It "worketh wrath, but the gospel grace," and since these "cannot co-exist" (*SM,* p. 1025) "the whole of the Mosaic law is abolished by the gospel." However, "the sum and essence of the law is not hereby abrogated. . . . It was with justice . . . that Christ asserted the permanence of the law" (p. 1026), and "so far from a less degree of perfection being exacted from Christians, it is expected of them that they should be more perfect than those who were under the law" (p. 1027). We have already noted the counterthrust of the word "grace" to the harsh concept of the "task Master" in Sonnet vii. To return to Sonnet xix — we may note the paradox that thousands of God's servants (angels of course) "speed / . . . without rest," yet no reader that I know of has ever thought of them as getting tired, though the lines themselves hurry along here. Milton is bending all his verbal resources to revealing a world which cannot, finally, be brought within the compass of human language. The last line — slower and more restful, aphoristic as

[89] Matt. 20:1-16. This parable too had been in Milton's mind for years: he alluded to it along with the one on the talents in that early letter already quoted, essentially a letter of self-analysis in which, at 23 or so, he tries to understand why he is so late-blooming. Is an "endlesse delight of speculation" causing him already to hide his talent? More likely, he thinks, it is the "very consideration of that great commandment," i.e. the one "set out by the seasing of him that hid the talent," that causes him to proceed with deliberation, "not taking thought of being late, so it give advantage to be more fit; for those that were latest lost nothing, when the maister of the vinyard came to give each one his hire." *SM,* p. 1128. On God's freedom cf. *SA,* 309: "Who made our Laws to bind us, not himself."

befits the close, and much quoted both in and out of context — gives us a new paradox, or more than one. To "serve" God is to do "his bidding"; for "thousands" that may mean ceaseless activity, but for some it may require — what is perhaps humanly speaking more wearing — inactivity. Not that "stand" and "waite" are entirely passive: stand fast in the faith (Ephesians 6), stand not sit, stand waiting to be hired (like the unemployed in Matthew 20), wait upon God — though the latter is not possible, I judge, in the sense of waiting at table, but only in that of enduring patiently until God acts, and meanwhile praying or, more likely, being on the lookout. Thus in his last line Milton returns to the allusion of the opening, the parable of the ten virgins, whose lesson is: "Watch therefore."[90] Patience has now provided a context of understanding in which the poet can interpret the parable of the talents aright. The servant who *cannot* multiply his talent, but bears as a yoke the fact that he cannot and waits faithfully, watching with spiritual eyes for God's "bidding" (which is also his blessing), is nonetheless a servant and may expect the reward for which he waits.

Implicit in this teaching is one final correction of the initial outcry. As before, the poet learns to trust in the divine vision, which both assigns the task and passes judgment on the result, rather than in his limited human vision. And in making this discovery he finds too that, though in one obvious sense his "light is spent," in a more important sense he has just gained access to a surer light than any he had before, to guide him through the "dark world." His outcry was a mark of spiritual blindness; he has been enlightened; perhaps the yoke-bearing itself is a continuing source of enlightenment, for (dare we deny a seventeenth-century poet the pun?) "my yoke is easy, and my burden is *light*."[91]

[90] Matt. 25:13. (The words *wait, watch* and *wake* share a common origin.) Still closer to the sonnet is a similar discourse in Luke, which admonishes, "Blessed are those servants, whom the lord when he cometh shall find watching" (12:37). (Cf. Matt. 24:45ff.) On the meaning of *wait* in this line see Roger L. Slakey, "Milton's Sonnet 'On His Blindness,'" *ELH*, XXVII (1960), 127. Of the many occurrences of the word in the Bible, especially relevant to this poem is Isa. 40:31, "They that wait upon the Lord shall renew their strength; they shall mount up with wings as eagles. . . ." We have noted in *SA*, 1695, how the eagle image and the idea of restoration of sight clustered in Milton's mind. Exactly the same ideas — including the figure of Samson — also appear together in a well-known passage in *Areopagitica* (*SM*, p. 750).

[91] A similarly punning allusion to Matt. 11:30 had been used in a poem with which Milton surely was familiar; see Leland Ryken, "Sidney's 'Leave Me, O Love Which Reachest But to Dust,'" *Explicator*, XXVI (1967), art. 9.

Thus trusting in a vision given him from above, Milton is able in a later poem to display a restored hope which has altered his view of both past and future. I refer to Sonnet xxii, "To Mr. Cyriack Skinner upon his Blindness." Like Samson in the play, once Milton can accept the fact that his service to God may amount to nothing more than standing and waiting — once he accepts this new self-image — then it becomes clear that he is indeed intended for greater accomplishments. The sonnet opens with a simple statement of his blind condition — not an outcry — and proceeds,

*Yet I argue not*
*Against heavns hand or will, nor bate a jot*
*Of heart or hope.*

This hope derives in part from the realization that his blindness is not a token of unprofitableness as a servant, as he feared in the earlier sonnet, but is actually evidence that he has already begun to show a profit: his early commitment to God's service *by notable achievements as a moral teacher* he has already in part fulfilled, having sacrificed his eyes

*In libertyes defence, my noble task,*
*Of which all Europe talks from side to side.*

The power this thought of fame has to console him betrays very humanly the continued presence of the "last infirmity"; but it is under control, as the concluding lines show:

*This thought might lead me through the world's vain mask*
*Content though blind, had I no better guide.*

Milton is here carefully distinguishing Greek from Christian comforts. He *has* a "better guide" but, like a thrifty housewife who puts butter on the table and uses margarine in cooking, is loth to call it into play when the lower comfort will do the job. In dealing with the "world" blindness is no handicap anyway, for sight would reveal only a "vain mask" — an empty masquerade. In such a context fame may be enough to bring "content," but the inward witness of the Spirit to divine guidance, judgment, and approval (for this is what I take him to mean by the "better guide") can go beyond "content" to bring "hope."[92] We know, of course, that this hope was fulfilled. The goal of epic poet and moral teacher of which he had been

[92] Possible glosses on the phrase "better guide" may be found elsewhere in Milton's poetry, from *Comus*, 380f., "He that has light within his own cleer brest / May sit i'th center, and enjoy bright day," through *PL*, III, 51-53, "Celestial light / Shine inward . . . / . . . there plant eyes," to *SA*, 1689, ". . . with inward eyes illuminated."

tempted to despair finally was attained — and foremost in what he taught in his epic was the lesson he had learned in his own crises. Having had his own eyes opened by grace to vision beyond them, he is anxious to pass this on to readers. Thus "in *Paradise Lost things* are not being clarified or ordered, rather *eyes* are being made capable of seeing things as they truly are already in the clarity of God's order."[93]

*Identity* is a curiously ambiguous word. To *identify* (something or someone) *as* is to emphasize separateness, individuality, uniqueness; to *identify* (something or someone) *with* is to submerge individuality in the mass. Casual modern sociological and psychological usage reflects the ambiguity. We speak of a person's finding his identity in the group or institution (family, club, church, corporation): he finds who he is by discovering where he *belongs*. We also say that one finds or asserts his identity in the things that differentiate him from the group — that take him out of the crowd and give him, in place of a punched card, his own face.[94] Milton's personal search for identity led him to see value in both of the word's valences, though on the level of human reasoning they remain mutually exclusive. The desire for glory presses the claims of the individual to be a unique self; Milton's ambition was to be outstanding, to "soar above" the crowd, even the small crowd of epic poets; he craved to have apply to him, as it seemed at first[95] to apply to Abdiel, the qualifying word "only." This aspect of Milton is dramatically reflected in the figure of Satan in *Paradise Lost*. But Milton was able to learn (as Satan never could) contentment with being one of the "thousands" of God's servants: with an identity based not on *differentiae* but on *genus*. This part of the lesson (unfortunately mistaken for the whole truth) appears, in terms strongly reminiscent of the Swedenborgian philosophy, as the concluding paragraph of Northrop Frye's *The Return of Eden* (Toronto, 1965):

> To use terms which are not Milton's but express something of his attitude, the central myth of mankind is the myth of lost identity: the goal

[93] Stanley E. Fish, "Discovery as Form in *Paradise Lost*," paper read at Modern Language Association convention, 1967. On God's eye in *PL* see further Rosalie L. Colie, *Paradoxia Epidemica* (Princeton, 1966), pp. 176-177.

[94] A similar ambivalence may be noted in the way we talk about *naming*, which can frequently be a synonym for *identifying*. To name is to classify, thus to tame and make computable. But a person's name is also a token of his uniqueness. See OED, s.v. *name*, sb., defs. 1 and 2; *identity*, defs. 1 and 2.

[95] *PL*, V, 897; but see Book VI and Fish, *loc. cit.* (note 86).

of all reason, courage and vision is the regaining of identity. The recovery of identity is not the feeling that I am myself and not another, but the realization that there is only one man, one mind, and one world, and that all walls of partition have been broken down forever.

Besides the allusion in the last clause to Ephesians 2:14, there are affinities between this statement and the New Testament teaching of the union of believers with Christ,[96] which was accomplished by God's becoming man, yet which means not the "conversion of the Godhead into flesh" but the "taking of the Manhood into God" (Athanasian Creed): in Pauline terms, Christ is "the firstborn among many brethren," who are to be "conformed" to his "image" (Romans 8:29). God's self-emptying is the antithesis of the Satanic self-aggrandizement. His descent into death in order to conquer death, his offering himself as a victim so as to be a victor, becomes a paradigm for the experience of all men. It is against this cosmic background that Don Cameron Allen urges us to see "Milton's poetic realization of the themes of descent and ascent, of the necessity of entering the dark in order to see the light, of the descent of the light itself so that men may see, and of the inner eye that knows only when the exterior sight is gone" — and, one may add, of the folly which is wisdom — a realization "constantly before us as we read him."[97] The profoundest significance of the Old Testament types of Christ, such as Samson, is not in what they as precursors give to him — though they do have a veiled kerygmatic function — but in the meaning *their* lives take on from the reality of which they were shadows. And the same relationship to Christ, the second Adam, is borne by persons who come after him in time. Whether of the Mosaic or the Christian era, Samson and Milton and thousands more *belong* to the great troop of those who, with Christ, descend, trusting in the faithfulness of God's eye, and reascend.[98] That is the one identity of over-

[96] On which cf. *CD*, I, xvi, xxi, xxiv; C. A. Patrides, *Milton and the Christian Tradition* (Oxford, 1966), pp. 155f., 160n., 172; Louis L. Martz, *The Paradise Within* (New Haven and London, 1964), pp. 140, 177, 180f., 200f.; C. M. Coffin, "Responsiveness of Milton's *Paradise Lost* to the important intellectual and spiritual concerns of its period," *Amer. Philos. Soc. Yr. Bk. 1955* (Philadelphia, 1956), pp. 375f.; and, more broadly, my article "Charles Williams, Novelist and Prophet," *Gordon Rev.*, X (1967), 55, 72f., 74f.

[97] *Op. cit.* (above, note 64), p. 628. On folly cf. above, p. 108, and I Cor. 1:18ff.; contrast Rom. 1:22; John 9:41; Mark 2:17.

[98] *Ibid.*, p. 630. Cf. the great hymn of *kenosis* in Phil. 2; and Erich Auerbach, *Mimesis*, trans. W. Trask (Garden City, N.Y., 1957), pp. 137f., 172. The pattern I have described is, of course, that of redemption from the Fall. Milton uses the eye imagery explicitly in *PL,* where man's attitude

riding importance. But the lesson Milton learned goes beyond identifying *with.* It must, to be in keeping with the pattern of descent and reascent we have just observed. The cry "My God, why hast Thou forsaken me?" is an essential part of Christ's paradigmatic experience: the choice made by Christ and his types is only a choice to descend; the ascending that follows has not been chosen, and could not follow if it had been chosen. Thus when Samson or Milton chooses to put aside self-identity, content to be simply *one who has descended,* that choice *is* the descent; and reinstatement of the unique identity of the person, fulfilling in their highest and purest form the self's abandoned claims and hopes — fulfilling the self, one may say — must follow. Truly the last shall be first.

toward God's eye changes from trust to fear because of sin; see N. Frye, p. 78. On Samson as one of the types see Krouse (above, note 53), pp. 68f., 119f.

# The Serpent and the Dove: "Christabel" and the Problem of Evil

ROBERT H. SIEGEL

*Be ye therefore wise as serpents and harmless as doves.*

Nearly all of Coleridge's narrative poems and fragments of narratives reflect his interest in the theme of vicarious suffering. From "The Wanderings of Cain" to "Alice du Clos" his protagonists, including the Ancient Mariner and Christabel, appear to suffer representatively for others. It is true that the roles of these last two are very different: the Mariner suffers, like Cain, for a crime, while Christabel suffers innocently, like Christ. Despite the apparently contrary nature of their roles, from another point of view there are profound similarities. That Coleridge to a certain extent associated Cain with the scapegoat of the Old Testament, a figure with which Christ is also traditionally associated, suggests the depths to which these poems plumb the intervolved currents of good and evil. The vision of interlocked good and evil at the heart of "The Ancient Mariner" and "Christabel" is found in Bard Bracy's dream of the serpent and the dove:

---

Robert H. Siegel is Assistant Professor of English at Dartmouth College. He has also taught at Trinity College, Chicago. After graduating from Wheaton College (A.B., 1961), he held a Gilman Fellowship and Junior Instructorship at Johns Hopkins University, where he earned an M.A. the following year as a member of the Writing Seminar. He holds the Ph.D. from Harvard University (1968), where he has been a teaching fellow. His dissertation traces through the whole body of Coleridge's poetry the theme studied in the present essay on "Christabel" alone. His poetry has appeared in *Poetry Magazine, The Atlantic Monthly, The Beloit Poetry Journal, America,* and *The Christian Century.*

*I saw a bright green snake*
*Coiled around its wings and neck.*
*Green as the herbs on which it couched,*
*Close by the dove's its head it crouched;*
*And with the dove it heaves and stirs,*
*Swelling its neck as she swelled hers!*
[549-554][1]

It is in "Christabel" that the theme of vicarious atonement and its relation to the mystery of good and evil finds the most complete expression.[2] His friend James Gillman and son Derwent agree that Coleridge conceived of Christabel as an innocent sufferer for the wrongs of others. According to the shorter Gillman account,

> the story of Christabel is partly founded on the notion, that the virtuous of this world save the wicked. The pious and good Christabel suffers and prays for
>
> *"The weal of her lover that is far away,"*
>
> exposed to various temptations in a foreign land; and she thus defeats the power of evil represented in the person of Geraldine. This is one main object of the tale.[3]

[1] All references to the poetry are to *The Complete Poetical Works of Samuel Taylor Coleridge*, ed. Ernest Hartley Coleridge (2 vols., Oxford, 1912). Poems are most easily located by reference to the year of composition. I have provided line references for the poem under discussion and other long poems.

[2] Most critics view the poem in these terms. "The poem was to have been founded on the doctrine of vicarious atonement, and in this way would have established its moral justification." Arthur H. Nethercot, *The Road to Tryermaine* (Chicago, 1939), p. 207. Werner Beyer agrees that "virtue or constancy emerges ultimately triumphant and redemptive." *The Enchanted Forest* (Oxford, 1963), p. 180. J. B. Beer believes that "*Christabel* might represent one of his most concentrated and powerful efforts to deal with the problem of evil. *The Ancient Mariner*, as we have seen, includes a redeeming principle, but only as one element in the poem. In *Christabel*, on the other hand, Coleridge makes a focal point of the redeeming principle, by personifying it in the heroine of his poem." *Coleridge the Visionary* (London, 1959), p. 177.

Everyone who studies "Christabel" is indebted to Ernest Hartley Coleridge's edition of the poem (London, 1907). Of subsequent studies — besides those quoted above — I might mention those by Humphrey House and G. Wilson Knight: *Coleridge: The Clark Lectures 1951-1952* (London, 1953) and *The Starlit Dome: Studies in the Poetry of Vision* (London, 1941; repr. New York, 1960). Richard H. Fogle includes an interesting essay on the poem in *The Idea of Coleridge's Criticism* (Berkeley, 1962) and Thomas R. Preston has done some suggestive work with "*Christabel* and the Mystical Tradition," in *Essays and Studies in Language and Literature*, Duquesne Studies: Philological Series 5, No. 23 (Pittsburgh, 1964), pp. 138-157. A complete list of important contributions to the study of "Christabel" would be too long to include here.

[3] The accounts of Gillman and Derwent Coleridge, as well as Coleridge's

Derwent Coleridge concurs in his account of the tale's main action:

> The sufferings of Christabel were to have been represented as vicarious, endured for her "lover far away"; and Geraldine, no witch or goblin, or malignant being of any kind, but a spirit, executing her appointed task with the best good will, as she herself says:—
>
> *All they, who live in the upper sky,*
> *Do love you, holy Christabel, &c.* (227-32).
>
> In form this is, of course, accommodated to "a fond superstition," in keeping with the general tenour of the piece; but that the holy and the innocent do often suffer for the faults of those they love, and are thus made the instruments to bring them back to the ways of peace, is a matter of fact, and in Coleridge's hands might have been worked up into a tale of deep and delicate pathos.

Coleridge himself claimed that Crashaw's lines on St. Teresa beginning,

> *Since 'tis not to be had at home,*
> *She'l travel to a martyrdome*

"were ever present to my mind whilst writing the second part of Christabel; if, indeed, by some subtle process of the mind they did not suggest the first thought of the whole poem." Christabel's martyrdom was not to be the stake that Joan of Arc foresees in Coleridge's "The Destiny of Nations" (1796), but a quiet one suffered at home while "abroad" in spirit. It was to end, according to the longer Gillman account, not only in the defeat of the power of evil but in reunion with her lover and reconciliation with her father:

> Over the mountains, the Bard, as directed by Sir Leoline, "hastes" with his disciple; but in consequence of one of those inundations supposed to be common to this country, the spot only where the castle once stood is discovered, — the edifice itself being washed away. He determines to return. Geraldine being acquainted with all that is passing, like the Weird Sisters in Macbeth, vanishes. Re-appearing, however, she waits the return of the Bard, exciting in the mean time, by her wily arts, all the anger she could rouse in the Baron's breast, as well as that jealousy of which he is described to have been susceptible. The old Bard and the youth at length arrive, and therefore she can no longer personate the character of Geraldine, the daughter of Lord Roland de Vaux, but changes her appearance to that of the accepted though absent lover of Christabel. Next ensues a courtship most distressing to Christabel, who feels — she knows not why — great disgust for her once favoured knight. This coldness is very painful to the Baron, who has no more conception than herself of the supernatural transformation.

remark about Crashaw's poem on St. Teresa, may be found in House, pp. 126-128.

> She at last yields to her father's entreaties, and consents to approach the altar with this hated suitor. The real lover returning, enters at this moment, and produces the ring which she had once given him in sign of her betrothment. Thus defeated, the supernatural being Geraldine disappears. As predicted, the castle bell tolls, the mother's voice is heard, and to the exceeding great joy of the parties, the rightful marriage takes place, after which follows a reconciliation and explanation between the father and daughter.

With essential agreement from two reliable sources as to the poem's basic theme and a rather detailed account of its projected ending, we may be confused as to why the author never kept the promise made in all editions of the Preface but the last: "But as, in my very first conception of the tale, I had the whole present to my mind, with the wholeness, no less than the liveliness of a vision; I trust that I shall be able to embody in verse the three parts yet to come, in the course of the present year." To recapitulate the endless speculation about the causes of his failure to complete the poem — the growing scarcity of inspired moments, the Wordsworths' discouragement of an effort to continue, his friends' general conviction that the finished part was too perfect to bear continuation — is not the task of this study.[4] Suffice it to say that, although he generally looked forward to completing the poem, his thoughts as to how to do so were not settled and his apprehension of the difficulty varied. A remark of 1833 represents quite justly his attitude in the later years:

> The reason of my not finishing Christabel is not, that I don't know how to do it — for I have, as I always had, the whole plan entire from beginning to end in my mind; but I fear I could not carry on with equal success the execution of the idea, an extremely subtle and difficult one. Besides, after this continuation of Faust, which they tell me is very poor, who can have the courage to attempt a reversal of the judgment against continuations?[5]

Some have used this confessed apprehension of difficulty to deny the validity of the accounts left with Derwent Coleridge and Gillman. Yet anyone aware of the perfection of the first two parts should understand that the mere *plot* of the continuation would hardly be the real problem. The author claims to have "always had the whole plan entire from beginning to end in my mind." The genuine difficulty would be to embody the evolving subtlety of the *idea* in verse as flawless as that already written. Others have sneered at what strikes them as the "vulgar, trivial

[4] See Nethercot's first chapter for a good summary of the speculation.
[5] *The Table Talk and Omniana*, ed. T. Ashe (London, 1923), July 6, 1833.

Gothic" nature of the proposed continuation.[6] Yet these last forget that it is not the plot as such that distinguishes Parts I and II. How cheap, vulgar and trivial might not these parts appear in the bare bones of a summary![7] At the risk of trying the reader's patience, I have written a summary of them to test this very point:

> The tale opens at midnight at Langdale Hall, a castle in the North Country surrounded by an aura of decay. Amid the striking of the clock, the howling of her guardian mastiff, and the premature crowing of the cock, the aged Baron's only daughter retires to a nearby grove to pray. There she comes upon a damsel in distress who claims to have been snatched from her father's home by a band of ruffians. Christabel assists her to the Baron's castle, entreating that she sleep that night in her room. Various signs — the dog's moaning and the fire's leaping up at her entrance — suggest that Geraldine is a witch or evil spirit. Paying no heed to them, Christabel takes her to her room. The lamp sputters at Geraldine's entrance and the ghost of Christabel's mother attempts to warn her daughter, but is driven off by Geraldine's unearthly power. Disrobing, the stranger reveals a hideous deformity on her bosom and side, and, lying down next to the helpless Christabel, presses "this mark of my shame, this seal of my sorrow" against her, muttering that henceforth Christabel will share the curse. The wicked nightbirds celebrate Geraldine's triumph. The next morning Christabel awakens remembering nothing from the night before....

And so on, through the recurring Evil Eye in Part II. A perhaps more valid objection to the projected continuations is their inconsistency as to Geraldine's character.[8] Both agree on the moral function of the heroine, but Gillman refers to "the power of evil represented in the person of Geraldine," while Derwent takes a more favorable view of her as "no witch or goblin, or malignant being of any kind, but a spirit, executing her appointed task with the best good will." But this objection also evaporates when we examine, as we shall later, the apparently intended ambiguity of Geraldine's character.

"Love," besides "The Ancient Mariner" the only finished ballad of Coleridge, is a brief but vivid rendering of the theme of vicarious suffering. This tale of a knight crazed by "cruel scorn" was written in 1799 as an "Introduction to the Tale of the Dark Ladie," a "sister tale/Of Man's perfidious cruelty" of which

[6] House, p. 128. His attitude is representative.

[7] E. H. Coleridge, p. 34, points out "that any *dénouement* of the story reduced to prose would sound *prosaic* and commonplace." Rossetti, whom he quotes, shared this insight: "The conclusion as given by Gillman from Coleridge's account to him was correct enough, only not picturesquely worded."

[8] See Nethercot, pp. 41-42.

Coleridge wrote only a few stanzas. It is apparent in both that a lover would suffer on account of the beloved. In "Love," a knight wanders crazed for ten years on account of the scorn he suffers at the hands of "the Lady of the Land." But his madness is indirectly the cause of his saving her from what would perhaps be a just reward for that scorn:

*And that unknowing what he did,*
*He leaped amid a murderous band,*
*And saved from outrage worse than death*
*The Lady of the Land!*

As a consequence, her disdain is overcome, but now that she too loves, she likewise suffers on account of her earlier scorn.

*And how she wept, and clasped his knees;*
*And how she tended him in vain—*
*And even strove to expiate*
*The scorn that crazed his brain.*

Suffering is always the liability, and sometimes the privilege, of love. Throughout his "ten long years" of wandering the knight has worn upon his shield a purgatorial emblem, a "burning brand." And we are told in the introductory stanza,

*All thoughts, all passions, all delights,*
*Whatever stirs this mortal frame,*
*All are but ministers of Love,*
*And feed his* sacred flame. [emphasis mine]

That the suffering of the knight finally saves the lady from an outrage worse than death (and, what is perhaps more important, from coldness of heart) is analogous to the salvation of her lover that Christabel effects in the projected ending. Part of the knight's ordeal is the visitations of a fiendish but beautiful spirit similar to Geraldine:

*There came and looked him in the face*
*An angel beautiful and bright;*
*And that he knew it was a Fiend,*
*This miserable Knight!*

"Love" does not have the happy ending intended for "Christabel": it ends with the knight "a dying man." Yet it is set within the framework of a happy love story. By telling the story of the knight and lady to "Genevieve" the narrator disturbs "her soul with pity" and wins her for his "bright and beauteous Bride." Like the helpless Wedding Guest, she is vicariously caught up in the tale, and at the end, sadder but wiser through pity, embraces her lover. "Few sorrows hath she of her own," the suitor confides,

*She loves me best, whene'er I sing*
*The songs that make her grieve —*

suggesting that one of the functions of art, like love, is to encourage sympathetic identification, even to the point of shared suffering.

The complication and ambiguous nuance of character possible in a story of vicarious suffering are only too apparent in "The Three Graves: A Fragment of a Sexton's Tale," written in part in 1797-98 and in collaboration with Wordsworth.[9] In this ballad three young people suffer — two to the death — from the curse of a jealous woman. The woman "drinks perdition" by cursing her daughter Mary, whom she envies the handsome Edward. Ellen, Mary's faithful friend, also suffers the mother's curse. The ever deepening shadow cast by the curse on the marriage of Edward and Mary is what originally interested Coleridge in the story, which he claims is based upon a true incident. In all their environment these feel the presence of that curse, just as the Mariner everywhere feels the curse of the dead men's eyes:

*"The Sun peeps through the close thick leaves,*
*See, dearest Ellen! see!*
*'Tis in the leaves, a little sun,*
*No bigger than your ee;*

*"A tiny sun, and it has got*
*A perfect glory too;*
*Ten thousand threads and hairs of light,*
*Make up a glory gay and bright*
*Round that small orb, so blue."*
["The Three Graves," 505-513]

In the Introduction Coleridge states that he finds in the curse and its aftermath "a striking proof of the possible effect on the imagination, from an idea violently and suddenly impressed on it," and that he "conceived the design of shewing that instances of this kind are not peculiar to savage or barbarous tribes." Here, as in the hypnotic hold of the Mariner over the Wedding Guest, there are strange seas of thought to charter.

Common-sense scepticism toward the curse and toward the notion that the innocent can suffer in strange ways for the guilty is voiced by Ellen, quite in vain, after she has been cursed:

*She smiled, and smiled, and passed it off*
*Ere from the door she stept—*

[9] The more important parts, III and IV, are Coleridge's. Edward E. Bostetter, *The Romantic Ventriloquists* (Seattle, 1963), p. 104. Coleridge published these parts in *The Friend.*

*But all agree it would have been*
*Much better had she wept.*

*And if her heart was not at ease,*
*This was her constant cry—*
*"It was a wicked woman's curse,*
*God's good, and what care I?"*
[336-343]

She is unwilling to see what the Wedding Guest learns: the implication of all men in the guilt of each.

Not only do these innocents suffer indirectly on the mother's account,[10] but, what is more interesting, they occasionally take on characteristics of the wicked woman against their will, as if they are forced to suffer the doing of evil as well as the effects of it. Ellen

*once her both arms suddenly*
*Round Mary's neck she flung,*
*And her heart panted, and she felt*
*The words upon her tongue.*

*She felt them coming, but no power*
*Had she the words to smother;*
*And with a kind of shriek she cried,*
*"Oh Christ! you're like your mother!"*
[440-447]

Not only does she feel compelled by an alien spirit to say an unkind thing to Mary, but her hateful words point to a similar metamorphosis in her fellow sufferer. Likewise, Edward literally does to the mother in a nightmare what she has done metaphorically to her daughter:

*But soon they heard his hard quick pants,*
*And the thumping in his breast.*

. . . . . . . . . . . . . .

*He sat upright; and ere the dream*
*Had had time to depart,*

[10] There is some suggestion that the suffering of the three young people is ultimately redemptive, even though the mother apparently dies unrepentant. For one thing, the three continue to revere her as a mother, "The holiest thing alive" (259). Second, one of the epitaphs reads, "The mercy of God is infinite" (Introduction). Finally, the thorn tree growing out of the graves persists in flowering, despite adverse conditions:

And 'tis a fearful, fearful tree;
The ghosts that round it meet,
'Tis they that cut the rind at night,
Yet still it blossoms sweet.
[216-219]

*"O God, forgive me!" (he exclaimed)*
*"I have torn out her heart!"*
[520-533]

Christabel too is forced at times seemingly to perform, as well as suffer, evil. Reacting to Geraldine's serpentine looks in the presence of Sir Leoline, she

*passively did imitate*
*That look of dull and treacherous hate!*
*And thus she stood, in dizzy trance,*
*Still picturing that look askance*
*With forced unconscious sympathy.*
["Christabel," 605-609]

All of these characters experience the nightmarish confusion recorded by the poet in "The Pains of Sleep" (1803), a confusion arising from

*Deeds to be hid which were not hid,*
*Which all confused I could not know*
*Whether I suffered, or I did.*

Vicarious suffering, it would seem, involves extremely close identification with the person for whose misdoing the suffering atones.

Like Christ, Christabel suffers for the weal of another. Although in this poem as in "The Ancient Mariner" suffering and the fruits of suffering are of central importance, they are not the entire point. What fascinates the reader of this poem as of that one is the complex intervolution of good and evil. Christabel's virtue at the beginning is cloistered and unfruitful, in danger of stagnating in an environment of senility and decay. It must be tested before it can flower from the decay like the slowly coming spring. By vicariously suffering for the temptation of her lover far away, she brings their love to union and the castle to new life. The spirit who takes the form of Geraldine is essentially ambiguous. Apparently evil, she drops hints that her trial of Christabel, like Satan's of Job, eventually serves the good. She is both a lamia and a dove-like double of lovely Christabel. When Bard Bracy finds the dove and serpent closely intertwined in a death-struggle, he momentarily mistakes the serpent's green for healing herbs! Geraldine, however dangerous, does bring vitality to the Baron and Christabel, and the encounter appears to be finally under the mysterious control of some cosmic hierarchy like that in "The Ancient Mariner."

In the verse-form of "Christabel" Coleridge discovered a flexibility appealing to a poet with an ear as sensitive as his: "This occasional variation in the number of syllables is not introduced wantonly, or for the mere ends of convenience, but in correspondence with some transition in the nature of the imagery or passion" (Preface). In this strongly rhythmical, usually rhymed verse he could achieve many of the effects of the ballad, while remaining free to modulate the rhythm even more than blank verse permits. The repetition and self-circling revery of the conversation poems are combined in a passage like the following with the incantatory rhythms of the ballad, until the detail singled out for attention becomes nearly hypnotic:

*There is not wind enough in the air*
*To move away the ringlet curl*
*From the lovely lady's cheek—*
*There is not wind enough to twirl*
*The one red leaf, the last of its clan,*
*That dances as often as dance it can,*
*Hanging so light, and hanging so high,*
*On the topmost twig that looks up at the sky.*
[45-52]

Yet the poet is not, as in the ballad, constantly having to walk a pitching deck.

The sense of immediacy in "Christabel" is not gained, as in "The Ancient Mariner," through identification with a visible narrator, but rather by gradual fascination with a nebulous voice, now slowly insinuating, now urgently incantatory. At the outset particularly, this elusive voice frequently employs the present tense both to set the action right before our eyes—

*'Tis the middle of night by the castle clock,*
*And the owls have awakened the crowing cock;*
*Tu–whit! — Tu–whoo!*
*And hark, again! the crowing cock,*
*How drowsily it crew*

— and to freeze it there, like a tableau, while it asks a question or makes an exclamation that expresses our own curiosity or feeling of suspense:[11]

*Is the night chilly and dark?*
*The night is chilly, but not dark.*
[14-15]
*What makes her in the wood so late,*
*A furlong from the castle gate?*
[25-26]

[11] As George Watson points out, "the trick of using a series of unanswered and, for the time being, unanswerable questions, massed together in nervous repetition" was a favorite of the Gothic novelists. *Coleridge the Poet* (London, 1966), p. 113.

*Hush, beating heart of Christabel*
*Jesu, Maria, shield her well!*
[53-54]

The author also convinces us of "the dramatic truth of such emotions as would naturally accompany such situations, supposing them real," by giving a kind of preternatural import to the most ordinary details: the leaf dancing, the dog howling, the bells echoing, the lamp sputtering. Within this context, Geraldine's hypnotic powers and apparent metamorphoses hardly seem out of place. So convinced are we by the voice that breathes this story to us that, as in Frost's "The Witch of Coös," no detail seems farfetched. The natural and supernatural are one. The colloquial tone of the opening stanzas establishes the imaginative truth of what we are about to hear in the same way the old witch's matter-of-fact mulling over of the past does — by understatement: "I struck the hand off brittle on the floor," the witch says, recollecting her struggle with the skeleton,

*The finger-pieces slid in all directions.*
*(Where did I see one of those pieces lately?*
*Hand me my button-box — it must be there.)*

Frost himself might be the author of, among other lines in "Christabel": "And the Spring comes slowly up this way" (22). Yet, unlike "The Witch of Coös," Coleridge's poem joins to the sometimes hair-raising effect of understatement the verse's aspiration, as it were, to incantation.

Like "Frost at Midnight" (1798), "Christabel" opens at a nadir of activity, both natural and human, in which all the "numberless goings-on of life" are as "inaudible as dreams." The time is chill April, when the decay of winter has nearly finished its work. There is not wind enough to twirl the one red leaf, the last of its clan, hanging in the bare grove of Langdale Hall. The "toothless mastiff bitch" (7) guarding the castle is impotent in several senses of the word and can but sterilely mark the passing of each hour. Even the moon "looks both small and dull" (19). A mist shrouds it, just as the death of Christabel's mother years before seems to have laid a permanent pall on the castle. Yet this stagnant landscape is pregnant with new life, if only adumbrated by the fact that it is April, that ambiguous month "of dark-brown gardens, and of peeping flowers," as it is described in "Dejection: An Ode." Here, the poet raises our hopes by introducing it as the "month before the month of May" (21). The spring is coming, however slowly.

Meanwhile there are other signs of something stirring at midnight. That bird of ambiguous omen, the owl, whose cry "came loud — and hark, again! loud as before" in "Frost at Midnight" and stirred the speaker's mind to a new perceptiveness, awakens this sleepy environment to an eery sort of activity:

*'Tis the middle of the night by the castle clock,*
*And the owls have awakened the crowing cock;*
*Tu—whit! — Tu—whoo!*
*And hark, again! the crowing cock,*
*How drowsily it crew.*

The cock is drowsy and strangely premature. Since "Christabel" "has Christ's name in 't,"[12] the cock may be heralding a betrayal analogous to the most famous of all. In the center of the poem, when we are told that Geraldine has her "will," these ominous night birds are

*jubilant anew,*
*From cliff and tower, tu—whoo! tu—whoo!*
*Tu—whoo! tu—whoo! from wood and fell!*
[308-310]

celebrating the completion of the dark work for which the opening prepares us. To complete this strange quartet of harbingers, as the clock tolls the midnight hour, the dog "maketh answer" to it with

*Sixteen short howls, not over loud;*
*Some say, she sees my lady's shroud.*
[12-13]

Even the dead are awake.

Well might the guardian spirit of Christabel and the watchdog be restless, for their ward has wandered a furlong from the protective castle gate to pray for her lover. There she discovers Geraldine. It is essential to our understanding of this strange creature to recognize that she is, among other things, Christabel's double.[13] The first vague intimation of Geraldine's presence startles Christabel, as if the sound came from within herself. Having knelt in prayer,

*The lady sprang up suddenly,*
*The lovely lady, Christabel!*
It moaned as near, as near can be,
*But what it is she cannot tell.*
[37-40, emphasis added]

[12] From the passage of Crashaw's poem, "A Hymn to the Name and Honor of the Admirable Sainte Teresa . . . ," that was on Coleridge's mind as he wrote "Christabel." See Nethercot, pp. 208-209.

[13] See Fogle, p. 131.

Geraldine's presence intrudes upon Christabel's prayer like an unholy thought disguised as an angel of light:

*There she sees a damsel bright,*
*Drest in a silken robe of white,*
*That shadowy in the moonlight shone:*
*The neck that made that white robe wan,*
*Her stately neck, and arms were bare;*
*Her blue-veined feet unsandal'd were,*
*And wildly glittered here and there*
*The gems entangled in her hair.*

[58-65]

Like our "lovely lady" (23) she is "beautiful exceedingly!" (68); the spotless white of her gown and complexion mirror the purity of the heroine. This similarity of appearance is ironically underscored in Part II when, after Bard Bracy's account of the dove Christabel's struggle with the serpent, the Baron turns to Geraldine and addresses her, "Sweet maid, Lord Roland's beauteous dove" (569). Conversely, in the course of the poem Christabel takes on, however unwillingly, characteristics of Geraldine. Their intertwined identities can suggest that the struggle here dramatically polarized in two individuals ordinarily finds its stage in a single bosom.

Geraldine resembles other ghostly "projections" and fatal, mysterious figures in Coleridge. Like the specter Life-in-Death whose skin is "white as leprosy," she too is exceedingly white. They share this extraordinary whiteness with the spirit who impersonates Abel in "The Wanderings of Cain" (1798): "Then the Shape shrieked a second time, and rent his garment, and his naked skin was like the white sands beneath their feet." Coleridge complains in *The Notebooks* of a nightmare haunted by "a frightful pale woman."[14] The whiteness of these figures is both fascinating and deathly, as ambiguous in its import as the white moonshine glimmering about the Albatross in the polar fog. It shares a wealth of mystery with such Romantic creations as Melville's white whale, Poe's white room below the House of Usher, or the latter's ghostly Ligeia.[15] Of course, it also was part of the stock-in-trade of romancers and Gothicizers, and even in 1797 Coleridge could spoof his own penchant for the effect:

[14] *The Notebooks of Samuel Taylor Coleridge*, ed. Kathleen Coburn, Bollingen Series 50 (2 vols., New York, 1957-1961), I, 1250.

[15] John Livingston Lowes quotes Melville's reference in the chapter on "The Whiteness of the Whale" to "that white phantom [which] sails in all imaginations." *The Road to Xanadu: A Study in the Ways of the Imagination*, new and enlarged ed. (Boston, 1930), p. 221.

*And thro' those brogues, still tatter'd and betorn*
*His hindward charms gleam an unearthly white.*[16]

Nevertheless, Coleridge reveals the genuine fascination whiteness had for him in a poem like "Lewti" (1798), as much an exercise in light and dark shading as it is a love lyric. This "Circassian Love-Chaunt" is an essay in the pseudo-oriental vein of Shelley's "The Indian Serenade." The scorned lover, "palely loitering" like Keats's knight-at-arms, finds everywhere in the moonlit landscape similes for Lewti's whiteness:

*The rock half-sheltered from my view*
*By pendent boughs of tressy yew,—*
*So shines my Lewti's forehead fair,*
*Gleaming through her sable hair.*

A rather unfortunate stanza, which the author excluded from later editions, shows that the lover's obsession verges, like Ahab's or the lover's in "Ligeia," on the pathological:

*I saw the white waves, o'er and o'er,*
*Break against the distant shore.*
. . . . . . . . . . . . . .
*Now disappearing from the sight,*
*Now twinkling regular and white,*
*And Lewti's smiling mouth can show*
*As white and regular a row.*

This obsession with her whiteness blends with his half-wish, half-complaint, that he die white of cheek for her. His desire for her whiteness becomes desire for a *Liebestod,* in which "die" has its Elizabethan connotation:

*Oh! that she saw me in a dream,*
*And dreamt that I had died for care;*
*All pale and wasted I would seem,*
*Yet fair withal, as spirits are!*
*I'd die indeed, if I might see*
*Her bosom heave, and heave for me!*

Lewti, to bear with the sexual connotations of the word "die," would offer him a kind of life-in-death. Similarly, the Mariner comes to new life through his symbolic death and Christabel through her deathly union with Geraldine brings new life to her lover and Langdale Hall.

The stealthy return of these two to Christabel's room emphasizes the unconscious complicity of the heroine in her own fate. We feel that Geraldine is stealing not only into the heart

[16] From "On a Ruined House in a Romantic Country," Coleridge's self-parody among the "Nehemiah Higginbottom" sonnets of 1797.

of the fastness, but into the very heart of Christabel. Their couching together represents symbolically the rape of good by evil — in the sense that any martyrdom is this. (Perhaps, given Christabel's cooperation, it more closely resembles a seduction.) There is an aura of assignation as the two, sandalless, creep by the Baron's room. Although Ernest Hartley Coleridge and several others have seen touches of Spenserian allegory in the poem,[17] none, surprisingly, associates this nocturnal betrayal with the long tradition symbolizing the soul as a besieged castle, a tradition given elaborate expression in the siege of the House of Alma (*The Faerie Queene*, Book II) and perhaps most familiar to us in Donne's "Holy Sonnet XIV." Christabel might be most willingly betraying her soul to the Devil:

*A little door she opened straight,*
*All in the middle of the gate;*
*The gate that was ironed within and without,*
*Where an army in battle array had marched out.*
*The lady sank, belike through pain,*
*And Christabel with might and main*
*Lifted her up, a weary weight,*
*Over the threshold of the gate.*

[125-132]

The sexual connotations of the gate do not seem incongruous in this context resonant of medieval allegory when we recall the sexual motive running through Donne's sonnet, as well as what afterwards transpires in Christabel's chamber. I am not suggesting that Coleridge inserted a short medieval allegory into his poem, but it seems equally absurd to think that he was not conscious of capitalizing on a medieval tradition prominently employed by both Spenser and Donne.

Christabel's room, like several in the House of Alma, is emblematic of the mind.[18] It is a

*chamber carved so curiously,*
*Carved with figures strange and sweet,*
*All made out of the carver's brain,*
*For a lady's chamber meet:*

[17] E. H. Coleridge, pp. 12-15; Nethercot, pp. 122-124; and Fogle, p. 133. They note only the resemblance of certain characters and incidents to some in Book I of *The Faerie Queene*.

[18] Cf. *FQ*, II. ix. 33:

Thence backe againe faire Alma led them right,
And soone into a goodly Parlour brought,
That was with royall arras richly dight,
In which was nothing pourtrahed nor wrought;
Nor wrought nor pourtrahed, but easie to be thought.

*The lamp with twofold silver chain*
*Is fastened to an angel's feet.*
[178-183]

All the images there are meet for a virgin's mind and lead, like the "inward beauty" of the bride in Spenser's *Epithalamion*, up to heaven. The chamber is pure, virginal, shut up; "not a moonbeam" (176) enters of the ambiguous light outside. But in Geraldine's presence, the silver lamp "burns dead and dim" (184). When its brightness is restored, she in turn sinks to the floor "in wretched plight" (188). The struggle has begun.

It is difficult to determine to what extent Geraldine is evil. While Gillman speaks of Christabel's defeating "the power of evil represented in the person of Geraldine," Derwent Coleridge contends that Geraldine is "no witch or goblin, or malignant being of any kind, but a spirit, executing her appointed task with the best good will." In a sense, she may be both good and evil. She may be one of those spirits described in "The Destiny of Nations" (1796), in one place as "rebellious," in another as "headstrong," who nevertheless "train up to God":

*Thus they make*
*Of transient Evil ever-during Good*
*Themselves probationary, and denied*
*Confess'd to view by preternatural deed*
*To o'erwhelm the will, save on some fated day*
*Headstrong, or with petition'd might from God.*[19]

Therefore, she may be considered a "neutral" spirit like the polar daemon who pursues the Ancient Mariner. And yet, insofar as she represents the evil impulse in the will of Christabel's lover, tempted in a foreign land, she *is* evil, even satanic. In Coleridge the satanic is always representative of the mystery of iniquity in the will of man. The Shape who misleads Cain in the wilderness seems a projection of his guilty self, and to the pilot's boy

[19] "The Destiny of Nations," 60, 61, variant 126-131. See Nethercot, pp. 202-207. Fogle warns against divorcing Coleridge's cosmology from his psychology and refers to a letter of 1806 in which Coleridge "infers from all he knows of the natural world a supernatural hierarchy between ourselves and God." Fogle, p. 136. See also *Collected Letters of Samuel Taylor Coleridge*, ed. Earl Leslie Griggs (4 vols., Oxford, 1956-1959), II, 1197. All we may venture here, however, is that Coleridge appears to be using this particular cosmology for poetic purposes.

[20] Coleridge reacted to the popular notion of a Devil in a remark on *Robinson Crusoe:* "The existence of a Personal intelligent evil Being the counterpart and antagonist of God is in direct contradiction to the most express declaration of Holy Writ!" *Coleridge on the Seventeenth Century*, ed. Roberta Florence Brinkley (Durham, N. C., 1955), p. 592. As he grew older, however, he came to value the personification of evil as a symbol, as

the Mariner himself appears satanic.[20] Like that of evil, however, Geraldine's ultimate status remains a mystery.[21]

Her alleged good will may account for her sometimes appearing reluctant to carry out her mission. On the other hand, her reluctance resembles Satan's in *Paradise Lost* upon drawing near to Eve and experiencing momentary regret in the presence of her goodness and beauty:

*That space the evil one abstracted stood*
*From his own evil, and for the time remained*
*Stupidly good.*
[IX. 463-465]

The rays of the silver lamp and the wildflower cordial (made by Christabel's mother) apparently have the same effect on Geraldine:

*And will your mother pity me,*
*Who am a maiden most forlorn?*
[194-195]

Momentarily Geraldine wishes the mother present, though the ghost's compliance with her wish calls her back to herself:

*But soon with altered voice, said she—*
*"Off, wandering mother! Peak and pine!*
*I have power to bid thee flee."*
[204-206]

Again she drinks the cordial, and again seems under the power of good:

*All they who live in the upper sky,*
*Do love you, holy Christabel!*
*And you love them, and for their sake*
*And for the good which me befel,*
*Even I in my degree will try,*
*Fair maiden, to requite you well.*
[227-232]

This confession may be interpreted several ways. It may express

this remark of about 1812 indicates: "With what contempt, even in later years, have I not contemplated the doctrine of a devil! but now I see the intimate connection, if not as existent *person*, yet as essence and symbol with Christianity — and that so far from being identical with Manicheism, it is the surest antidote (that is, rightly understood)." *Anima Poetae*, ed. E. H. Coleridge (London, 1895), p. 260.

[21] Of interest here may be the later note on Donne's Sermon XVII: "Pain is not necessarily an *ultimate* evil, as the means of ultimate good, it may be a relative good — but surely that which makes Pain, Anguish, Heaviness, necessary in order to Good, must be Evil. . . . but God's infinite mercy raises them into sacraments, means of Grace." Brinkley, p. 195.

her realization that the attempt on Christabel is only possible, like Satan's on Job, with "petition'd might from God," that "they who live in the upper sky" will turn her evil design to a good end. If such is the case, there may be the irony born of despair in the last three lines: the good — the cordial — only aggravates her malice by reminding her of that from which she is cut off. Satan experiences a similar reaction to his momentary enchantment by Eve (*PL*, IX, 473-479):

> *Thoughts, whither have ye led me? with what sweet*
> *Compulsion thus transported to forget*
> *What hither brought us? hate, not love, nor hope*
> *Of Paradise for Hell, hope here to taste*
> *Of pleasure, but all pleasure to destroy,*
> *Save what is in destroying; other joy*
> *To me is lost.*

Yet, that this is a neutral or good spirit forced to do a loathsome task because of the "various temptations" to which Christabel's lover is exposed and executing it, as Derwent says, "with the best good will," is a theory that receives support from Geraldine's apparent attempt at delay.

> *Ah! what a stricken look was hers!*
> *Deep from within she seems half-way*
> *To lift some weight with sick assay,*
> *And eyes the maid and seeks delay;*
> *Then suddenly, as one defied,*
> *Collects herself in scorn and pride,*
> *And lay down by the Maiden's side!*
> [256-262]

Yet, however lenient we are to Geraldine, it is obvious that she still "represents" the power of evil. Its deformity is manifested in her body as she disrobes and reveals "her bosom and half her side/ . . . lean and old and foul of hue" (to use the more explicit language of an early version of 252-253). Taking the maid in her arms, Geraldine utters the spell that initiates Christabel's vicarious atonement for the weal of her lover far away:

> *In the touch of this bosom there worketh a spell,*
> *Which is lord of thy utterance, Christabel!*
> *Thou knowest to-night, and wilt know to-morrow,*
> *This mark of my shame, this seal of my sorrow.*[22]

During the hour she lies entranced, Christabel assumes in some

[22] 267-270. Cf. Satan's resolve (*PL*, IV, 375-377):
League with you I seek,
And mutual amitie so streight, so close,
That I with you must dwell, or you with mee.

mysterious fashion the weight of her lover's guilt, while Geraldine, sleeping "still and mild" (300), is apparently relieved of an equivalent burden. The jubilation of the nightbirds marks the end of this evil hour along with one suggestive astronomical detail: "A star hath set, a star hath risen" (302).

The hour of trial does not appear to have materially harmed Christabel. The experience seems to have been cathartic, if anything, and the tears it brings are followed by an intuition of impending good:

*Her limbs relax, her countenance*
*Grows sad and soft; the smooth thin lids*
*Close o'er her eyes; and tears she sheds—*
*Large tears that leave the lashes bright!*
*And oft the while she seems to smile*
*As infants at a sudden light!*
[313-318]

This last image may remind us of the infant Hartley's reaction to the moon at the end of "The Nightingale" (1798):

*He beheld the moon, and, hushed at once,*
*Suspends his sobs, and laughs most silently,*
*While his fair eyes, that swam with undropped tears,*
*Did glitter in the yellow moon-beam!*

In each case grief is transfigured. Weeping and smiling are mixed as Christabel continues the religious vocation initiated by her going to pray in the grove:

*Yea, she doth smile, and she doth weep,*
*Like a youthful hermitess,*
*Beauteous in a wilderness,*
*Who, praying always, prays in sleep.*
[319-322]

Those in the upper sky apparently have things well in hand:

*No doubt, she hath a vision sweet.*
*What if her guardian spirit 'twere,*
*What if she knew her mother near?*
*But this she knows, in joys and woes,*
*That saints will aid if men will call:*
*For the blue sky bends over all!*
[326-331]

Her relief, like the Mariner's, is only temporary, and she recurrently succumbs to the spell, helplessly reflecting evil when fascinated by Geraldine's serpent eye:

*So deeply had she drunken in*
*That look, those shrunken serpent eyes,*
*That all her features were resigned*

*To this sole image in her mind:*
*And passively did imitate*
*That look of dull and treacherous hate!*
[601-606]

Leaving to one side the question whether Geraldine is a lamia,[23] her serpentine metamorphoses in Part II are the source of irony that underscores the complex intervolution of good and evil in an act of vicarious suffering. Speaking of Geraldine's abductors, Sir Leoline vows to dislodge "their reptile souls / From the bodies and forms of men!" (442-443), ironically unconscious that as he embraces the supposed daughter of his friend, she reveals her own "reptile soul" to Christabel. When Bard Bracy recounts his dream in which a green snake coils about

*that dove,*
*That gentle bird, whom thou dost love,*
*And call'st by thy own daughter's name*
[531-533]

ironically Christabel's father turns to Geraldine and boasts,

*Sweet maid, Lord Roland's beauteous dove,*
*With arms more strong than harp or song,*
*Thy sire and I will crush the snake!*
[569-571]

His reference to Geraldine as "Lord Roland's beauteous dove" suggests not merely the confusion of identities noted earlier, but what amounts to an exchange of identities. For at this moment Christabel helplessly imitates a snake:

*Christabel in dizzy trance*
*Stumbling on the unsteady ground*
*Shuddered aloud, with a hissing sound.*
[589-591]

The substitution of the innocent for the wicked is complete as the Baron, Geraldine on his arm, turns away from his only daughter.

Although Geraldine obviously has a disruptive effect on Langdale Hall, she also brings new life to the castle and its inhabitants. This creative intervolution of good and evil is adumbrated from the beginning. The wanly shining moon forecasts showers which will stir "dull roots with spring rain" in this, "the cruellest month," to borrow words describing a later wasteland. In the grove of Langdale Hall "naught was green upon the oak / But moss and rarest mistletoe" (33-34), both parasitic plants that bring new life out of decay in a relation-

[23] See Nethercot, Ch. iii, for a discussion of this question.

ship analogous to Geraldine's parasitic attachment to the castle and its inhabitants. In this regard we may recall from "The Ancient Mariner" (521-522) the Hermit's cushion of "moss that wholly hides / The rotted old oak-stump." We also know that the oak's "one red leaf, the last of its clan" (49-50) will make room for a new leaf when the season of decay, which necessarily precedes the spring, is complete.

Geraldine's inability to pass the threshold or to praise the Virgin Mary, like the fire's leaping up at her presence, are traditional signs of the presence of an evil spirit. Yet, the fire's new vigor is unusually suggestive of the breath of fresh air she introduces into this atmosphere of suffocation:

*The brands were flat, the brands were dying,*
*Amid their own white ashes lying;*
*But when the lady passed, there came*
*A tongue of light, a fit of flame;*
*And Christabel saw the lady's eye,*
*And nothing else saw she thereby,*
*Save the boss of the shield of Sir Leoline tall,*
*Which hung in a murky old niche in the wall.*
[156-163]

In the flame glitter Geraldine's hypnotic eye and, what in better days would symbolize Christabel's security, the shield of Sir Leoline, now hanging useless upon the wall. Even though the shield may suggest the decrepitude of the castle's and Christabel's defenses, one can argue that the gleaming boss anticipates the new burst of martial vigor — however illusory — the Baron experiences in Part II. The meeting of the eye and the shield burnishes both.

Even more suggestive of ultimate good, the time and conditions of the opening foreshadow the wedding which, according to Gillman, was to seal Christabel's victory. The nocturnal meeting with Geraldine at the stroke of midnight and the consequent retirement to the couch is a grotesque parody of this union at noon, but nevertheless looks forward to it. At midnight the ghost of Christabel's mother is abroad and makes an attempt (thwarted by Geraldine) to warn her daughter; later, according to Gillman, the mother's voice was to be heard at the wedding. His account receives corroboration from within the poem where Christabel reveals that her mother "should hear the castle-bell / Strike twelve upon my wedding-day" (200-201).[24]

[24] An early unpublished review (probably written by John Morgan) also remarks this consistency. E. L. Griggs, "An Early Defense of 'Christabel,'"

If Geraldine is a grotesque parody of the lover (and according to Gillman the spirit was to assume the absent lover's shape once the disguise as Sir Roland's daughter was no longer feasible), she is also presented as a gross perversion of the mother.[25] While she holds Christabel in her arms, she

*Seems to slumber still and mild,*
*As a mother with her child.*
[299-300]

Instead of nourishing Christabel, the touch of the shrunken bosom appears to *draw* life from her, as in the morning Geraldine's girded vests newly "tight beneath her heaving breasts" (380) suggest. Yet this perverse madonna-and-child may be seen as emblematic of the principle that evil or rebellious spirits, despite themselves, evolve the process of eternal good. For Christabel, either despite or because of Geraldine's depredations, is equally nourished. After the hour of trial she is more than sustained by "a vision sweet" (326) from those who live in the upper sky, a vision that has salutary effects physically:

*Her limbs relax, her countenance*
*Grows sad and soft; ...*
. . . . . . . . . . .
*And, if she move unquietly,*
*Perchance, 'tis but the blood so free*
*Comes back and tingles in her feet.*
[313-325]

Likewise, after the first recurrence of the spell she experiences "a rapture in her breast" (467). The virgin goodness of Christabel becomes fruitful when impregnated with the sorrow and shame of Geraldine.[26]

Geraldine has herself confessed that all is in the control of those in the upper sky and said, however ironically, that she means to requite her rescuer "well." And when, during the first recurrence of the spell, the Baron asks the heroine what is troubling her, the vision with which she is immediately comforted allows her to say, "All will yet be well!" (472). Like

in *Wordsworth and Coleridge: Studies in Honor of George McLean Harper*, ed. E. L. Griggs (1939; repr. New York, 1962), p. 190.

25 Fogle feels that they are "in some occult sense the same" (p. 142).

26 Nethercot, p. 209, notices the elaborate sexual metaphors with which Crashaw describes St. Teresa's religious vocation in the poem that influenced Coleridge. These lines, for instance:

She never undertook to know
What death with love should have to doe;
Nor has she e're yet understood
Why to show love, she should shed blood.

Julian of Norwich, with whom as a "youthful hermitess" (320) she may have more than accidental affinities, she can assure us through the vision that crowns her suffering that "sin is behovable, but all shall be well, and all shall be well, and all manner of thing shall be well."[27]

At the beginning of Part II, the sprightliness of Geraldine contrasts with the "world of death" (333) to which the tolling matin bell wakens the castle. She

*rises lightly from the bed;*
*Puts on her silken vestments white,*
*And tricks her hair in lovely plight.*
[363-365]

To Christabel she appears "fairer yet! and yet more fair!" (374) than the night before. Charming the Baron, she inspires him not only with illusory martial vigor, but with the false hope of reunion with the friend whose daughter she purports to be:

*Sir Leoline, a moment's space,*
*Stood gazing on the damsel's face:*
*And the youthful Lord of Tryermaine*
*Came back upon his heart again.*
[427-430]

However illusory the hope will prove, and however pernicious to his relationship with his daughter, it does move him to contrition for an age-old quarrel and to an impulsive act of love:

*And now the tears were on his face,*
*And fondly in his arms he took*
*Fair Geraldine, who met the embrace,*
*Prolonging it with joyous look.*
[447-450]

His awakened longing is so strong that he imaginatively creates the reunion while commissioning Bard Bracy to go to Tryermaine. His speech reflects the new energy that Geraldine has called forth from him:

*Bard Bracy! bard Bracy! your horses are fleet,*
*Ye must ride up the hall, your music so sweet,*
*More loud than your horses' echoing feet!*
*And loud and loud to Lord Roland call,*
*Thy daughter is safe in Langdale hall!*
[498-502]

But the hope was to have proved illusory: "Over the mountains, the Bard, as directed by Sir Leoline, 'hastes' with his disciple;

[27] *Revelations of Divine Love,* ed. Grace Warrack, 6th ed. (London, 1917), pp. 55-56.

but in consequence of one of those inundations supposed to be common in this country, the spot only where the castle once stood is discovered, — the edifice itself being washed away." This intended turn of events is predictable, however, from what we already know of Geraldine as well as from the first description of the rift between Leoline and Roland:

*They stood aloof, the scars remaining,*
*Like cliffs which had been rent asunder;*
*A dreary sea now flows between.*
[421-423]

The Baron, tricked into forgetting his age by Geraldine, is trying to restore the good of bygone days. The suggestion that part of the torpor of Langdale Hall is caused by his desire to hold on to the past is implicit in his commanding that each matin bell be a death-knell for his wife, dead since Christabel's birth. His energy is here rather like that of the one red leaf clinging to the oak, "with which," as Coleridge describes the phenomenon elsewhere, "the Gust . . . strikes up a mockery of life."[28] The old must be "washed away" before the new — in this case the union of Christabel and her lover — can be accomplished. There is in this the mystery of the seasons, as the April setting implies. The Baron's energy hastens the death that leads to new life. The oftener the leaf dances, the sooner it will fall that a new may replace it.

While Leoline is turning away from Christabel to Geraldine, the narrator protests,

*Thy only child*
*Lies at thy feet, thy joy, thy pride,*
*So fair, so innocent, so mild;*
*The same, for whom thy lady died!*
. . . . . . . . . . . . . . .
*She prayed the moment ere she died:*
*Prayed that the babe for whom she died,*
*Might prove her dear lord's joy and pride.*
[622-631]

The mother's death in childbirth to bring "joy and pride" to her husband is parallel to Christabel's martyrdom for her absent lover. This detail suggests as well that just as the mother's suffering benefited not only her lord but her daughter, so Christabel's suffering will not only benefit her lover but bring "joy and pride" to her father. The Baron will find his lost

28 "The Dry Bones, are dancing and eddying like the fallen leaves, with which the Gust of November strikes up a mockery of Life." Quoted by Beer, p. 186, from a notebook.

youth restored and the pall lifted from the castle in the only way possible: through the safe return of Christabel's betrothed and the lovers' joyful union.

The "Conclusion to Part II" has no apparent connection with the action except the rather tenuous one of the child's rebuff by its father.[29] Yet the fact that Coleridge used this fragment as the conclusion shows that he must have thought it related integrally to "one main object" of the tale. To generalize, this analysis of a father's reaction to his happy child is involved with one main object of both "The Ancient Mariner" and "Christabel": to represent the mystery of iniquity, particularly the dim intuition that the good implies its opposite and that evil is somehow complementary to the good.[30]

*A little child, a limber elf,*
*Singing, dancing to itself,*
*A fairy thing with red round cheeks*
*That always finds and never seeks,*
*Makes such a vision to the sight*
*As fills a father's eyes with light;*
*And pleasures flow in so thick and fast*
*Upon his heart, that he at last*
*Must needs express his love's excess*
*With words of unmeant bitterness.*
[656-665]

The father's strange reaction shares the absurdity (if not the seriousness) of the Mariner's slaying the Albatross. Why should an excess of good, like the Albatross' love for the Mariner, evoke a swift and irrational manifestation of its opposite? The poet speculates, "Perhaps 'tis pretty to force together / Thoughts so all unlike each other" (666-667). As an excuse for the Mariner, rather than for a teasing father who dallies "with wrong that does no harm" (669), this would be nothing short of horrible. Yet in it we may glimpse some of the dynamic of the story of "Christabel." Ernest Hartley Coleridge saw in the confronta-

29 "The nexus between this so-called Conclusion and the closing lines of the Second Part is to be found in the implied comparison between Sir Leoline's wrath, the excess of love transformed into the excess of bitterness and the mock resentment of love playing at wrath, which is none the less 'a fault and corruption' of this world of sin." E. H. Coleridge (above, note 2), p. 32.

30 "Like *The Ancient Mariner,* it was to have represented evil as something which was not completely separate from good, but a distortion of it." Beer, p. 197. Bostetter (above, note 9), p. 130, sees in the conclusion "a cryptic attempt to suggest that 'Christabel' is no mere Gothic tale but the dramatic exploration of the nature of evil and its ambiguous interrelation with good."

tion of Geraldine and Christabel "the antithesis of the beauty of innocence to the beauty of sin" (p. 15). The poet next attempts another rationalization, related to the previous:

*Perhaps 'tis tender too and pretty*
*At each wild word to feel within*
*A sweet recoil of love and pity.*

It is, after all, the Mariner's evil act and its consequences that move him to learn "love and pity" and Cain's murder of Abel that teaches him to groan over Enos. A darker thought, however, concludes the brief introspection:

*And what, if in a world of sin*
*(O sorrow and shame should this be true!)*
*Such giddiness of heart and brain*
*Comes seldom save from rage and pain,*
*So talks as it's most used to do.*

The father's motive, however innocent the act, is here viewed in the least favorable light. He finds pleasure in destructive feelings. There is in this idyl the implicit suggestion that the child's innocence may drive the father to mar what he cannot share, the ability to "always find and never seek" that is the perfect happiness of childhood. Such is Satan's reaction to his glimpse of Paradise and (perhaps) Geraldine's response to Christabel's kindness:

*And for the good which me befel,*
*Even I in my degree will try,*
*Fair maiden, to requite you well.*
[230-232]

In his examination of the motive is implied the still more comprehensive question of why "a world of sin" exists at all. While "Christabel," like "The Ancient Mariner," bows before the mystery, it leaves us with strong intimations that good and evil are related in ways that we can hardly begin to comprehend and that, through the mystery of sacrificial love, evil is finally subservient to good. Not only do Derwent Coleridge and Gillman agree that "Christabel" was intended as a divine comedy, but the existing parts can leave us in little doubt. The elaborate description of the bell-ringing which opens Part II offers an objective correlative of the relationship of good and evil in the poem.[31] Each matin bell tolls in the new day with a death-

[31] The bell motif is important. The stroke of midnight opens the poem and presumably the stroke of noon on Christabel's wedding day would have marked its close. Thus the elaborate description of the matin bell opening Part II more than incidentally underscores the changes from night to day,

knell reflecting the "world of death" (333), of stagnant age and untried youth, that Langdale Hall has become:

> *At dawn the sacristan,*
> *Who duly pulls the heavy bell,*
> *Five and forty beads must tell*
> *Between each stroke — a warning knell,*
> *Which not a soul can choose but hear*
> *From Bratha Head to Wyndermere.*
> [339-344]

This knell inspires a strange response:

> *Saith Bracy the bard, so let it knell!*
> *And let the drowsy sacristan*
> *Still count as slowly as he can!*
> *There is no lack of such, I ween,*
> *As well fill up the space between.*
> *In Langdale Pike and Witch's Lair,*
> *And Dungeon-ghyll so foully rent,*
> *With ropes of rock and bells of air*
> *Three sinful sextons' ghosts are pent,*
> *Who all give back, one after t'other,*
> *The death-note to their living brother;*
> *And oft too, by the knell offended,*
> *Just as their one! two! three! is ended,*
> *The devil mocks the doleful tale*
> *With a merry peal from Borodale.*
> [345-359]

The lifeless knell of the good but drowsy sacristan finds a strange echo in the lively tintinnabulation of the devilish crew, at whose merry peal, by the way, Geraldine rises and goes about her work with energy. Like her, the evil sextons with their ropes of rock and bells of air are only a shadow, parasitically drawing their semblance of reality from a substantial double. Yet their parasitic activity, like Geraldine's, paradoxically wakens the castle to new life. The antithesis that Ernest Hartley Coleridge saw in the poem is dynamic. To borrow Coleridge's own words for this dynamic, in Geraldine and the ghostly sextons we can perhaps see "an *evil* Power striving against, yet controlled by the Great Spirit — in this there is the chiaro-oscuro, the working of the modifying Energy in the dim combination of contraries."[32] Indeed, the devil's "merry peal from Borodale" — which struck one early reviewer like "the sudden transition of a dream"[33] —

from winter to spring, from one generation to the next, which are integrally related to the theme of the poem.

[32] From a late, unpublished notebook cited by Beer, p. 105.

[33] Griggs (above, note 24), p. 188.

is an inadvertent harbinger of the happy ending as it "mocks the doleful tale" like the bells that shall ring out on Christabel's wedding day.

# III. Inklings and Ancestors

# The Joy of the Absolute: A Comparative Study of the Romantic Visions of William Wordsworth and C. S. Lewis

DANIEL K. KUHN

From time to time in the cursory unfolding of human affairs certain men of highly creative powers appear who, gifted with extraordinary and unique genius, are able to present to us the vision of a higher order of life and being, an order immanent in practical living and everyday cares but undisclosed to usual modes of perception. Two such men are William Wordsworth and C. S. Lewis, whose ontological visions embodied in the corpus of their literary work we wish to compare. It may be said at the outset that both men knew similar romantic conceptions of the nature of being which, however, evolved along quite different lines — in fact rather opposite approaches. Wordsworth's genius awakened to the immanent immediacy of essential being in the universe while Lewis, over a much more circuitous route, realized first the utter transcendence and only later the immanent nature of unconditioned being. Both, however, were "surprised by Joy" in their initial awakening to the

---

Daniel K. Kuhn graduated from Wheaton College (A.B., 1965). In his final year at Wheaton he was elected a Varsity Scholar and studied closely with Professor Kilby on an Honors project in the general area of myth and symbol. After a brief period of graduate study he entered the U. S. Army and served in Vietnam until 1968, attaining the rank of captain. Since leaving the service, he has studied in West Germany and at the University of Chicago. Of his immediate plans he writes: "I hope to concentrate privately on developing myself as a writer and poet. The challenge of the creative life passed on to me by Dr. Kilby and other romantics of similar vision is a challenge that will remain with me the rest of my life."

transcendental mode, and were so profoundly changed and creatively moved by their envisioning that English literature has been forever enriched as a result.

William Wordsworth from the dawning years of his life seemed filled with an unusual capacity to sense the innate beauties of nature. In childhood his soul and sense received the panoply of nature with an undifferentiated wonder. The images that filled his eyes were implanted and fused with intuitions that colored his perceptions in a singularly meaningful manner. These vivid sensual experiences early in life found later correspondence with his inner modes of being; they stirred his creative faculties to the production of poetry in which he celebrates his experience of the Spirit, who

*from my first dawn*
*Of childhood didst . . . intertwine for me*
*The passions that build up our human soul;*
*Not with the mean and vulgar works of man,*
*But with high objects, with enduring things —*
*With life and nature — purifying thus*
*The elements of feeling and of thought.*[1]

His aesthetic sensitivity to nature clothed the ontological reality that he intuited with a profuse wealth of natural imagery. Wordsworth writes in *The Prelude* that even at the age of ten his spirit responded to the moods and patterns of nature, holding "unconscious intercourse with beauty" (I, 562); these images and luculent sensations were conjuring up in his mind transcendental longings, "first-born affinities that fit / Our new existence to existing things" (I, 555f.). He does not confuse this with the normal pleasures of childhood experience but notes that

*even then I felt*
*Gleams like the flashing of a shield; — the earth*
*And common face of Nature spake to me*
*Rememberable things.*
[I, 585-588]

All the moods, shades, colors, motions, and events of nature assumed for him evocation of an unseen, divine reality. With further growth he came to differentiate more clearly between sense and soul, between phenomena and noumena. It was Wordsworth's genius to find creative correlations between natural ap-

[1] *The Prelude,* I, 405-411. All quotations from the *Poetical Works* of Wordsworth follow the text in the edition of Thomas Hutchinson, rev. E. de Selincourt (London, 1904), and unless otherwise noted are from *The Prelude.*

pearances and the ontological Spirit, which he felt gave them meaning and worth. And finally it was his sense of the immanency of this Spirit which produced his rapport with nature and which intensified and exhilarated his existence.

By contrast C. S. Lewis's childhood intuitions of a transcendental realm seem much more fleeting and elusive. He remembers his childhood as being rather barren of beauty. His attention was seldom, if ever, drawn to the effects of beauty by his parents, and he was unable to recall any striking views from his childhood or even any pictures on the walls. Compelling aesthetic experiences were rare for him and religious experience almost nonexistent. However, both his father and mother read a great deal, and Lewis from an early age formed a passion for books, which became a constant means of entertainment and enjoyment. This developed in him a keen inventive imagination more attuned to the evocations of the phantasmagoric and the rich symbolisms of fantasy than was that of Wordsworth. Lewis's dialectical mind relied more on reason than upon such intense intuitions as Wordsworth felt, and his romantic awakening was prompted by only the most fleeting of intuitive experiences.

He claims it first began when he was six, seven, or eight years of age. He does not recall precisely when. He does remember standing by a blooming currant bush the first time when a memory of another memory burst into his consciousness. He says of it—

> ...There suddenly arose in me without warning, and as if from a depth not of years but of centuries, the memory of that earlier morning at the Old House when my brother had brought his toy garden into the nursery. It is difficult to find words strong enough for the sensation which came over me.... It was a sensation, of course, of desire, but desire for what?...And before I knew what I desired, the desire itself was gone, the whole glimpse withdrawn, the world turned commonplace again.[2]

As this was to prove the germinal beginning of his metaphysical quest, Lewis thought it to be the most significant thing that ever happened to him. The second glimpse was much the same. Through a reading of *Squirrel Nutkin* by Beatrix Potter it came, as a sudden intense longing and yearning for autumn, then was gone — something quite apart from ordinary experience, leav-

[2] C. S. Lewis, *Surprised by Joy* (New York, 1955), p. 16. All further references are to this edition. Lewis's title, of course, was borrowed from Wordsworth's sonnet which begins, "Surprised by joy — impatient as the Wind" (*Poetical Works*, p. 257).

ing a lingering sense of deep significance. The nature of the desire was such that one wished to awaken it again, only to find it not subject to volition. A third such experience came with Lewis's first reading of Longfellow's *Saga of King Olaf* at the point where Balder is declared dead. Lewis says,

> I knew nothing about Balder; but instantly I was uplifted into huge regions of northern sky, I desired with almost sickening intensity something never to be described (except that it is cold, spacious, severe, pale, and remote) and then, as in the other examples, found myself at the very same moment already falling out of that desire and wishing I were back in it [p. 17].

Lewis calls this intense desire which he experienced a kind of joy, but points out that it is a sensation that one wants to have perpetually and to have more than anything else. It is a conative reaching forth to unite with a transcendent mode of being, and for Lewis it became the spur to grasp consciously the ontological meaning of life — such meaning as later appeared in the astonishing perceptions found in the final pages of *Perelandra* and *Till We Have Faces.*

From this point on Lewis's sensibility seemed to respond to anything that smacked of mythopoeic "northernness." In the ensuing years Lewis adopted Christianity for a period, but only succeeded in plunging himself into pessimism by forcing his imagination to stir him emotionally in the effort to find significance and conviction in his religious practices. He seems to have had little awareness of faith during this period and made rather desperate attempts to create religious meaning for himself through psychic compulsions. Such behavior soon ended in a scepticism of religion altogether, and outright atheism followed in logical sequence. On the heels of atheism came a general degeneration of moral fiber. He recalls himself as snobbish, lustful, and more than ever alienated from the joy once glimpsed.

Of this low ebb in his life Lewis writes, "The authentic 'Joy' (as I tried to describe it in an earlier chapter) had vanished from my life." Suddenly one day, however, he read in a literary periodical the words "Siegfried and the Twilight of the Gods" and the words found immediately in his soul the old longing for northernness and the mythopoeic quality of those vast cold reaches. With this longing came back the memory of joy haunting his soul with an "unendurable sense of desire and loss" (pp. 72-73). It was this experience through which he discovered an unquenchable craving to immerse himself in Norse mythology. He also discovered great delight in Wagner's music and bought as many Wagnerian records as he could afford.

Later Lewis's interest in mythology broadened, partly as the result of his classical studies, to include Greek and Roman mythology. Following the completion of his academic preparation when his creative powers came into their own, Lewis's philosophic convictions moved into idealism, to the concept of the Absolute and finally to theism.

There appears a parallel theme running through the visions of both Wordsworth and Lewis. It may be described as a theomorphic conation for the godlike — not in the Dionysian or satanic sense, but an urge for man in his personal being to partake of the divine quality of life. Wordsworth writes:

> *for there's not a man*
> *That lives who hath not known his god-like hours,*
> *And feels not what an empire we inherit*
> *As natural beings in the strength of Nature.*
> [III, 190-193]

For Wordsworth the hypostatization of godlikeness derives from powerful mystical intuitions which elevate man's existence with heightened sensations of power, freedom, joy, creative rapport with nature, and creative union with the ontological Spirit of the universe. Lewis, on the other hand, seems to apprehend godlikeness through the reflection of a divine form of human personality evanescent in mythology. Lewis believes that mythology at its highest levels reveals human nature in its theomorphic state. For him mythology becomes the symbolic manifold of the divine reality. It contains the visionary revelation of what man's personality could be if it were not for the moral guilt that has enslaved him in his rejection of God. This understanding, for instance, comes forcibly to Ransom as he contemplates the nature of life in Perelandra.

> Ransom had been perceiving that the triple distinction of truth from myth and of both from fact was purely terrestrial — was part and parcel of that unhappy division between soul and body which resulted from the Fall. Even on earth the sacraments existed as a permanent reminder that the division was neither wholesome nor final. The Incarnation had been the beginning of its disappearance. In Perelandra it would have no meaning at all. Whatever happened here would be of such a nature that earth-men would call it mythological.[3]

This passage also points out Lewis's belief that mythology bears the hypostatization of man's primordial being before sin alienated him from the universe. Man in his present terrestriality is tragically estranged from his primordial being and thus thinks

[3] C. S. Lewis, *Perelandra* (New York, 1944), pp. 143-144.

mythology to be unreal when actually it symbolizes a fuller reality. Lewis believes it is shortsighted to view mythology exclusively as chimerical representations of surrogate wish-fulfillment instincts, as evident as these may be, for mythology also holds up to our vision the penetrating life-symbols of godlikeness, and these may become the hieroglyphics of revelation leading us to an epiphanic grasp of the divine being. He sees in Christianity the culminating synthesis of truth and myth capable of restoring fallen man to a concretized spiritual existence in divine freedom, a return of man through faith in Christ to union with his essential being.

We have seen thus that for both Wordsworth and Lewis the transcendental awareness grew from intuitions experienced in early childhood. Wordsworth's intense intuitive faculties turned his consciousness first to a heightened awareness of being in its immanental immediacy, while Lewis through greater philosophical acuity turned first to a conscious belief in the absolute transcendence of God in the universe, in much the same visionary tradition as Dante, Spenser, Bunyan and Milton. Now it would be profitable to examine more closely the metaphysics of both men and to note the similarities and differences of their presuppositions and conclusions.

The metaphysics of both Wordsworth and Lewis find their philosophical roots not so much in either empirical philosophy or traditional rationalistic idealism but rather in a philosophical vitalism of the sort articulated by Henri Bergson fifty years after Wordsworth's prime. It will be well to refer to Bergson here since his thought gave a supreme philosophic expression to romantic intuitional metaphysics. Lewis, of course, clearly recognizes the influence of Bergson on his own thinking when he states,

> He did not abolish my old loves, but he gave me a new one. From him I first learned to relish energy, fertility, and urgency; the resource, the triumphs, and even the insolence of things that grow.[4]

A basic premise of vitalism and a common theme in Wordsworth's work is that human intellect — the rational, logical, and analytical faculties of man's mind — cannot yield absolute or metaphysical knowledge because it does not participate in the flux, mobility, and process that time, or duration as Bergson prefers to categorize it, imposes on reality. When intellect seeks to understand an aspect of experience through rational categories, it immobilizes the perception for purposes of measure-

[4] *Surprised by Joy*, p. 198.

ment and calculation and usually imposes some artificial unit upon the subject which splits it up and robs it of its wholeness, temporality, and inner process. Intellect analyzes experience into static existents, and logic determines the structural relationships between these immobilized units. Therefore rubricated and scientific thinking do not grasp the essence of experience because they ignore its duration, flux, and growth. At a metaphysical level this results in a falsification of the meaning of experience, for while rational paradigms may be efficacious on a practical level, they never grasp the total reality.

Metaphysics for the vitalist is man's act of grasping the ultimately real, and as such it must view reality as it occurs in duration, caught up in the living, moving, changing flux of time. It does this by intuitions born out of the manifold of perception. This should be understood in the Bergsonian sense as

> an act or a series of acts, of direct participation in the immediacy of experience. It can be accomplished only by making an effort to detach oneself from the demands of action, by inverting the normal attitude of consciousness and immersing oneself in the current of direct awareness.[5]

The romantic vitalist holds that the key to absolute knowledge rests in the fact that one exists in process, that he is caught up in the stream of living, and that his very source of life is rooted in the creative ground of being. Such is Bergson's famous *élan vital* or vital force. Man is the highest conscious expression of this fountain of life which burgeons forth in a continuing creative evolution. It is by living consciously, growing, feeling, and intuiting, that we are able to identify with the absolute cosmic life.

It is in this sense that Wordsworth builds his metaphysical conceptions. Caught up in the very motions of nature, Wordsworth invoked the earth and sky to

> *teach me what they might;*
> *Or turning the mind in upon herself,*
> *Pored, watched, expected, listened, spread my thoughts*
> *And spread them with a wider creeping; felt*
> *Incumbencies more awful, visitings*
> *Of the Upholder of the tranquil soul.*
> [III, 112-117]

Such words demonstrate the vitalist's inversion of perception to correlate with his ontological intuition and the resulting

[5] Henri Bergson, *An Introduction to Metaphysics*, trans. T. E. Hulme, Library of Liberal Arts 10 (New York, 1955), p. 12.

epiphany of the unconditioned Spirit which he witnesses. This epiphany reaches an acute realization, filling his mind with

*a sense sublime*
*Of something far more deeply interfused,*
*Whose dwelling is the light of setting suns,*
*And the round ocean and the living air,*
*And the blue sky, and in the mind of man;*
*A motion and a spirit, that impels*
*All thinking things, all objects of all thought,*
*And rolls through all things.*
["Tintern Abbey," 95-102]

Bergson himself did not describe the *élan vital* in more accurate or sublime terms. This consciousness of Spirit was no intellectual concept merely, but one that welled up from deep inner conations and flooded his mind and thought consumingly. In his mature powers there is no longer that innocent identification of soul and sense that we noted in his early childhood. Unconditioned forms of being are now distinguished from the images that once subsumed them. In his more profound intuitions, sensual images fade out in a manner characteristic of mystical experience. Here imagination lifts the world of sense into the world of Spirit.

*. . . even the motion of our human blood*
*Almost suspended, we are laid asleep*
*In body, and become a living soul;*
*While with an eye made quiet by the power*
*Of harmony, and the deep power of joy,*
*We see into the life of things.*
[ibid., 44-49]

There is some evidence to indicate that Wordsworth never fully understood the relation of his sensual experience to his moments of lucid, mystical insight which seemed so completely to transcend his sensual perceptions. In "Tintern Abbey," for instance, he states that his sensual awareness dies out when subsumed by the intuition of ontological Spirit; but later in the same poem nature and phenomenal perceptions become the governing forces of his soul. Be it as it may, his primary metaphysical conception is of transcendental cosmic Spirit animating both the universe and the mind of man.

*Wisdom and Spirit of the Universe!*
*Thou Soul that art the eternity of thought,*
*That givest to forms and images a breath*
*And everlasting motion.*
[I, 401-404]

Implicit in this vision of a supranatural Spirit are the age-old philosophical concepts of being and becoming. Wordsworth's Spirit is the eternal sustainer of the universe, immutable in its essential nature, but always changing in that it is in a constant, creative motion and flux. It cannot rest immobile or static. It is a kaleidoscopic movement always emerging in new and fresh patterns but always composed of the same permanent essence of life. The years of Wordsworth's greatest creativity are dominated by the mode of becoming in the eternal motion of the universal Spirit. He felt this motion of Spirit stirring through nature and all things. Consequently, his metaphysical thought emphasized the immanence of Spirit in nature. Later as Wordsworth's mystical powers gave way to a more conceptual frame of mind, this sense of the vital, dynamic ebbing and flowing of Spirit around him also gave way to a more fixed conception of the transcendence of God in all things and of the divine immutability.

Wordsworth's vision of God's immanence in nature cannot justifiably be passed off as pantheism. It is never the rocks, trees, rivers, flowers themselves that are univocally identified as the intuited Spirit. Rather he sees an encounter of nature with Spirit resulting in life, energy, growth, and fertility. Theologically, Wordsworth's preoccupation with God's immanental manifestations reflects no more than the natural and logical end of the Christian doctrine of divine omnipresence.

Lewis's interest in this regard makes an interesting contrast to Wordsworth because, though he never quite seems to approach Wordsworth's immanental immersion in Spirit, he emphasizes vividly that human spirit does confront the reality of divine Spirit. When this occurs, the effect on human personality is always a dramatic transformation. Nowhere does Lewis portray more vividly this transforming impact of God on man than in his chapter in *That Hideous Strength* on "The Descent of the Gods." It happens suddenly that Glund-Oyarsa (Lewis's mythical theomorphism of Divine Majesty) appears to Ransom in the blue room of the spacious house inhabited by himself and his few followers. The effects are immediate. Those who are waiting in the kitchen begin naturally to dance, leaping high, gracefully, beautifully. Lewis describes the aura:

> It seemed to each that the room was filled with kings and queens, that the wildness of their dance expressed heroic energy and its quieter movements had seized the very spirit behind all noble ceremonies.[6]

Upstairs in the blue room the immediate presence of Glund-

[6] C. S. Lewis, *That Hideous Strength* (New York, 1946), p. 387.

Oyarsa fills the room with a blazing furnace of light. Before this radiant intensity of Spirit man must perish or be metamorphosed to a higher existence in order to bear the piercing reality of the divine presence. If he does anything in his transfiguration, he must laugh with absolute joy, for such is the infinitely exhilarating effect of the divine presence on human personality. And as for Glund-Oyarsa himself,

> Kingship and power and festal pomp and courtesy shot from him as sparks fly from an anvil. The pealing of bells, the blowing of trumpets, the spreading out of banners, are means used on earth to make a faint symbol of his quality. It was like a long sunlit wave, creamy-crested and arched with emerald, that comes on nine feet tall, with roaring and with terror and unquenchable laughter. . . . For this was great Glund-Oyarsa, King of Kings, through whom the joy of creation principally blows across these fields of Arbol [p. 387].

If for Wordsworth sensations of Spirit come to man from nature and find a córroborating affinity with his own spirit within the mind, for Lewis the impact of absolute Spirit is to raise man to a higher, mythological level. It is a renovation of man's natural being into the godlike echelon of life. For Wordsworth transcendental consciousness actualizes the inherent potential for goodness in man, intensifying his perspicacity of soul and energizing it to communicate its depth more creatively. But for Lewis the divine Spirit imparts godlikeness *to* man. This is an important distinction between Wordsworth's metaphysics and that of Lewis. Wordsworth, especially in his years of poetic power, held to the inherent goodness of human nature and believed devoutly in its perfectibility. But Lewis recognizes in man a fundamental moral and psychological alienation from God and godlike existence.

This basic difference in viewpoint figures largely in the metaphysical development of both men. Wordsworth perhaps thought human nature to be inherently good because of his own sublime accomplishments. He admits in *The Prelude* that his early circumstances were favorable to the development of a positive view of man because he was sheltered from many of the evils of society:

> *first I looked*
> *At man through objects that were great or fair;*
> *First communed with him by their help. And thus*
> *Was founded a sure safeguard and defense*
> *Against the weight of meanness, selfish cares,*
> *Coarse manners, vulgar passions, that beat in*
> *On all sides from the ordinary world.*
> [VIII, 315-321]

Coupled with this early affirmation of man's goodness was Wordsworth's abundant confidence in the human mind. He believed all men would respond positively to life if given the freedom to do so. Like most men of genius he hated to regard himself as a man of extraordinary endowments. He always identified with the common man and empathized deeply with his concerns. Doubtless he hypostatized many of his lofty ideals in men of lesser mind who in reality could scarcely have comprehended them. Newton P. Stallknecht in his brief essay, "The Tragic Flaw in Wordsworth's Philosophy,"[7] has assessed Wordsworth's view of man as a basic inadequacy in his thought. While he looked on the common man as the exponent of goodness and strength of character, Wordsworth looked with suspicion on leaders and rulers because he assumed that only despots would seek ascendancy over other men. Influenced by the catastrophic events of the French Revolution, Wordsworth came to believe that evil and tyranny in the world were the result of powerful men seeking sovereignty and position over their fellow man. He refused to accept the fact that some men are endowed with superior abilities which legitimate their desire to rule and give order to society. This ultimately led him to an archconservatism and a resistance to any of those moved to revolt against the status quo. This amounted to a denial of any philosophy of revolution or even of liberal change. In his later years Wordsworth came to deny his romantic philosophy of self-realization embodied in *The Prelude* and to adopt the stiff moral imperatives of allegiance to duty and God as shown in his "Ode to Duty." It is perhaps significant that with the development of his conservatism, his poetic creativity diminished accordingly. It is also an irony that his belief in the inherent goodness of man should have resulted in such support for the existing social hierarchy in England at that time — a hierarchy that hardly lent credence to this conviction. More significantly this myopia prevented Wordsworth from penetrating to a vision of the tragic source of evil and alienation in the world.

Despite this flaw Wordsworth was sensibly aware of man's suffering and estrangement in the universe. He repeatedly decried all enslavement and servitude to artificial codes and institutions and lamented man's tragic loss of freedom and spontaneity under society's heavy-handed conventions. He attributed such evil to the abuse of natural instincts which in themselves are good. This, of course, did not solve the problem of why any

[7] In *Wordsworth and Coleridge,* ed. Earl Leslie Griggs (Princeton, 1939), pp. 47-61.

man should be moved to such abuse; or, in other words of the origin of evil. One senses this ironic helplessness as he reads:

*Little we see in Nature that is ours;*
*We have given our hearts away, a sordid boon!*
*This sea that bares her bosom to the moon;*
*The winds that will be howling at all hours,*
*And are up-gathered now like sleeping flowers;*
*For this, for everything, we are out of tune.*[8]

Wordsworth's remedy for such estrangement is to immerse oneself in nature and respond to the vivid communication of beauty through the senses. Thus one may be receptive to the intuitions of the universal Spirit through the stimulated imagination. But the testimony of his later life is that intuition fades, the glory that pervades nature dims, and the imagination must resort to finding

*Strength in what remains behind;*
*In the primal sympathy*
*Which having been must ever be;*
. . . . . . . . . . . . . . . .
*In the faith that looks through death,*
*In years that bring the philosophic mind.*[9]

Such words indicate that Wordsworth's romantic vision of man's receptivity to nature and his spiritual response to the intuited ontological reality is still somewhat vitiated by his inadequate reconciliation with the problem of evil.

Lewis's more Christian vision provides a firmer solution to the problem of evil both metaphysically and existentially. Lewis recognizes in man a condition of moral separation from God. He is inherently evil although he retains a vestige of his primordial *Imago Dei.* He no longer lives as a creature in divine freedom. In his allegorical fantasy *Out of the Silent Planet* Lewis illustrates his position with great metaphorical clarity. He relates allegorically how the spirit of earth rebelled against the Great Spirit of Deep Heaven and became bent. In this condition the Bent One led man to rebel against the decrees of Maleldil, the Great Oyarsa, and man too became bent. This bentness fastened itself to earth. The planet was silenced, and has been out of touch with the universe ever since. On earth bentness passed on all creatures, and man became a grasping instead of a giving personality. To continue the metaphor, if man is to regain his former existence, he must be straightened out. Wordsworth

[8] "The world is too much with us," 3ff.

[9] "Ode: Intimations of Immortality from Recollections of Early Childhood," xi.

has no such concept. To him man is already straight, and the occurrence of evil is simply due to a faulty juxtaposition of individuals within the framework of society. But following through in his Christian doctrine, Lewis affirms the need for the Incarnation and the work of Christ to transfigure man's bentness and bring him into tune again with nature and essential being. To experience such transfiguration Lewis insists that an individual must in faith release his monomanias of self-interest and surrender himself to the Spirit of God. He writes thus of his own conversion:

> I had always wanted, above all things, not to be "interfered with." I had wanted (mad wish) "to call my soul my own." I had been far more anxious to avoid suffering than to achieve delight. . . . But now . . . what might not be expected of one? . . . Not the slightest assurance on that score was offered me. Total surrender, the absolute leap in the dark, were demanded. The reality with which no treaty can be made was upon me. . . . Now, the demand was simply "All" [*Surprised by Joy*, p. 228].

In all Lewis's illuminating descriptions of characters confronting this crisis of spiritual transfiguration the struggle is much the same, entailing the necessity to let go of one's own petty desires and trivial preoccupations, to surrender oneself up to absolute love, to choose to let the final vision of reality remove from one's clutching grasp all the lesser realities narcissistically clung to with such fractionalizing effects. When such hindrances are put aside and consumed by the divine Spirit, the "pilgrim" can begin his "regress" back to God and to a realization of his own mythical essence. For Lewis there is no other means to the real other than surrender to the "glory of God in the face of Jesus Christ" (II Corinthians 4:6). Only thus can man recover his true godlike existence. In his own words —"The hardness of God is kinder than the softness of men, and His compulsion is our liberation."[10] Thus it is, that when Psyche leads Orual to meet her Prince by the pillars before the pool *(Till We Have Faces)*, Orual finds the exuberant joy of surrender to unconditioned love as the Prince approaches in all his divine luminosity. She bows her head in humility and sees to her surprise that her reflection in the pool is not of the old ugly Orual but of another beautiful Psyche. Surrender to Love Himself has transformed her existence. The veil has been removed. Her godlike existence is recovered and her myth made concrete in her life.

Having seen the central position of the unconditioned Spirit in the metaphysical thought of both Wordsworth and Lewis and

[10] *Surprised by Joy*, p. 229.

how both men viewed the nature of man and his relationship to the Spirit, we must now broaden our scope and examine the visionary character of the universe both men inhabit. To retain the perspective of comparison we turn our attention again to Wordsworth.

In Wordsworth's *Weltanschauung* there is a strong anthropocentric emphasis. He sees everything, nature and Spirit, in its bearing upon man and his experience. In human experience infinity and concreteness are merged and find their synthesized expression in creative imagination. In turn through creative imagination the universe becomes available to man — a spiritual abyss of infinite possibilities for words, music, and mystical intuitions of power, motion, and joy; the dynamics of romantic self-transcendence. Such is

*a mind*
*That feeds upon infinity, that broods*
*Over the dark abyss, intent to hear*
*Its voices issuing forth to silent light*
*In continuous stream.*
[XIV, 70-74]

The "voices" or intuitions that emerge from this abyss constitute the creative imagination in its full power: as this power arises "from the mind's abyss/Like an unfathered vapour that enwraps" (VI, 594f.) the entire field of consciousness, the mystical apperception of ontological reality is brought fully into one's mind, and one's imagination is elevated to a participation in unconditioned being. It becomes imbued with the same inexorable fecundity, taking on such creative energies that

*They from their native selves can send abroad*
*Kindred mutations; for themselves create*
*A like existence. . . .*
. . . . . . . . . . . . . .
*. . . they build up greatest things*
*From least suggestions; ever on the watch,*
*Willing to work and to be wrought upon,*
*They need not extraordinary calls*
*To rouse them; in a world of life they live,*
*By sensible impressions not enthralled,*
*But by their quickening impulse made more prompt*
*To hold fit converse with the spiritual world.*
[XIV, 93-95, 101-108]

This describes the mode Wordsworth holds to be the human aptitude for godlikeness. Imagination awakened and intensified in creative action: thus is man brought to his fulfillment. There is no tragic moral barrier to be overcome as there is in Lewis.

There is simply a self-reliant resort to natural spontaneity and powerful emotive response to nature, man, and God. The identification of the individual's human spirit in the spiritual universe is grasped in creative imagination.

Through imagination Wordsworth's *Weltanschauung* becomes a diverse and colorful environment characterized by activities of motion, change, growth and the ebb and flow of energy. It is made living by the immanent Spirit that "rolls through all things."[11] It is a pageantry of life in which man is vitally involved through his perceptions, feelings, and sympathetic participation in the life processes of nature. Wordsworth is convinced that his vitalistic epistemology bears within itself the panacea for man's ills:

*Ye motions of delight, that haunt the sides*
*Of the green hills; ye breezes and soft airs,*
*Whose subtle intercourse with breathing flowers,*
*Feelingly watched, might teach Man's haughty race*
*How without injury to take, to give*
*Without offense.*

[XII, 9-14]

Oscar Campbell has pointed out that for Wordsworth man's awareness of his own appointed place in a universe so qualified by mutability is found in his aesthetic experience. It is when he finds a common identity between his intuitions of unconditioned being and his sensory perceptions of the same presence redolent in nature that aesthetic experience lifts man above the apparent mutability of nature and emancipates him "from the world of eye and ear, and also from his ties with his fellow men. Wordsworth's political and social conservatism was thus a natural result of his deeply felt independence of all manifestations of mutability."[12]

A further aspect that must be noted about Wordsworth's universe is his treatment of the freedom-necessity paradox. It is significant that Wordsworth's passion for freedom and liberty as voiced so powerfully in such sonnets as "It is not to be thought of" and "Thought of a Briton on the Subjugation of Switzerland" is balanced consistently by a concept of philosophic necessity. In Wordsworth's romanticism it is the *élan vital* that is the determining agency in human destiny. This is an evident meaning in the "motion and a spirit, that impels/All thinking things,"[13] for it

11 "Tintern Abbey," 102.

12 Oscar Campbell, "Wordsworth's Conception of the Esthetic Experience," in Griggs, p. 45.

13 "Tintern Abbey," 100-101.

is the impelling spirit that creates human fortunes. His treatment of the paradox is stated clearly in the following excerpt from Book IV of *The Excursion* (1264-70):

*So build we up the Being that we are;*
*Thus deeply drinking-in the soul of things,*
*We shall be wise perforce; and, while inspired*
*By choice, and conscious that the Will is free,*
*Shall move unswerving, even as if impelled*
*By strict necessity, along the path*
*Of order and of good.*

It is evident here that Wordsworth seeks to reconcile free will and necessity by identifying them both as differentiated modes of the creative Spirit that sustains the universe. To participate in the *élan vital* is to be at once both free and predestined, for freedom means to Wordsworth living in harmony with nature much as Spinoza predicated. Tyranny and oppression are not modes of necessity to be passively accepted, however. They are evils to be resisted since they disrupt the harmony and wholeness of society.

A fourth aspect of Wordsworth's *Weltanschauung,* one frequently noted, has been called his preexistence theory. The clearest statement of it is in his famous "Ode: Intimations of Immortality from Recollections of Early Childhood" and appears to be based rather closely on Plato's theory of prenatal existence. As Wordsworth looks back on life he remembers how in his childhood years nature seemed imbued with a special radiance and splendor which faded with the onset of years and adult responsibilities. With advancing age the glory of infancy and youth was extinguished — a glory of childhood's vivid sense perceptions when sense and soul seemed to him to be a single, undifferentiated radiant consciousness. Wordsworth believed that such heightened sensibility is smothered to a large extent by social conventions, expectancies, institutions, and pragmatics, "A wedding or a festival,/A mourning or a funeral" (93-94). He found himself in his more advanced and forlorn years to be cast on philosophic reflection as a means to recover the lost glory of his existence.

To explain this phenomenon that he experienced, he asserted that the soul of man partakes of the same spiritual essence as does the divine Spirit and that in birth the human individual soul leaves the cosmic oversoul, as it were, and incarcerates itself in the infant. Infancy and childhood are more freshly animated by the life of the divine Spirit. Before the desiccated conventions of adulthood smother this divine animation, the child experiences the glories of a godlike perceptibility and receptivity to nature.

Memory of preexistence is almost, but not quite, obliterated by the infant mentality.

*Not in entire forgetfulness,*
*And not in utter nakedness,*
*But trailing clouds of glory do we come*
*From God, who is our home.*
[62-65]

Wordsworth has been criticized for this transcendentalist view of immortality, probably more than is warranted since he never meant to defend it as a religious dogma. The obvious pantheistic tendencies entailed by the concept Wordsworth did in fact later try to avoid when he said,

> It is far too shadowy a notion to be recommended to faith as more than an element in our instincts of immortality. [But] there is nothing in Revelation to contradict it, and the fall of man presents an analogy in its favour. A pre-existent state has entered into the popular creeds of many nations. . . . I took hold of the notion of pre-existence as having sufficient foundation in humanity for authorizing me to make for my purpose the best use I could of it as a Poet.[14]

This is certainly a cautious apology, perhaps too cautious, for Wordsworth's theory of immortality fit in quite well with other tenets of his metaphysical thought. He believed in God as an absolute, spiritual life full of vital energy, motion, and creativity, or in ontological terminology, as the ground of being to all manifestations of life in the universe. An individual human existence is a standing out from this ontological ground both objective to and participating in the ground. In the dawn of the individual's life he manifests that pristine purity of the Spirit from which all forms of life derive their source. He is not estranged from this source because of depraved existence; estrangement is an aftereffect. Thus, theologically speaking Wordsworth's view of immortality equates the *Imago Dei* with human nature. Man enters the world and actual existence directly from the form-giving essence of the divinc Spirit. Spiritual fractionalization occurs only later, as a result of deplorable practices assumed as part of adult socialization patterns and adaption to the pragmatic necessities of life. As in the rest of his philosophy, human being is related to divine Being directly, spontaneously, intuitively. The exuberant joy of childhood is an existential proof of it.

Lewis's grasp of the universe stands as a remarkable complement to Wordsworth's view. The reaches of space are no longer quite the vast, spiritual symbol of the imaginative infinite

[14] Quoted by Helen Darbishire, *The Poet Wordsworth* (Oxford, 1950), p. 65.

that they are for Wordsworth. Rather, in Lewis's writings we find a startling synthesis of the actual and the spiritual universes harmonized in the mythopoeic mode. For Lewis the realm of stars and suns is the realm where myth and reality are merged absolutely in a kind of mythic belief. The universe described in the trilogy finds earth isolated from the cosmic reaches of the heavens, cut off from the celestial abodes by the Fall of man and Satan. This is why the universe appears so appalling and hostile to man, because it is of an unconditioned order — an order so intense that man in his natural state cannot bear to exist under its conditions. This unfitness of man for the divine order is vividly portrayed in *The Great Divorce.* The ghosts up from Hell for a visit hobble around painfully on the grassy fields in front of Heaven unable to find comfort because the solid heavenly reality of the grass and rocks pierces the less real phantom substance of their ghostly bodies. Unlike Wordsworth, Lewis believes that a real ontological cleavage exists between the human order and the divine order. Man must be unbent, reoriented psychologically and recreated spiritually before he can freely participate in the divine order of being. The belief in man's need for spiritual regeneration to overcome the cleavage between earthly existence and divine essence is a central difference between the romantic visions of Wordsworth and Lewis.

In other ways, though, their visions are similar. For Lewis the universe is a panoply of light, beauty, individuated living personalities, struggle, love, and sinister evils. Away from earth there is a Wordsworthian harmony. No sooner, for example, does Ransom leave the silent planet Earth, than he awakens to the fluid warmness and astonishingly intimate glories of the celestial panorama. The host of stars before his eyes beam brilliantly like a field of sapphires shining in puissant splendor. The sun is a blazing bath of ethereal glory and the universe stretches out rapt in a warmth of harmony and joy. Ransom senses the exhilaration and realizes suddenly how different space has become to him:

> Now . . . the very name "Space" seemed a blasphemous libel for this empyrean ocean of radiance in which they swam. He could not call it "dead"; he felt life pouring into him from it every moment. How indeed should it be otherwise, since out of this ocean the worlds and all their life had come? He had thought it barren: he saw now that it was the womb of worlds, whose blazing and innumerable offspring looked down nightly even upon the earth with so many eyes.[15]

It is evident that Lewis here is looking on space much as Words-

[15] C. S. Lewis, *Out of the Silent Planet* (New York, 1946), p. 29.

worth looked on nature. Where Wordsworth finds a "splendour in the grass," a "glory in the flower,"[16] Lewis sees a similar resplendency in the cosmos; but where focussed on earthly nature, Lewis speaks of a warped perception, one allowing only shades and flashes of the essential glory to meet the eyes. Earthly perception for him is truncated by its dependence on only five senses, by the physiological limitations of mere nerves and synaptical connections, and by the manner in which causal necessity habituates responses, channelling perception into dull, repetitive orbits.

Lewis's mythopoeic approach to theology with his emphasis on the total transcendence of God offers a remarkable contrast to Wordsworth's immanental viewpoint, while the end result is much the same. As might be expected Lewis has not just a broad, categorical Spirit present in the universe, but myriads of spirit personalities with whom "light is instead of blood."[17] They are, of course, much like the angels and spirits of Scripture, powers and forces of divine being. Lewis believes in a heavenly hierarchy too. There are eldils who seem to be local, geographical spirits. There are Oyarsas — spirits who seem to dominate an entire celestial body (Satan is the Oyarsa of earth). There is, finally, Almighty God, who is known as the great Maleldil. To Lewis the *eldila* constitute a representation of divine existence, unfettered freedom in the spiritual hierarchy. They are bigger beings in a metaphysical sense than men, in that they operate on a higher ontological frequency than mortals are attuned to. This is the reason they appear invisible or phantom-like to men just as men do to them. They are beautiful, strong, ebullient — real gods, mythical beings more real perhaps to Lewis than corporeal beings. Traditionally man fears them as shadowbrutes when in actuality they are handsome Cupids rippling with Herculean muscles and sinews and radiant with heavenly well-being. The universe is their playfield — the Solar System a mere "indoor affair."[18] All exist and coexist in the cosmic harmonics for the purpose of glorifying the Creator, the great Maleldil.

Maleldil is for Lewis the unconditioned, eternally creative Spirit whose nature and will direct the universe in its freedom. We have already emphasized that Lewis is forcibly impressed by the doctrine of total divine transcendence. While for Wordsworth God was primarily a subjective perception, Lewis starts by viewing God as an objective fact to be dealt with. Neither

16 "Ode: Intimations of Immortality," 182.
17 *Out of the Silent Planet*, p. 129.
18 C. S. Lewis, *The Great Divorce* (New York, 1946), p. 18.

viewpoint seems complete in itself, for throughout history man has confronted God in both modes. So it is significant that both writers reach the opposite perspective at some point in their romantic vision. This progression is evident in Wordsworth's poem "Ode to Duty," where he speaks of the Deity's exalted and elevated position; and Lewis reaches the perspective of the divine immanence in one of literature's most profound and sublime passages — the final chapter of *Perelandra.* Here Ransom is given a vision of the essential nature of Maleldil's plan and purpose in the universe. It is presented as a kind of epiphanic panegyric to Maleldil, and in it the subjective and objective modes of perceiving the divine reality are united to evoke a grand sense of universal participation — a participation in Maleldil's Great Dance which fills the universe with a great, gay, ringing diversity and the unchanging refrain "Blessed be He!" Here God, the supreme object, becomes the vital subject. He is at once both the center and circumference, the Creator and Consummator, the rhythm and the harmony of the Dance.

> He thought he saw the Great Dance. It seemed to be woven out of the intertwining undulation of many cords or bands of light, leaping over and under one another and mutually embraced in arabesques and flower-like subtleties . . . wherever the ribbons or serpents of light intersected, minute corpuscles of momentary brightness: and he knew somehow that these particles were the secular generalities of which history tells — peoples, institutions, . . . arts, sciences, and the like — ephemeral coruscations that piped their short song and vanished [p. 218].

And amidst the rush and sweep of the Dance comes the moment of supreme immanence.

> Where Maleldil is, there is the centre. He is in every place. Not some of Him in one place and some in another, but in each place the whole Maleldil, even in the smallness beyond thought. There is no way out of the centre save into the Bent Will which casts itself into the Nowhere. Blessed be He!
>
> Each thing was made for Him. He is the centre. . . . Each thing, from the single grain of Dust to the strongest eldil, is the end and the final cause of all creation and the mirror in which the beam of His brightness comes to rest and so returns to Him. Blessed be He! [pp. 216f.]

In such sublime terms Lewis evokes the activity of God in and through all creation. Being and becoming are fused and woven together in this exalted metaphysical vision. Vitalism — the metaphysic of becoming — is lambent in the constant motion, continual eruption of energy, the seething turmoil of varying patterns ebbing and flowing, waxing and waning, never repeating itself twice, all consummated in the kaleidoscopic nature of the creative spirit. Yet, the underlying permanence, the immutable transcendence of the Creator is not forgotten. Always, he remains Maleldil, the objective supreme essence and presence of (as Lewis might say) Being Himself. Here the divine immutability subsumes the constant evolution of change, the persistent burgeoning forth of wave upon wave of creative love. In this the divine Spirit never ceases to express its absolute and unconditioned character while its infinite resources never permit monotony or repetition to tarnish the freshness of its self-expression. Its manifestations are always new, and in this aspect Wordsworth and Lewis meet in one accord. This spontaneous freedom and self-expression are part of the godlike existence they both envision. Both affirm that man is never truly free until his individuated spirit partakes of the freedom of the divine Spirit. Only thus may his essential freedom be actualized.

But Lewis goes on to impress us with another of his fascinating metaphysical convictions. This is his concept of transcendental genders — something to which Wordsworth has no real corollary. Lewis intuits the nature of being to be composed of macrocosmic modalities of masculinity and femininity and even of other genders beyond human analogy. Lewis is careful to note that he does not conceive of these universal genders as rooted in the biological level of male and female. He believes that such organic distinctions are mere expressions physiologically of higher and broader modalities inclusive of far more than just sex. They are more like primordial characterological syndromes expressing and venting the fundamental, ontological feelings abroad in the universe. What we know as male and female are only partly expressive of their respective genders since man's fallen nature and corrupted perception never render a clear picture of the harmonious complementation that exists between the genders essentially. This distorted perception results in much disorder, sorrow, and evil in the human order, and such problems as marital tensions, divorce, jealousy, possessiveness, rage, and hatred are due to a misunderstanding of the complementation existent between the genders. Lewis is developing this point in *That Hideous Strength* when Jane discusses her strained relationship to Mark, her husband. Ransom tells her:

> Your trouble has been . . . Pride. You are offended by the masculine itself: the loud, irruptive, possessive thing — the gold lion, the bearded bull. . . . The male you could have escaped, for it exists only on the biological level. But the masculine none of us can escape. What is above and beyond all things is so masculine that we are all feminine in relation to it [p. 374].

Lewis ascribes gender to all spirited personalities and points out in *That Hideous Strength* (p. 385) that there are seven genders in his scheme of things, two of which are somewhat understandable to men as they bear a direct analogy to the biological sexes. (His number seven may be derived from the mention of seven spirits of God in Revelation 5:6.) The concept of cosmic genders makes Lewis's treatment of spiritual harmony more profound and heterogeneous than Wordsworth's, and it should be noted in passing that Lewis thus achieves a deeper cognitive identification with universal harmony than does Wordsworth, who never pursued to any extent his reflections on the nature of harmony itself.

Science — or at least its eternal companion, scientism — has always been a beam in the romantic's eye. It is not surprising, therefore, to find Wordsworth and Lewis sharing similar views on science, and particularly on the universal claims of its methodology. Both men opposed science as a means of grasping the ultimate values and metaphysical truths of life. This opposition for both men seems to be based on the vitalist assumption that scientific methodology perceives only quantitative values and disregards qualitative ones. Science immobilizes reality and isolates it from the continuum of life for purposes of observation and measurement; and in so doing, it falsifies reality to the extent of achieving only a relative, pragmatic knowledge as opposed to its absolute claims of verifiability. Moreover, the knowledge gained by science appears to the vitalist-romantic to be rather irrelevant to the deep, primary intuitions of qualitative value that he experiences. In this light Wordsworth's attitude toward science in the following lines is quite understandable.

*Science appears but what in truth she is,*
. . . . . . . . . . . . . . . .
*. . . a succedaneum, and a prop*
*To our infirmity. . . .*
*. . . that false secondary power*
*By which we multiply distinctions, then*
*Deem that our puny boundaries are things*
*That we perceive, and not that we have made.*
[II, 212-219]

Lewis is just as outspoken against science as a method of gaining metaphysical knowledge as is Wordsworth. This is, in fact, a central theme of *That Hideous Strength* — the hideous strength being a godless scientism striving to gain knowledge of absolute existence through the creation of a super-brain of suprahuman powers. Lewis fears the tendency in science to reduce all reality, even the complex processes of thought, to objective, mathematical facts which can be tested against each other, rearranged, and manipulated to produce calculated results. A power such as this could, he believes, emasculate human nature and leave it barren of existential, creative power and spiritual meaning. Should spiritual and emotional experiences come under a manipulative, outside control through artificial stimuli, human nature would then have to be reconditioned to complete objectivity. To illustrate this, Lewis has Frost, the N.I.C.E. scientist, explain to Mark Studdock why

> a systematic training in objectivity must be given to you. Its purpose is to eliminate from your mind one by one the things you have hitherto regarded as grounds for action. It is like killing a nerve. That whole system of instinctive preferences, whatever ethical, aesthetic, or logical disguise they wear, is to be simply destroyed [p. 350].

This description aptly demonstrates Lewis's bias against science in general.[19] Such objectifying of spiritual faculties undermines the whole basis of Lewis's metaphysics of value. In fairness to Lewis it should also be noted that he has no quarrel with a science that confines its activities to the study of natural phenomena, but both he and Wordsworth are united in their opposition to a science that presumes to impose its methods on metaphysical questions.

Wordsworth even proceeds to consign the existence of social evils to the nefarious effects of scientific reasoning. It was his conviction that when man imposes his rational problem-solving thought-processes onto the spontaneous and subjective responses that he feels coming to him from nature and the mind, he dissolves his own freedom and subjects himself to the heteronomous control of conventions and institutions. As the individual learns conformity and imitation, his imagination is smothered by the vicious education. He is left insensitive to the presence of Spirit in nature and himself, and more and more he is led to depend on intellect to structure his behavior. Thus, man is alienated from a creative union with the divine Spirit and left to his own devices; he inevitably ends up being "confounded, more and more misguided, and misguiding . . . dragging all precepts, judgements, maxims, creeds, like culprits to the bar" (XI, 292-295). In short, he considers scientific reasoning an evil insofar as it builds up an antipathy toward intuitional participation in the life process, which is his basis for a metaphysics of value.

Lewis attributes the source of evil in the world to man's rebellion in freedom against God's moral purposes in creation.

[19] Philip Deasy, "God, Space, and C. S. Lewis," *Commonweal*, LXVIII (July 25, 1958), 422.

But he agrees with Wordsworth that reason alone produces a damning objectivity, cold, stark and bereft of value. Reason is a primary value for Lewis, but it must be founded on man's essential spirituality and his consciousness of reason's subjective roots. If intellect ignores man's spiritual nature, then it becomes materialistic and inevitably sets out to become God and fashion its own universe. With this insight, then, Lewis's consideration of good and evil takes on a historical perspective. It appears to be a kind of evolutionary view of good and evil, for in his thinking,

> Evolution means species getting less and less like one another. Minds get more and more spiritual, matter more and more material. Even in literature poetry and prose draw further and further apart.[20]

This burgeoning pattern of evolution is a continual splitting up of and diversification of reality, much like a tree's branches split off into smaller and more numerous branches the higher one goes. The evolution proceeds from unity toward ever greater differentiation and specialization. Accordingly, Lewis believes that good becomes better, more distinct, more clearly defined just as evil becomes more hideous, more distantly bifurcated from goodness and more diabolic. "Good, as it ripens, becomes continually more different not only from evil but from other good."[21] This position has two noteworthy metaphysical implications: the first is that it seems to presuppose a primordial neutrality as a source of the original unity, a kind of subconscious cosmos. Differentiation began with the advent of human self-consciousness. Lewis describes in *The Problem of Pain*[22] how in the ontological evolution man was prepared by God through long ages of time to assume the scope and burden of human self-consciousness. He envisions the primordial entrance of man into the divine cosmos of freedom, and witnesses again his tragic rebellion which plunged man into the curse of selfishness, where the first bifurcation of good and evil took place. In the immediately ensuing generations of history the distinction between good and evil was still blurred. "Mental processes were much more physical actions."[23] Merlin in *That Hideous Strength* is Lewis's resurrected prototype of the old order in which the distinction between spirit and matter was still confused. The second important implication this theory has for Lewis is his predication that evil cannot be transmuted into good. It can only be rectified by tracing it back to the original decision that perpetrated it and by reversing the

[20] *That Hideous Strength,* p. 334.
[21] *The Great Divorce,* p. vi.
[22] (London and Glasgow, 1957), pp. 65-72.
[23] *That Hideous Strength,* p. 335.

decision. Evil must be expunged at its source. In *The Great Divorce* we find case histories of individuals confronted with the opportunity to go back to the source of their evil; and by allowing the divine Grace to purge away their original decision through pain, they are allowed to enter into glory. Hell, Lewis maintains, can become Purgatory to anyone willing to be purged of monomania and to surrender to the divine Glory.

In the final synthesis of their visions both Wordsworth and Lewis find love to be the unifying power of the universe. It is love that brings together spirit and matter into creative, godlike existence. Wordsworth says simply, "By love subsists/All lasting grandeur" (XIV, 168f.), and then goes on to assert that only love can achieve that ultimate union between man and the unconditioned Spirit —

*love that breathes not without awe;*
*Love that adores, but on the knees of prayer,*
*By heaven inspired; that frees from chains the soul,*
*Lifted, in union with the purest, best,*
*Of earth-born passions, on the wings of praise*
*Bearing a tribute to the Almighty's Throne.*
[XIV, 182-187]

Wordsworth believed such spiritual love to be wholly contingent upon the creative imagination for its power and content. It was for him the supreme expression of Spirit, emanating from the eternal Spirit to meet the kindled imagination of man and meld all things into an effusion of joy and harmony. Lewis holds similarly that the function of love is to reunite the ontologically separated; but for him more perhaps than for Wordsworth love is distinctly a transfiguring hypostatization of personality in its godlike being. He always identifies love with a person who has been spiritually liberated. In *That Hideous Strength* love comes in the personality of Perelandra or Venus, its more than mythical embodiment, who restores Ransom's followers to godlike being.

> Perelandra is all about us and Man is no longer isolated. We are now as we ought to be — between the angels who are our elder brothers and the beasts who are our jesters, servants and playfellows [p. 453].

Or, as in *The Great Divorce* we find the heavenly Lady telling her earthly lover the dwarf,

> I am full now, not empty. I am in Love Himself, not lonely. Strong, not weak. You shall be the same. Come and see. We shall have no *need* for one another now: we can begin to love truly [p. 116].

This affirmation of love beyond need becomes the perfect fulfillment of all possible need. It strengthens what is weak, makes whole what is wanting, sheds joy on what is mournful. It has no trace of grasping, is not based on craving, but is courted by exuberance and sheer bounty. Thus, Lewis writes of Maleldil that he is at once "infinitely necessary" and "infinitely superfluous."[24] Of his sufficiency there is no lack; of his plenty no end.

In conclusion we would note that Lewis's road to metaphysical maturity was longer and harder than Wordsworth's. Lewis pursued the fleeting glimpse of transcendental joy throughout a lifetime of increasing perception and creativity. His childhood vision drove him on until at last the elusive joy was realized for him in his unique synthesis of Christianity and romantic myth creation. Furthermore, there is no doubt that Lewis had the benefit of Wordsworth's wisdom and through it expanded the depth and embrace of his own romantic vision. As he himself acknowledged in later years, "*The Prelude* has accompanied me through all the long stages of my pilgrimage: it and the *Aeneid* . . . are the two long poems to which I most often return."[25] Wordsworth's romanticism, by contrast, was noted for its enigmatic failure in his later years. His teeming intuitions waned with age and left him bereft and without creative power. That loss he seems to have anticipated even while writing one of his greatest lyrics, the "Immortality" ode.

> *The things which I have seen I now can see no more.*
> . . . . . . . . . . . . . . . . . . .
> *Whither is fled the visionary gleam?*
> *Where is it now, the glory and the dream?*

These words bear eloquent testimony to the final inadequacy of an anthropocentric romanticism with its easy recourse to human intuition and feeling. For, as Wordsworth found, feelings are capricious and indeterminate: when undisciplined by a creative reason, they often vanish when they are most required. Wordsworth's romanticism failed in that it did not reveal an objective overcoming of man's tragic conflict between being and nonbeing. Lewis, however, can say on the final page of his autobiography, "I cannot indeed, complain, like Wordsworth, that the visionary gleam has passed away." Lewis's vision, founded in the truths of Christian revelation, led him to hope for the future and joy in his day-to-day life. His faith sought to reunite man with a power transcendent to himself — he was caught up in its ebullient stride, its dashing panoply of life, light, love and spirit, its penetrating joy — the joy of the absolute.

[24] *Perelandra*, p. 217.
[25] *Letters of C. S. Lewis*, ed. W. H. Lewis (London, 1966), p. 228.

# The Fantastic Imagination in George MacDonald

GLENN EDWARD SADLER

"...*A Spirit seemed*
*To stand beside him*..."
—Shelley's Alastor[1]

It was in Clyde Kilby's spring class on Romanticism, I think, that I first entered the "undulating woods" of Shelley's *Alastor*. That particular class session started with a devotional reading from C. S. Lewis's *George MacDonald: An Anthology* (1946). Vividly I recall one student's persistent exposure of Wordsworth's so-called pantheism and another's ecstatic appraisal of "Ode to the West Wind." (Both students received a generous and modest reply.) But it was Mistress North Wind who had, unknowingly then, wafted me, with Alastor and Diamond, to her icy blue cave of dreams. Boldly I would soon

[1] MacDonald quotes this section of *Alastor* as his caption for Ch. i of *Phantastes*. *The Complete Poetical Works of Percy Bysshe Shelley*, ed. Thomas Hutchinson (London, 1934), p. 25.

---

Glenn E. Sadler is Assistant Professor of English, Westmont College (Santa Barbara). He received his A.B. from Wheaton College in 1958; his M.A. in English in 1960 from UCLA; and his Ph.D. from the University of Aberdeen, Scotland in 1967. His poetry has appeared in *Christian Life, Eternity Magazine*, the *Aberdeen University Review*, and other journals. Presently he is preparing an edition of the letters of George MacDonald and a full-length study of Charles Williams. He has spoken widely, both in this country and in Britain, on the Oxford Christians and related fantasy writers. He is active in the Mythopoeic Society, a group interested in the Oxford circle. In 1968 he held a postdoctoral Junior Fellowship at Edinburgh University, and he has been nominated for inclusion in the forthcoming edition of the *Dictionary of International Biography*.

walk, in fact, down the narrow granite-set streets of Old Aberdeen, Scotland, where — 125 years ago — George MacDonald listened dreamily to "the sough of the Norlan' Seas" on his way to King's College.

* * *

Because I believe MacDonald to be the nineteenth-century innovator of the current revived interest in fantasy literature, represented by the Oxford Christians[2] and others, I should like to trace the emergence of his Christianized Romantic idea, so admirably rediscovered by C. S. Lewis. In MacDonald's ten-volume *Works of Fancy and Imagination* (1871) we have, it seems to me, the modern beginnings of a fantasy school — if we can suppose that one now exists — which has its mimetic roots in the Blue Flower tradition of the English-German Romantic poets. MacDonald kept that inflorescent dreamland alive. Its youthful enchantments shimmer throughout his *Phantastes* (1858); its apocalyptic wonders flash throughout his old man's vision in *Lilith* (1895). In his two adult spiritual romances MacDonald richly repaid his lifelong debt to his Romantic masters.

Frequently I have tried, without success, to conjure up for myself what Lewis says baptized his imagination "that night" he omnivorously read *Phantastes.* But like all spiritual discoveries, this MacDonaldesque quality cannot be manufactured; Lewis has called it Holiness.[3] In spite of my failure to experience it in *Phantastes,* I have talked with scores of people — on both sides of the Atlantic (two of whom knew MacDonald) — who claim an almost legendary allegiance to the power his fantasies and novels hold over them. Some heartily confess that his novels, especially *Sir Gibbie,* make them weep; others remember, with childlike trepidation, having felt the spell of his poems ("Baby") and fairytales. "To hear him speak to a snowdrop or a primrose reminded one of Wordsworth," recalls an elderly lady who, as a child, listened to MacDonald spin his native Strathbogie flora into fluttering beings like Anodos's garden carnival of flower-fairies. "For the first time," says Lewis about his encounter with

[2] Significantly Charles Moorman, in his recent study of the image of the city in the writings of Charles Williams, C. S. Lewis, J. R. R. Tolkien, T. S. Eliot, and Dorothy Sayers, concludes: "I think it is possible to maintain that the Oxford Christians most certainly can be described as a literary group and perhaps in days to come as a movement" (*The Precincts of Felicity: The Augustinian City of the Oxford Christians* [Gainesville, 1966], p. 138).

[3] *Surprised by Joy: The Shape of My Early Life* (New York, 1956), p. 179.

*Phantastes*, "the song of the sirens sounded like the voice of my mother or my nurse."[4] He experienced self-identity. In MacDonald's "faerie romance for men and women" Lewis as an adolescent listened passionately to the same chorus of spiritual rivals which faced him in his own imaginative life. Hopefully, he followed Anodos into the dark woods.

In *Surprised by Joy* Lewis tells us that before he was six years old he was seized by an insatiable longing which seemed, like the deep pain of incurable Delight, endless. Following Novalis and MacDonald, he later became "a votary of the Blue Flower."[5] Novalis, describing this romantic sensation, calls it "home-sickness, an impulse to be at home everywhere."[6] For Lewis it meant (among other things) reaching "the Green Hills" of Castlereagh in Ireland, beyond the borders of his brother's toy garden.[7] "It is a climbing and striving," suggests MacDonald, "to reach that point of vision where the multiplex crossings and apparent intertwistings of the lines of fact and feeling and duty shall manifest themselves as a regular and symmetrical design. . . ."[8] For MacDonald there were the "blue hills" of his own Celtic birthplace, surrounding "the little grassy brae" of his "father's house."[9] This religious syndrome of Desire or *Sehnsucht* gave birth to the imagination of all three men. They envisioned it simply as Nature's maternal "home-centre,"[10] where lived the Landlord and his Son, feared by John in Lewis's *Pilgrim's Regress*. MacDonald depicts this archetypal image well in his verse-parable "The Hills":

*For I am always climbing hills,*
*From the known to the unknown—*
*Surely, at last, on some high peak,*
*To find my Father's throne. . . .*[11]

To objectify the spiritual implications of this common Christian scene through natural images and symbols is the central purpose of everything MacDonald and Lewis wrote; it is what kept Anodos in Fairyland.

[4] *Ibid.*
[5] *Ibid.*, p. 7.
[6] Quoted by MacDonald in his essay "Browning's 'Christmas Eve,'" *A Dish of Orts, Chiefly Papers on The Imagination, and on Shakespeare*, enlarged ed. (London, 1893), p. 211.
[7] *Surprised by Joy*, p. 7.
[8] See note 6.
[9] "The Hills," in *The Poetical Works of George MacDonald* (London, 1893), II, 3—hereafter cited as *PW*.
[10] See note 6.
[11] *PW*, II, 4.

*Phantastes,* like most dream romances, is peopled by the disguised inhabitants of the imagination. Its title, taken from Canto vi of Phineas Fletcher's *Purple Island,* and the two lines which MacDonald extracts from it —

> *Phantastes from "their fount" all shapes deriving,*
> *In new habiliments can quickly dight*[12]

— hint at a seething array of semi-material beings, all of which "can quickly dight" themselves before us. We discover a colorful cosmology of talkative (sometimes ornery) garden flower-fairies, greedy and kind tree-spirits, a voluptuous marble maiden, dancing statues, a beautiful-wise old woman, an ominous Shadow, and other lively citizens of Faerie. The eye-catching power of *Phantastes* is derived, at the start, from the speed and smoothness of the transformations and from its teasing symbolism throughout. With wide sweeps MacDonald crosses in Chapter i the "peach-colored" horizon of morning slumber and manages in three short pages in Chapter ii to skillfully shift Anodos ("pathless") from his Victorian bedroom, with its green marble washbasin and heavily carved black oak dresser, to the timeless "path into Fairy Land." Thus Anodos — followed by Lewis's John — leaves the land of Puritania. Both are overcome, however, like Novalis's Hyacinth, by the sickness of the young man's quest: " 'I must away to a foreign land!' he said: 'the strange old woman in the wood has told me what I must do to get well. . . .' "[13]

MacDonald's infectious mentor was Novalis,[14] to whom he paid repeated tribute. Commenting on an essay on biography by T. T. Lynch, MacDonald exclaimed: "It is, indeed, well with him who has found a friend whose spirit touches his own and illuminates it. . . . Shall I not one day, 'somewhere, somehow,' clasp the large hand of Novalis, and, gazing on his face, compare his features with those of Saint John?"[15] The sudden loss of his adolescent Madonna, his mystic confidence in the prophetic

[12] *Phantastes, A Faerie Romance* (London, 1858), epigraph. Subsequent references are taken from Wm. B. Eerdmans' paperback edition, *Phantastes and Lilith* (Grand Rapids, 1964).

[13] George MacDonald, *Rampolli: Growths from a Long-Planted Root, being translations chiefly from the German . . .* (London, 1897), pp. 37-41.

[14] MacDonald quotes from Novalis's *Heinrich von Oftendingen* as his caption for Ch. ii of *Phantastes;* interestingly Lewis describes, in an unpublished letter (Aug. 13, 1930), his own translation of Novalis; he says: "— indeed Novalis is perhaps the greatest single influence on MacDonald — full of 'holiness', gloriously German-romantic (i.e. a delicious mingling of earthy homeliness and magic, also of a sort of spiritual voluptuousness, with innocence). . . ."

[15] "Essays on Some of the Forms of Literature," *A Dish of Orts,* p. 230.

worth of dreams, his emphasis on immortality and, above all, Novalis's peculiar belief in "magic idealism" (which became for him something more than metempsychosis)[16] and his untimely death — these biographical facts influenced MacDonald to follow his German master closely.

Through the rigors of translating Novalis's poetry MacDonald acquired his own prosodic skills. In 1851, while at his Arundel pastorate in Sussex, he printed privately his "Twelve of the Spiritual Songs of Novalis" (his first published work) as a Christmas gift for his friends. "The mystic pietism of these songs," says his son Dr. Greville MacDonald, "had gripped my father's imagination in, I think, his student days."[17] Possibly he had begun them in 1842, while, at age eighteen, he had spent the summer at Sinclair Castle, owned then by Sir George Sinclair, a fine linguist and German scholar who had studied at Göttingen. At Thurso, if Greville MacDonald's supposition is correct, George MacDonald learned German as he polished his translations and catalogued the Sinclair library, which contained the poetry of the German and English Romantic poets. Certainly Thurso, with its treeless skyline, rocky coast, and icy winds reminds one of the country to which Diamond is taken. There he found "North Wind on her doorstep . . . like one of the great figures at the door of an Egyptian temple."[18] And like Hyacinth and Anodos he entered for the first time "the white hall of Phantasy"[19] and unveiled, with a song, his marble Isis. Alastor had been there before him.

Perhaps every poet, especially a writer of fairytales, has his own symbolic vision of life's tale with which he delights young and old alike. The Romantic poets cradled theirs in dreams. Wordsworth dreamed, to the end, of laughing childhood — Shelley and Byron of raging, disconsolate, adolescence. Perhaps the greatest dream of all, however, is the *Märchen* of Eternal Youth. Without it Romanticism could not exist. It is difficult, in fact, to think of any dream-world in which a handsome youth does not eventually meet and wed his Rosebud. This Romantic

[16] See Ralph Tymms on Novalis's "magic idealism" in his *German Romantic Literature* (London, 1955). Briefly Novalis's term expresses his own type of Fichtean solipsism, which is the philosophical source for much of MacDonald's mysticism.

[17] *George MacDonald and His Wife* (London, 1924), p. 159 — hereafter cited as *GMAW*.

[18] George MacDonald, *At the Back of the North Wind* (New York: Macmillan, n.d.), p. 104.

[19] *Phantastes*, p. 114.

ideal, with its optimistic longing, nurtured the imagination of the Blue-Flower offspring. Sexual desire pursued them all. Alastor, for instance, is driven to destruction by the "veiled maid" who in a dream sequence confronts him with the poet's ideal of relentless satisfaction. She appears, fleetingly, to Anodos as his "white lady" and, also in a dream, to Lewis's John as his "divinely fair" Media. She is identified in Novalis's *Hyacinth and Rosebud* as "the virgin with the veil" or "the sacred goddess Isis."[20] In *Perelandra* Lewis calls her "the Green Lady."[21] In Novalis's fairytale, which MacDonald entitled "A Parable," we see her transformed from a Pagan goddess into Christian love, the traditional symbol of holiness. The pursuit of her is the theme of *Phantastes*.

MacDonald's *Phantastes* is a poet's artistic diary of youthful dreams. Like Lewis's *Pilgrim's Regress*, it is the record of a young man's spiritual contest with the "false objects" which taunt his thirst for the fulfillment of "Sweet Desire."[22] Both Anodos and John search bravely for a realization in their actual life of dream-world aspirations. Both must forsake parental ties. Having strayed "far away from home," John hears the plucking sound of the Aeolian harp beckoning him to "Come" (p. 32). Through a glassless window he sees, for the first time, the primrose woods of Desire:

> ...there came to him from beyond the wood a sweetness and a pang so piercing that instantly he forgot his father's house, and his mother, and the fear of the Landlord, and the burden of the rules. All the furniture of his mind was taken away....
>
> [p. 24]

And he wept. So Lewis, at thirty-four, recalls reading, eighteen years before, of Anodos's look through the "old castle" window into Fairyland:

> ...as soon as I looked out of the window, a gush of wonderment and longing flowed over my soul like the tide of a great sea. Fairy Land lay before me, and drew me towards it with an irresistible attraction.
>
> [*Phantastes,* p. 61]

Like John, Anodos is immersed in Nature's maternal stream:

> The trees bathed their great heads in the waves of the morning, while their roots were planted deep in gloom; save where on the borders the sunshine broke against their stems, or swept in long streams through

[20] *Rampolli*, p. 41.

[21] Describing his creation of the Green Lady, Lewis wrote: "She's got to be in some ways like a Pagan goddess and in other ways like the Blessed Virgin" (*Letters of C. S. Lewis*, ed. W. H. Lewis [London, 1966], p. 195).

[22] Preface to *The Pilgrim's Regress,* rev. ed. (London, 1943), p. 9.

> their avenues, washing with brighter hue all the leaves over which it flowed. . . .

At thirty-three, MacDonald was, like Lewis, far from home when he wrote of his adolescent fears and fantasies.

The composition of *Phantastes* took place in 1858 at Huntly Cottage, Hastings. "It had taken," comments Greville MacDonald, "but two months to write" (*GMAW*, p. 290). On January 2 of that year MacDonald wrote confidently to his father: "I am writing a kind of fairy tale in the hope it will pay me better than the more evidently serious work. This is in prose" (p. 288). Beyond this, we know almost nothing about the actual writing of the romance.[23] A guest in the MacDonald home at the time described how "in the evenings, when the children were all in bed, Mr. MacDonald would still be writing in his study . . . and Mrs. MacDonald would go down and sit with her husband, when he would read to her what he had been writing; and I would hear them discussing it on their return to the drawing-room" (p. 289).

MacDonald's imagination was, Lewis notes, haunted by "the image of a great house."[24] It became his Cosmic Image of life. Within this lofty "half castle, half farmhouse"[25] (or sometimes in a magical hut) an inquisitive, lonely, and spiritually orphaned child learned some of life's hardest lessons. A certain Norman castle was, I believe, the boyhood source of MacDonald's imaginative house of instruction. Frequently as a bairn in Huntly, Aberdeenshire, he had visited it. George MacDonald was born in a stone-built house next to his grandmother's, on December 10, 1824. Not far from his birthplace is The Farm, "Howglen" or Bleachfield Cottage as it was known then. And near it, hidden now in tall trees, stand the partially restored ruins of Huntly (Strathbogie) Castle. Young George never forgot the supernatural meaning for him of its strange markings, forbidding locked wooden door, spiral stairs, earthen-floor dungeon, and round tower vantage point, surveying the Strathbogie valley and winding Deveron river beyond. While exploring its perilous stairway (mostly then in ruins) MacDonald looked heroically into primitive rooms which still echoed ruthless tales of his father's brutal ancestry. And at night, asleep alone in

[23] MacDonald was indebted for the idea of *Phantastes* to his reading, while in Manchester, of Carlyle's translation of E. T. A. Hoffmann's *The Golden Pot* (*GMAW*, p. 297).

[24] *George MacDonald: An Anthology*, p. 12.

[25] From the opening chapter of MacDonald's *The Princess and the Goblin* (Baltimore, 1964), p. 11.

his sky-light garret room at The Farm, he dreamed like Ranald Bannerman of God's cosmic family:

> — Mr. Sun nodding and smiling across the intervening space to Mrs. Moon, and she nodding back to him with a knowing look, and the corners of her mouth drawn down. ... In one corner of the ceiling there was a hole, and through that hole came down a ladder of sun-rays — very bright and lovely. Where it came from I never thought, but of course it could not come from the sun, because there he was, with his bright coat off, playing the father of the family in the most homely Old-English-gentleman fashion possible. ...

And with great care he managed at last to climb up its fragile "ladder of rays."[26] At the top he dashed into the arms of the Father-King and was at home. Consistently we sense in MacDonald's best poems and tales of fantasy a certain Scottish clannishness — "a warm atmosphere," as he defined it in his parable "The Castle," "like the children of a household when the mother is at home."[27] The vision of his own family always securely "at home" continued to be MacDonald's source of literary inspiration. Whenever he wrote fairytales, there were children at his feet or sleeping nearby. At Hastings, where he finished *Phantastes,* there were five.

MacDonald's literary career is marked by periods of spiritual introspection and unrest. *Phantastes* is, as I have suggested, an imaginative journey into MacDonald's poetic consciousness. In a sense it is his fortress of dreams. Anodos's fear of his shadow-self and at the end his heroic fight against the worshippers of apostate religion reflect conflicts dating from MacDonald's own student days at King's College. At sixteen, in 1840, he left the "busy Squar' " of Huntly for city life in Aberdeen, acquiring "digs" in a large granite boarding house overlooking "the grey sand dunes on to the cold North Sea."[28] But though the natural and intellectual austerity at King's sparked his active imagination, neither his mastery of chemistry and natural philosophy nor the dissenting sermons he heard on Sunday adequately filled his need for spiritual kinship with the universe. There rose in him waves of melancholy and anxiety which never totally subsided. He could be seen taking long evening walks to the local Links where, pacing "backwards and

[26] George MacDonald, *Ranald Bannerman's Boyhood* (London, 1886), p. 6.

[27] George MacDonald, *Works of Fancy and Imagination* (London, 1905), x, 6.

[28] *Alma Mater,* University of Aberdeen (October 18, 1905), p. 2.

forwards on the sands amid the howling winds and the beating spray,"[29] the student-poet consigned himself longingly to the storm. Later, in a suicidal moment MacDonald would send Anodos into the deep:

> ...I stood on the shore of a wintry sea, with a wintry sun just a few feet above its horizon-edge.... A cold, death-like wind swept across the shore, seeming to issue from a pale mouth of cloud upon the horizon. Sign of life was nowhere visible. I wandered over the stones, up and down the beach, a human embodiment of the nature around me. The wind increased; its keen waves flowed through my soul; the foam rushed higher up the stones; a few dead stars began to gleam in the east; the sound of the waves grew louder and yet more despairing.... I could bear it no longer.
>
> [p. 127]

Death, its sensations and significance, drives Anodos onward. Through dying he learns "that it is by loving, and not by being loved, that one can come nearest to the soul of another" (p. 179). MacDonald's Shelleyan sea-flight produced, however, unlike Alastor's, deep religious commitment; it fostered Anodos's unguarded belief "that good is always coming; though few have at all times the simplicity and the courage to believe it" (p. 182). In poetry, MacDonald told of his call to discipleship.

MacDonald's first published poem "David," in 1846, typifies his early excitement over religious themes, this time the theme of a broken family. In a blank-verse narrative of 114 lines he describes the grief-stricken King David who, having lost his son Absalom, wanders aimlessly through the "desolate streets" of dark conscience. Finally David sees in a vision the restored filial scene:

> *The form of Absalom; as when a child*
> *He sat upon his mother's knee, whose brow*
> *Bent cloudless over his upturned cheek....*[30]

In 1855, after his marriage to Miss Louisa Powell, MacDonald repeated the child-son-ship theme in his verse-drama *Within and Without,* a five-act operatic poem in which he treats the inner strife between dedication to an active intellectual life and outward duty to his wife and child. Count Julian, a highly sensitive monk, escapes from the monastery in order to join his "long-lost-lady" Lilia, who against her will is about to marry a villainous Count Nembroni. A duel follows in which Julian kills Nembroni, thus adding murder to his ecclesiastical guilt. Julian and Lilia are married and move from Italy to London where they

[29] Quoted in *GMAW*, p. 80.
[30] *The Scottish Congregational Magazine* (Feb. 1846).

have a child, Lily. But husband and wife become estranged over Lilia's misunderstood relationship to a certain Lord Seaford and Julian's subsequent neglect of her. She is exonerated, however, and the Lamballa family are at the end united in "God's big house," as Count Julian, the father-figure, gratefully concludes:

> *O God, thy thoughts, thy ways, are not as ours;*
> *They fill our longing hearts up to the brim.*
> [*PW*, I, 131]

This vigorous search for a balance between intellectual aspiration and filial duty continues as the mainspring of MacDonald's poetic imagination.

In 1857 MacDonald published his first collection of poems. Included in it are narratives on love, age, and death, parables of fanciful excursions (one to find the Grail), other lyrics on traditional subjects, sonnets on the nature of Jesus Christ, and sixteen devotional poems on New Testament women. In its diversity of themes and versification, *Poems* is what one would expect from a beginning poet. By far the best poem in the collection is MacDonald's semi-autobiographical narrative on his student days, "A Hidden Life," in which he returns to the family theme: a Scottish farmer's son discovers the world of thought and aesthetics through his visionary encounter with a beautiful lady. Aside from its poetic merits, "A Hidden Life" has sections revealing what I think is MacDonald's greatest talent, his childlike fascination with the spirit of living things. All of MacDonald's major poems (and frequently passages in his prose) have in them Wordsworth's universal spirit and Shelley's windblown child. It is the visionary and moralist perfectly balanced: the "hidden life" of the imagination speaking without offense. I can define it only by quoting from his writings; for example Anodos's final vision of Fairyland:

> As I lay, with my eyes closed, I began to listen to the sound of the leaves overhead. At first, they made sweet inarticulate music alone; but by-and-by, the sound seemed to begin to take shape, and to be gradually moulding itself into words; till, at last, I seemed able to distinguish these, half-dissolved in a little ocean of circumfluent tones: 'A great good is coming — is coming — is coming to thee, Anodos'; and so over and over again. I fancied that the sound reminded me of the voice of the ancient woman, in the cottage that was four-square. I opened my eyes, and, for a moment, almost believed that I saw her face, with its many wrinkles and its young eyes, looking at me from between two hoary branches of the beech overhead. But when I looked more keenly, I saw

> only twigs and leaves, and the infinite sky, in tiny spots, gazing through between....
>
> [p. 182]

And it is this emergent myth of Christian cosmology proliferated through Romantic symbolism which, I believe, dominated Lewis's mind and imagination as he read *Phantastes*. "I know nothing that gives me such a feeling of spiritual healing, of being washed," Lewis wrote, "as to read MacDonald."[31] As Lewis eagerly followed Anodos's encounters and deadly march toward individuation, MacDonald's "bright shadow" of optimism assailed him. His "popular realism"[32] vanished; he was almost converted.

Some of MacDonald's best work appears in his 1871 small-octavo set of "fancy and imagination," which he reissued at the peak of his literary fame. Volume I contains *Within and Without* and "A Hidden Life," followed by other reprints, in Volumes II-IV, from *Poems* and *The Disciple and Other Poems* (1867); *Phantastes,* in two volumes, and *The Portent* (1864) make up Volumes V-VII; and his most celebrated fairytales, including "The Light Princess," "The Golden Key," and "Cross Purposes," comprise Volumes VIII-X.

MacDonald was always a poet. Although convinced by poverty and a growing family to become a novelist, fairytale-writer, and editor, he never stopped writing poems. His "poetical gifts were," after the publication of *Phantastes,* "fully recognized by all the critics," claims his son; yet for five years his father published nothing. But "with tireless, minutely painstaking energy" he did continue to write, all the while troubled "by bronchitis, asthma and wretched headaches" (*GMAW,* p. 317). In *Phantastes* MacDonald had given as much of his fairytale-vision as he could then articulate. Thus he turned, somewhat regretfully, from his Ossianic muse and wrote novels; his genius was truncated. Before he fully exhausted it, however, he once again used his myth-making talent, this time in *Lilith,* his "mandate direct from God" (*GMAW,* p. 548). Finally in 1891 he wrote wearily to his daughter: "I have still one great poem in my mind, but it will never be written, I think, except we have a fortune left us, so that I need not write any more stories

[31] I am indebted for this quotation and the one cited in note 14 to Professor Kilby, who pointed them out to me from his reading of Lewis's unpublished letters, now in the Wheaton College collection.

[32] Preface of *Pilgrim's Regress,* p. 5. Says Lewis: "On the intellectual side my own progress had been from 'popular realism' to Philosophical Idealism; from Idealism to Pantheism; from Pantheism to Theism; and from Theism to Christianity."

— of which I am beginning to be tired . . ." (*GMAW*, p. 518). His great poem was never written.[33]

Every fairytale must have, I suppose, some kind of ending. MacDonald's is graphically given in *Lilith,* his "A Tale of the Seventh Dimension," as it was subtitled in its shortened manuscript version. The theme of *Lilith* is conversion.[34] We are introduced to Mr. Vane (Anodos on his return journey through Fairyland), this time to rescue the Little Ones from their depraved giant kin and from Lilith the night queen, snatcher of babies and Adam's rebellious first wife. Throughout the tale MacDonald interweaves his strong belief in the immortality of all creation. At the end, in "The Waking," Adam exults:

> Hark to the golden cock! Silent and motionless for millions of years has he stood on the clock of the universe; now at last he is flapping his wings! now will he begin to crow! and at intervals will men hear him until the dawn of the day eternal.
>
> [p. 410]

Such golden passages are balanced by equally fine scenes of Dantesque grotesqueness; for example the glittering moonlit "Gruesome Dance" of the skeletons in the pinewood hall or Lilith's struggle against repentance, symbolized by her tightly ingrowing hand which Adam severs. Admittedly *Lilith* is overcrowded with religious symbols (at times so is Dante's *Divine Comedy*); and yet, there is nothing written in the nineteenth century to equal, I think, its rapturous portrayal of resurrection life. There are passages in it, in fact, which almost break into poetry. To awaken into the *real* life was MacDonald's fairytale ending; thus he quoted from Novalis: "Our life is no dream, but it should and will perhaps become one."[35]

I have taken considerable space to discuss MacDonald's poetry, because it is there and in his fantasies that one finds the sources of his genius. What Lewis has defined as MacDonald's "pure vision"[36] appears only occasionally in his novels — although there are sections there which sparkle with it — but MacDonald's greatest literary claim is not, I am convinced, that of a novelist. Primarily he is, as Louis MacNeice has suggested,

[33] MacDonald's "great poem" would undoubtedly have been devotional in content, perhaps like his *The Diary of an Old Soul* (1880).

[34] See R. M. Schieder, "Loss and Gain? The Theme of Conversion in Late Victorian Fiction," *Victorian Studies*, IX (Sept. 1965), 42, for reference to MacDonald's importance as a writer and influence on 19th-century religious fiction.

[35] Quoted at the end of *Phantastes and Lilith.*

[36] Unpublished letter (Aug. 31, 1930); see note 31.

a "parable writer." "... In the realm of parable writing no one went further than MacDonald," says MacNeice, "in the whole of the nineteenth century."[37] He will be remembered, I think, as the founder of a modern circle of fantasy writers all of whom use, in varying degrees, the parable form. *Phantastes* and *Lilith* will stand as touchstones of the fantasy craft in fiction. Finally, MacDonald gave to Lewis, Charles Williams, and Tolkien their simple definition of the function of the imagination — the definition he quoted in his *A Cabinet of Gems* (1891) from Sir Philip Sidney:

> With a tale forsooth the poet cometh unto you, with a tale which holdeth children from play, and old men from the chimney-corner; and pretending no more, doth intend the winning of the mind from wickedness to virtue.

For George MacDonald, Diamond's soaring ride over chimney-tops and icebergs with North Wind had no end; she waited always for him on her doorstep.

[37] *Varieties of Parable* (Cambridge, 1965), p. 95.

# Coinherence, Substitution and Exchange in Charles Williams' Poetry and Poetry-Making

ALICE MARY HADFIELD

Charles Williams considered that the most important concept of his writing was that which he called coinherence, or, in full, coinherence, substitution and exchange. He himself became more aware of it as it developed through the middle years of his work, but anyone looking through his early writings can see shoots of the growth from the beginning. In a pamphlet called "The Way of Exchange," reprinted in *The Image of the City* (London, 1958), C. W. pulled the concept out of his writings into a single focus. He says there is a union of existences, and everywhere an interdependence in social life for mutual benefit or survival. But the Christian church holds a promise by our Lord of a "particular and intense union with each other through Himself" (p. 149), a union of the same nature as that which he has with his Father, a coinherence in which the Son exists in the Father and the Father in the Son and the Spirit correspondingly in each. This is the Christian imagination of the authority and origin of all things. Depending directly on this coinherence,

---

Alice Mary Hadfield won a history scholarship to St. Hilda's College, Oxford, where she took her degree, and then went on a scholarship to Mount Holyoke College in Massachusetts for her master's. Returning to England she joined the Oxford University Press at Amen House, London, to edit the *Oxford Dictionary of Familiar Quotations,* and later became the Amen House librarian. She spent six years in close working association with Charles Williams, who among many other duties was adviser on the *Dictionary of Quotations.* She left Amen House in 1939, and returned in 1944 to work for Charles Williams in the seventeen months before his death. She is the author of *An Introduction to Charles Williams* (1959) as well as books of history, topography, and juvenile interest, and is presently working on a book on Williams' poetry.

the Son has substituted his manhood for ours in the Incarnation and the Atonement, and we can if we choose accept this exchange of our life in all our awarenesses and activities.

From the highest imagination of perfected life to the basic condition of human existence, exchange, substitution, and coinherence are not a matter of faith but of fact, a single principle. The root of all human facts is an example of it — childbearing. "The masculine seed has to be received by the feminine vessel. . . . By the substitution of the woman for the man the seed fructifies" (p. 150). New life is begun, and must coinhere with the mother's for nine months to be fully formed.

The rest of life follows the same principle. We live from others — aware of it or not — and we can do so with far more intense energy than is common. It is not a matter only of married people loving each other, however deeply, or of dedicated communal communities. A greater life lies about us and holds us all. Awareness of this life can affect our emotions and our wills, and in time our actions. A new life can spring in us, which is known in the coinherence of the greater life and ourselves. Lovers know a little what it is to live the other's life, to live her family troubles, his fear of failure at work — not sharing but living from these conditions as if they were one's own, a true substitution, coinherence and exchange. What we can do and know as lovers, love teaches we can spend our lives becoming able to do and know in a few more instances and circumstances.

All this is not new. Most religions and humanists have considered much of it. But as religion or practical help it was largely dead stuff to between-the-wars generations. Charles Williams saw the living element in it, unstifled by religious accretion. He spoke of an awareness of burdens carried, of lives substituted, not blurred or suppressed, but a redeemed life living the unredeemed life, not dodging or rising above it, but producing in it a new life of the nature of creative power that holds us all. The ability to assent to this and to do it comes from the life of Christ, which experienced the life of us all and was substituted for each of us at the final agony. But C. W. was no man of religion, and did not press a creed. He was a man of ideas, and a poet. Insofar as he was a poet he was not a Christian, and his presentation of Christ's work in man was acceptable to people who could tolerate no religious creed. How prophetic his approach was! He presented unchurched Christianity a generation before the search for it became conscious.

Ideas of this scope are often too big to make much impact. We need detail to put flesh on the pattern, and this was C. W.'s method. He did very little abstract writing, but rather showed ideas as visible effects in will and word and action in his characters or images. He never in conversation thought of himself as inventing or thinking up an idea, but always as finding it. He observed in lives or events a relationship or principle which he declared was there for all to see — and indeed his friends used to imagine that the idea was obvious once he had pointed it out, and his insistence on the perfectibility of each and all of us made it easy to fancy that we should have thought of it ourselves if he had not said it first.

His poetry chose for its continuing theme the Arthurian myth, and in this his meditations on coinherence led him to a significant interpretation. In the central story of the myth, the birth of Galahad was the result of Lancelot's being deceived into lying with Helayne instead of with Guinevere. By a shift of words, Williams saw that, unintended by Lancelot or Guinevere, Helayne was substituted for the Queen in the act of conceiving. Thus by substitution, an unwilled, say, a heavenly substitution, the healer of the Dolorous Blow, the achiever of the Grail, the figure of man's capacity for Christ, was born, as by substitution Christ in his manhood brought into time the healing of the nature of man. Instantly Galahad is central to the myth, which everywhere lacked him till he was born, instead of being a late development or coda.

The substitution took place in a dark room, one of many in the stories of the myth. Williams took the image to represent not only an interior rather than an external activity, but also a mind completely in the dark about it — and not only the mind of the knight or lady concerned but in a deeper sense the mind of the writers who through many centuries were unaware of their own ignorance about this kind of scene. Williams held that myths, ideas and the like could be used only by a generation or mind for which they were valuable, and lay dormant in knowledge until another such generation arrived. They are not vitiated by those who ignore them or even who "debunk" them. He used to quote of such dormant ideas, "He will not suffer his holy one to see corruption."

His early verse is not regarded as important, but interesting signs can be seen in the young and still derivative writing. *Poems of Conformity* was published in 1917, when he was thirty-one, and *Divorce* in 1920. He was serving his apprenticeship to poetry and to married love during their writing, climbing slowly up through the lower grades of editorial staff in the Oxford University Press, married to the love dreamed of in his first book of sonnets, *The Silver Stair,* living in a small-street flat in a crowded north London district, exempt from war service by weaknesses of physique, anxiously supporting the war effort, anxious for his two friends serving in France. The strongest attraction of the books is the experience of friendship; and, shadowing it, substitution and exchange move through the verse unfocussed, just below the surface in many poems, and rising to it in some. I have quoted Poem II of "Christmas" in *Poems of Conformity* in my *Introduction to Charles Williams* (London, 1959), but it will bear quoting again in this connection. It speaks of love newly arrived at daily married life, and the newly incarnate Christ.

*The Child lies not alone:*
*His voice, his eyes, his fingers and his heart*
*Catch at his mother lest she should depart;*
*Who being gone*
*He should be hungry soon and naked-cold.*

*Saved is he, yea, and shown, —*
*Both held a secret and professed at large*
*In this committal for a most dear charge*
*To her, his throne;*
*Upon her breast he threatens and is bold.*

*O Infancy! — to us*
*Himself hath he presented in no less*
*Protection of another's littleness.*
*He safely thus*
*Dares, till time strengthen him and he grow old.*

*Clings the Immanuel still*
*Unto some mortal office; he is girt*
*With use of a familiar soul from hurt,*
*And holy will:*
*On human love the new-born Love lays hold.*

In "The Continuing Doctrine," also in *Poems of Conformity,* he speaks of the nature of war as being common to us all, in public or in private.

*Who then but ourselves may know*
*The beginning of this woe,*
*Sloth or wry activity*
*To so swift catastrophe*
*Gay intention bringing low?*

. . . . . . . . . . . .

*Never malice to us clung*
*But through bloody heart or lung*
*Of our fellows now hath torn,*
*Never apathy or scorn*
*Or hypocrisy of tongue.*

In *Divorce* the war poems are particularly heavy with the feeling of substitution, not always the full doctrine of it but approaches to it. Both of C. W.'s friends, Ernest Nottingham and Harold Eyers, were killed. He knew substitution unchosen but experienced. Poem II of "In Time of War," lovers consenting to the war speaking to lovers parted by it, says:

*Our wills, that dare not break with war's will, thus*
*Are made the agents of your sole divorce:*
*To you the rent, the agony; to us*
*Salvation, hardly tinctured with remorse.*

*Yet doubt not soon, in some new wrath immersed,*
*On us our Lord Love shall avenge your pain,*
*When, smitten with disaster, we shall thirst*
*For consolation, — and shall thirst in vain.*

And in poem IV of the same group, written to his two friends, "In Absence":

*So we, 'neath strangers' footsteps, hear*
*Your heavy marches sounding near;*
*And in your silent listening post*
*Are their confused noises lost.*

*To walls and window-curtains cling*
*Your voices at each breakfasting,*
*As the cups pass from hand to hand,*
*Crying for drink in No Man's Land.*

In "Commentaries," poem IV, on Galatians 4:1-7, being made adult in love:

*Duly, the Sunday after Christmas, we*
*Heard the epistle read, and suddenly*
*A great voice cried within my heart: Behold,*
*This is the doctrine ye have proved of old,*
*And in your bodies bear the signs thereof;*
*This is the knowledge of the sons of love.*

*Windows of Night* is the book where the ground swell of Williams' new kind of poetry moves and disturbs the early forms. Night-colored, laboring in a darkness of existence, the book's life is lit from beneath with a rage of disastrous substitution and coinherence, known in misery and breaking. Read the terrible "Domesticity," which links back to "In Absence" just quoted. Here

*Hate steams like a pestilence upward, though far above*
*They build the millennium.*

Or read "Prisoners," which declares

*what each one singly would,*

*The commonwealth of all hates, and for fear*
*Of her own lusts hath clutched you with rough hand.*

Or "The Two Domes," which are St. Paul's Cathedral dome in London, and the nearby dome of the Old Bailey, England's Central Criminal Court. Or "A Cup of Water": when lying awake the poet saw fire and war devastating the earth, inescapable, necessary to Christendom and all aimed-at good. Or the long poem "To a Publisher," where he speaks of words which are drudges until a poet recharges them with power and they are released into poetry.

*They have their life, but at what cost of death,*
*Out of such dark impassioned moment born*
*As when young Browning met Elizabeth,*
*Or, turned from watching on Niphates' head*
*Milton lamented blindness, or forlorn*
*Catullus mourned above his brother dead!*

After *Windows of Night* in 1925 came the long break in published poetry, while he wrote and published continuously but kept his new style in verse a secret growth. When *Taliessin Through Logres* appeared in 1938, he had become aware of the range of coinherence and substitution, and how deep the concept penetrated into poetry, history, religion, social studies and love.

"Prelude"*[1] in *Taliessin* establishes it. The poem opens on the coinherent life. The physical body of man and of the universe are intended in the image of Caucasia; the activities, government, and commerce of man in Camelot; visions, dedications and ecstasies in Carbonek — all points of the Empire coinhering in each other and in the Emperor by the operation of holy wisdom expressing the Logos. Man's life is quick with glory and light. But men began to teach that coinherence need not be, that man could live by his own effort, cultivating his own rational virtue, subduing the flesh which made him less than himself and visions which showed him something greater. Christ had lived and shown the way of union, but the longing of man to be subject to no one, grateful to no one, which longing Mahomet illumined and uplifted, led men into the struggles and processes which the poems in this book go on to explore. In man and in events union of being was breached.

The third poem, "The Vision of the Empire," closely develops the idea. In the first eleven lines it is made clear that

[1] Poems marked with an asterisk are excerpted more extensively in the appendix to this article. Also included in the appendix are selections from other relevant poems not cited in the article.

the Emperor is coinherent with the world by his choice to be known only through men's lives. Stanzas *b*, *c*, and *d* develop this knowledge through the body, the actions and the thoughts and creeds of man. Stanza *e* unites all ways — but only in some moments and conditions. Union everywhere and at all times is breached, by the desire of man to "grow to the height of God and the Emperor" (stanza *g*), not through the union of manhood exchanged with Christ, but denying the union, independent, doing it himself.

Many and many a conversation did C. W. hold on what happened next, walking up and down his little office in the narrow space between the desk and the wall of bookshelves, or sitting with his feet on the desk, smoking. He believed that only good had reality, but he was met and torn everywhere by the experience of pain or deadly absence of meaning. Through years of experience, poetry, thought, and conversation he came suddenly to his clarification, and went walking round the passages of Amen House with the page from his little writing pad in his hand, looking for a friend, and meeting one, said,

"Look, I've just settled the problem of Adam. He was a modern fellow, bored, as he thought, with what he called good. He wanted something different. There wasn't anything different for him to know, as there isn't now, though you might not think it, but since he had chosen it he had it, a projection, you see, not a reality, but enough for Adam or you, of existence and each situation as potentially evil, if he wanted it, instead of, or as well as, actually good. See?" In his hand was stanza *g* of "The Vision of the Empire."

*The Adam in the hollow of Jerusalem respired:*
*softly their thought twined to its end,*
*crying: O parent, O forkèd friend,*
*am I not too long meanly retired*
*in the poor space of joy's single dimension?*
*Does not God vision the principles at war?*
*Let us grow to the height of God and the Emperor:*
*Let us gaze, son of man, on the Acts in contention.*

"Don't you like 'the poor space of joy's single dimension'?" he said cheerfully.

The reply, after reading, was "Who the devil is his forkèd friend?"

C. W. chuckled. "Certainly not, you've got it wrong. *Not* the devil; he couldn't be in this poem, but Adam's other half. All the old stories carry the idea of Adam and Eve being one form divided. I must say that I personally am entirely willing to be

*meanly retired*
*in the poor space of joy's single dimension."*

Stanza *h* pursues the deadly horror of life known in separation — actions pointless, body dreary, events hostile, and over all a sense of fate without intelligence or will. The last stanza recovers the vision in a rapture of identity and detail of glory.

Detail indeed is one of Charles Williams' glories. He knew the doctrine of the whole Christ, whole in every broken particle of bread or nerve or myth — and absent so also. In "The Calling of Arthur" King Cradlemas in the bitter cold weather

*polishes his emerald, misty with tears for the poor.*

We need no more information about him. "The Crowning of Arthur" shows us the detail of the whole condition as it might have been, coinherence restored — or so it seemed to Arthur, but it was not securely so.

*Taliessin beheld a god lie in his tomb.*

In the myth, representing all human process, the restoration must be continuous, must reckon to start again as soon as breath is drawn after an effort. In other words, it must be a life. This lacks drama, is not popular. The people who plug on, are they not bourgeois, does not every newspaper ignore them while the cultural weeklies sneer? What about Bors, explaining economic policy to Elayne ("Bors to Elayne: on the King's Coins"*) ? He would be a disaster — if he did not pursue the coinherence of organization with ideas and nerves and with the organization of heaven.

*Cleared the branched jungles*
*where the unthumbed shapes of apes swung and hung.*
*Now when the thumbs are muscled with the power of goodwill*
*corn comes to the mill and the flour to the house,*
*bread of love for your women and my men;*
*at the turn of the day, and none only to earn;*
*in the day of the turn, and none only to pay;*
*for the hall is raised to the power of exchange of all*
*by the small spread organisms of your hands; O Fair,*
*there are the altars of Christ the City extended.*
*I have ridden all night from organization in London,*
*ration and rule, and the fault in ration and rule,*
*law and the flaw in law, to reach to you,*
*the sole figure of the organic salvation of our good.*

In "Bors to Elayne: The Fish of Broceliande" Bors also perceives clearly the double nature of events and the deep pull of instincts. He has a feeling for politics. He has worked to restore peace and rebuild the administration, living all activities by his knowledge of the exchanged life of love in marriage.

*I have seen the branches of Broceliande.*
*Though Camelot is built, though the king sit on the throne,*
*yet the wood in the wild west of the shapes and names*

*probes everywhere through the frontier of head and hand;*
*everywhere the light through the great leaves is blown*
*on your substantial flesh, and everywhere your glory frames.*

The simplest aspect of the concept of coinherence is exchange, and this produced two of Williams' most charming poems, one in the serious collection and one not. In *Taliessin Through Logres,* in "The Star of Percivale," Taliessin is standing in the palace courtyard, touching the strings of a harp to the music that Percivale was making in the king's hall. A serving maid was smitten with adoration, for Taliessin she thought, but, as he showed her, rather for the power in the words he sang. The Archbishop saw her face radiant with adoration, but

*she answered: The light of another, if aught, I bear,*
*as he the song of another.*

It was the situation which C. W.'s power was constantly provoking with the young, and which he as constantly turned away from himself to a passion for poetry, for goodness, with himself as fellow worker.

*More than the voice is the vision, the kingdom than the king.*

It is the saving doctrine of relationship, but bitter in the mouth at first. Williams rightly made it unacceptable in his poems to most knights and to the king.

In lighter vein, but quite as serious, he took the simple situation further in his "Apologue on the Parable of the Wedding Garment," which was published in December, 1940, in a weekly newspaper.[2] The Prince Immanuel gives a fancy dress ball; a guest, high in the administration and of good family, dislikes all forms of dressing-up and prefers his own simple worth. He arrives, and is not admitted. The footman allows him a glimpse of the gathering.

*He saw along*
*the Great Hall and Heavenly Stair*
*one blaze of glorious changes there.*
*Cloaks, brooches, decorations, swords,*

[2] *Time and Tide,* repr. in *The Image of the City,* pp. 166-168.

*jewels — every virtue that affords*
*(by dispensation of the Throne)*
*beauty to wearers not their own.*
*This guest his brother's courage wore;*
*that, his wife's zeal, while, just before,*
*she in his steady patience shone;*
*there a young lover had put on*
*the fine integrity of sense*
*his mistress used; magnificence*
*a father borrowed of his son,*
*who was not there ashamed to don*
*his father's wise economy.*
*Nor he or she was he or she*
*merely: no single being dared,*
*except the Angels of the Guard,*
*come without other kind of dress*
*than his poor life had to profess,*
*and yet those very robes were shown,*
*when from preserval as his own*
*into another's glory given,*
*bright ambiguities of heaven.*

This is the style of verse Williams used for poetry that he did not see as his *Collected Poems,* of which he regarded *Taliessin Through Logres* and *The Region of the Summer Stars* as the only components. He wrote this other kind rapidly with the upper surfaces of his mind. In his younger days it produced fairly easy, running verse, but as his mind achieved mastery of access to the sources of his power his light verse flashed its own communication.

The result of Adam's choice in "The Vision of the Empire" is explored in a long poem in *Taliessin Through Logres,* "The Son of Lancelot." This son is Galahad, who, by expressing in himself the assent to coinherence in Christ, restores the union broken by Adam. The old stories tell of Lancelot's madness when he realized that he had lain with Helayne, tricked into unfaithfulness to his love. He ran, they say, as a wolf, savage and starved. In the poem he knows there will be a child, and he lives only to destroy it.

*All the winter the wolf haunted the environs of Carbonek;*
*now what was left of the man's contrarious mind*
*was twinned and twined with the beast's bent to feed;*
*now it crept to swallow the seed*
*of love's ambiguity, love's taunt and truth.*
*Man, he hated; beast, he hungered; both*
*stretched his sabres and strained his throat; rumble*
*of memories of love in the gaunt belly told*
*his instinct only that something edible might come.*

*Slavering he crouched by the dark arch of Carbonek,*
*head-high howling, lusting for food, living*
*for flesh, a child's flesh, his son's flesh.*

Hate and hunger devastated the world. Only a few strongholds held the witness of a better life, and they were encircled and menaced. The child Galahad was born. Merlin, as Time, that power which offers to every man his moment, came to the beast-man at the season of Quinquagesima, for which the collect of the church shows

*the manner of the second working*

whereby man's self-sufficiency is caught up into "that most excellent gift of charity, without which whosoever liveth is counted dead before thee." The forces of the second working move to the release of man from his own oppression and his own division. Lancelot's attack on his infant son is defeated; the capacity for Christ is saved in man.

*Gaudium multum annunciamus;*
*nunc in saecula servi amamus;*
*civitas dulcis aedificatur;*
*quia qui amat Amor amatur.*

*We proclaim great joy;*
*now for ever we servants can love;*
*the sweet city is being built;*
*because Love who loves is loved.*

More wary than the medievals, more faltering than the Romantics, we ponder how to love, how to coinhere. On a few occasions in our lives it needs no asking, for we are swept along. But all day and every day? And especially on bad days? In "The Coming of Galahad" when the High Prince came to Arthur's court it was one of those times when we are in no doubt, for our love and our capacity run before our instruction and our duty. For that occasion Galahad superseded the King and his power, and was ceremonially laid in the King's bed. The palace staff watched astonished. Word flew round to the kitchens and stables. Taliessin went down through the lower corridors, out to the stable yards and

*saw*
*through the unshuttered openings of stairs and rooms*
*the red flares of processional torches and candles*
*winding to the king's bed.*

Gareth, prince and menial, doing turn as night-soil man, asks him what the coming of the High Prince means for him in the jakes. Taliessin answers by asking, What builds the City? Choice, always and everywhere choice and will.

*Question and digestion, rejection and election,*
*winged shapes of the Grail's officers, double*
*grand equality of the State, common of all lives,*
*common of all experience, sense and more;*
*adore and repent, reject and elect.*

A serving maid says she has heard that at the appearing of the Grail everyone found on his plate the food he loved best, and asks what food Taliessin chose. "The good that was there," he answered. She queried the sense of this.

*Has all food one taste?*
*felicity does not alter?*

He answers that felicity alters from its center, and joy comes from what the Grail offers, not what man dreams of. It is always hidden in the life of the moment. "Where I find you," says the old apocryphal word, "there will I judge you." All approaches but this are doubtful: desire, which is symbolized by the planet Mercury, weakening or strengthening, urging to dodge or snatch instead of coinhering; preference, symbolized by Venus, always defining one's own choice and lessening one's ability to love where one would not choose; irony of detachment which is Jupiter, where one reserves always the final committal and imagines a security thereby. Beyond is the state of Galahad, symbolized by Saturn, "circled, girdled by turned space," free to all points and moments.

But as Kierkegaard said, there are times when to know that it is a loving God who is offering you this pain only makes it harder, not easier, to bear; and Charles Williams knew it well. Much of his own life was painful and restricted, and his powers made poverty, obscurity, and emotional isolation more intensely grievous. To believe that the whole system was operated by love and joy only made it worse. In "Percivale at Carbonek" he wrote from the center of his own heart.

*Joy remembered joylessness; joy kneeled*
*under the arch where Lancelot ran in frenzy.*
*The astonished angels of the spirit heard him moan:*
*"Pardon, lord; pardon and bless me, father."*

*Doubtfully stood the celestial myrmidons, scions*
*of unremitted beauty; bright feet paused.*
*Aching with the fibrous infelicity of time,*
*pierced his implacability, Galahad kneeled.*

. . . . . . . . . . . . . . . . . . . .

*the subdued glory implored the kingdom*

*to pardon its power and the double misery of Logres.*

*Under the arch the Merciful Child*
*wept for the grief of his father in reconciliation;*
*who was betrayed there by Merlin and Brisen*
*to truth; he saw not; he was false to Guinevere.*

. . . . . . . . . . . . . . . . . . . . . .

*The High Prince shivered in the cold of bleak conjunction.*

*His head shook; pale were his cheeks;*
*his head the head of a skull, flesh*
*cleaving to bone; his dry voice rattled;*
*"Pardon, Lord Lancelot; pardon and blessing, father."*

Galahad asks pardon for his world of ideas and creeds of love (Carbonek) from the world of daily life and common experience of sin (Camelot).

*"Forgive Us," the High Prince said, "for Our existence;*
*forgive the means of grace and the hope of glory.*
*In the name of Our Father forgive Our mother for Our birth."*

This is the dry season, the grey afternoon when he would saunter slowly in to the library where I worked, which gave a longer stretch in which to pace up and down, and there he would sigh and smoke and walk and turn, and look out of the tall windows at the court full of vans and horses and cars, seeing none of them through the thin line of cigarette smoke, and talk a little, maybe repeat,

*This she? no, this is Diomed's Cressida.*
*If beauty have a soul, this is not she.*

. . . . . . . . . . . . . . . . . . . . . .

*. . . O madness of discourse,*
*That cause sets up with and against itself;*
*Bi-fold authority! where reason can revolt*
*Without perdition, and loss assume all reason*
*Without revolt.*[3]

All the voices and trampings of a big office building seemed to fall away, and stillness would settle round the tall slim figure pacing up and down, hands in his pockets, shapely head with thick grey hair and gold-rimmed spectacles tilted back to keep the smoke out of his eyes. In a little while he would say, "Well, I must catch the post with that *Ring and the Book* commentary for Oxford," and be off up the step and through the swing door in a long stride. The dry season was never allowed to deny the spring of joy. "Percivale at Carbonek" goes on to Bors' answer to Galahad:

[3] Shakespeare, *Troilus and Cressida,* V.ii.137-146.

*"Sir," Bors said, "only God forgives.*
*My lord Sir Lancelot my cousin is a lover and kind.*
*I assent to all, as I pray that my children assent*
*and through God join with me in bidding their birth."*

The last long poem in *Taliessin*, "The Last Voyage,"* gathers all the poems' knowledge of substitution and exchange into the ship where

*the necessity of being was communicated to the son of Lancelot*

as the three knights sped toward Sarras. Here too is gathered the sense of time that moves so powerfully in Williams' verse. It needs a special study of its own, for it is used in the poetry more as a sacrament than a symbol, an aesthetic expression of an interior process. It appears in stanza *e* of "The Vision of the Empire"—

*The mist rolled down the edge of an old sun;*
*mammoth and bear prowled on the broad ledge of the shoulders*

— and in "Mount Badon" where Taliessin commanded the King's cavalry reserve in the decisive battle with the barbarians, and drew on the interior decisions with which Virgil built the hexameters of the *Aeneid*. The battle went against the King. Motionless on their horses Taliessin's company waited the word to charge.

*In the silence of a distance, clear to the king's poet's sight,*
*Virgil was standing on a trellised path by the sea.*
*Taliessin saw him negligently leaning; he felt*
*the deep breath dragging the depth of all dimension,*
*as the Roman sought for the word, sought for his thought,*
*sought for the invention of the City by the phrase.*

. . . . . . . . . . . . . . . . . . . .

*Civilized centuries away, the Roman moved.*
*Taliessin saw the flash of his style*
*dash at the wax; he saw the hexameter spring*
*and the king's sword swing; he saw, in the long field,*
*the point where the pirate chaos might suddenly yield.*

. . . . . . . . . . . . . . . . . . . . .

*The Aeneid's beaked lines swooped on Actium;*
*the stooped horse charged; backward blown,*
*the flame of song streaked the spread spears*
*and the strung faces of words on a strong tongue.*
*The household of Taliessin swung on the battle;*

. . . . . . . . . . . . . . . . . . .

*The tor of Badon heard the analytical word;*
*the grand art mastered the thudding hammer of Thor,*
*and the heart of our lord Taliessin determined the war.*

Again, in the battles ravaging Europe in the war of 1939, the hates and cruelties of the past are conscripted as units into the forces of the war — in "The Prayers of the Pope"* in *The Region of the Summer Stars.*

Time is only one of the phenomena, subject to change, in need of redemption. "The Departure of Merlin" shows a different knowledge of process. The method of phenomena is indrawn to Broceliande and sequence is translated into simultaneity.

*Moons and suns that rose in rites and runes*
*are come away from sequence, from rules of magic;*
*here all is cause and all effect; the laws*
*of Merlin's boyhood are unknown in Numue's wood.*

Now grace

*through each membraned and tissued experience*
*smites in simultaneity to times variously veined.*

Time itself must be redeemed. In "Taliessin at Lancelot's Mass" the process of the Grail and the effort of Arthur are over. The Table is broken, most of the knights are dead. All had been twisted and lost, and yet was found restored in the heart of man.

*In Blanchefleur's cell at Almesbury the queen Guinevere*
*felt the past exposed; and the detail, sharp and dear,*
*draw at the pang in the breast till, rich and reconciled,*
*the mystical milk rose in the mother of Logres' child.*

*Out of the queen's substitution the wounded and dead king*
*entered into salvation to serve the holy Thing;*
*singly seen in the Mass, owning the double Crown,*
*going to the altar Pelles, and Arthur moving down.*

*Lancelot and Arthur wove the web; the sky*
*opened on moon and sun; between them, light-traced on high,*
*the unseen knight of terror stood as a friend;*
*invisible things and visible waited the end.*

At the Epiclesis, all time before it and after it is recalled back into the moment of substitution when Christ's body was broken for man. Probably this operation underwrote all Williams' use of time in his poetry.

The last slim volume of verse, *The Region of the Summer Stars* (1944), has not the feeling of struggling to birth that *Taliessin* often has, and which has proved sympathetic in many younger writers. *Summer Stars* is written from achievement, from a stage struggled to and reached, even if unconsciously, a stage not for resting at but for launching out into the ether. The same is true of *The Figure of Arthur,* the prose work written in the same period, which he had not time to finish. I could envy a later generation which will read these advanced poems simply as poems, without stumbling over contemporary detail and personal words like "shy." Williams himself heavily deprecated the searching of biographies of poets, and efforts to enter a man's poetry by way of his life's events. To him a poet lived in the printed word. Even a chronological table of English poetry should almost be built up from that alone.

His own life would be hard to deduce. The argument from absence might say that so fixed a use of exteriorized myth and symbol spells an interior lack or block, but I think his power and his belief dissolved any such block, and carried any such lack through all his work to deepen its richness, as he did deliberately in "The Prayers of the Pope."* I do not know if there was such a lack, but I am sure that if there had not been, the needs of his thought would have presented it to him. By the time of *Summer Stars,* the convention of the Arthurian myth, which was a real world throughout *Taliessin Through Logres,* has become a setting, a thin historical veil for the poet's experience. He wrote a few direct poems at this late stage, to Sir Humphrey Milford the head of the Oxford University Press, and to occasional friends. He continued to drop sonnets as he had always done, like flakes of light, on office events, a performance by the firm's dramatic society, for which he was always an active adviser, a birthday, a publication, a joke. I wish he had written more of the longer non-myth poems. Certainly *Summer Stars* could never have been written outside the myth altogether, or it would have been a different poetic experience. It is very much of its age, however singular the handling, for the formality of it has a relationship with the world of Hemingway, and the Arthurian experience of a world disintegrating and having to be continuingly and personally rescued and remade is perfectly contemporary.

Coinherence and substitution and exchange are operative throughout. In "Prelude"* they are specifically Christian, since the Incarnation is named in the fixed stars: Theotokos, Anthropotokos — God-bearer, Man-bearer. No doubt the opponents of unchurched Christianity rightly observe how near Williams came in his novel *Descent into Hell* to saying that coinherence and exchange could operate with no Christian basis of fact, though he never reached the point of saying it. At the time of writing the novel he was leading a busy literary life in London, and was much exposed to intellectual nonbelievers. He used to say that educated ignorance of Christian dogma was so great that they would be hard put to say what it was that they did not believe in. Except for the title, he could not have ranged much wider from an explicit Christian position than in *Descent into Hell.*

In "Prelude" we are firmly based on the "twyfold Nature" and "physiological glory." We are secure from the wiles of "professing only a moral union" of flesh and spirit, where flesh and matter only get a small allowance of glory. On the other hand, of course, flesh is involved in both glory and spirit and cannot discard either from laziness or pride. C. W. often found himself at odds with modernists of the 1930s and '40s over this, as Christians did with Nestorius in the 430s and '40s. "Flesh" includes in its meaning all matter, and the world of nature on this earth. In the third stanza of "Prelude," "the zone of visionary powers" refers to Wordsworth's poetic insight into nature. So, in that stanza, coinherence of flesh and spirit includes under the concept of flesh the "Roman polity" or man's organization of society in the world, nature and poetry, and the almost materialized glimpse of the divine Person in beauty or in the form of the beloved. The images persist, hazel of all man's measurement and control, corn of the body's physical well-being, vine of inspiration and expansion of power.

Williams' verse is nearly all narrative. Invocation, lyric exclamation, and lament are woven in so finely that they are easily missed. Like most poets of his time he uses conversation in his poetry, but the main style is narrative. At a literary meeting recently where his poetry was being read, a young man said that he found C. W. too didactic, and that this alienated him. Certainly C. W. did not intend to teach or found a school — more than once he had to fight for his freedom with a band of devotees who were insisting on his founding one — and to the very end continued to present his ideas and thoughts, even meditations, as events and processes of his Arthurian medium. Perhaps a didactic flavor is given by his observation of principles in operation through events. "The Calling of Taliessin,"* which is a poem on his process of becoming a poet, is a closely coinhering substance of event and reaction and meditation, at once Taliessin's and Charles Williams'. Stanza five begins,

*Dangerous to men is the wood of Broceliande.*

This is the region of primal forces, in the mind, and the subconscious, in the body, and in history. Here man feels after God and poetry, in which all art is to be understood.

*Many a mile of distance goes to the making.*

Did he not know it? Not only the inflexible discipline of art and morals and experience, but the drag of time — four unsuccessful little books of verse published by the time he was forty, and the first outward recognition — the invitation to write *Thomas Cranmer of Canterbury* — when he was fifty.

The title of *Summer Stars* is taken from this poem. A line recurs,

> *The stones of the waste glimmered like summer stars.*

We were the stones of the waste. We, the clerks, secretaries, junior editors, electricians, mechanics, nurses, mostly young, a few older, who came to his lectures at first because we felt the lack of education, culture, or opportunity, or meaning, in our lives. We felt ourselves stones of the waste, even if few of us had heard of *The Waste Land*. Later on, when the world widened for him, he spoke chiefly to university students, who had been given all these things that his early students lacked, and to older people who were conscious of wastes far wider than we had pined in.

But in the 1930s the stones lay in the less well-off suburbs, in the semidetached villas, in wastes of long monotonous streets and long monotonous years with a small pension at the end. They lacked the robustness and importance of the "working class," and poverty was always at hand to disable hopes.

To Charles Williams they were his friends, his household. They accepted his ideas without having the general knowledge to judge them or find them difficult. They were the food on their plate when enlightenment appeared. Scattered at the desks in the chilly classrooms after a day's work, they ate, and lived and grew. In their varying degrees they grew into the life Williams showed them, the life of love and poetry, of coinherence and exchange. Often he declared that they taught him, and that they did what he only showed and spoke of.

He offered no comfort, cure, or change, no personal magic. He offered the way to find a new life in our old conditions. The stones were not brought in from the waste, the waste was not illumined or cultivated. He showed us poetry and theology, and the life within them, and we accepted that we could take it and be taken by it seriously. He pressed no religious faith or practice, but presented dogmas just as he presented Wordsworth's poetic concept of imagination or Keats's of beauty. He took them seriously, and taught us to do so. We were ready to try out a dogma which we had truly grasped, but would not have been ready to accept a faith. Yet looking back, I think that coinherence presumed a faith and created the faith it presumed. The stones grew to coinhere with the life of substitution and exchange, and a new life grew up in the old, so that conditions pressed less heavily, abilities developed and prospects held new emphases, incurable conditions like the coming of old age found that the life inhered also in them. At moments the stones began to glimmer, and at those moments the waste could be seen as the vault of sky in which the stars move. Lack and deprivation were met, and

*Taliessin*
*began then to share in the doctrine of largesse.*
["The Calling of Taliessin," stanza 11]

Williams knew that throughout cities and countries everywhere, in people of all seasons of life, there existed this "wide waste." But he saw the wide waste now lit

*by the clear assuaging fires; in the shadow*
*the stones of the waste glimmered like summer stars.*
[stanza 11]

As life grew among them it was known more and more in its nature of exchange and coinherence, with each other, with C. W., with Christ in the nature of the world; and though a few could not accept a creed of Christ, they did accept the fact.

*All that stood*
*at the height of the brain faded into the space*
*again of a starry night; through the reach of Logres*
*the stones of the waste glimmered like summer stars,*
*as if the king's poet's household of stars*
*shone, in a visible glory, on the dreaming Taliessin.*
[stanza 13]

The very word "suburb" can be part of that restoration.

*They who shall be called and thralled*
*by Taliessin's purchase and their own will*
*from many a suburb, many a waste; say*
*that they are a wonder whose origin is not known,*
*they are strown with a high habit, with the doctrine of largesse,*
*who in his house shall be more than the king's poet*
*because of the vows they take.*
[stanza 13]

Vows not to him, he never would allow them, but to the life he showed.

*They only can do it with my lord who can do it without him,*
*and I know he will have about him only those.*[4]

Once more he deliberately drew suburbia into verse. In "The Departure of Dindrane"* Taliessin says to Dindrane,

[4] "The Departure of Dindrane," last lines, in *Region of the Summer Stars.*

*I will ride through the suburbs beside you. Advance, companions.*
[stanza 6]

And they ride together until "the last villas of Camelot lay behind," along the city road,

*on the high road of the hazel*
*between city and convent, the two great vocations.*

Williams spent no time looking for an ideal reader or an intelligent circle. His knights do not ride the streets of university towns, and spend very little time in Carbonek. He lived and worked directly through each day and the people and jobs it brought. But instead of the details becoming less and less alive to him, and more and more stones in a waste, he caused them by his attention and work to live more fully, until in him the life of love might open naturally at any moment through any of them, writing a note for Production, sitting in a World's Classics committee, a joke on the stairs, signing a check, turning the key in the flat door, going to lecture yet again.

As his writings made their way, other people began to get in touch with him, famous men like Lewis and Eliot, writers like David Jones and Dorothy Sayers, and the ordinary men and women who make up the public. All came sooner or later to talk or write about coinherence. The Anglican Church made its own approaches. I remember him strolling in to say that he had crossed the Atlantic, an American had written to him. All ages, interests, and problems came. There was no difference between old friends and new; everyone exchanged talk and friendship as was needed, with equal genuineness.

Perhaps the poetic dispersal of the household developed from the discovery that there were no bounds. Coinherence and exchange will not live a selected life between one pair or group of lovers, nor between members of one sect or one church only. That is an image of it only, which can be for good, often is for bad. Coinherence comes from and moves through the web that holds us all. Emotional domination and emotional dependence alike have no hold there, nor intellectual or spiritual seniority. Only the fact of coinherent union stands, and the will toward it. Thus, in *The Region of the Summer Stars,* in "The Prayers of the Pope,"* Taliessin dispersed his household before they were inevitably scattered by war, and in the act of dispersal the members recognized that, outwardly sealed or loosed, the coinherence endured for ever. Taliessin said,

*We dissolve*
*the outer bonds; We declare the Company still*

*fixed in the will of all who serve the Company,*
*but the ends are on Us, peers and friends; We restore*
*again to God the once-permitted lieutenancy;*

. . . . . . . . . . . . . . . . . . . .

*We restore it to God in each singly and in all.*
*Receive it in God.*

Time has gone by, and some have died, and the rest grow old, but new names come freshly on. There are theses being written on detailed aspects of Williams' work at the present time in England, the United States, France, and Germany. Indeed, a strange new growth appears everywhere, for while coinherence, substitution, and exchange sustain our inward hearts, the outward world increasingly demands that politics, economics, religion, and life in society shall be slanted toward that life. It is no easier way than any other, no more certain of general success. What will the world make of it?

*If skill be of work or of will*
*in the dispersed homes of the household, let the Company*
*pray for it still.*[5]

[5] "Taliessin at Lancelot's Mass," last lines, in *Taliessin Through Logres.*

# Appendix: Selections from the Poetry of Charles Williams

Passages from Charles Williams' *Taliessin Through Logres* and *The Region of the Summer Stars,* additional to those quoted in the essay, which show the working of coinherence, substitution, and exchange.

## *TALIESSIN THROUGH LOGRES*

### from "Prelude"

*Carbonek, Camelot, Caucasia,*
*were gates and containers, intermediations of light;*
*geography breathing geometry, the double-fledged* Logos.

*The blind rulers of Logres*
*nourished the land on a fallacy of rational virtue;*
*the seals of the saints were broken; the chairs of the Table reeled.*

*Galahad quickened in the Mercy;*
*but history began; the Moslem stormed Byzantium;*
*lost was the glory, lost the power and kingdom.*

. . . . . . . . . . . . . . . . .

*Caucasia fell to the Moslem;*
*the mamelukes seized the ancient cornland of Empire.*
*Union is breached; the imams stand in Sophia.*

Good is God, *the muezzin*
*calls, but lost is the light on the hills of Caucasia,*
*glory of the Emperor, glory of substantial being.*

### from "Taliessin in the School of the Poets"

*'At the huge and heavy stair's head*
  *all measures, to infinite strength,*
*from sapphire-laced distances drawn,*
*fill the jewel-joint-justiced throne;*
*adored be God and the Emperor*
  *for the gathering of the* n*th.*

. . . . . . . . . . . . . .

*Each moment there is the midmost*
  *of the whole massive load;*
*impulse a grace and wonder a will,*
*love desert, and sight direction,*

*whence the Acts of Identity issue*
*in the Pandects and the Code;*

*while in the opposite shires of Logres*
*the willows of the brook sway*
*by the tribal tracks and the Roman roads*
*in the haze of the levels and the lengthening lines,*
*and the nuts of the uncut hazel fall*
*down the cut hazel's way.'*

. . . . . . . . . .

*Infinite patterns opened*
*in the sovereign chair's mass;*
*but the crowned form of anatomized man,*
*bones, nerves, sinews,*
*the diagram of the style of the Logos,*
*rose in the crimson brass.*

from "Taliessin on the Death of Virgil"

*Virgil fell from the edge of the world,*
*hurled by the thrust of Augustus' back; the shape*
*he loved grew huge and black, loomed and pushed.*
*The air rushed up; he fell*
*into despair, into air's other.*
*The hexameter's fullness now could find no ground;*
*his mind, dizzily replete with the meaningless sweet sound,*
*could found no Rome there on the joys of a noise.*
*He fell through his moment's infinity*
*(no man escapes), all the shapes of his labour,*
*his infinite images, dropping pell-mell.*

. . . . . . . . . . . . . . .

*Unborn pieties lived.*
*Out of the infinity of time to that moment's infinity*
*they lived, they rushed, they dived below him, they rose*
*to close with his fall; all, while man is, that could*
*live, and would, by his hexameters, found*
*there the ground of their power, and their power's use.*
*Others he saved; himself he could not save.*
*In that hour they came; more and faster, they sped*
*to their dead master; they sought him to save*
*from the spectral grave and the endless falling,*
*who had heard, for their own instruction, the sound of his calling.*
*There was intervention, suspension, the net of their loves,*
*all their throng's songs:*
Virgil, master and friend,
holy poet, priest, president of priests,
prince long since of all our energies' end,
deign to accept adoration, and what salvation
may reign here by us, deign of goodwill to endure,
in this net of obedient loves, doves of your cote and wings,
Virgil, friend, lover, and lord.

*Virgil was fathered of his friends.*
*He lived in their ends.*
*He was set on the marble of exchange.*

from "The Coming of Palomides"

*Blessed for ever be the hour*
*when first the intellectual power*
*saw triple angles, triple sides,*
*and that proceed which naught divides*
*through their great centre, by the stress*
*of the queen's arm's blissful nakedness,*
*to unions metaphysical;*
*blessed the unity of all*
*authorities of blood and brain,*
*triply obedient, each to twain,*
*obedience in the mind, subdued*
*to fire of fact and fire of blood;*
*obedience in the blood, exact*
*to fire of mind and fire of fact;*
*to mind and blood the fact's intense*
*incredible obedience,*
*in the true equilateral ease.*

from "Bors to Elayne: on the King's Coins"

*The Archbishop answered the lords;*
*his words went up through a slope of calm air:*
*'Might may take symbols and folly make treasure,*
*and greed bid God, who hides himself for man's pleasure*
*by occasion, hide himself essentially: this abides —*
*that the everlasting house the soul discovers*
*is always another's; we must lose our own ends;*
*we must always live in the habitation of our lovers,*
*my friend's shelter for me, mine for him.*
*This is the way of this world in the day of that other's;*
*make yourself friends by means of the riches of iniquity,*
*for the wealth of the self is the health of the self exchanged.*
*What saith Heracleitus? — and what is the City's breath? —*
dying each other's life, living each other's death.
*Money is a medium of exchange.'*

. . . . . . . . . . . . . . . . . . . . .

*What can be saved without order? and how order?*
*Compact is becoming contract; man only earns, and pays,*
*the house outside the City burns but the house within is enslaved.*
*What without coinage or with coinage can be saved?*
*O lady, your hand held the bread*
*and Christ the City spread in the extensor muscles of your thumbs.*

from "The Last Voyage"

*A saffron pall*
*over the bier and the pale body of Blanchefleur,*

*mother of the nature of lovers, creature of exchange;*
*drained there of blood by the thighed wound,*
*she died another's death, another lived her life.*
*Where it was still to-night, in the last candles of Logres,*
*a lady danced, to please the sight of her friends;*
*her cheeks were stained from the arteries of Percivale's sister.*
*Between them they trod the measure of heaven and earth,*
*and the dead woman waited the turn and throe of the dance*
*where, rafting and undershafting the quadruplicate sacrum,*
*below the saffron pall, the joyous woe of Blanchefleur,*
*the ship of Solomon (blessed be he) drove on.*

. . . . . . . . . . . . . . . . . . . . .

*But the Infant's song was thick with a litany of names*
*from the king and the king's friend to the least of the slaves.*
*He was borne through the waves to his end on a cry of substitution.*

## *THE REGION OF THE SUMMER STARS*

from "The Calling of Taliessin"

*In Elphin's house he grew and practised verse;*
*striving in his young body with the double living*
*of the breath in the lung and the sung breath in the brain,*
*the growing and the knowing and the union of both in the showing,*
*the triune union in each line of verse,*
*but lacking the formulae and the grand backing of the Empire.*
(stanza 2)

. . . . . . . . . . . . . . . . . . . . .

*As he came on the third day down the way to the coast*
*he saw on his left a wilderness; Logres lay*
*without the form of a Republic, without letters or law,*
*a storm of violent kings at war — smoke*
*poured from a burning village in the mid-east;*
*transport had ceased, and all exchange stilled.*
(stanza 4)

. . . . . . . . . . . . . . . . . . .

*The weight of poetry could not then sink*
*into the full depth of the weight of glory.*
*For all the codes his young tongue bore*
*Taliessin could not think in Merlin's style,*
*nor his verse grow mature with pure fact.*
*Many a mile of distance in the Empire was to go*
*to the learning, many a turn of exchange in the need*
*of himself or others or the Empire, much speed*
*in chariots and ships by the Golden Horn, and the high*
*cliffs and gardens of Caucasus, and the sky of Rome*
*where the hands of the Pope are precise in the white sacrifice.*
(stanza 11)

. . . . . . . . . . . . . . . . . . . . .

*'Sarras is free to Carbonek, Carbonek to Camelot;*

*in all categories holds the largesse of exchange,*
*and the sea of Broceliande enfolds the Empire.'*

(stanza 12)

from "Taliessin in the Rose-Garden"

*'I*
*everywhere study and sigh for the zodiac in flesh —*
*scandal to men, folly to women! but we,*
*Palomides and I, see everywhere the hint,*
*in a queen's shape or a slave's; we bid for a purchase;*
*the purchase flies to its aim in the heart of another;*
*our fame is left us darkling, and our mind to find*
*a new law; bitter is the brew of exchange.*
*We buy for others; we make beauty for others;*
*and the beauty made is not the beauty meant;*
*shent is pride while the Rose-King bleeds at Carbonek.'*

(stanza 3)

*The zodiac of Christ poorly sufficed the Adam;*
*they bade the Scorpion sting; they looked wildly*
*on the crookt curves of identity; venom is hereditary,*
*and the Adam's children endure the Adam's blood.*
*Cain, seeking a cure, was driven farther*
*into the pit; at a blow he split the zodiac.*
*He called into being earthly without heavenly justice,*
*supposing without his brother, without the other,*
*he solely existed.*

(stanza 7)

from "The Departure of Dindrane"

*The slave-girl looked; well she knew the princess,*
*who in a year and a day had grown dear*
*to the king's poet's house; she knew the vows*
*Dindrane rode to take, for the sake of Christ;*
*she guessed the sword of schism that pierced her lord,*
*dew-bright as the chrism of dedication*
*shining already there in Dindrane's brow.*
*She measured herself against her, in a suddenly now*
*new-treasured servitude; she saw there*
*love and a live heart lie in Dindrane*
*and all circumstance of bondage blessed in her body*
*moving to a bondage — to a new-panoplied category.*
*The cell of her own servitude was now the shell*
*of the body of the princess; therefore, closer, of hers.*
*The jointed and linked fetters were the jointed bones,*
*manacles of energy were manipulations of power.*
*The hazel of the cattle-goad, of the measuring-rod,*
*of the slaves' discipline, of Logres' highway, of Merlin's*
*wand of magic, of her lord's line of verse,*
*of the octave of song, of the footpace under the altar,*

*straight and strong, was in Dindrane's bare arm,*
*fair measure in the body of the body's deeds.*
*Love and a live heart lay in Dindrane;*
*love and a live heart sprang in the slave.*

from "The Founding of the Company"

*What says the creed of the Trinity?* quicunque vult;
*therefore its cult was the Trinity and the Flesh-taking,*
*and its rule as the making of man in the doctrine of largesse,*
*and its vow as the telling, the singular and mutual confession*
*of the indwelling, of the mansion and session of each in each.*

*Grounded so in the Acts and pacts of the Empire,*
*doctrine and image — from rose-lordly Caucasia*
*to the sentences sealing the soul through the whole of Logres*
*by the mouth of London-in-Logres; from the strong base*
*of maids, porters, mechanics, to the glowing face*
*of Dindrane (called Blanchfleur*) and the cells of the brain*
*of the king's college and council — were the wise companions.*

. . . . . . . . . . . . . . . . . . . .

*At the first station,*
*were those who lived by a frankness of honourable exchange,*
*labour in the kingdom, devotion in the Church, the need*
*each had of other; this was the measurement and motion*
*of process — the seed of all civil polity*
*among Esquimaux or Hottentots, and in any turbulent tribe*
*the ceasing of strife; only rejected in P'o-l'u,*
*but only by a nightmare could the household know P'o-l'u.*
*This the Acts of the Emperor decreed to the world,*
*losing or loosing none, of the heathen without*
*or the slaves within; nay, servitude itself*
*was sweetly fee'd or freed by the willing proffer*
*of itself to another, the taking of another to itself*
*in degree, the making of a mutual beauty in exchange,*
*be the exchange dutiful or freely debonair;*
*duty so and debonair freedom mingled,*
*taking and giving being the living of largesse,*
*and in less than this the kingdom having no saving.*

*The Company's second mode bore farther*
*the labour and fruition; it exchanged the proper self*
*and wherever need was drew breath daily*
*in another place according to the grace of the Spirit*
*'dying each other's life, living each other's death.'*
*Terrible and lovely is the general substitution of souls*
*the Flesh-taking ordained for Its† mortal images*
*in Its† first creation, and now in Its sublime self*

* So spelled in *Summer Stars (Blanchefleur* in *Taliessin Through Logres).*
† 1944 text: its.

*shows, since It deigned to be dead in the stead of each man.*
*This to be practised the hidden contemplatives knew*
*throughout the Empire, and daily slew and were slain;*
*this to be practised the whole Company believed*
*and gently and sweetly received in the shining air*
*even at Camelot; at Caerleon it became common —*
*there when they removed they loved easier.*
*This now out of the cells of contemplatives*
*walked for a little in the sun; none of the Company —*
*in marriage, in the priesthood, in friendship, in all love —*
*forgot in their own degree the decree of substitution.*

. . . . . . . . . . . . . . . . . . .

*Few — and that hardly — entered on the third*
*station, where the full salvation of all souls*
*is seen, and their co-inhering, as when the Trinity*
*first made man in Their image, and now restored*
*by the one adored substitution; there men*
*were known, each alone and none alone,*
*bearing and borne, as the Flesh-taking sufficed*
*the God-bearer to make her a sharer in Itself.*

*Of the lords — Percivale, Dindrane, Dinadan, the Archbishop;*
*of the people — a mechanic here, a maid there,*
*knew the whole charge, as vocation devised.*
*More rarely, at a moment, the king's poet saw*
*in the large vision of verse, at once everywhere*
*the law willed and fulfilled and walking in Camelot;*
*as from a high deck among tossing seas*
*beyond Broceliande he had seen afar*
*a deep, strange island of granite growth,*
*thrice charged with massive light in change,*
*clear and golden-cream and rose tinctured,*
*each in turn the Holder and the Held — as the eyes*
*of the watcher altered and faltered and again saw*
*the primal Nature revealed as a law to the creature;*
*beyond Carbonek, beyond Broceliande,*
*in the land of the Trinity, the land of the perichoresis,*
*of separateness without separation, reality without rift,*
*where the Basis is in the Image, and the Image in the Gift,*
*the Gift is in the Image and the Image in the Basis,*
*and Basis and Gift alike in Gift and Basis.*

from "The Prayers of the Pope"

*The tale spread,*
*till the governors of the themes knew it in their own dreams;*
*forsaking the Emperor, they chose among themselves,*
*here one and there one, foes*
*among themselves, puppets of reputation,*
*void of communicated generation of glory;*
*clouds covered the Imperial Throne in Byzantium;*

*and the Acts of the Throne were let by infidels; none*
*cared how men were shaped in body or mind,*
*nor pined for the perfect Parousia; all gave*
*their choice to the primal curse and the grave; their loves*
*escaped back to the old necromantic gnosis*
*of separation, were it but from one soul.*
*Frantic with fear of losing themselves in others,*
*they denounced and delivered one another to reprobation —*
*Mordred or the Khan of the Huns or the Khalif of Asia*
*or any neighbour they envied in labour or love.*
*They rejected the City; they made substitutes for the City;*
*mutes or rhetoricians instead of the sacred poets,*
*cheating for charity, exposition for experience,*
*braggadocio or burlesque for faith and hope.*

(stanza 2)

*The line faltered along the Danube and the Rhine;*
*pale in London and Lutetia grew the tale of peace,*
*and bloody the Noel-song; the towns of Logres*
*felt the sliding planes of the raiders' sails,*
*and Gaul all the push of the Northern woods,*
*savage growths, moods infinitely multiplied*
*across the bleak plains, under rains and snows*
*of myths bitter to bondage, where in race*
*by sullen marshes separated from race*
*virtue is monopolized and grace prized in schism.*
*The consuls and lords fought for the fords and towns,*
*but over the Rhine, over the Vistula and Danube*
*pressed the grand tribes; the land shook*
*as band after band stamped into darkness cities*
*whose burning had lamped their path; their wrath grew*
*with vengeance and victory; they looked to no returning.*

(stanza 4)

*The Pope prayed: 'O Blessed, confirm*
*not thee in thine images only but thine images in thee.*
*Bestow now the double inseparable wonder,*
*the irrevocable union: set in each thy term.*
*The formulae of glory are the food of intellectual love,*
*from the rose-gardens to the wardens of the divine science,*
*and so to the sacred Heart; the Flesh-taker*
*with the God-bearer, each the off-springing of other,*
*the Maker a sharer only and the making as much.*
*Let the chief of the images touch the Unimaged, and free*
*the Love that recovered Itself, nor only an image,*
*nor only all the images, but wholly Itself;*
*free It that we, solely the rich, may pray*
*send not, send not, the rich empty away.'*

(stanza 9)

*'Keep thy word in thine unknown elect:*

*no wise their supernatural parts sundered*
*from their natural hearts; little shall those hearts suffer —*
*so much shall the healing metaphysic have power upon them —*
*from evil and mischief and the crafty assaults of the devil.*
*Purely their souls shall go and their bodies securely,*
*whether in body or soul they drink deadly,*
*or handle malice and slander as they handle serpents,*
*by the magnificence in modesty, the modesty in magnificence*
*that the doctrine of largesse teaches; what recovers*
*lovers in lovers is love; let them then*
*go into every den of magic and mutiny,*
*touch the sick and the sick be healed, take*
*the trick of the weak devils with peace, and speak*
*at last on the coast of the land of the Trinity the tongue*
*of the Holy Ghost. O Blessed, for ever bring*
*thine own to thyself and for ever thyself to thine own.'*

(stanza 11)

# The Vision of Cosmic Order in the Oxford Mythmakers

MARJORIE EVELYN WRIGHT

The mythic realms mapped out by C. S. Lewis, Charles Williams, and J. R. R. Tolkien are clearly defined regions organized by an intricate system of cosmic order — order, that is, which embraces the whole world in which each myth is set.[1] We

[1] Charles Williams, Arthurian Poetry: *Taliessin through Logres* (Oxford, 1938), referred to in the text as *Taliessin,* and *The Region of the Summer Stars* (London, 1944); Fiction: *War in Heaven* (London, 1930, repr. Grand Rapids, 1965), *Many Dimensions* (London, 1931, repr. Grand Rapids, 1965), *The Place of the Lion* (London, 1931, repr. Grand Rapids, 1965), *The Greater Trumps* (London, 1932), *Shadows of Ecstasy* (London, 1933, repr. Grand Rapids, 1965), *Descent into Hell* (London, 1937, repr. Grand Rapids, 1965), and *All Hallows' Eve* (London, 1945).

C. S. Lewis, Science Fiction Trilogy: *Out of the Silent Planet* (London,

---

Marjorie Evelyn Wright graduated from Wheaton College *summa cum laude* in 1954. From 1954 to 1956 she held a graduate assistantship in English at the University of Illinois, earning an M.A. meanwhile, and in 1957 she was appointed George A. Miller Fellow in English. The following year she began her teaching career at Hood College. Returning to Maryland for her second year of teaching, she was killed in an automobile accident on September 16, 1959. She had completed Ph.D. work at Illinois pending final typing and oral defense of the thesis; the degree was awarded posthumously in 1960. The present article is a very slightly edited version of Chapter iii of her dissertation, *The Cosmic Kingdom of Myth: A Study in the Myth-Philosophy of Charles Williams, C. S. Lewis, and J. R. R. Tolkien* (Ann Arbor: University Microfilms 60-4025), © 1961 Dr. Paul McCoy Wright, with whose permission it is included in this volume. Professor Kilby took a great interest in Miss Wright's project, having first interested her in Lewis and suggested the idea for the dissertation, and having in turn been persuaded by her to read Tolkien's trilogy, *The Lord of the Rings*. Other publications by Miss Wright include poems in the 1949 and 1950 volumes of *Anthology of Private High School Poetry*.

shall also find that all follow basically the same pattern, as we should expect from the similar orientation of the three Mythmakers.

The cosmic patterns of the myths can be divided into two groups. First is the passive system of order, the stable, unchanging organization in which each thing, person, and event has its own proper place. Then there is the active system, governing the movements, actions, and exchanges of those who make up the kingdom. We might call the former the geography of the cosmos, and the latter the commerce of the cosmos.

The basic cosmic pattern of these myths is hierarchy. The hierarchy, of course, can be as intricate or as simple as the particular myth demands, but the pattern is the same. Once the idea of the kingdom enters, the hierarchy is inescapable. It is true, of course, that hierarchy is usually associated with religious government or military government, but the principle applies whenever there is absolute power at the top and intermediate ranks exercising authority toward those below and obedience toward those above. It is a pyramidal structure, emphasizing relationship, place, function, order. In a hierarchy, everything or everyone in it can be located, is there for a particular reason, and can be related to everything else in the structure. The structure is both horizontal and vertical. A thing can be above or below another, or it may be on the same horizontal plane or level, but in a different vertical order.

One naturally tends to think of hierarchy applied to cosmic order as a characteristic of medieval thought, fading out gradually after the Renaissance. It certainly does fit well with the Ptolemaic universe, and is indeed the philosophic counterpart of the scientific system. The system is complete and detailed in Dante, but the principle is still there in Ulysses' degree speech in Shakespeare's *Troilus and Cressida.* Even Pope, though living in a different universe, finds at least the hierarchy of being still useful in explaining the nature and function of man. But

1938), *Perelandra* (London, 1943), and *That Hideous Strength: A Modern Fairy-Tale for Grown-ups* (London, 1945); NARNIA SERIES: *The Lion, the Witch and the Wardrobe* (New York, 1950), *Prince Caspian* (New York, 1951), *The Voyage of the "Dawn Treader"* (New York, 1952), *The Silver Chair* (New York, 1953), *The Horse and his Boy* (New York, 1954), *The Magician's Nephew* (New York, 1955), and *The Last Battle* (New York, 1956); OTHER: *Till We Have Faces: A Myth Retold* (New York, 1956, repr. Grand Rapids, 1964).

J. R. R. Tolkien, *The Hobbit* (London, 1937), *The Lord of the Rings* (3 vols., London, 1954-56) (referred to in text as *Ring*).

since then hierarchy as either a reality or an imaginative force seems to have almost died out, except in directly Christian references to God and the angels, or to the church on earth, and then only in the more ritual-minded sector of Christianity.

However, to the three Mythmakers, hierarchy is not something dead and gone, applying only to a worn-out scientific theory. The Mythmakers are, of course, identified with that part of Christianity which is familiar with the hierarchic structure, but to these three, and especially to Lewis, goes much of the credit for a reidentification of hierarchy with cosmic imagination. But they are not alone in this. D. E. Harding's *The Hierarchy of Heaven and Earth* (London, 1952), although it comes too late to be an influence on any of them, is an interesting attempt to orient the modern scientific universe to a hierarchic philosophical perception. Lewis, indeed, has written the preface to the book, and as he points out, one of its most significant features is that the hierarchic system expounded attempts to reverse a long-standing trend of philosophy toward the separation of being and the universe.

The principle of hierarchic order is inherent in each of the myth-worlds we shall consider, but its most complete expression is in Lewis's space trilogy. Maleldil is the creator of all the worlds, and he can, of course, have direct dealings with any of his creatures. But in general, each planet is controlled by an eldil who is appointed the Oyarsa or tutelary ruler. The Oyarsa is in turn served by the other eldils in his sphere, and the eldils are responsible for the creatures on their planet. There are various species of intelligent creatures, including man, some existing together on the same planet. These creatures have authority over the dumb animals, especially those which can be tamed.

This is the basic vertical structure of the hierarchy, but there can be, in fact must be, variations among different strands. The pattern cannot be quite the same on any two planets. Malacandra has three intelligent species, none subservient to the others, all under the Oyarsa and on the same plane, yet not exactly equal, either. Each species has a different function, each complementing the others. The *pfifltriggi* are miners and skilled manual workers; the *hrossa* poets, fishers and hunters; the *séroni,* scientists and scholars.

In Perelandra man is the only intelligent species, and the hierarchy undergoes a reversal when the eldil yields the duties of Oyarsa to the King and places himself under the command of the King. For although we have spoken of the hierarchy as stable so far as structure goes, the place of any individual within it may change, but the structure remains.

When the Oyarsa of Earth became corrupted, Earth ceased to have contact with the rest of the universe, except through the intervention of Maleldil himself. But the Oyéresu of other planets have nothing to do with it, for it is not their province. Power must be exercised only in its own realm. But when the bent Oyarsa of Earth interferes with the affairs of Malacandra and Perelandra, then a way is opened up for the eldilic power to enter the domain of Earth, as it does in *That Hideous Strength.* For though any eldil is on a higher plane of being than man, each eldil has his own sphere of action. These spheres of action we may call provinces, which may be equal in rank but are different in function.

This is true also in Williams' Empire. The Emperor is primary and over all, but the Empire is divided into provinces. Each province has again its own ruler, that of Logres, our main interest, being Arthur. Taliessin, the court poet, is under Arthur, but he in turn becomes the head of a Company which is a sort of inner nucleus of Logres in the latter days of the kingdom. None of the provinces could exist without the core of the Empire at Byzantium, but neither could Byzantium exist without its provinces, nor could the intellectual unity of Logres exist without the sensuous life of Caucasus.

Hierarchy is closely bound up in Williams with the doctrine of coinherence, each existing in the other, and in this way he avoids the one-way exercise of power which would be tyranny. As he explains in *The Figure of Beatrice* (London, 1956), "The hierarchy admitted, there is, it seems, no hierarchy at all; no higher or lower; all is here, in the first" (p. 196). Because all exist in all, none can be injured without hurting the whole. And, like Lewis, he allows for changing function within the structure. "It is the recognition of the change in the hierarchies — now one rank above another according to one mode, now reversed according to another — which prevents it becoming fixed and tyrannical" (p. 156). This, I think, adequately defends Williams from charges of totalitarianism. He insists on hierarchy, but he insists equally on a republic within the hierarchy. Everything has a place in the structure, higher or lower, but the function may change, and any place may be, for the moment, the center of the system.

This principle of the Empire is well illustrated in the roles of Lancelot and Galahad in Logres. Galahad is one who achieves the Grail and thus the means of grace for the fallen kingdom of Logres. Therefore Lancelot is indebted to him and dependent on him. But Galahad is Lancelot's son and therefore dependent upon him for life. The fact that one is a spiritual matter and the other material makes no difference; each derives from the other. Thus in the poem "Percivale at Carbonek" (*Taliessin,* p. 81) Galahad will not enter Carbonek to view the Grail without the pardon and blessing of his father Lancelot, who was grieved by deception at Galahad's birth. But Lancelot is not there, and so Bors, representing the house of Camelot, answers for him, so providing yet another act of coinherence. It would seem clear that with this type of interrelationship of function, which is continuous throughout the system, there is little room for misuse of power. In fact, in some ways hierarchy itself is a protection against totalitarianism, which often arises out of a pretense of equality when there is none.

In Middle-earth we do not see the hierarchy as a whole, but only certain parts of it. It is the higher ranks, mainly, that are hidden. We know that every good thing in Middle-earth derives from the Valar, or powers, in the Far West. But who or what the Valar are we do not know, whether creators, or lesser gods, or simply the highest ranks of elves with responsibility for Middle-earth. The elves are, as a rule, the only creatures allowed passage back and forth between the two shores. There is a sharp-cut distinction between the elves and other creatures. They are immortal. The descendents of an elf and a man may choose which race they will be of, but it means being cut off from the other.

The elves are clearly the foremost of beings on Middle-earth, and taught to mortal races their language, calendar, and astronomy. In spite of this, they are not rulers of men. They remain in their own lands, where the elf-lords rule their own people. In fact, each of the races seems to be a separate province and each has its own rulers, whether it be simply a Mayor in the Shire of the hobbits or the lordly King of men in Gondor from the long line of Númenor. Any long-range guidance that is necessary is given through the White Council, a group composed of the noblest of elf-lords and the wizards. They act as overseers for all of Middle-earth, though rarely interfering directly in the business of a particular province.

The wizards themselves are attached to no particular province. They are sent directly from the Valar to protect Middle-earth from the enemy Sauron. For in times of trouble, there may be danger if any land or ruler forgets its place. Gondor has long been without a king, and the land is ruled "till the king comes" by a steward. But since Gondor is on the borders of Mordor, the steward Denethor has come to think that his is the last hope and defense, and that nothing else matters if Gondor falls. He has lost the perspective of order and hierarchy. Gandalf, the wizard, has to tell him: "The rule of no realm is mine, neither of Gondor nor any other, great or small. But all worthy things that are in peril as the world now stands, those are my care. And for my part, I shall not wholly fail of my task, though Gondor should perish, if anything passes through this night that can still grow fair or bear fruit and flower again in days to come. For I also am a steward" (*Ring,* III, 30-31). The wizard is a steward of the whole of Middle-earth. But he is there only for a particular time, the third age. When Sauron is overthrown and the king returns, Gandalf's time of stewardship is over, and he goes back over the sea to the Far West. The next steward of Gondor, Denethor's son Faramir, does what his father could not have brought himself to do, turns over the realm to the new king, Aragorn.

In Narnia the top of the hierarchy is the rarely mentioned Emperor-Beyond-the-Sea; but it is Aslan the lion, the Emperor's son, who created Narnia and guides it, either from near or from far. As we already know, Aslan made Narnia a land to be ruled by human beings. The kings of Narnia are established by Aslan and rule under him. Then, in the various communities of talking beasts and other creatures that live in Narnia, each group has its own chief under the king. Even the talking mice are led by the High Mouse, Reepicheep. In Narnia, as in the other myths of the study, every race, every person, has a place; and if one function is disturbed it upsets the whole order.

In hierarchy as we have been discussing it, authority is passed down from one plane to the next below it. But one of the key features to the system is the single hierarchical relationship, the ruler-creature relationship, which exists on every level. It is a natural principle of a hierarchic world that some should be rulers and some subjects, and the idea of kingliness is taken very seriously. A king is different from his subjects, nobler and wiser, or he may be different in kind altogether. And yet, with all the nobility of kingship, there is always the feeling in the background that the king himself is only a steward or guardian to another even more kingly.

In Narnia, for instance, it is assumed that man is the natural ruler of the animal world, even of talking animals. And Narnia must have human kings for its own health. The kingliness of these people is apparent, even if they had been only ordinary children in England. But the children are themselves subjects when Aslan comes. Aslan, as a lion, is also the natural king of beasts. And as Narnia is his world, he is above any creatures who come in from other worlds, even though they be men. A curious example of authority arises in the last days of Narnia, as told in *The Last Battle,* after the monkey has disguised the unwitting donkey, Puzzle, as Aslan. Rumors begin coming to the people and to the king about the grievous damage being done in the west of the land, supposedly by the orders of Aslan. It does not make sense to those who believe that Aslan is good, but a traditional phrase keeps recurring: "Aslan is not a tame lion." One dare not predict what he might do. Even the king, Tirian, nearly beside himself with sorrow, knows that if Aslan has come back he can do nothing but obey. Not till the attempt is made to identify Aslan with Tash does Tirian realize that there is a trick and that he may rebel with justice.

In the battle that ends the old Narnia, the dwarfs refuse to take sides either with the king or with the usurpers and traitors. They have decided that there is no ruler and no Aslan, and keep repeating, "The Dwarfs are for the Dwarfs" (*The Last Battle,* p. 114). When the end comes and the Narnians are brought into their new country in the sight of Aslan, the dwarfs are blinded and can see nothing of their new surroundings. They have isolated themselves from the kingdom, and thus are cut off from the real life that is around them.

In Middle-earth, of course, the ruler-creature pattern is very strong. In Gondor, the realm of men is ruled by men, but the royal line is of higher descent than most of the subjects, for it is the last remnant of the race of Númenor. Even in the line of stewards there is some noble blood of Númenor, though not the royal strain of the kings. But the steward of Gondor is actually more kingly than the king of the neighboring country of Rohan, for Rohan is of lesser lineage than Gondor. Even the elves are distinguished by those who had gone over the sea and those who had not, and the elves of lesser line, such as the Wood-elves of Mirkwood, are ruled by elf-lords of the race of High-elves.

But some of the most interesting ruler-creature relationships are found in the forest provinces. Two of the oldest beings on Middle-earth are Tom Bombadil and Treebeard. Tom Bombadil is manlike in appearance, but it is hard to say just what he really is. He lives in the Old Forest near the Shire. When questioned by the hobbits, he says that he is the master of the forest but that it does not belong to him. He has control over all the trees of the forest, and especially keeps an eye on the half-alive trees, which are likely to be dangerous. He has dealings with elves and wizards, but will not go outside of his realm, not because he has an exaggerated sense of importance, like Denethor, but because his is a far older dominion and he has no place or concern in the affairs of the Third Age.

Treebeard, or Fangorn, is the other forest-master. He is the chief ent in the forest of Fangorn, to which he has given his name. There are other ents in the forest, but Treebeard is the oldest and original. There are, besides ents and trees in the forest, creatures called huorns, ents that have grown more like trees. All these are governed by the ents, with Fangorn as leader. Fangorn is, like Bombadil, mainly concerned with the welfare of his forest; but he realizes the importance of the events in the rest of the world, though he knows that he himself can have little to do with it. But in guarding his own land he is aroused to destroy the works of the traitorous wizard Saruman and thus gives indispensable aid to the cause of the allies.

In fact, one of the chief reasons for Saruman's downfall was that he tried to usurp power that did not belong to him. He, like Gandalf, was supposed to be a sort of steward-at-large, guarding the interests of Middle-earth in whatever way he could. But he was not satisfied with that role. He established a place of his own, made fortifications, and gathered forces of whatever creatures he could find, mostly orcs and evil men. Then he tried to encroach on the domains of Fangorn and Rohan, and eventually desired domination of Middle-earth. Rulership cannot be assumed unless it is given; otherwise it results in disorder, confusion, and evil as bad as that of the original enemy.

The nature of the hierarchy, being one of order on successive levels, also involves the principle of correspondences. Although no two patterns are exactly alike, the events in one plane or province may foreshadow or reflect the pattern of events in another. We find a good many of these correspondences in Lewis's space myth of Deep Heaven. One of them explains the nature of the gods. Ransom, on his space travels, meets the ruling eldils of Mars and Venus, who are obviously the originals of the gods in the old myths of earth. After long study and conversation with the eldils, he discovers the reason for the similarity, that each planet is represented in each. Thus "it was these earthly wraiths of the high intelligences that men met in old times when they reported that they had seen the gods" (*That Hideous Strength,* p. 375). These wraiths, since ours is a corrupted planet, naturally appear in distorted form, but still bearing some resemblance to their heavenly counterparts. On the other hand, there is an unfallen image of the corrupted Oyarsa of earth on each of the other planets. Thus the correspondences between planets keep the fallen earth from being completely without knowledge of the rest of Deep Heaven.

As there are correspondences between forms, so are there correspondences between events. We have such a repetition of pattern in Ransom's trip to Perelandra. Here Satan's temptation of Eve is reenacted with the Green Lady of Perelandra and Satan in Weston's body. The similarity is indeed so striking that Lewis thought it well to preface the story with a statement that it is *not* allegorical. It is not a "what might have been" account of the Garden of Eden if Eve had not yielded. It is a correspondence to the same pattern, but the events differ as they must in a new location, with the preparation of the old pattern. For the Green Lady is not left to withstand the temptation alone. After many days of trial, Ransom realizes that unless the temptation is stopped, the Lady will inevitably yield. And the only way to stop it is for him to kill the body of Weston. Thus in Perelandra, the pattern of temptation is mingled with the pattern of redemption. But since there has been no fall, redemption is not achieved by the sacrifice of Maleldil but by the action of the man Ransom. Ransom, a member of a redeemed race, follows the pattern established by Maleldil in another world. There is no duplication, but there is correspondence.

Another type of correspondence is found in the myth of Narnia. After the last battle, which ends with friends and enemies alike being thrown through the stable door of the false Aslan, the loyal Narnians find themselves in a pleasant open space where they meet Aslan. Aslan empties and finishes the old Narnia, and then gives the command to follow him "further up and further in." They do so, and soon discover that the geography around them is the geography of Narnia, and that this Narnia is better and "more real" than the old one. They keep proceeding past the Western Wilds, till they find the walled garden where Digory, the first boy in Narnia, was once sent to pluck an apple for Aslan. When they get inside the garden, they find that it also contains Narnia, and still better than the one before. At last they get far enough up into the mountains of Aslan's country to see that Narnia is a spur jutting off from the mountain, and that another spur leads to the world of England — the real world, that is, and not the England the children had been familiar with. The old worlds of Narnia and England had both been faint and imperfect copies of the real worlds joined to Aslan's country. In those old worlds, too, one could only pass from one to another by magic; but here there is easy access by the mountains of Aslan. They only reach this country, however, by death, by a railway accident in England and the battle in Narnia, and only then are enabled to see the correspondences between the worlds.

It is not only the great things of the hierarchy of the universe but also the lesser that are bound by correspondence. In *The Greater Trumps,* Williams states the principle that "all things are held together by correspondence, image with image, movement with movement: without that there could be no relation and therefore no truth" (p. 53). In this case there is special attention to the correspondences between the four suits of the Tarot pack, deniers, cups, sceptres, and swords, and the four elements, earth, water, air, and fire. Various ways of handling the cards will produce the activities of the elements. The shuffling of the deniers makes earth; the pattering of the cups, water; the beating of the sceptres, wind; and the pointing of the sword, fire. These movements can, of course, be used for good or bad purposes; but if the purpose is evil, the proper balance is destroyed and the result is chaos. The cards also correspond to their matching images, and by observing their relationships one can see and foretell events in the world, though not without danger if the cards are selfishly used. For these correspondences are part of the order of the universe, and tampering with that order may bring a chain of unexpected reactions. One of Williams' teachers of occult lore, MacGregor Mathers, relates the Tarot cards to an even more complicated system of correspondences, and quotes Eliphas Lévi's comment that "the absolute hieroglyphical science had for its basis an alphabet of which all the gods were letters, all the letters ideas, all the ideas numbers, and all the numbers perfect signs."[2] Correspondences, then, provide a relationship of affinity between images and events on different planes and, along with the other relationship of ruler and creature, give a balance and order to the system of hierarchy.

There is another side, however, to the system of correspondences. All three writers hold the view that evil is not a thing in itself, but a corruption of, or denial of, the good. Therefore evil cannot create, but only copy and pervert the good. It can do this by what we may call a reverse system of correspondences. So, in Middle-earth, the creatures of Sauron, trolls and orcs, are but counterfeits of ents and elves, and though horrible, are not so powerful (*Ring,* II, 89). Also, the winged, bird-like monster that serves as steed of the captain of the Ringwraiths is probably a counterfeit of the great and noble eagle-lord, Gwaihir, who comes to Gandalf at his need and bears him where he chooses to go. The succubus made by Wentworth in *Descent into Hell* might also be considered as a deathly, and therefore evil, correspondence to the girl Wentworth once desired. And in Narnia the White Witch is a descendant of Lilith and the Djinns (*The Lion, the Witch and the Wardrobe,* pp. 65-66). Thus she is counter-

[2] *The Tarot: Its Occult Signification* (New York, n.d.), p. 57.

feit human, as all evil is counterfeit, and on the strength of tnat she usurps the rule of Narnia.

We have been speaking of the hierarchy as if it were a system of planes and provinces, of spheres of rule and correspondences, and this certainly is the structure of the system. And it is, in a sense, stable, and gives a framework for the various possible types of relationship within it. But the picture would be inaccurate unless we stressed the fact that the system is primarily one of movement and activity. The active and passive systems are not separate, but are different aspects of the same thing. The commerce of the cosmos is simply the geography in movement.

Two of the most important types of movement in the cosmic order are the upward and downward actions of obedience and the use of power. The proper exercise of these functions yields harmony, but it is obvious that there are greater temptations to their misuse than in almost any other part of the system. Inequality must be carefully handled, and it is admittedly not very popular in modern democratic thinking. But once the principle of varying place for varying functions is established, equality does not mean so much. Furthermore, in these hierarchies of myth, obedience is not based on force but on love, and the use of power is the same. Lewis likens these actions as Ransom sees them on Perelandra to the movements of a dance, the Great Dance of Deep Heaven:

> All is righteousness and there is no equality. Not as when stones lie side by side, but as when stones support and are supported in an arch, such as His order; rule and obedience, begetting and bearing, heat glancing down, life growing up. . . . Thus each is equally at the centre and none are there by being equals, but some by giving place and some by receiving it, the small things by their smallness and the great by their greatness, and all the patterns linked and looped together by the unions of a kneeling with a sceptred love [*Perelandra,* pp. 229-230, 323].

The exchange of rule and obedience forms the pattern of the dance.

It is not, of course, necessary that the rule and the obedience should all go in the same direction all the time. Ransom himself finds this true on Perelandra. He yields place to the king and queen, although they are not of his race, because he is a guest on their planet and they are royal, and to the Oyarsa because eldils are of a greater race than man. But the king also does reverence to Ransom, because Ransom has saved his world from breaking Maleldil's commandment. The Oyarsa yields the planet to the king, for it has been prepared for his rule; but the king acknowledges the gift of the Oyarsa and asks for help in ruling his new world.

When Ransom goes back to earth, he finds new duties. He becomes the Pendragon of Logres and the Director of a Company which has been gathered to thwart the attack of the macrobes on England. Jane Studdock, when she comes to the group, finds an equality she had not looked for — her cleaning woman is on an equal footing with the others — but the word of the Director is obeyed, even by the sceptical and logical Scotchman, MacPhee. Jane herself has difficulties. In the first place, she is expected to get permission from her husband to join the Company, for the hierarchy also includes the obedience of a wife to her husband. When danger comes, she is asked to put herself under the protection of Maleldil. But Jane is not ready for this step of obedience, and is allowed to place herself under the protection of the Director as her immediate and temporary master. Both natural and supernatural obedience must be learned, but inequalities based on pride are done away with.

Williams' Taliessin in the Logres of the Empire has a similar role to that of Ransom, the Director. It seems safe to say that Ransom is for Jane Studdock a representative of Maleldil, and he receives her obedience until she is mature enough to transfer it to its proper sphere, to her husband and to Maleldil. Taliessin, as a poet, is a carrier of vision. In "The Star of Percivale" (*Taliessin,* p. 46), a slave-girl sees Taliessin, and through him, his vision. She is tempted to worship him. He warns her, "More than the voice is the vision, the kingdom than the king," and accepts her obedience to show her the source of the vision. Later she acknowledges that "the light of another, if aught, I bear,/as he the song of another; he said: I obey." Taliessin must not take the obedience for himself, but neither must he refuse the responsibility of one placed in authority.

The preceding examples illustrate not only the exercise of obedience and rule but also the principle of substitution that pervades both Williams' and Lewis's concept of cosmic order. Because of the correspondences and relationships of all things, it is often the function of one person to take the place of another, either higher or lower in the hierarchy.

Taliessin also is the head of a Company which arises when Logres is in need. Taliessin does not found the Company; it grows from the mutual acknowledgment of the coinherence of the Empire, and its purpose is to practice substitution and exchange on whatever level the individual member might find himself. And Taliessin does not wish to be the head of the Company, fearing that if he sets himself up as master he will be in danger of pride and of the tyranny of P'o-Lu. But Dinadan persuades him that, although he may feel unworthy and superfluous, it is necessary that someone take the place. It might be anyone's function, but it happens to be his. He has no choice but to "take the largesse; think yourself the less; bless heaven" (*Region of the Summer Stars,* p. 38). Rule is to be accepted in the spirit in which it is given, and all will be well.

In *Many Dimensions,* obedience not to a person but to an object is required. Chloe Burnett, secretary to Lord Arglay, the Chief Justice, is confronted by the Stone of Suleiman, which is composed of the First Matter and is marked by the Tetragrammaton. An Arab leader who knows the lore of the Stone sees the mark of the Tetragrammaton on Chloe's forehead, and realizes that she is already in the process of conforming to the Way of the Stone. When the necessity arises for something to be done with the Stone, it becomes Chloe's task to place herself in obedience to the Way of the Stone. She does not do this, however, until her master, Lord Arglay, requests it. She becomes the path by which all the types flow back into the Stone, and then the process is reversed and she receives the matter of the Stone. The process causes her death, but her obedience has allowed the Stone to go back to its source, and it is believed that she has gone there too. The bond between Chloe and Lord Arglay is based on a book he is writing called the *Survey of Organic Law.* The title expresses for both of them the nature of universal order and their relationship within it.

For Williams, the hierarchy is not complete without the republic; the two are simultaneous and coexistent. The republic could not be without the order of the hierarchy, and its equality is based upon balance and exchange within that hierarchy. When Peter Stanhope, in *Descent into Hell,* asks Pauline Anstruther to give him the burden of her fear of the *Doppelgänger,* she hesitates for fear of imposing on him. But he explains that the order of the universe is not built on pride and self-sufficiency but upon the acceptance of exchange. Later as she is thinking of this and of Stanhope's play in which she has a part, she realizes that "in her very duty the doctrine of exchange held true, hierarchical and republican. She owed the words to Stanhope; he owed the utterance to her and the rest. He was over her in the sacred order, and yet in the sacred equality they ran level. So salvation lay everywhere in interchange" (p. 202). The inherent demand for one's rights does not yield equality; it comes by mutual submission to the aid of another.

In the *Ring* trilogy rule and obedience are continually present in shifting relationships, but some of the most important examples are connected with the Ring itself. The Ring has no master but Sauron, who made it, but it will master anyone else who tries to use it. In fact, anyone who keeps it for a time begins to have an unbalanced sense of ownership and will do almost anything rather than lose possession of the Ring. It even works on those who merely desire the Ring, like Boromir and his father Denethor, and tempts them with ideas of the power they could wield if they had it. All the greatest and wisest lords of Middle-earth, especially the holders of the Elven-rings, Gandalf, Elrond, and Galadriel, realize that they are already too powerful to be entrusted with the Ring, because the temptation to use it would be too great. This is the reason it is thought best to let it remain till its destruction in the keeping of the small hobbit, Frodo. And even so, when Frodo actually does reach the Mountain of Fire after an almost impossible journey, the desire to use the Ring overcomes him, and he is only saved by the treachery of the creature Gollum.

Gollum is a furtive, selfish underground creature who for many years kept the Ring hidden in the caverns he roamed in. It is found by Bilbo, Frodo's uncle; and Gollum, unable to stand being without it, comes out of the dark and begins to hunt for it. He even goes to Mordor and is tortured by Sauron to get information. Eventually he is captured by Gandalf and Aragorn; but even though they confine him, they will not kill him in spite of the evil he has done. There is still possibly some remnant of good left that the Ring has not destroyed, or a task that Gollum must yet perform. Later he escapes, follows Frodo, and is caught again. Frodo will not kill him either, though his servant Samwise has doubts. Gollum does prove treacherous again, but in the end that treachery causes Gollum to destroy himself accidentally with the Ring, and so averts disaster for Frodo and the rest of Middle-earth. Thus if it were not for pity and the moderation of power, the whole quest might have failed.

Neither do power and victory permit the destruction of the traitor Saruman. He is allowed to leave his broken fortress and wander at will. Even after he does some last damage to the Shire, he is not harmed by the hobbits, but he is murdered by his equally treacherous servant, Wormtongue. As long as there is a possibility of good left, the rulers never harm an enemy but offer him the choice of pardon. Only the entirely evil creatures of Sauron are destroyed.

In both Narnia and the kingdom of Glome of *Till We Have Faces* the obedience of substitution is practiced, but in a slightly different form from that in the myths of Deep Heaven and the Empire. In both cases there is a confusion of the real God with a monstrous false god. In Narnia the situation is fairly clear-cut. The Narnian plotters and the Calormenes announce that Aslan and Tash are the same god. And Tash, whom none of them really believes in, comes to them, an ugly shape looking something like a monstrous pterodactyl. Those who foolishly called on Tash find him and perish. But one young Calormene warrior has loved and served Tash honestly all his life. When he is thrown to the god, he finds not Tash but Aslan. Instantly he recognizes Aslan as his true master and is afraid because he has served Tash. But Aslan tells him that any true service done can only be done to the true God, for the false god can accept no good; therefore Aslan accepts the true worship of the Calormene even though he did not know it was Aslan he was serving.

In Glome the relationship is a little more complicated. There has been a struggle between the older and more common people and the newer Greek influences about the nature of the goddess Ungit. The old Ungit is ugly, shapeless, and bloody. The new Ungit is beautiful, Greek, bloodless and sophisticated. Yet when the people are really in need, they pray to the old Ungit, and rejoice in the sacrifice of cocks and the yearly rite of the birth of Ungit's son. When Orual, after years of suffering, finds out the truth about herself and Psyche and the God of the Mountain, she learns that neither of the Ungits is the true goddess. The Greek one is too intellectual and knows no suffering; she can offer no comfort. The old, ugly, cruel Ungit is not true either, but she is closer to life. She is partly an image of the demonic and evil side of man, but she is also witness to the fact that the true gods demand obedience and sacrifice, not aesthetic admiration. The knowledge of Ungit is the beginning of truth. She must be superseded but she cannot be completely denied.

The acts of exchange and substitution in the story are intricately worked out. Orual discovers in a vision that she has become Ungit. She undergoes many hardships and Psyche reaps the benefit, being enabled to perform her appointed tasks. In her last task, that of bringing a casket from the underworld, Orual tries to stop her. But Psyche perseveres, for the casket is to make Ungit beautiful. Orual has been Ungit; it is she who is transformed by the casket and becomes like Psyche herself. And both Orual and Psyche owe their new existence to the God of the Mountain, for whose sake Psyche has been made a goddess.

Some of these examples of exchange and substitution wander a bit from the area of rule and obedience and mingle with other types of hierarchic movement. Besides vertical exchange of ruler and creature, there is horizontal exchange, and it is sometimes hard to tell where one ends and the other begins. The horizontal exchange takes place in those aspects of the hierarchy where there is no question of rule or obedience, and we may refer to it as the action of courtesy. Courtesy exists between two creatures in the same province, between creatures from different provinces, and between rulers of equal standing, especially in the province of one. It consists in the acknowledgment of the rightful place of the other and of exchanges offered not out of necessity but out of graciousness.

The deliberate submission of a ruler to his subjects might also be classified as courtesy, as it is one of the processes that make for equality. Its absence means the rigid, fixed system of Hell, according to Williams, for the "hierarchy of the abyss does not know anything of equality, nor of any lovely balance within itself, nor (if indeed he be) does the lord of that hierarchy ever look up, subordinate to his subordinates, and see above him and transcending him the glory of his household" (*All Hallows' Eve*, p. 128). For that too would be yielding without the necessity of doing so.

On Malacandra Ransom has a chance to observe the courtesies between the three intelligent races on the planet. The three have different functions and do not mix much, living on different parts of the planet. It takes Ransom a long time to understand that none of the groups controls the others. Each group gladly yields precedence to the others in the things they are best fitted for, although each race has a rather amused tolerance for the others' inabilities in its own particular specialty. In fact, Ransom notes on his visit to Meldilorn, the court of Oyarsa, that the gathering of the members of the three races produces the most pronounced forms of humor on Malacandra. The differentness of the species is accepted without question, but it is also a source of delighted enjoyment.

During his adventures on Perelandra, Ransom discovers the need for a graver type of courtesy. After his fight with Weston, he is making his way through underground caverns when a chariot carrying a strange but majestic form passes him. He senses that this is not a region for men. He wonders if "there might, if a man could find it, be some way to renew the old Pagan practice of propitiating the local gods of unknown places in such fashion that it was no offense to God Himself but only a prudent and courteous apology for trespass" (*Perelandra*, p. 196). Whatever their relative standings in the universe, this creature is in his own domain and Ransom is only a permitted guest.

In Middle-earth, the creatures of the various provinces prefer for the most part to let each other alone, but when they do meet there are always interesting results. In the old days, there had been some rather serious quarrels between the elves and the dwarfs, and at the time of the war of the Ring some hostility remains. When the Company of the Ring reaches Lorien, the most secret of the elf-woods, the dwarf Gimli has difficulty gaining admittance. But once there, he becomes the staunchest admirer and defender of the elf-lady, Galadriel, and he and Legolas, the elf member of the Company, resolve their differences and become renowned friends. Their mutual courtesy goes so far that Legolas agrees to go with Gimli to visit the Glittering Caves of Rohan; and still more surprising, the dwarf accompanies Legolas to the forest of Fangorn where no dwarfs have been allowed.

The differences of creatures are a source of amusement here too, but there is no lack of respect. Even the hobbits, the smallest of the peoples, are not treated too lightly, for many have had cause to discover that hobbits are tougher than they look. Even the ents, startled at first because hobbits are so hasty, are impressed by their abilities. And certainly it is a great exchange when the hobbits Frodo and Sam successfully complete the quest of the Ring and so repay elves and wizards and rangers of men for their long years of protection of the Shire. It would be ironic in another framework that after the heroic efforts of so many peoples the coming of the Fourth Age should bring the dominance of men, and that all the other creatures, including hobbits, should gradually fade from Middle-earth. But here, though there is inevitably sorrow at the passing of an age, it is recognized that there is a time for each people to flourish and that it can be a joy to pass on a domain after successful occupancy.

We have already spoken of the Great Dance of Deep Heaven by which the whole universal hierarchy moves in order. This dance is reflected even in the smallest aspects of that order. The Great Snow Dance of Narnia is a result of the harmony and courtesy of the varied creatures who inhabit that kingdom. Fauns and dryads are the dancers, and dwarfs circle round and throw snowballs between the dancers while musicians keep time. As the girl Jill sees the dance, "they were throwing them [snowballs] through the dance in such perfect time with the music and with such perfect aim that if all the dancers were in exactly the right places at exactly the right moments, no one would be hit.... Of course, it is a kind of game as well as a dance, because every now and then some dancer will be the least little bit wrong and get a snowball in the face, and then everyone laughs" (*The Silver Chair,* p. 186). The Snowball Dance may seem like a trivial example, but actually it is an exact description of the way in which the movement of the hierarchy works.

And, of course, it is a principle of the hierarchy that it applies equally in everyday and minor affairs and in the great events of the universe, if such a distinction can be made at all.

Rule, obedience, courtesy, exchange are the natural activities of the hierarchy. There are others that are less common and perhaps less acceptable. Under this category in general come the exercises of magic, which are brought about by the control of correspondences. There is both good magic and bad magic, but even good magic must be used with care. The Merlin of Lewis's space trilogy knew the kind of magic that depended upon a different relationship of mind and matter than now exists on our planet. This would mean a closer, more direct correspondence between the spiritual and material planes. However, Merlin's magical activity, while effective, was dangerous even in his own day; and when he comes out of his trance into present-day England, the time is completely past for the safe use of his magic. Merlin wants very much to try to cure the wound Ransom received in Perelandra, and Ransom has a difficult time explaining that the magic must not be used, especially not for personal convenience. And that is probably one of the chief dangers of magic. By using correspondence, it achieves a sort of shortcut to hierarchical power and gives the magician a great temptation to transfer that power to his own ends, especially if he becomes impatient with the normal operations of that power. This is what happens to Digory's uncle, the magician in the Narnian series, to Mr. Lee, the gypsy in *The Greater Trumps,* and to Sir Giles Tumulty in *Many Dimensions.* If magic can be used in due proportion of authority, as it is by the wielders of the Elven-rings in Middle-earth, all is well.

The myths of cosmic order are not dull and dreary police states. They are kingdoms full of life, movement, ceremony, courtesy. They are ordered in changing equalities and inequalities, in exchanges of love and obedience. The members of the hierarchy are all, depending on how one looks at it, superfluous or significant, for the whole system coinheres in each.

# Past Watchful Dragons: The Fairy Tales of C. S. Lewis

WALTER HOOPER

## I

"When I was ten," said C. S. Lewis, "I read fairy tales in secret and would have been ashamed if I had been found doing so. Now that I am fifty" (that was in 1952) "I read them openly. When I became a man I put away childish things, including the fear of childishness and the desire to be very grown up."[1]

Readers of Lewis's fairy tales are not likely to understand, simply from reading these books, how deeply his imagination slept as a boy, or how momentous was his liberation in losing "the desire to be very grown up." His boyhood was, nevertheless, a period of great fecundity: he wrote many stories about his invented world of Animal-Land at the time, and was, without knowing it, training himself to be the future chronicler of Narnia. Yet grown-up matters, which were all-in-all to Lewis

[1] C. S. Lewis, "On Three Ways of Writing for Children," *Of Other Worlds: Essays and Stories*, ed. Walter Hooper (London, 1966), p. 25.

---

Walter Hooper received a B.A. from the University of North Carolina in 1954 and an M.A. there in English in 1957. Prior to the death of C. S. Lewis in 1963, Mr. Hooper was Lewis's personal secretary; since then he has edited several books of Lewis's unpublished and uncollected works: poems, essays, stories, and correspondence. He has also published a bibliography of Lewis's writings and, most recently, an article on Lewis in *The Franciscan*, Vol. IX (1967); he is working on a biography. He has read theology at St. Stephen's House, Oxford, and is an Episcopal priest now serving as Assistant Chaplain of Jesus College, Oxford.

when he wrote about Animal-Land, find no mention whatsoever in the Narnian books.

In Lewis's autobiography, *Surprised by Joy*,[2] we get the impression of two lives — the "outer" and the "inner," the life of the intellect and the life of the imagination — being lived over against each other, albeit at the same time. The "outer" life is chiefly concerned with those things which he spoke and wrote about openly: namely, Animal-Land. The "inner" life — and this is what *Surprised by Joy* is mainly about — is essentially the story of Joy (i.e. intense longing) working on his imagination. Narnia would never have come into existence had Lewis not come to understand the meaning and purpose of Joy.

What drove Lewis to write was his extreme manual clumsiness from which he always suffered: he had only one joint in his thumb. This disability kept him from taking up the hobbies and sports that occupy most young boys. (I have seen him try to remove the cellophane wrapping from a pork pie: first with his fingers, then with a knife, then with a fork, then with both, until he finally handed it over for me to unwrap.) And so, when his family moved into their new house, "Little Lea," in 1905, he staked out a claim in one of the attics and there he wrote his first stories, stories that combined his two chief literary pleasures — "dressed animals" and "knights in armour." He was, from the first, a systematizer, a characteristic that caused him eventually to become a historiographer of his invented world of Animal-Land. When his brother was home it was necessary that it become a country shared with him. "India" (his brother's world) was lifted out of its place in the real world and became geographically related to Animal-Land. In time they became the single state of Boxen.

The earliest piece of juvenilia, *The King's Ring,* is about the theft of the crown jewels of Animal-Land in the reign of Benjamin I. This is very early Boxoniana indeed, for Benjamin I succeeded Bublish I in 1331 and the last Boxen stories take us down to 1903 (Boxen time). If the stories are ever published, the year 1856 will give Boxonologists occasion for much celebration: Lord Big is born in that year. He is that frog of powerful personality who as Little-Master (i.e. Prime Minister) carries on his shoulders not only great matters of state, but responsibility for the young kings, Benjamin VI and Hawki IV.

Some of the Boxen stories are very good and one cannot help boggling at the sheer invention and patience that went into the creation of seven hundred years of Boxoniana. Yet, con-

[2] *Surprised by Joy: The Shape of My Early Life* (London, 1955).

trary to what readers of Lewis's Narnian Chronicles might expect, the juvenilia are surprisingly prosaic. There is not the slightest hint of faerie or other worlds. The dominant theme is politics: to get into the "Clique" is the ambition of almost every character. Yet none of the characters, to say nothing of the author, seems to have a clear idea of what the "Clique" is. Ambitions run high and are almost solely concerned with money. The daily newspaper is of major interest.

When you consider that romances and fairy tales were the young Lewis's favorite form of reading, it seems odd that so much interest and energy went into stories about things that Lewis was later to detest. Yet politics and money, Lewis told me, were the chief topics of conversation between Lewis's father and his friends. Doubtless, the young Lewis wanted his stories to reflect as nearly as possible the words that fell from the lips of grown-ups and the things that to them seemed important.

I think I can best illustrate this by quoting a passage from a "novel" entitled *The Locked Door*.[3] It is rather late Boxoniana — written I should think when Lewis was about twelve. Although there are obvious traces of grown-up conversation and nights out at parties and the hippodrome, it illustrates the ease and pleasure he found in writing. Mr. James Bar, a "hock-brown" bear, and Captain Samuel Macgoullah, a horse, are on their way to a ball given by Their Majesties, Benjamin VII and Hawki V (both rabbits). I have retained Lewis's original spelling and punctuation:

> Great was the preparation of Bar and Macgoullah when the eventful evening arrived. Bar had hired a handsome to be ready for them both outside the 'Schooner' where they had arranged to meet.
>
> As they drew near the palace, Regency Street became a mass of moving lights dancing to the music of horses' hoofs and the powerful purr of motors: and it was not without difficulty that the hireling Jehu navigated them to the portals of Regency St. Palace. Stepping out they were conducted by suave domestics to the cloak room, which, as is usually the case on these occasions, was crowded with knots of whispering guests fiddling with their gloves. There of course is Puddiphat immaculately clad; there is Reginald Pig the Shipowner dressed in solid and plain evening dress; there is Quicksteppe looking finer than ever as the electric light catches his glossy curling locks; there is Colonel Chutney, formerly head of the war office, but now removed to give place to Fortescue who is also present. After some time of nervous fumbling and hushing, Pig, the most couragious person present, led a sort of forlorn hope to the salon where their Majesties were recieving their guests and where stout domestics dispensed tea etc. The two kings were throwing

[3] Lewis MS. 6. In the collection of W. H. Lewis.

all their histrionic powers into an imitation of enjoyment, and behind them stood the Little-Master looking rather worried. The boys kept up a continual flow of conversation:—

"Good evening, My dear Pig! How are the ships? Ah, Viscount Puddiphat, very glad you came."

"Good evening Your Majesties. Ah my dear Little-Master I see you've been having busy times in the Clique"

"Yes" said Big drily

The Duchess of Penzly came up, a heavy woman whom they all abominated.

"Good evening Duchess. Hasn't Miss Penzley—oh! Influenza? I am very sorrey to hear that" The Duchess passed on to Big,

"Ah, Lord Big, this is a pleasure. How delighted I was to hear you had had some excitement in politics, it does liven things up so, doesn't it?"

"It certainly does", responded the frog brusquely, and engaged a dance [fols. 31-34].

I shall return to Lewis's "outer" life presently, but it is important at this point to say something about Joy. In his autobiography Lewis defines Joy by first recording three experiences from his early childhood. While standing by a flowering currant bush on a summer day there arose in him the memory of a yet earlier morning in which his brother had brought into the nursery a toy garden. The memory of this memory caused a sensation of desire to break over him. Before he could know *what* he desired, the desire itself was gone and he was left with a "longing for the longing that had just ceased" (*Surprised by Joy,* p. 22). The second glimpse of Joy came through *Squirrel Nutkin.* This little book troubled him with the "Idea of Autumn" (p. 23), and again he was plunged into the experience of intense desire. The third glimpse came to him while reading Longfellow's translation of *Tegner's Drapa.* When he read

*I heard a voice that cried,*
*Balder the beautiful*
*Is dead, is dead—*

his mind was uplifted into huge regions of northern sky. At the very moment he was stabbed by desire, he felt himself falling out of that desire and wishing he were back in it.

Lewis tells us that Joy, the quality common to these three experiences, is an unsatisfied longing which is itself more desirable than any other satisfaction. The authentic Joy vanished when he went off to school. When, however, a year or so later while looking at a periodical, his eyes fell on the words *Siegfried and the Twilight of the Gods* and one of Arthur Rackham's illustrations to the book, it returned. In a single moment he was plunged back into the past of Balder and sunward sailing cranes, and felt the old inconsolable longing. The memory of his own past Joy and the Twilight of the Gods "flowed together," he said, "into a single, unendurable sense of desire and loss, which . . . had eluded me at the very moment when I could first say *It is*" (p. 75).

Lewis made many mistakes in his pursuit of Joy. As the old thrill became less and less frequent, he attempted most desperately to "have it again." In his impatience to snare it, to tear the veil and be in on the secrets of the universe, he turned from one medium of Joy to another, hoping always to find permanent satisfaction. He shifted from Northernness (a frequent and early transmitter of Joy) to erotic pleasure, only to find that the hounds had (again) changed scent and that though "Joy is not a substitute for sex, sex is very often a substitute for Joy" (p. 161).

Lewis lost his virginity while a student at "Chartres";[4] but it was often the "potent, ubiquitous, and unabashed"[5] eroticism of William Morris's romances that led him to believe that sex might be the substance of Joy. Interestingly enough, it was a romance of a very different sort that served as a check for this mistake. Everyone knows the book I refer to: George MacDonald's *Phantastes: a faerie Romance* which he bought at Leatherhead station when he was the pupil of W. T. Kirkpatrick at Great Bookham in Surrey. Lewis was as smitten by MacDonald as many people are by Lewis. Hitherto, each visitation of Joy had momentarily left the common world a desert. But from the pages of *Phantastes* there emerged a "bright shadow" (later known to be holiness) that transformed all common things — the bread on the table and the coals in the grate — without itself becoming changed. His imagination was, he said, "baptised" and he was carried one step closer to that which he had so long desired.

At about the same time that Lewis was beginning to understand something of the nature of Joy, he was losing interest in his political stories of Boxen. His interests were now mainly poetical. Before going to Great Bookham he began writing *Loki Bound,* a pessimistic Norse tragedy. Commenting later on the contradictions in this poem, he said: "I maintained that God did not exist. I was also very angry with God for not existing. I

[4] "Chartres" is the fictitious name he gave to Cherbourg House, a school in Malvern, Worcestershire which he attended from 1911 to 1913.

[5] C. S. Lewis, "William Morris," *Selected Literary Essays,* ed. Walter Hooper (Cambridge, 1969), p. 222.

was equally angry with Him for creating a world" (*Surprised by Joy,* p. 113). I am a bit surprised that he failed to notice the contradictions at the time, for he was even then quick to spot illogicalities. Still, I meet people every day who, though they have no real knowledge of Christianity, are nevertheless convinced that whatever they say about God *must* be true. Lewis may have been enjoying the mood, if not the fact, of infallibility.

It was while Lewis was at Great Bookham that he began corresponding with his friend, Arthur Greeves. Both were enthusiastic letter-writers, and each was anxious to share with the other the discoveries he was making. One of their first quarrels was about Christianity. Lewis did not like to talk about this but Greeves forced him to state his position. Lewis wrote:

> You know, I think, that I believe in no religion. There is absolutely no proof for any of them, and from a philosophical standpoint Christianity is not even the best. All religions, that is, all mythologies to give them their proper name, are merely man's own invention — Christ as much as Loki. Primitive man found himself surrounded by all sorts of terrible things he didn't understand.... Thus religion, that is to say mythology grew up. Often, too, great men were regarded as gods after their death — such as Heracles or Odin: thus after the death of a Hebrew philosopher Yeshua (whose name we have corrupted into Jesus) he became regarded as a god, a cult sprang up, which was afterwards connected with the ancient Hebrew Jahweh-worship, and so Christianity came into being — one mythology among many.... Of course, mind you, I am not laying down as a certainty that there *is* nothing outside the material world: considering the discoveries that are alway being made, this would be foolish. Anything MAY exist.[6]

In truth, between Lewis's imaginative life and that of his intellect — what I term his "inner" and "outer" life — there yawned a great chasm. And there did not appear to be any way of bridging the two. His imagination, over which brooded his "immortal longings," was peopled with gods, nymphs, fauns, satyrs, giants, paradises. His intellect — and especially now that Boxen with its friendly "dressed animals" had dropped out — was stark and practical. As Lewis said: "The two hemispheres of my mind were in the sharpest contrast. On the one side a many-islanded sea of poetry and myth; on the other a glib and shallow 'rationalism.' Nearly all that I loved I believed to be imaginary; nearly all that I believed to be real I thought grim and meaningless" (*Surprised by Joy,* p. 161).

When he went up to Oxford after the war he was deter-

[6] From an unpublished letter to Arthur Greeves, probably written October 12, 1916.

mined that there were to be no flirtations with the idea of the supernatural. All the images he associated with Joy were, he concluded, sheer fantasies. He had at last "seen through" them. The important thing was to get ahead with the "good" life without the Christian "mythology." But he could not be left alone. In almost every book, in almost every conversation, a chance reference to Christianity threatened to unsettle his solid philosophical position. Early in 1926 Lewis entertained in his Magdalen rooms a man whom he considered the "hardest boiled of all the atheists." He was amazed when the atheist remarked on what surprisingly good evidence there was for the historicity of the Gospels. He was shattered when the man went on to say, "Rum thing. All that stuff of Frazer's about the Dying God. Rum thing. It almost looks as if it really happened once" (p. 211).

I could not in this short paper recount how, one by one, his reservations about accepting the Christian faith were swept away (it is all admirably recounted in *Surprised by Joy*). But so they were. After long searching, yet with much reluctance, he was brought to his knees in the Trinity Term of 1929 and forced to admit that God was God. He who is the Joy of all men's desiring came upon him and compelled him by divine mercy to surrender a long-sieged fortress. His surrender, however, was to what seemed at the time a purely nonhuman God. He became a theist. The next step occurred in 1931 on the way to Whipsnade Zoo, Lewis riding in the sidecar of his brother's motorcycle. When they left Oxford he did not believe that Jesus Christ was the Son of God: when they reached the zoo he did. After that, the old bitter-sweet stabs of Joy continued as before. But he never gave them the importance they once had. That would have been impossible: he knew to what — or, rather, to *Whom* — they pointed.

## II

Now, what is the relevance of all this to the Narnian Chronicles? In the last few pages I have concentrated on those things — "dressed animals," mythology, Joy — which I feel played an especially important part in Lewis's youth and which, in various ways and degrees, contributed to his conversion to Christianity. There is a stretch of a good many years, however, between his conversion and his writing of the Narnian books. So, before jumping prematurely into a discussion of the fairy tales, I intend in the next few pages to show how Lewis's conversion helped him to rethink these same elements before they appear transformed and regenerate in the world of Narnia.

### Dressed Animals

When Lewis first put pen to paper in his Animal-Land stories, he seemed to have little understanding of the true nature of beasts. This may not have been so much his failure to observe as rather the ignorance or unconcern of some of the writers whose stories he read. And, of course, when he wrote about Animal-Land, the only animals with which he had any real intimacy were a pet mouse, Peter, and his dog, Tim. If one were not told in advance, how many of us would have guessed the nature of the animals who are speaking in the passage I quoted from *The Locked Door?* Although I have read Lewis's juvenilia, my knowledge of who is what is partly derived from the pictures Lewis drew to illustrate his Boxen stories.

His acute observations of wild and domestic animals and his old childhood fear of pain led him, years later, to devote a chapter to "Animal Pain" in his book *The Problem of Pain.* His thoughts on the matter are roughly these:[7] As beasts are incapable of either sin or virtue, they can, therefore, neither deserve nor be improved by pain. On the other hand, we must not allow the problem of animal suffering to become the center of the problem of pain because God has not given us data about the suffering of beasts. As animals presumably preceded man in the order of creation, Satan should be thought to have corrupted the brutes first. After man's own creation, it may have been one of his functions to restore peace to the animal world. This he might have done to an almost unimaginable extent had he himself not joined the enemy and, in his fall, furthered Satan's malice toward the animal kingdom. Lewis believed that animals have consciousness, though not as we know it in ourselves; and this leads to the question of whether they are, like men, immortal creatures. The answer in a nutshell is, "We don't know." As the doctrine of *human* immortality comes late in the history of Judaism, it seems unlikely from what we can discern of God's method of revelation that he would have revealed whether animals are, or are not, immortal.

The greatest difficulty about supposing all animals to be immortal, Lewis went on to say, is that immortality has almost no meaning for a creature that has no unity of consciousness. For instance, if the life of a newt is no more than a succession

[7] *The Problem of Pain* (London, 1940), pp. 117-131. See also the essays on "Vivisection" and "The Pains of Animals" in Lewis's *God in the Dock,* ed. Walter Hooper (Grand Rapids, 1970).

of sensations, it is anyone's guess whether the newt that died today would, if it were recalled to life by God, recognize itself as the same newt. Lewis believed that there is no question of immortality for creatures like newts that are merely sentient. The survival of higher animals he felt to be a more open question.

He believed that the beasts are to be understood only in their relation to man and, through man, to God. As man is appointed by God to have dominion over the beasts, those animals that man *tames* become the only "natural" animals — that is, the only ones that occupy the place God intended for them if men and animals had not fallen. If a tame animal has any real self or personality, Lewis believed that it owes this almost entirely to its master. If it is raised to life eternal, its identity will reside in its relation to the master or to the whole of humanity of which he was a member. That is, as the personality of the tame animal is largely the gift of man, then their mere sentience would be reborn to soulhood in *us* as our mere soulhood is reborn to spirituality in Christ.

One of the most interesting speculations in the chapter on "Animal Pain" is one that seems to anticipate the character of Aslan, King of Narnia. Lewis believed that creatures so remote from us as wild beasts may have no separate selves or sufferings but that each species may have a corporate self. He uses the lion as an example.

Lewis by no means always thought of animals in the collective. He had an eye for their individual beauties and differences. In his poem "Impenitence" he speaks of the

*cool primness of cats, or coney's*
*Half indignant stare of amazement, mouse's*
*Twinkling adroitness,*
*Tipsy bear's rotundity, toad's complacence....*[8]

His eyes were also open to those physical similarities that men and beasts have in common. This is why he felt that Kenneth Grahame in *The Wind in the Willows* made the right choice when he gave his principal character the form of a toad.[9] The toad's face, with its fixed "grin," bears such a striking resemblance to a certain kind of human face that no other animal would have suited the part so well. Lewis saw these physical similarities as extending even further: some animals can be most interestingly used in pictures and literature as representing the actual archetypes of some human and animal charac-

[8] C. S. Lewis, *Poems,* ed. Walter Hooper (London, 1964), p. 2.
[9] "On Stories," *Of Other Worlds,* pp. 13-14.

teristics. If they do not rise to the archetypal level, many at least, as he says in the poem quoted above,

*cry out to be used as symbols,*
*Masks for Man, cartoons, parodies by Nature*
*Formed to reveal us.*

Perhaps I might be forgiven a small digression about Lewis's relation to his own pets. When I was living at The Kilns (his home in Oxford), Lewis was affectionately termed "The Boss" by everyone there: his brother, secretary (myself), housekeeper, and gardener. Yet I never remember him speaking a sharp word or giving an order: it was his house, but he was "Boss" by virtue of his unfailing kindness and courtesy. The Kilns "family" also included two cats, an old ginger named Tom (a mighty hunter of mice when he was young, but then living on a pension of fish) and Snip (a Siamese which Lewis inherited from his wife and referred to as his "step-cat"). There was also a young boxer pup named Ricky.

They recognized Lewis as the undisputed head of the house, but he never made an elaborate fuss over them. He greeted Tom in the morning, stroked Snip when she jumped in his lap, and passed the time of day with Ricky. Live and let live: just what they wanted. If the door to his study was open, they knew they were welcome within: otherwise not. One summer morning when Lewis was writing at his desk by the open window, Snip took a great spring and shot through the window. She landed with a great thump on top of his desk, scattering papers in all directions, and skidded into his lap. He looked at her in amazement. She looked at him in amazement. "Perhaps," he said to me, "my step-cat, having finished her acrobatics, would enjoy a saucer of milk in the kitchen." I opened the door for poor Snip and she walked slowly out, embarrassed, but with the best grace she could manage.

## Mythology

In one of Lewis's notebooks, I found this definition of myth: "A *Myth* is the description of a state, an event, or a series of events, involving superhuman personages, possessing unity, not truly implying a particular time or place, and dependent for its contents not on motives developed in the course of action but on the immutable relations of the personages."[10] Stories such as those of Balder, Osiris, and Orpheus are examples of what

[10] Lewis MS. 15, fol. 138. (All of Lewis's unpublished MSS quoted are, unless otherwise specified, in the collection of Walter Hooper.)

he means. They are not dependent on fine details or eloquent language, although they usually reach us in story form. In enjoying great myths, Lewis believed, we come nearest to experiencing as concrete what could otherwise only be understood as an abstraction. For example, when we read or hear the myth of Osiris we have a concrete experience. In other words, concrete reality flows into us as we listen to the myth — like the passing of food from the mouth of a mother bird to its chick. When we attempt to "taste" it — to know the meaning of it — what we taste turns out to be truths, or universal principles. Or to put it another way, myth is a mountain from whence streams flow down into the valley. What reaches us down here in the valley is truth.[11]

I have already quoted Lewis's letter to Arthur Greeves in which he equates Christ with other gods such as Odin and his own Loki. He believed that Christianity was only one of many mythologies — a belief he held up to the time of his conversion. How on earth, he wondered, have Christians the cheek to claim their mythology true and the others false? In *The Pilgrim's Regress* he attempted to explain not only why the Pagan mythologies are not (totally) false, but how the truths in all of them *cohere.* History (an allegorical character) explains to the Pilgrim that God sent "pictures" which stir up "sweet desire" to both the ancient Jews and Pagans. The Jews were given not only pictures but Rules (the Law of Moses) as well. Both the Jews' and the Pagans' pictures contained the divine call, but the Pagans made up untrue stories about the pictures. They sought the end of "sweet desire" (i.e. Lewis's Joy) in one thing after another, trying to believe that what they found was what they wanted. There was no absurdity that they did not commit. And just when their own stories seemed to have overgrown the original message, God would send a new message and their fanciful stories would look stale. If they grew contented with lust and "mystery-mongering," a new message would arrive and the old desire would sting them again. They were, as it were, attempting eloquence before they had learned grammar.

The Jews, on the other hand, were too narrow. Of course the thing they had charge of was narrow: the Road. Once they found it they kept it clear and repaired and sign-posted: but they did not follow it. The Jew was only half a man, and the Pagan was only half a man, so that neither was well without

[11] C. S. Lewis, "Myth Became Fact," *God in the Dock,* p. 66.

the other, nor could either be healed until Christ came into the world.[12]

It was, then, no longer a matter of finding the one true religion among many, but rather finding where religion had reached its true maturity. "Paganism," he saw, "had been only the childhood of religion, or only a prophetic dream. Where was the thing full grown? or where was the awaking?" (*Surprised by Joy,* p. 221). The whole matter is summed up in an invaluable footnote in Lewis's book on Miracles:

> As, on the factual side, a long preparation culminates in God's becoming incarnate as Man, so, on the documentary side, the truth first appears in *mythical* form and then by a long process of condensing or focusing finally becomes incarnate as History. This involves the belief that Myth . . . is . . . at its best, a real though unfocused gleam of divine truth falling on human imagination. The Hebrews, like other people, had mythology: but as they were the chosen people so their mythology was the chosen mythology — the mythology chosen by God to be the vehicle of the earliest sacred truths, the first step in that process which ends in the New Testament where truth has become completely historical.[13]

Although the Gospels have what we called a moment ago the mythic "taste," they are themselves History. They are the end of the focusing. As myth transcends thought, so Incarnation transcends myth. We pass from a Balder and an Osiris, dying we know not when or where, to the great myth becoming Fact when the Virgin conceived.

## Joy

I believe there is an important connection between Lewis's personal experience of intense longing and the Narnian Chronicles. *Surprised by Joy* is the story of how this longing led to Lewis's conversion. But one of his reasons for writing the book is that he felt it to be a *common* experience, easily misunderstood, difficult to bring to the forefront of consciousness — and of immense importance. *The Pilgrim's Regress,* which is partly autobiographical, is the story of the Pilgrim's quest for a far-off island, the vision of which has stung him with sweet desire. When Lewis realized that the word *Romanticism* in the subtitle was misunderstood, he wrote a preface to the third edition (1943) explaining the meaning he gave the word. It means

[12] *The Pilgrim's Regress: An Allegorical Apology for Christianity, Reason and Romanticism,* 3rd ed. (London, 1943), pp. 152-155.

[13] *Miracles: A Preliminary Study* (London, 1960), pp. 137-138. (I quote from the Fontana paperback edition because it contains Lewis's revision of Chapter iii. The original edition was published by Bles in 1947.)

Joy — as in *Surprised by Joy*. Indeed, the same Joy, or longing, that you and I feel for our own far-off country: "the secret we cannot hide and cannot tell."[14] A longing which, though painful, is felt to be somehow a delight. A hunger more satisfying than any other fullness: a poverty better than all other wealth. A desiring which, if long absent, is itself desired so much that the new desiring becomes an instance of the original desire.

A peculiar mystery hangs over the *object* of this desire. We feel we know what it is we desire, but in the final achievement of that desire — when it is actually in our hands — we know the real object of our desire has moved farther afield, eluding us like the cuckoo's voice or the rainbow's end. *All* I want, someone will say, is a university degree, or a happy marriage, or a steady job, or to get the book that has been in my head for years onto paper. But when he is married or settled into the right job, or gets whatever it is he wants, it proves itself to be a cheat. It is not what he is actually looking for.

Lewis reasons that we are not born with desires unless satisfaction for those desires exists. And if we find in ourselves a desire that no experience in this world can satisfy, the most probable explanation is that we were made for a different world. A happy marriage, a successful career — these things were never intended to satisfy our desire for the far-off country: more likely they were meant to arouse it, to suggest the real thing. That far-off country is of course Heaven.[15] Not indeed that our desire for Heaven proves that you or I shall enjoy it — we can of our own free wills reject it — but it is a good indication that it exists and that nothing other than God can be our ultimate bliss.

## III

As I suggested a moment ago, there is, I believe, a connection between our longing for Heaven and fairy tales such as those of Lewis. I am quite aware that it is difficult for most of us to want "Heaven" at all. Almost every aspect of modern life fixes our minds on this world, and if the desire for Heaven is in us we rarely recognize it. We are encouraged to seek all our good in "this dim spot." Indeed, to bring up the subject at all is more likely than not to be howled down as nostalgic, romantic, sentimental, or adolescent, all meant in a contemptu-

[14] C. S. Lewis, "The Weight of Glory," *Transposition and Other Addresses* (London, 1949), p. 23.
[15] C. S. Lewis, *Mere Christianity* (London, 1952), p. 108.

ous sense. And those who accuse us of being obsessed with Pie-in-the-sky-by-and-by usually consider fantastic literature a means of escapism (hateful word) and wishful thinking. What I am suggesting is that our critics see a connection between our desire for the far-off country and fantastic literature. And I am convinced they are right. I think there is one.

Lewis admits that marvelous literature evoked his desire for Heaven, but at the same time he believes that no literature is less likely to give a person a false impression of this present world than are fairy tales. His thoughts on this subject are set out in his essay "On Three Ways of Writing for Children." He first of all draws our attention to a point made earlier by Professor J. R. R. Tolkien[16] that fairy tales were not originally written for children, but gravitated to the nursery when they became unfashionable in literary circles. Some children *and* adults like them: some children *and* adults do not. So-called "realistic" stories, Lewis maintains, are far more likely to deceive than are fairy tales because, though the adventures and successes in them are possible (e.g. they do not break the laws of nature), they are almost infinitely improbable. It is possible to become a duke or a millionaire with a yacht and rooms in a posh hotel, or to be the idol of irresistible beauties — anything is possible — but things of this sort are for most of us improbable. On the other hand, no one expects the real world to be like that of the fairy tales.

As for the popular charge of escapism and wish-fulfillment, school stories and fairy tales both arouse and imaginatively satisfy wishes. In one we long to go through the looking glass and reach fairyland (or through the wardrobe to Narnia?). In the other we long to be a rich, popular, successful schoolboy who discovers the spy's plot or rides the horse that none of the cowboys can manage. The two longings are, however, very different. The one directed on something so close as school life is, Lewis argues, ravenous and deadly serious. On the level of imagination it is compensatory and we run to it from the disappointments and humiliations of the real world: and we return to the real world "undivinely discontented" for it is all flattery to the ego. One has been, all along, picturing oneself as the object of admiration. The longing for fairyland is a different sort of longing for it cannot be supposed that the boy who longs for fairyland really longs for the dangers and discomforts of a fairy tale. "It would be much truer," says Lewis,

[16] "On Fairy-Stories," *Essays Presented to Charles Williams*, ed. C. S. Lewis (Oxford, 1947), pp. 58ff.

> to say that fairy land arouses a longing for he knows not what. It stirs and troubles him (to his life-long enrichment) with the dim sense of something beyond his reach and, far from dulling or emptying the actual world, gives it a new dimension of depth. He does not despise real woods because he has read of enchanted woods: the reading makes all real woods a little enchanted. This is a special kind of longing.[17]

I have before me one of Lewis's notebooks containing a fragment of a story about a boy who, in his garden, has been having an imaginary joust in the "unchartered forests of Logres." It was written, I believe, before Lewis's conversion, and is a good illustration of the point made above: fairyland, even when it has no conscious connection with Heaven, throws a little enchantment upon the present, actual world. The joust ended, the boy is returning home:

> To remember suddenly that this was all a game was like hearing the voice of a friend: all the details of that "real" world that lay behind the game — the holidays just begun, the lighted, carpeted rooms, and, presently, the sound of teacups.... It was the strangest systole and diastole — no sooner was home regained, than that other world of desert hills and distant, ominous castles enisled in haunted woods, rose up, clothed in its turn with all the alluring colours of the long-lost. And so one swung backwards and forwards. Each world was best just as you left it for the other, as if to blow out these cloudy worlds and then to suck them in again were as functional as the rising and falling of the breast in sleep.[18]

Lewis goes on, in the essay "On Three Ways of Writing for Children," to defend fairy tales against the charge that they are far too frightening for children. He agrees that we must not do anything that would give a child those "haunting, disabling, pathological fears against which ordinary courage is helpless: in fact, *phobias*" (p. 31). But he thinks we would give children a false impression of the world if we withheld from them the knowledge that they are born into a world of death, violence, wounds, adventure, heroism, and cowardice, good and evil (all these things occur, by the way, in the Bible). And, therefore, since we are born into a world of violence and the atomic bomb, children ought at least to hear of brave knights and heroic courage. Otherwise, he insists, we make their destiny not brighter, but darker. As for all the hullabaloo talked about children being frightened by fairy tales, Lewis says, "I think it possible that by confining your child to blameless stories of child life in which nothing at all alarming ever happens, you

[17] "On Three Ways of Writing for Children," *Of Other Worlds*, pp. 29-30.
[18] Lewis MS. 26, fols. 2-3.

would fail to banish the terrors, and would succeed in banishing all that can ennoble them or make them endurable. For in the fairy tales, side by side with the terrible figures, we find the immemorial comforters and protectors, the radiant ones; and the terrible figures are not merely terrible, but sublime" (p. 32).

I think it worth recording that I have met some adults who, having merely dipped into Lewis's fairy tales, considered them far too violent for children: of the many children I have met who had read the Narnian stories (many six or seven times over), all were eager to read them again.

## IV

"All my seven Narnian books, and my three science fiction books," said Lewis, "began with seeing pictures in my head. At first they were not a story, just pictures. The *Lion* all began with a picture of a Faun carrying an umbrella and parcels in a snowy wood. This picture had been in my mind since I was about sixteen. Then one day, when I was about forty, I said to myself: 'Let's try to make a story about it.' "[19]

When Lewis wrote the first few chapters of his book in 1938, Aslan did not appear in it. He put the manuscript aside, but by March 1949 he was working on it again and reading the chapters to his friend, Roger Lancelyn Green. Meanwhile, as Lewis continues, Aslan came "bounding" in, "pulled the whole story together," and the other six Narnian stories after him. *The Lion* was published in 1950. Roger Lancelyn Green, who read all seven stories in manuscript and who is the most reliable authority in the world on the writing of the Narnian Chronicles, tells us:

> The sequel, *Prince Caspian,* was written by the end of the year [1949], and 1950 must have been spent by Lewis largely in exploring and living in the new world which had, as it were, been shown to him: for by the time *The Lion, the Witch and the Wardrobe* was published that autumn, *The Voyage of the "Dawn Treader"* and *The Horse and his Boy* were finished, and *The Silver Chair* nearing completion. After this there was a pause, much longer being spent on *The Magician's Nephew,* which was not completed until the end of 1951, to be followed by the final instalment, *The Last Battle,* written two years later.[20]

Lancelyn Green's information about when the fairy tales were *written* (1938, 1949-1953) as opposed to when they were *published* (1950-1956) suggests something worth remembering: the

19 "It All Began with a Picture," *Of Other Worlds,* p. 42.
20 *C. S. Lewis,* A Bodley Head Monograph (London, 1963), p. 37.

publication of a book does not always follow so close on the heels of the writing of a book as critics sometimes imagine.

It would, perhaps, have been an intelligent guess to suppose that Lewis began with things he wanted to say about Christianity and then fixed on the fairy tale as a way of saying them. But this is not what happened. Lewis says he could not and would not write in that way; that he has never exactly "made" a story. It all began with seeing "pictures": a faun carrying an umbrella, a queen on a sledge, a magnificent lion. It was more like bird-watching, he says, than talking or building. Sometimes a whole set of pictures would join themselves together but it was necessary to do some deliberate inventing, contrive reasons as to why characters should be in various places doing various things. Lewis says that at first there was nothing Christian about the pictures he was seeing in his head: that element pushed its way in of its own accord.[21]

In his essay "Sometimes Fairy Stories May Say Best What's to be Said" (in *Of Other Worlds*), Lewis tells us that he chose the fairy tale as the form for his stories because of its "brevity, its severe restraints on description, its flexible traditionalism, its inflexible hostility to all analysis, digression, reflections and 'gas'" (pp. 36-37). It is a form he had long been in love with, and now he felt he would burst if he did not write one. Choosing the *form,* he says, was allowing the Author in him to have its say. But then the Man in him began to have his turn.

He thought he saw how stories such as he had in mind could steal past certain inhibitions that had paralyzed much of the religion he had had in childhood. He believed that the reason we find it so hard to feel as we are told we ought to about God and the sufferings of Christ is because an *obligation* to do so freezes feelings. "The whole subject," he says, "was associated with lowered voices; almost as if it were something medical. But supposing that by casting all these things into an imaginary world, stripping them of their stained-glass and Sunday school associations, one could make them for the first time appear in their real potency? Could one not thus steal past those watchful dragons? I thought one could" (p. 37).

Lewis had not drawn out a scheme for the whole Narnian series before writing *The Lion, the Witch and the Wardrobe,* although he wrote "An Outline of Narnian history so far as it is known" after all the books were in print. Because there was no definite scheme from the beginning, there are a few incon-

[21] This paragraph conflates parts of two essays by Lewis (*Of Other Worlds*, pp. 32, 36).

sistencies in the stories. Like many others, I read the stories in the order in which I could get them from the book store. It is, I think, best to read them in their proper chronological order but, as each is a separate story, they can be enjoyed in any order. However, the proper sequence according to Lewis is: *The Magician's Nephew* (published in 1955), *The Lion, the Witch and the Wardrobe* (1950), *The Horse and his Boy* (1954), *Prince Caspian* (1951), *The Voyage of the "Dawn Treader"* (1952), *The Silver Chair* (1953), and *The Last Battle* (1956).

For the purpose of following, as it were, the mental processes of the author, I have chosen to summarize the books in the order in which they were written.

In *The Lion, the Witch and the Wardrobe* the four Pevensie children, Peter, Susan, Edmund, and Lucy, are sent out of London during the war to visit old Professor Kirke who lives in a large country house. While there, Lucy hides in the wardrobe in the spare room and discovers it to be an entrance into the world of Narnia. She meets there a faun, Mr. Tumnus, from whom she learns that Narnia is ruled by the White Witch, who has cast the country into perpetual winter. Later Edmund goes through the wardrobe into Narnia and meets the White Witch, who promises that, if he will bring his brother and sisters to her, she will make him a Prince and feed him on Turkish Delight every day. Following this, all four children find their way into Narnia and meet the Beavers, from whom they learn that Aslan, the great Lion and Lord of Narnia, is on the move, and that the White Witch will be overthrown when four "sons of Adam and daughters of Eve" are enthroned at the castle of Cair Paravel. While they are talking, Edmund sneaks out in order to betray them to the White Witch. When his absence is marked, the others flee to the Stone Table, where they are to meet Aslan. Edmund, on reaching the house of the White Witch, learns her true nature. The Witch, with Edmund and her followers, hastens toward the Stone Table hoping to catch the other children. But Spring begins to melt the ice and snow, thus forecasting her doom. The Witch then prepares to kill Edmund in order that the prophecy of the thrones shall not be fulfilled. Aslan, however, offers his life for Edmund's, thus satisfying the Magic which the Emperor-Over-Sea put into Narnia at the beginning: that every traitor belongs to the White Witch and that for every treachery she has a right to kill. In Edmund's stead, Aslan is slain with the Stone Knife on the Stone Table. Lucy and Susan witness his vicarious death, but while they are sorrowing the Stone Table is cracked and Aslan, resurrected from the dead, returns to them. He explains to them the "Deeper Magic from before the dawn of Time": if a willing victim who had committed no treachery were killed in a traitor's stead, the Table would crack and Death itself would start working backward. Aslan and his followers then defeat the Witch and the four children are enthroned as Kings and Queens of Narnia. They reign for many years until one day while following the White Stag (who would give you wishes if you caught him) they chase him into the thicket past the Lamp Post, and — soon come tumbling out of the wardrobe into the spare room.

*Prince Caspian: The Return to Narnia* opens with the four Pevensie children waiting on a station platform one year after their earlier adventure. They are suddenly drawn back into Narnia and find themselves in the ruins of Cair Paravel. After rescuing Trumpkin, the Dwarf, they are led by Aslan to the mound, Aslan's How, which covers the ancient Stone Table. Centuries have passed and the human descendants of some Earthly pirates (now called Telmarines) rule Narnia. The old Narnians have been driven into hiding by the usurper king, Miraz. The rightful heir, Prince Caspian (who has blown the Magic Horn and thereby drawn the children into Narnia) joins the old Narnians and, with the help of Aslan and the English children, conquers Miraz' army and brings order and peace to the country. He is then crowned King Caspian X by Aslan.

In the third book, *The Voyage of the "Dawn Treader,"* Lewis introduces a new character from our world: "a boy called Eustace Clarence Scrubb, and he almost deserved it" (p. 9). Eustace and his cousins, Edmund and Lucy, are drawn into Narnia through a picture of an ancient ship and sail with Caspian X in search of the seven Narnian lords whom the wicked Miraz sent to explore the unknown Eastern Seas beyond the Lone Islands. Reepicheep, the valiant Mouse, hopes that by sailing to the eastern end of the world they will find Aslan's own country. On one island the selfish Eustace is turned into a dragon. Only after he has learned humility does Aslan restore him to human form. They go on to discover the island of the invisible Monopods and Lucy helps them regain their visibility by daring the adventure of the Magician's Book. By a hair's breadth they miss landing on the Dark Island where dreams come true. At last they come to "The Beginning of the End of the World" where they discover the last three Narnian lords for whom they have been searching, in an enchanted sleep at the mystic table on which is lying the Stone Knife with which Aslan was slain by the White Witch. As they approach the End of the World, Reepicheep and the three children go forward, although only Reepicheep is allowed to enter Aslan's Country. The children meet Aslan, who tells them, before sending them home, that though Edmund and Lucy will never come back to Narnia they shall thereafter know him better under a different name in their own world.

Seventy Narnian years pass, but only a few months to Eustace, before he and Jill Pole are called away from their horrible coeducational school to Narnia. In *The Silver Chair* Aslan sends Eustace and Jill with instructions as to how they are to find Caspian's only son, Prince Rilian. They bungle the first step by Eustace's failure to recognize the now aged Caspian. One of Lewis's most delightful creations, the marsh-wiggle, Puddleglum, leads Eustace and Jill into giants' country in search of Prince Rilian. They are waylaid in the giants' city, but eventually discover Underland where a Witch, who has the Prince under her power, is preparing to invade Narnia with her army of Earthmen. Before they can escape, the Witch, by the use of enchantment, almost brings them to a state in which they are ready to disbelieve Aslan's existence. By a great effort of the will and faith in Aslan, Puddleglum breaks the enchantment. Rilian kills the Witch (now in serpent form) and they escape to Narnia — just in time for the Prince to bid farewell to Caspian before the old king dies. Eustace and Jill are taken back to the Mountain of Aslan overlooking Narnia and, by the blood of Aslan, Caspian is resurrected from the dead. He is allowed to step into this world for a few minutes in order that he and the children may give the bullies at the coeducational school a sound thrashing before he is recalled to Aslan's Country.

*The Horse and his Boy* is a story that takes place during the reign of Peter, Edmund, Susan, and Lucy as described at the end of *The Lion, the Witch and the Wardrobe.* It is, in fact, a story within a story. It tells how Shasta of Calormen runs away to avoid being sold as a slave. He takes with him — or, more correctly, is taken *by* — Bree, a Talking Horse of Narnia. Spurred on by Aslan, who appears in various guises, he reaches Archenland in time to warn them of the plot by Prince Rabadash of Calormen to kidnap Queen Susan. Rabadash is defeated and Shasta discovers that he is the son of King Lune of Archenland.

In the penultimate volume, *The Magician's Nephew,* Lewis turns back to seek the origin of all the other stories. Digory Kirke (who grows up to become Professor Kirke) and Polly Plummer are carried by magic rings into the dying world of Charn. Digory gives way to a temptation there which results in their taking Jadis Queen of Charn (later the White Witch) and Uncle Andrew (the Magician) with them to Narnia. They arrive just in time to see Aslan creating it. Digory brings back the Magic Apple from whose seeds grow the tree out of which the wardrobe is made.

*The Last Battle* recounts the end of Narnia, many centuries after Aslan was last seen moving visibly through the world. Shift the Ape dresses the simple ass, Puzzle, in the skin of a lion and deceives the Talking Beasts and Dwarfs into thinking that it is Aslan himself. By that deception the Calormenes who worship the devil Tash are enabled to overrun the country. Tirian, the last king of Narnia, prays to Aslan for help and is rescued from the Calormenes by Eustace and Jill, who are mysteriously pulled into Narnia while on a train journey. They steal Puzzle from the stable, and the Calormenes discover there the odious Tash (in whom they have lost faith), who carries off the Calormene leader and Shift. Tirian and the remnant of the faithful Narnians are either slain or make their way into the stable. Those who live to go in find it to be the door into Aslan's Country and meet there all the kings and queens of the former stories, with the exception of Susan, who is no longer a friend of Narnia. Aslan comes to the door and holds his Last Judgment. Those who are counted worthy pass in, the others into darkness. Narnia is then destroyed by water and fire and the stable door is closed upon it forever. Those who are beyond the door discover themselves in the *real* Narnia of which the other had only been a copy. Aslan leads them to the Garden of Paradise, where they are united with their friends and see from that height all that was worth saving from all worlds joined onto Aslan's Country.

## V

A few pages back I mentioned that after Lewis had written all seven Narnian Chronicles he drew up an outline of the history of that world. He gave the outline to me, and I shall reproduce it here after pointing out a peculiarity of Narnian time and what use Lewis made of it in his stories. All told, there are 2555 Narnian years between its Creation and its End: only fifty-two Earthly years pass during those 2555 Narnian years. But there is no exact Narnian equivalent of an Earthly year. As you will see, between 1940 and 1941 of our time 1303 Narnian years go by: between 1941 and 1942 (our time) only three Narnian years. Lewis knew what he was doing and had long entertained the thought that other worlds might enjoy a time not so linear as ours, a time that has thicknesses and thinnesses.

In his *Letters to Malcolm* (London, 1964) he suggests that the blessed dead in Purgatory might experience just such a thing:

> The dead might experience a time which was not quite so linear as ours — it might, so to speak, have thickness as well as length. Already in this life we get some thickness whenever we learn to attend to more than one thing at once. One can suppose this increased to any extent, so that though, for them as for us, the present is always becoming the past, yet each present contains unimaginably more than ours [p. 141].

The "thickness" of Narnian time not only provided the children with more interesting and varied adventures than they might otherwise have had, but Lewis found in it, I believe, a means of pointing out a great truth to his characters (and readers). When the four Pevensie children left Narnia the first time, the White Witch was dead and everything was shipshape. If Peter, back in this world, had written of the adventures he had there he might have been tempted to say, "And all the Narnians lived happily ever after." But they did not. And a second adventure helped him to see how ignorant he might have been of the health and future of Narnia and (it is hoped) of this world as well. The point Lewis is trying to drive home is that, as we do not know what stage in the history of the world we are in at the moment, we cannot possibly see the meaning of the whole thing. Are we at the beginning? the middle? or the end? We cannot know until it is over; and we have no way of knowing when *that* will be. To use Lewis's favorite analogy: "We do not know the play. We do not even know whether we are in Act I or Act V. We do not know who are the major and who the minor characters. The Author knows."[22] But here finally, as I promised, is Lewis's outline.

Outline of Narnian history so far as it is known[23]

| Narnian years | Narnia | English years | England |
|---|---|---|---|
| | | 1888 | Digory Kirke born. |
| | | 1889 | Polly Plummer born. |
| 1 | Creation of Narnia. The Beasts made able to talk. Digory plants the Tree of Pro- | 1900 | Polly and Digory carried into Narnia by magic Rings. |

[22] "The World's Last Night," *The World's Last Night and Other Essays* (New York, 1960), p. 105. An interesting use of this idea is also found in the essay on "Historicism" in Lewis's *Christian Reflections*, ed. Walter Hooper (London and Grand Rapids, 1967), p. 106.

[23] Lewis MS. 51. This MS, consisting of three loose sheets, is printed here in full.

| Narnian years | Narnia | English years | England |
|---|---|---|---|
| | tection. The White Witch Jadis enters Narnia but flies into the far North. Frank I becomes King of Narnia | | |
| 180 | Prince Col, younger son of K. Frank V of Narnia, leads certain followers into Archenland (not then inhabited) and becomes first King of that country. | | |
| 204. | Certain outlaws from Archenland fly across the Southern desert and set up the new kingdom of Calormen. | 1927<br>1928 | Peter Pevensie born<br>Susan Pevensie born. |
| 300. | The empire of Calormen spreads mightily. Calormenes colonise the land of Telmar to the West of Narnia | 1930<br>1932 | Edmund Pevensie born.<br>Lucy Pevensie born. |
| 302. | The Calormenes in Telmar behave very wickedly and Aslan turns them into dumb beasts. The country lies waste. K. Gale of Narnia delivers the Lone Islands from a dragon and is made Emperor by their grateful inhabitants. | 1933 | Eustace Scrubb and Jill Pole born. |
| 407. | Olvin of Archenland kills the Giant Pire. | | |
| 460. | Pirates from our world take possession of Telmar. | | |
| 570 | About this time lived Moonwood the Hare. | | |
| 898. | The White Witch Jadis returns into Narnia out of the far North | | |

| Narnian years | Narnia | English years | England |
|---|---|---|---|
| 900 | The Long Winter begins | | |
| 1000 | The Pevensies arrive in Narnia. The treachery of Edmund. The sacrifice of Aslan. The White Witch defeated and the Long Winter ended. Peter becomes High King of Narnia. | 1940 | The Pevensies, staying with Digory (now Professor) Kirke, reach Narnia through the Magic Wardrobe. |
| 1014 | K. Peter carries out a successful raid on the Northern Giants. Q. Susan and K. Edmund visit the Court of Calormen. K. Lune of Archenland discovers his long-lost son Prince Cor and defeats a treacherous attack by Prince Rabadash of Calormen | | |
| 1015. | The Pevensies hunt the White Stag and vanish out of Narnia. | | |
| 1050 | Ram the Great succeeds Cor as K. of Archenland. | | |
| 1502 | About this time lived Q. Swanwhite of Narnia. | | |
| 1998. | The Telmarines invade and conquer Narnia. Caspian I becomes King of Narnia. | | |
| 2290. | Prince Caspian, son of Caspian IX, born. Caspian IX murdered by his brother Miraz who usurps the throne. | | |
| 2303. | Prince Caspian escapes from his uncle Miraz. Civil War in Narnia. By the aid of Aslan and of the Pevensies, whom Caspian summons with Q. Susan's magic Horn, Miraz is defeated and killed. | 1941 | The Pevensies again caught into Narnia by the blast of the Magic Horn. |

| Narnian years | Narnia | English years | England |
|---|---|---|---|
| | Caspian becomes King Caspian X of Narnia. | | |
| 2304. | Caspian X defeats the Northern Giants. | | |
| 2306.-7 | Caspian X's great voyage to the end of the World. | 1942. | Edmund, Lucy, and Eustace reach Narnia again and take part in Caspian's voyage. |
| 2310 | Caspian X marries Ramandu's daughter. | | |
| 2325 | Prince Rilian born. | | |
| 2345. | The Queen killed by a Serpent. Rilian disappears. | | |
| 2356 | Eustace and Jill appear in Narnia and rescue Prince Rilian. Death of Caspian X. | 1942 | Eustace and Jill, from Experiment House, are carried away into Narnia. |
| 2534. | Outbreak of outlaws in Lantern Waste. Towers built to guard that region. | | |
| 2555. | Rebellion of Shift the Ape. King Tirian rescued by Eustace and Jill. Narnia in the hands of the Calormenes. The last battle. End of Narnia. End of the World. | 1949 | Serious accident on British Railways. |

I wish Lewis had written at least two more stories of the same sort as *The Horse and his Boy,* adventures of specifically Narnian heroes such as Prince Col, who became the first king of Archenland; or, better still, the story of how King Gale delivered the Lone Islands from a dragon and was made Emperor by the islanders. If he ever did see "pictures" in his mind of King Gale's adventures, he apparently did not find them interesting enough to make a story of, for you may recall that in *The Voyage of the "Dawn Treader"* Caspian, Edmund, and Lucy were wondering how the Lone Islands ever came to belong to Narnia. And Lewis offers the tantalizing comment: "By the way, I have never yet heard how these remote islands became attached to the crown of Narnia; if I ever do, and if the story

118

Plots.

SHIP. Two children somehow get on board a ship of ancient build. Discover presently that they are sailing in time (backwards): the captain will bring them to islands that have not existed for millennia. Atlantean islands. Attacked by enemies. Children captured. Discover that the ship's captain was really taking them because his sick king needs blood of a boy in the far future. Nevertheless prefer the Capt. and his side to their soi-disant rescuers. Escape and return to their first rocks. The blood giving, not fatal, & happy ending. Various islands (of Odyssey and St Brendan) can be thrown in. Beauty of the ship the central spell. To be a v. green & pearly story.

PICTURE. A magic picture. One of the children gets thro' the frame into the picture and one of the creatures gets out of the picture into our world.

INVERTED Ordinary fairy-tale K., Q. and court, into wh. erupts a child from our world.

SEQUEL TO L.W.W. The fascist tyrant to be Miraz. Interesting history of Narnia told nominally by the Dwarf but really an abstract of his story wh. amounts to telling it in my own person.

An early outline of *The Voyage of the "Dawn Treader"* (Lewis MS. 15, folio 118, in the collection of Walter Hooper) is at all interesting, I may put it in some other book" (p. 38). When I did ask for more stories about Narnia, Lewis's answer was much the same as he gave to others: "There are only two times at which you can stop a thing: one is before everyone is tired of it, and the other is after!"

Unfortunately, Lewis almost always destroyed the manuscripts of his published writings. This, as far as I know, is true of all the manuscripts of the Narnian stories, with the exception of a few bits scribbled in his notebooks. The little that I find in them is sufficient to give us an idea of the "deliberate inventing" that was sometimes necessary when his mental pictures did not group themselves into a whole story. It is obvious as well that his first pictures were sometimes supplanted by others, and that pictures that were not used in one story often found a place in some other. In one notebook the following piece is written in what looks a very hurried hand, as if it were dashed off the moment it came into his head.

PLOTS.

SHIP. Two children somehow got on board a ship of ancient build. Discover presently that they are sailing in time (backwards): the captain will bring them to islands that have not existed for millennia. Approach islands. Attack by enemies. Children captured. Discover that the first captain was really taking them because his sick king needs blood of a boy in the far future. *Nevertheless* prefer the Capt. and his side to their *soi-disant* rescuers. Escape and return to their first hosts. The blood giving, not fatal, and happy ending. Various islands (of Odyssey and St.-Brendan) can be thrown in. Beauty of the ship the initial spell. To be a v. green and pearly story.

PICTURE. A magic picture. One of the children gets thro' the frame into the picture and one of the creatures gets out of the picture into our world.

INVERTED. Ordinary fairy-tale K., Q. and court, *into* wh erupts a child from our world.

SEQUEL TO L.W.W. The present tyrants to be Men. Intervening history of Narnia told nominally by the Dwarf but really an abstract of his story wh. amounts to telling it in my own person.[24]

What we have here is quite obviously a very rough sketch of *The Voyage of the "Dawn Treader"* which was, when this was written, meant to be the sequel to *The Lion, the Witch and the Wardrobe.* The "intervening history of Narnia told nominally by the Dwarf" comes, not in the *Dawn Treader,* but in *Prince Cas-*

[24] Lewis MS. 15, fol. 118.

*pian,* which was, we learn from Roger Lancelyn Green, the second story to be written. After telling us in Chapter iii of *Prince Caspian* how the Pevensie children rescue Trumpkin the Dwarf, Lewis goes on to say: "So the Dwarf settled down and told his tale. I shall not give it to you in his words. . . . But the gist of the story, as they knew it in the end, was as follows" (pp. 38-39). In Chapters iv-vii Lewis tells us what Trumpkin said.

I have a few scraps of the galley proofs of one fairy tale from which we learn a little. It is of no great importance, but the title of this story was, as printed on the proofs, *The Wild Waste Lands.* This was amended to read *Night Under Narnia,* and finally *The Silver Chair.* In Chapter v of *The Silver Chair* the very sleepy Jill is riding on an owl's back. According to the proofs, Lewis wrote:

> Jill was once more pinching herself to keep awake — for she knew that if she dosed on Glimfeather's back she would probably fall off — long before the two owls ended their flight. She tumbled off and found herself on flat ground.

It sounds, of course, as if Jill did in fact fall off the owl's back, and so was amended to read in the printed text (p. 63):

> Jill had to pinch herself to keep awake, for she knew that if she dozed on Glimfeather's back she would probably fall off. When at last the two owls ended their flight, she climbed stiffly off Glimfeather and found herself on flat ground.

In one of Lewis's exercise books there is a fragment that appears to be an early version of *The Magician's Nephew,* although there is not exactly a magician or a nephew as we know them in the book by that title. It begins:

> Once there was a boy called Digory who lived with his Aunt because his father and mother were both dead. His Aunt, whose name was Gertrude, was not at all a nice person. Years ago she had been a schoolmistress and bullied the girls. Then she became a headmistress and bullied the mistresses. Then she became an inspector and bullied headmistresses. Then she went into Parliament and became a Minister of something and bullied everybody.[25]

The story goes on to say that Digory would have led a very unhappy life except that Cook, who "was as nice as Aunt was nasty," befriended him. More important still, ever since Digory could remember he had had the gift of being able to understand the trees and animals. He is never so content as when talking with those in his back garden, especially a great oak in whose

[25] Lewis MS. 46, fol. 5.

5

Once there was a boy called Digory who lived with his Aunt because his father and mother were both dead. His Aunt, whose name was Gertrude, was not at all a nice person. Years ago she had been a schoolmistress and bullied the girls. Then she became a headmistress and bullied the mistresses. Then she be- -came an inspector and bullied headmistresses. Then she went into Parliament and became a Minister of something and bullied everybody.

It might have been expected that Digory who had to live with this Aunt would have led a very unhappy life. But there were two things that very nearly made up for it. One was that his Aunt was very seldom at home, and even when she was she got up late and went out in the afternoon and usually did not come back till long after Digory's bed-time. People in Parliament are often like this. And when Aunt Gertrude was away Digory did not have a bad time. The only other ~~person~~ people in the house were a secretary called Miss Spink whom he had nothing to do with and Cook. Cook was as nice as Aunt was nasty. She was rather old and had been cook in Grand mother's house long ago when Digory's mother and his Aunt had been girls together. Aunt did not approve of Cook, but she knew that no one else would stay with her, so

First page of the "Lefay Fragment" by C. S. Lewis (Lewis MS. 46, folio 5, in the collection of Walter Hooper)

branches he is invited to sit and a red squirrel called Pattertwig. One day while Digory is sitting in the oak looking over the wall at the house next door, a girl comes out and is soon "busily engaged in doing something with planks and sticks and string and nails and a hammer." He and the girl, Polly, are soon talking; and all goes well until she asks him to cut a limb from the oak he is sitting in so that she can complete the raft she is building. This puts Digory into a terrible fix; but rather than tell her of his marvelous gift or allow her to assume that he is afraid of his aunt's disapproval, he consents to cut a limb from the tree.

The next day Digory learns that his godmother, Mrs. Lefay, whom he never remembers seeing, is coming to visit him. Before she arrives, he goes into the garden to apologize to the oak whose limb he cut off. Despite his begging and imploring and apologizing, the trees and animals will not answer. With a shock he realizes that he has lost his wonderful gift and become like everyone else. Miserable, he returns to the house. As he walks into the drawingroom he hears his Aunt saying:

> "Always felt the boy needs taking out of himself."
>
> Another voice, a deep, dry voice that sounded more like a man's than a woman's, replied
>
> "Taking out of himself, eh? How do you do that? by skinning 'em?"
>
> And of course Digory knew they were talking about him. Then he came out into the middle of the room.
>
> The visitor was the shortest and fattest woman he had ever seen. When you saw her face from in front it looked almost square, and very big. When you saw it from the side the long nose and the long chin stuck out so that they almost met. She was dressed in black and her chest seemed to be all covered with some kind of yellow dust.
>
> "Don't be afraid you're going to have to kiss me," said the old woman staring at Digory with very keen eyes under very fierce grey eyebrows. "I'm too ugly for that and ten to one you don't like snuff. I do, though" — and she took out a little gold box and took a big pinch of snuff up one of her wide nostrils and then another big pinch up the other.
>
> "How do you do, godmother?" said Digory politely.
>
> "I won't ask how *you* do," said Mrs. Lefay "Because I see you do very badly."
>
> "He is just getting over influenza," said Aunt G. "We are quite satisfied —"
>
> "I dare say you are," said Mrs. Lefay "And I wasn't talking about that"
>
> "I thought," said Aunt G., with her lips getting thinner and whiter as they always did when she was angry, "that if you were interested in the boy you might like to hear —"
>
> "Well, I wouldn't," said Digory's godmother. "Of course he'll get over influenza. They all do except the ones that die, and I can see he didn't."

"I will leave you together for a little while," said Aunt G. with her iciest voice, getting up, and leaving the room.

Digory was standing all this time in front of his godmother and staring at the large black bag which hung over her arm. Two long biscuit-coloured objects projected from it . . .

"Well!" said Mrs. Lefay, "*She's* gone. Now for you. I'm not going to ask what's wrong with you —"

"But there's nothing wrong, Godmother," said Digory.

"That's a good lie," said Mrs. Lefay (not in a scolding voice but rather as one might say, "That's a heavy shower") "And you needn't tell any more because, as I said, I'm asking no questions. But I'll tell you how you look. You look exactly like what Adam must have looked five minutes after he'd been turned out of the Garden of Eden. And you needn't pretend you don't understand. And — drat the boy, what do you keep staring at?"

"Its — its your bag, Godmother"

"Oh *him,*" said Mrs. Lefay. "Well you can see him, but Hands Off." She loosened the mouth of the bag and out popped the head of a live rabbit: it was his ears, projecting from the bag, that had so puzzled Digory.

"That's Coiny, that is," said Mrs. Lefay. "Out for his afternoon ride. And he's not a present for you, whatever you may think."

"I never thought anything of the sort," said Digory indignantly.

"I see you're telling the truth this time," said Mrs. Lefay "And I know you didn't expect to be given Coiny. A nice house this would be for a sensible, experienced rabbit and he a founder of a family! I only wanted to make you angry."

"Why, Godmother?", asked Digory.

"To see what you'd look like, of course. To see if you'd the right flash in the eye. And you haven't lost that, anyway, though I think you've lost something else in the last day or so. And now, I don't want to waste any more time. Here's my card with my address on it, and if ever you want to see me, take in all these directions because I don't mean to say everything twice over. You can catch a tram outside this house that will take you to Ravelstone Circus. Then look all round the Circus till you see Little Antrim Street. Then go along that on the left side till you come to Cuckoo Court. Then go down the Court on the right side till you come to a furniture shop that sells birds and pictures. Then you must go into the shop and you'll see" [fols. 16-18].

I do not know what we should have seen in the shop, for the manuscript ends at this point. A pity, for the matter-of-fact Mrs. Lefay was beginning to be a very interesting old woman. But what kind of woman? She appears indirectly in *The Magician's Nephew* as Uncle Andrew's *bad* fairy godmother from whom he "inherits" the Atlantean dust out of which the Magic Rings were made. My guess is that she would have been Digory's *good* fairy godmother.

I said a moment ago that this fragment "appears to be an

early version of *The Magician's Nephew"*; and if I had not read the four stories that were composed in between *The Magician's Nephew* and *The Lion, the Witch and the Wardrobe* I would have guessed it to be an early draft of *The Magician's Nephew* which Lewis rejected before going on to write the book by that title. But there is reason to believe that this fragment — which I shall henceforth refer to as the Lefay fragment — was written before *any* of the last six Narnian Chronicles. (The Lefay fragment runs to a little over twenty-six pages in an exercise book measuring seven by nine inches.) Here are my reasons for thinking so:

(1) After the Lefay fragment ends abruptly at the top of page 27, Lewis dropped down a few lines and wrote an early version of Eustace's diary, which is found in *The Voyage of the "Dawn Treader."* Quite obviously, then, "Lefay" was written before the diary.

(2) The picture of Aunt Gertrude with which "Lefay" opens is remarkably like the Head of Experiment House who, after the excitement at the end of *The Silver Chair,* was seen to be "no use as a Head, so they got her made an Inspector to interfere with other Heads. And when they found she wasn't much good even at that, they got her into Parliament where she lived happily ever after" (p. 216). Did Aunt Gertrude serve as the original for the Head of Experiment House? I am inclined to think so.

(3) In the second chronicle of Narnia, *Prince Caspian,* we meet a talkative red squirrel named Pattertwig who offers Caspian a nut from his winter store. As he bounds off to fetch it, Trumpkin whispers in Caspian's ear, "Don't look. Look the other way. It's very bad manners among squirrels to watch anyone going to his store or to look as if you wanted to know where it was" (p. 68). In the Lefay fragment Digory is offered a nut from a red squirrel, Pattertwig, and when the squirrel goes off to get it "Digory at once looked the other way; it is considered very [bad] manners among squirrels to watch anyone going to his hoard. To ask where it is would be simply outrageous." Because it is unlikely that Lewis would have named a Narnian squirrel Pattertwig and afterward duplicated the name and almost the same context in a story that takes place in *this* world, I believe the Lefay Pattertwig to be first in the order of invention.

(4) In the Lefay document, Digory has the unique gift of being able to talk with the trees and animals in *this* world. As none of the children in any of the published fairy tales possesses this gift, I am inclined to think it was an idea Lewis toyed with

in the very early stages of his writing of the Narnian stories, but decided against using.

I believe, then, that the Lefay fragment was written soon after *The Lion, the Witch and the Wardrobe* and before the final draft of *Prince Caspian* which contains one of its ingredients (Pattertwig). Lewis probably wrote many other such fragments which eventually found their way into his wastepaper basket. This fragment survived because the exercise book in which it is written contains some notes on English literature which he intended to preserve. I have felt it worthwhile devoting some space to it because it tells us something worth knowing about the workings of Lewis's imagination. The fragment is rather like a fuzzy ball of dandelion seeds which, when struck by the wind, were scattered in many directions. Some of the seeds, or "pictures," found root in other books, and some remained on the parent stem and became the basis for *The Magician's Nephew* as we now have it.

The five pages of Eustace's diary that follow the Lefay fragment are essentially the same as the diary found in Chapters ii and v of *The Voyage of the "Dawn Treader."* The dating is, however, slightly different. The manuscript I have before me reads: "*Tue. Aug 20* — This is positively the first day since we left L. I. on which it has been possible to write anything. We have been driven before the storm for 26 days and nights, as I know because I have kept a careful count; though the others all say it is 28" (fol. 18). (Was there only *one* Lone Island at first?) In the book we read: "*September 3.* The first day for ages when I have been able to write. We have been driven before a hurricane for thirteen days and nights. I know that because I kept a careful count, though the others all say it was only twelve" (p. 68). It would appear that Lewis originally planned for the "Dawn Treader" to dock at Narrowhaven for a shorter while than it in fact does in the finished book, and to have the ship brave a *storm* for twenty-eight days, rather than a *hurricane* for twelve (I reckon, you notice, on "the others" being more accurate than Eustace). There is one other difference worth noting. In *The Voyage of the "Dawn Treader,"* Eustace's adventures as a dragon last about six days. In the manuscript version, Eustace is a dragon for only one day. The manuscript ends with this final entry from Eustace's diary: "*Aug. 29.* The most terrible and queerest day of my life but all's well that ends well (Here follows Bill Birdbittle's dragon story and the writer's change of heart)" (fol. 20).

Having reread the preceding pages on my dating of the Lefay fragment and Eustace's early diary, I am seized with

The original map of Narnia by C. S. Lewis (Bodleian Library, MS. Eng. Lett. c. 220, folio 160)

doubts about all I have written. I was not looking over the author's shoulder when he wrote the Narnian stories, nor have I seen any of the bits and pieces (if there were any) that were thrown away. I may have guessed right about the fragments I have; but I do not know. I may never know. For this reason, I feel it only fair to admit that my conjectures are a long shot. But something warns me that if I begin to conjecture about my conjectures, someone other than Prince Rabadash will turn into an Ass, so I sternly draw rein and return to the more profitable realm of fact: the seven Narnian Chronicles which Lewis meant for us to see.

## VI

From the mental picture of a Faun carrying an umbrella and parcels in a snowy wood, Lewis went on to imagine a country which has become as real and familiar to many people as the world we live in. After Miss Pauline Baynes had been commissioned to illustrate *The Lion, the Witch and the Wardrobe,* Lewis sent her his own drawing of a map of Narnia. On it are marked the sites we come to know in all the stories set in Narnia proper (Lantern Waste, the Castle of Miraz, Beruna, Cair Paravel, etc.) as well as the fringes of the Wild Lands of the North and Archenland, which lies south of Narnia. Miss Baynes' redrawing of Lewis's original map appears on the end papers of the Geoffrey Bles and Puffin editions (both British) of *Prince Caspian.* Lewis had foreseen the story of *The Silver Chair,* for marsh-wiggle country is clearly indicated on his original map with a note to Miss Baynes pointing out that "a future story will require marshes here. We needn't mark them now, but must not put in anything inconsistent with them."[26]

[26] Miss Baynes' map on the end papers of *Prince Caspian* is, except for some small details, almost an exact copy of Lewis's original map. The pictures of the Monopods on pages 152 and 154 of *The Voyage of the "Dawn Treader"* are based on a drawing by Lewis of a Monopod asleep (its foot raised aloft) and a Monopod standing. Lewis's map, his drawing of the Monopods, and his letters to Miss Baynes are in the Bodleian Library, Oxford. Lewis was very pleased with Miss Baynes' illustrations to his fairy tales, with the exception, however, of the children in *The Lion, the Witch and the Wardrobe* which he considered slightly ill-proportioned. In a letter dated August 15, 1967, Miss Baynes described to me the three meetings she had with Lewis. Of his criticism of her work, she said:

> ... Dr. Lewis and I hardly corresponded at all over the illustrations to his books; he was, to me, the most kindly and tolerant of authors — who seemed happy to leave everything in my completely inexperienced hands! Once or twice I queried the sort of character he had in mind — as with Puddleglum and then he replied, but otherwise he made no remarks or criticisms.... When he *did* criticise, it was put over so

Lewis's close observations of nature and his ability to describe what he saw, heard, and smelled, are nowhere so evident as in the Narnian stories. His description of Narnian countryside, weather, and food are, I expect, more effective than we first realize in contributing to the astonishing sense of reality achieved in these books. They are based essentially on the countries Lewis knew and liked best: Ireland and England. If you want to plunge into what seems to me the very quiddity of some Narnian countryside, you must go to what Lewis considered the loveliest spot he had ever seen. It is in the Carlingford Mountains of southern Ireland. There the grass is almost emerald green and the heather a delicate purple. Beyond the tiny sheepcotes you will see, looking north, down below you a narrow bay of water stretching inland

charmingly, that it wasn't a criticism. i.e. I did the drawings as best as I could — (I can't have been much more than 21 and quite untrained) and didn't realise how hideous I had made the children — they were as nice as *I* could get them — and Dr. Lewis said, when we were starting on the second book, "I know you made the children rather plain — *in the interests of realism* — but do you think you could possibly pretty them up a little now?" [Bodleian Library, MS. Eng. Lett. C. 220, fols. 162-163].

By the time Miss Baynes had completed the illustrations to the fifth book, Lewis was more satisfied than ever with the quality of her work. Indeed, he felt that whatever praise the fairy tales were entitled to was partly owing to Miss Baynes' illustrations. His enthusiasm is evident in the following letter (dated from Magdalen College, Oxford, January 21, 1954):

Dear Miss Baynes

I lunched with Bles yesterday to see the drawings for *The Horse* and feel I must write to tell you how very much we both enjoyed them. It is delightful to find (and not only for selfish reasons) that you do each book a little bit better than the last — it is nice to see an artist growing. (If only you cd. take 6 months off and devote them to anatomy, there's no limit to your possibilities).

Both the drawings of Lasaraleen in her litter were a rich feast of line and of fantastic-satiric imagination: my only regret was that we couldn't have both. Shasta among the tombs (in the new technique, wh. is lovely) was exactly what I wanted. The pictures of Rabadash hanging on the hook and just turning into an ass were the best comedy you've done yet. The Tisroc was superb: far beyond anything you were doing 5 years ago. I thought that your human faces — the boys, K. Lune etc. — were, this time, really good. The crowds are beautiful, realistic yet also lovely wavy compositions: but your crowds always were. How did you do Tashbaan? We only got its full wealth by using a magnifying glass! The result is exactly right. Thanks enormously for all the intense work you have put into them all. And more power to your elbow . . . [*Ibid.*, fol. 155].

Miss Baynes' helpful maps of the countries and sea surrounding Narnia are found on the end papers of the Bles and Puffin editions of *The Voyage of the "Dawn Treader"*, *The Silver Chair*, and *The Horse and his Boy*. Unfortunately, the Macmillan editions (American) of the Narnian books do not contain these maps; nor do they contain all the illustrations found in the English editions.

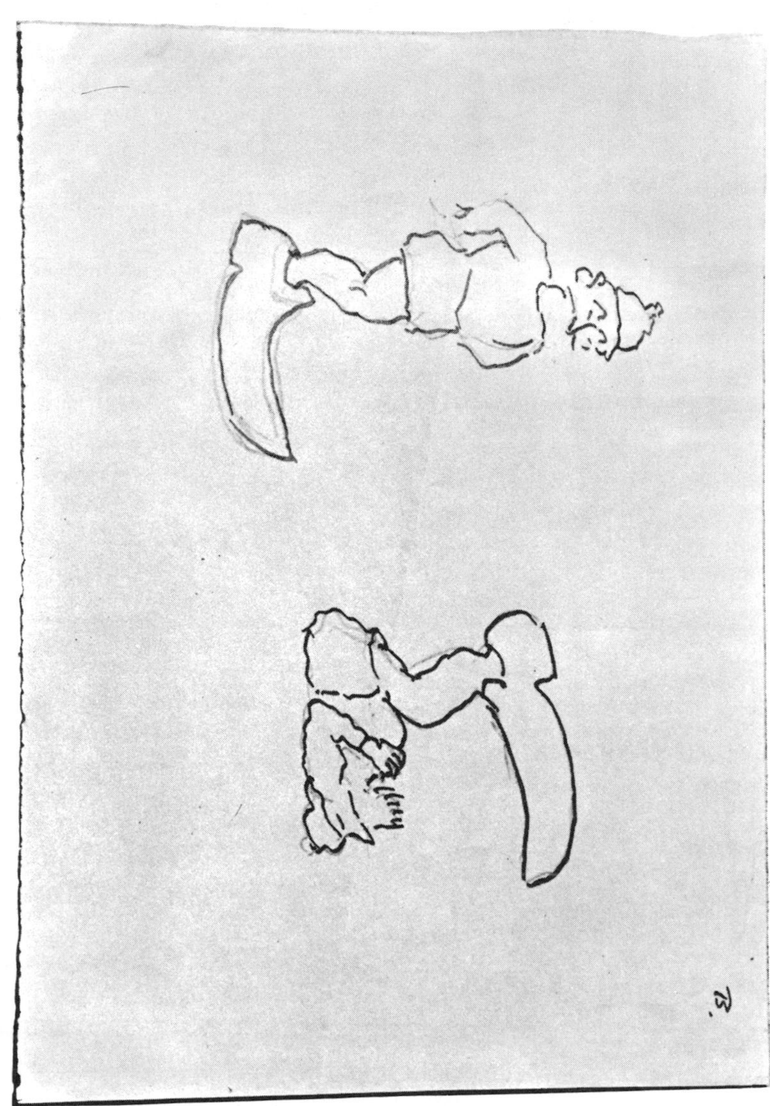

C. S. Lewis's drawing of Monopods (Bodleian Library, MS. Eng. Lett. c. 220, folio 161)

to Warren Point. And visible beyond that, on a clear day, are the Mourne Mountains, which really do give the appearance of rolling down to the sea. The Narnian weather is pretty much the same as that of the British Isles (except that there is less rain): cool, dewy, fresh. It might be worth recording that Lewis absolutely detested hot weather. Believe it or not, I have heard him describe a summer's day with temperatures in the high seventies as "suffocating," "blistering," "scorching." It is not difficult to understand why the Calormenes lived in the South.

What about Narnian food? Is that a concession to children? As we all like to, and must, eat (it is usually adults who are forced to diet), the answer ought to be clear. The descriptions of Narnian foods remind us that we are in a *real* world, and that we would enjoy living in Narnia if we could get there. Sumptuous feasts very properly follow coronations and victories, but I am not sure if most of us aren't more vulnerable to the descriptions of the more ordinary Narnian fare. What about the huge jug of beer and the freshwater fish which was "alive half an hour ago and has come out of the pan half a minute ago" in the Beavers' house (*Lion,* p. 74)? Or the meaty, spicy sausages "fat and piping hot and burst and just the tiniest bit burnt" in the Dwarfs' cave (*The Silver Chair,* p. 204)?

I said earlier that it would be difficult to know what kind of "dressed animals" Lewis was writing about in his boyhood stories without the benefit of his illustrations. In the Narnian books his animals appear in their natural beauty and interesting differences. They are the real thing. Although you will not have read Lewis's juvenilia, chances are you will have seen a Walt Disney film. I find much of Walt Disney's work very pleasant, but his dressed animals do not seem to me much like the animals they are intended to represent. Perhaps they are not supposed to. Nevertheless, it cannot be claimed, I think, that Mickey Mouse is very mousy, or Pluto very doggy. If we sat in the cinema with our eyes closed and *heard* a Walt Disney film, would we be able to guess what kinds of animals the characters are? On the other hand, the Narnian animals, whether they can talk or are dumb, retain the qualities that endear them to us. Anyone who has owned a dog will recognize the realistic touch when he reads about the adventures at the Giants' Castle, where there are "wagging tails, and barking, and loose, slobbery mouths and noses of dogs thrust into your hand" (*The Silver Chair,* p. 115). The Giants' dogs were dumb, but even the Talking Dogs in *The Last Battle* "joined in the conversation but not very much because they were too busy racing on ahead and racing back and rushing off to sniff at smells in the grass till they made themselves sneeze" (p. 160). In the same chapter everyone is waiting to hear what Aslan said to Emeth the Calormene; and when "the Dogs had all had a very noisy drink out of the stream they all sat down, bolt upright, panting, with their tongues hanging out of their heads a little on one side to hear the story" (p. 162).

But why did Lewis choose to make his characters Talking Animals and mythological creatures (or *Longaevi,* as Lewis calls them[27]) ? Would not people have done as well? Talking Animals and *Longaevi* such as giants, dwarfs, fauns, centaurs, dryads, naiads and other creatures which are not human, but which behave in varying degrees humanly, are, Lewis believes, the "expression of certain basic elements in man's spiritual experience . . . the words of a language which speaks the else unspeakable."[28] He is, then, speaking the proper language of the fairy tale, the only language there is for the type of stories he was writing. To have used people instead, or to have given these creatures anything other than their traditional characteristics, would have been, he thought, *ungrammatical.* Besides this, Talking Animals and *Longaevi* are, he says, "an admirable hieroglyphic which conveys psychology, types of character, more briefly than novelistic presentation."[29] Eustace, Jill, and Puddleglum have among the Northern Giants a quality of experience that would have been impossible among any other sort of creature. All those twenty-ton, earthshaking, unpredictable morons, just as likely to laugh as cry, are the only creatures who could have frightened and exasperated them in just that way. Could the greedy and vulgar Shift have been anything but an ape? Could any *person* have made us understand bravery so well as the gay and martial Reepicheep? Lewis was not fond of talking about his own books, but when he did, it was usually with as much detachment as when speaking of other writers' works. We agreed that Puddleglum and Reepicheep were the best of his creations. Puddleglum, the marsh-wiggle, is modelled, Lewis told me, after his gardener, Paxford — an inwardly optimistic, outwardly pessimistic, dear, frustrating, shrewd countryman of immense integrity. But unlike Paxford, Puddleglum is so much *more* the type of man of which Paxford is typical.

As Lewis points out in his essay "On Stories,"[30] there is a

[27] See the chapter on "The *Longaevi*" in Lewis's *The Discarded Image: An Introduction to Medieval and Renaissance Literature* (Cambridge, 1964), pp. 122-138.

[28] *A Preface to "Paradise Lost"* (Oxford, 1942), p. 56.

[29] "On Three Ways of Writing for Children," *Of Other Worlds,* p. 27.

[30] *Of Other Worlds,* p. 14.

convenience in making your characters animals (and, in his case, *Longaevi* as well). As they are not human, so many economic difficulties are avoided. They do not have to be either children or adults. There is no struggle for existence, no domestic worries. They come and go as they please. There is plenty of good eating in Narnia, but where does it all come *from?* The Dwarfs are very clever, but I never heard of them keeping pigs. Who, then, made the sausages? or the wine, beer, and cheese?

I mentioned some of Lewis's ideas on animal immortality several pages back because I think we can see some application of those ideas in the Narnian stories. Nevertheless, we must remember that we are talking about imaginative fiction, and I think it would be disastrous to push the analogies too far. It would appear that part of Lewis's purpose was to create a world in which the relation between men and beasts is as nearly as possible like that which might have existed before both were corrupted at the beginning of this world. He even gives us an idea of what the Narnian animal kingdom was like before men or evil came into their lives (the people are there only as witnesses at first). Instead of animals being subordinate to men, the dumb beasts are subordinate to the Talking Animals (this is all in Chapters ix and x of *The Magician's Nephew*). The biblical parallels are obvious. After the Creation, Aslan chooses from the beasts (all of which are dumb) two of every kind and gives them speech and reason: Noah is commanded to take into the Ark "every living thing of all flesh, two of every sort" (Genesis 6:19). Aslan then gives the Talking Beasts dominion over the dumb beasts: as God gave Man "over every living thing that moveth upon the earth" (Genesis 1:28). Aslan commands the Talking Beasts to treat the dumb ones gently lest they become like them and lose their reason, "for out of them you were taken and into them you can return" (p. 116). The nearest parallel to this — although, like the first, the context is not the same — is the curse that falls on Man after the Fall: "In the sweat of thy face shalt thou eat bread, till thou return unto the ground; for out of it wast thou taken: for dust thou art, and unto dust shalt thou return" (Genesis 3:19).

However, after the Coronation of King Frank I, all Narnian beasts become subordinate to Man. Though Man is responsible for the corruption of Narnia (Digory brought the evil Jadis there on the day of Creation), the Kings and Queens of Narnia must always be *human*. This is not their privilege, but their responsibility: "As Adam's race has done the harm, Adam's race shall help to heal it."[31] It is, then, part of Man's redemptive function to help raise the beasts to their derivative immortality in the eternal Narnia. And — who can deny it? — the beasts play some part in the redemption of Man ("Either other sweetly gracing").

Most of Lewis's children are quite unattractive before they visit Narnia, and they come back much improved. That is one of the reasons they are taken there. Some of their faults can be traced to their schools. "I wonder what they *do* teach them at these schools," Professor Kirke asks himself in *The Lion, the Witch and the Wardrobe* (p. 51). Eustace Clarence Scrubb, we learn in *The Voyage of the "Dawn Treader"*, "liked books if they were books of information and had pictures of grain elevators or of fat foreign children doing exercises in model schools." He also liked bossing and bullying other people (p. 9). When he takes shelter in the dragon's uncomfortable cave, the author says: "Most of us know what we should expect to find in a dragon's lair, but, as I said before, Eustace had read only the wrong books. They had a lot to say about exports and imports and governments and drains, but they were weak on dragons" (p. 83). At the beginning of *The Silver Chair*, Eustace and Jill Pole are students at the same school: "It was 'Co-educational', a school for both boys and girls, what used to be called a 'mixed' school; some said it was not nearly so mixed as the minds of the people who ran it. These people had the idea that boys and girls should be allowed to do what they liked" (p. 11).

Lewis is here attacking the modern theory of "democratic education" as envisaged by the Board of Education and the schools of education in the United States. The attack began with two articles[32] directed at the Norwood Report.[33] It was continued in a later article[34] and reached its fullest expression in *Screwtape Proposes a Toast*. In the last two instances he reminds us of Aristotle's belief that democratic education ought to mean, not the education that democrats like, but the education that will preserve democracy. Lewis believes that educators and parents

[31] *The Magician's Nephew*, p. 134. Cf. Rom. 5:19 and I Cor. 15:22.

[32] "Is English Doomed?" *The Spectator*, CLXXII (Feb. 11, 1944), 121; and ["The Parthenon and the Optative"] "Notes on the Way," *Time and Tide*, XXV (March 11, 1944), 213. (Lewis wrote titles on his private copies of "Notes on the Way," and I have reproduced them here within square brackets so that we can distinguish one essay from another.)

[33] *Curriculum and Examinations in Secondary Schools: Report of the Committee of the Secondary School Examinations Council Appointed by the President of the Board of Education in 1941* (London: H. M. Stationery Office, 1943).

[34] ["Democratic Education"] "Notes on the Way," *Time and Tide*, XXV (April 29, 1944), 369-370.

have confused the two. They want an education that is democratic only in the sense of being egalitarian — one that smudges over the inequality of the intelligent and diligent boy and the stupid and idle one. There are two ways of doing this: one is to abolish those compulsory subjects that show up the real differences between the boys; the other is to make the curriculum so broad that every boy is bound to find something he can do well. The main object is that no boy, and no boy's parents, will feel inferior. This demand for equality, which is now by no means confined to schools, results in the inferior person's resentment of anything that is stronger, subtler, or better than himself. And, as Envy is insatiable, the more you concede to it the more it will demand. As Screwtape says, it induces a man "to enthrone at the centre of his life a good, solid resounding lie" — a lie that is often expressed in the familiar phrase *I'm as good as you.*[35]

Eustace Clarence Scrubb is the product of a social education and home that have made him the truculent, selfish coxcomb we meet at the beginning of *The Voyage of the "Dawn Treader"*. Desperate diseases require desperate remedies. It is in the form of a dragon, the outward semblance of his inner spiritual condition, that he learns humility and the beginnings of self-knowledge. Afterward, Aslan helps him strip off the "old Adam" and he emerges a much better person. This is one example of what is repeated throughout the books. None of the children simply "develops" into a better person. They are strongest when they are most dependent on Aslan, and it is all those Lion's kisses (imparting divine grace) that make the otherwise impossible possible.

It is Peter who, in my opinion, best fulfills the chivalric ideal. Lewis devoted an essay to this special contribution of the Middle Ages to our culture.[36] This ideal is perfectly expressed in Sir Ector's lament over his dead brother, Sir Launcelot: "Thou wert the meekest man that ever ate in hall among ladies; and thou wert the sternest knight to thy mortal foe that ever put spear in the rest" (Malory, XXI, xiii). The important thing about this ideal is the *double* demand it makes on human nature. "The knight," says Lewis, "is a man of blood and iron, a man familiar with the sight of smashed faces and the ragged stumps of lopped-off limbs; he is also a demure, almost a maidenlike, guest in hall, a gentle, modest, unobtrusive man. He is not a

[35] *The Screwtape Letters and Screwtape Proposes a Toast: with a new Preface* (London, 1961), p. 149.

[36] ["The Necessity of Chivalry"] "Notes on the Way," *Time and Tide*, XXI (Aug. 17, 1940), 841.

compromise or happy mean between ferocity and meekness; he is fierce to the *n*th and meek to the *n*th." Unfortunately, it is not natural for a man to be both heroic and meek. Heroism is most often found in the noisy, arrogant bully: and meekness usually found in the weak, defenseless man. Though the two tendencies do not live well together, it is, nevertheless, important that a man embody both. It is the ideal embodied in Sir Launcelot, as Lewis sees it, that "offers the only possible escape from a world divided between wolves who do not understand, and sheep who cannot defend, the things which make life desirable."

At our first meeting of the four Pevensie children in *The Lion, the Witch and the Wardrobe,* it is Peter whom we would choose as the meekest, the most courteous and fair-minded. But would he be any good at defending Narnia (to say nothing of himself)? But then, what about the impetuous and cowardly Peter of the Gospels? If we had not read Acts, would we have believed that after the resurrection he would become one of the most courageous defenders of the Faith the world has ever known? When Susan winds her horn, the slightest prompting from Aslan is sufficient to send Peter to her rescue. He feels sick at the thought of fighting the Wolf, but he rushes into battle. For a while it is all "blood and heat and hair" (p. 122), but he slays the Wolf and is afterward knighted Sir Peter Wolf's-Bane. After this the seed of courage is planted in all of them. Even the one-time traitor, Edmund, after some words from Aslan (which he never forgets), fights the White Witch until he falls wounded.

In this and all the other Narnian books, the greatest feats of arms are inseparable from the most perfect courtesy. Some of the most thrilling are recounted in *The Voyage of the "Dawn Treader"*. The young king, Caspian, overthrows the slave trade in the Lone Islands by sheer pluck and courage. How it must cheer the heart of anyone who is himself not a politician to see the hideously complicated, lazy bureaucracy overturned by Caspian, who, an instant later, his naked sword across his knees, is facing the bilious Governor. " 'My Lord,' said he, fixing his eyes on Gumpas, 'you have not given us quite the welcome we expected. We are the King of Narnia' " (p. 57). Then follows the (all too familiar) bilge from Gumpas about economics, interviews, appointments, graphs, trade, statistics, ending in the question, "Have you no idea of progress, of development?" "I have seen them both in an egg," Caspian replies. "We call it Going Bad in Narnia" (p. 59).

It is on this same voyage that the adventurers sight what

appears to be a cloud of infinite blackness resting on the sea. It is decided that they will not venture into the ominous Darkness, and all speak with hushed voices as they prepare to avoid this frightening enterprise. "And why not?" comes the clear voice of Reepicheep. "Will someone explain to me why not." No one is anxious to explain and so Reepicheep continues: "If I were addressing peasants or slaves, I might suppose that this suggestion proceeded from cowardice. But I hope it will never be told in Narnia that a company of noble and royal persons in the flower of their age turned tail because they were afraid of the dark" (pp. 163-164).

These and all other heroic achievements are centered around the castle of Cair Paravel, the hereditary seat of Narnian kings. It is modelled on a medieval court such as that of King Arthur at the beginning of *Sir Gawain and the Green Knight.* Lewis has restored all the fragments of an old unity: coronations, feasts, rich clothes, courtly language, merriment, friendship, hawking. There is one detail of the medieval (indeed, even earlier than the medieval) court which Lewis, as an admirer of epic poetry,[37] was certain to include. Before Eustace and Jill set off in search of Prince Rilian, they are entertained in the great hall of Cair Paravel where after "all the serious eating and drinking was over, a blind poet came forward and struck up the grand old tale of Prince Cor and Aravis and the horse Bree, which is called *The Horse and his Boy*" (*The Silver Chair,* p. 48). They are listening to a Narnian epic which is well over a thousand years old. Though the setting of all the Narnian stories is essentially medieval, it is *Narnian* medieval. Lewis has so perfectly blended the high court of Cair Paravel with the ancient *Longaevi* of Greek and Roman myths that we are hardly aware that it has a dimension no real medieval court ever had. It seems the most natural thing in the world to see a centaur come galloping up to court, and some of Lewis's own marsh-wiggles doing most of the "watery and fishy kinds of work" (*The Silver Chair,* p. 209) nearby.

Narnia is a monarchical society, one in which there is a joyful and loyal obedience to those above one in the hierarchic scale of being. From top to bottom, the order of precedence would run something like this: The Emperor-Over-Sea and Aslan — the High King Peter — the Kings and Queens of Narnia — the minor nobility — Talking Beasts and *Longaevi* — the dumb beasts. One would be very far wrong to suppose that because Narnia is monarchical it is a society of slaves. Before his corona-

[37] "Primary Epic," *A Preface to "Paradise Lost,"* pp. 12ff.

tion Frank, the first king of Narnia, promises Aslan that he will "rule and name all . . . creatures, and do justice among them, and protect them from their enemies," rule the creatures "kindly and fairly, remembering that they are not slaves . . . but Talking Beasts and free subjects," that he will not "have favourites either among [his] own children or among the other creatures or let any hold another under or use it hardly," and if enemies come against the land, to "be the first in the charge and the last in the retreat."[38] These solemn promises are binding on every king of Narnia and Archenland: Tirian, the last king, offers his life in the service of his subjects.

I expect there are some people who cannot understand why Lewis would make the Narnians free subjects, yet at the same time answerable to the Monarch. Aslan knows that evil is already at work on the day of Creation, and he is insuring Narnia against an absolute, tyrannical rule such as the Calormenes chafe at under their Tisroc. This will possibly become clearer if I mention Lewis's own "political" position. (1) He believed that most people are democrats because they think themselves so wise and good as to deserve a share in the government. He was himself a democrat for the opposite reason: he believed that mankind is so fallen that no man can be trusted with unchecked power over his fellows. It follows from this that they ought to have equal rights (equal *rights* is a very different thing from the "good, solid resounding lie" that all men are equal beings). But having equal rights is not something we should be proud of. It is, more properly, something we ought to be ashamed of, something to be treated as a medicine for our fallen condition, rather than as a food. (2) Lewis defends the ceremonial monarchy on the grounds that it is, among other things, a reminder that we are not equal beings:

> There, right in the midst of our lives, is that which satisfies the craving for inequality, and acts as a permanent reminder that medicine is not food. Hence a man's reaction to Monarchy is a kind of test. Monarchy can easily be "debunked"; but watch the faces, mark well the accents, of the debunkers. These are the men whose tap-root in Eden has been cut: whom no rumour of the polyphony, the dance, can reach — men to whom pebbles laid in a row are more beautiful than an arch. Yet even if they desire mere equality they cannot reach it. Where men are forbidden to honour a king they honour millionaires, athletes, or film-stars instead: even famous prostitutes or gangsters. For spiritual nature,

[38] *The Magician's Nephew*, pp. 136-137. Cf. "Rulers are not a terror to good works, but to the evil. Wilt thou then not be afraid of the power? do that which is good, and thou shalt have praise of the same: For he is the minister of God to thee for good" (Rom. 13:3-4).

like bodily nature, will be served; deny it food and it will gobble poison.[39]

## VII

Lewis believed that there are three elements in all developed religions, and in Christianity one more. The first is the experience of the *Numinous.* If you were told that there is a mighty spirit in the room with you, you would feel wonder and a sense of inadequacy to cope with such a visitant. This shrinking feeling which the numinous object excites in you is *awe.* A good example is Jacob's vision of a ladder reaching from earth to heaven on which ascend and descend the angels of God. When Jacob woke from sleep he exclaimed, "Surely the Lord is in this place; and I knew it not. And he was afraid, and said, How dreadful is this place!" (Genesis 28:16-17). The second element in religion is the consciousness of a moral law, and the third element appears when we realize that the numinous power is the guardian of the morality to which we feel an obligation. The fourth is a historical event, such as the recognition that the incarnate Son of God is the "awful haunter of nature and the giver of the moral law" (*The Problem of Pain,* p. 11).

All these elements are vested in the person of the great, golden Lion of Narnia, but it is the Numinous, the dreadful, that at first strikes us the most directly. When the Pevensie children first hear the name of Aslan, something jumps in their insides (*Lion,* p. 67). When they see him they know that they are face to face with one who is both good and terrible. The sight of his great, royal, solemn, overwhelming eyes causes them to go "all trembly" (p. 119). He is a figure of immense power and beauty. When, after his resurrection, "he opened his mouth to roar his face became so terrible that they did not dare to look at it. And they saw all the trees in front of him bend before the blast of his roaring as grass bends in a meadow before the wind" (p. 151). The greed of Caspian and Edmund over the magical properties of Deathwater pool (which turns all that touches it to gold) gives way to fear and wonder when, across the gray hillside "without noise, and without looking at them, and shining as if he were in bright sunlight though the sun had in fact gone in, passed with slow pace the hugest lion that human eyes have ever seen" (*"Dawn Treader",* p. 119). Two qualities Lewis told me he borrowed from the Holy Grail, that of brightness and a sweet odor, contribute to Aslan's numinous effect. Both are

39 "Equality," *The Spectator,* CLXXI (Aug. 27, 1943), 192.

present in the manifestation of Aslan's glory to Shasta in *The Horse and his Boy.* When the boy fell at the Lion's feet, the "High King above all kings stooped towards him. Its mane, and some strange and solemn perfume that hung about the mane, was all round him. It touched his forehead with its tongue. He lifted his face and their eyes met. Then instantly the pale brightness of the mist and the fiery brightness of the Lion rolled themselves together into a swirling glory and gathered themselves up and disappeared" (pp. 148-149).

There is never any doubt in anyone's mind that Aslan is the Lord of that world. Even his enemies believe this ("the devils also believe, and tremble," James 2:19). If I had not read the Narnian Chronicles, I could not have believed an author could concentrate so much goodness into one being (I am not forgetting the author's Model). None of the mushy, goody-goody sort of thing we sometimes find in people we feel we ought to like, but cannot. Here, in this magnificent Lion, is absolute goodness beyond anything we could imagine. Qualities we sometimes think of as opposites meet in him and blend.

He can be very stern. When the White Witch questions whether he will keep his promise (to die in Edmund's stead) his great roar sends her running for her life. After the rude and saucy Jill has pushed Eustace off the cliff, she turns toward the stream to get a drink. Her way is blocked by the Lion, who she knows has seen her, "for its eyes looked straight into hers for a moment and then turned away — as if it knew her quite well and didn't think much of her." When she asks him to move out of her way, she is answered by a look and a growl. She knows she may as well have asked a mountain to move aside for her convenience. Nor will he bargain with her. Desperate for a drink of water, she asks, "*Do* you eat girls?" "I have swallowed up girls and boys, women and men, kings and emperors, cities and realms," says Aslan. "I daren't come and drink," says Jill. "Then you will die of thirst," the Lion tells her. When she proposes to look for another stream, he tells her, "There is no other stream" (*The Silver Chair,* pp. 26-27).

It does not occur to Jill to disbelieve the Lion. And Aslan's sternness, as she and all the other children come to see later, is the only thing that could have helped them past their pride and ignorance to some good which he planned for them. It is the proof, not the weakness, of his love. He always wants for them something so much better than they could have wanted, or thought they wanted, for themselves. As the master of an unwilling donkey knows when to apply the whip, and when the carrot, so Aslan in his omniscience knows when tenderness is best. At the end of the quest for Prince Rilian, the sight of Aslan causes Jill to remember all her snappings and quarrellings and how she muffed nearly all the signs he had given her. She tries, but is not able, to say "I'm sorry." The Lion, understanding this, draws Jill and Eustace to himself, and touching their pale faces with his tongue, says, "Think of that no more. I will not always be scolding" (*The Silver Chair,* p. 211). Shasta did not know that Aslan had been caring for him since his birth. Nor does he realize that he would never have reached King Lune in time to warn him of Rabadash's treachery had not the Lion spurred him on. When the tired and dispirited boy complains that he is the unluckiest person in the world, he feels the warm breath of Aslan on his hands and face and the great Lion says, "Tell me your sorrows" (*The Horse and his Boy,* p. 146).

Nowhere in the Narnian books is the large, embracing love of Aslan for every creature in all worlds so poignantly felt as when Digory, anxious to draw the Lion's attention to the fact that his mother lies dying, blurts out:

> "But please, please — won't you — can't you give me something that will cure Mother?" Up till then he had been looking at the Lion's great front feet and the huge claws on them; now, in his despair, he looked up at its face. What he saw surprised him as much as anything in his whole life. For the tawny face was bent down near his own and (wonder of wonders) great shining tears stood in the Lion's eyes. They were such big, bright tears compared with Digory's own that for a moment he felt as if the Lion must really be sorrier about his Mother than he was himself.
>
> "My son, my son," said Aslan. "I know. Grief is great. Only you and I in this land know that yet. Let us be good to one another."[40]

There are others whom Aslan is unable to help. Like many of us in this world, the Dwarfs in *The Last Battle* are so determined not to be taken in that they stop their ears and close their eyes against anything that can do them good. When a glorious feast is spread before them, they see and taste only such fare as they would expect to find in a stable. "The Dwarfs are for the Dwarfs," they constantly reiterate to their false comfort and to their eternal undoing. "They have chosen," says Aslan, "cunning instead of belief. Their prison is only in their own minds, yet they are in that prison; and so afraid of being taken in that they cannot be taken out" (p. 150). When the self-imposed blindness of Uncle Andrew erects a barrier between himself and the comfort Aslan longs to give him, the

[40] *The Magician's Nephew,* pp. 139-140.

Lion says, "Oh Adam's sons, how cleverly you defend yourselves against all that might do you good!" (*The Magician's Nephew*, p. 168). Similar words were spoken by this same Lion over Adam's sons in the land of Judah centuries ago: "O Jerusalem, Jerusalem, thou that killest the prophets, and stonest them which are sent unto thee, how often would I have gathered thy children together, even as a hen gathereth her chickens under her wings, and ye would not!" (Matthew 23:37).

Yes, the *same* Lion, for Aslan is Christ. It is, however, with reluctance that I mention this fact, whether you already knew it or not. I am reluctant because I do not want in any way to damage Lewis's success in getting "past those watchful dragons" which freeze many people's feelings about Christ and orthodox Christianity. I am sympathetic with those well-intentioned Christians who in Sunday schools, and writing for periodicals, draw attention to the fact that Aslan is meant to be the Son of God; and I know only too well the temptation, when all our evangelistic efforts seem to fail, to hand out to non-Christians the fairy tales with the comment, "Just you read these, and you'll know what I mean." Let us, by all means, give away as many copies of the fairy tales as we can afford: but not, please, with any explanation about who Aslan is. An "explanation" on our part is, I am convinced, very unwise, as it would very likely frustrate Lewis's purpose and blunt the effectiveness of the books. It is often precisely because many readers do *not* know who Aslan is that the Narnian stories have been so successful in getting into the bloodstream of the secular world. Hints about who is what and so forth have already caused many readers to regard the fairy tales as codes that need deciphering. They were written to give pleasure and (I think) as an unconscious preparation of the imagination. And this they do most effectively without our extra efforts. If the fairy tales succeed in breaking down the partition of prejudices that prevent nonbelievers from thinking of the Christian faith (and they appear to be doing this), then our efforts will be very much needed.

"But why," you might well ask, "are you at this very moment talking about the forbidden subject?" The kind of essay I am writing is not intended for the ordinary reader of the tales but only for specialists, people deeply interested in C. S. Lewis himself. When I heard that the fairy tales were, in some places, being taught as a kind of systematic theology, I felt that someone ought to attempt an explanation of why this is impossible. We will not find an exact, geometrically perfect equivalent of Christ's incarnation, passion, crucifixion, and ascension in the

Narnian stories. We are not meant to. This is why we should not press the analogies too closely, or expect to find in the fairy tales the same logic we find in the Christian story. If we do press the analogies too closely, we will, I think, go a long way toward spoiling our receptivity for what the stories have to give us. Here are some examples of what I mean.

(1) First, in what way is Aslan the Son of God? I once thought we could say that he is the Son of God *incarnate* as Lion. This may have been because Lewis himself says that Aslan "is an invention giving an imaginary answer to the question, 'What might Christ become like, if there really were a world like Narnia and He chose to be incarnate and die and rise again in *that* world as He actually has done in ours?' "[41] Lewis is, however, using the term rather loosely here for Aslan is never incarnate as Lion in the same way that Christ was Man. Let us consider what the Incarnation means.

According to the Athanasian Creed, Christ is: "God and Man; God, of the Substance of the Father, begotten before the worlds: and Man, of the Substance of his Mother, born in the world; Perfect God, and Perfect Man . . . Who although he be God and Man: yet he is not two, but one Christ; One; not by conversion of the Godhead into flesh: but by taking of the Manhood into God." This means that in some mysterious way the eternal Son of God is united with a natural, human organism so as to become one person; the union, as the Creed says, of Perfect God and Perfect Man. The Christian story goes on to say that, by his incarnation, Christ is able to taste death on behalf of all others, and by his rising to life again restores us to everlasting life. He then ascends into heaven in his glorified Manhood — which Manhood he keeps for all time.

When Christ became Man, his divine Nature was united with that of a natural, human mortal. But Christ as Aslan is never incarnate as a natural, dumb lion; never a cub suckled by a lioness. Indeed, he is not always found in the fashion of a Talking Lion, although if Chapter xiv of *The Horse and his Boy* were the only part of the fairy tales we possessed we might be led to think so. In that chapter Bree the Horse maintains that Aslan (whom he has never seen) is not a *real* lion, but resembles a lion only in his strength and fierceness. While Bree is talking, Aslan walks up from behind him and nearly startles the Horse out of his wits (or, more correctly, into *better* wits). "Now, Bree," says Aslan, "you poor, proud, frightened Horse, draw near. Nearer still, my son. Do not dare not to dare. Touch

[41] *Letters of C. S. Lewis,* ed. W. H. Lewis (London, 1966), p. 283.

me. Smell me. Here are my paws, here is my tail, these are my whiskers. I am a true Beast" (p. 179). This episode is quite obviously modelled on John's account of the risen Lord's appearance to the doubting Thomas. And Aslan's answer to Bree (which I have just quoted) is meant to parallel Our Lord's answer to Thomas: "Then saith he to Thomas, Reach hither thy finger, and behold my hands; and reach hither thy hand, and thrust it into my side: and be not faithless, but believing" (John 20:27).

The passage from John and the passage from *The Horse and his Boy* are remarkably similar, but they nevertheless mean something quite different. Thomas had been with Jesus for several years and he is saying (John 20:25) that only by handling his physical body will he believe (a) that Jesus is risen, and (b) that the risen Lord is the same person as the incarnate and crucified Jesus. Bree, on the other hand, is more like the Bishop in *The Great Divorce* who thought of Jesus as "something purely spiritual."[42] Bree denies that Aslan has the body of an animal: "If he was a lion he'd have to be a Beast just like the rest of us."[43] Aslan makes it quite clear that he is not a man, not a phantom, but — like Horses, Squirrels, Rabbits, Dogs and so on — he is a true *Beast.* And *that* — and no more than that — is what Lewis means when he talks about Christ being "incarnate" in Narnia.

By taking upon himself the form of a Man, Christ was (I presume) never free to change his nature into something other than a Man. Aslan is not thus restricted. Quite obviously, it is as a Lion that Lewis usually thinks of Aslan. John the Baptist, after all, thought of Christ as a Lamb ("Behold the Lamb of God"),[44] and in the same Gospel Our Lord speaks of himself as bread, water, light, a vine — even a door.[45] There are, of course, biblical writers who picture him as a Lion.[46]

[42] C. S. Lewis, *The Great Divorce: A Dream* (London, 1945), p. 42.
[43] *The Horse and his Boy*, p. 178.
[44] John 1:29.
[45] John 6:35; 7:37; 12:46; 15:1; 10:7.
[46] I have been given much help on this point by Dr. Austin Farrer, the late Warden of Keble College. In response to my request, Dr. Farrer honored me with the following note, written for inclusion here (the translations of biblical texts are Dr. Farrer's own): "The Seer of Revelation is shown Christ as a Lamb, not a Lion. But it is to be observed that at his first appearance the Lamb-Christ is introduced as a paradoxical substitute for a Lion-Christ. 'One . . . saith unto me, Weep not: behold, the Lion from the Tribe of Judah, the Scion of David, has conquered; he can open the Book. . . . And I saw in the midst of the Throne . . . a Lamb standing as though slaughtered' (Rev. 5:5-6). A Jewish seer of much the same date pre-

Quite apart from the biblical parallels, Narnia is after all predominantly a world of animals, and the Lion, the King of Beasts, seems the most natural and appropriate choice for Lewis to make. But — and this is where the incarnation of Christ in this world differs chiefly from Aslan's "incarnation" in Narnia — Aslan does not always appear as a Lion. In *The Voyage of the "Dawn Treader"* Aslan takes the form of an albatross (p. 170) and a lamb (p. 221). In *The Horse and his Boy* he assumes the form of a cat (p. 80) and on several occasions of an ordinary, dumb lion. And, finally, in the new Narnia, "He no longer looked to them like a lion."[47] What then? What else but in his resurrected Manhood. It is fortunate, I think, that Lewis does not actually say this, for that fact belongs to all the "chapters" that followed, of which the Narnian Chronicles had been "only the cover and the title page."[48] There may be others besides myself who would have been the tiniest bit sorry to have seen the last of that magnificent leonine form.

(2) In order to satisfy God's demand for perfect justice, Christ, the Perfect Man, died upon the Cross for the sins of the whole world. Aslan died on the Stone Table for Edmund Pevensie. We might deduce from this that Aslan would have died for the whole of Narnia, but we are not in fact told that he would or did do so. Try as we might, I simply do not see how we could work out a doctrine of the Atonement from Aslan's vicarious sacrifice for one boy — a boy, not from Narnia, but from this world. I should be very sorry to hear that anyone was attempting to do so, for I think he would have to read into the fairy stories all sorts of things that are not there, and were not meant to be there. What Lewis tells us is that Aslan is obedient to the will of the Emperor-Over-Sea, and that he loves Edmund so much that he is willing to pay his penalty for him. It is moving and beautifully clear, easier for most minds to grasp than the fact that Christ died for all mankind. *And* it gets "past those watchful dragons."

(3) The Gospels represent Christ as passing after death

sents the straight picture of the royal Aslan: 'And I beheld, and lo, as it were a lion roused out of the wood roaring; and I heard him send forth a human voice.... This is the Messiah whom the Most High has kept unto the end of the days, who shall spring up out of the seed of David' (II Esdras 11:37; 12:32). The Lion-Messiah of Jewish tradition derives from the Oracles of Jacob on his twelve sons. He praises Judah as the royal stem, a lion none does rouse, a hand from which the sceptre will never depart (Gen. 49:9)."

[47] *The Last Battle,* p. 183.

[48] *Ibid.,* p. 184.

into a life that has its own new Nature: he is still corporeal, can eat broiled fish, but finds locked doors no obstacle for him (John 20:19) and can ascend bodily into heaven. He is related to Nature in such a way that Spirit and Nature are fully harmonized. As Lewis says, "Spirit rides Nature so perfectly that the two together make rather a *Centaur* than a mounted knight."[49] I tremble at the thought of what I should say if I were forced to explain how Aslan's preresurrection body differed from that which he had after his death. Aslan undergoes something like the passion of Christ: "But how slowly he walked! And his great, royal head drooped so that his nose nearly touched the grass. Presently he stumbled and gave a low moan" (*Lion,* p. 138). What does it mean? It means exactly what it says. Nevertheless, I cannot see that any physical change is caused by his resurrection: he was omniscient and omnipotent both before and after the event. But is it not pointless to make such heavy weather about a theological problem that is not even posed? Especially when the fairy tales have something so much better to give us. If you want them, the real hints about the new, resurrected Nature are found, not in *The Lion, the Witch and the Wardrobe,* but in the final chapter of *The Last Battle* where the blessed Narnians swim up a waterfall and run faster than an arrow flies.

In his essay on "The Genesis of a Medieval Book" Lewis says:

> The text before us, however it came into existence, must be allowed to work on us in its own way and must be judged on its own merits. . . . And while we are reading or criticizing we must be on our guard against a certain elliptical mode of expression which may be legitimate for some other purpose but is deadly for us. We must not say that the Grail "is" a Celtic cauldron of plenty, or that Malory's Gawain "is" a solar deity, or that the land of Gome in Chrestien's *Lancelot* "is" the world of the dead. Within a given story any object, person, or place is neither more nor less nor other than what that story effectively shows it to be. The ingredients of one story cannot "be" anything in another story, for they are not in it at all.[50]

We know Lewis meant for Aslan to be Christ, but I do not think we can say anything so definite as this of all the parallels we find between the Narnian Chronicles and the biblical and nonbiblical stories from which Lewis may have drawn ideas. We cannot say that the sacrifice of Aslan "is" the cruci-

[49] *Miracles,* p. 164.

[50] *Studies in Medieval and Renaissance Literature,* ed. Walter Hooper (Cambridge, 1966), pp. 39-40.

fixion. It reminds us — or, rather, some of us — of the crucifixion, but the two events have different meanings. You can learn a good deal about centaurs from encyclopedias of mythology, but you will not read of any exactly like those in *The Silver Chair* which have a man-stomach and a horse-stomach, both of which want a different breakfast (p. 207). Thus, one would be wrong in saying that the crucifixion and the centaurs of Greek mythology are "in" the Narnian stories.

I think we can appreciate fully the use Lewis made of biblical parallels when we consider the two opposite dangers into which he could have fallen. Had the biblical parallels been very obvious, he would not, I think, have nearly so many readers. Nonbelievers would have felt they were being "got at" and rejected them at once. On the other hand, our imaginations would not have been attuned to the Everlasting Gospel had he been too subtle — especially as so many people today have never read the Bible. Some middle way was needed. This *via media* came easily to Lewis because he did not begin with morals or the Gospels at all, but wrote stories in which those ingredients pushed themselves in of their own accord. This is understandable if you have spent some time in Lewis's company. He could talk about the saints as naturally and unembarrassedly as you or I could talk about next-door neighbors. "Poor Lazarus," I recall him saying, "he had to die all over again!" And because Lewis's primary intention was to tell a story, rather than get a "message" across, the biblical elements blend into the stories. They are more like leaven in dough than raisins in a cake. It is difficult to say where they begin and where they end. But it is not solely the biblical elements that cause us to think of them as Christian books. Almost every page of every book is illustrating some aspect of eternal truth. There must be many priests and teachers who wish they could get their flock to understand the nature of pride and jealousy as well as Lucy does during her session with the Magician's Book.[51] And not once does Lewis use theological jargon. Here is an ingredient from the Old Testament that takes on a rather different meaning from that which it originally had.

While on Mount Sinai, Moses asks to see God's glory, the full manifestation of himself. Because no man can see the Lord's face and live, the Lord says, "There is a place by me, and thou shalt stand upon a rock: And it shall come to pass, while my glory passeth by, that I will put thee in a clift of the rock, and will cover thee with my hand while I pass by: And I will

[51] *The Voyage of the "Dawn Treader"*, Ch. x.

take away mine hand, and thou shalt see my back parts: but my face shall not be seen" (Exodus 33:21-23). At the end of *The Silver Chair* Aslan comes with Caspian, Eustace and Jill into this world to visit Experiment House. "They shall see only my back," he says. After he caused the wall of the school to fall down, "he lay down amid the gap he had made in the wall and turned his golden back to England, and his lordly face towards his own lands" (p. 215). The bullies from Experiment House rush toward them, but when they see the back of the Lion and the figures in glittering clothes they are filled with terror. After they are given a sound thrashing they run and get the Head, who, when she sees the Lion and the others, becomes hysterical. All this eventually results in Experiment House's becoming a better school. God's manifestation causes Moses to worship and pray for the Israelite nation. The golden back of Aslan strikes terror into the hearts of the children and the Head, who had previously been not unlike those "stiffnecked people" for whom Moses prayed.

This next example illustrates not so much a particular biblical element as a theological overtone. The Narnian stories might perhaps have succeeded just as well without any mention of the Emperor-Over-Sea, but Lewis, it seems, wanted to hint at the Trinity of Persons in the Godhead. The Emperor-Over-Sea is meant, I assume, to suggest the Father. The Holy Ghost is hinted at more subtly. In the Nicene and Athanasian creeds we confess that the Holy Ghost *proceeds* eternally from the Father and the Son. After his resurrection, Christ "breathed" on the Apostles saying, "Receive ye the Holy Ghost" (John 20: 22). I believe Lewis means to suggest something like this when Aslan breathes on the children, imparting strength for the tasks they are to undertake. A broader hint is found in *The Horse and his Boy:* "Who *are* you?" Shasta asks the Lion who has been walking beside him. " 'Myself,' said the Voice, very deep and low so that the earth shook: and again 'Myself,' loud and clear and gay: and then the third time 'Myself,' whispered so softly you could hardly hear it, and yet it seemed to come from all round you as if the leaves rustled with it" (p. 147). The reader who knows some theology, and whose mind is turned, as it were, in a certain direction when he reads these words, may catch an echo of eternal truth reverberating from Aslan's words: *Myself* (the Father)... *Myself* (the Son)... *Myself* (the Holy Ghost). If, on the other hand, the reader does not "know the doctrine" the passage will by no means be spoiled for him. He will take the Lion to mean what he says, even if he (the reader) does not know the depths of meaning behind the Lion's words. One of the excellences of the fairy tales is that their ability to entertain and edify does not depend on "explanation" from outside the books. Indeed, I am inclined to believe that the kind of essay I am writing at the moment could, in some hands, have a detrimental effect. It is better to read *nothing* more into the books than to view them as a vast complex of "ideas," "influences," "images," "allegories," and "symbols" which we are expected to explain.

## VIII

Before it was established who Aslan is, we discussed how Lewis's movement from atheism to Christianity involved an answer to the question of where religion reached its full maturity. Paganism, he came to see, had been only a "prophetic dream" of that which became fact in the Incarnation. But just as God, by becoming Man, underwent a certain humiliation, so the old, richly imagined myths, Lewis believed, must succumb to rational analysis; they must undergo a kind of death before they can be reborn in glory. But "those who attain the glorious resurrection," Lewis wrote, "will see the dry bones clothed again with flesh, the fact and the myth re-married, the literal and the metaphorical rushing together."[52] In his interplanetary novels Lewis attempts to bridge the gap that, in this world, exists between fact and myth. On Malacandra (Mars), Lewis's hero, Ransom, meets creatures who use the same method of shepherding as did the Cyclops in Homer.[53] He sees on Perelandra (Venus) the Garden of the Hesperides, mermaids, mermen, Mars and Aphrodite, and realizes that the "triple distinction of truth from myth and of both from fact was purely terrestrial — was part and parcel of that unhappy division between soul and body which resulted from the Fall. Even on earth the sacraments existed as a permanent reminder that the division was neither wholesome nor final. The Incarnation had been the beginning of its disappearance."[54] At the end of the third novel, the planetary Intelligences come down from their spheres to destroy a modern Tower of Babel in England.[55] In the short story "Forms of Things Unknown," the astronauts discover something on the moon that, on earth, they had considered "mere mythology."[56]

[52] *Miracles*, p. 165.
[53] *Out of the Silent Planet* (London, 1938), p. 105.
[54] *Perelandra* (London, 1943), p. 163.
[55] *That Hideous Strength* (London, 1945).
[56] In *Of Other Worlds*, pp. 119-126.

But nowhere in all of Lewis's fiction are we so likely to forget that there ever has been an estrangement between fact and myth as in the Narnian stories. This is, I should think, especially true of those young readers who are brought up on the Narnian stories before they know there are such things as "ancient myths"; they will consider the *Longaevi* just as much a part of Aslan's original creation as are the animals. But Lewis had been closing the gap between fact and myth in ways other than his interplanetary novels. A good example is found in his chapter on "Miracles of the Old Creation" in which he points out that when Our Lord makes water into wine at the wedding feast in Cana he is doing "close and small and, as it were, in focus what God at other times does so large that men do not attend to it." This miracle, he says, "proclaims that the God of all wine is present. The vine is one of the blessings sent by Jahweh: *He is the reality behind the false God Bacchus.* Every year, as part of the Natural order, God makes wine. He does so by creating a vegetable organism that can turn water, soil, and sunlight into a juice which will, under proper conditions, become wine."[57]

But if Christ (Aslan in Narnia) is the *reality* behind the false god, why does Lewis bring into *Prince Caspian* Bacchus, Silenus, and the Maenads? Because now that we know who the God of wine really is, there is no danger of confusion: Bacchus "can do nothing of himself, but what he seeth the Father do" (John 5:19). Now that we no longer *need* Bacchus, it is *safe* to have him. Besides this, how else could we have a proper romp before the Battle of Beruna Bridge if we forego such a wealth of imaginative experience as we get from Bacchus and his madcap followers? Although Lewis has divested him of his power to cause madness and murder, the god retains his essential wildness. In his retinue is his old tutor, Silenus, who "began calling out at once, 'Refreshments! Time for refreshments,' and falling off his donkey and being bundled on to it again by the others, while the donkey was under the impression that the whole thing was a circus, and tried to give a display of walking on its hind legs. And all the time there were more and more vine leaves everywhere" (p. 140). After the festivities Susan says to Lucy, "I wouldn't have felt very safe with Bacchus and all his wild girls if we'd met them without Aslan." "I should think not," replies the sensible Lucy (p. 141).

Without enfeebling his own power, Aslan does through Bacchus that which he did "close and small" centuries ago in

[57] *Miracles,* pp. 139-140 (italics mine).

Cana of Galilee. "Here you are, mother," said Bacchus, dipping a pitcher into the cottage well and handing it to the little old woman. "But what was in it now was not water but the richest wine, red as red-currant jelly, smooth as oil, strong as beef, warming as tea, cool as dew" (p. 178). The same is true of the other mythological creatures in Narnia: all are extensions and expressions of the power and fecundity of their Creator. "Hail, Lord," says the River-god to Aslan (p. 173). That gets it just right: there never has been a permanent divorce between fact and myth.

## IX

Professor Kilby, in his excellent book, *The Christian World of C. S. Lewis,* draws our attention to the "motif of joy and longing, and the greater joy in possessing"[58] which runs through the Narnian books. You may recall from my preliminary remarks about Joy, that Lewis believed that if we find in ourselves a desire no experience in the world can satisfy, the most probable explanation is that we were made for a different world. In *The Last Battle* the faithful Narnians pass through the Stable door into the world of their hearts' desire. I am quite aware that some nonbelievers use Lewis's reasoning about desire, and the fulfillment of that desire in the real Narnia, to illustrate their stock argument that "people *want* heaven to be real, so they make up religion and try to believe it." But there is good reason for distrusting the nonbelievers' argument.

(1) Like Lewis, most Christians have found that in their search for one thing they were being *sought* by Something else. The Hound of Heaven was tracking them down even as they were sniffing along the path that led to him. They were not so much the hunters as the quarry. "God closed in on *me,*" Lewis said of his own experience.[59] If those nonbelievers who speak so freely about "man's search for God" would read the Bible they would find there a surprise. There is not nearly so much in it about man's search for God as there is about God's persistent wooing of man, his efforts to give man some great richness without which he will die of poverty. One impression I sometimes get from reading the Old and the New Testament is that of a man coaxing his sick pup into his lap in order to put some medicine down his throat. The pup may love his master and want to be well, but because he would almost rather

[58] "The Kingdom of Narnia," *The Christian World of C. S. Lewis* (Grand Rapids, 1964), p. 144.
[59] *Surprised by Joy,* p. 211 (my italics).

die than surrender to the will of someone else, he snaps and snarls and bites his master's wrists until the pill is safely inside him. Or, to use Austin Farrer's superb analogy: "God takes my head between his hands and turns my face to his to make me smile at him. And though I struggle and hurt those hands — for they are human, though divine, human and scarred with nails — though I hurt them, they do not let go until he has smiled me into smiling."[60]

(2) Is it, then, a lucky accident that God turns out to be what we want more than anything in the world? It is neither luck nor accident. Our appetite for God is one of his gifts. Paul has a good deal to say about this in his letters. Lewis shows us what this desire (God's for man: man's for God) is like in action by illustrating how the three-personal Being operates in a Christian's life when he is saying his prayers:

> God is the thing to which he is praying — the goal he is trying to reach. God is also the thing inside him which is pushing him on — the motive power. God is also the road or the bridge along which he is being pushed to that goal.... He is being pulled into God, by God, while still remaining himself.[61]

My reason for discussing this here is that something very similar happens in the Narnian stories and is articulated on several occasions. But before we think of them, it might be illuminating to look at a passage that I find (though it says nothing of *mutual* desire) stabs with "sweet desire" — stabs me, at any rate — more powerfully than do any other words in the fairy tales. After the White Witch is dead, Aslan leads the children to Cair Paravel. The castle towered above them and "before them were the sands, with rocks and little pools of salt water, and seaweed, and the smell of the sea and long miles of bluish-green waves breaking for ever and ever on the beach. And oh, the cry of the sea-gulls! Have you heard it? Can you remember?"[62]

I can, of course, speak only for myself, but, taken in their context, these words — especially the questions — set me yearning for that "unnameable something"[63] more powerfully than any bluish-green waves and the cry of seagulls in this world

[60] "Forgiveness of Sins," *A Faith of Our Own*, with a Preface by C. S. Lewis (Cleveland and New York, 1960), p. 68. This is an adaptation of Dr. Farrer's book *Said or Sung: An Arrangement of Homily and Verse* (London, 1960), which does not contain Lewis's Preface.

[61] *Mere Christianity*, p. 129.

[62] *The Lion, the Witch and the Wardrobe*, pp. 166-167.

[63] Preface to *The Pilgrim's Regress*, p. 9.

have ever done. In this particular instance I do not feel sorry for the children in Narnia (they remain there for five years), but for myself. I can tell from the feel of the book in my hands that, for me, the adventure is almost at an end. And (forgetting the other fairy tales momentarily), how can *I* live never meeting Aslan? What I am suggesting is that, for both the reader and those who get into Narnia, the joys of that world (the place, the people, the castles, the landscape) are inseparable from the joy of knowing the Lion. We want to be there because *he* is there. We desire the Lion because — well, not only because Aslan is in himself desirable, but because the desire is one of the things he has given us, one of the things of which we are made.

From what we know of Experiment House, it seems pretty unlikely that any of the students there would have read the kinds of books that evoke a desire for anything outside this world. (I doubt that they had books like the Chronicles of Narnia in their library.) Thus, poor Jill is puzzled when Aslan speaks of "the task for which I have called you and [Eustace] here out of your world."[64] She explains to the Lion that nobody called them into Narnia: it was they who asked to go there, hoping that "Somebody" there would let them in. To which the Lion replies, "You would not have called to me unless I had been calling to you" (p. 29). At the end of their quest for Prince Rilian, Jill and Eustace are taken to Aslan's Country where they see Caspian X resurrected from the dead. Longing to be, like Caspian, forever united to Aslan, "A great hope rose in the children's hearts." "No, my dears," said Aslan, reading their thoughts. "When you meet me here again, you will have come to stay. But not now" (p. 214).

There is a particularly moving example of the children's love for Aslan in *The Voyage of the "Dawn Treader"* (p. 222). When they learn they must return to their own world, the truth dawns upon them that it is not so much the change in *worlds* they dread, but separation from the Lion.

> "It isn't Narnia, you know," sobbed Lucy. "It's *you*. We shan't meet *you* there. And how can we live, never meeting you?"
>
> "But you shall meet me, dear one," said Aslan.
>
> "Are — are you there too, Sir?" said Edmund.
>
> "I am," said Aslan. "But there I have another name. You must learn to know me by that name. This was the very reason why you were brought to Narnia, that by knowing me here for a little, you may know me better there."

[64] *The Silver Chair*, p. 28.

That, by the by, is as frank a statement as Lewis makes anywhere about his evangelistic purpose in writing the Narnian Chronicles.

Edmund, Lucy, Jill and Eustace are, I suppose, from a Narnian point of view, "Gentiles" from an unknown world who become Narnians by adoption. There are, however, true Narnians who, when they see the Lion for the first time, feel a natural and spontaneous devotion to the person of the divine Aslan — as, for instance, Caspian's old nurse, who when she sees Aslan bending over her sick bed says, "Oh, Aslan! I knew it was true. I've been waiting for this all my life."[65] Hwin, the mare, on seeing the Lion, trots up to him and says, "Please, you're so beautiful. You may eat me if you like. I'd sooner be eaten by you than fed by anyone else."[66]

Numbered among the blessed in the real Narnia is Emeth the Calormene. I have never heard any denunciation of Lewis for allowing him this beatitude, but it might be worthwhile seeking some justification. "Is it not frightfully unfair," Lewis asks, "that this new life should be confined to people who have heard of Christ and been able to believe in Him? But the truth is God has not told us what His arrangements about the other people are. We do know that no man can be saved except through Christ; we do not know that only those who know Him can be saved through Him."[67] Like the Pagans in *The Pilgrim's Regress,* which I mentioned earlier, the "pictures" the Calormenes received probably contained the divine call, but through a passage of time they were all but overgrown with Calormene inventions. The fact remains that Emeth, stung with desire, acted on as much truth as he could perceive through the "dirty lens" of the Calormene religion.[68] He sought Aslan with all his heart even when circumstances made it all but impossible to find him. And though he did not know Aslan *until* he went through the Stable door, it is Aslan, nevertheless, who became his savior *there.* The beautiful retelling of Emeth's meeting with Aslan[69] echoes many dominical utterances. One passage I think Lewis might have had in mind is, "And other sheep I have, which are not of this fold: them also I must bring, and they shall hear my voice; and there shall be one fold, and one shepherd" (John 10:16).

65 *Prince Caspian,* p. 178.
66 *The Horse and his Boy,* p. 179.
67 *Mere Christianity,* p. 51.
68 "Horrible nations have horrible religions: they have been looking at God through a dirty lens." *Mere Christianity,* p. 130.
69 *The Last Battle,* pp. 165-166.

Speaking of the desire for heaven as part and parcel of the desire for God, Lewis says, "The proper rewards are not simply tacked on to the activity for which they are given, but are the activity itself in consummation."[70] The old Narnia flows, as it were, into the real Narnia. Jewel the Unicorn, arriving on the other side of the Stable door, expresses the feelings of the others. He stamped his hoof, neighed, and cried, "I have come home at last! This is my real country! I belong here. This is the land I have been looking for all my life, though I never knew it till now" (*The Last Battle*, p. 172).

The Unicorn's words recall for me Lewis's own reaction to death at a crucial time in his life, and I end on this personal note. On July 15, 1963, Lewis was taken to the Acland Nursing Home in Oxford. Immediately upon arrival, he went into a coma and the doctors expected that he would die at any moment. After a priest had given him Extreme Unction, I, among other friends, waited close by for the sad news. To our astonishment and delight, Lewis awoke and asked for his tea, completely ignorant that he had been so close to death. During the weeks that followed, I sat by his bed talking with him about many things. His conversation was as lively and interesting as I ever remember it. I can still hear his great, booming voice quoting the English poets, joking with his friends, and taking me to task for deficiencies in my logic.

Despite Lewis's high spirits, I began to feel that I was wrong in not telling him how close he had come to dying after entering the nursing home, especially as the doctors felt he might not live much longer. I was tortured as well when I remembered Screwtape's belief that it is better for us to die *unprepared* in costly nursing homes amid friends who lie about our condition, than for a soldier to go, *prepared* for death, into battle.[71] In the end I gave in and told him about the coma from which it was not expected that he would recover, his anointing — everything I knew. And all the while I attempted to comfort him as best I could. He listened spellbound, his eyes glowing with excitement. "Dear Walter," he said when I finished, "I am glad you have not left me a stranger to that which concerns me most deeply." And then, seeing how afraid I was that he might die soon, he set about comforting *me*.

Although Lewis's illness caused him little pain at this time, he knew he would never be completely well. And knowing that this is a world in which none of us tarry long, he longed for

[70] "The Weight of Glory," *Transposition and other Addresses*, p. 22.
[71] *The Screwtape Letters and Screwtape Proposes a Toast*, p. 38.

those "lenten lands"[72] beyond which something better and permanent awaited him. Observing his peaceful acceptance of death — there was nothing regretful about it — I said, "You know, you really do believe all the things you've written." He looked a bit surprised. "Of course!" he said. "That's why I wrote them." I know he was tantalized by the fact that he had almost passed the last frontier separating him from our true country, and after he came home he dictated many letters describing his feelings about the experience in the nursing home. He began one: "The door was open, but as I started through it was closed in my face." Then, turning to me, he added, "I would rather have died, but apparently it is my duty to live. I am happy to do either, but — oh, I would like to have gone through that door!" A few months later — the same day, almost the same hour that John F. Kennedy was killed in Dallas — the door opened again. This time he went through.

[72] As far as I know this is Lewis's own expression. It occurs in "Epitaph 17" of *Poems*, p. 137, and *Letters to Malcolm*, p. 158.

# C. S. Lewis on Eros as a Means of Grace

CORBIN SCOTT CARNELL

Some people like to tell us that knowledge is doubling every ten years. They speak as if with the passage of the years we know more about how to be a whole person, how to love, how to be rational and loyal. It is true that quantitative and scientific data is multiplying at an incredible rate, but how much it contributes to knowledge is another matter.

C. S. Lewis, whose roots were in the classical and medieval world, was generally uneasy about the social sciences on the grounds that they were new subjects, at times too brash to know their limitations. His greatest disagreements were not with the scientists but the social scientists and social engineers who assume too readily that people can and should be conditioned in the light of "new discoveries." His particular wisdom owed much, of course, to the many insights one gains from knowing Plato, Augustine, Chaucer, and Milton. He would have been the last to advocate sending out questionnaires or using interviews to analyze attitudes and problems. Yet he understood much about the causes of our discontents in this century, and though he was a bachelor until the last few years of his life, he wrote profoundly on a subject with which our culture is greatly preoccupied, the love relation between man and woman.

---

Corbin Scott Carnell holds an A.B. degree from Wheaton College (*magna cum laude*), M.A. from Columbia University, and Ph.D. from the University of Florida, where he was elected to Phi Beta Kappa. He has done postdoctoral study in theology and literature and serves on the national Advisory Council of the Danforth Foundation. He has published a reader for students of English as a second language as well as articles in *Modern Drama* and *Eternity*. Associate Professor of English at the University of Florida, he teaches not only in his specialty but in the general humanities course as well.

In *The Four Loves* Lewis refers to that state which we call "being in love" as Eros. It includes the animally sexual element, which he calls Venus; but he points out that sexual experience can occur without Eros and that Eros includes other things besides sexual activity.

Eros causes the lover to center his thoughts on the Beloved. He is full of desire for her; but the sexual interest is only part of a total desire to contemplate, possess, and give pleasure to his beloved. There have been those from Lucretius down to Orwell's Winston Smith in *1984* and Hugh Hefner's Playboy who want the physical sensation above all. They theorize that emotional involvement and talk of love will dull the sheer physicality of Venus. Yet the majority of human beings sing songs, write verses, give gifts and otherwise behave as if sexual activity should *mean* something. This meaning may be outrageously sentimental, but meaning is sought — witness almost any of the week's "Top Twenty" tunes.

Lewis points out that without Eros sexual desire becomes simply a fact about ourselves, that the most beautiful mountain view is "killed" when one begins to locate it in his "own retina and optic nerves" (p. 89).[1] But he is quick to challenge the view that Eros is noblest when Venus is reduced to the minimum. Though some of the Church Fathers depreciated sexuality, they did not see the greatest danger in soul-destroying surrender to the senses but rather in seeking to please one's partner to the neglect of "waiting uninterruptedly upon God."[2]

Lewis goes on to say that the Scriptures do not speak disparagingly of the marriage bed. In fact, St. Paul discourages prolonged abstinence from Venus in I Corinthians 7. Lewis might have added at this point that Luther commended marriage as a way to chastity, for since the sexual impulse is so strong and few have the power to sublimate it completely, a married man may be more chaste than a monk in that he is free from the obsession of sex. Luther here stresses the remedial nature of marriage, which C. S. Lewis does not settle for.

I find in Lewis's thought four basic emphases concerning the benefits of married love. First, in marriage one has the opportunity to develop a disciplined awareness of another person,

[1] All citations of Lewis's books are from the first American editions: *Out of the Silent Planet*, 1943; *The Problem of Pain*, 1947; *Arthurian Torso*, 1948; *Mere Christianity*, 1953; *Surprised by Joy*, 1955; *The Four Loves*, 1960; *A Grief Observed*, 1963; *Letters* (ed. W. H. Lewis), 1966.

[2] See Roland Bainton's *What Christianity Says About Sex, Love, and Marriage* (New York, 1957).

to get to know that person in his or her uniqueness. In this respect, marriage is like friendship, and it is risky to marry someone with whom you have had no real friendship. But the marriage relationship is mediated by a constancy of association and a physical closeness not to be found in friendship. In *A Grief Observed,* writing anonymously on the death of his wife, Lewis says: "The most precious gift that marriage gave me was this constant impact of something very close and intimate yet all the time unmistakably other, resistant — in a word, real" (p. 18). He speaks of the "rough, sharp, cleansing tang" of the otherness of one's beloved. He says that even after she has died, there rushes upon one's mind "her full reality . . . not . . . foreshortened and patheticized and solemnized by my miseries but as she is in her own right." He finds this awareness, even when it is accompanied by grief, a "good and tonic" thing (p. 45).

It is good and tonic because one cannot love another until he has given that person the right to be himself in his uniqueness (this is Erich Fromm's definition of love). We are commanded to love our neighbor, and, as Luther taught, one's wife is his nearest neighbor. One loves her when she is attractive and when she is not, because one has discovered and affirmed her in her otherness. In this sense then, Eros can teach us to be self-giving, for as Lewis observes in *The Four Loves,* Eros is not prudential. Even a lawless love can teach a person something of the uniqueness of another. In speaking of prep school homosexual affairs Lewis says in *Surprised by Joy* that for some boys it was the "only chink left through which something spontaneous and uncalculated could creep in. Plato was right after all. Eros, turned upside down, blackened, distorted, and filthy, still bore traces of his divinity" (pp. 109-110). Lewis here and elsewhere follows Dante and Aquinas in believing that sins of the body are the least bad of all sins. They arise, he says in *Mere Christianity* (p. 80), out of the "Animal self"; and though they may become involved with the "Diabolical self," such pleasures as "putting other people in the wrong . . . back-biting . . . the pleasures of power, of hatred" are worse. They are worse because the mind and the will conspire in their gratification. This view, of course, is in marked contrast to the current American tendency to equate "morality" with sexual morality.

Lewis finds a second gift bestowed in marriage in the opportunity it affords to celebrate sexuality as a kind of pagan sacrament. Good sex thus offers a way to be more physically and intensely alive; it brings a sense of well-being, of unity with the world of living things. I have wondered how much of the illicit sexual activity of our time reflects precisely a quest after this quality of aliveness. People who live and work in insulated high-rise capsules, surrounded by cement and smog, lose contact with the earth and living things. Such people are bound to feel less and less alive, less and less male or female. Perhaps sex and violence are the two most available ways for city-dwellers to be aware of their physicality.

Lewis believes Christianity to be "almost the only one of the great religions which thoroughly approves of the body—which believes that matter is good, that God Himself once took on a human body, that some kind of body is going to be given to us in Heaven and is going to be an essential part of our happiness, our beauty, and our energy" (*Mere Christianity,* p. 77). In this connection he observes that nearly all the greatest love poetry in the world has been produced by Christians. In the light of these facts it is curious that Christianity has generally avoided the celebration of human sexuality in its teachings and ceremonies. Highly rhythmic music, dancing, and scant clothing have generally been taboo in Christian worship. Perhaps the best explanation is seen in the fear that practices associated with paganism would lead to idolatry. For example, the early Christians buried their dead, partly because of the belief in bodily resurrection but partly because their pagan neighbors cremated their dead. Therefore, it would have been equally undesirable to celebrate Easter with liturgical dancing, which called to mind Bacchanalian rites, or to glorify the female form in any way, a practice too reminiscent of the cults of Venus and Diana.

It is regrettable that church history gives ammunition to those who find in Christianity a suspicion about sex and a tendency to connect the transmission of original sin with sexual function. Though this uneasiness about sex is not without sound reason (Eros *can* be badly perverted by the Diabolical self or the Animal self), it is unfortunate in that it obscures the thing pagan cultures have glimpsed by means of what theologians have called "general revelation." Observing the rejuvenation of the earth in spring, sensing heightened powers in sex relationship, and experiencing the amazement of parenthood must have led various pagan societies to their celebration of sexuality. Lest we disparage their insight we should remember that "pagan" comes from the Latin *pagani,* which literally means "worshippers in the fields." Better to be a worshipper in the fields than to worship at the altar of Militarism, Race, or even the American Way. The Psalms and the Epistle to the Romans remind us that there is a revelation of God in nature.

The fiction and theological writings of Lewis are filled with images that capture the joy of Maleness and Femaleness. Knowing that sex is not something we do but something we are, he celebrates it in descriptions that relate to the totality of our being (the Green Lady in *Perelandra,* Mark Studdock in *That Hideous Strength,* the tribute to femininity in *A Grief Observed:* "a nest of gardens, wall within wall, hedge within hedge, more secret, more full of fragrant and fertile life, the further you entered" [p. 50]).

Such an approach causes much of the glorification of intercourse, so frequently encountered today, to appear tawdry and mechanical. With respect to sex as with other subjects (government, art, worship), Lewis had a way of discovering profound insight in pagan cultures, for he did not believe that divine truth came only through the Hebrews and the Christians. Lewis finds in the phenomenon of myth-making itself evidence of a divine reality. Clyde Kilby has an important summary of Lewis on this point:

> What is the cause of myth-making? There is a great, sovereign, uncreated, unconditioned Reality at the core of things, and myth is on the one hand a kind of picture-making which helps man to understand this Reality and on the other hand the result of a deep call from that Reality. Myth is a "real though unfocussed gleam of divine truth falling on human imagination" which enables man to express the inexpressible.[3]

In teaching literature I have found that students generally have difficulty with the relation of the Christian myths and symbols to other myths and symbols. They either want to say one is as good as another, levelling everything out, or they cannot fit Christian and pagan insights together. Perhaps the church has directed too much energy against paganism and not enough against the idolatries in our own culture, including the churches.

Lewis says that in the "pagan sacrament" of sex the man plays the Sky-Father and the woman the Earth-Mother. But, he adds, we must give full value to the word "play"— it is "play" in the sense of playing a part in a larger whole and also in the sense of happy abandon, as in a game. Lewis quotes Charles Williams in *Arthurian Torso:* "The maxim for any love affair is 'Play and pray; but on the whole do not pray when you are playing and do not play when you are praying.' We cannot yet

[3] *The Christian World of C. S. Lewis* (Grand Rapids, 1964), p. 81.

manage such simultaneities" (pp. 58-59). In *That Hideous Strength* Ransom warns Mark and Jane against that daintiness in love which would intellectualize the bodily instincts away. In *The Four Loves* Lewis says, "The highest does not stand without the lowest. A plant must have roots below as well as sunlight above and roots must be grubby. Much of the grubbiness is clean dirt if only you will leave it in the garden and not keep on sprinkling it over the library table" (p. 20). A gloss on this statement appears in *Mere Christianity* in the warning against confusing propriety with chastity (p. 74). Primness has nothing to do with virtue and bodily functions do not in themselves connote anything immoral.

Perhaps our confusion here comes from the zeal of two extremes: one saying, with the Victorians, that the body must somehow be disowned or at least ignored (nineteenth-century girls didn't have legs, they had limbs); the other extreme saying, with the sex cultists, that human sexuality is far too magnificent to be associated with domesticity, pregnancy, or mundane body functions. Both groups need to be reminded of St. Francis' name for the body, "Brother Ass," which in Lewis's view strikes just the right note theologically.

The Victorians and sometimes the Pietists before them treated human love in vague and airy terms, exalting "ideals" at the expense of any mention of the body. On the other hand, a composer like Wagner or novelists like D. H. Lawrence, Hemingway, and Norman Mailer expect too much from Eros. They make it carry much more of life than it is able to bear. (The same may be said of television serials and Hollywood films whose subject is the constant toying with love and the search for the perfect love. These dramatic fantasies are produced through the talents of small armies of cosmetologists, costumers, script writers, musicians, and camera specialists — all aiming to create images of desirable man and woman, in impossible technicolor in the case of the films and with omnipresent tremolo organ accompaniment in the case of the serials.) While the current Christian interpretation of sex fully appreciates its pleasures, it has a profound sanity and humility in it that refuse to make sex an idol.

Perhaps only in this way can the perils of romantic love be avoided. Denis de Rougemont argues in *Love in the Western World* that romantic love by its very nature must be thwarted and unfulfilled, that the only "happy" fruition is for the lovers to die together. This is true because romantic love promises more than can be given in this world, as Emma Bovary and

Anna Karenina discovered. De Rougemont observes that "love ceases to be a demon only when he ceases to be a god" (quoted by Lewis in *The Four Loves,* p. 17).

Lewis finds a third gift in marriage in the way one person completes the other, helping to heal the wounds encountered in living, helping to overcome the limitations of being one person sealed in one skin. Here we can be kinder to the Victorians, who inherited from their Puritan forebears a genuine understanding of the companionable aspects of marriage. The Victorians had a special appreciation for these least exciting and least glamorous aspects of the relationship; and perhaps many of them understood that if Eros included falling in love, it also included the contemplation of the beloved — not simply over candlelight on the wedding trip but on humdrum journeys when a couple who have been long married can communicate by sharing the care of children or, occasionally, good silence. There is a total relationship which involves many common experiences in a total commitment. And this is precisely what is wrong with premarital or extramarital coition — it is an attempt to have part of the relationship out of context. It is not simply on whim that illicit lovers like to make breakfast for each other or in some way play at keeping house.

Stressing the companionable side of marriage may seem to favor the idea of the platonic marriage or the marriage of convenience. But because sex may not be to the fore does not mean that it has not been crucial in sealing the relationship. Venus need not, however, be as magically blissful as it was during the first year of marriage when the couple were young and unencumbered. In Lewis's thought it is the touchstone of lust to want "to have *it* again," whatever it may be — sexual ecstasy, money, or praise. He assumes that only in focussing on persons can we expect to avoid thing-centered lust. (He would not go so far as some, however, in arguing that we should never love things; there is a legitimate love of things — for God's sake, as St. Augustine urged. For someone to love a beautifully tended garden that no one else ever saw might be immoral in the eyes of those who argue that we must use things and love people, never the reverse. But in Lewis's context the gardener might be responding, in a dim way perhaps, to the love of God and cooperating in the work of creation.)

The role of memory is also important in understanding the difference between longing and lust. In *Out of the Silent Planet* Ransom discovers that to the unfallen *hrossa* on Malacandra, longing is not painful. "A pleasure is full grown only when it is remembered," they tell him. Thus the things that come only once in a *hross*'s life, such as mating, are not only enjoyed in anticipation but are remembered and "boiled inside" and made "into poems and wisdom" (p. 76). And in a letter he wrote as a young man while on vacation in southern England, Lewis says: "I still feel that the real value of such a holiday is still to come, in the images and ideas which we have put down to mature in the cellarage of our brains, thence to come up with a continually improving bouquet" (*Letters*, pp. 71-72).

Thus it may take many years of living and remembering to make a marriage. The traditional Christian stand against divorce reflects not only the belief that two have sacramentally become one but that it takes a lifetime to know some of the uniqueness of another person. And not the least value of the discovery of the other is the degree to which his or her being complements, challenges, and enlarges one's own being. "Five senses; an incurably abstract intellect; a haphazardly selective memory; a set of preconceptions and assumptions so numerous I can never examine more than a minority of them — never become even conscious of them all. How much of total reality can such an apparatus let through?"[4] Lewis argues that when two become one flesh their capacities for hearing and feeling and tasting the multitudinous variety of creation are enhanced. There is still the temptation to mold the other person, to deny his "personhood"; but there is help in sexual and companionable incentives to expose oneself, to enjoy the otherness of one's spouse. It is in the nature of Eros to promise loyalty and constancy (*Mere Christianity*, p. 83). To that extent, Lewis would accept Luther's understanding of marriage as remedial. But agents used to alleviate human ills — the legal doctrine of equality, depth psychology, the peace efforts of the United Nations — are medicines, not foods. If we try to make them into systems that will in themselves provide nourishment, we commit the error of trying to make medicines into foods. The well-springs of law and health and peace lie deeper than remedies. And so it is with love, whose springs are deeper than domestic comfort or sexual sublimation.

This leads to a final insight about marriage which Lewis crystallizes so memorably in climactic passages in several books and essays: earthly love as a reflection of divine love. Others before Lewis have explored the first three benefits that I have discussed (though seldom with as much clarity as Lewis brings to the subject). In dealing with these earlier points he focusses and synthesizes much that theologians, literary scholars, and

[4] *A Grief Observed*, p. 51.

others have said. But with respect to the last point he seems to me to be breaking fresh ground. Plato, Augustine, Dante, and St. Teresa have surveyed this land, but no other writer that I know has communicated as much about Eros as a preparation for heaven—many of the saints who have glimpsed this either lapse into mystical raptures (St. Teresa) or seem to renounce the body (St. John of the Cross).

Lewis had first become interested in the ideological implications of Romanticism when he was a student at Oxford, as we discover from *The Pilgrim's Regress* and the edition of letters done by his brother (quoted above). *The Allegory of Love,* published in 1936, applied Lewis's thinking on the rise of romantic love to the development of literature. And then in *Surprised by Joy* he tells, autobiographically, how nameless longing and "Joy-Melancholy" entered into his religious pilgrimage. A fairly subtle point emerges when we trace Lewis's treatment of romantic questing and longing: there are many good things to be enjoyed in this life, among them beauty, friendship, and love, but they are never quite what we anticipate nor quite what we remember. We are beckoned on continually toward that which will satisfy our hearts. This may sound like only a paraphrase of Augustine's "We are restless till we rest in Thee." But Lewis says somewhat more, with more careful analysis. He is arguing that God is present in every good but is not to be identified with that good. To echo Ingmar Bergman's Isak in *Wild Strawberries,* he woos us in "the twilight . . . an ear of grain and the fragrance of flower . . . in every sign and breath of air his voice is there. His voice whispers in the summer breeze. . . ."

Augustine shies away from sexual imagery in speaking of the vision of God, perhaps because in Augustine's experience sex was associated with a bondage that kept him from God. But Lewis celebrates the fact that in Hebrew-Christian thought God is always *he,* that God is definitely male in relationship to us. Before him we are all feminine, in physical strength, in dependence, and in needing him to define our being. It is significant in this connection that many psychologists now believe a woman is fulfilled most completely not in sex itself but in motherhood. (This does not necessarily mean literal maternity — I have met nuns who were fully feminine and motherly in a most winsome way, though their willingness to give up conventional motherhood is not to be taken lightly.) We are not only dependent upon God to define our being, but we look forward expectantly to union with him, though it is not to be a Nirvana sort of union in which our selfhood is lost. Lewis is quick to point out, however, in *The*

*Problem of Pain* that the sexual analogy of divine-human relationship is not one that can be pressed too far. The analogy has a long history; there is evidence of it in the early church response to *The Song of Songs* and in the continuing metaphor of the church as the Bride of Christ; it is also a consistent thread running through much of devotional literature. But the analogy cannot be pressed because there are no adequate analogies for the divine, and the erotic inevitably suggests that God has a body, an idea that has no real basis in Scripture.

While he does not press the erotic analogy, Lewis does make a strong case for Eros as a way to learn love both for God and other people. As he reasons in *The Four Loves,* we have no metaphors for the resurrection or heaven except as we find images in nature, and as nature offers images for heaven so Eros offers images for love. He presents the different kinds of love as intermingling, each leading toward Charity, which is God-directed love (directed toward God and by God toward others). It can be roughly pictured this way: (Lewis is not disturbed by the idea, which Freud endlessly adumbrated, that there is an erotic element in friendship, religious experience, and many sorts of affection. Lewis in several books offers some telling rebuttals to Freudian arguments, but in *The Four Loves* he is content to stress the intermingling of our various loves.)

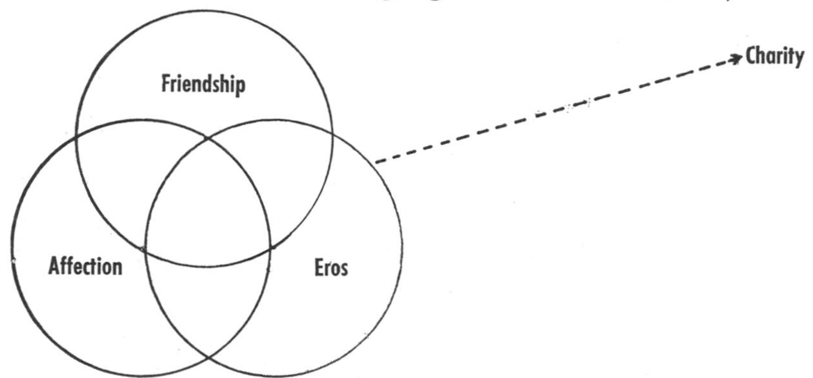


Love is not the same as unselfishness. It may proceed out of an ample ego, but it develops in the person who learns to bend, to be vulnerable, and at times to be silent in order to affirm the well-being of the other person. This sort of behavior reflects a fidelity to God in that it involves loyalty to the realm of being—in fact, to very concrete other beings.

The fact that human loves can be images of divine love does not assure any man salvation through Eros or Affection or

Friendship, even at their highest. Proximity of likeness is not the same as proximity of approach (*The Four Loves,* p. 20). Just as a man does not need a college education to respond to God's love, so he need not to have deeply experienced Eros. There are many ways to know God. It is remarkable that Lewis as a rationalist and a scholar could recognize so humbly that reason is not enough, that simple "need-loves" can lead some people to God when their minds do not. Lewis's understanding of Eros does justice to the sacramental, companionable, and romantic aspects of marriage. Yet what is most helpful to me in his approach is that he rejects any concept of grace that abolishes nature (*Arthurian Torso,* p. 175).

I do not recall Lewis making comment on that troubling passage in Matthew 22: "For in the resurrection they neither marry, nor are given in marriage, but are as the angels of God in heaven." At first Jesus' reply to the Sadducees appears to set aside earthly relationships and even sexuality — as if some of earth's goods would be lost to heaven. But the context indicates that the basic issue is not the extent of a continuum between earth and heaven (the Sadducees did not believe in the resurrection). Jesus' reply to their mocking question about the woman who was married seven times seems to be about love, rather than legality and institutions. Perhaps Christ is saying that in heaven there is no marrying or giving in marriage in the sense of exclusive, possessive love but there is rather a mutuality of loves. Perhaps these will complete rather than set aside those loves that were growing on earth.

Divine grace therefore does not set aside the creation. This world is real and human loves are real harbingers of a love that draws us toward a dance of life. In his memorable conclusion to *The Problem of Pain* Lewis describes this gamelike dance, which he envisions as a part of heaven. There the "golden apple of selfhood" is not an apple of discord which the greedy scramble for. Every dancer must by all means touch the ball (i.e., he must not deny his selfhood) and then pass it on:

> To be found with it in your hands is a fault; to cling to it, death. But when it flies to and fro among the players too swift for eye to follow, and the great master Himself leads the revelry, giving Himself eternally to His creatures in the generation, and back to Himself in the sacrifice of the Word, then indeed the eternal dance "makes Heaven drowsy with the harmony." All pains and pleasures we have known . . . are initiations in the movements of that Dance.

# IV. Aspects of the Contemporary Scene

# The Classical Revival in Contemporary British Poetry

CALVIN D. LINTON

After more than a century and a half of more or less triumphant romanticism in British poetry, with periods of only slightly relieved intensity, there has emerged within the past decade a group of young British poets whose conscious reflection of the principles and practices of eighteenth-century neo-classicism justifies our granting the movement definition and official recognition. The purposes of this paper are to specify the identifying characteristics of the movement, to identify its chief members, and to hazard a general comment on its contemporary significance and possible future.

## I

In the opinion of some, T. E. Hulme's famous 1913 prediction of a classical revival[1] has already been fulfilled in the poetry of Eliot, Auden, Spender, Day Lewis, and MacNeice in the 1930s. This view may be denied on many grounds, including the tendency of the "Macspaunday" group toward obscurity, symbolism, metrical complexity, emotional, religious, and political commit-

[1] *Speculations: Essays on Humanism and the Philosophy of Art* (New York, 1961), pp. 119-120.

---

Calvin D. Linton is Professor of English Literature and Dean of the College of Arts and Sciences at the George Washington University. Educated there and at Johns Hopkins (Ph.D. 1940), he has published three books on writing and articles on literary, religious, and educational topics in *ELH, Southwest Review, Saturday Evening Post, Educational Journal, Christianity Today,* and other periodicals. In progress is a study of T. S. Eliot's use of the Bible. He is American Secretary of the Modern Humanities Research Association and Editor of the MHRA-Duquesne University Press Monograph Committee.

ment, and a passion for self-analysis. Above all, perhaps, they exhibited the trait that George Sherburn has identified as basically inimical to the temper of the Enlightenment: "A disputatious, and hence ungenteel, love of logic."[2] There was vastly more of the intellectualism of Donne than of Pope in the poetry of the 1930s; a great deal more of Hobbes and Marx than of Shaftesbury and Locke in their ideas. Even Eliot's 1921 rehabilitation of Dryden to the depreciation of Milton (a temporary lapse; Eliot recanted in 1947) praised Dryden for personal poetic powers rather than for his reflection of neoclassicism; for his differences from, not his similarities to, Pope.[3]

In contrast, the situation of the past decade exhibits many unmistakable evidences of a genuine revival of the poetic purposes, principles, and forms which, in English literary history, we associate with the eighteenth-century Enlightenment. The surface evidences are there in abundance: objectivity; cool rationalism; metrical regularity; suspicion of enthusiasm and missionary fervor; literary erudition; urbanity and wit; clarity of communication; search for the general truth rather than the personal vision; engagement with the contemporary social and intellectual environment — the list could be extended.

Granted, of course, that all of these ingredients may, by the determined seeker, be found in some degree in almost any body of poetry, yet the authenticity of these signs as genuine hallmarks may be demonstrated by a deeper examination of the purposes lying behind them. Chiefly, the purposes grow out of the manifest failure of romanticism over a period of 160 years or more to produce a stable society by means of revolution, utopian vision, military force, technology, Freudian psychology, or any other means that does not take as its center the search for the norms of Reason, Nature, and Truth. So comprehensive a statement as this is obviously susceptible to query and attack from a hundred positions; but my purpose in making it is to suggest that the new classicism is not *merely* a petulant reaction against the cosmic roars of the poets of the Apocalypse. At the same time, there is no doubt but that the death of Dylan Thomas in November 1953 released a pent-up antagonism against what was, to many (notably to the "University wits," later to be rather facetiously

[2] "Eighteenth-Century Quality," in *A Literary History of England* (New York and London, 1948), p. 828.

[3] "Much of Dryden's unique merit consists in his ability to make the small into the great, the prosaic into the poetic, the trivial into the magnificent. In this he differs not only from Milton, . . . but from Pope." "John Dryden," *Selected Essays of T. S. Eliot* (New York, 1932), p. 269.

called the "Movement"), a particularly sloppy kind of pseudo-romanticism. In so brief a study as this, the larger dimensions of the history of ideas cannot, of course, be dealt with. But it may be well to preface our observation of specific manifestations of classicism in recent poetry by selecting from among many instances two significant general observations about the intellectual temper of our time.

Looking at a world politically remade by three revolutions, the American, the French, and the Russian; and a world continually being refashioned by a fourth revolution, the scientific, British historian A. L. Rowse, for one, refuses to join Eliot, Betjeman, the Sitwells, and Evelyn Waugh (his list) in playing butler to the New Barbarism. On the contrary, he foresees an end of the "fires of ideological conflict" and a new "age of prose and sense, of cool investigation and rational enjoyment." He hails the return of "the spirit of the later seventeenth and early eighteenth century rather than of the earlier period, something of the age of Newton and Locke rather than that of Milton and Oliver Cromwell."[4]

Speaking as a poet and of poetry, Stephen Spender, writing in the same journal as Professor Rowse and within three weeks of the historian's pronouncement, sees poetry "undergoing a kind of strategic withdrawal from the great ambitions of the poets of the modern movement early in the present century. . . . It is . . . a period of consolidation. There is a narrowing of aims. . . ."[5] Spender, no doubt looking nostalgically back to a time when he "stamped his words with emphasis" in the service of a utopian social revolution, deplores the tendency he sees toward limited goals, direct, rational observation, and limited engagement instead of total commitment.

## II

The definite emergence of the new classicism is fairly easy to date. It appeared in an increasing number of poems and critical statements in the early 1950s, and achieved its official status in 1956 with the publication of an anthology, *New Lines,* edited by Robert Conquest.[6] Included in the volume is the work of nine poets: Elizabeth Jennings, John Holloway, Philip Larkin, Thom Gunn, Kingsley Amis, D. J. Enright, Donald Davie, Robert Conquest, and John Wain. At the center of the group are three products of St. John's College, Oxford — Amis, Larkin, and Wain,

[4] "Is Our Age Unique?" *Saturday Review,* June 2, 1962, pp. 11-13.
[5] "For a Wider View of Poetry," *Saturday Review,* May 19, 1962, p. 19.
[6] First edition, London, June 1956. Reprinted October 1956 and 1957.

the core of the group named the "Movement" as early as 1954. Similarly academic, "intellectual," and antiromantic are Davie, Enright, and Holloway. Dr. Davie, particularly, had even earlier made his voice heard in protest against excessive admiration of Dylan Thomas.[7]

Within an atmosphere of intellectualism, reminiscent of the *philosophes* (and perhaps with an audience equally limited to the educated classes), Robert Conquest in his Introduction enunciates the creed of the Movement. He begins by pointing out that no significant anthology of new poetry produced by poets with common convictions had appeared for more than a decade prior to *New Lines*. "It is in the belief that a general tendency has once again set in, and that a genuine and healthy poetry of the new period has established itself, that this collection has been made." He quickly pinpoints the enemy: the impulsive, nonrational, subjective center of romantic creativity.

> In the 1940s the mistake was made of giving the Id, a sound player on the percussion side under a strict conductor, too much of a say in the doings of the orchestra as a whole. As it turned out, it could only manage the simpler part of melody and rhythm, and was completely out of its depth with harmony and orchestration. This led to a rapid collapse of public taste, from which we have not yet recovered.... Poets were encouraged to produce diffuse and sentimental verbiage, or hollow technical pirouettes: praise even went to writers whose verse seemed to have been put together from the snippets in the "Toward More Picturesque Speech" page of the *Reader's Digest*.[8]

In such a formless poetic environment, " 'objection, reason, proof — all would be swamped in the universal mess,' as Mr. Geoffrey Grigson put it" [p. xiv].

Mr. Conquest passes on to the positive position of the new school:

[7] His antagonism toward poetic pretension continues: "Even when it is properly professional, pretension is a price that the best British taste (in contrast to American taste, or French) is unwilling to pay: we like our poet in a roomy old jacket, not in his singing-robes" (from a review of Samuel Beckett's *Poems in English*, in *New Statesman*, January 5, 1962, p. 21).

[8] *New Lines*, pp. xi-xii. In reading the scattered critical comments of the *New Lines* poets, one often feels that he has turned back to the writings of Pope and Addison, Joseph Warton and William Duff, Archibald Alison and David Hume. There is the same dismay at the crudeness of popular taste, the same appeal to Truth *(rien n'est beau que le vrai)*, Nature, and Reason as superior to passion and impulse. There is, too, a good deal of the cool disdain and intellectual superiority that irritates such contemporaries as Dannie Abse and Howard Sergeant (editors of *Mavericks*, 1957, a slap at the Movement) as much as its eighteenth-century manifestation did the new generation of romantic poets of that time.

> If one had briefly to distinguish this poetry ... from the predecessors, I believe the most important general point would be that it submits to no great theoretical constructs, nor agglomerations of unconscious commands. It is free from both mystical and logical compulsions and ... is empirical in its attitude to all that comes. This reverence for the real person or event is, indeed, a part of the general intellectual ambience ... of our time....
>
> On the more technical side, though of course related to all this, we see refusal to abandon a rational structure and comprehensible language, even when the verse is most highly charged with sensuous or emotional intent....
>
> The most glaring fault awaiting correction when the new period opened was the omission of the necessary intellectual component from poetry.... Some years ago Mr. John Wain advocated the methods of Mr. William Empson in poetry. Other writers revived eighteenth-century forms.... [But] intellectual forms can be filled out with bad materials as well as good, and Empsonianism has been almost as much a vehicle for unpleasant exhibitionism and sentimentality as the trends it was designed to correct.... An intellectual skeleton is not worth much unless it is given the flesh of humanity, irony, passion, or sanity ... [pp. xiv-xv].

Praise is also given to the stylistic lessons taught by Robert Graves, whose recent resurgence is another, if tangential, evidence of the new classicism. "Reading through *Poems and Satires* (1951) and *Poems 1953,* it is obvious why the younger 'University wits' approve of him," writes Geoffrey Moore of Graves.[9]

Turning to the poems themselves, it is of passing interest that of the seventy-eight poems included by the nine authors, forty-two are in iambic decasyllabic verse. Four more are octosyllabic. The consistent tone is one of clear statement, natural syntax, and absence of poetic diction. Such conversational lines as "You talk fast without thinking what to say" (Amis), "By now I've got the whole place clearly charted" (Larkin), "Really no moral point attaches to this tale" (Holloway), and "All travellers escape the mainland here" (Jennings) abound. It is difficult to find a single passage of pretension or obscurity, and there is a complete absence of all seven forms of "pseudo-reference" which

[9] *Poetry Today* (London, 1958, published for the British Council and the National Book League), p. 19. Whatever may be the degree of personal idiosyncrasy, of involvement in continuing elements of Georgianism, or of imaginative extravagance, Robert Graves has held firm to simple diction, unambiguous syntax, and universal themes. He has neither roared with the Apocalypse nor retreated, murmuring, into his subconscious. See a particularly acute estimate by W. H. Auden, in *The Mid-Century,* No. 28 (July 1961), pp. 3-9. Graves, Orwell, and Empson are all judiciously and rather selectively admired by the Movement.

Yvor Winters specified some years ago as among the key distinguishing marks of the experimental, "modern" poetry of the 1920s and 1930s.[10] The difference becomes dramatic when one compares the *New Lines* poets with those represented in one of the most typical collections of the verse of the 1940s, *The New British Poets* (1948),[11] in which molten passion, Freud and Jung, "explicit references to a non-existent or obscure principle of motivation" (Winters' sixth type of pseudo-reference), and "reference to purely private symbolic values" (the seventh type) abound. There is, in short, ample justification for the recent designation of the new classical poets as "the common sense school," writing in "the new, plain, non-visionary style" in this "our sub-Augustan age. . . ."[12]

Any attempt to categorize the poems in *New Lines* by type is necessarily more difficult than to specify their verse forms and stylistic features. Even a rough pattern, however, is rather significant. For example, the greatest number of poems (approximately thirty-one) may be classified as critical-satiric. The next largest group (about twenty-five) is made up of generally philosophical poems without distinct personal, subjective elements. (Another half-dozen philosophical poems come closer to being contemplative personal lyrics.) There are a half-dozen descriptive pieces (four distinctly topographical), three or four personal lyrics (only one out-and-out love poem), and a couple of occasional poems. From beginning to end, the poems advance by syllogistic progression, appeal to the common reason, and readily permit of paraphrase. They do not, perhaps, comply fully with the Jonsonian classical dictum that the first requirement of good poetry is that it should possess the qualities of good prose, but they clearly reflect the four qualities specified in *Timber: ingenium, exercitatio, imitatio,* and *lectio.*[13]

[10] "Primitivism and Decadence," *In Defense of Reason* (New York, 1937).

[11] Edited by Kenneth Rexroth (New York). One may also compare the cool intellectuality of Conquest's introduction to *New Lines* to the passionate emotionalism of Rexroth's introduction. The latter, for example, speaks approvingly of that fact that "Thomas is far more shameless than Barker. He doesn't wear his heart on his sleeve. He takes you by the neck and rubs your nose in it" (p. xviii). And again of Thomas: "Most of his early poetry is about the agony and horror of being born and of childbirth" (p. xix). He also says, with regard to the alleged classicism of the poetry of the 1930s, that "I think it is as misleading to describe Auden as a Classicist as it is so to describe Byron" (p. x).

[12] Anonymous review of Elizabeth Jennings's *Every Changing Shape,* in *The Times Literary Supplement,* October 6, 1961.

[13] Herford and Simpson, *Ben Jonson* (Oxford, 1925), II, 437-451.

## III

A single volume makes a slim basis for announcing the presence of a significant trend, granted; but I have concentrated on *New Lines* only to gain specificity while remaining brief. There are many broad evidences of the typicalness of this particular anthology, among them, first, the fact that many of the best known of the younger poets are represented therein; second, the fact that each of the poets represented has published significantly in the same vein in separate volumes; and, third, the fact that scattered poems of classical form and tone now appear in great numbers in literary periodicals, magazines, and even newspapers, suggesting a certain general popularity. And a fourth reason may be cited, namely, the vocal antagonism to the new classicism on the part of the "older" spokesmen of the Apocalypse and neoromanticism.[14]

Occupying a niche by himself, but clearly located in Classical Poets' Corner, is John Betjeman, whose topical, topographical, ironic, rational verse has received a degree of popular approval denied even Dylan Thomas (who was never, as Betjeman is alleged to be, the favorite poet of Princess Margaret!).[15] Adding his name to those mentioned in this paper (and many more necessarily omitted), we find ample warrant for a recent summary (excluding, perhaps, the adverse critical judgment at the end):

[14] G. S. Fraser, for example, writes in *Poetry Now* (London, 1961), pp. 22-23: "These young poets [the new classicists] had often been influenced by the teachings and writings of Dr. Leavis and by the poetic example of Mr. Empson. Their arrival on the scene represented what might, perhaps, be described as an ousting of the bohemians by the pedants. Many . . . were teachers of English, or sometime librarians. They . . . were at once more scholarly (with certain reservations, and within certain limits) and also much more cautious. They worked almost entirely in the typical Augustan line, the end-stopped iambic pentameter."

And Hilary Corke (quoted by Fraser) writes: "The recipe for this type of poetry is simple. Read five hundred lines of Dryden till you have the 'noble, frank, and manly' rhythms pat; choose any theme more proper to critical prose; garnish with two *chic* philosophical terms, three classical references (*minor* writers, please!) and half a dozen rather naughty ones; deluge in an *espagnole* of Total Knowingness, and serve up in a *villanelle* or *terza rima*." ("The Bad Old Style," *Encounter*, June 1955.)

[15] Of Betjeman, W. H. Auden writes: "His poetry has very little in common with what is generally thought of as 'modern Poetry,' the ancestors of which are the English metaphysicals and the French *symbolistes*. . . . There is complexity of feeling in his verse, but no ambiguity of image or metaphor; . . . he has never felt the slightest need or desire to write free verse or experiment with unconventional prosodies." "John Betjeman's Poetic Universe," *The Mid-Century*, No. 1 (July 1959), p. 13.

> It becomes more and more clear as the years go by and the books pile up that the one thing the poets of the 1960s can do extremely well is to create an impression of honest, unpretentious, but often wryly ironic, concern. The poets of the 1930s were poets of the passionate conscience. The 1940s gave us poetry of the symbol-obsessed imagination. In the 1950s and 1960s we are more sober, more reliable, and, maybe, a little bit dull.[16]

As to dullness, many of us would willingly give up any number of "highly-charged Freudian sex-symbols" in favor of more such sharp, Popean lines as the following:

Attack on the Ad-Man

*This trumpeter of nothingness, employed*
*To keep our reason dull and null and void,*
*This man of wind and froth and flux will sell*
*The wares of any who reward him well. . . .*[17]

What of the future of the movement — and the "Movement"? Are we likely, ten years hence (assuming that we remain unincinerated), to have accumulated a sizable body of verse genuinely reminiscent of the Enlightenment? In all honesty, it does not appear likely, for many reasons. For one thing, literary history suggests that the typical Englishman is not temperamentally disposed toward classicism. For another, with all the hope in the world that Professor Rowse's prediction of the coming of the new age of reason proves correct, one would have to be a born optimist to count on it. For a third, there is little evidence that the great Cult of Irrationalism of our century, with Lawrence as its Prophet, has yet been interred in an unsung grave. Indeed, there are those who at the moment hope to lay the axe to the root of the new classicism by advocating and practicing a kind of poetry growing out of the "psycho-linguistic" school, which insists that poetry (and art in general) must be interpreted psychologically rather than rationally.[18] A more

[16] Anonymous review of four new books of poems (*Control Tower*, by Richard Kell; *A Row of Pharaohs*, by Patrick Creagh; *The Night of the Hammer*, by Ned O'Gorman; and *A Garland for the Green*, by Ewart Milne), *The Times Literary Supplement,* June 22, 1962.

[17] The first four lines of a 38-line poem by A. S. J. Tessimond, in *The Times Literary Supplement*, July 6, 1962.

[18] *The New Poetry* in the Penguin Modern Poets series (London, 1962) is edited by A. Alvarez, who believes that the new classicism is sterilizing English poetry by "the disease so often found in English Culture: gentility," the belief that holds "that life is always more or less orderly, people always more or less polite, their emotions and habits more or less decent and more or less controllable; that God, in short, is more or less good." Quoted by Walter Allen in "A Literary Letter from London," *The New York Times Book Review,* July 15, 1962. Essentially, the Alvarez position is that "crit-

subtle and prevalent antagonist is the spiritual malaise of our age, exaggeratedly but pointedly summed up by Samuel Beckett in *Malone Dies:* "I cannot think and do not know, therefore I am — or am I?" The cry of Helvetius' Oromaze, "Hell is no more; 'tis heaven now on earth," rings oddly in an age that, although it has eliminated its fear of hell-fire, confronts the fear of nothingness, the "nonbeing" of Paul Tillich. It is hard to get a favorable hearing for the Philosopher of Dr. Johnson's *Rasselas:* "To live according to nature is to act always with due regard to the fitness arising from the relations and qualities of causes and effects; to concur with the great and unchangeable scheme of universal felicity; to cooperate with the general disposition and tendency of the present system of things."[19]

The young poets we have spoken of are, of course, children of their time. The quality of our age colors their thinking and writing, and it would be idle to pretend that they represent a precise little rebirth of the Enlightenment. But in spite of all, it is not a little thing in our time to have a poetic movement to which we may apply, with at least a degree of accuracy, Sir Harold Nicholson's definition of the overall aims of the great ones of the Age of Reason:

> They created an ideal of sincerity, both toward oneself and toward one's fellow human beings. They certainly did inspire a passion for good sense, balance, moderation, order, taste, intellectual truthfulness, and tolerance. They believed in cosmopolitanism and regarded nationalism, whether political or intellectual, as uncivilized.... They denounced war as a method of settling international disputes, and although the century [the eighteenth] was marked by several wars that enhanced, or diminished, glory, the intellectual reaction against militarism was increased by their teaching.[20]

icism of poetry must ... be in a sense primarily psychological rather than merely ethical, and political rather than merely social." (Editorial, "Language and the Self," *The Times Literary Supplement,* June 29, 1962.) There clearly continues in this point of view the conviction of the 1930s that the artist is obliged to commit himself to a positive political position, although Alvarez himself is not a member of the so-called "New Left." But rather oddly mingled with this position is the existentialist insistence that the inner self must experience the anguish and pain common to all human awareness so as to "express the complexity, the bastardy of being human and having to face all the pain ... and remain sane...." This last quotation is from the first issue of a new critical magazine, *The Review,* June 1962, edited by Ian Hamilton, 39 Woodstock Road, Oxford. An important feature of this issue is a discussion of these matters between Dr. Donald Davie and Mr. Alvarez.

[19] *Rasselas,* ed. Warren Fleischauer (New York, 1962), pp. 21-22.

[20] *The Age of Reason* (New York, 1961), p. 15.

# Such Stuff as Dreams: The Poetry of Howard Nemerov

DOUGLAS H. OLSEN

*The serious and the funny are one. The purpose of Poetry is to persuade, fool, or compel God into speaking.* —Howard Nemerov, in a letter to Robert D. Harvey.[1]

The poetry of Howard Nemerov is conventional and conversational; it has been called "academic" and even prosaic. His best poetry, however, is among the best American poetry written since World War II, partly because it is poetry that comes so close to being prose. Much postwar poetry, in reaction to the Eliot-Pound influence, attempts to communicate outside the classroom by using colloquial idioms and even slang, a conversational and even flippant tone, and contemporary subjects, such as Old Dutch Cleanser, television, Merritt Parkway, and J. Edgar Hoover. The danger in such poetry, of course, is that it may communicate to our time and our time only. It may be only Instant Poetry or Disposable Poetry (reflecting perhaps a fear that there will be no centuries to communicate to after ours). Howard Nemerov's best poetry, however, succeeds in being both contemporaneous and universal; it succeeds often in being both prosaic and poetic — prosaic on the surface for our prosaic

[1] Robert D. Harvey, "A Prophet Armed: An Introduction to the Poetry of Howard Nemerov," *Poets in Progress*, ed. Edward B. Hungerford (Evanston, 1962), p. 126.

---

Douglas H. Olsen graduated from Wheaton College (A.B. 1960), taught at Trinity College in Chicago, then attended Johns Hopkins University with a scholarship and junior instructorship, and received his M.A. in the Writing Seminars in 1964. He taught literature and creative writing (including the writing of poetry) at Wheaton College for six years, then left to be a free-lance writer.

times, yet intensely poetic beneath. Hayden Carruth in a review (*The Nation,* January 21, 1961) said that he was not tempted to reread Nemerov's poems because they had "strayed into prose." Though the statement may be true of some of the poems, such a wholesale dismissal is unwarranted; it is almost as unfair as dismissing Eliot's poetry because it strays into nonsense.

Nemerov, it is true, is quite at home with prose. He has published three novels *(Melodramatists, Federigo, The Homecoming Game),* a collection of delightful short stories *(A Commodity of Dreams),* an autobiographical journal-novel *(A Journal of the Fictive Life),* and a collection of essays and literary criticism *(Poetry and Fiction).* But he is at his best in his six volumes of poetry (of which the last two are best): *The Image and the Law* (1947), *Guide to the Ruins* (1950), *The Salt Garden* (1955), *Mirrors and Windows* (1958), *New and Selected Poems* (1960), and *The Next Room of the Dream* (1962). The last volume includes two biblical plays (modernized) in verse.[2]

His poems comment on a great range of subjects — dandelions, autumn, snowmen, TV cartoon shows, a dial tone, modern religious attitudes, war, a town dump, lovers, the fairy tale "Sleeping Beauty" — with the calm, sometimes gently ironic voice of a leisurely observer out for a stroll. This quiet style, which is sometimes mistaken for prose, is achieved with much art. Consider, for example, one of Nemerov's best poems, "Storm Windows."

*People are putting up storm windows now,*
*Or were, this morning, until the heavy rain*
*Drove them indoors. So, coming home at noon,*
*I saw storm windows lying on the ground,*
*Frame-full of rain; through the water and glass*
*I saw the crushed grass, how it seemed to stream*
*Away in lines like seaweed on the tide*
*Or blades of wheat leaning under the wind.*
*The ripple and splash of rain on the blurred glass*
*Seemed that it briefly said, as I walked by,*
*Something I should have liked to say to you,*
*Something . . . the dry grass bent under the pane*
*Brimful of bouncing water . . . something of*
*A swaying clarity which blindly echoes*
*This lonely afternoon of memories*
*And missed desires, while the wintry rain*
*(Unspeakable, the distance in the mind!)*
*Runs on the standing windows and away.*[3]

[2] Since the above paragraph was written, Nemerov has published (Fall 1967) a seventh book of poems, *The Blue Swallows.*

[3] *New and Selected Poems,* p. 41.

Despite the iambic pentameter — most of Nemerov's poetry is in blank verse — the entire poem has a looseness of sentence structure and rhythm associated more often with prose than with poetry. The first four lines especially seem like prose: there is no paradox, no metaphor, no original phrasing, no vivid imagery, no compression of thought. So far it is what you might notice about Frost's

*Whose woods these are I think I know.*
*His house is in the village though;*
*He will not see me stopping here*
*To watch his woods fill up with snow.*[4]

But Frost's lines have rhyme and a more definite meter, instantly identifying it as verse. In Nemerov's lines even the iambic pentameter does not distinguish it as verse, since iambic pentameter is so close to natural speech rhythm. There is, however, slant rhyme in these lines — *now, rain, noon, ground* — an arrangement that would not occur in prose. These slant rhymes further chime with other words — *windows, indoors, windows.* Also the sound *or* is in each of the lines — *storm, morning, indoors, storm* — and there are repetitions of *m* and long *o*. If it is prose, it is a pleasantly skillful prose.

In addition to these subtle rhythmic effects, there are two subtle tensions of thought in the four lines. The first is the qualification, "Or were, this morning, until the heavy rain/Drove them indoors." This qualification may cause the reader to suspect Nemerov of wordiness, for these four lines can easily be condensed to three:

*People were putting up storm windows when*
*The heavy rain drove them indoors. At noon*
*I saw storm windows lying on the ground, . . .*

Apparently the meaning has not been changed, but does the revision improve the lines? If it does, obviously the poem is flawed, and we can call Nemerov's original lines prose. In this case, however, one thing that the revision changes is the style. Nemerov's style is a relaxed style; the revised lines, on the other hand, seem to rush too fast — they are not as graceful, as natural, as the original. Also, something quite important to the meaning has been left out: the qualification has been removed. Still it might seem that the qualification was pointless in the first place, since it seems to contradict and even negate the idea of the first line, that "people are putting up storm windows *now*." The *now* is essential to the whole poem, however: the people are still in

[4] *Complete Poems of Robert Frost* (New York, 1962), p. 275.

the process of putting up storm windows; when the rain stops, they will come out and finish the job. The qualification, therefore, only qualifies; it does not negate. The situation, therefore, as in many poems, is a frozen moment, an eternal now. Another of Nemerov's poems, "Moment," illuminates this idea.

*Now, starflake frozen on the windowpane*
*All of a winter night, the open hearth*
*Blazing beyond Andromeda, the sea-*
*Anemone and the downwind seed, O moment*
*Hastening, halting in a clockwise dust,*
*The time in all the hospitals is now,*
*Under the arc-lights where the sentry walks*
*His lonely wall it never moves from now,*
*The crying in the cell is also now,*
*And now is quiet in the tomb as now*
*Explodes inside the sun, and it is now*
*In the saddle of space, where argosies of dust*
*Sail outward blazing, and the mind of God,*
*The flash across the gap of being, thinks*
*In the instant absence of forever: now.*[5]

The people are putting up storm windows *now,* the poet is writing the poem *now,* we are reading the poem *now* — art blends the time differences into a single *now.* Furthermore, putting up storm windows is as seasonal as the fall of leaves; in a sense, therefore, people are always putting up storm windows, as there always is an autumn.

The second tension of thought in the first four lines of "Storm Windows" is the irony that the people, while trying to protect their houses from storms, were driven indoors by a storm. Man's constant struggle against Nature and the ultimate futility of that struggle are thus symbolized at the poem's outset.

"Frame-full of rain" in line 5 is the first slightly unusual, more "poetic" (because compressed) phrasing in the poem. It comes as a mild surprise after the relaxed lines preceding it; moreover, the image is set at the beginning of the line and followed by a caesura. It is the central image of the poem, and Nemerov makes us see it. Then the image is described in four lines as though the frame contained a painting. The poet, however, paints the picture with similes. The observed fact of crushed grass is transformed into an underlying reality — the natural kinship of grass with wheat and seaweed. Likewise, the storm and glass become tide and wind as the imagination of the poet

[5] *New and Selected Poems,* p. 3.

takes us from the original scene to the sea and country, and even into elemental Nature.

The similes make sharp pictures, but they are, nevertheless, only similes. The grass *"seemed* to stream." The grass is "crushed," the glass is "blurred," the clarity sways and "blindly echoes." In Nemerov's poetry windows and mirrors are used frequently as metaphors or symbols for the way we perceive the world: in a mirror reversed or distorted (as through a glass darkly) or through a window in which the glass is a tangible, though invisible, barrier between the observer and reality. So in this poem the image seen through the glass is not seen clearly, it seems in imagination to be what it is not in fact (though the imagination may be closer to Reality than the fact is). In the next six lines the image of rain on glass *seems* to be even more. It seems to say something very important, some truth perhaps. But what it says is not nearly so clear as the seaweed and wheat. It is only *something*. It is an intuition, a memory, a longing, a note of beauty or nostalgia perhaps, but unformed. How can one describe a sunset or love or rain on storm windows? "If only we had words," we often think. The poet is one whose job it is to have words, but here he can only record the fact itself and say it said "something." The situation, therefore, comes to stand for abstract truth itself. We sense a greater reality behind observable fact, but cannot ultimately define it, cannot know it forever into words. But it is there; it is *something*. "Unspeakable the distance in the mind!" Within itself the mind can travel infinitely far from the storm window starting place; but when it returns, it is like the man who saw heaven and was unable to tell about it. For Nemerov this "secret of life," which can be known intuitively but not empirically verified, is often symbolized by water, itself a mysterious source of life. For example, Section xv of "Runes":

*To watch water, to watch running water*
*Is to know a secret, seeing the twisted rope*
*Of runnels on the hillside, the small freshets*
*Leaping and limping down the tilted field*
*In April's light, the green, grave and opaque*
*Swirl in the millpond where the current slides*
*To be combed and carded silver at the fall;*
*It is a secret, but to have it in your keeping,*
*A locked box, Bluebeard's room, the deathless thing*
*Which it is death to open. Knowing the secret,*
*Keeping the secret — herringbones of light*
*Ebbing on beaches, the huge artillery*

*Of tides — it is not knowing, it is not keeping,*
*But being the secret hidden from yourself.*[6]

Here this intuitive knowledge is transformed into *being*, which paradoxically is unknowable (it can only be *experienced*).

In "Storm Windows" the key phrase is "swaying clarity." That is, after all, what the rain on the glass seemed to say something of. The phrase is similar to "swaying form" in Nemerov's essay "The Swaying Form," which discusses the relationship of art and religion. The term, *une forme maistresse*, comes from a passage by Montaigne, as translated by Florio; Nemerov applies it to poetry and explains,

> The form ... is simultaneously ruling and very variable, or fickle; shifting and protean as the form of water in a stream, where it is difficult or impossible to divide what remains from what runs away.[7]

The "swaying clarity," therefore, is first of all that which the combination of grass, window, and rain evokes in the observer— the memories, desires, feelings, mood — and, second, a term appropriate for the poem itself. The poem as an objective correlative creates the same clear yet vague feelings in the reader: the situation, the imagery, the sense of loneliness are clear; yet any message of truth, any "moral," runs away like seaweed on the tide or water on windows. According to Nemerov, this is often the nature of poetry. It is art working against itself to reveal and yet not reveal. The reason for this is that the "truth" in poetry is not a theology, not a systematic philosophy, not an outline of any doctrine, but a re-creation of a situation.

> The poet's business ... is to name as accurately as possible a situation, but a situation which he himself is in. The name he gives ought to be so close a fit with the actuality it summons into being that there remains no room between inside and outside; the thought must be "like a beast moving in its skin" (Dante) [*Poetry and Fiction,* p. 13].

The situation named in "Storm Windows" is "This lonely afternoon of memories/ And missed desires." More specifically, the situation may be one of unrequited love or a broken love affair with the "you" of line 11. "The dry grass bent under the pane/ Brimful of bouncing water" reflects the mood of the speaker, a protected (though bent) condition, a numbness perhaps — "After great pain a formal feeling comes," to quote Emily Dickinson. The temptation toward an outpouring of emotion bounces off and away. That the windows in the last line are not the ones lying on the ground, but are standing, suggests a

[6] *New and Selected Poems,* p. 11.
[7] *Poetry and Fiction* (New Brunswick, N. J., 1963), p. 7.

resoluteness of the speaker, a squaring of the shoulders and walking on (undoubtedly under an umbrella). Even our deepest emotions affect us with a "swaying clarity." Grief is often mixed with relief.

Further "meaning" is suggested by the seasonal setting, the tide, the water running off the windows, the poet's passing by the scene. The "message" of the poem is that life goes on, thank goodness, whether we like it or not. This is the message of many great poems. By itself it is a rather banal message; in the great poems it is profound truth. That is why naming a situation is so important: the new name is fresh, and the situation is more than an abstract generalization — it becomes life itself. The poem attempts to give us life itself so clearly that if there is any meaning to life we can read that meaning from the poem. Actually, therefore, the entire poem is the named situation; the meanings of its words should evoke a response similar to that observed by the poet from the real situation. Poems ideally should mean no more than trees do, but

*Poems or people are rarely so lovely,*
*And even when they have great qualities*
*They tend to tell you rather than exemplify*
*What they believe themselves to be about,*
*While from the moving silence of trees,*
*Whether in storm or calm, in leaf and naked,*
*Night or day, we draw conclusions of our own,*
*Sustaining and unnoticed as our breath,*
*And perilous also — though there has never been*
*A critical tree — about the nature of things.*

This didactic excerpt from "Trees" (*New and Selected Poems,* p. 47), is — like MacLeish's "A poem should not mean/ But be" — unfaithful to its own advice. "Storm Windows" more effectively names a situation.

It may still seem to some, however, that "Storm Windows" does not name the situation accurately, that the diction and sentence structure are still too prose-like. So many of the great poets of this century — Eliot, Cummings, Thomas, Roethke, Stevens, Hart Crane, Robert Lowell — pack so many implications into each word and line that a readily readable poet like Nemerov, especially in a period dominated by the New Criticism, seems to have the same fault of wordiness as some of the popular nineteenth-century poets, such as Bryant and Longfellow. Or his diction may seem too colloquial and commonplace for poetry. In some of his poems the diction does fail, but that is not a fault of the diction. "To be, or not to be: that is the question" is not intrinsically less poetic than "The slings and arrows of outrageous fortune," despite the former's plain language. Since Wordsworth, at least, there has been a line of poets — such as Whitman, Frost, and even Eliot — who have sought to write in a common language. Nemerov is in this tradition; he uses ordinary words, avoiding both poetically contrived phrasing and, as a general rule, colloquialisms and slang. He uses a communicative and enduring language. His method is summed up in "Vermeer" (in *The Next Room of the Dream,* p. 37):

*Taking what is, and seeing it as it is,*
*Pretending to no heroic stances or gestures . . .*

*If I could say to you, and make it stick,*
*A girl in a red hat, a woman in blue*
*Reading a letter, a lady weighing gold . . .*
*If I could say this to you so you saw,*
*And knew, and agreed that this was how it was*
*In a lost city across the sea of years,*
*I think we should be for one moment happy.*

That is exactly what "Storm Windows" does, and in reading it we are, despite the loneliness in the poem, "for one moment happy." It is an aesthetic happiness that comes from our being able to agree that that was exactly how it was; Nemerov has succeeded in naming the situation accurately.

Some of Nemerov's verse appears to be less than poetry because of a seeming lightheartedness, a tendency toward wit and satire. For example, "Absent-Minded Professor":

*This lonely figure of not much fun*
*Strayed out of folklore fifteen years ago*
*Forever. Now on an autumn afternoon,*
*While the leaves drift past the office window,*
*His bright replacement, present-minded, stays*
*At the desk correcting papers, nor ever grieves*
*For the silly scholar of the bad old days,*
*Who'd burn the papers and correct the leaves.*[8]

Some of his poems satirize materialistic religious attitudes. "Boom!" is based on an actual statement by President Eisenhower's pastor that we are in a time of "unprecedented religious activity." After describing some of this activity, Nemerov sums it up:

*Never before, O Lord, have the prayers and praises*
*from belfry and phonebooth, from ballpark and barbecue*
*the sacrifices, so endlessly ascended.*

Then he comments,

[8] *New and Selected Poems,* p. 56.

*It was not thus when Job in Palestine*
*sat in the dust and cried, cried bitterly;*
*when Damien kissed the lepers on their wounds*
*it was not thus; it was not thus*
*when Francis worked a fourteen-hour day*
*strictly for the birds; when Dante took*
*a week's vacation without pay and it rained*
*part of the time, O Lord, it was not thus.*

The long satiric prayer ends with a promise to

*give to Thee,*
*if Thee will keep us going, our annual*
*Miss Universe, for Thy Name's Sake, Amen.*[9]

Another poem, "Santa Claus," attacks in a fresh way the commercialization of Christmas.

*Somewhere on his travels the strange Child*
*Picked up with this overstuffed confidence man,*
*Affection's inverted thief, who climbs at night*
*Down chimneys, into dreams, with this world's goods.*
. . . . . . . . . . . . . . . . . . . . .
*. . . His name itself*
*Is corrupted, and even Saint Nicholas, in his turn,*
*Gives off a faint and reminiscent stench,*
*The merest soupcon, of brimstone and the pit.*
. . . . . . . . . . . . . . . . . . .
*Played at the better stores by bums, for money,*
*This annual savor of the economy*
*Speaks in the parables of the dollar sign:*
*Suffer the little children to come to Him.*

*At Easter, he's anonymous again,*
*Just one of the crowd lunching on Calvary.*[10]

A few of Nemerov's poems gently poke at literary attitudes. For example, "On the Threshold of His Greatness, the Poet Comes Down with a Sore Throat" has, in parody of "The Waste Land," sixteen footnotes and a "Note on the Notes":

> These notes have not the intention of offering a complete elucidation of the poem. Naturally, interpretations will differ from one reader to another, and even, perhaps, from one minute to the next. But because Modern Poetry is generally agreed to be a matter of the Intellect, and not the Feelings; because it is meant to be studied, and not merely read; and because it is valued, in the classroom, to the precise degree of its difficulty, poet and critic have agreed that these Notes will not merely adorn the Poem, but possibly supersede it altogether.[11]

[9] *New and Selected Poems*, pp. 18-19.
[10] *The Next Room of the Dream*, p. 5.
[11] *The Next Room of the Dream*, p. 65.

Carruth calls such poems "wisecracks," which he defines as poems of wit in which the two parts — a joke and a moral — "fail to cohere" (*Poetry*, September 1963, p. 390). This very criticism shows a serious intention behind such poems, and Nemerov has stated, "In general, to succeed at joking or at poetry, you have to be serious."[12] A poem in which the humorous and serious combine for effect is "Make Big Money at Home! Write Poems in Spare Time!"

*Oliver wanted to write about reality.*
*He sat before a wooden table,*
*He poised his wooden pencil*
*Above his pad of wooden paper,*
*And attempted to think about agony*
*And history, and the meaning of history,*
*And all stuff like that there.*

*Suddenly this wooden thought got in his head:*
*A Tree. That's all, no more than that,*
*Just one tree, not even a note*
*As to whether it was deciduous*
*Or evergreen, or even where it stood.*
*Still, because it came unbidden,*
*It was inspiration, and had to be dealt with.*

*Oliver hoped that this particular tree*
*Would turn out to be fashionable,*
*The axle of the universe, maybe,*
*Or some other mythologically*
*Respectable tree-contraption*
*With dryads, or having to do*
*With the knowledge of Good and Evil, and the Fall.*

*"A Tree," he wrote down with his wooden pencil*
*Upon his pad of wooden paper*
*Supported by the wooden table.*
*And while he sat there waiting*
*For what would come next to come next,*
*The whole wooden house began to become*
*Silent, particularly silent, sinisterly so.*[13]

The title immediately gives away the humorous intent, and the colloquial phrase "all stuff like that there" establishes the speaker's mocking attitude toward Oliver. The poem appears to be light verse satirizing many would-be creative writers who find they have nothing to say. But it is not light verse; by the time the last line is reached, the tone has changed. As "Storm

[12] "Bottom's Dream: The Likeness of Poems and Jokes," *Virginia Quarterly Review*, XLII (Autumn 1966), 566.
[13] *The Next Room of the Dream*, p. 62.

Windows" begins casually and ends profoundly, this poem begins lightly and ends chillingly. The mocking tone is aimed not only at Oliver, but at his high moral intentions in the third stanza (contrast Nemerov's attitude in the passage from "Trees" quoted above). Oliver, therefore, represents at the end any poet who tries to make meaning from the silent universe. It may be that there is nothing to say. Compare Ferlinghetti's "poet like an acrobat" who is "constantly risking absurdity/and death" in his attempt to catch Beauty.

*And he*
*a little charleychaplin man*
*who may or may not catch*
*her fair eternal form*
*spreadeagled in the empty air*
*of existence.*[14]

This is the modern existentialist attitude: because God is dead, the artist creates in a vacuum of meaning, "the empty air of existence." This note occurs in other Nemerov poems; for example, his four-line "The Poet at Forty."

*A light, a winged, & a holy thing,*
*Who if his God's not in him cannot sing.*
*Ah, Socrates, behold him here at last*
*Wingless and heavy, still enthusiast.*[15]

A recent poem, "Projection" (*The Atlantic*, May 1967), also pictures the existentialist attitude of making the best of the world despite the loss of God.

*They were so amply beautiful, the maps,*
*With their blue rivers winding to the sea,*
*So calmly beautiful, who could have blamed*
*Us for believing, bowed to our drawing boards,*
*In a large and ultimate equivalence,*
*One map that challenged and replaced the world?*

*Our punishment? To stand here, on these ladders,*
*Dizzy with fear, not daring to look down,*
*Glue on our fingers, in our hair and eyes,*
*Piecing together the crackling, sticky sheets*
*We hope may paper yet the walls of space*
*With pictures any child can understand.*

Note the underlying humor, the slight tongue-in-cheek tone that is in tension with the seriousness. The suggestion is that the effort to wallpaper space is futile, but the effort itself is called

[14] Lawrence Ferlinghetti, *A Coney Island of the Mind* (New York, 1958), p. 30.
[15] *The Next Room of the Dream*, p. 60.

a punishment. Is Nemerov claiming universal absurdity and Divine Injustice — that the punishment is really not deserved? ("Who could have blamed/Us," he asks.) Is the punishment for having once believed in the maps, or is it for now rejecting them? In any case, the actions of "Us"— modern mankind — are ludicrous, absurd. They are only a new (and apparently inferior) version of the old attempts to find meaning. It is like Oliver's trying to make his imagined tree into the axle of the universe: it is going about things the wrong way. What Oliver failed to observe was the relationship between the wooden pencil, the wooden paper, the wooden table, and the wooden house — the essential "woodenness" of these things. Section xi of "Runes" illuminates this.

*A holy man said to me, "Split the stick*
*And there is Jesus." When I split the stick*
*To the dark marrow and the splintery grain*
*I saw nothing that was not wood, nothing*
*That was not God, and I began to dream*
*How from the tree that stood between the rivers*
*Came Aaron's rod that crawled in front of Pharaoh,*
*And came the rod of Jesse flowering*
*In all the generations of the Kings,*
*And came the timbers of the second tree,*
*The sticks and yardarms of the holy three-*
*masted vessel whereon the Son of Man*
*Hung between thieves, and came the crown of thorns,*
*The lance and ladder, when was shed that blood*
*Streamed in the grain of Adam's tainted seed.*[16]

Nemerov's existentialism, therefore, seems to be mixed with a form of transcendentalism. God may be silent in that He does not speak to us personally, but He is not dead; God is the very process of life, the Life Force we might call Him. The clearest embodiment of this idea is perhaps "Mrs. Mandrill" (*New and Selected Poems,* p. 21). The lady, busy with activities, believed not in God, until she died and became part of Nature. The poem ends,

". . . . . . . . . . . . . . .
*It hasn't been easy," Mrs. Mandrill cried*
*to the crickets and other creatures who now silenced*
*their conversations at her heart, "for though*
*I knew the lead behind my looking-glass*
*better than some, I was the more deceived*
*by the way things looked. But for the love of God*

[16] *New and Selected Poems,* p. 9.

*all's one, I see that now, since I shall be*
*converted even against my will, and my will*
*converted with me, hearing this creature cry*
*before her wet heart spills and goes to seed."*

In being converted to seed (the source of life) she is converted to belief in God. Rather, all that remains of her is that which is God. Her personality is lost, and it is not life after death as we usually dream of it. In fact, it seems ultimately to be a joke, for such a "meaning" is virtually a lack of meaning: such a "God" may as well not exist as far as any individual human soul's awareness is concerned. Such a God may be impersonal, but at least he is not the burned-out star that many of the existentialists seem to make him. And such paradoxical faith in God is not a giving up to absurdity, despair, negation; it is a positive commitment to life.

One of Nemerov's most frequent metaphors for life, however, is that of the dream. Life is a dream, or *like* a dream; God is the Great Dreamer; our little lives are rounded by a sleep. But men are also dreamers; we dream by imagining things and by wishing for things, but also by trying to interpret the Dream with science, philosophy, history. But "As with a dream interpreted by one still sleeping,/ The interpretation is only the next room of the dream."[17]

Poetry also is "the next room of the dream." In "Bottom's Dream: The Likeness of Poems and Jokes," an amusing essay, Nemerov quotes as a definition of poetry Bottom's line: "It shall be called Bottom's Dream, because it hath no bottom." The definition suggests the resonances of meaning a good poem can sound in interpreting the complexities of life.

Nemerov's poems are not dreamlike themselves in the sense that those of Poe, Edwin Muir, or Walter de la Mare are. That is, except for a few — such as "Fables of the Moscow Subway," "The Stare of the Man from the Provinces," and "Brainstorm"[18] — they do not use fantastic and surrealistic imagery. If real life itself is considered a dream, if the stuff of life is dreamlike, then even a poem using realistic images can be considered dreamlike. As an example read Nemerov's "Death and the Maiden."

*Once I saw a grown man fall from a tree*
*and die. That's years ago, I was a girl.*
*My father's house is sold into a home*
*for the feeble-minded gentlefolk who can't*

[17] "To Clio, Muse of History," *The Next Room of the Dream*, p. 3.
[18] These three are in *New and Selected Poems.*

*any longer stand the world, but in those days*
*there was money to maintain the mile or so*
*of discipline that kept the hungry grass*
*parading to the lake, and once a year*
*bring men to prune the files of giant trees*
*whose order satisfied and stood for some*
*euclidean ancestor's dream about the truth:*
*elms, most of them, already dying of*
*their yellow blight, and blackened with witches' broom*
*in the highest branches — but they could die for years,*
*decades, so tall their silence, and tell you nothing.*
*Those men came in October every year,*
*and among the last leaves, the driven leaves,*
*would set their ladders for assault and swarm*
*like pirates into the shrouds, thrusting with hook*
*and long-handled bill against the withered members*
*of those great corporations, amputating*
*death away from the center. They were called*
*tree surgeons, on the ground they were surly-*
*polite and touched their caps, but in the air*
*they dared. I would watch one straddle a branch*
*on a day of rainy wind, his red shirt patched*
*on the elm's great fan of sky, his pruning-claw*
*breaking the finger-bones from the high hand*
*which held him, and I'd dream of voyages.*
*My father said: "It looks more dangerous*
*than really it is." But if your hand offend,*
*I thought, cut off the hand, and if your eye*
*offend, pluck out the eye. I looked at him*
*out of my window all one afternoon,*
*and I think he looked back once, a young man*
*proud and probably lecherous, while I —*
*was a maiden at a window. Only he died*
*that day. "Unlucky boy," my father said,*
*who then was dying himself without a word*
*to anyone, the crab's claw tightening*
*inside the bowel that year to the next*
*in a dead silence. I do not know if things*
*that happen can be said to come to pass,*
*or only happen, but when I remember*
*my father's house, I imagine sometimes*
*a dry, ruined spinster at my rainy window*
*trying to tally on dumb fingers a world's*
*incredible damage — nothing can stand it! — and*
*watching the red shirt patched against the sky,*
*so far and small in the webbed hand of the elm.*[19]

[19] *New and Selected Poems,* pp. 25-26.

In one sense the whole poem is a dream in that it is a product of the imagination. In a kind of daydream the poet plays the role of a spinster. The man falling from the tree may or may not have been actually witnessed once by Nemerov; within the poem, however, the incident itself is "real," while the poem is imagined, or "dreamt." That it was dreamt differently from "Kubla Khan" makes it no less a dream.

The first reference to a dream —"euclidean ancestor's dream about the truth"— is apropos. The ordering of the trees is analogous to the poet's ordering of words; a poem is also a "dream about the truth." And does not the line imply that Euclid's theories were likewise dreams — intangible, impermanent products of imagination?

The other reference to a dream —"I'd dream of voyages"— is interesting because it comes immediately after the image of the red-shirted man in the tree. The tree has already reminded the speaker of a ship; now she dreams of voyages. Again we see the unspeakable distance in the mind. In the same moment she is safely in her house, up in the tree with the man, and far away from both. How like a dream! How like a poet to transform by means of metaphors one thing into another, trees into ships, tree surgeons into pirates, himself into a spinster.

Her dreaming of voyages, of course, has another meaning: she wishes to escape the reality of the man's death. But she cannot, for as her mind voyages, her body goes nowhere. This is significant because the poem is very much about the limitations of the human body. The trees, for example, are likened to the body collectively in "the withered members of those great corporations," and the one tree is likened to a hand. The disease of the trees is paralleled by the cancer killing the father. The metaphor for the cancer —"crab's claw"— connects it with the tree surgeon's "pruning claw/breaking the finger bones from the high hand which held him." The hand-claw similarity suggests that blight is universal throughout Nature, affecting trees, crabs, human beings. The trees, the tree surgeon, the father, and the spinster "trying to tally on dumb fingers a world's incredible damage" are all caught in this slow grip of death. The allusion to the words of Christ suggests the wrath and judgment of God, especially since the tree surgeon's eye is "probably lecherous." Christ's original words were a warning against adultery.

> You have heard that it was said, "You shall not commit adultery." But I say to you that every one who looks at a woman lustfully has already committed adultery with her in his heart. If your right eye

> causes you to sin, pluck it out and throw it away; it is better that you lose one of your members than that your whole body be thrown into hell. And if your right hand causes you to sin, cut it off and throw it away; it is better that you lose one of your members than that your whole body go into hell.[20]

This reference to lust in the poem fits in with the rest of the references to the body; however, Nemerov's point here is not a traditional condemnation of the sinner to hell. The point is that everything dies, perhaps because of original sin, perhaps regardless of sin — the emphasis is on death, not sin. The allusion to Christ's words is, therefore, ironic. The disease cannot be cut out, the lecherous eye will not be plucked out for its lechery. The trees and the father will die anyway; the tree surgeon will die, not because he is "probably lecherous" (and only probably) but, if anything, because he is an "Unlucky boy." Chance is suggested, not Divine Purpose; and it is only *suggested.* It remains an open question, for the speaker says, "I do not know if things/that happen can be said to come to pass/ or only happen." Interpretations, after all, are only "the next room of the dream."

*What* comes to pass or only happens is clear, however; in the poem everything disintegrates. "Among the last leaves" the geometric order of the estate has been given over to feeblemindedness, disease, and death. The speaker has gone from maiden to "dry, ruined spinster," an indication of the fruitlessness of things. As geometry and surgery could not save the trees or her father, she is left to imagine herself trying to tally up the damage — the Euclidean theorems are reduced to counting on the fingers, the surgeon's skill is reduced to "dumb fingers."

Notice that she only *imagines* — dreams. And again the observing is separated from reality by a window. It is a picture of human noninvolvement in tragedy; yet it is *involved* noninvolvement. She is like the poet who can record and try to make some order from a situation he is in but cannot completely comprehend, even if that order he creates is only a "swaying clarity." Or if she cannot make order from it, she can at least feel it —"nothing can stand it!" she thinks. Still, like the poet, she is only an observer, a recorder. It is interesting that "if your eye / offend, pluck out the eye" is followed immediately by "I looked at him." The implications are, (1) her eye offends her by the tragedy it sees; (2) she too, not only the proud and lech-

[20] Matthew 5:27-30 (RSV).

erous tree surgeon, will die (have her eye plucked out); (3) her eye offends because it can only see and not understand.

That which she sees at the end of the poem is the image that ties the poem together; it is, therefore, important to understand it. Nemerov may have meant to evoke Stephen Crane's "The red sun was pasted on the sky like a wafer" and the death of Jim Conklin that precedes it. In any case, the synecdoche "red shirt" disembodies the man, making him an effigy or merely a remembered image. "Patched" implies an attempt to repair the sky, as the daring tree surgeon by pruning trees was in effect trying to correct nature. The "webbed hand" may suggest an insect in a spider web, but it is more likely to mean an amphibious hand (like a claw of a crab). At this point in the poem we are in a rainy world, as we were in "Storm Windows." Whether the world is wet or dry (notice the spinster is called "dry"), this hand of blight and death is acclimated to it.

Another poem, "The View from an Attic Window," helps us interpret two of the symbols involved — the tree and the rain.

*But what I thought today, that made me cry,*
*Is this, that we live in two kinds of thing:*
*The powerful trees, thrusting into the sky*
*Their black patience, are one, and that branching*
*Relation teaches how we endure and grow;*
*The other is the snow,*

*Falling in a white chaos from the sky,*
*As many as the sands of all the seas,*
*As all the men who died or who will die,*
*As stars in heaven, as leaves of all the trees;*
*As Abraham was promised of his seed;*
*Generations bleed,*

*Till I, high in the tower of my time*
*Among familiar ruins, began to cry*
*For accident, sickness, justice, war and crime,*
*Because all died, because I had to die.*
*The snow fell, the trees stood, the promise kept,*
*And a child I slept.*[21]

The rain in "Death and the Maiden" has associations similar to the snow and the seeds in the lines just quoted. Nemerov further clarifies the imagery in *Poets on Poetry* (edited by Nemerov, the book contains contemporary poets' answers to a questionnaire); he says that water images represent for him "an emblem for human life and the life of the imagination" as opposed to stone images, which he associates with monuments and

[21] *New and Selected Poems*, pp. 23-24.

statues "as representing the rigid domination of past over present."[22] Rain, running streams, and snow are also all representative of the natural flux of life — they suggest the seasons, erosion, growth. The life of the imagination must partake of this natural flux; it cannot be rigid, conservative, tradition-bound. The life of the imagination must adapt to change, even to tragedy and death.

Trees, on the other hand, are immovable like stone; yet they are alive and growing. They seem to represent human endurance, which resists for a time the natural flux but finally succumbs to it. In "Learning By Doing" (*The Kenyon Review,* XXVI [Spring 1964], 387-388) Nemerov describes the cutting down of a supposedly diseased tree, which when sectioned turns out to be healthy. The poem concludes:

> *There's some mean-spirited moral point in that*
> *As well: you learn to bury your mistakes,*
> *Though for a while at dusk the darkening air*
> *Will be with many shadows interleaved,*
> *And pierced with a bewilderment of birds.*

It is a "mean-spirited moral" because the moral is, in effect, that we can do nothing about the seeming injustices of life except endure them; they are a natural and inevitable part of life. In the many interleaved shadows of life man is bewildered as the birds. He can try to tally the injustice on his fingers, he can put up storm windows, he can cry, he can write poems, but he cannot stop the flux of life. He will be driven indoors, he will die trying.

M. L. Rosenthal, in *The Modern Poets: A Critical Introduction* (New York, 1960), p. 259, comments concerning "Storm Windows" that "the rain falling on the windows and grass crushed beneath them are seen in a momentary frame that gives the whole thing the illusion of having a point — though what is really being seen in the frame is essential chaos." This is true, but what must be emphasized is that the chaos for Nemerov is *essential.* Man may be caught in the web of death, and his attempts to prune out the death may be as futile as trying to patch the sky with red cloth; the "world's incredible damage" may seem like chaos as we perceive it through our windows; yet this chaos is not necessarily evil, is not even necessarily chaos. For Nemerov this chaos is the ongoing process of life; it is the working of God himself. Man is "far and small" compared to it, but like the daring tree surgeon in the elm he is

[22] "Attentiveness and Obedience," *Poets on Poetry,* ed. Howard Nemerov (New York, 1966), pp. 247f.

caught up in it. He is himself caught and yet a vital part of the process. He might be considered — in a sense similar to that meant by Emerson, Thoreau, and Whitman —"divine." That is, man as a part of Nature is a part of God. Nemerov is not so optimistic as the transcendentalists — there is no indication that the process is constantly improving itself — yet neither is he so pessimistic as the naturalists and the existentialists.

The poet in this scheme of things could perhaps be thought of as a priest serving the God who is Being Itself (as the transcendentalists tended to think of the poet).

> Poetry and institutionalized religion are in a sense the flowing and the static forms of the same substance, liquid and solid states of the same elemental energy....
>
> So the work of art is religious in nature, not because it beautifies an ugly world or pretends that a naughty world is a nice one — for these things especially art does not do — but because it shows of its own nature that things drawn within the sacred circle of its forms are transfigured, illuminated by an inward radiance which amounts to goodness because it amounts to being itself.[23]

The poet is, in a sense, a spokesman for God; his vocation is to capture, not in stone but in a living form, life itself.

Therefore, it is appropriate that Nemerov's poetry is so like prose, so like jokes, so like dreams. Distinctions between prose and poetry, comic and tragic, dream and reality, pass away. Life appears to us as prosaic, yet Nemerov reveals it full of poetry — of correspondences, metaphors, essential order; life appears to us as tragic, yet for Nemerov the tragedy is ultimately not so terribly serious — death is the inevitable and necessary order of things; life appears to us as fixed and tangible reality, yet Nemerov sees it as kaleidoscopic and evanescent as dreams — the only reality is flux, Being, Aliveness.

All this may perhaps seem to be making too much of the philosophy behind Nemerov's poems. It is, of course, not a systematic philosophy but rather a viewpoint, an attitude toward life; besides, Nemerov again and again shows the futility of drawing any final philosophic conclusions — that almost becomes his philosophy, in fact. Nevertheless, Nemerov's viewpoint unifies his poems; almost all of them show in different lights his way of looking at the world as though it were God. Furthermore, in each individual poem this "philosophy" is virtually another of his poetic devices: like metaphors, iambic pentameter, alliteration, it helps hold the poem together and give it form.

[23] "The Swaying Form," *Poetry and Fiction,* pp. 13, 16.

It is not a moral tag applied at the end of each poem, but an integral part of the art of each poem. To misunderstand his outlook is to misread the poems. Many of them at first glance may appear to be saying the opposite — that is, have the opposite attitude toward the situation — from what they actually say. They seem to show universal loneliness, meaninglessness, alienation. But Nemorov treats these contemporary attitudes with a tone of irony and paradox and transcends them. The spinster's attitude in "Death and the Maiden"— her attitude of helpless hand-wringing anguish at the world's injustices — is not wholeheartedly Nemerov's. (That she is not really wringing her hands, but counting on them, is a clue to her insincere sincerity.) If anything, he is on the side of the tree surgeon daring death (and probably on the side of the absent-minded professor who would correct the leaves — does not the poet "correct" nature, too?). He may regret, he may dream, he may wish it were otherwise, but he does not cry about it; he does not sit in sackcloth and ashes like so many modern Jobs who have not heard the Voice from the Whirlwind. Nemerov has apparently heard the Voice and seeks to comfort (or perhaps discomfort) our modern Jobs. As "The View from an Attic Window" (quoted above) suggests, it is even better to sleep than to cry. Or as the narrator of one of his short stories, "A Commodity of Dreams," says concerning the collection of dreams, over three thousand of them filed and cross-referenced in a museum, of Capt. Frank Lastwyn,

> They would at the British Museum look at it all twice, and imperturbably file it away under Dreams . . . which was probably where everything, after all, belonged. We were all, I thought sleepily, going down in history, whether as Tamerlane or Genghis Khan, Beethoven, St. Francis or Nesselrode who invented the pudding. Or as Capt. Frank Lastwyn, R. A. (ret.), or as anonymous nobodies, such as myself. And ho-hum to it all.[24]

But that, too, needs to be taken with a grain of irony. Nemerov's attitude is usually not so flippant.

Wallace Stevens' "Men Made Out of Words" comes very close to summing up Nemerov's poetry.

> *Life consists*
> *Of propositions about life. The human*
>
> *Revery is a solitude in which*
> *We compass these propositions, torn by dreams,*

[24] *A Commodity of Dreams* (New York, 1959), p. 68.

*By the terrible incantations of defeats*
*And by the fear that defeats and dreams are one.*

*The whole race is a poet that writes down*
*The eccentricities of its fate.*[25]

But for Nemerov defeats and dreams *are* one; he has thus overcome the fear. His propositions will seem eccentric to those of us whose center is different from his, yet within his poems the eccentricity — the apparent conflict between good and evil, dream and defeat — is at the center. There good and evil, dream and defeat, are paradoxically *One.*

[25] *The Collected Poems of Wallace Stevens* (New York, 1955), pp. 355-356.

# Fantasy and the Fiction of Bernard Malamud

ROBERT W. WARBURTON

The best Jewish writers of our time, Alfred Kazin has remarked, are those like Isaac Bashevis Singer, who uses "all of the old Jewish capital of folklore, popular speech and legendry, yet from within this tradition itself is able to duplicate a good deal of the conscious absurdity, the sauciness, the abandon of modern art."[1] In this sense, Bernard Malamud is one of the best Jewish writers of our time. In his somewhat gloomy and grotesque stories dealing with urban Jewish life and experience, Malamud translates some of the moral and spiritual truths of an ancient tradition into contemporary idiom. Like Singer, Babel, Kafka, Bellow, Salinger, Roth and others, Malamud's fictional materials and vision of human existence are deeply steeped in the Jewish ethos. Jews and Jewishness permeate the atmosphere of his fictional worlds. "A wonderful thing, Fanny," says Manischevitz, the Job-like suffering tailor of "Angel Levine." "Believe me, there are Jews everywhere." Most of Malamud's Jews are the vulnerable and alienated *nudniks* and *schlemiels* of the inner-city ghettos, the ludicrous and luckless failures who collect

[1] "The Saint as Schlemiel," *Contemporaries* (Boston, 1962), p. 283.

---

Robert W. Warburton is Professor of English at DuPage College in Illinois. He has previously taught at the University of Southern California (1955-57) and at Wheaton College (1958-68). He holds the B.A. and M.A. degrees from the University of Michigan and the B.D. from Fuller Theological Seminary. Presently he is a candidate for the Ph.D. at the University of Chicago, where his dissertation is on the theories and forms of fantasy in modern fiction. He has been a Danforth Teaching Fellow from 1962 through 1965, and was Junior Teacher of the Year at Wheaton for 1966-67.

injustices and run the tortuous labyrinthine mazes of contemporary existence. They are the gaunt, skeletal, hollow-eyed storekeepers, the poverty-ridden light bulb peddlers, the freakish egg-candlers and marriage-brokers — the unnoticed nobodies and fixers and outsiders of modern urban society. They are what Saul Bellow has called the "Jewish *cafoni,*" the "burlap heroes" of modern fiction. Their scrawny existence is one of "rusty caftans and rusty black derbies, decrepit tenements, gloomy grocery stores smelling of poverty, of age, and of inviolate failure."[2]

Unlike many of his contemporaries, however, Malamud's Jewishness is not primarily ethnic and socially oriented. In his fiction he is not particularly preoccupied with what Leslie Fiedler has described as "the need of the Jew in America to make clear his relationship to that country in terms of belonging or protest."[3] And as Ihab Hassan has pointed out, Malamud does not easily fit into the scheme that Fiedler has devised for Jewish authors of the past two decades: highbrow (Bellow), upper middlebrow (Salinger), middle middlebrow (Shaw), and low middlebrow (Wouk).[4] Among contemporary Jewish writers, Malamud is what Marcus Klein describes as a "special case," a Jewish writer who is himself alienated from "the ordinary contingencies of American middle class culture," and consequently exhibits in his fiction a knowledge that is "parochial, isolated, and exotic."[5] Partly for this reason he has been criticized (Philip Roth in *Commentary,* for instance) for his neglect of public issues and preoccupation with the "private life." Kazin, who admires Malamud's "magic" and ability to come "so close to the bone of human feeling," nevertheless mourns his failure to believe in society enough "to deal with it not merely as it is but as something that *is.*"[6] In his first three novels his perspective is strictly from within "the dark prison of the self."[7] As for his latest novel, *The Fixer,* one reviewer complains that the novel owes too much to "the cult of Jewish sensibility in U. S. fiction,

[2] Marcus Klein, *After Alienation: American Novels in Mid-Century* (Cleveland, 1962), p. 247.

[3] Leslie Fiedler, "Saul Bellow," *Prairie Schooner,* XXXI (Summer, 1957), 104.

[4] *Radical Innocence: The Contemporary American Novel* (New York, 1961), p. 161.

[5] Klein, pp. 248-249.

[6] Alfred Kazin, "The Magic and the Dread," *Contemporaries,* pp. 206-207.

[7] Ben Siegel, "Victims in Motion: Bernard Malamud's Sad and Bitter Clowns," originally published in *Northwest Review,* V (Spring, 1962), and reprinted in *Recent American Fiction: Some Critical Views,* ed. Joseph J. Waldmeir (Boston, 1963), p. 203.

and most significantly, nothing whatever to the current U. S. scene."[8]

At the same time, it is difficult to understand how Malamud's fiction can be validly criticized for its Jewish isolation and parochialism. If not making "the U. S. scene" has become a cardinal literary sin, vey is mir! If there is anything Malamud shares more readily with the tradition of Yiddish writers like Singer and Aleichem, or if there is anything more plainly evident throughout almost all of his stories, it is the point that all men are Jews. In *The Assistant* the rabbi at Morris Bober's funeral declares, "There are many ways to be a Jew." And Morris was "a true Jew because he lived in the Jewish experience.... He suffered, he endu-red, but with hope." And Frank Alpine, the Italian-American who sins against Morris and enacts his own painful expiation by assimilating Morris's suffering and endurance, thus fittingly becomes a Jew at the end of the novel. Jewishness for Malamud is the spiritual dignity achieved in a painful and mundane existence by all men who share their common suffering and endurance. In this way, Malamud himself felt, the Jew was "the very stuff of drama," and the purpose of the modern writer was not to promote the Jewish ethos but "to keep civilization from falling apart."[9]

It is Malamud's peculiarly enigmatic and poignant perspective of the ambiguities of human suffering and endurance that distinguishes his fiction, not its isolation and parochialism. In all of the four novels and two collections of short stories he has published since 1952, he has managed to create a precarious and haunting fusion of what seems most painful and despairing and at the same time most permanent and hopeful in the human condition. His fictional milieu is invariably a bittersweet gray-world of decay and endurance, a kind of quasi-spiritual limbo existing somewhere between the drab banalities of daily frustrations and the faint hopes of redemptive blessings. By blending the mundane and the mystical into a coherent shape of fictional reality, Malamud is able to achieve the kind of paradoxical moral vision that Klein has aptly called "the sadness of goodness." In his themes of drudging failure, ineffective and unreturned love, chronic suffering, guilt and expiation, and ironic hope, Malamud transcends the parochial conditions of his fictional materials and probes into some of the most profound aspects of the American Dream and the human heart.

[8] *Time*, LXXXVIII, ii (Sept. 9, 1966), 106.

[9] *Current Biography Yearbook, 1958*, ed. Marjorie Dent Candee (New York, 1958), p. 272.

Malamud's fiction deals, then, not with Jewishness as such, but with the extremities of human suffering and endurance as dramatically embodied in the Jewish ethos. His concern is not strictly with private or public issues in human existence, but with the precarious, tenuous and unprotected state of human existence itself. In his worlds we are continually impressed by the fact that ordinary, everyday existence is itself the most incredible of all human experience. Our own "realities" cannot be assumed. The so-called actuality and solidity of this life is airy and suspect and must be held in problematical suspension. For Malamud, this actual world is near allied to madness, out of joint, almost incomprehensible. To this extent, he reflects the puzzlement that Philip Roth once expressed over the frustrating problem faced by the modern novelist of understanding and informing a contemporary reality that seemed almost daily to toss up its own images of actual human existence that are so much more infuriating and stupefying than any that the meagre imagination of the novelist had the power to invent. "Who, for example," Roth asks, "could have invented Charles Van Doren?"[10]

The answer to Roth's question must be that Van Doren has already been "invented," at least in the minimal terms of journalistic reconstruction. However incredible — or credible — human existence may be, it must be mediated in some terms before it achieves the condition of what we call "reality." As novelists, neither Roth nor Malamud can be concerned only with the puzzlement of an incredible existence. Their fiction necessarily also embodies and implies an informed response to their puzzlement. Malamud, too, must at one time have wondered what kind of national insanity could have invented Mendel Beiliss, the Kiev Jew wrongly accused in 1911 of murdering a Christian child and milking his blood for the purposes of making Passover matzos. His response was eventually the "Yakov Bok" of *The Fixer*. Likewise, the "Perry Smith" and "Richard Hickock" of *In Cold Blood* are Capote's responses (contrary perhaps to his theories of fiction) to the puzzlement of the historical Smith and Hickock. The same is true of Styron's "Nat Turner" of *The Confessions*, and of all fictional inventions not just recently but since the beginning.

Undoubtedly, many such contemporary fictional responses despair over both the substance and form of the response itself, but Malamud's basic response to the infuriating and stupefying

[10] "Writing American Fiction," *Commentary*, XXXI (March 1961), 223-233 and XXXII (Sept. 1961), 250-252.

conditions of human existence is neither philosophical nor aesthetic despair. In his fiction he abandons neither life nor art. His response to the ambiguities of the human condition is essentially that of fascination and wonder. His work possesses a peculiar blending of irony and compassion, a capacity to marvel in the spirit of both despair and hope at the desperate and precarious conditions of human suffering and endurance. Malamud's capacity to marvel and wonder at the enigmas of human existence is what, in a general sense, I mean by fantasy in this discussion. It is his artistically conscious shaping of the marvelous and his directing of the motion of his fiction toward a sense and significance of life that includes the marvelous that give substance and form to his fantasy. I contend that it is Malamud's sense of the fantastic that makes up his essential intellectual and artistic response to the puzzlements of contemporary reality. And in his fiction, the forms and functions of fantasy are some of the significant means by which he gives that response expression and direction.

In suggesting the uses and purposes of fantasy in relation to some of the larger artistic and moral concerns of Malamud's fiction, I realize that I am at the same time raising some difficult problems of definition. So far I have not intended anything more than a general notion of fantasy in Malamud's work, nor have I meant to imply that Malamud makes consistent and steady use of fantasy in each and every one of his stories, at least in any traditional or explicit sense. I am also aware that for some readers of Malamud almost any discussion of fantasy in his fiction would seem about as incongruous and peripheral as a discussion of European politics in the novels of Jane Austen. For them, perhaps, short stories like "Black Is My Favorite Color" and "A Choice of Profession" or novels like *A New Life* and *The Fixer* read more like examples of realistic than fantastic fiction. But even these impressions imply some general concept of fantasy or of realism, and such concepts are hard to come by. The essential problem in defining concepts like fantasy is, I believe, in the way we look at most literary definitions and what we usually expect from them.

In this sense it may be appropriate to recall Northrop Frye's advice that "no literary critic of any experience will make much effort to define his terms."[11] Such efforts seem particularly useless and disconcerting when we apply lexical and psychological definitions to fantasy. One of the difficulties with lexical defini-

[11] *Fearful Symmetry* (Princeton, 1947), p. 316.

tions of literary terms is that they tend to proliferate into other terms even more abstract and obscure than the original. Thus, when I spoke earlier of Malamud's fantasy in terms of "wonder" and "marvel," I was merely shifting slightly the terms of the discussion, not developing any concept of fantasy itself. In the same way, *fantasy* can be defined as anything from the "fanciful" and "extravagant" to the "unusual" and "unreal." In fiction it usually means anything "different - from - realism." Such approaches, however, will have as much trouble with "realism" or "fanciful" — or whatever term — as with *fantasy.* The very nature of lexical definitions is that they move in circles, the size of the circle depending upon the size of the dictionary or handbook available. We come into the circle at some point where we can associate the unknown with something better known. C. S. Lewis, for example, defined fantasies as narratives dealing in "impossibles" of various kinds, the only thing in common among them being "the fantastic."[12] Which is one way to complete the circle (and incidentally add another term like "impossibles"). The truth is, that while definitions of fantasy can tell us something about the meaning of fantasy as a word, they can in fact tell us very little about the nature of fantasy as a literary experience to which the word refers.

Psychological definitions of fantasy have been about as confusing as lexical ones. Originating in scholastic psychology, *fantasy, phantasy,* and their derivative, *fancy,* were terms used to designate a mental apprehension of things not actually present — functions of *imagination.* Such terms eventually came to connote not only the mental apprehension itself but also a deluded belief in the reality of the mentally apprehended object. In time, this psychological connotation of mental imbalance or distortion carried over into poetics, where *fantasy* came to be associated with the nonrational, the capricious, an extravagance and incoherence of ideas, and the operation of a delusive imagination in the making of literary works. Even as late as the eighteenth century, Dr. Johnson in his *Dictionary* of 1755 maintained this scholastic distinction between *reason* and *imagination / fantasy.* And although Coleridge shortly thereafter liberated *imagination* from its pejorative context he did so at the expense of *fantasy* (*fancy*), which maintained its more-or-less secondary place throughout the nineteenth century as a mere "mode of memory."

Many modern psychologists and literary critics have continued the scholastic confusion of literary and psychological

[12] C. S. Lewis, *An Experiment in Criticism* (Cambridge, 1961), p. 50.

fantasy. In Sigmund Freud, for example, there is little or no distinction between the psychic and inventive processes of fantasy, or phantasie: both processes are controlled by "wish-fulfillment." The "insight gained from phantasies leads us to expect" something similar in the artistic process: "some actual experience which made a strong impression on the writer had stirred up a memory of an earlier experience, generally belonging to childhood, which then arouses a wish that finds a fulfillment in the work in question, and in which elements of the recent event and the old memory should be discernible."[13] A critic like Simon Lesser takes the same tack in *Fiction and the Unconscious* (1957). Fantasy is a substitute gratification that rearranges "the facts of reality to mold phantom worlds more harmonious, more gratifying and less fearful than the world of experience" (p. 56). C. S. Lewis has perhaps been the most lucid in attempting to distinguish between psychological and literary fantasy. Psychological fantasy, he suggests, is either self-imposed delusion, which is unconscious and makes up some form of mental sickness, or it is "Morbid Castle-building," which is usually conscious and egoistic. In such conscious and egoistic psychological fantasy, "the day-dreamer himself is always the hero and everything is seen through his eyes." In contrast to this, literary fantasy is disinterested and the "day-dreamer is not the hero of the day-dream or perhaps not present in it at all." Such literary daydreams (like those of the Brontë children) "may feign a whole world and people in it and remain outside it. But when that stage is reached," Lewis asserts, "something more than reverie has come into action: construction, invention, in a word, *fiction*, is proceeding."[14] Lewis's distinctions between the psyche and the imagination are more helpful than his translation of fantasy into "fiction." He tells us something of what fantasy is not but very little about what fantasy is. But then this is perhaps the most that any definition can do.

In Lewis's struggle with the meaning of literary fantasy, however, his emphasis upon the procedure of fiction points us in the right direction. If we wish to understand Malamud's uses of fantasy, we must begin not with any general definition or concept of *fantasy*, but with Malamud's "invention" and "construction" of the fantastic itself in his fiction. In fact, no single concept, quality, process, or structure of fantasy accounts entirely for all of Malamud's uses of the fantastic. Throughout his fiction he employs fantastic action, episode, character, language

[13] *On Creativity and the Unconscious* (New York, 1958), p. 52.
[14] Lewis, pp. 52-53.

and idea in a variety of patterns and functions. However, by examining the different uses Malamud makes of these elements of fantasy, as well as the contrasting structural relationships between the fantastic and the natural in his stories and novels, it is possible, I believe, to distinguish at least three separate kinds of fantasy in Malamud's work: objective or traditional fantasy, subjective fantasy, and reciprocal fantasy. It will be worthwhile, then, to discuss these kinds of fantasy not only within the context of Malamud's fiction but also within the larger historical and generic context to which each of these is related.

Objective fantasy is the fantasy of Other-Worlds. This is the traditional kind of fantasy, with which we are most familiar. In such fiction, a writer constructs and uses separate, objective fantastic worlds, worlds radically unlike our own, removed by time or space or some other feature from the ordinary realities of this actual world. This is the kind of fantasy typical of most fairy stories, utopian, anti-utopian, and science fictions, legends, folktales, myths, stories of the supernatural, medieval fables, bestiaries, and other kinds of apologues. Such fictional narratives include within themselves representations of both this world and the Other-World, the ordinary and the extraordinary, the natural and the preternatural. In such stories we usually journey from one world to the other, through interstellar space, down a rabbit's hole, back or ahead in time, through a door, or through a dream. We may, of course, be already "there" and spend our time entirely in the Other-World, in what J. R. R. Tolkien calls the "Primary World," but all the time the ordinary, or "Secondary," world is implied and is present somewhere. One of the significant purposes and pleasures of objective fantasy is simply the sheer wonder cultivated in the Other-World, in the suspension, extension, or modification of the physical and moral laws that we accept as natural or conventional in our own world. And because of the parallel and contrasting structure of the natural and preternatural worlds, objective fantasy is particularly useful for satiric, comic, and moral purposes. Examples of such fantasy extend from Homer to Huxley, and are as diverse in nature and purpose as Carroll's *Alice in Wonderland,* MacDonald's *Lilith,* and H. G. Wells's *Time Machine.*

There is very little objective and traditional fantasy in Malamud's fiction. In most of his work, as we shall see, the natural and the fantastic tend to blend and reciprocate rather than separate and contrast. The fantastic acting within or upon the natural order of things is rarely explicit or sustained; its action is more oblique and temporary. However, in two of his short stories, "Take Pity" and "The Jewbird," Malamud has produced two interesting examples of the uses of objective fantasy.

"Take Pity" is a fantasy set within the framework of some kind of post-mortal existence, a sort of dreary and drab limbo consisting of a cold, dimly lit room (top-floor, back) with only a cot, a folding chair, an "institutional soap," and a single narrow window with a drawn shade. Occupying the room is Rosen, an ex-coffee salesman, who is visited by an indifferent, limping "census-taker," Davidov, to whom Rosen wearily reports, for the record, the earthly experience that has brought him to this place. Davidov knows the ending but not the beginning of Rosen's story, and so Rosen tells how it all began with Eva Kalish, the widow of a poverty-ridden grocer friend of Rosen, who died leaving Eva with only a failing business and two small children. Rosen offered Eva his advice, money, protection, but she proudly refused them and clung to the failing business. Out of what he thought was pity and compassion, he even offered her his name in nominal marriage, so that his property and security could benefit her and the children. Eva spurned this even more emphatically and cut off all relations with Rosen. A sickly man, Rosen gets even sicker over his inability to express pity. "Here is a very strange thing," he came to realize, "a person that you can never give her anything. — *But I will give.*" So after making out his will leaving everything to Eva and the children, Rosen puts his head in the gas oven and dies. "Let her now say no," he tells Davidov, who is by now somewhat bored and, knowing the end of the story, has stopped taking notes. Before Rosen can stop him, the census-taker reaches over and raises the window shade. There, dimly through the window, out across the twilight of space, Eva stands with haunted, beseeching eyes, and arms outstretched toward Rosen. "Whore, bastard, bitch .... Go home to your children," Rosen shouts, and rams down the shade.

Although "Take Pity" has no fairies, witches, or fairyland, it has basically the same structure as a fairy-tale — and some of the same moral toughness of classical fairy-tales. We go from this world to the Other-World and back again to this world. This parallel and contrasting two-world structure allows Malamud to develop a double irony that reinforces his moral point of view. Ironically, in his earthly life, Rosen could not experience the fulfillment of his own need for pity and compassion toward Eva because she selfishly refused to take them. And with the same irony, now intensified and reversed by the perspective of the Other-World, Rosen can succeed in expressing his pity only in his death, but after death, in his dreary limbo, it is too late. Pity can be an experience only of life. Outside, far off and untouchable, Eva now desires to take his pity, but Rosen, eternally frustrated by his realization that her desire is too late and also by his own unfulfilled experience, bitterly refuses it to her. For both, their agony and hell is the unfulfillment of shared compassion and love. The fantasy thus provides both the perspective and the distance necessary to reinforce the irony that in turn sustains and impresses upon us the imperative of compassion and pity. The result is that this ironic relationship between Rosen's two worlds serves to embody and give dramatic emphasis to the moral paradox that informs the story: we can experience only the compassion and love that we are able to share with each other.

In "The Jewbird" an old frazzle-feathered and rumply-dignified black bird named Schwartz, who talks in a Jewish dialect and smells of herring, flies into the top-floor, East-side apartment of Harry Cohen, frozen foods salesman, skeptic, and progressive Jew. Before Cohen can swat the bird and chase him out, Schwartz yells (or caws), "Gevalt, a pogrom!" and Edie, Cohen's wife, and Maurie, their "not overly bright" ten-year-old son (whom Cohen, more than anything, wants to get into the Ivy League) are more sympathetic. Schwartz tells the family he is flying from "Anti-Semeets" — eagles, vultures, hawks, and "once in a while some crows." But aside from the absolute unbelievability of a talking Jewbird, Cohen does not like Schwartz from the outset. The two have an innate suspicion and hatred of each other, and this antagonism and the outcome of it make up the movement and meaning of the fable.

Schwartz is orthodox, pious, fussy with age, and irritatingly proud. Cohen is ambitious, unbelieving, earthly, and somewhat cruel. Schwartz is of an ancient moral order. He wants compassion for his plight and respect for what he represents. Cohen is of the new order. He wants success and the future, and no reminder of any connections he may have with the past. Because Schwartz proves to be of help in Maurie's schoolwork, Cohen begrudgingly and temporarily tolerates him, at least as far as a birdhouse on the outside balcony. Schwartz freezes, endures Cohen's scorn, and holds on with herring and pity from Edie and friendship from Maurie. However, when Schwartz declares to Cohen that Maurie will never be a scholar, "although maybe a good mechanic," the end is in sight. Cohen mixes watery cat food with the finicky Jewbird's herring slices, and finally buys a full-grown cat, supposedly for Maurie, that drives

Schwartz to terror-ridden days and sleepless nights. For Cohen, Schwartz is always there, "even in his dreams." And "what's more, whoever heard of a Jewbird?" The end comes the day after Cohen's mother dies and Maurie scores a zero on an arithmetic test. Alone with Schwartz, Cohen grabs the bird by the legs, whirls him in a circle, and throws him off the balcony to the street below, but not before Schwartz catches Cohen's nose in his beak and leaves a permanent scar. The next spring when Maurie, "moved by a memory," looks for Schwartz, he finds a dead black bird in an empty lot with its wings broken and its eyes plucked clean. "Who did it?" he asks. "Anti-Semeets," Edie replies.

There are several advantages and effects that Malamud gains in embodying his typical theme of suffering and endurance in this kind of fantasy. In "The Jewbird" the natural and the fantastic exist independently alongside of each other, but not so far apart as they are in "Take Pity." Schwartz comes into Cohen's world, and because neither is able to assimilate the other, the clash between them is dramatically sharp, immediate, and intuitively felt by us. Moreover, their antagonism is primarily one of moral values. Schwartz's look of dissipation, his petty dignity, and his rumpled piety at once embody and express his alien and tattered spiritual values in the unsympathetic and materially-bounded world of Cohen — our world, the ordinary world. At the same time, the fantasy makes it difficult for us to sympathize too closely with the plight and values of Schwartz, or to be altogether unsympathetic with the cruelty of Cohen. The very nonhumanness of the bird, however humanized, compels us to maintain a certain distance from both antagonists. Thus, while we can understand and sympathize to some extent with the sufferings of Schwartz, at the same time we can also recognize in him a picture of a fated, self-defeating, tattered, and admirable religious orthodoxy. He is, as he tells Cohen, "an old radical." And likewise, while we can understand the cruelty and coarseness of modern humanity in the character of Cohen, we can also recognize the dream that lies beneath the callous and sensual exterior. To Cohen, Schwartz is a visible and constant reminder of an old, forgotten ethnic and religious faith. In the tactics of Schwartz's traditional wisdom against the modern shrewdness of Cohen, in Schwartz's tolerance and patience with the dull Maurie, or in his small expectations from existence — his request for the *Jewish Morning Journal* and "now and then a schnapps, thanks God" — he radically and irritatingly cuts across the fixities of Cohen's existence. He is Cohen's prick of spiritual conscience. He calls up dreams, not of himself but of something beyond himself. He is the unwelcome reminder of a formalized and yet compassionate grace that resides still in the antiquated shell of traditional faith.

"The Jewbird" provides not only the kind of moral distance we need in order to grasp Malamud's values but also the kind of comic distance we need in order to share in those values. The idea of a domestic squabble between animals, or birds, as any medieval allegorist or fabulist would know, is as effective as it is ridiculous in throwing light upon our own squabbles. But a domestic squabble between a bird and man is even more ridiculous. And the incongruity of an orthodox Jewbird piously praying in Jewish, sulking, and maintaining his ruffled place like a petty patriarch in the household of his wayward children, is not only weird and grotesque but also sardonically humorous and outrageously funny. In Cohen's progressive household it is even funnier. Malamud is able to use the very comic incongruity of the situation to draw our compassion and pity toward the antagonism between Schwartz and Cohen. While it always borders on the violent, it also borders on the ludicrous and impossible. The very fact that it could not be possible in these terms seems to make it all the more realizable. Each comic thrust brings us into congenial response to the moral point of view that controls it. Thus, Edie suspiciously wonders if Schwartz could be an old Jew changed into a bird by somebody. "Who knows," answers Schwartz. "Does God tell us everything?" And when Cohen says that he has heard of a Jewfish but never a Jewbird, Schwartz replies, "We're once removed." Comedy and theology are neatly combined when Schwartz complains to Edie about the hazards of Maurie's cat. Edie, who believes in patience and cleanliness as much as she does in godliness, assures Schwartz that "when the cat gets to know you better he won't try to catch you anymore." But Schwartz knows better: "When he stops trying we will both be in Paradise." The perspective of the lamb might provide a different view of the problem of suffering than that of the lion, or than our own. For Malamud, suffering and fatality are daily staples of existence. Compassion wears a wry smile. And love is an almost impossible grace in a grim, inhuman world.

The second kind of fantasy Malamud employs in his fiction is what may be described as subjective fantasy. This kind of fantasy lies at the other end of the spectrum from traditional and objective fantasy. It is closer to "The Jewbird" than to "Take Pity." It is not explicit but implicit, subtly diffused throughout the atmosphere of many of Malamud's worlds, and often indistinguishably blended within the elements of ordinary reality. The faery and the human are usually not set so radically apart from or opposed to each other as they are in objective fantasy. In subjective fantasy the predominant movement is from the Other-World to this world. Rather than our journeying to Wonderland, or to Perelandra, or to the Primary World, the preternatural comes to our own kind of ordinary world and acts subjectively within it. In this sense, the fantastic is a coloring, a tone, a gesture, a mood, a word. It infiltrates the natural world but does not become a permanent part of it. It comes close to what E. M. Forster had in mind when he discussed fantasy as the "spirit of Muddle" in Sterne's *Tristram Shandy* or Beerbohm's *Zuleika Dobson,* cutting like a bar of light across the ordinary lines of fictional probabilities.[15] Other forms of subjective fantasy can be found in the ghostly stories of Gogol or James, the "gothic" and horror tales of E. T. A. Hoffman or Ann Radcliffe, the grotesques of Poe, and stories of the supernatural as widely differing in tone and effect as those of Sheridan Le Fanu and Charles Williams.

In these examples of subjective fantasy, as well as in Malamud's fiction, there are undoubtedly several similarities to what we call fictional Romance. This is what Charles Hoyt, for example, has in mind when he speaks of Malamud's attitudes as "overwhelmingly Romantic" or of the "Romantic drive that supplies the impetus of Malamud's greatness" and "can be found, in one form or another, in each of his works to date." In Malamud, Hoyt asserts, this Romantic attitude is essentially the "Rejection of Objectivity," the refusal to accept "despair" and "order," and the desire to reorder "a new solution." It is this attitude that distinguishes Malamud and other contemporary writers from what Hoyt calls the "athletic fatalism of Hemingway, the closed 'realism' of the Naturalistic school, the chipped classicism of Eliot and T. E. Hulme."[16] By dealing with Malamud's fiction in these conceptual terms of Romance, Hoyt gains, I am sure, certain values and insights. But the critical value of this kind of thematic analysis depends almost entirely upon the arbitrary exclusiveness of Hoyt's definition of Romance. Whatever he builds into and preconceives about such terms as "objectivity" and "order" he builds into and preconceives about Malamud's fiction. And the same would be true of almost any of the seemingly endless definitions of Romance available. For

15 *Aspects of the Novel* (New York, 1927), pp. 105-123.

16 "Bernard Malamud and the New Romanticism," in *Contemporary American Novelists,* ed. Harry T. Moore (Carbondale, Ill., 1964), pp. 66-67.

instance, I am not altogether sure that Malamud's fiction rejects all forms of objectivity or reorders experience primarily in terms of new solutions — whatever these terms may mean to Hoyt or to Malamud or to myself. Nor am I sure how Hoyt's concept of Romance can help us to decide such issues. In any case, however we might differ in interpretation, it is necessary for us to go behind the terms themselves to more basic distinctions in Malamud's uses of fantasy, or romance, in order to resolve our differences.

One of these basic distinctions can be discovered, I believe, by asking why Malamud uses fantasy at all in his fiction. And why objective fantasy in one story and subjective fantasy in another? Objective fantasy begins, it seems, when the writer has an idea or vision of human experience that could or should be realized in some world, but not necessarily our world. Objective fantasy originates with the Other-World. Subjective fantasy, however, originates with this world, with some idea of human existence as the writer feels it to *be*. The fusion of the extraordinary and the ordinary, the incredibility of actual life, the fading line between fantasy and reality that the writer represents in his world of fiction is an artistic reflection and shaping of the same conditions of human life that he feels and responds to in our real world. Thus, subjective fantasy begins with a view of the ludicrous, precarious, and absurd conditions of our real world, where the real and the nonreal seem to blend and fade into each other indistinguishably. The normalcies and probabilities of our ordinary world, the natural laws that we assume to be fixed and unchangeable, are in fact unexpectedly and unpredictably changed, interrupted, reversed, twisted, suspended, distorted. Actual existence is irrational, stupefying, embarrassing.

In many ways, the modern tradition of subjective fantasy begins with Dostoevsky, who felt that it was in the exceptional happenings of existence that reality could be found. "What most people regard as fantastic," Dostoevsky declared, "I hold to be the inmost essence of truth."[17] More recently, in his Foreword to *Black Humor* (1965) Bruce Friedman has expressed a similar view from a contemporary perspective:

> There *is* a fading line between fantasy and reality, a very fading line... almost invisible line.... If you are alive today, and stick your head out of doors now and then, you know there is a nervousness, a tempo, a near-hysterical new beat in the air, a punishing isolation and loneliness

[17] From *Letters*, tr. Ethel Colburn Mayne (1914), quoted in Miriam Allott, *Novelists on the Novel* (London, 1959), p. 68.

> of a strange, frenzied new kind. It is in the music and the talk and the films and the theater and it is in the prose style of Joe Heller and Terry Southern. You can find it in Gogol and Isaac Babel, too.
>
> [p. viii]

What do we say when *The New York Times* reports that "five hundred captured Congo rebels are ushered into a stadium before their Free World captors. The ones who are booed have their heads blown off. Those with good acts who draw applause go free."[18] Or when more recently an American general declares that U. S. forces have destroyed a South Vietnamese village in order to save it?

By tracing the source of subjective fantasy to a similar belief in the incredibility of actual reality, I do not mean to imply that the forms or uses or effects of subjective fantasy are all of one kind. Malamud's own subjective fantasy is quite varied and is related to at least three distinguishable kinds of such fantasy evident in the fiction of the last hundred years or so, such distinctions depending upon the manner in which the natural and the fantastic are blended and fused.

When the fantastic flits playfully and lightly on the surface of reality, fluttering in and out, we have the kinds of light-comic fantasies and divertissements typical of novels like Chesterton's *The Man Who Was Thursday* or Meredith's *The Shaving of Shagpat*. These types of light comedies are about the only kind of fiction for which some readers exclusively reserve the term fantasy. They are what Tolkien has somewhat disparagingly called "Chestertonian" or "*Mooreeffoc*" fantasies, a reversed "Coffee-room" view of this world, seen through a glass window from the inside out on a dark London day as Dickens would have seen it.[19] The effect can be anything from the nostalgia and sentiment of a warm brown tone to the freedom and frivolity of a silvery volley of laughter.

Subjective fantasy can also be shaped into shocking, bitter, biting kinds of comedy. It is more black than silver or brown. The fantastic functions to expose the extreme harshness and cruelty of the incongruities of actual existence; it cuts deeply into the exterior of the ordinary world. Its methods are wit, sarcasm, hyperbole, sardonic humor. This type of dark-comic fantasy ranges from Nathanael West's *Day of the Locust* and Joseph Heller's *Catch-22* to John Barth's *Sot-Weed Factor* and Kurt Vonnegut's *Cat's Cradle*. In Bruce Friedman's *Sterne*, for

[18] Friedman, p. ix.

[19] J. R. R. Tolkien, "On Fairy-Stories," in *Essays Presented to Charles Williams*, ed. C. S. Lewis (Oxford, 1947; repr. Grand Rapids, 1966), p. 74.

example, an urban Jewish status-seeker, a transplanted *schlemiel* who tries to make it in gentile suburbia, goes from his train to his home each night with each wrist clamped in the jaws of a large dog. Such weird, distorted, and grotesque images and episodes attempt to embody the madness of contemporary existence as the writer feels it. It is like the dwarf in one of Ray Bradbury's short stories, who goes alone each evening to a Fun House after hours to watch his body metamorphosed into proportion and beauty within the variously shaped mirrors, only to have someone switch mirrors on him one evening. This use of fantasy seems all the more shocking, both dramatically and emotionally, because the mundane ordinariness of reality is there all the time, it *is* and it goes on. We feel that the fantastic eruption in the midst of the steady beat of existence is not enough even to arouse our sensibilities or to arrest the normalcy of our cruelties.

Somewhere between these light and dark comic uses of subjective fantasy lies in the fantasy of writers like Gogol, Dostoevsky, Isaac Babel, and, for the most part, Bernard Malamud as well. The blend of the fantastic and the ordinary in these writers is less extremely playful or violent than in the other kinds of subjective fantasy mentioned. The comic absurdities can be just as incongruous and disparate, but they are characterized also by a pity and compassion for the human victims involved in their own ludicrous conditions. Their uses of subjective fantasy not only jolt us out of the ordinary but return us to it. There is something to return to, something intrinsically valuable in the most absurd of experience, a value which lies behind existence itself and allows, as it were, the absurd to be known as the absurd. In this sense, subjective fantasy, like objective fantasy, looks within, through, and beyond the surface realities of life to a greater Reality. Like the writer of objective fantasy, the writer of this kind of subjective fantasy must, as C. S. Lewis has put it, "draw on the only real 'other world' we know, that of the spirit."[20] For these writers the sensation of the unreal and impossible in the most extreme conditions of ordinary life is infused with the spiritual qualities of wonder and hope. And thus while Malamud shares the playfulness and the ironies of both light and dark comic uses of subjective fantasy, his own most characteristic blending of the fantastic and the natural is usually conditioned by this residue of spiritual and enduring life underlying the most desperate and hopeless of human experiences.

[20] "On Stories," in *Essays Presented to Charles Williams*, p. 98.

Malamud's subjective fantasy adopts several forms and devices throughout his short stories and novels: preposterously exaggerated episodes and endings, grotesque twists of characterization or description, dreams, annunciations, epiphanies, and possibly most of all, the wry ironies of what Kazin calls the "Doomsday terseness" of Yiddish speech rhythms. "The Loan" is a grotesque on the sufferings of Lieb, a baker, his estranged friend, Kobotsky, who comes to request a loan, and Bessie, Lieb's wife, a victim of Europe's pogroms and incinerators. All three are sickly, desperately poor. Lieb wishes to give the loan, Bessie refuses. As the sadness and tension grows, the woes of all three are chanted and interwoven like a litany of confession and mourning for their mutual suffering, rising to a morbid climax as Bessie screams over the blackened "charred corpses" of bread burned as they talked, and as the two old friends embrace in a bizarre kiss, mouths pressed together, and then part forever. The grotesque images of the charred loaves and the two friends kissing embody and focus the compassion of human suffering. The deft touches of fantasy here at the end of the story seem to arrest and suspend before us in an appropriately effective manner the poignant search for compassion in the drab hopelessness of daily suffering. The same kind of subtle and deft distortion of mundane existence is present in "The Death of Me." Marcus, a benevolent and compassionate tailor, employs a Polish presser and a Sicilian tailor who quarrel constantly and violently. Marcus continually separates them, appealing for peace and showing them in their own ethnic traditions as well as in his personal life an example of suffering greater than hatred. One day Marcus steps between them during a particularly bloody battle, his withered arms flailing, wailing with anguish and appealing desperately to each of them, only to collapse between them at the top of a stairs, then topple "like a fragile pitcher" from the shelf, bumping down the stairs, "cracking at the bottom, the shards flying everywhere." Marcus's glazed, accusing eyes staring in death from the bottom of the stairs up at the horror-stricken presser and tailor is an image similar in function to Rosen's accusations shouted from death at Eva in "Take Pity." In contrast to the supernatural perspective provided by the objective fantasy, the subjective fantasy here provides an implicit, earthly perspective of the same frustrations of pity, from the point of view of the accused and noncompassionate. The image of the falling, bumping, shattering pitcher, like that of the two old friends locked in a mouth-to-mouth kiss, suspends the motion and arrests our attention on it. The casually absurd motion of the falling pitcher suggests that in the casual absurdity of Marcus's death, it is only the fragility and helplessness of compassion that can arrest even for the moment the cruelties of existence.

In another story, "The Mourners," Malamud uses fantasy to embody the idea of not only the efficacy but also the assimilation of suffering. It is the story of a loud, fat landlord, Gruber, who evicts an egg-candler nobody, Kessler, from a top-floor flat of his decrepit tenement. Kessler sits in the rain and snow on the sidewalk in front of the tenement, his dispossessed furniture around him, until he is carried back into the flat by neighbors. When Gruber comes storming over to throw the old man out again, he finds him sitting on the barren floor of the smelly, run-down flat, white from fasting, bunched up in his frailty, and rocking back and forth in mourning. At first demanding, then pleading, Gruber comes to realize that the egg-candler is not mourning for himself but for him, Gruber — "it was *he* who was dead." Frightened and sweating, Gruber grabs up an old sheet and throws it around his bulk, sinking on the floor alongside Kessler to become a fellow-mourner. Like Kobotsky and Lieb kissing, the two grotesquely related mourners work out their almost hopeless redemption in the assimilation of each other's suffering.

In "The Lady of the Lake" Henry R. Freeman, alias Henry Levin, ex-floorwalker from Macy's basement, hides his Jewishness and escapes to Old Italy to seek wit, love, adventure, and freedom (he considered adopting the name Le Vin). But alas! his only true love turns out to be an orthodox Jewish maiden, a lady of the lake once tortured at Buchenwald. Wanting only a Jew and spurning Freeman's "non-Jewishness," she disappears forever into the mist, leaving Freeman / Levin to embrace "only moonlit stone." The fantasy of the story not only reflects the irony of abandoned identity (in *The Fixer* Malamud builds a whole novel around the idea) and the fusion of the real and unreal, but it also reflects the airy, disappearing quality of life in general. The real is continually becoming unreal, and the unreal, real. The supernatural and the trivial, as Kazin puts it, "jostle each other." It is difficult to know for sure which aspect of experience is the dream, the mundane or the mysterious. "Life is never very solid for these Jews, these people 'who live on air'; they are always on the verge of saying good-by and departing for the other world."[21] In several of these stories the effect is one of suspending only momentarily the already established probability of action. In suspending the natural action,

[21] Kazin, p. 206.

Malamud does not require that we "suspend our disbelief" (as though this Coleridgean dictum were an unquestionable Commandment for the appreciative reading of all fantasy!) but instead cultivates new belief. To believe in the reality of the spiritual that occasionally filters through the dense atmosphere of our mundane and incredible existence is no more impossible than believing in the reality of that existence itself.

Malamud's last three novels, *The Assistant* (1957), *A New Life* (1961), and *The Fixer* (1966), appear more "realistic" than fantastic. On the surface at least, they read like naturalistic treatments of the drab experiences and harsh realities of their heroes, an Italian-American drifter, a thirty-year-old academic failure, and a Russian-Jewish handyman. We may agree with Leslie Fiedler that in the "muted, drab" worlds of such novels, Malamud has turned away from the "magical universe" and the "lovely absurd madness" of some of his earlier short stories and his first novel, *The Natural,* and now in this later fiction has adapted the quality of his prose to a "denial of the marvelous" to which he had earlier committed himself.[22] This distinction, however, may be too sharply drawn; the marvelous can be invested as effectively in the muted and drab as in the mad and absurd, perhaps even more so. In the sometimes somber, sometimes comically ludicrous worlds of these later novels, the uses of subjective fantasy are more diffusive and in this way more appropriate to Malamud's implicit and repeated theme of the spiritual values of self-expiation through suffering. The sense of the marvelous is cultivated by the extremities of human experience that are already an implicit part of the fictional situation and frame of each novel.

In the somewhat somber world of *The Assistant,* for example, Morris Bober's grocery store — smelling "like a open grave" — is situated precariously on the edge of a poor, often hostile gentile neighborhood, like a woodsman's cottage in a fairy tale situated precariously on the edge of a dark and dreaded forest, marginal and isolated. Strange wraith-like creatures, such as a bony bulb peddler with bobbing adam's apple or a red-haired firemaker in a soundless whisper and dark overcoat down to his ankles, appear and disappear — like elves and goblins, all living, like the store, on the edge of existence. An eerie air of unreality hangs over the density of Morris's poverty and suffering, and it clings to all who share Morris's life with him. In *A New Life,* it is Seymour Levin, like his namesake, Henry Levin / Freeman of "The Lady of the Lake," who tries

[22] *Love and Death in the American Novel* (New York, 1960), pp. 469-470.

to leave his Jewishness and thirty-odd years of failures behind him in New York City and find a new identity in the midst of the gentile peace, plenty, and conformity of a provincial state agricultural college in the Pacific Northwest. The situation itself is comically incongruous, and within it Levin's picaresque pursuit of a new life begins and ends in absurdity. And yet it is this very absurdity that makes up the necessary condition of Levin's discovery. In his comic and ludicrous predicaments, in the petty insanities of his college world, and in the primordial beauties of the Northwest forest (where you can get lost), Levin discovers that reality eludes whatever version we place upon it. Happiness, he rediscovers, is a "grace settled on the spirit in desire of life . . . how magnanimously beautiful even to have been is." And much of what Levin discovers within his comic situation, Yakov Bok of *The Fixer* discovers within his more somber and tragic situation. Bok's flight from the squalid conditions of the ghetto and his Jewish identity, his ironic criminal predicament, and his long imprisonment are an entire study in the seemingly impossible and incredible. Bok's prison world, a nightmare of cruelty and sadism, is difficult to distinguish from the nightmare of life outside the prison. And both seem equally unreal. Almost the only reality that remains is Bok's endurance. Like Bober, Alpine, and Levin, Bok discovers that only in our endurance of the incredible disparities and sufferings of ordinary existence do we grasp and experience the more fundamental spiritual reality and identity of our lives.

A similar pattern of absurdity and paradox characterizes the action of the protagonists of all three novels. Each hero fulfills what Sy Levin calls "Levin's Law II: One becomes his victim's victim." Frank Alpine of *The Assistant* becomes Morris Bober's victim by adopting the poverty and suffering of the man he once robbed. Sy Levin makes a victim of his department chairman by lusting after his wife, Pauline, and then becomes a victim himself by inheriting Pauline, whom he no longer loves, her two adopted children, his own child inside her, and the loss of his job and the possibility of teaching college again, something he does love. If Levin is a victim of his own deception, Yakov Bok is a victim of his own self-deception. Deceiving himself by disclaiming his Jewish identity and living like a non-Jew, Bok is found out, imprisoned for a murder he did not commit, and tortured like a Jew. The absurdity of his experience is that in his suffering as both an ethnic Jew and a self-claimed non-Jew, he in fact becomes a true Jew, a *mensch,* an Everyman. Likewise, Frank Alpine, the alien and goy, becomes a Jew literally and spiritually, "after" Passover. And Levin rediscovers his new life of hope and endurance in the old life of alienation and suffering.

Thus, what I have tried to suggest is that Malamud blends the fantastic into the basic fictional constituents of plot and character in each novel. And he reinforces this underlying sense of the marvelous by making use also of various minor and interjecting elements of fantasy, including visions and "dream-fantasies," exaggerated episodes and situations, close juxtapositions of the extremely mundane and extraordinary, twists of language, and all sorts of outrageous humor ranging from slapstick to puns and jokes. Sy Levin, for example, chases grapefruit down the street with his college dean while discussing departmental politics, delivers a fascinating first-day lecture with his fly open, and walks back to town in only his beard after having his clothes stolen during an adventure of love in the country. Levin is not only *schlemiel* but *schlimazel,* too — the bumpkin, the blundering fool who gets "for every pleasure, pain." Frank Alpine follows the same kind of law, is the same kind of *schlimazel.* At Morris's burial he loses his balance and falls into Morris's open grave. In such incidentals the fantastic informs the obvious symbolism and changes it from a mere abstraction to a concrete experience of pathos, absurdity, and wonder. Just on the verge of a meaningful relationship with Helen Bober, for whom he gives his life in toil and suffering, Frank saves her from cruel rape, only to end up raping her himself and thus destroying his dream at the very moment of securing it. In a vision at the end of the novel, Malamud uses fantasy to blend the mundane and the spiritual. In his vision, Frank saw

> St. Francis come dancing out of the woods in his brown rags, a couple of scrawny birds flying around over his head. St. F. stopped in front of the grocery, and reaching into the garbage can, plucked the wooden rose out of it. He tossed it into the air and it turned into a real flower that he caught in his hand. With a bow he gave it to Helen, who had just come out of the house. "Little sister, here is your little sister the rose." From him she took it [she had formerly taken the rose Frank carved for her and thrown it in the garbage can], although it was with the love and best wishes of Frank Alpine.

In such grotesque gambolings, slight and momentary as they are, Malamud represents the small incredibilities of our daily human existence, and blends them credibly into the unified experience of each fictional world. Their sometimes surprising, sometimes restrained near-impossibility is what arrests our attention and shapes the drabness of ordinary existence into the wonder of life itself.

Malamud's only non-Jewish novel, *The Natural,* includes his most sustained and frequent uses of subjective fantasy. It is a fantasy of folklore and morality embodying the age-old story of the hero's fall into temptation and corruption. The hero in this case is Roy Hobbs, an All-American baseball "natural," who wanted to be and could have been "the best there ever was," but who failed because he wanted success too desperately, too much for his own sake, and too much as an end in itself. In the novel, Roy falls not only once but twice. He comes from the backwoods full of promise, innocence, pride in his natural gift. But he soon falls prey to his own pride and lust and the silver bullet of an erratic temptress.

After seventeen years of wandering and obscurity, Roy gets a second chance, this time with the New York Knights. Soon his glistening magical bat, Wonderboy, breaks all kinds of records and Roy rises to glory and fame. But this is short-lived, and he ultimately falls again because he neither understands his natural gift nor knows how to apply it. His tempters this time are not only his own pride and moral flabbiness, but also the corrupters of society who justify their ambitions, frustrations, and dreams just as much in Roy's failures as in his successes (for in the destruction of our heroes we can still believe in the future possibility of our own unfulfilled dreams). There are corrupters like Max Mercy, a sportswriter who lives like a grubby parasite off the heroes he helps make and destroy; Memo Paris, Roy's inaccessible and unlovable love-goddess; the fans, like Otto Zipp, who attend only the games in which Roy loses; and the fat, greedy Judge who owns the Knights and bets against them, bribing Roy. Roy also fails to heed the wisdom of those already scarred by personal and societal corruption — Sam Simpson and Pop Fisher, Roy's teachers and managers; Red Blow, his coach; and Iris, a tainted "goddess" who loves Roy. By the end of the season, Roy has fallen prey to all of the ancient sins: sloth, gluttony, lust, greed, and deceit. Although he changes his mind too late from accepting the Judge's bribe and wants desperately to win the last crucial game, he is too weak from his self-corruption and pathetically strikes out. "He coulda been a king," sigh the fans. "Say it ain't true, Roy," shouts a newsboy, parodying the famous line supposedly said to Shoeless Joe Jackson of the 1906 Chicago Black Sox scandal. But Roy knows it is true, and that what is even more true is the loss of his irredeemable dream, the beautiful but painful trust of his inner, natural Self. Roy's final insight, which is ironically both desperate and hopeful, is that he has in fact learned nothing from his past life and now will "have to suffer again."

In Malamud's more characteristic uses of Jewish folklore and the "legend of the wandering Jew," he creates in most of his stories a poignant, mellow, somewhat leaden and gloomy atmosphere. Humor and pain are somehow twisted together. The comedy is ambiguous. In *The Natural,* however, Malamud uses American folklore and the legendry of baseball to create a more saucy and flippant comedy. It is both biting and compassionate. Things jostle and clash and bounce off one another. The novel still serves the purposes of moral comedy, but in a more caustic and casual sense. The reason for this effect, I believe, is that the comic form of the novel is shaped out of two disparate and yet related levels or movements. There is on one level the movement of Roy's story, his rise and fall in the world of baseball. And there is on another level the movement of a recurrent (especially the parallels between "Pre-Game" and "Batter-Up!") series of loosely connected images, dreams, legends, and myths that intersect the story movement and relate meaningfully to it. It is the action that tacks between these two movements and fuses them together that, in large part, makes up the fantasy of the novel.

It would seem foolish, of course, to read the novel as only a story of baseball adventure, with the hero's struggle for fame and fortune. Very few readers would be satisfied with the novel as such. At the same time, it would seem just as foolish to read the novel primarily in terms of its symbol and myth. And yet this is the tendency of most criticism and interpretation of the novel. There are, of course, numerous allusions to myth — Percivale, the Holy Grail, Greek goddesses, nature cycles, the Fisher-King, and so forth. And myth-hunters have made the most of them.[23] In addition, there are images and dreams and other kinds of allusions that Malamud uses to symbolize more abstract goals and moral qualities within Roy's experiences: a recurrent white rose of purity (or impurity); golden bats, golden baseballs, golden wheat; distant yowls of train-whistles; and so on. Such symbols and mythic allusions, however, are significant not in themselves but only in so far as they give shape to the meaning of Roy's moral quest. Percivale or Babe Ruth may illuminate the meaning of Roy's rise and fall, but it is also true that Roy may illuminate the meaning of Percivale or Babe

[23] Cf. Norman Podhoretz, "Achilles in Left Field," *Commentary,* XV (March 1953), 321-326; and Fiedler, *No! In Thunder* (Boston, 1960), pp. 104-105.

Ruth — even more so. The point is that myth and story intersect and reinforce each other, and their fusion is significant as it helps to shape the moral doctrine that Malamud embodies within the total structure of *The Natural,* a doctrine of self-fulfillment through suffering and endurance. And to a large extent, Malamud informs this doctrine by his uses of fantasy.

One of the functions of fantasy in the novel is that of preventing us from getting too one-sidedly involved with either story or symbol (myth, and so forth). For example, on the level of the baseball story, when Roy hits the ball he either knocks the cover off or sends it up into the heavens infinitely out of sight. When he strikes out he strikes out with the roar of a freight train. Out in center field he snags down birds. This is no game for serious or literal-minded baseball fans. When it comes to myth and Harriet Bird, the first "goddess" who ensnares Roy, Malamud makes sure she is a "snappy goddess" — with a veil no less. Ready to shoot our hero, Harriet "pulled the trigger (thrum of bull fiddle)" and then "danced on her toes around the stricken hero." After being fondled by Roy in a railroad-tunnel of love (!) Harriet shrieks, jumps up, crooks her arms like broken branches, hangs her head grotesquely between her shoulders, and dances like a twisted tree. It is not so much the symbol of the tree of good-and-evil (and/or of knowledge — I suspect many readers pay no attention to the symbol at all) that we focus upon, but a parody of the symbol itself, a parody not clearly reasoned out. The very absurdity of Roy's temptation prevents it from being either abstract or literal. It has the reality of a pain that we cannot compare to anything else. "I have," Harriet informs Roy, "a fantastic imagination."

The very paradoxical and absurd quality of Malamud's morality (suffering brings happiness) makes fantasy not only appropriate for giving this morality form and expression but also effective for impressing it upon our sensibilities. The images of gold or moon-hazed mountains or white-faced lost boys in Roy's dreams are fantasies of a vague, haunting beauty that reinforce Roy's yearning and desire for purity and self-fulfillment. They are like reappearing pictures of forgotten and yet never forgotten truths — just as Frank Alpine does not know why he never forgets the stories about St. Francis. Thus, fantasy gives a preconscious form to Roy's moral quest. The grotesquely fantastic image of the dark, faceless judge, sitting in darkness and surrounded by shadows, puffing black smoke from a black cigar, and hypocritically spouting the dark wisdom of moral platitudes, is the kind of absurdity that makes evil both ludicrous and hellishly awesome at the same time. The comic absurdities of Memo, the Temptress, awaiting her lover while chewing on a turkey drumstick in bed; of Roy grinding a stream of moral platitudes, is the kind of absurdity that makes evil both nose until he screams and squeals like a pig; of Pop Fisher in a two-piece bathing suit trying to catch a grapefruit dropped from an airplane (but beaned instead) — all have the effect of a suddenly stopped home movie, catching a ridiculous pose, a crazy angle, a gaping grin, a wry smile.

Such fantasy, whether grotesque or humorous, focuses on the absurd and unprotected condition of man's nature. It shapes the variety of images, symbols, allusions, and myths into a changing pattern of suspending, shimmering, self-reflecting mirrors that at once illuminate and distort the image of man in Roy's experiences, blur and yet sharpen that image into new focus. And the same fantasy that reflects compassionately on the absurd condition of human nature also prevents us from taking Roy's moral quest too piously or soberly, or Malamud's mythic gambolings too literally or seriously. This very play of fantasy helps to make Roy's corruption itself appear absurd. The paradox of Malamud's morality implies that we gain fulfillment not primarily in the things we learn nor in the moral truths we discover, but through the acceptance and endurance of suffering. Our myths and symbols, and even our moralities, are less significant than the incarnated grace of life itself. At one time Roy rejected Iris's wisdom that "Experience makes good people better . . . through their suffering." In the end, Roy accepts neither the inevitability of his goodness nor the finality of his failure, but only the necessity of his suffering.

In the kinds of objective and subjective fantasies analyzed thus far in Malamud's fiction, the preternatural — in some sense and in varying degrees — acts *upon* the natural. The fantastic intersects and suspends the movement of ordinary existence. The Other-World is the prime mover. Its influence may be from outside or from within this ordinary world, but nevertheless the fantastic is the active force. In some of Malamud's fiction, however, the preternatural not only acts upon the natural order of things, but is in turn acted upon by the natural. That is, the fantastic and the ordinary act reciprocally upon one another. Their actions are confluent and interrelated. They interpenetrate each other and qualify the meaning of each other's existence and purpose. The result is to give form and direction to a view of men and God and things that is not so predominant or possible in Malamud's other kinds of fantasy. This limited but creative use of Malamud's fantasy is present in at least three of his best short fictions, "The Magic Barrel," "Idiots First" (titles also given to his two collections of short stories), and "Angel Levine."

"The Magic Barrel" is the story of a rabbinical student, Leo Finkle, who for practical purposes hires the services of Pinye Salzman, a sad-eyed marriage broker smelling of fish. Salzman is one of Malamud's most memorable burlap heroes, hanging on the edge of existence, both comic and pathetic, in every way fantastic and yet realizable. Salzman's one devotion is to the ideal of matching lovers, of creating love. But he is too devoted, he exaggerates the ideals of his clients, and his business is poor. He has his office "in the air," appears and disappears, eats his fish meals out of his worn portfolio of prospects — the magic barrel of love. Leo Finkle is young, intellectually aloof, and somewhat embarrassed over seeking a matchmaker. When Salzman offers him several selections from the magic barrel, Leo cannot find any girl that suits him. After some finagling, Salzman persuades Leo to meet Lily Hirschorn, a high school teacher with breeding and ten thousand in savings. Leo and Lily meet, with Salzman hovering unseen in the vicinity — "perhaps a cloven-hoofed Pan, piping mystical ditties as he danced his impossible way before them, strewing wild buds on the walk and purple grapes before them." Leo soon realizes, however, that Salzman has also piped Lily an exaggerated idea of his orthodoxy and mystical piety. Furiously, he tells her, "I think that I came to God not because I loved Him, but because I did not." Exit Lily. But the experience shocks Leo into the realization that he is incapable of human relationships with either God or man, that "he had never loved anyone. Perhaps it went the other way, that he did not love God so well as he might, because he had not loved man." Thus, the moral insight that Leo's divinity studies could not provide, Salzman's fantastic magic barrel did provide.

Leo's illumination, however, brings suffering, not salvation. He wants no more of Salzman, but the broker leaves behind a packet of pictures of other prospects that Leo ignores for a long while but finally, in desperation, opens. None of the pictures interests him, except one that he almost overlooked. Then his heart sang. Some unremembered desire was aroused. When Salzman sees the picture, he is startled and tells Leo it was only accidentally included in the packet. "She is not for you," he woefully informs the student. "She is a wild one — wild without shame. . . . Like an animal. Like a dog." Still, Leo's love is persistent. Why not this girl? Because, Salzman replies, "This is my baby, Stella, she should burn in hell." At first Leo hides in despair, but then decides that loving Stella will be for her, conversion to goodness, and for himself, conversion to God. Salzman is now as cynical and unbelieving as Leo once was, even mocks himself and his magic barrel. But when Leo suggests that he might be of some help to the fallen Stella, the broker arranges a meeting. Leo and Stella meet under a street light, with Salzman again hovering nearby, this time leaning against a wall, chanting prayers for the dead. Leo sees in both the hardness of Stella's corruption and the "desperate innocence" of her eyes the picture of his own "redemption." And in his redemption, and Stella's, there is ultimately Salzman's own hope and redemption.

The reversal of the story's action effectively embodies Malamud's truth that love and suffering are reciprocal. If the magic of Salzman is necessary to bring love into the life of Leo Finkle, then the suffering of Leo is equally necessary to bring hope into the life of Salzman. Salzman's magic and love and Leo's misery and suffering are thus reversed, exchanged, intertwined. Moreover, they are not only fellow-victims, as Lieb, Kobotsky, and Bessie of "The Loan," nor only fellow-mourners, as Gruber and Kessler of "The Mourners" — they are also fellow-redeemers, redeeming each other in their shared suffering and mourning.

The reciprocal fantasy of "Idiots First" is more explicit and grotesque than the fantasy of "The Magic Barrel." All of the action takes place during one cold, bleak November night. Mendel, a sick man left with only an idiot son, Isaac, of thirty-nine years, and the harsh memories of a poverty-ridden life, desperately tries to get enough money to send Isaac to an uncle in California. Throughout the night Mendel and Isaac are hounded and haunted by a strange, devilish supernatural creature, Ginzburg, and it is not until the end of the story that we discover that Mendel is apparently dying, that this night is his last chance to care for Isaac, and that Ginzburg is the supernatural harbinger of his death. After many failures, Mendel secures the money, only to find that Ginzburg, now in the form of a ticket collector, has closed the gate to the waiting train and refuses to let Isaac aboard. "It just left — in one more minute." Mendel pleads with him to have pity, if not for his own miserable life, at least for Isaac. But Ginzburg informs Mendel that his only responsibility is "to make happen what happens. I ain't in the anthropomorphic business." Rather, his business is the law, "the cosmic universal law . . . the one I got to follow myself." Mendel lunges at the unpitying Ginzburg: "Don't you understand what it means human?" Then, as Mendel locked himself in his death struggle with Ginzburg, he saw

> reflected in the ticket collector's eyes the depth of his terror. But he saw that Ginzburg, staring at himself in Mendel's eyes, saw mirrored in them the extent of his own awful wrath. He beheld a shimmering, starry, blinding light that produced darkness.
>
> Ginzburg looked astounded. "Who me?"
>
> His grip on the squirming old man slowly loosened, and Mendel, his heart barely beating, slumped to the ground.
>
> "Go," Ginzburg muttered, "take him to the train."

In the fantasy of "Idiots First," the supernatural and the trivial do more than merely jostle; they are locked in a profound struggle in which they qualify the existence and action of each other. The God-man struggle reveals each one to the other, as well as each to himself. Mendel sees his own terror, his mortality, but also his furious insistence on justifying the significance of his life. Like Rosen of "Take Pity," he *will* give pity. Even the cosmic universal law can be changed under the influence of man's precarious and tenacious hold upon life. And in Mendel's endurance and compassion Ginzburg has revealed the limits of his own wrath. It is Mendel's compassion that reveals and fulfills the divine compassion, as though only in man's suffering and struggle can God's love and redemption be known and experienced.

"Angel Levine" poses the absurd situation of a visitation by Alexander Levine, a Negro-Jewish angel, to Manischevitz, a pious orthodox Jewish tailor, who has suffered the loss of just about every worldly and spiritual good — a ruined business, a son killed in war, a wayward daughter lost forever to him, a wife, Fanny, wasting away in a sick bed, and himself in pain at every step. And also like Job, Manischevitz finds the sheer quantity of his woes incomprehensible and "an affront to God."

Even more of an affront to Manischevitz's orthodox God is the sudden appearance of Levine, claiming to be a "bona fide angel of God" but in fact looking more like a case worker from the Welfare Department in frayed cuffs and ill-fitted suit. Manischevitz has heard of black Jews but never of black Jewish angels. And why doesn't Levine have wings, or why should God send a black angel rather than a white one? When Manischevitz demands more proof, maybe a miracle, Levine explains that his recent disincarnation into an angel is not yet complete and that he is actually now in a "condition of probation" which limits his powers for the present, everything depending upon the outcome of his probation. But to Manischevitz it all seems like some grim Yiddish joke; he remains skeptical, and Levine, deeply disappointed at his rejection, goes off to Harlem.

For a few days after Levine's appearance Fanny's pain subsides and Manischevitz feels hopeful, but these blessings are short-lived, and, more desperate than ever, Manischevitz decides to look up Levine in Harlem. After some difficulty he spots the angel in a lurid honky tonk, looking more deteriorated than before and dancing with a wild, sexy Negress. Levine slyly winks at Manischevitz peering in from the outside, and the tailor flees home. Things get worse: Fanny is near death, Manischevitz seeks but fails to find God's deliverance in the synagogue, he curses his disbelief, and dreams of Levine. Still disbelieving, he goes once more to Harlem and stumbles into a Negro Jewish synagogue where he learns that God puts his Spirit into all things of all colors. He again locates Levine at the honky tonk, but now dressed in bright, flashy colors, worldly and cocky. Hobbling and humiliated, Manischevitz requests a private word with Levine, but the angel tells him to speak his piece publicly. In the midst of the sudden hush that falls on the place, and in blinding tears and cracked voice, Manischevitz confesses, "I think you are an angel from God." And through his own tears Levine cries, "How you have humiliated me." By the time they get back to Manischevitz's flat, Fanny is cured and up cleaning the place. Manischevitz just catches sight of a dark figure borne aloft on a pair of magnificent wings, a white feather falling to earth and turning to snow.

The principle of exchange and assimilation that informs so much of Malamud's fiction is intellectually and artistically reinforced and brought into its clearest focus in the reciprocal fantasy of these stories. Not only man and man, nor victim and victimizer, but also God and man exchange suffering and assimilate each other's compassion. The supernatural not only parallels or intersects the human, but shares in the pain and endurance of men. In this way Malamud reflects much of the mood of contemporary Jewish and Christian theology that finds in man's struggle with the Divine, even in his rejection of God, both the reality of God and the meaning of human suffering. For Malamud, God is both the condition and the redeemer of man's suffering, an existential paradox that can be best conceived in poetic terms. In theological terms, human suffering in his fiction is an aspect of God's prevenient grace. In his struggle with God, man confirms not only his own human integrity but also his ultimate redemption. In his struggle with man, God confirms his reality and grace.

The art of Malamud's fantasy, then, cannot be explained in

simple humanistic or transcendental terms. Sy Levin's "grace settled on the spirit in desire of life" is neither pure desire nor pure spirit. The grace of human endurance and hope is neither identified with nor detached from the absurdities of human existence. The fantasy of Malamud's fiction shapes the interaction between the frustration of desire and the redemption of spirit within the context of absurdity and focuses it upon the grace of endurance and hope. Unlike many other contemporary existentialist writers and dealers in the absurd, Malamud believes in the significance of human suffering and endurance not simply because life is itself absurd (*Credo quia absurdum*) nor primarily because of the human will to endure in the face of absurdity. Rather, Malamud believes through the absurdities of life into the spiritual grace that sustains absurdity itself, and beyond this, ironically and yet compassionately, to the hope and redemption that confirms and sustains the quest of faith itself. In all of this, Malamud's basic fictional resource is, after all, an ancient Judeo-Christian tradition that has long accepted the redemptive value of suffering and endurance. In the contemporary idiom of his worlds, he still appeals to this strength, and within their grotesquely, compassionately glowing life, his fantasy serves to heighten and intensify the paradoxically painful and yet noble condition of man in both his depravity and salvation.

# A Good Writer Is Hard to Find

MELVIN E. LORENTZEN

A literary evaluation of a piece of contemporary fiction that described it as a "Christian short story" might seem to some quite helpful, but would doubtless draw from others accusations of irresponsible criticism. The noun "Christian" used as an adjective modifying "short story" creates an ambiguity that much vigorous debate has not resolved.[1] The problem grows more complex when the author of such a story is lauded as an outstanding "Christian writer" in our era. It goes beyond a matter of opinion on the merit of an author and story. The point at issue is how the word "Christian" can properly be used. Often in such discussions, someone gets around to saying: There

[1] See the column "Dialog" in the *Newsletter of the Conference on Christianity and Literature*, XVI, i (Autumn 1966) through XVII, ii (Winter 1968), with contributions by R. Warburton, N. Vos, C. Seerveld, V. Mollenkott, E. C. Vanderlip, K. Richardson, O. C. Daub, and L. A. King. Also passim in the essays presented in December, 1967, at the Modern Language Association, Conference 13 (Literature and Religion), and edited by C. Huttar in a mimeographed booklet, "Can There Be a Christian Criticism of Literature?" More generally on the problem of terminology see Randall Stewart, *American Literature & Christian Doctrine* (Baton Rouge, 1958), pp. viii-ix, 14ff.

---

Melvin E. Lorentzen is Assistant Professor of English at Wheaton College where he has taught since 1958. He is a graduate of Wheaton College (A.B.), The Johns Hopkins University (M.A.), and Northern Baptist Theological Seminary (B.D., Th.D.). During 1967-68 he was Visiting Lecturer in Writing Seminars at Johns Hopkins while on leave of absence from Wheaton under a Faculty Research Grant. He is Executive Director of the Bedford Center for Creative Study, which he founded, and an ordained minister in the American Baptist Convention. He has in progress a historical novel and a textbook in church administration.

is no such thing as a "Christian story"; or, even, There is no such thing as a "Christian writer."

At this point, one is tempted to dismiss the whole affair as "antics with semantics." The extreme position is often represented by an analogy: There is no such thing as a "Christian" bookcase — the materials of cabinetmaking are the same for a skeptical craftsman as for a devout one; likewise, a story utilizes certain literary contrivances common to all writers — therefore, as a thing in itself, it has no distinguishing character beyond its form. Someone else may attempt a fine distinction: "Christian" may be a suitable term to apply to an individual as a *person,* but not as an *artist,* nor to his work. (Strangely, other modifiers are not so strictly confined: we speak acceptably of "romantic" poets and poems, "naturalistic" novelists and novels, "existentialist" dramatists and dramas.)

As the discussion goes on, all except the most occult minds (or the McLuhanized) agree that "Christian writing" does not pertain to metrical patterns, plot devices, and syntax any more than it does to ink, paper, or typography. If the term has any justification at all, they conclude, it must refer somehow to content rather than to forms and techniques. A tale which contains elements of Christian truth may, perhaps, be called a Christian story, it is half-heartedly conceded.

Can we do no better than that? Many stories contain statements, or even seem to convey messages, that accord with aspects of New Testament teachings. A piece of fiction that faithfully represents the sinful depravity of man, for instance, is true as far as it goes — but is that doctrine by itself distinctively and definitely "Christian"?

For discussion to proceed profitably, there should be brought in for analysis an example of an excellent story purporting to be Christian by a writer who is a Christian. Such an example is "A Good Man Is Hard to Find," whose author is the late Flannery O'Connor.

The uncanny craftsmanship of this young woman from Milledgeville, Georgia, who died in 1964 at the age of thirty-nine, has evoked from fellow writers, literary critics, teachers of literature, and discriminating readers such extravagant praise that the temptation to discount it inevitably arises. Can one take seriously such tributes as these: "one of the most important writers of our age"... "a verbal magician whose phrases flamed like matches in the dark" ... "an incomparable craftsman who wrote, let it be said, some of the finest stories in the language" ... "like Sophocles" ... "To create perfect short fiction is an art that few have mastered; Flannery O'Connor did it again and again"?[2]

Even a reviewer who takes stringent exception to Miss O'Connor's stories says she "has created a masterpiece: every line counts, every word; her tone is right and her vision is multi-leveled" — and further credits her with being "highly gifted" and possessing "a fine talent."[3]

Flannery O'Connor received no less than four major literary grants, and her stories appeared in the foremost annual collections (*O. Henry Prize Stories* and *Best American Short Stories*) in seven different years. Within two years of her death, a 300-page critical assessment of her work was attempted in *The Added Dimension,* edited by Melvin J. Friedman and Lewis A. Lawson (New York: Fordham University Press, 1966).

All of this recognition is for a body of work that includes two short novels (*Wise Blood,* 1952; *The Violent Bear It Away,* 1960) and two collections totaling nineteen short stories (*A Good Man Is Hard to Find,* 1955; *Everything That Rises Must Converge,* 1965, posthumous).

Here, then, is a rare phenomenon in any century: an articulate Christian who is also a literary artist. To discover whether she can be called a "Christian writer" of "Christian stories" requires consideration of several aspects of her work, beginning with her conviction of the value of story.

## I

A Christian who writes fiction must not harbor misgivings or reservations about the validity of storytelling. If he has any feeling, however slight, that fiction is a "lie," he ought either to avoid it altogether or to evaluate its merits so that he can choose his course intelligently with respect to it. A Christian has no right to attempt the art of storytelling with an uneasy conscience about the form itself.

When a Christian minister stated at a writers' conference, of all places, that he thanked God for delivering him from the vice of reading novels, he betrayed his ignorance of what a novel is. On the other hand, the editor of a Christian magazine in Southeast Asia may have gone a bit far, intriguing as his

[2] Caroline Gordon in *Critique,* II, ii (Fall, 1958), 3; *Time,* June 4, 1965, p. 92; *Newsweek,* May 31, 1965, p. 86. Thomas Merton, quoted on back of dust jacket of O'Connor's *Everything That Rises Must Converge;* Louis D. Rubin, *Esprit* (University of Scranton), VIII, i (Winter 1964), 44.

[3] Lillian Smith, "With a Wry Smile Hovering Over All," review of *Everything* ... in *Chicago Tribune Books Today,* June 6, 1965, p. 5.

idea is, when he wrote: "Evangelism through fiction might yet save the day for Christ."

Somewhere between these two, and surely much nearer to the second, lies a genuine appreciation for fiction. A young Christian writer who had established an enviable literary reputation with three works of nonfiction turned to fiction. When asked whether she was enjoying writing a novel more than the other books, she replied that she was finding it easier to tell the truth in the novel.

Professor Henry Zylstra of Calvin College expressed the matter cogently:

> . . . we know what fiction is. We know that it is not abstract; it is concrete. We know that it is not a principle; it is an embodiment. It is not a theory but a manifestation. In fiction the skeleton of life takes on the body. This is a little frightening. We know that the real and the ideal in us are poles apart. We remember that except we be covered by the righteousness of Christ we shall cower, naked all, from the eyes of God. So it is a little frightening to think that in this world of fiction we leave our theoretic norms and abstract ideals and enter into the arena of experience. But we see that fiction is just this, and that we cannot, may not alter it. For, if this is the danger, this is also the worth of fiction, that it is close to life, to life concretely embodied, and to life that goes down to the root-reaches of our moral experience. We ought not, therefore, as a way out of our predicament, convert fiction into something which is not fiction by making it a disembodied ghost of life.[4]

Another unrestrained endorsement of fiction comes from Gordon Keith Chalmers: "To know a story and why it is a story and why it cannot be translated into exposition and remain the same, and that the rarest and mightiest possessions of the human spirit can be discovered only by means of story and by no other process of thinking — to know all this and to have it as your own is to have much."[5]

Each of these is saying that fiction is not only an acceptable artistic form for the embodiment of truth, but actually an indispensable one. Flannery O'Connor would have no difficulty consenting to the full import of these statements. The concluding paragraph of her essay "The Fiction Writer and His Country" is as forceful a declaration of belief as can be found anywhere:

> St. Cyril of Jerusalem, in instructing catechumens, wrote: "The dragon

[4] *Testament of Vision* (Grand Rapids, 1958), p. 49.

[5] *The Republic and the Person* (Chicago, 1952), p. 77, as quoted by Nels Ferré, *Christian Faith and Higher Education* (New York, 1954), p. 210 n.

sits by the side of the road, watching those who pass. Beware lest he devour you. We go to the Father of Souls, but it is necessary to pass by the dragon." No matter what form the dragon may take, it is of this mysterious passage past him, or into his jaws, that stories of any depth will be concerned to tell, and this being the case, it requires considerable courage at any time, in any country, not to turn away from the storyteller.[6]

The Master Storyteller of all time, Jesus Christ, created parables which have survived for two thousand years as gems of the art of story and vehicles for the profoundest truths the human spirit can yearn for and come to know. He could have said: A loving father will forgive his wayward son any foolishness if he will just come home — and we would have lost the parable of the Prodigal Son, regarded by many as the perfect short story. While not "true" in the same sense that it is a factual report of an actual occurrence in the lives of real people, the story is timelessly and universally true in the sense that it pictures, through imaginative creation of an illusion of reality, man's need and God's provision.

At least four reasons have been suggested for Christ's using this method in his public teaching: (1) the inherent power of a story to attract and hold attention; (2) the intrinsic advantage of story over sermon for depicting truth in the concreteness of real-life situations rather than through theoretical abstractions; (3) the mnemonic value of story; and (4) the effectiveness of story in separating discerning hearers from insensitive ones.

In his use of parables, Jesus not only sets an example of superb storytelling, but also endorses this art form. His telling of stories did not establish the legitimacy of the art; he chose storytelling because it was a legitimate art. If Christian writers are to produce great fiction, they must believe in storytelling — and they must know how to do it.

## II

Flannery O'Connor knew how to tell stories. On this all the critics agree, whether or not they sympathize with her philosophical viewpoint, sociological focus, or technical procedures. She said that when she began her work in the graduate writing program at the University of Iowa in the 1940s, she "didn't know a short story from an ad in a newspaper."[7] Nearly twenty years later, she described a "good" story as "one which con-

[6] *The Living Novel*, ed. Granville Hicks (New York, 1962), pp. 163-164.
[7] *The Added Dimension*, pp. 250-251.

tinues to rattle on at a great rate at the same time that it reaches a profound level of meaning."[8]

She would have little patience with the sophisticated disdain of many talented young writers today toward such basic concepts as Aristotle's "beginning, middle, end." Many of them "write" merely by putting words (or non-words) on paper, failing to comprehend that the *art* of writing entails selecting and arranging words to create an effect foreseen in the writer's imagination. Some of the young moderns in literature might make excellent journalists or researchers or clinical analysts with their near-pathological attentiveness to minute details of surfaces. If their writing were to appear in the daily papers, or in textbooks, or in professional journals, it might be acceptable as good work; but when it is offered as the art of literature, one may seriously question the validity of much of it.

Flannery O'Connor knew and respected the "mechanics" of fiction. In every one of her stories, a character or set of characters is involved in a crisis-conflict which builds in intensity until a climactic turning point occurs and the situation resolves. This is not "formula fiction," but the essential pattern of "story": fiction is an imaginative creation of an illusion of reality, and "real life" is an unending series of critical ups and downs, some more intense than others, which either climax and resolve, or destroy characters one way or another. Call it by that much-maligned term "plot," if you wish; the fact is that in all O'Connor fiction, something happens to somebody.

In "A Good Man Is Hard to Find,"[9] a family on vacation has an auto accident and is slaughtered by three escaped convicts who happen upon the scene. Those twenty words tell what happens in that story; but they do not disclose what this classic O'Connor story is saying. The twenty words, amplified with further facts, would make a good news story; but it took Miss O'Connor about 7,000 words to make a good short story. Building scene by scene, she led readers to a vicarious experience of stark tragedy.

It is always interesting to observe the reactions of an audience to whom the story is being read aloud. At first, they chuckle or even guffaw with a kind of self-conscious amusement as the typical squabbles of a family are delineated. But they grow increasingly sober as the story moves swiftly from the opening episode of domestic tension to the serio-comic occurrences of

[8] *Ibid.*, p. 255.

[9] All references to this story are from *Three by Flannery O'Connor* (New York: The New American Library, 1964).

the trip (including a lunch stop at a rundown roadside cafe and the Grandmother's futile attempts to keep the children entertained), to the sudden drama of the accident and the slow-gathering tragedy in the encounter with the convicts, to the split-second climax and the sharp falling off in resolution.

Or, consider Miss O'Connor's artistry in characterization. In the first fifteen lines of the story, she uses at least six literary methods for characterizing the Grandmother without one word telling us directly what kind of person the woman is. We are informed of the situation and the Grandmother's frame of mind by an expository statement or two. Then we hear her speak, watch her move, observe the reactions of other characters to her, hear what other characters say about her, and are shown one detail about her physical appearance. From this we learn that the woman is an angular, wiry old lady rather than the plump, "comfy" kind; that she is energetic, strong-willed, self-centered; that she plays people against each other, and is proud. But none of these qualities is stated.

Incidentally, through this opening scene of less than one page, which focuses on the Grandmother to establish her as the central figure in the story, all the other characters are introduced and characterized as well, including the one not yet present who will become the antagonist. This deftness in setting the stage, presenting the characters, and starting the action creates the same sudden and complete effect as the raising of the curtain on a play in the theater.

Miss O'Connor's "cast" in this story — domineering Grandmother, taciturn son, totally resigned daughter-in-law, incorrigibly bratty children, a bland baby, and three murderous convicts — is typical of her much-discussed "grotesques." Whenever a writer creates distorted or comic characters, a question is raised about his attitude toward them, and even toward humanity. Are these exaggerated figures being ridiculed by a contemptuous creator, or are they spawned in a compassionate heart that wants them to be regarded with sympathetic concern?

Representing those critics who charge that Flannery O'Connor lacks compassion, a reviewer of her collection *Everything That Rises Must Converge* wrote: "Acrid laughter is her response to the struggles of these flies whom she pins down and watches so carefully. The author's point of view begins to be questionable. It is so nearly right, but it is so bereft of the warmth of compassion and empathy that it becomes so wrong somehow."[10]

[10]Lillian Smith (above, note 3).

Such an indictment cannot be overlooked, especially since further comments by this critic imply that Miss O'Connor has substituted spiritual and cultural arrogance for the old racial arrogance which is no longer acceptable in writing.

The accusation was perennial, and Flannery O'Connor responded to it forthrightly in a lecture at Wesleyan College on October 28, 1960:

> Even though the writer who produces grotesque fiction may not consider his characters any more freakish than ordinary fallen man usually is, his audience is going to; and it is going to ask him, or more often tell him, why he has chosen to bring such maimed souls alive. Thomas Mann has said that the grotesque is the true anti-bourgeois style, but I believe that in this country, the general reader has managed to connect the grotesque with the sentimental, for whenever he speaks of it favorably, he seems to associate it with the writer's compassion.
>
> It's considered an absolute necessity these days for writers to have compassion. Compassion is a word that sounds good in anybody's mouth and which no book jacket can do without. It is a quality which no one can put his finger on in any exact critical sense, so it is always safe for anybody to use. Usually I think what is meant by it is that the writer excuses all human weakness because human weakness is human. The kind of hazy compassion demanded of the writer now makes it difficult for him to be anti-anything. Certainly when the grotesque is used in a legitimate way, the intellectual and moral judgments implicit in it will have the ascendancy over feeling.[11]

In another notable statement, she gave her rationale for creating grotesques:

> The problem may well become one of finding something that is *not* grotesque and of deciding what standards we would use in looking. My own feeling is that writers who see by the light of their Christian faith will have, in these times, the sharpest eyes for the grotesque, for the perverse, and for the unacceptable.... The reason for this attention to the perverse is the difference between their beliefs and the beliefs of their audience. Redemption is meaningless unless there is cause for it in the actual life we live, and for the last few centuries there has been operating in our culture the secular belief that there is no such cause. The novelist with Christian concerns will find in modern life distortions which are repugnant to him, and his problem will be to make these appear as distortions to an audience which is used to seeing them as natural; and he may well be forced to take ever more violent means to get his vision across to this hostile audience.[12]

Because Flannery O'Connor was afflicted for fourteen years

[11] "Some Aspects of the Grotesque in Southern Literature," in *Cluster Review* (Mercer University), vii (March 1965).

[12] *The Living Novel*, pp. 162-163.

with a disease (disseminated lupus) that made her a partial invalid, she eschewed sentimental pity for herself or others. How patently foolish it would be, however, to suggest that she was without feeling, this woman who was forced to endure physical grotesquery in herself. Her expressions of that feeling were always salty rather than syrupy, but the wryness of her celebrated humor is not to be confused with cynicism.

As a matter of fact, deeper concerns aside for the moment, her "feeling" for the two central characters in "A Good Man" is not completely unsentimental. The Grandmother is undeniably a nagging, self-centered, strong-willed, sly old biddy toward whom we feel little sympathy. Yet we sense the justifiable hurt in her reply to sassy June Star, "All right, Miss. . . . Just remember that the next time you want me to curl your hair." Her attempts to keep the children entertained in the car with instructive comments, funny stories, and game-playing surely evoke the sympathy of any grandmother, or aunt, or older child, who has had to assume oversight of obstreperous children when a sullen father and a silent mother do nothing. And when her son Bailey rebukes her for recognizing the Misfit, using language "that shocked even the children," the old lady cries, and slaps at her eyes with a clean handkerchief removed from her cuff.

The Grandmother's dialogue with the Misfit, assuring him that he must be a good man at heart, that he could be honest if he would try, that he would find help from Jesus if he would pray, depicts a desperate woman who is instinctively defending herself and her brood by focusing attention on the one who threatens. And despite the cartoon quality of the description, there is no dearth of sentiment and genuine pity in a scene like this: "There were two more pistol reports and the Grandmother raised her head like a parched old turkey hen crying for water and called, 'Bailey Boy, Bailey Boy!' as if her heart would break."

However much a reader may dislike the Grandmother, he is compelled to "feel" for her in some degree because she is sympathetically drawn by the author. In her tragic plight, she is not the ridiculous clown her grotesque appearance and behavior superficially suggest; she is a terror-stricken human being.

What about the Misfit? He is the villain of the piece; if Flannery O'Connor writes without compassion, surely here the characterization should reveal her at her biting, unsympathetic best. This is not the case. Although no normal reader can condone the mass slaughter instigated by the Misfit (and if a reader does sanction it simply because he finds this Southern family highly disagreeable, *then* who lacks compassion?), he cannot help but identify to a degree with the Misfit, to have some sympathy for him, not as a murderer but as a man: a man who is made nervous by the presence of belligerent children, who is embarrassed at his semi-nakedness in front of women, who expresses high regard for his parents, who is confused and hurt by the turns his life has taken, who has a chivalrous thought for the distraught mother, and who finally loses emotional control of himself as he wrestles with the problem of his ignorance and unbelief. He may be a cold-blooded murderer, but he is not a hardened criminal. He is a human soul — troubled, tormented, doomed. Anyone who scoffs at such a pitiful creature is without compassion. The author surely does not do so. Through the eyes of the Grandmother (who is the story's protagonist, after all — the one whom the author is "for"), Flannery O'Connor sorrowfully beholds the unrealized possibilities in this wasted life which is condemned by its own refusal to render faith and commitment.

But Miss O'Connor's compassion is evident at a much deeper level than sentimental feeling for the characters, and here it is not at all soft or permissive. To her, man has but one existential option: believe and be saved, or reject and be damned. Perhaps it is because she, like the Lord himself, cherished such compassion for the unbelieving damned, that some readers mistake the Misfit for the "hero" of the story.

Jesus Christ said, "The Son of man is come to seek and to save that which was lost" (Luke 19:10). Miss O'Connor looks on the woeful human heart, grotesquely distorted by its misalignment with the Divine plan for human life (the glorification and enjoyment of God), and shows us that such grotesquery is not a laughing matter, but is profoundly tragic. Because the Misfit had some "redeeming qualities" (perceived by the Grandmother, incidentally), and because the Grandmother's goodness by grace was obvious even to the Misfit, who denied that such existed, the story closes with a cry fraught with compassionate understanding of man's lostness apart from Jesus: "It's no real pleasure in life."

Christ used his knotted sash to scourge religious racketeers out of the Temple; he exposed the hypocrisies of pious frauds with scathing denunciation and name-calling; he drew story-pictures of tormented souls. Yet, no one charges this Man with lacking compassion, this Man who prayed at the site of his execution, "Father, forgive them, for they know not what they do."

Flannery O'Connor, with her sacramental view of life, looks on humanity with Christian compassion, which is anything but a mushy sentimentality that excuses corruption and winks at weakness. Mercy and forgiveness and love, given at the cost of one's life, are the Christian virtues expressed by the Grandmother, and repudiated by the Misfit. These virtues are bestowed on her by Flannery O'Connor, the essentially compassionate literary creator who sees the Misfit as one of God's prodigal sons. The Grandmother does not say to the Misfit, "You poor boy," but rather, "You're one of my own boys." The Misfit might have been able to take pity; but compassionate identification was impossible for him to accept. ("He came unto his own, and his own received him not" — John 1:11.)

Given such a profound message, a lesser artist than Flannery O'Connor might have stumbled into the pitfall of preaching (many have!). She is saved from this fatal artistic error by her mastery of the techniques of fiction. The climax and resolution of "A Good Man" deserve close scrutiny.

Having introduced into her conversation with the Misfit the assurance that Jesus will help him if he will pray, the Grandmother becomes obsessed with this thought; but in her absolute horror at what is transpiring as the Misfit's henchmen, Hiram and Bobby Lee, take other members of the family off into the woods to shoot them, she is reduced to near incoherence, mouthing only the name "Jesus."

The Misfit picks up the suggestion and speaks about Jesus as throwing everything off balance. While he rambles on, telling why he has named himself the Misfit ("I can't make what all I done wrong fit what all I gone through in punishment"), a scream and pistol shots from the woods throw the Grandmother into a frenzy. Shouting the name of Jesus and admonitions to pray, she appeals to the Misfit's sense of pride ("You've got good blood!"), decency ("I know you wouldn't shoot a lady!"), family honor ("I know you come from nice people!"), and finally his supposed cupidity ("I'll give you all the money I've got!").

The Misfit then explains that it was by raising the dead that Jesus threw everything off balance. In a succinct and graphic manner, he poses the existential option:

> If He did what He said, then it's nothing for you to do but thow away everything and follow Him, and if He didn't, then it's nothing for you to do but enjoy the few minutes you got left the best way you can — by killing somebody or burning down his house or doing some other meanness to him. No pleasure but meanness. . . .

Now occurs a most crucial artistic crisis, as well as the final complication of the plot. The Grandmother must remain "in character" and at the same time be confirmed as a true believer. This is how Flannery O'Connor handles it. " 'Maybe

He didn't raise the dead,' the old lady mumbled, not knowing what she was saying and feeling so dizzy that she sank down in the ditch with her legs twisted under her." Thus, the Grandmother, in panic and confusion, verges on a denial of her faith — which would put her on the side of the Misfit, who has obviously chosen to disbelieve Jesus.

Triggered by this suggestion, the Misfit explodes in the frustration of his ignorance and uncertainty, revealing his soul torment. As the Grandmother notices this, Flannery O'Connor is careful to tell us, her "head cleared for a instant." Gone momentarily are her hysteria and confusion. With a clear mind, she identifies with the Misfit, and reaches out and touches him on the shoulder. He springs back and shoots her three times through the chest.

Of course! In that one moment of clarity, of sanity in these insane proceedings, the Grandmother epitomized goodness, the opposite of meanness. Thereby, she validated the truth about Jesus — that he *did* do what he said — and proved the Misfit wrong. He killed her in literal self-defense. That he knew why he had killed her is made vividly clear in his words to Bobby Lee: "She would of been a good woman if it had been somebody there to shoot her every minute of her life."

Perhaps no characters in American fiction reveal more strikingly than do the Grandmother and the Misfit what François Mauriac had in mind when he wrote: "If there is a reason for the existence of the novelist on earth it is this: to show the element which holds out against God in the highest and noblest characters — the innermost evils and dissimulations; and also to light up the secret source of sanctity in creatures who seem to us to have failed."[13]

## III

Flannery O'Connor's definitive statement of her Christian belief is classic:

> . . . I am no disbeliever in spiritual purpose and no vague believer. I see from the standpoint of Christian orthodoxy. This means that for me the meaning of life is centered in our Redemption by Christ and that what I see in the world I see in its relation to that. I don't think that this is a position that can be taken half-way or one that is particularly easy in these times to make transparent in fiction.[14]

*Redemption by Christ* — this is the keystone of all her work,

[13] *God and Mammon* (London, 1946), p. 59.
[14] *The Living Novel*, pp. 161-162.

the sure clue to what her stories are saying. Imbued with a sacramental view of life by her commitment to Christian orthodoxy, Flannery O'Connor did not try to explain divine redemption at work in the sinful human heart; she merely tried to expose the action of redemption — thereby urging us to faith that goes where reason cannot — and therefore using situations and symbols which defy rational explanation. She wrote under figures of the mysterious. In fact, she cherished her religious commitment on this very score:

> I have heard it said that belief in Christian dogma is a hindrance to the writer, but I myself have found nothing further from the truth. Actually, it frees the storyteller to observe. It is not a set of rules which fixes what he sees in the world. It affects his writing primarily by guaranteeing his respect for mystery.[15]

Thus, her grotesques become meaningful: they cannot be explained or understood; their meaning has to be sought beneath their surfaces — and that meaning turns out to be the mystery of iniquity and the mystery of redemption.

The mystery of iniquity is made meaningful not in communion but in alienation. When a man is resistant to the Spirit of Christ, he is a Misfit in human society. The mystery of grace puts him in touch with his fellowman (the Grandmother); the mystery of iniquity ruptures all relationships with humanity (the Misfit). In her moment of grace, identifying with the Misfit's soul need for restoration and redemption, the Grandmother "thows away everything" and follows Jesus, fulfilling the "royal law" (James 2:8). The Misfit, accordingly, does some meanness to her and no longer finds any pleasure in it because he has been confronted by goodness and has been touched by that grace whose existence he tried to deny.

How is the mystery of iniquity to be overcome in the existential dilemmas? Only by a sacramental view of life. This view is not limited to the historic Incarnation of God in Christ and his atoning death on the cross; it is, by logical extension and application, an awareness of the Real Presence in *all* of life. Immanuel is the name of Christ: God not only *was* but *is* with us. The sacramental view of life sees the Redeemer at work in human lives, redeeming, and sees all things as potential means of grace. Saints have been redeemed and are being redeemed; lost sinners are objects for redemption. They are without Christ in the sense that they remain passively or actively alien to him; but they are not without his Spirit, whose work in the world

[15] *Ibid.*, p. 161.

is to convince men of sin, righteousness, and judgment (the great mysteries, again). Thus, in the most evil of men, the Real Presence makes itself manifest one way or another, as it does in the most saintly. "A Good Man" pictures the mystery of sin (the Misfit, meanness, alienation, and death) and the mystery of godliness (the Grandmother, helpfulness, identification, and death — with a smiling upward into a cloudless sky from a pool of one's own blood).

Nor is the sacramental view of life confined to the words instituting the Sacrament of Holy Communion. It is also in the Lord's words of comfort to the disciples ("I will come again") and in the promise accompanying his commission to them ("Lo, I am with you alway"). This is the essential doctrine of the Real Presence; the sacramental view of life sees the Real Presence of God at work in the lives of sinful men to bring them to redemption.

There is another spirit at work in the lives of men, that of the Evil One, the fallen Lucifer, whose sole obsession is to thwart the purpose of God and thereby deprive him of glory that is his due. Therefore, wherever the activity of the Real Presence is focused on, the manifestation of evil resistance will be particularly evident.

Divine grace is at work in the Grandmother, and it culminates in her triumph over the Misfit because she accepts it. Grace is at work in the Misfit, and it culminates in his complete despair because he rejects it. She is redeemed and triumphant; he is lost and defeated. Her triumph is not simply a final eluding of his power by dying under his exercise of that power; her triumph is a final vindication of her faith over his unbelief by her dying with a smile, while he is forced to self-condemnation with every word he speaks. His evil becomes the testimony to her goodness.

So, the mystery of evil — that man should defy his Creator — is countered with the mystery of redemption — that the Holy God should seek and save the sinner. Wherever the saving has not yet been consummated, the seeking goes on: "Where sin abounded, grace did much more abound" (Romans 5:20).

Even the Misfit, despite all he had decided against Jesus, and despite all he had done against mankind, was not beyond the hope of this grace: "Jesus will help you if you pray," the Grandmother told him. His answer was not unbelief, but defiance: "I don't want no hep." The Grandmother did not condemn the Misfit; she said, "I know you're a good man." The Misfit condemned himself: "Nome, I ain't a good man."

"A Good Man" is the Grandmother's story — the account

of a "good" woman turned in on herself who needed to "act" redeemed if what she professed to believe was to have validity. In story terms, her "problem" was to live up to her faith, to behave in accordance with her deepest convictions, to give instead of to receive. But her living by such a faith was unendurable to those who did not share it and had deliberately repudiated it. Hence, when she lived her faith, she died for it — "If any man will come after me, let him deny himself, and take up his cross daily, and follow me" (Luke 9:23).

The sacramental view of life becomes a vital consideration in exploring a persistent literary question: Why is contemporary fiction by Catholics generally better and more significant than current stories by Protestants?

Professor Tom F. Driver of Union Theological Seminary, New York, advances this thoughtful comment: "Although Protestantism has at its center the principle of protest, the arts function primarily as celebration. Therefore Protestantism has been more effective at voicing critical judgments (which does not necessarily mean acting upon them) than at expressing the body of the faith in works of the imagination."[16]

The idea of "celebration" is as germane to the Sacrament as it is to art; consequently, the sacramental view of life may be inherently more conducive to artistic expression than the propositional stance of nonliturgical traditions. Remembering that the Sacrament is essentially a mystery, however one interprets the communion meal itself, Protestants in general and Fundamentalists or Conservatives in particular do well to think twice about these words from the late Dr. A. W. Tozer, Christian and Missionary Alliance pastor and editor:

> [The beginner in Christ] may consult some of the rationalistic-orthodox theologians who in fancied near-omniscience presume to resolve all Biblical difficulties with a wave of their typewriter. . . . They proceed on the false assumption that everything in heaven and earth can be explained. . . .
>
> Far better than the attempt to understand is the humility that admits its ignorance and waits quietly on God for His own light to appear in His own time. We will be better able to understand when we have accepted the humbling truth that there are many things in heaven and earth that we shall never be able to understand.
>
> The pitiable attempt of churchmen to explain everything for the smiling unbeliever has had an effect exactly opposite to that which

[16] "Thesis for a Playwright Still in Hiding," in *Christian Faith and the Contemporary Arts*, ed. Finley Eversole (New York, 1962), p. 142.

was intended. It has reduced worship to the level of the intellect and introduced the rationalistic spirit into the wonders of religion.

No one should be ashamed to admit that he does not know, and no Christian should fear the effect of such a confession in the realm of things spiritual. Indeed the very power of the cross lies in the fact that it is the wisdom of God and not the wisdom of man. The day we manage to explain everything spiritual will be the day that we have (for ourselves) destroyed everything divine.

...Mystery lies all about us from the atom to the soul of man, and all any of us can do is to bow and say, "O Lord God, thou knowest."[17]

## IV

A deeply committed Christian such as Flannery O'Connor was, once having mastered the techniques of fiction because of a firm belief in the value of story, faced the ultimate challenge to artistic integrity when the reader reactions began to filter back. Since she wrote not only for her readers' enjoyment, but also for their engagement with her vision of truth and reality, she was widely unappreciated and misunderstood.

Numbers of her fellow Roman Catholics found Miss O'Connor too ecumenical for their liking, missing in her writing the parochial flavor which marks so much of the work of Powers, Mauriac, and even Greene. If they do give proper consideration to the fact that she was writing out of her own "country," which was not simply rural Georgia but the Protestant Bible Belt as well, they are uncomfortable that her heroes and heroines are Fundamentalists and Independents, leading some to dismiss her as "a mere chronicler of the decadent South."

Fundamentalists and conservative evangelicals, on the other hand, generally seem to have great difficulty in appreciating her artistry in fiction, having grown accustomed to "Christian novels" that spin out formula romances replete with clichés and jargon. Two questions invariably raised by some readers in this group are these: (1) How can you call that story Christian? (it contains "swear words," or it doesn't present "the way of salvation," etc.); and (2) Will the average reader of stories get the point of what she is trying to say?

It is ironic that Fundamentalists so frequently miss the point in Miss O'Connor's work when she herself felt a strong kinship with them. Alluding to a speech she had given at Loyola University in New Orleans on the subject "The Catholic Writer in the Protestant South," she wrote to me:

[17] *The Root of the Righteous* (Chicago, 1955), pp. 77-80.

> The gist of the lecture was that the Protestant South had more to give such a novelist than anywhere else in this country because in the South belief could still be made believable in relation to a coherent body of manners and a definite idiom, and also because the Biblical background is there to give the writer the extension into sacred history that he must have if he is going to make the Christian message anyway intelligible; and I also said that as far as basic religion went, the Catholic had more in common with the Fundamentalist than with other varieties of Protestant.

It needs to be said also in this connection that we must be fair to a Christian artist, not requiring him to do the whole job of evangelism in a single work any more than we expect the preacher to do it in a single sermon. Some works, like some words, catch attention for God; some expose the plight of the soul without God; some display the wonders of life in God; some *do* show the way — but they *all* make a man pause and consider God.

As for that "average reader," he does often fail to get the message in the O'Connor stories, probably because they were not written for the average reader, but for the discriminating and thoughtful one. The initial publication of her stories was always in the "quality" magazines or the literary quarterlies, never in the mass circulation "slicks." She would not compromise her basic convictions for the sake of sales.

> The Christian writer will feel that in the greatest depth of vision, moral judgment will be implicit and that when we are invited to represent the country according to survey, what we are asked to do is to separate mystery from manners and judgment from vision, in order to produce something a little more palatable to the modern temper. We are asked to form our consciences in the light of statistics, which is to establish the relative as absolute.... In the greatest fiction, the writer's moral sense coincides with his dramatic sense, and I see no way for it to do this unless his moral judgment is part of the very act of seeing, and he is free to use it.[18]

The fact that teachers of literature so often missed the point in her stories was a source of anguish to Miss O'Connor. She wrote to me:

> I've talked to a lot of people who teach "A Good Man Is Hard To Find" and I'm always horrified at what I find they turn it into. I've never been able to convince them that what makes the story work is the grandmother's moment of grace when she reaches out to touch the Misfit. Take that out and the story is nothing. They teach it that the grandmother is a witch, even down to the cat, and that the Misfit is a hero and at no point more so than when he shoots the old lady. It's

[18] *The Living Novel*, pp. 160-161.

> the bias of the age and particularly of the schools and it disturbs me considerably to think that I am feeding it. So you can see that when I find the story understood, as you have understood it, I feel a good deal better about what I am doing. This is the dilemma of the Christian writer—that he doesn't have a believing audience, or if they do believe it's a sentimental kind of belief, not very logical and not capable of facing any unadorned alternatives. . . .

Still, she was not dissuaded from her goals by the misinterpretations. She cherished understanding, but she did not require it in order to believe in what she was doing. A friend quotes her as saying: "I can wait fifty years, a hundred years for it to be understood. It will take awhile for people to see what I mean."[19]

Some do understand. A college teacher wrote to her: "True: 'a good man is hard to find.' But there is *One* (who 'thown everything off balance'); and having seen Him, we can never again find any pleasure in meanness. Without Him, we are all misfits."

A Canadian artist, an avowed atheist, read all of Flannery O'Connor's stories and conceded that "maybe Christianity is real," sensing "the drastic impact of sin and salvation — the inevitability of death — and the violent urgency pervading every story."

A university graduate student came to an O'Connor admirer and said, "I read Flannery O'Connor's two novels last weekend, and I want you to explain to me about salvation."

Literary critics, of whatever religious persuasion or degree of skepticism, seemed to know what Miss O'Connor was driving at, though some of them had trouble finding words for it since it did not fit into their thought patterns. (It is worth noting that while her first novel received fewer than twenty reviews, her second eight years later received nearly sixty.)

## V

One April afternoon in the year before her death, Flannery O'Connor and I visited together on the wide screened porch of the white farmhouse at "Andalusia." Speaking gratefully of François Mauriac, I commented on what seemed to me a striking spiritual resemblance between her work and his. Immediately she replied that he was the greatest single influence on her as a writer, and she shared with me three favorite volumes of his which she fetched from the massive old bookcase in the parlor.

In 1952, the year that Miss O'Connor's first novel was pub-

[19] *Esprit*, VIII, i (Winter, 1964), 27.

lished, Mauriac said, in accepting the Nobel Prize for Literature:

> A writer who focuses his work on human being made in the image of the Father, redeemed by the Son, and illumined by the Holy Spirit could never, possibly, as I see it, be considered a master of despair, no matter how somber a picture he paints.
>
> True, the coloring still remains somber. That is because he sees human nature as wounded, if not corrupted. It stands to reason that the human story as told by a Christian novelist is no idyll, since he is forbidden to shut his eyes to the mystery of evil.[20]

This, surely, was the vision of Flannery O'Connor. Whatever other questions may remain unresolved, this one is answered by a resounding *Yes* in her work: Can a Christian who is thoroughly committed to orthodoxy write, in times like these, imaginative fiction of first quality that bears witness to the Gospel of Jesus Christ? Flannery O'Connor was a "Christian writer" (not just a Christian who wrote) whose viewing of everything in life in the singular light of Redemption by Christ inspired her to produce "Christian stories" in which her storytelling genius made the very materials of fiction serve to reveal the mystery of God's redeeming grace.

[20] *Words of Faith* (New York, 1955), p. 74.

# The Writer That Is to Be

## WARD S. MILLER

Once it was customary, especially in this country, to think of writers as original, creative spirits who would have been damaged by exposure to college disciplines, even literary. This was the era when lawyers learned their profession by apprenticeship and the colleges offered little more than a very basic schooling in languages, especially in Latin and Greek, in literature, and in "natural" science. There existed a widespread prejudice against college education for most nonprofessional purposes, which continued well into the present century. It was encouraged by self-made men of many varieties, including numerous writers like Horatio Alger, Jr., who have slipped into well-earned oblivion.

For aspiring authors, Shakespeare, with his allegedly "small Latin and less Greek," was the classic example of what a writer could become if he did not let the college system shrink his head to humanistic size. Defoe, Steele, Samuel Johnson, Lamb, Keats, Burns, Dickens, George Eliot, and numerous second-rate authors

---

Ward Searing Miller is Professor of English and currently chairman of the department at the University of Redlands. A Phi Beta Kappa graduate of Denison University in 1929, he taught and supervised publications in a Rochester, New York, high school in the 1930s and served in the U. S. Navy from 1942 to 1946 as a technical writer and editor. After the war he taught at the University of Rochester before moving to Redlands in 1949. Ph.D. work (Iowa, 1955) led to publication in the *Huntington Library Quarterly*. In addition to *Word Wealth* and *Word Wealth Junior,* vocabulary-building textbooks for secondary schools, he has written a manual on article-writing and many professional and popular articles. As chairman of Writer's Week at Redlands for more than ten years and as teacher and later Dean of the Extension School of Writing at Green Lake, Wisconsin, he has come to know many professional writers personally. He held a Fulbright Lectureship in Finland (1962-63) and another in Jordan that ended in evacuation in 1967.

of the twentieth century, especially in the United States, helped to bolster the list. The fact that Milton, Dryden, Addison, Swift, Sterne, Fielding, Wordsworth, Byron, Carlyle, Tennyson, Arnold, and most of the American writers who figured in the "flowering" of New England were college trained — not to mention Henry James — was not publicized. Nor was the very evident fact that Pope (with tutors, because he was ineligible for the universities on religious grounds) compensated or overcompensated for his handicap and in so doing became a conspicuously learned man. Yet Herman Melville, Mark Twain, Walt Whitman, and Jack London are conspicuous among those who make it difficult for Americans to think of writers as learned persons, as college graduates, or as professional men.

Today one can hardly insist that the image is changing. Americans are attending college in phenomenal numbers, but writers are almost invariably pictured in the *Saturday Review* as earthy, muscular, proletarian, with their sport shirts open at the collar and with an apparent contempt for things intellectual, traditional, or "bourgeois."

Thirty years ago Bernard DeVoto could still claim with perhaps some justice that "College is a foolproof device for destroying originality and crippling individuality."[1] No longer does this ringing half-truth carry conviction, however. The New Criticism in the 1940s and 1950s made scholars more resourcefully analytic than they were before, and a rising tide of liberating influence has since made the colleges, if anything, too tolerant of every conceivable kind of innovation in the fine arts.

The truth is that the four leading novelists who emerged in the decade of Mr. DeVoto's dictum do not quite corroborate it. Ernest Hemingway and William Faulkner did not go to college, it is true,[2] but Willa Cather took an A.B. degree at the University of Nebraska, and John Steinbeck studied for five years at Stanford. William Faulkner, however, though he did not finish high school, nevertheless acquired a Yale training in literature at second hand through his friend Phil Stone in Oxford, Mississippi.[3] His intensive studies subsequently of Twain, Hawthorne, Dostoevsky, James, Joyce, and others — not to mention the Bible — could conceivably have qualified him for an earned doctorate. He was thus a man "learned" in literature, and

[1] This quotation comes down in written as well as oral form from my own college years. I have not been able to trace it to any printed source.

[2] Faulkner did have a single rather fruitless year at the University of Mississippi.

[3] Robert Coughlan, "The Man Behind the Faulkner Myth," *Life*, XXXV, xiv (Oct. 5, 1953), 55ff.

these studies make his writings a worthy projection of the Western literary heritage in perspective and techniques to a probably greater degree than Cather, Hemingway, or Steinbeck could claim. Hemingway had a deeper knowledge of literature than most readers would suspect; and Steinbeck hardly surpasses either, though he was unusually well read. His familiarity with the Bible rivals Faulkner's.

Whatever the popular image of the writer may be today, it is clear that the future of literature belongs more and more to the universities. This is true not merely because there have arisen since DeVoto's day such writing centers as Stanford, Iowa, Michigan, and Missouri, but because increasing numbers of colleges offer increasingly competent courses in creative writing. At times in such courses, and even outside of them, a talent like that of Jesse Stuart will encounter a teacher like Henry Harrison Kroll, and two important names will emerge in literary artistry and literary history. The very large percentage of our most capable youth who now go to college, the greatly augmented number of literate readers since the 1930s, and the intricacy of our inner and outer worlds all but guarantee that future writers of enduring fame will come almost wholly from those who have attended college.

There is, after all, no better place to absorb the history, the literature, and the philosophies of the past. There is no better place to explore the literary heritage and relate oneself to it. There is no better place to investigate the contemporary world in all of its protean aspects, including a cross-section of its future participants.

In such an atmosphere, with the right teachers, one can discover and experiment with the modes, techniques, and structures of writing art as one can do nowhere else. One can find out what he wants to say, and learn how to say it; the greatest obstacle is immaturity. A student may subsequently need several years of comparative solitude to find himself, as Steinbeck did — along with Hawthorne, Melville, Tennyson, Pope, Wordsworth, and numerous others, all the way back into Bible history. In most cases the years of solitude came after the best that schools could give, even though the schooling itself offers an example of Toynbee's principle of withdrawal and return.

## II

Obviously, if writing is increasingly centered in the colleges, it follows that the colleges need to be concerned more than ever with their responsibility in this as in other creative fields. A majority have courses in creative writing, though sometimes it is still called "advanced composition." Some bring visiting writers and critics or maintain a series of writers in residence. One question is asked almost daily, however: Can creative writing be taught?

The simple answer that chokes off all argument and silences almost all of the sceptics is probably a truthful one: No. Yet somehow Henry Harrison Kroll played midwife or catalyst to Jesse Stuart, the Paris expatriates launched Ernest Hemingway, Ezra Pound cut *The Waste Land* almost in half, and Booth Tarkington wielded a beneficent blue pencil on the early works of Kenneth Roberts. If editing is a method of "teaching," all four examples are germane; and one could compile dozens more. It seems highly probable that those who write well the kind of thing the student wants to write are best qualified to train him.

One may argue by analogy also. Presumably painting can be taught, musical composition has a place in the curriculum of most music schools, and teaching — which is also an art — is everywhere thought a fit subject for instruction. Why, then, cannot creative writing be taught?

The exact truth seems to be that the craftsmanship of writing *can* be taught, but not the ultimate artistry or perceptivity by which specific writings are formed. One can teach story structure, but not in such a definitive way that it provides anything more than guidelines, road signs, or topographical maps for a freely ranging imagination with its clouds of controlling insights both artistic and thematic. There can be little question that, somehow or other, writing classes, writing exercises, writers' conferences, and writers in residence are not in vain, that all may prove helpful to emerging creativity if competently carried out by well-qualified persons. Whether these methods help or not, however, it is clear that writing talent can at least be cultivated; and that is the safest way to approach the problem.

The garden analogy is an especially fortunate one for the art and the artistry of writing. A garden is, first of all, a place of beauty. Its plantings are varied, and each grows according to inner laws and necessities which the gardener can change but little. He can only cultivate them, furnishing encouragement in the form of nutrients of just the right kind, pruning them judiciously, adjusting their conditions according to the season, and helping them in other ways to fulfill to the utmost their inherent capacities. He can suppress hindrances, protect plants from pests, and hasten their growth in various other ways. He can uproot and destroy them, too, either wantonly or by accident.

A gardener is well trained in his field of activity. He is not necessarily a botanist, though it is probably better that he be an expert in this related field. Yet there are many gardening skills and insights that a botanist does not possess unless he has studied and practiced gardening.

If the analogy is valid, it clarifies the problem of being a teacher of creative writing. It implies that teaching requires skills, experience, and interests that are no necessary or normal part of purely literary scholarship or of a doctoral training. It implies also that the professor who cultivates writing talent needs a firm grasp of whatever laws or principles exist for the guidance and care of emerging talent and also for the detection of such talent. The theory is likely to prove easier than the practice, however; and a teacher-writer needs more than his own creative experience and practice — which one assumes to be prerequisite, but which is hardly a broad enough base for the duty of sponsoring a diverse assortment of young writers.

The limitation inherent in the teacher who is merely a published writer may well be that he can cultivate only images of himself or that he will somehow induce young writers to conform to his own practices and insights. He may try unsuccessfully to avoid this. The more fully he knows literature as scholarship, however, the wider will be his knowledge of the varied patterns, experiences, and problems of emerging writers in various eras and under various conditions. He will be less likely to conceive of himself, even unconsciously, as a matrix, and more as a gardener. Obviously a doctor's degree is an asset rather than a handicap.

Unfortunately, little has been written that will help the professor of creative writing directly. A compilation like Brewster Ghiselin's *The Creative Process*[4] is helpful, but it belongs more to the botanist than the gardener. It tells how certain writers work, how their creations took shape and grew, and what experiences have been relevant. Only by implication does such a book tell how one may foster creativity. The *Paris Review* interviews a few years ago offer a more practical approach.[5] They provide stimulating accounts of how authors live, think, and work. They tend to be superficial, however, providing only material from which inductions may be drawn about creativity rather than the kind of carefully tested principles and precepts that a teacher needs and can generate for himself only at great risks to the "plants" in his "garden." The long series of paper-

[4] New York, 1955 (Mentor Books).

[5] Published under the title *Writers at Work* (New York, 1963).

backs called *New World Writing*[6] presented, perhaps prematurely, the work of young writers under cultivation but showed more of the need than of methods of cultivation.

Another fact must be recognized. The kind of paternalism that Booth Tarkington, Ezra Pound, and others bestowed on their respective protégés functioned as a semifinal stage in the production of important literary works rather than in any sense a formative one. The relationship of Maxwell Perkins to Thomas Wolfe and other writers comes nearer to being a case study in cultivation;[7] but it, too, is only an intermediate stage in the productivity of a talent already well past its crucial early stages.

From the now standard theory of creativity and from much accumulated experience with young writers, it is possible to deduce a number of useful precepts that do in practice prove useful. It is also possible to list some of the dangers a teacher of creative writing needs to avoid. First of all, however, it is necessary to determine, from the accumulated dicta of literary criticism and from the broadest attainable spectrum of values, *what are the ultimate objectives of the talent one proposes to cultivate.* One can approach these objectives only by attempting to demonstrate the breadth and extent of the garden one proposes to cultivate. One must survey literally the whole of the world's literary heritage before he can offer principles or precepts by which to treat the flora or fauna he finds in the garden he is to cultivate.

## III

To put it more simply, the gardener needs a wide knowledge of and a wide tolerance for many kinds of creativity, both in artistic and in thematic terms. As professor of creative writing, he is far more than a talent scout, born to make the fittest survive and relegate the rest to one of the nine circles. He is looking first of all for geniuses, capable of the highest creative attainments, but in his realistic moments he knows he can hardly expect to find more than one or two in a lifetime. This one or these two will be for most laymen the summit of his achievement and the sole justification of a lifetime of endeavor, if he helped them; they will be his nemeses if he failed to help them or they failed to appreciate what he did for them. In

[6] No longer published (15 vols., New York, 1951-58; 7 vols., Philadelphia, 1959-64), but see *New Writings in S-F*, ed. John Carnell (London, I [1964].-.

[7] It was something more than mere editing. See Richard S. Kennedy, *The Window of Meaning* (Chapel Hill, 1962), pp. 173-178 and, especially, 259-262.

either case, he cannot build a career or teach a course every year for one or two persons in a lifetime.

Obviously, he must work over hundreds of tons of pitchblende to find one gram of radium; but the analogy fortunately is a false one. He is looking for one prizewinner in several thousand specimens, but he cultivates all of them because each is worth the trouble. He is, above all else, serving human beings, not just one but many, all of whom have aspirations, talent, inner needs, or all three. It is his duty to help each one fulfil his own potentialities, in this as in every other field of human endeavor.

In doing this, the professor of creative writing can scarcely fail to realize that there are at least four major motives for literary creativity, all of them equally respectable. They may overlap, and a literary achievement of the highest merit may be the product of all four motives. It may have arisen chiefly or initially from any one of the four. They must be examined separately, however.

The first and the most immediate motive for creative writing, especially in the terms of college objectives, is cultural; and it is this motive or result that chiefly justifies existence of a course or of course credit for creative writing. Writing still maketh a clear man, and few activities foster the finding of one's identity or an initiation into life's depths and values more effectively. It sharpens one's observations of surface and motive alike, it generates wisdom, and it preserves experience as a kind of laboratory record, if nothing more. It enriches every area to which it is applied.

A second motivation not always or necessarily recognized as such is therapeutic. Writing is the student's couch, and the teacher of creative writing must play the role, not so much of artistic taskmaster as of father confessor, without having a degree in either theology or psychiatry. If he is worthy of a teaching post at all, however, he possesses a certain amount of practical competence as a counselor, and a vast amount of tolerance. He has a responsibility which he may often need to share with a person professionally more able. But no one else can serve better than the trusted teacher as a catalyst, so that the student's writing attains primarily the author's purpose, rather than the teacher's. In so doing it attains the values most important for the student.

The third motivation is commercial, and it calls for a tolerance not always available in college English departments. It also calls for a kind of competence professors sometimes take more pride in not possessing than in acquiring. Commercial requirements are very exacting and very specialized. They do not always align themselves well with the highest principles of artistic integrity. Nevertheless, commercial writing is as respectable and honest a way to earn a living as any other, for the few who have the faith and determination. Moreover, commercial writing provides, more often than not, a way station on the route to loftier attainments. Teachers who discourage commercial motives in writing can hardly claim they are serving humanity or their students to the fullest, especially in the case of writers with talent suited to this kind of creativity.

The fourth or artistic motive is naturally the ultimate and the most gratifying to the teacher. He will readily accept as a solemn duty the professional obligation to cultivate the finest aspirations of literary art, adapting himself as fully as possible to the artistic individuality of the author. He will inject just the right amount of constructive criticism and just the right amount that is derogatory, if he can find out how much is just right. He will do this with a degree of perceptivity and rapport that enables him at times to participate in the author's creativity, modulating and perfecting it. It is at this point that he needs the largest possible degree of cultural breadth and depth, even that of a Ben Jonson or a Cervantes.

Before considering the ultimate boundaries of the writing professor's cultural adequacy, however, it is necessary to point out a fact not always recognized by professional writers. It is more important for the teacher than the professional, if he is to serve his students and his world to the best advantage. The fact is simply stated: There are not three or five but a hundred kinds of writing that require talent, art, training, and a pragmatic adaptation of the means to the end.

It is all too easy for inmates or apprentices in the groves of Academe to imagine that trade fiction, poetry, and essays are the only kind of writing to which a self-respecting student should address himself. These are merely the most familiar of the traditional routes to literary fame, however.

Actually, trade fiction is one of the less promising routes, if only because it is overtrodden today and somewhat overshadowed by nonfiction. If a first novel is published at all, it may be the only one accepted out of hundreds submitted. Once published, it has five chances in one hundred of becoming a best seller. If it is one of the ninety-five that do not become best sellers, it will linger on the bookstore shelves only a few months, bringing the publisher at best barely enough to pay the cost of publication. It will bring the author anything from a few hundred to perhaps three thousand dollars, usually a small return for the time he has spent on it. He will be expected to plow under even this small sum in advertising for his second or third novel. He will get little or no literary recognition, probably, and his hopes of becoming known are still quite limited.

Nonfiction in our day has outstripped fiction in range and demand. The chances of finding a wide readership in this field are therefore greater than in fiction, and it offers a more promising foundation for a writing career as well as a training ground and even a meal ticket while one is exploring the rarer air of a literary Parnassus. In nonfiction, a new book is less likely to be pushed aside in a few weeks. It may go on for years. Also, its topic will attract buyers, and the author does not have to depend wholly upon his unknown name.

Periodical fiction is another large field, in which dozens of writers have made a name and remained or moved on to less perishable achievements. It is worth the art to do it well, it is useful to society, and it ranges all the way from pulp fiction to the little magazines. Included are children's stories, juvenile fiction, romances for women's magazines, and adventure stories for a dozen different men's magazines. The field also includes psychological stories, mystery stories, science fiction, and literary stories such as one finds in the *Atlantic* and the *New Yorker*. These "literary" stories are always more character-minded and more sophisticated but not necessarily more artistic than action stories with their "round" or "flat" characters in middle-range and "lowbrow" periodicals.

Church periodicals, which use hundreds of stories a month in every age range, have helped to impel several writers of note toward distinguished later careers; even confession stories have an unquestioned educational and guidance value for teenagers and young married women. It is narrow-minded, if not fanatical, to imagine that only stories for the *Atlantic* and the little magazines are worth doing in the field of short fiction.

Essays are rewarding to read and to write, but the magazine article is no less so. It is more informative, more viable, and also more vendible. If art is as much a matter of skillfully applied psychology as it clearly is in fiction, from Homer on down, the article form is no less artistic than the essay. It has been perfected in the intense competition among magazines today in their struggle for survival. Unlike newswriting and mere journalism, the magazine article requires amazing unity, coherence, and emphasis. It uses all the techniques of fiction to make it attractive, readable, compelling, and at times comprehensive. Moreover, well-written magazine articles of every kind serve a democratic society in a way that makes them indispensable throughout the entire range of topics, coverage, and style in the hundreds of periodicals in which they appear. Why should English departments take so little interest in a form that owes much more to the timeless canons of good "literary" writing than to the disjointed journalistic writing of which it is alleged to be the offshoot?

Even textbooks offer a large field for creative ability to those who possess or will acquire the necessary knowledge and teaching skill. Textbooks need to be as well done as edited texts of literary classics. A majority are not, however, especially on the college level, as Oscar Handlin demonstrated with singular forcefulness some years ago.[8] A really excellent textbook may go on — with revisions to keep the copyright date fresh — for ten, twenty, or thirty years. It may serve humanity and even art more handsomely than a dozen stories in the little magazines or half a dozen published novels. The income it provides may liberate the author and enable him to do something more belletristic and possibly less valuable, if he has the will and the skills.

To say all this is not to deny or minimize the fact that a work of fiction, a book of poems, or a play that attains the highest levels of literary excellence is still the supreme achievement of writing talent and the one most to be desired of a person who has the ability to produce it.

As already pointed out, however, hardly one in twenty or even one in a hundred of the conventionally talented students who elect a class in creative writing is likely to attain such a summit. There is neither the room nor the oxygen at that level for more than a handful. Many feel called, and many undoubtedly have the technical ability, but only two or three in a hundred have the perseverance, the faith, the daring, the endurance, or whatever it is that determines. No doubt luck is a factor. Birth is a factor too. So is happening or contriving to know the right people along the way.

In surveying the many kinds of writing that are useful and satisfying, then, one must be more objective and less selective. Art is to a very large extent a matter of degree, and the crucial difference between the kind of published literary creativity a professor of English likes or reads and the kind he does not like, read, or know about is a matter of how fully the material was adapted to his particular intellectual capacities and tastes rather than to artistic values as such. He often thinks there is more art in that which addresses itself to him than in that which makes the esoteric complexities of our life and world more intelligible to

[8] "Textbooks That Don't Teach," *Atlantic*, CC, vi (Dec. 1957), 110-113.

millions of literate but unliterary readers. The issue is at least debatable.

## IV

Having established a perspective from which a thousand varieties of creative writing need to be seen by him who would cultivate adequately all of the talents that offer themselves, one must now concentrate on the few rather than the many. What is good for the few can scarcely harm the many if artistry is a matter of degree rather than kind. Therapeutic or cultural motivation must not be discouraged, of course, by being compelled to attain beyond its desire or capacity. The methods of attaining excellence are the same for all, however, as in any other class a student might select. Each student progresses as far as he can or will toward the subtlest and most complex attainment. He finds satisfaction either subjectively or objectively — or both.

Fortunately, one does not need to identify a future Hemingway or Willa Cather even if he has one in his class. The professor can be fairly sure that this person will not resemble Hemingway or Cather in a superficial way, and presumably will not give any clearer evidence of genius than these two did in the published but quite undistinguished writings of their youth.

One is not surprised, for example, that William Cullen Bryant at sixteen was writing graveyard poetry or that he never got beyond or differed much from the kind of nature poetry that was being written in England a few decades before his time. Nor is one surprised that Dryden at nineteen wrote an elegiac poem in the tradition to which *Lycidas* belongs or that it overstepped the bounds of good taste to an almost ludicrous degree because the author had not learned to control his metaphoric gift more judiciously.[9] In fact the best writers are usually fortunate if their youthful work is destroyed instead of being preserved and even published many years later when creativity begins to lag.

The truth is that young writers of great talent are almost invariably imitative and rarely, if ever, brilliantly original. Also, first novels are virtually certain to be autobiographical, and at least a majority may be justified solely on the value that each has for its author in release or self-discovery.

Is there any way to recognize genius, as opposed to mere talent? The question is trite, but one must ask it in the process of discovering what causes a novel, a play, or a poem to be called

[9] The poem is "Upon the Death of the Lord Hastings," with its "blisters . . . / Like rose-buds, stuck i' th' lily skin about." The next line reads: "Each little pimple had a tear in it."

a work of genius. If one can find out on the top level in a work like *Don Quixote* or *The Sound and the Fury* what skills and knowledge are required, it is possible to encourage or inculcate them in young writers. If they are primarily inborn, one knows what to watch for. But how can one know?

The familiar saws about genius are as trite as the question. Is genius "a compelling desire to work along a given line"?[10] Obviously, the desire is a prerequisite to the attainment — and obviously little more. A dozen, indeed a hundred young writers have the desire, and many of them will consider it compelling, but only one or two will turn out to be the author of "a distinguished work of genius."

Is genius "an infinite capacity for taking pains"?[11] Almost invariably, one would think, among other things. It is other qualities that must concern us most.

Does genius consist of 99 percent perspiration and only 1 percent inspiration, as Edison maintained?[12] The confessions of numerous authors, including Hemingway, bear this out — without offering a really illuminating answer to the question.

The only way to attain a definitive concept of genius is obviously the inductive method. One must examine persons or works widely recognized as examples of the highest levels of genius and try to discover why they are so regarded. In English literature, Chaucer, Shakespeare, and Milton would be among the first to be named, and there would be great difficulty in agreeing on a fourth — for reasons that may prove explainable. In world literature, works like *Don Quixote, The Divine Comedy, Moby Dick,* the *Aeneid,* the *Iliad,* the *Odyssey,* Plato's *Dialogues* and probably the best plays of Sophocles would be listed on the top level, and there would be a second level, clearly distinguishable but more difficult to analyze.

If we take Shakespeare as exemplar because he is quite generally considered the greatest of all English writers (except by Marxists, and this is significant),[13] how can we account for

[10] I have not been able to locate the source of this familiar definition.

[11] A correspondent for *Notes and Queries,* Sept. 13, 1879, claims that Miss Jane Hopkins, a social reformer, was the first to use these words. The definition has also been attributed to Charles Dickens. Thomas Carlyle, J. M. Barrie, and Samuel Butler the Younger said substantially the same thing in slightly different words, according to the *Home Book of Quotations.*

[12] In a newspaper interview quoted in *Golden Book,* April 1931. It was William Hogarth who offered the supreme oversimplification: "Genius is nothing but labour and diligence."

[13] See, for example, Herbert Read, "Surrealism and the Romantic Principle," and Ralph Fox, "Marxism and Literature." Both are included in

his preeminence? Is his "genius" reducible to a combination of traits, skills, sensitivities, and knowledge? What does he have in common with Cervantes or Milton and not with an admitted genius on the second level, like Shelley or Dryden?

At first the task seems hopeless. Critics for centuries have been trying to analyze Shakespeare. It is the very diversity of their conclusions that provides the most promising clue, however, and makes a long, exhaustive analysis unnecessary. The clue is this: if the explanations are hopelessly diverse, it is because all or most of them are valid. In other words, Shakespeare had all the capacities, skills, sensitivities and knowledge attributed to him by widely assorted and often quite contentious admirers, but these admirers have behaved very much like the six blind men of John Saxe's poem who were trying to describe an elephant.

The soundness of this clue can be shown by pointing out five major facets of Shakespeare's dramatic supremacy. The first is his talent for structure. It stands out especially when any of his later plays is compared with, say, *The Duchess of Malfi.* It is implicit in the stories he selected — in contrast with stories he did not undertake — as well as in the skill with which he altered or adapted them to his purposes. His structural genius shows perhaps most clearly in these purposes as they may be deduced. It was presumably this facet of his genius and not merely conformity to custom that led him to utilize well-known and well-proved stories rather than to invent his own; and yet he showed in *The Tempest* what he might have done had he chosen to be more audaciously original in creating plots.

A second facet of Shakespeare's genius is his unequalled mastery of theatrical devices, effects, illusions, and spectacles. In these he displayed a distinctly different kind of superiority, one for which the stage experience of all the preceding centuries could hardly equip him as it could with plots.

One must add to his theatrical talent a third and even more impressive fact: merely as a poet Shakespeare has few if any peers. This facet, like the others, has been too widely recognized to need any demonstration. George Bernard Shaw oversimplified it memorably: Shakespeare's power lies in his "enormous command of word music."[14]

*Criticism: The Foundations of Modern Literary Judgment,* ed. Mark Schorer *et al.* (New York, 1948).

[14] Archibald Henderson, *George Bernard Shaw* (New York, 1956), p. 697. Shaw also said, "In manner and art nobody can write better than Shakespeare" (p. 709). He has been quoted as saying, "It's simply the way he has of putting things," but I have not been able to verify this specific quotation.

Not less important than his way of putting things were the things he put, and it is these in which the knowledge and wisdom of genius seem to inhere most conspicuously. It is the realm of what is sometimes called learning, but learning is merely its body, not its spirit or soul, and it arises from life as much as from books and often more. Knowledge is an ingredient of genius, but only as a reservoir or means, a kind of surrounding sea in which one lives, moves, and has his being.

More than anything else, Shakespeare's genius culminates in his characters, the marvelous way in which he understands, projects, adapts, motivates, humanizes and individualizes them. So great is this talent for imaginative projection that it is difficult (though not impossible) to find Shakespeare in his plays. More validly than Whitman he could boast, "I contain multitudes." At the very least, he could project them all with consummate skill. It is doubtful if any other playwright has projected so many so well.

A final facet of Shakespeare's genius is his use of contrasts to heighten his effects — characters, light and dark scenes, prose and poetry, wise man and fool, the scholar and the practical man, and comic scenes to relieve yet heighten tragic situations. This facet is familiar enough, but it attains a special pervasiveness or resourcefulness in Shakespeare.

The definitive fact of Shakespeare's genius thus turns out to be his well-rounded wholeness, and it is that wholeness that helps one understand why his very conspicuous faults have marred his fame and his currency so little. It also suggests a hypothesis or theory of the nature of genius which is hardly new but needs to be examined to discover if it is not, after all, the ultimate explanation. It may be stated in five words: In literature genius is synthesis.

On the highest levels, it is invariably more than one or two kinds of superiority that one discovers; it is a configuration of several quite different kinds. Does this hypothesis help to explain the preeminence of, say, Cervantes in Spanish literature? Many volumes have been written about Cervantes, but the ultimate facts are simple and clear. In his maturity Cervantes wrote one book that stands among the top ten in world literature.

In the last analysis, *Don Quixote* stands out by virtue of the *totality* of its achievement. The unmatched magnitude and symmetry of its structure is only one facet, with Part II ingeniously counterbalancing and complementing Part I, and Part I enlivened, enriched, and illuminated by the novellas. These novellas in turn present as comprehensive and orderly a study of the varieties of amorous adventure as one can find anywhere. These give the work, simply in structural terms, a leavening effect enhancing what might otherwise become a monotonous, overblown sequence of quixotic absurdities.

The book at the same time rivals Shakespeare's best in its range and variety of well-realized characters, its pervasive use of contrasts, and its protean knowledge, insight, wisdom — with Sancho Panza's unfailing proverbs as a particularly memorable feature. *Don Quixote* thus proves in these and a number of other ways to be a work of the most ambitious synthesis, excelling all comparable works at almost every point where comparison may be made. By its combination of knowledgeability, structural skill, character projections, variety, and comprehensiveness it thus well deserves the reputation it has gained and is not likely to lose that reputation.

One may appraise a dozen other such works of similar or somewhat lesser magnitude in the same way with comparable results. Thus under this kind of analysis *Paradise Lost* turns out to be a well-integrated synthesis of the Hebraic and the Hellenic heritage in an era that almost compelled a writer to overemphasize one or the other. It combines a timeless subject with the highest kind of poetic genius and structural skill, including contrasts in an era averse to them. The result is an epic on the level of the classical epics, the only one of a score or more of Renaissance epic efforts that lives today. It has a universal appeal because it has proved uniquely rewarding, whether approached primarily as a literary work or as a biblical treatise.

One could go on for many pages. *Tom Jones* is a work like *Don Quixote* but indigenously English, less ambitious in structure but well provided with memorable characters in a wide variety of actions, and wonderfully knowledgeable. *Moby Dick* is even more indigenously American on an epic level and much less like *Don Quixote* except in its comprehensiveness. In the most celebrated works of Greek literature like *Oedipus Rex* one finds the same combination of structural genius, characterization, poetic talent, human appeal, and profound wisdom. The *Iliad* and the *Odyssey* are achievements in the same kind of synthesis, which no one seems likely to surpass.

## V

If this synthesis principle is sound, what significance does it have for young writers and their professor-gardeners? Especially for their professors, because a full realization of the nature of genius is as likely to discourage as it is to inspire the fledgling. Although at best only one young writer in hundreds will attain the highest level, the precepts by which young writers live must be soundly based on the ultimate nature of literary achievement, as we have seen. Several precepts may be deduced from such studies.

In the first place, *basic techniques are important to the point of being indispensable*—all of the devices that make characters come alive, all of those which stir feeling, lend variety, and foster insight. They include live verbs, sharp images, sense appeals, fresh figures of speech, good dialogue, thought transcription, and various devices of depth psychology. Student writers are often impatient with techniques, and writers often learn them best from their reading. Yet the greatest writers have rarely succeeded in any generation without techniques as the basic level of communication.

These techniques are scarcely less necessary on a merely professional level of writing, whenever it seeks to be affective.[15] No other means have been devised; and these cannot change until human nature does, because each is an application of applied psychology. The only innovation of the twentieth century in techniques has been an elaboration of stream-of-consciousness and other devices for the communication of thoughts, and these scarcely go beyond the ones employed in *Tristram Shandy.*

A second precept, universally recognized but not always accorded its full importance, is that *character study is the core of all fiction writing* as well as much nonfiction. This principle can hardly change, though its focus may. The preoccupation in our day with deranged, disorganized, and even monstrous characters marks such a change of focus, and it may prove justifiable. The cult of the antihero has its familiar and doubtless valid rationale.

The methods of communicating character are not often set down and are probably not sufficiently stressed. Douglas Bement and Ross M. Taylor in *The Fabric of Fiction* listed nine;[16] young writers do not readily learn to use all of them resourcefully. Practice is important as they gain skill appropriate to their years in observing behavior like a scientist, in contrasting the outward

[15] The best presentation I have seen of these basic techniques is found in a book by L. A. Sherman, *How to Describe and Narrate Visually* (Garden City, N.Y., 1928). Though out of print, it is one of the very few writing books published before 1950 which are now of any value.

[16] New York, 1948. The methods are these: by exposition, by description, by action, by setting and tastes, by dialogue, by opinion of other people or reputation, by thought, and by a mixture of the other seven methods (pp. 93-326). A ninth is added: the inverse method by which a first impression is shown to be dramatically wrong.

with the inward, and in resourcefully utilizing every scrap of evidence in imaginary and in real life. Moreover, skill in imaginative projection must be cultivated in every conceivable way by students and their teachers in persistent conspiracies of empathetic adventure. They must together learn all the ways of understanding and projecting character. These certainly include wide reading and personal experience of many kinds as well as tireless note-taking and practice. Skill will come if not great art, and cultural or therapeutic benefit will accumulate.

The third precept is more controversial: *The values and verities that literature celebrates and by which it lives are very ancient.* They come from classical as well as Hebraic sources, and it is doubtful that they can, will, or should change greatly. As far as *mores* and effects are concerned, it is quite clear from much historical study that societies that reject these values and verities do not endure. Yet to say this is not to deny that social renewal and creativity is one of the values. Arnold Toynbee in discussing the "Nemesis of Creativity" affirms its value on a quasi-theological level, tracing the loss of social, spiritual, industrial, and literary creativity to three kinds of stagnation: idolization of (1) the ephemeral self, (2) the ephemeral institution, and (3) the ephemeral technique.[17] In his view surfaces and exteriors change, but not basic values. New means must at intervals be devised, but not new ends.

A fourth precept needs not recognition so much as emphasis in the fullest and broadest sense of the term: *Knowledge is far more important than techniques or literary skill,* if only because it is so much harder to attain in sufficient quantities and because it takes so much longer. "Knowledge" is not a good word, "learning" is even more academic in its connotations, and "wisdom" is too much a result rather than the source of a writer's normal and necessary medium. Obviously, knowledge means all kinds of information and insight from all kinds of sources and experiences, and not merely knowledge gained in literature or even in college textbooks generally. *This principle makes it desirable that widespread reading play as large a part as it can in writing courses* to enhance but not to overshadow the practice of writing, and to permit a variety of experiences.

A fifth precept pertains to writing as such and it stands out prominently in the study of genius: *Structure is of the utmost importance* in every kind of literary art. It is far more vital than students can sometimes be induced to believe, and often it is

[17] *A Study of History* (Somervell Abridgment of Vols. I-VI, Oxford, 1947), pp. 307-336.

crucial. All too often students are led to believe that genius is marked by its eagerness to break all the rules and thus produce a masterpiece. This notion is a half-truth which must be patiently and repeatedly corrected. A vigorous and original young writer will frequently break one or two "rules" out of a dozen or two that apply; and these are likely to be rules that have but limited relevance, or even none at all, as in the case of the Neo-Classic rules for writing plays. Shakespeare was set down as an iconoclast because he did not know or observe them. The truth is, of course, that Shakespeare's method of creating plays was better founded alike in classical practice and ultimate principles of psychology than the Neo-Classic "rules" of seventeenth-century French drama; his vigorous survival has vindicated both the classical practice (at its best) and the psychological principles, while the highly artificial rules resulted in dozens of English plays now almost forgotten.

It is also hard for students to understand that a work of literature never fails *because* it has good structure or other virtues. It is shortcomings in some other area, including audience appeal or universality, that prevent a work from attaining viability or vendibility. Butler's *Hudibras* is a convenient example of a work that has unusually good structure and characters. Voltaire called it the wittiest work in English. It fails largely because it is too monotonously witty, as well as too specialized. It does not stir the kind of sympathy for the protagonist that makes the reader feel and care as he does in *Don Quixote*. The Don attains tragic overtones, with strong pathos at times, because the reader admires and to some degree identifies with him as he never does with Sir Hudibras.

The next precept proves especially controversial. It will be denied volubly by many English majors and their professors: *Partisanship is a hazardous and damaging condition for a writer.* It has its place in the forum and the marketplace as a stance — political, social, literary, religious, or whatever else may be needed. The best writers are like Tiresias, however. They thrive on controversy, tension, and conflict, of course, but they do not take sides on anything less than good versus evil in its most timeless and most universal frames of reference; and they may even come to see evil the way God himself must, as a timebound and transient means toward eternal good. They portray both sides, without committing themselves, often at quite a cost. They live and think as God himself may be thought to do, permitting evil in order that good may come or that the evil will destroy itself.

Chaucer is a good example, and his impartiality shows most

clearly in his churchmen. He portrays the best and the worst. He includes stories of every type for his remarkably varied assortment of pilgrims. On the same highly sensitive topic of religious figures, George Bernard Shaw is similarly impartial and objective. His Morell in *Candida,* his Anderson in *The Devil's Disciple,* and his Major Barbara are neither promoted to sainthood nor subtly denounced as villians. They are presented objectively if not sympathetically.

It is significant that Shakespeare, Cervantes, Milton, and others of the highest literary magnitude cannot be classified readily as romantic, realistic, or naturalistic. They rise above such compartmentalization for the very reason that they lived the kind of synthesis that they created, refusing to yield their vision of the whole of life and art or let it be narrowed by overemphasis or imbalance in any major way. They serve as perhaps unwitting witnesses to the impressive fact that most partisan views in any area of living or thinking are half-truths. It is difficult to state the whole truth of any major issue in anything less comprehensive than a paradox. Man is potentially good, and man is naturally evil. Similarly, man is mortal and he is immortal.

Ben Jonson is an excellent example of a lesser figure whose literary equal is hard to find because, like Milton, he magnificently combined humanistic learning with Renaissance religious knowledge and displayed a versatility that made him the greatest common denominator of seventeenth-century classicism. He wrote plays and poetry of such variety and genius that none of his followers to the end of the century equalled his attainments as a person and as a writer. He was more classicist than romantic, and he fell short of Shakespeare, it appears, chiefly in the ability to create and project individualized, lifelike human beings.

A seventh precept is: *Enduring works of literature of wide impact nearly always have a strong human appeal,* the kind of appeal that well-organized compilations like *The Anatomy of Melancholy* or even *The Remembrance of Things Past* lack. Important works of literature like *The Faerie Queene* may lack it too, but it is a necessary ingredient of most works that attain a high degree of currency, including popular nonfiction.

The eighth precept has to do with *originality: It is not eccentricity, self-indulgence, or revolt so much as innovation.* It involves a departure from the conventional or expected on substantial grounds, usually rational. Typically, it is a departure resulting from an analysis of the values, objectives, or ends to be served. It analyzes them as a chemist does a solution, only to assemble the ingredients in slightly different amounts or a more adequate configuration in order to obtain new results or properties.

Poe's *Raven* is a good example, if one accepts his own account of its composition. He wanted to write a superior poem that would have a wide popular appeal. In order to do this, he listed the elements or ingredients he would include, and his analysis of the "problem" led him to choose a beautiful woman, loved and lost, as his subject. He then sought out the saddest word and devised a variable refrain to go with his raven symbol. The originality of his poem thus consisted in having a configuration of ingredients with well-known properties put together in musical lines with several distinctive features rarely all found in a single poem, and not in the originality of any one of them separately.

Why should such deliberateness in art be incredible or unthinkable, as a number of poets have declared it to be in Poe's case?[18] Certainly only because of a very narrow concept that puts poetry and mathematics into altogether separate categories. Poetry is more than rational formulas, to be sure. It is vastly more, but is there any good reason for denying it the benefit of the synthesis process Poe claims to have employed? Why not even in poetry produce superior work by the same process a chemist uses — analysis, experimentation, and synthesis?

Is poetry instead to be thought of wholly as "the spontaneous overflow of powerful feelings" or as "emotion recollected in tranquillity"?[19] One has but to consider the source of these phrases and Coleridge's criticism of Wordsworth's theory to discover their fallaciousness as inflated half-truths.[20] It would of course be equally fallacious to make poetry wholly the product of dispassionate calculation or computation. Poetry may originate by either method. It is definable by its effects, not by its methods of creation.

A ninth and final precept effectually subsumes and amplifies the other eight: *Creative writing is both an art and a science.* It essays "a grace beyond the reach of art."[21] Science, that of

[18] Robert Spiller *et al.*, *The Literary History of the United States: History*, 3rd ed. (New York and London, 1963), p. 335, leans toward the disingenuous view and rather stresses Baudelaire's misgivings. This work does not mention, for example, the three critics cited by Killis Campbell in *The Poems of Edgar Allen Poe* (New York, 1917; repr. 1962), p. 250, as having accepted Poe's account. Campbell cites only Brownell as rejecting it. Poe's account is in his essay *The Philosophy of Composition.*

[19] Preface to the 2nd ed. of *Lyrical Ballads*, in *Wordsworth's Poetical Works*, ed. E. de Selincourt, 2nd ed. (Oxford, 1952), II, 400.

[20] *Biographia Literaria*, xvii; ed. J. Shawcross (Oxford, 1907), II, 28-43.

[21] Pope's *Essay on Criticism*, 155.

psychology in particular, overlaps and to a large degree corroborates what "art" has known and practiced for several thousand years. By its comprehensive thoroughness, it can make fiction and poetry — as well as nonfiction — more effective and more enduring than they would otherwise be, in knowledge as well as in art.

The great danger of mixing art with science is that art will become subservient, limiting itself to that area of life in which science can claim competence; that it will lose its subjectivity and its emotional appeal; or that it will let itself be induced to abandon the simplicity of its ancient universal language or its mystical sense of mission and become infected by the ephemeral terminologies of a too aggressive science, to the neglect of its own unique prerogatives.

## VI

If the nine precepts at first seem overgeneralized and not extremely or immediately relevant to the cultivation of writing talent, they nevertheless provide the kind of groundwork that must exist if the horticultural process is to operate with confidence and competence. They serve to indicate the kind of ingredients which plants and shrubs need and which the soil must therefore contain. Only after such preliminary factors have been set down may one legitimately ask either of the questions the teacher of creative writing must at length answer when he selects his class and when he works with any person in it. The two questions are these: (1) How can he recognize talent; and (2) how can he cultivate it most effectively?

In general, there are at least five major criteria of writing talent that are generally accepted. Of these five the first two are more crucial than the next two, but the last is like the strait and narrow way, and "few there be that find it."

The first criterion is obviously *motivation.* Writing talent is not something static but dynamic. It waxes and wanes, and motivation is a variable, not a constant factor. The gestalt approach to educational psychology makes motivation more significant than any kind of intelligence quotient or rating in knowing how well a pupil will do in school. Maturation is equally important but can hardly be a practical factor in gauging creative ability at a specific time.

Motivation toward literary creativity may change as a person matures. More often than not it decreases as a student finds emotional release in other ways. Under encouragement, publication, or other recognition, it is likely to increase. It is certainly in this area that a teacher has the greatest leverage, even to the power of life and death, and thus the greatest responsibility.

The second criterion is *intelligence,* or, more properly, a student's capacity to absorb and to apply knowledge. Its importance has already been noted. The intelligence scores by which it is normally measured are often thought unreliable or even inversely related to literary creativity; and college admissions officers have in fact tended more and more to use high school grades as the most reliable measure of college performance.

Actually, intelligence tests are to a very large degree vocabulary tests. The verbal factor that these tests measure is one very specific test of a student's knowledge and comprehension, and also of his aptitude to use words and the concepts they convey.[22] Thus they provide an index that should be more reliable as a gauge of young writers than for students generally. Especially is this true if the greatest writers of any era are, among other things, projectors of a tradition and heritage that comes to them chiefly in words and verbal mosaics.

Even the math-science factor on tests of intelligence and scholastic aptitude indicates whether a student is well rounded, with a good grasp of quantitative concepts and cause-and-effect relationships of many kinds. These elements are not indispensable to a writing career, of course, and Ralph Waldo Emerson is a conspicuous example of one who was by his own account a dunce in math. He had amazing quasi-mystical gifts to compensate, but one can name many writers who give evidence of having been better rounded and more versatile, with far greater powers of constructive imagination. One thinks of Donne, Dryden, Goethe, Carlyle, and other literary figures who were notably familiar with the science and theology of their day.

An exact, comprehensive study of this intelligence factor in writing careers needs to be made, but the principle is generally accepted that without the native capacity for wide knowledge and subtle perceptivity a writer is not likely to get beyond journalism, potboilers, or formula fiction, if he gets that far. He may not earn high grades in college, but he will have the capacity if applied to this end. At the very least he will need the ability to

[22] Johnson O'Connor, director of the Human Engineering Laboratory of Stevens Institute of Technology, Hoboken, N.J., and one of the ablest investigators in the field of vocabulary, once said: "An extensive knowledge of the exact meanings of English words accompanies outstanding success in this country more often than any other single characteristic which the Human Engineering Laboratory has been able to isolate and measure." *Time,* XXXI, i (Jan. 3, 1938), 32, quoting from "Vocabulary and Success," *Atlantic,* CLIII, ii (Feb. 1934), 160-166.

get into college and to get by. Beyond such a point, however, it is other criteria that distinguish writers from laymen.

The third criterion is *imagination,* whatever that may be. In this context imagination consists not so much of unrestrained, undisciplined fancifulness, useful though that is, as it does of something corresponding to the qualities an architect must possess. Creative imagination in any field is an ability to conceive a well-proportioned artistic whole and then to devise and assemble the structural elements that, when put together skillfully, fulfill the artist's conception. This is the rational, mathematical process of analysis and synthesis by which Poe created *The Raven.*

Imagination is also the spontaneous, sometimes mystical process of building an idea, a character, a problem, a situation, or even a setting into a story or other literary form. One does this at times in a sudden, subconscious way that one cannot explain. One looks at the result and knows that it is good or not good, whether he can analyze it critically or not. However much a story or poem may spring full-blown out of a writer's psyche as Minerva allegedly sprang from the forehead of Jove, it more often goes through a critical-rational process which adapts, modifies, and heightens it for greater effect.

In this connection it is significant that skillful structural imagination marks the works of the Neo-Classic era more clearly than it does the Romantic in English literary history. Thus, three of the most widely read works in English are products of this era dominated by the urge for order, control, form, and structural regularity rather than by relatively uncontrolled, quite emotionalized productions such as those of the Lake poets. The three works are *Paradise Lost, The Pilgrim's Progress,* and *Gulliver's Travels.*

Some students have more of this imaginative capacity than others, with its structural, projective, and decorative potential. It seems to find its fullest flowering in the Celtic temperament or under strong Celtic influence. For English literature, this Celtic quality is exemplified to a notable degree in Spenser, Congreve, Swift, Wilde, Shaw, Joyce, and Yeats.

Imagination manifests itself primarily in three ways: the ability (1) to "see" the thing that is not and crystallize it in a unified artistic structure or whole, as in patterns of action we call plots; (2) to project well-realized persons and situations that create and at the same time dominate the fiction in which they appear; and (3) to recognize the kind of relationships that find expression in figures of speech, especially similes and metaphors, and to put them to good decorative or even structural use.

This ability to conceive the thing that is not is actually the one quality, more than any other, that raises human beings above the animal level. It is the source of the most terrible feats of evil as well as the most angelic forms of good. On its highest levels in fiction it sometimes proves prophetic, as Thomas Mann in his *Doctor Faustus* demonstrated of Goethe's masterpiece.

In its various ways, then, imagination is a very special ingredient of writing talent, vital but not quite indispensable. The well-advertised Famous Writers School uses a talent test which centers in a series of pictures. The candidate must project and describe the action of which each picture is a stage. Certainly any valid measure of writing talent will include such an exercise, testing one's perceptivity as well as his powers of projection. Reportorial writing can subsist without it and can attain perhaps the magnitude of *The Grapes of Wrath,* yet not entirely without imaginative reshaping and the adaptation of materials to artistic imperatives.

A fourth criterion involves the *material* or *experience* a writer possesses. This material may be largely subjective, as it was in the case of Emily Dickinson, or it may be external, as it is for most writers today. Typically, imagination suffuses reality, and reality is transformed by imagination into the kind of conceivable experience that best fulfills the demands of artistic form and effects.

In an absolute sense, any life has enough experience to produce great art, but only those with the motivation to persevere, the knowledge to interpret, the imagination to dissolve and reshape the experience, and the technical skill to express it are likely to find a place in literary history. The reshaping process can become so photographic and so mechanical that the result is of small literary value, however, as in sociological case studies. This condition results from the lack of imagination or the lack of some complementary quality, commonly called originality.

*Originality,* the fifth criterion, is the crucial quality without which the other four are of little use. Originality may be perverse, however. It is likely to be nonconformist in ways that are rational, erratic, or idealistic, or all three. It is at least that derivative or form of imagination that insists on innovation of one or more kinds. The innovation may be called reaction, revolt, accident, whim, or conscience. At its utmost, if literary genius expresses itself most fully in synthesis, originality is, as we have seen, the capacity to supply the element(s) or ingredient(s) that are missing or to rectify those which are misconceived in a literary project. It aligns itself with ultimate principles of "art" and of life (which are as timeless as the theorems of Euclid's geometry) and endeavors to project these more perfectly.

Can one measure originality? The differential it imposes on a young writer's earliest efforts may be insignificant, and its most memorable achievements may have to await the independence of maturity, as in the case of Shakespeare himself. Originality is a quality difficult to identify in youth, yet recognizable in a tendency to think for oneself and to arrive at values or solutions different from those existing or proposed. Mere revolt or rejection not related to rational or aesthetic principles is likely to be perversity rather than originality, particularly if it springs from one of the idols of Plato's cave. One can hardly hope to be sure which it is in every case; and he does not know when revolt may prove to be truly creative.

To these five criteria one might add *initiative,* if it is not included in motivation. That *self-confidence* which is "the substance of things hoped for"[23] might also be listed, but it is either too intangible or too implicit in motivation and other qualities to be inserted as a separate criterion.

## VII

If these five criteria, each with two or three satellite qualities, are the major ingredients of creativity, they are useful less as tools of selection than as guideposts in the daily cultivation of writing talent. In fact, the cultivation process is merely a series of applications and ramifications of these precepts and criteria. Listing them is more a matter of recapitulation than of culmination; they may be ticked off rather briefly.

Having accepted a group of young writers for whatever benefits they or society may derive from their labors, a teacher's first duty is to enhance and reinforce the motivation they already possess. He will find his own ways of doing so, remembering, as pointed out above, that some need it more than others and that it is quite possible to overstimulate students who give relatively little promise or who might be damaged by forcing their talents.

The most obvious motivation consists of putting before one's students the delights, rewards, and privileges of having written well, in terms of either outward or inward results. He will motivate them by holding up the lives, the work, and the satisfactions of others who have written well in the present as well as the past. He will provide motivating experiences like trips to court, inter-

[23] Heb. 11:1.

views with successful writers, and other varied adventures of numerous kinds. If they need guidance, he will help them find topics to write about and motives for writing each. He will understand them as individuals and adapt his strategies to each, according to the need.

A second method is encouragement — as long and far as he sees benefits to be gained. He will of course avoid building excessive expectations where abilities are limited. His discouragement may occasionally provide just the challenge a complacent or perverse temperament requires. He will encourage, not merely with platitudes or uncritical optimism but by showing the student what he can do best and teaching him the techniques he needs. A wide spectrum of literary tolerance is important as already pointed out.

The teacher of writing must challenge all his students to the highest attainments of which they are capable. Contests and writing competitions, both local and national, often serve to bring out the teacher's and the student's best efforts and are especially valuable for those who have the most talent and vitality. Too much challenge, like too much rain in a garden, may discourage, but a strategy that draws out a talent gradually or by stages is generally the best kind. The challenge to think for themselves, to experiment, to search out the ways in which other writers have solved technical problems, and to meet all the verifiable criteria of ancient and modern critics is obviously a part of the process.

Discipline is an undeniable duty of the teacher, as much discipline as the student needs in terms of the teacher's prognosis and as much as the student's temperament can stand. A wise gradualness is clearly better than peremptory demands at an early stage. This discipline should be self-imposed. Naturally, unless the teacher can induce the student to discipline himself, he has little ground for expecting much after the student completes the course. Sometimes a teacher can inspire impressive achievements by the constraining power of his own personality, but too often a student can write only under the spell of the teacher and often only in an imitative way. His work may project the teacher's creativity more than his own.

One of the most difficult duties of the professor of creative writing is to criticize constructively. In each paper he will usually find something that needs to be improved, often much, and something to commend. It is far harder to show a student how he can do a piece of work better than to point out its shortcomings. To do so he must have not only creative talent himself but the ability to project himself into the student's problem as if it were his own. And he must do this with a humility that hesitates to impose his ideas, however good, on a student. He may well hesitate to participate at all in the student's creativity.

As indicated already, a teacher needs to understand each student as well as possible — what his interests and capacities appear to be, how he responds to criticism, what his problems and objectives are, and what is his range of writing abilities in material, forms, and techniques. If, for example, a student persistently handles dialogue better than narration, he should certainly write plays. If he does not have a poet's intensity, he should not be badgered into writing serious poetry. The teacher will be especially considerate of the bruised reed and of smoking flax. Yet he must be as grim as judgment day at times.

The subject of a writer's reading cannot be too strongly stressed. Often a teacher must set up specific schedules or, better, induce students to set up their own, directing a student toward the kind of material that will help him most in content and technique alike. Some students need to read the kind of writing they wish to produce and will react to it in a fine way, while others would slip into imitation. The natural imitators need to read material quite different in style, form, and content. All need to read the best books there are, and yet it not infrequently happens that one learns more from the defects of a work poorly done than from the finest achievements.

If a teacher can do all these things and much more in terms of the precepts and criteria suggested in this article, he will be the kind of teacher that may become as celebrated as his best student. He will deserve the kind of accolade a still-familiar poem by Rudyard Kipling bestows on the kind of person who has succeeded to the fullest degree merely in becoming "a man, my son."

The opportunity of the teacher to lead out his students, each in his own way, is indeed most challenging. He can become a literary Pygmalion who does not reshape young writers in his own image, and he can do more to make the literature of the year 2000 what it needs to be and may indeed become than one can readily imagine. He can point out topics and themes that beg for treatment; he can help a few of the writers of the future to regain something of the wholeness in themselves and in their productions that was lost in the seventeenth century and has hardly been recovered since. He can do all this and much more if he is as versatile and knowledgeable a teacher as Ben Jonson was as a writer. He will not be a writer of Ben's magnitude if he gives his best creativity or even most of his time to teaching, but he will be well versed and well convicted in the principles, precepts, criteria, and methods that undergird the writing process. They have always done so, and will not cease to do so as long as human nature remains what it now is and long has been. He will stress the role of imagination, the importance of techniques, the indispensability of form, the heights and depths of knowledge, the need for discipline, and the summits of spherical synthesis in a thousand ceaseless, subtle ways, year in and year out.

# V. Clyde S. Kilby: The Man and His Writings

# Clyde S. Kilby: A Sketch

PAUL M. BECHTEL

The opening words of *Poetry and Life,* Clyde Kilby's first book, published in 1953, declare: "Every good poem leads us on a journey of discovery." In this book and four others to follow, together with many reviews and articles, it is clear that poetry — indeed, literature at large — has been for Kilby a vast arch leading into a lifetime of exciting discoveries.

Life began for Professor Kilby in the hill country of Eastern Tennessee. The forenoon and afternoon hours of life carried him to many assignments both in this country and abroad. Now the later days have come, and with this volume his friends wish to honor him for his distinguished achievement as teacher, author, critic, man of good will, and Christian scholar.

To his class in biography, a popular course which he taught for many years at Wheaton College, Dr. Kilby frequently offered the aphoristic judgment that it is as hard to write a good life as to live one. He has achieved both. But to catch the quintessence of this many-faceted life is not easy. For him life is an art to be lived with grace, purpose, and creative activity. Always he has brought to his academic concerns an intellectual rigor touched with amiability, patience, and humility.

Clyde Kilby was born in 1902 just outside Johnson City, Tennessee, along the Nolichuckey River. He was the youngest of the eight children of Sophronia and James Lafayette Kilby, a carpenter. His oldest sister, Lula, eighty-five and still living in

---

Paul M. Bechtel is Professor of English and Chairman of the English Department at Wheaton College. He received his A.B. from Juniata College, M.A. from Cornell University, and Ph.D. from Northwestern University. He has published articles and reviews in *Christianity Today, Asbury Seminarian, Eternity, His,* and elsewhere. In 1968-69 he was Fulbright Professor of American Literature at Istanbul University, Turkey.

Johnson City at the time of this writing, told me that her father could make anything from a coffin — which he often did for people along the river — to a piece of fine furniture. She further observed that he always maintained an honorable home where the children "never heard any rough or evil talk."

Dr. Kilby's education in the local schools was conventional, though in the later years somewhat marked by economic stress, for the father died when his son was twelve. Without resources to go to college, Clyde entered a lawyer's office after high school and for four years also served as a court reporter and public stenographer. During these years the vision of a college education became a compelling dream, and in 1929 he graduated from the University of Arkansas, the only member of his family to graduate from college — not an unusual thing in the 1920s.

In 1930 he married a Mississippian, Martha A. Harris, who was to become the gracious hostess of the Kilby household and whom many students over the years have known and cherished. Without children of their own, the Kilbys have found a special delight and a distinctive gift in entertaining and counseling students. And Dr. Kilby's devotion to small children has made him a fast friend of many a faculty youngster.

A fellowship at the University of Minnesota, which required him to work in the Registrar's office, enabled him to complete a Master's degree in 1931. He came to Wheaton College as Assistant Dean of Men and Assistant Professor of English in 1935. In 1938 he received a Ph.D. at New York University, where his dissertation was a study of Horace Walpole as literary critic. In 1970 he completed thirty-five years of service at Wheaton.

Dr. Kilby served as Chairman of the English Department at Wheaton College from 1951 to 1966. During part of this time he was also Chairman of the Division of Languages and Literature. While he directed the work in English, the Department grew steadily in student esteem and in the numbers of students electing to major in the field. At the time of his retirement from the Chairmanship, the English Department was the largest in the college. By then the number of senior English majors had grown so large that it was no longer possible for the weekly seminar on Monday nights to meet in the Kilby home, as it had for many years. There students had read papers, analyzed literary problems, relaxed with cookies and punch or cocoa, and listened to the genial yet penetrating promptings of their mentor. Such evenings were always made lively by the irrepressible Kilby humor and his anecdotes.

His colleagues in the English Department remember Professor Kilby as a tireless worker, a genial and relaxed leader, a good team man who never wanted to appear to run the show. Departmental problems he always shared with his associates, and major decisions were made in conference with them. Affability, humor, and humility never seemed to desert him. As something of an evangelist at large for evangelical culture, he never lost these qualities of spirit that made his proddings acceptable preachments.

In 1956 he laid plans for a Christian Writers' Conference. For a number of years he had been distressed by the quality of evangelical writing. He felt that it lacked both technical competence and vivifying power. Too often it was earthbound — it did not take wings. What he wrote in the Wheaton College *Alumni Magazine* in 1961 represents the convictions that had prompted him to initiate such a conference:

> I am afraid that the problem of Christian writing is not so much that of making it Christian as making it structurally and intellectually sound. ...I believe one reason contemporary evangelicals have done so badly in creative writing is that they simply do not believe in it. They have done badly not because of innate lack of ability.... They have never become persuaded that good writing is worthy of their efforts.... As long as we suppose writing to be an after-dinner exercise in sentimentality, we shall continue to produce trash.

The last sentence has a certain shock value which he believed essential if evangelicals were to become aware of a major area of deficiency. The first conference was held June 12-14, 1956, in conjunction with the college Inter-Session, a two-week summer program. Among the speakers at the first conference were Chad Walsh, who spoke on "Poems Across an Editor's Desk" and "How Not to Convert an Artist"; Frank Gaebelein, whose subject was "The Bible and the Christian Writer"; and Frederick Babcock, then Book Editor of the *Chicago Tribune*, whose talk was titled "Return to Decency in the Novel." Present also and participating in the program were Mae Tenney, Virginia Grabill, Ward Miller, Charles Huttar, Kenneth Taylor, and Ralph Hone.

A meticulously kept file reveals that nearly a hundred personal letters were written in organizing that first conference. It is no disparagement of Dr. Kilby's letter writing to note that composition comes easily for him, with a steady and natural flow of ideas. Moreover, his shorthand and typing mastery, gained when he was a court reporter, has been immensely valuable. Anyone who has watched his typewriter sing with its amazing rhythm and speed understands how he has been able to maintain a very extensive correspondence over the years.

It is perhaps an additional tribute to his administrative ability to observe that the first Writers' Conference was managed on a budget of $300.

The need for capable writers and dedicated Christian scholars among evangelicals was strongly set forth at the first conference. The high quality of the papers and the sense of mission aroused among those in attendance encouraged Dr. Kilby to envision a second conference almost from the moment the first adjourned.

Over the years the conference has grown steadily in its influence and in the number of attendants it has attracted. In the last several years faculty representatives and students have come from twenty-five to thirty colleges, and observers from fifteen to twenty publishing organizations have attended, as well as many area residents and Wheaton students and faculty. From time to time there have been suggestions that the conference broaden its concerns by including discussions of literature. But the original purpose — to serve writers and those who wish to write — has been steadily maintained.

There is no way of measuring the consequences of an enterprise like this. One can only assume on the basis of expressions of appreciation that the conferences have been a time of information and inspiration. Some young attendants certainly have had a vocational vision created or solidified. One would like to think, without having the means to assure himself that it is so, that the conferences have had a meaningful impact upon evangelical writing today, and that in this there has been some fulfillment of Dr. Kilby's original dream.

In 1948-49 Dr. Kilby was awarded the Wheaton College Alumni research grant to help him assemble materials for a biography of Jonathan Blanchard, first president of Wheaton College. In preparation for the writing, he visited the cities associated with Blanchard's birth and young manhood in Vermont, the colleges which had been a part of his life before his arrival in Wheaton — Middlebury, Oberlin, Knox — and other stopping points in his crusading odyssey. The two and a half pages of acknowledgement which preface this biography, *Minority of One*, published by Eerdmans in 1959, suggest the painstaking meticulousness with which the investigation for the book was carried on. It is characteristic of Dr. Kilby's scholarly workmanship; he is an unrelenting foe of shoddy efforts.

The biography reads like a novel. Blanchard was a man of restless energy with a great interest in projects for the betterment of society. His life was diversified, often adventuresome, frequently fraught with peril; he was a man of rigorous independence and fearless courage. These qualities emerge from the biography because the writing is vital, enthusiastic. It crackles with life and draws energy and interest from its anecdotal quality. It exemplifies Dr. Kilby's own convictions about biography. One feels from the beginning that the biographer believes in his subject and has found in him a hero. Yet, the work is above all honest, revealing the man as he was; it is never merely adulatory.

In the late spring of 1953, Dr. and Mrs. Kilby were in Dothan, Jordan, where Dr. Joseph Free, Professor of Archaeology at Wheaton College, had for some years been carrying on excavations. From Dothan the Kilbys went to England during the summer. Like many others, Kilby had been immensely impressed by several of the early writings of C. S. Lewis. "It was almost a quarter of a century ago," he was later to write in the Preface to *The Christian World of C. S. Lewis,* "that I picked up at my college book store a little volume by an Oxford don named C. S. Lewis. It was called *The Case for Christianity,* and when I sat down to read it I realized a new planet had sailed into my ken." He determined, if at all possible while he was in England, to meet this Oxford literary scholar turned Christian lay apologist. A note to Lewis requesting an opportunity to chat with him when the Kilbys came to Oxford was the means of bringing the two men together.

Professor Kilby likes to recall that he asked the porter at Magdalen College, Oxford, whether there was any truth to the report that Lewis disliked women and was told that there was "some truth in it." Consequently Mrs. Kilby did not join her husband in the visit to Lewis's office. There in the course of a congenial hour on a July afternoon Lewis and his guest chatted about the Renaissance (he thought it was not nearly so much a "rebirth" as some scholars claimed), the relation of Christianity and art, the opinions of C. E. M. Joad and D. S. Savage, and Kilby's recent experiences in the Holy Land. The American visitor observed that his host had "a pleasant, almost jolly face, full though not fat, with a double chin. . . . Actually, he is a much better looking man than the published picture of him."

Although this was the only meeting between the two men, there followed a lively correspondence which continued until Lewis's death in 1963. Dr. Kilby's reading of Lewis and his personal encounter and correspondence with him were to lead to an intellectual turning point in his life. The Wheaton professor found in the Englishman a Christian scholar writing with a simple yet eloquent profundity about many of the same questions that had long interested him. Here was a man saying significantly positive things about the relation of Christianity and art, about the value of mystery in religious experience, about the uses of myth in the creation of moral vision. Lewis's was the kind of mind evangelicalism ought to be producing and was not. Here was a sort of modern Pascal, who could persuade the twentieth-century intellectual to belief in Jesus Christ in spite of all the contemporary compulsions to disbelief. "My impression was of a man who had won, inside and deep, a battle against pose, evasion, expedience, and the ever-so-little lie and who wished with all his heart to honor truth in every idea passing through his mind."

Dr. Kilby's enthusiasm for Lewis led him to become a champion and defender of his work. Many evangelical students whom Kilby guided through the structure of Lewis's thought found the same vivification of the fabric of Christian ideas. Lewis's distinctively fresh approach and his lucid style gave the ancient declaration of the faith a new muscularity and relevance. Confident in the rightness of his own estimate of the value of Lewis's thought to contemporary Christianity, Kilby was nonetheless encouraged by the confirming judgments of others.

When W. Norman Pittenger mounted a strong attack on Lewis's theological competence and the mode in which his ideas were cast, Kilby challenged the attacker's judgments.[1] To Pittenger's opinion that Lewis's writings have little value, Kilby responds: "My own judgment is that Lewis has done more to clear the theological atmosphere of our time than many theologians together." When Pittenger charged Lewis with vulgarity for trying to demonstrate the idea of the Trinity by referring to a cube as having both diversity and oneness, Kilby noted that Jesus was constantly simplifying the complex through the use of things near at hand. "I believe that one of Lewis's greatest contributions to orthodox Christianity is his demonstration that a sanctified imagination is a legitimate tool for any Christian apologist."

Pittenger's severest attack was directed against *Miracles,* where, he charged, Lewis clung to a long-outmoded cosmology. In meeting this argument Kilby reveals one of his finest gifts: his ability to come to the center of a complex issue and open it up with simple clarifications. This interpretive skill, together with an honest conviction of the worth of the whole body of Lewis's work, has had a substantial influence upon the develop-

[1] W. Norman Pittenger, "A Critique of C. S. Lewis," *The Christian Century,* LXXV (October 1, 1958), 1104-07; Clyde S. Kilby, "C. S. Lewis and His Critics," *Christianity Today,* III, v (December 8, 1958), 13-15.

ment of a large Lewis readership in this country. Here also he exhibits his ability to handle a theological argument without becoming verbose, contentious, or obscure.

In 1964 *The Christian World of C. S. Lewis* was published. This summary criticism was the result of a quarter-century of thoughtful reflection on the Englishman's achievement. In the Preface to the book Professor Kilby declared his purpose to be "to evaluate Lewis's Christian works one by one, to compare them with each other and sometimes with books by other writers, to discover the themes which made up the main body of his writing, and to consider the consistency of Lewis's works as a whole." The volume was generously acclaimed by the popular and periodical press. The *Chicago Tribune* called it "a definitive analysis of Lewis's writings."

It is hardly possible to say that one work or one group of Lewis's works has interested Kilby more than any other. It is clear, however, that the fiction has intrigued him greatly, especially *Out of the Silent Planet, Perelandra, That Hideous Strength,* and the Narnian tales. The use of the mythic as a means of conveying the truth intrigued him, and his interest in modern myth and mythmakers grew in no small measure out of his study of Lewis, as well as out of his interest in the creative process as an aspect of aesthetics — a study in which he became increasingly absorbed after he began to teach a course in that field.

In myth Kilby sees something fundamental to the human process of cognition, especially as men yearn for those deeper reservoirs of truth that the familiar routes of learning will not open. "What is the cause of myth making?" he asks. To this inquiry he replies:

> There is a great, sovereign, uncreated, unconditioned Reality at the core of things, and myth is on the one hand a kind of picture-making which helps man to understand this Reality and on the other hand the result of a deep call from that Reality. Myth is a "real though unfocussed gleam of divine truth falling on human imagination" which enables man to express the inexpressible. The glory of the Morning Star is somehow not enough glory for us. We want much more, and it is at this point that poetry and mythology come to our aid.[2]

Lewis's disposition to make an "unorthodox presentation of strict orthodoxy," to insist on concretizing theological abstractions, interested Professor Kilby greatly. Lewis was orthodox about heaven and hell in a time when it was not fashionable in academic circles to be orthodox. Few men have written with

[2] *The Christian World of C. S. Lewis,* p. 81.

more cogency, Kilby holds, on the transcendent glories of heaven and on the terrors of hell.

In 1956 the Conference on Christianity and Literature was organized with Clyde Kilby as its first president. He and others had for some time been interested in creating a professional organization of Christian teachers of college literature. The purpose of the group, with its few charter members, was to encourage scholarship among Christian teachers and to provide an agency of fellowship for those who share a common vocational vision. The organizational meeting took place at Wheaton College and annual meetings for several years were held there. In 1967, however, the annual meeting was held in Chicago in conjunction with the Modern Language Association; and it is likely that the CCL will continue to tie in with this large, national organization of college teachers.

In the early years of its history in the 1950's, Dr. Kilby was also for a time Executive Secretary of Lambda Iota Tau, a students' national honor society. This organization, too, over the years had grown substantially.

In 1955 Professor Kilby, at the invitation of the Philosophy Department of Wheaton, began to teach a course titled "A Christian Philosophy of the Arts." In this study he and his class were able to come to grips with some of the problems that had long interested him: What is the relation of form to beauty? How does the creative process work? How can the creative imagination be exercised to the glory of God? What is art's distinctive approach to human concerns? He saw in art, nurtured by the Christian vision and guided by its imperatives, the highest expression of the human spirit. The pity of it was that too few evangelicals were gripped by this kind of conviction. The class pursued its vision and struggled with its formulations with a kind of missionary zeal.

The fruit of Kilby's thinking about aesthetics found expression in a short work, *Christianity and Aesthetics,* published in 1961. Here he points out how art differs from the logical proposition, the scientific formulation, the achievements of empirical investigation. "Art," he notes, "grows restive under the slow and laborious method of expository statement, chooses instead the penetrating insight gained through symbol and metaphor" (p. 14). The basic assumption in the book, from which all other declarations arise, is in this statement: "For the Christian, God is the supreme artist" (p. 18). The world fashioned by this supreme artist is "no tight little rational one, but rather a world of magic and mystery in which anything can happen with impressive disregard to human norms" (p. 37).

If the Christian artist has his sanction from God, he is "therefore greatly responsible." But his opportunities are wondrously awesome: "Christianity makes it possible for the artist to depict with sharpened contrasts both the anxiety and despairing agony, and the possibility of their healing — both a paradise lost and a paradise to be regained" (p. 35).

One of the students in the aesthetics class recently published an account of his intellectual and spiritual pilgrimage through college and beyond. He observes:

> In my last semester at college, I studied aesthetics under a great and good man named Kilby. . . . We began, in this class, to read Benedetto Croce, Jose Ortega y Gasset, Roger Fry, Herbert Read, Bernard Bosanquet, and I. A. Richards, and we shouted at each other and tore our hair and tried to define beauty and truth and goodness and wrote great splashy papers and looked at paintings and listened to Mozart and wondered if we would ever be able to pull ourselves together. . . . But I felt that once again a door had been blown open and that I could never again insist that there was nothing on the far side.[3]

In 1964 Professor Kilby met in Oxford for the first time J. R. R. Tolkien, author of *The Hobbit* and *The Lord of the Rings*. The occasion for the meeting was Kilby's desire to have Tolkien publish in this country an early, unpublished children's story. The mission failed, but an acquaintanceship with the Oxford professor had been initiated. Kilby's long interest in myth, and his conviction that Tolkien was one of the most effective of modern mythmakers, led him in the spring of 1966 to offer his services to Professor Tolkien to help make ready for publication *Silmarillion,* a sequel to *The Lord of the Rings*. The invitation was accepted, and the two men met regularly several mornings a week from early June until the end of August. Kilby's effort was to encourage Tolkien, then aging and somewhat unwell, to make the final effort to complete and ready his work for publication. Progress was made and the Oxonian expressed warm appreciation to his visiting friend, but the book was never finished; nor has it yet been published.

During the academic years 1966-67 Professor Kilby was on a leave of absence made possible by a grant from the class of 1962 at Wheaton College, to complete an anthology of the works of C. S. Lewis. This volume, called *A Mind Awake,* was published in 1968. But much of the leave time was devoted to a second project, an effort which Professor Kilby had begun in a quiet way several years earlier. From his acquaintanceship with Lewis, he knew that the English author had been a prolific

[3] Thomas Howard, *Christ the Tiger* (Philadelphia, 1967), pp. 44ff.

letter writer. There must be, he thought, hundreds of these letters, perhaps more than a thousand scattered around the world — in spite of Lewis's professed dislike of letter writing. Possibly Wheaton College could become the repository for some of these if the owners might be encouraged to lodge them there. Quietly Kilby began to disclose his vision to some of Lewis's associates — Major W. H. Lewis, the author's brother; Owen Barfield, Lewis's attorney and closest friend; J. R. R. Tolkien; and a few others. Some of the letters and papers of Charles Williams have also found their way into the Wheaton collection.

In 1967, selections from one of the collections of Lewis letters given to the college were published, with an introduction by Dr. Kilby, in a book entitled *Letters to an American Lady*. A *Chicago Tribune* critic called the book "a literary gem." At this writing more than 60,000 copies are in print.

There have been many other workmanlike performances in Professor Kilby's many-faceted career that this brief sketch has not described. From his pen have come, for example, dozens of reviews, appearing in such publications as *The New York Times*, the *Herald Tribune*, the *Chicago Tribune*, *Christianity Today*, *Eternity*, and *His*. The insights and arresting phraseology characterizing these reviews are well represented in his *New York Times* review of Lewis's *Poems*, published in 1966. Speaking of the varied qualities of the verse, he wrote:

> The music is often on the brittle side, something like the crackle of a bitten apple, as though Lewis wishes to discourage a reader from being lulled by mere cadence into thoughtlessness. But again there is poetry smooth as a flower's petal or the sinuosity of a flowing stream.

But however large the area of his concerns, however full his sheaf of talents, it must be clearly declared that the thousands of students who have moved through his classes have had the first claim upon Professor Kilby's energies and wisdom. One of his recent students expressed the hope that this volume might be a tribute "to the unique intellectual legacy which was Dr. Kilby's inimitable contribution to his students." Another former student, now fifteen years out of college, speaks of him as "a provocative bringer-to-birth of gestating ideas in young minds." To all, he has conveyed with an easy humility his own passion for the intellectual quest. The heart of his work has been bequeathing to others the treasures of knowledge and certitude which he had come upon. For the goodness of life, the exuberant beauty of the world, and the astonishing gift of grace, he evidences a vital rejoicing.

Throughout his long career Clyde Kilby has been a faithful

servant of the Lord Jesus Christ. For him the Word made flesh, the revelation in Scripture, and the radiance of divine love have been wondrous realities. He has continuously borne witness to his soaring vision of the God of the cloud chambers — a vision too commonly snuffed out, he holds, by modern liberalism and propositional statement. Many will thank him for having reinvoked in his teaching and writing the larger vision of the Divine which the creative and imaginative spirit is capable of appropriating.

# Bibliography of Clyde S. Kilby


### 1930

"The Intelligence Test as a College Entrance Medium for Adult Students." *Journal of Arkansas Education,* VIII, viii (May), 12-13.

"Intelligence Tests for Adult Admission." *Junior College Journal,* I (December), 135-139.

### 1933

"College Bulletins." *Journal of Higher Education,* IV (February), 54-58.

"John Brown College Success." *Junior College Journal,* III (January), 210-211.

### 1935

"Rochester Library." *Junior College Journal,* V (March), 322.

"Success of Rochester Junior College Transfers." *Junior College Journal,* VI (December), 127-129.

"Went to Jail and Wrote a Book." *Milwaukee Journal,* April 8, sec. 1, p. 8.

### 1937

"College Catalogues — Some Shortcomings." *Bulletin of the American Association of Collegiate Registrars,* XII (April), 244-249.

"Famous Books Written in Jail." *World Digest.*

### 1938

"Horace Walpole as Literary Critic." Ph.D. dissertation, New York University.

### 1941

"Horace Walpole on Shakespeare." *Studies in Philology,* XXXVIII (July), 480-493.

### 1942

(ed.) *Life Writing: Essays on the Technique of Biography*. Wheaton, Ill.: Wheaton College.

### 1943

"Browning's CRISTINA." *The Explicator,* II (November), art. 16.

### 1944

"Study of Freshman Tests Repeated in the Sophomore Year." *Journal of the American Association of Collegiate Registrars,* XIX (January), 217-224.

### 1946

*Review*

Fremont Rider, *The Scholar and the Future of the Research Library. News Letter of the College English Association.*

### 1947

"Keats' Ode to a Nightingale, Line 35." *The Explicator,* V (February), art. 27.

"Moral Values in Literature." *CMS News* (Christian Medical Society), No. 48 (April), pp. 1, 5-6.

### 1953

*Poetry and Life.* New York: Odyssey Press.

"E. E. Cummings' Memorabilia." *The Explicator,* XII (November), art. 15.

"A Visit with C. S. Lewis." *Kodon* (Wheaton College), VIII, ii (December), 11, 28, 30.

### 1955

"The Meaning of 'Fiction.'" *Wheaton College Faculty Bulletin,* XVIII, i (Winter), 1-4.

"Of Roses and Field Mice and 9 x 8." *His,* XVI, i (October), 10-14, 28-29, 33.

"Signs in Great Britain." *Word Study,* XXXI, ii (December), 7.

### 1956

*Reviews*

C. S. Lewis, *Surprised by Joy. New York Herald Tribune Book Review,* February 5, p. 5.

William Sansom, *A Contest of Ladies. New York Herald Tribune Book Review,* March 25, p. 5.

Alberto Moravia, *Bitter Honeymoon, and Other Stories. New York Herald Tribune Book Review,* August 26, p. 2.

Frederick Wight, *Verge of Glory. New York Herald Tribune Book Review,* October 14, p. 1.

Joan Reverzy, *The Crossing. New York Herald Tribune Book Review,* November 4, p. 7.

Augusta Walker, *The Eating Valley. New York Herald Tribune Book Review,* December 9, p. 13.

### 1957

"Form in Religion." *Christianity Today,* I, xxiii (September 2), 15-17.

"Old Reuben: An interview with a 108-year-old Mississippi patriarch." *This Day,* VIII, vi (February), 37.

"Till We Have Faces: a review of the C. S. Lewis book" [review-article]. *His,* XVIII, iii (December), 16-20. Reprinted in the *Wheaton College Faculty Bulletin,* XXI, iii (Winter 1958), 6-10.

*Reviews*

Jack Shuler, *The Valley of Silence. Christianity Today,* I, vii (January 7), 38.

Carl Jonas, *Our Revels Now Are Ended. New York Herald Tribune Book Review,* January 20, p. 4.

*Winter's Tales Two. New York Herald Tribune Book Review,* February 3, p. 3.

Blair Fuller, *A Far Place. New York Herald Tribune Book Review,* February 10, p. 5.

C. S. Lewis, *Till We Have Faces. Eternity,* VIII, iv (April), 24.

Bernard Malamud, *The Assistant. New York Herald Tribune Book Review,* April 28, p. 8.

Elisabeth Elliot, *Through Gates of Splendor. Eternity,* VIII, vi (June), 5, 36-37.

Jerome Bahr, *The Linen Suit and Other Stories. New York Herald Tribune Book Review,* June 2, p. 7.

Geoffrey Wagner, *Rage on the Bar. New York Herald Tribune Book Review,* July 28, p. 8.

Themistocles Hoetis, ed., *Zero Anthology No. 8 of Literature and Art. New York Herald Tribune Book Review,* August 18, p. 8.

Helen Frazee-Bower, *Garment of Praise,* Johnstone G. Patrick, *Above the Thorn,* and B. B. and Edna Allen Edmiaston, *Rhythm and Rhyme. Christianity Today,* I, xxiv (September 16), 36-37.

Harvey Swados, *On the Line. New York Herald Tribune Book Review,* October 6, p. 3.

Herbert Simmons, *Corner Boy. New York Herald Tribune Book Review,* October 27, p. 5.

Tereska Torres, *The Dangerous Games. New York Herald Tribune Book Review,* November 17, p. 11.

Phyllis Woodruff Sapp, *Small Giant. Christianity Today,* II, v (December 9), 34-35.

## 1958

"C. S. Lewis and His Critics." *Christianity Today,* III, v (December 8), 13-15.

"What About C. S. Lewis and His Writings?" *Sunday School Times,* C (March 1), 158.

*Reviews*

Jack Kerouac, *The Subterraneans. New York Herald Tribune Book Review,* February 23, p. 4.

Christmas Carol Kauffman, *Hidden Rainbow. Eternity,* IX, iii (March), 42.

Francois-Regis Bastide, *Les Adieux. New York Herald Tribune Book Review,* June 1, p. 8.

Hubert Kubly, *Varieties of Love. New York Herald Tribune Book Review,* June 22, p. 8.

Gordon Langley Hall, *The Gypsy Condesa. New York Herald Tribune Book Review,* June 29, p. 4.

Henry Zylstra, *Testament of Vision. Christianity Today,* II, xx (July 7), 34.

Leon Edel, *Literary Biography. The Gordon Review,* IV (Summer), 98-99.

Duncan Thorp, *Only Akiko. New York Herald Tribune Book Review,* August 31, p. 6.

Elisabeth Elliot, *Shadow of the Almighty. Eternity,* IX, ix (September), 38.

James Aldridge, *I Wish He Would Not Die. New York Herald Tribune Book Review,* October 5, p. 6.

Alfred Andersch, *Flight to Afar. New York Herald Tribune Book Review,* October 19, p. 8.

Ernest Frankel, *Band of Brothers. New York Herald Tribune Book Review,* November 9, p. 3.

**1959**

*Minority of One.* Grand Rapids: William B. Eerdmans Publishing Company.

"Three Antislavery Prisoners." *Journal of the Illinois State Historical Society,* LII (Autumn), 419-430.

*Reviews*

C. S. Lewis, *The Pilgrim's Regress. Chicago Tribune Magazine of Books,* January 4, p. 7.

Harold E. Kohn, *Thoughts Afield. Christianity Today,* III, xxii (August 3), 39.

M. H. Abrams, *Literature and Belief. The Gordon Review,* V (Fall), 134-135.

Roy F. Nichols, *Religion and American Democracy,* and Joseph A. Sittler, *The Structure of Christian Ethics* (review entitled "Studies in Christian Learning"). *Modern Age,* IV (Winter), 99-101.

**1960**

"Introducing Mrs. Lewis" [letter]. *Christianity Today,* IV (July 4), 825.

"A Perfect State of Society." *Wheaton College Faculty Bulletin,* XXIII, iii (Spring), 1-7.

*Reviews*

C. S. Lewis, *The World's Last Night. Christianity Today,* IV (April 25), 632-633.

Francois Mauriac, *The Son of Man. Christianity Today,* IV (June 20), 802-803.

**1961**

*Christianity and Aesthetics.* Chicago: Inter-Varsity Press.

"A Further Clarification, by C. S. Lewis" [correspondence]. *Newsletter of the Conference on Christianity and Literature,* XI, vii/viii (December), 6.

"Writing at Wheaton." *Wheaton College Alumni Magazine,* XXVIII, vii/viii (July-August), 6.

*Reviews*

J. B. Phillips, *God Our Contemporary. Eternity,* XII, ii (February), 43.

Ola Elizabeth Winslow, *John Bunyan. Christianity Today,* VI (November 10), 157.

Merton L. Dillon, *Elijah P. Lovejoy, Abolitionist Editor. Journal of the Illinois State Historical Society,* LIV (Winter), 431-432.

## 1962

*Review*

Oscar Sherwin, *John Wesley, Friend of the People. Christianity Today,* VI (January 5), 345.

## 1963

"The Novel — Yes/No." *His,* XXIII, v (February), 11-14. Reprinted in *Light and Life Evangel,* August 25, 1963.

## 1964

*The Christian World of C. S. Lewis.* Grand Rapids: William B. Eerdmans Publishing Company. Published in Abingdon, England: Marcham Manor Press, 1965.

"Between Hell and Heaven." *Panorama, Chicago Daily News,* July 4.

"C. S. Lewis: Everyman's Theologian." *Christianity Today,* VIII (January 3), 313-315.

*Reviews*

Olov Hartman, *Holy Masquerade. Christianity Today,* VIII (January 31), 415.

Richard E. Kim, *The Martyred. Christianity Today,* VIII (June 5), 846-847.

## 1965

"The Artistic Poverty of Evangelicalism." *Eternity,* XVI, xii (December), 16-18.

"The Decline and Fall of Christian Imagination." *Eternity,* XVI, iii (March), 15-17, 46.

"Knowledge Versus Wisdom." *Stony Brook Bulletin,* XXXIII, iii (July), 7-8.

"Preface," in John Bunyan, *Pilgrim's Progress* (Chicago: Moody Press).

"Preface" and "Introduction," in Daniel Defoe, *Adventures of Robinson Crusoe,* abr. ed. (Chicago: Moody Press).

*Reviews*

Maurice J. Quinlan, *Samuel Johnson: a Layman's Religion. The Gordon Review,* VIII (Spring), 170-171.

Edward Wagenknecht, *Harriet Beecher Stowe* (review entitled "Is Uncle Tom's Cabin Really a Classic?"). *Eternity,* XVI, viii (August), 42.

Charles Williams, *Shadows of Ecstasy, War in Heaven, Many Dimensions, The Place of the Lion, Descent into Hell, The Descent of the Dove. Eternity,* XVI, xi (November), 43.

## 1966

"David Brainerd: Knight of the Grail," in *Heroic Colonial Christians,* ed. Russell T. Hitt (Philadelphia and New York: J. B. Lippincott Company), pp. 151-206.

"'I Thirst.'" *Christianity Today,* X (April 1), 661.

"Kilby Works with Tolkien" [correspondence]. *Newsletter of the Conference on Christianity and Literature,* XVI, i (Autumn), 6-7.

"That Sunday Touch." *His,* XXVII, iii (December), 32-33.

*Review*

C. S. Lewis, *Poems,* ed. Walter Hooper. *New York Times Book Review,* January 23, p. 34.

## 1967

(ed.) C. S. Lewis, *Letters to an American Lady.* Grand Rapids: William B. Eerdmans Publishing Company. Published in London: Hodder and Stoughton, 1969.

"The Aesthetic Poverty of Evangelicalism." *Wheaton College Faculty Bulletin,* XXXI, i (Fall), 1-14. Reprinted in the *Wheaton College Alumni Magazine* in two installments, XXX, x (November 1967), 3-6; xi (December), 6-7.

"Tolkien as Scholar and Artist." *The Tolkien Journal,* III, i (Spring), 9-11.

*Reviews*

Lycurgus M. Starkey, *James Bond's World of Values,* and Ann S. Boyd, *The Devil with James Bond. Christianity Today,* XI (March 3), 564-566.

C. S. Lewis, *Christian Reflections,* ed. Walter Hooper. *Books Today, Chicago Tribune,* April 9, p. 8.

## 1968

*A Mind Awake: An Anthology of C. S. Lewis.* London: Geoffrey Bles. Published in New York: Harcourt, Brace and World, 1969.

"Many Meetings with Tolkien: An Edited Transcript of Remarks at the December 1966 TSA Meeting." *Niekas* (Center Harbor, N.H.), No. 19, pp. 39-40.

## 1969

"Christian Imagination." *The Christian Herald,* XCII, ii (March), 17-20.

"Logic and Fantasy: Christian Thought in the World of C. S. Lewis." *Christian Action,* I, v (January).

"The Lost Myth." *Arts in Society,* VI, ii, 155-163.

"Meaning in *The Lord of the Rings,*" in *Shadows of Imagination: The Fantasies of C. S. Lewis, J. R. R. Tolkien, and Charles Williams,* ed. Mark R. Hillegas (Carbondale and Edwardsville: Southern Illinois University Press; London and Amsterdam: Feffer & Simons), pp. 70-80.

*Review*

Owen Barfield, *Romanticism Comes of Age. The Gordon Review,* XI (Summer), 250-251.

## 1970

*Review*

Neil D. Isaacs and Rose A. Zimbardo, *Tolkien and the Critics, Essays on J. R. R. Tolkien's The Lord of the Rings. The Gordon Review,* XI (Spring), 311-312.

Malcolm Muggeridge, *Jesus Rediscovered. The Catholic World,* CCXI (April), 37.

## 1971

"Charles Williams' Supernatural World." *His,* XXXI, vi (March), 24-25, 32.

"The Creative Logician Speaking," in *C. S. Lewis, Speaker and Teacher,* ed. Carolyn Keefe (Grand Rapids: Zondervan Publishing House), pp. 15-34.

"Poetry," in *Encounter with Books: a guide to Christian reading,* ed. Harish D. Merchant (Downers Grove, Ill.: Inter-Varsity Press), pp. 189-191.

*Review*

C. S. Lewis, *Selected Literary Essays,* ed. Walter Hooper. *Christian Scholar's Review,* I (Winter), 174-177.

# Index nominum

The bibliography has not been indexed. Names appearing only in the footnotes are omitted. Names of fictional, mythological, and biblical characters are included in the *Index rerum.*

# Index rerum